Python 3

Rheinwerk Computing

The Rheinwerk Computing series offers new and established professionals comprehensive guidance to enrich their skillsets and enhance their career prospects. Our publications are written by the leading experts in their fields. Each book is detailed and hands-on to help readers develop essential, practical skills that they can apply to their daily work.

Explore more of the Rheinwerk Computing library!

Veit Steinkamp
Python for Engineering and Scientific Computing
2024, 511 pages, paperback and e-book
www.rheinwerk-computing.com/5852

Philip Ackermann
JavaScript: The Comprehensive Guide
2022, 982 pages, paperback and e-book
www.rheinwerk-computing.com/5554

Sebastian Springer
Node.js: The Comprehensive Guide
2022, 834 pages, paperback and e-book
www.rheinwerk-computing.com/5556

Christian Ullenboom
Java: The Comprehensive Guide
2023, 1126 pages, paperback and e-book
www.rheinwerk-computing.com/5557

Jürgen Wolf
HTML and CSS: The Comprehensive Guide
2023, 814 pages, paperback and e-book
www.rheinwerk-computing.com/5695

www.rheinwerk-computing.com

Johannes Ernesti, Peter Kaiser

Python 3

The Comprehensive Guide

Editor Rachel Gibson
Acquisitions Editor Hareem Shafi
German Edition Editor Anne Scheibe
Translation Winema Language Services, Inc.
Copyeditor Melinda Rankin
Cover Design Graham Geary
Photo Credit Adobe Stock: 65543369/© Sergey Skleznev
Layout Design Vera Brauner
Production Graham Geary
Typesetting SatzPro, Germany
Printed and bound in the United States of America, on paper from sustainable sources

ISBN 978-1-4932-2302-2
1st edition 2022, 3rd reprint 2025
6th German edition published 2021 by Rheinwerk Verlag GmbH, Bonn, Germany

---

© 2025 by:
Rheinwerk Publishing, Inc.
2 Heritage Drive, Suite 305
Quincy, MA 02171
USA
info@rheinwerk-publishing.com

Represented in the E.U. by:
Rheinwerk Verlag GmbH
Rheinwerkallee 4
53227 Bonn
Germany
service@rheinwerk-verlag.de

Library of Congress Cataloging-in-Publication Control Data
Names: Ernesti, Johannes, author. | Kaiser, Peter (Computer programmer),
  author.
Title: Python 3 : the comprehensive guide / by Johannes Ernesti and Peter
  Kaiser.
Description: 1st edition. | Bonn ; Boston : Rheinwerk Publishing/SAP Press,
  2022. | Includes index.
Identifiers: LCCN 2022029178 | ISBN 9781493223022 (hardcover) | ISBN
  9781493223039 (ebook)
Subjects: LCSH: Python (Computer program language) | Computer programming.
Classification: LCC QA76.73.P98 E76 2022 | DDC 005.13/3--dc23/eng/20220812
LC record available at https://lccn.loc.gov/2022029178

Contents at a Glance

Dear Reader,

I am a self-proclaimed minimalist.

I have been known to go on day-long decluttering sprees, and actively try to reduce my consumption and the amount of possessions I own. Just the thought of digging through a jam-packed junk drawer of half-dead batteries, takeout menus, and long-forgotten mail to find a single, usable pen? It makes my blood pressure spike. While I might never get to the stage of owning a sleek, all-white house with just one set of dishes and bare-bones furniture, having a streamlined, calm environment significantly boosts my productivity and lowers my stress levels.

If there was ever a programming language made for minimalists, Python fits the bill. Python was built around simplicity. Every element is treated as an object, which makes coding straightforward; developers are encouraged to write clean and easy to read code; and even the official Python principles carry an essence of serenity (the "Zen of Python"). Plus, it's the ultimate multi-purpose tool: it's not specialized and can be used to code just about anything you can think of.

With this book, you're getting everything you need to know about this simple but powerful language, all in one place. So what did you think about *Python 3: The Comprehensive Guide*? Your comments and suggestions are the most useful tools to help us make our books the best they can be. Please feel free to contact me and share any praise or criticism you may have.

Thank you for purchasing a book from Rheinwerk Publishing!

Rachel Gibson
Editor, Rheinwerk Publishing

rachelg@rheinwerk-publishing.com
www.rheinwerk-computing.com
Rheinwerk Publishing · Boston, MA

Contents

4   The Path to the First Program

5   Control Structures

6 Files

7 The Data Model

12 Sequential Data Types

15 Date and Time

16 Enumerations and Flags

Part III Advanced Programming Techniques

17 Functions

18 Modules and Packages

19 Object-Oriented Programming 341

20   Exception Handling

21   Generators and Iterators

22 Context Manager

23 Decorators

24 Annotations for Static Type Checking

25 Structural Pattern Matching

Part IV The Standard Library

28 Regular Expressions

29 Interface to Operating System and Runtime Environment

30   File System 569

33   Network Communication

34   Accessing Resources on the Internet

35 Email

39 Virtual Environments

40 Alternative Interpreters and Compilers

41   Graphical User Interfaces

42   Python as a Server-Side Programming Language on the Web: An Introduction to Django   893

43   Scientific Computing and Data Science   935

44   Inside Knowledge

45   From Python 2 to Python 3

Appendices

Chapter 1

Introduction

Welcome to our comprehensive guide to the Python programming language. Because you're holding our book in your hands at this moment, you've already made a decision: you want to program in Python. Whether you're a programming novice or already have programming experience, our goal throughout this book is to introduce you to the Python language itself and its related background, concepts, and tools. But first, we want to congratulate you on your decision: Python is simple, elegant, and powerful; in short, programming in Python is pure fun.

Before we take you into the wonderful world of Python, we'd like to briefly introduce this book. This will provide basic information on the way the book is structured and give advice on how to read it depending on your individual level of experience. We also outline the goals and concepts of the book so that you know upfront what to expect.

1.1 Why Did We Write This Book?

We, Peter Kaiser and Johannes Ernesti, became aware of the Python programming language by chance in 2002 and have stayed with it ever since. We were particularly impressed by Python's simplicity, flexibility, and elegance. With Python, an idea can be developed into a working program in a short time. Short, elegant, and productive programs for complex tasks can be written, not least with the help of the extensive standard library, which considerably simplifies everyday programming. In addition, Python code runs unmodified on all major operating systems and computer architectures. For these reasons, we now use Python almost exclusively for our own projects.

Our first encounter with Python also had its downsides: While there were many books on the subject, and documentation and tutorials could also be found on the internet, these texts were either very technical or only intended to get you started with the Python language. The abundance of tutorials makes it easy for a beginner to get a taste of the Python world and take their first steps. With good introductions, it's even possible to build up a sound basic knowledge within a few days, which makes it quite possible to get started quickly. But the transition to advanced programming is a bit of a problem: you can't get ahead with the introductory tutorials, and at the same time you're still not able to use the predominantly very technical documentation of Python for further education.

The aim of this book is to fill this gap. In addition to a comprehensive introduction to the Python language, it offers many advanced chapters that will ultimately enable you to use Python professionally. In addition, the book always provides reference points and terms you can use for further research—for example, in the Python documentation.

1.2   What Does This Book Provide?

This book will provide you with in-depth Python knowledge that will enable you to tackle professional tasks. For this purpose, the Python language is introduced comprehensively and systematically from the first simple program to complex language elements. The book focuses on the practical use of Python; it should enable you to understand and develop Python programs yourself as quickly as possible.

Apart from the introduction to the language itself, large parts of the Python standard library are discussed. This is a collection of tools available to the programmer to develop complex programs. The extensive standard library is one of Python's greatest strengths. Depending on the importance and complexity of the respective topic, concrete sample programs are created for demo purposes, which on the one hand train you in the use of the Python language and on the other hand can serve as a basis for your own projects. The source code of the sample programs is immediately executable and can be found in the online offerings for this book, which are described in Section 1.5.

Even if the practice-oriented introduction and practical work with Python are in the foreground, a lot of background knowledge about programming is imparted as well. We'll refrain from overly theoretical explanations.

1.3   Structure of the Book

This book is divided into five parts, the contents of which are briefly summarized ahead. Should you not be able to make any sense of the terms at the moment, don't worry; at this point, all the terms mentioned are for orientation purposes and will be explained in detail in the respective chapters.

Part I provides an introduction to working with Python. We attach importance to the fact that you can develop and test your own first programs at an early stage. We recommend that you apply the knowledge gained in this part to your own Python programs. We believe that as with programming in general, learning by doing is the most promising learning method in Python.

Part II covers in detail the data types available in Python. Among other things, numeric data types, sequential data types, mappings, sets, and data types for dates and times are covered.

Part III focuses on important concepts that make working with Python very enjoyable, but can also be completely new territory for the inexperienced reader. The major overarching themes are functions, modularization, and object orientation, which play a central role in Python. It also covers modern programming techniques such as exception handling, iterators and generators, and annotations.

Part IV focuses on Python's "batteries-included" philosophy: if possible, Python should have everything in the standard library that is required for developing your own applications. We'll discuss many of the included modules in this part, as well as one or two third-party modules.

It's worthwhile to browse and experiment a bit here to know later which tools of the standard library are available to solve a problem.

Finally, in **Part V**, we cover more advanced topics, such as the distribution of finished Python programs and modules to end users or other developers, the programming of graphical user interfaces with Tkinter and Qt, or an introduction to scientific computing with Python. Other central topics in this part are web development with the Django framework and an overview of alternative interpreters and compilers—for example, for interoperability with programs written in C or C++. At the end of the book, we discuss the differences between Python generations 2 and 3.

1.4   How Should You Read This Book?

This book is essentially aimed at two types of readers: those who want to get started programming with Python and ideally already have a basic knowledge of programming, and those who are already more or less familiar with the Python language and want to deepen their knowledge. For both types, this book is ideally suited, providing both a complete introduction to the programming language and a comprehensive reference for how to use Python in many areas.

In the following paragraphs, we recommend how to read this book—depending on your level of knowledge.

- As a beginner programmer or a newcomer with basic knowledge of another programming language, you should carefully work through the first two parts of the book. The introduction will enable you to write your own Python programs early on. Take this chance and program as much as you can while you are still reading the introduction. Be prepared for the demands to increase rapidly from Part II onward, as this book is designed to enable you to use Python professionally.

- If you're already good at programming and want to use this book as a transition from another language to Python, you should read the first three parts of the book to learn the syntax and concepts of Python and fill any gaps in your knowledge. Depending on your skill level, learning the Python language won't be difficult. Subsequently, you can deepen your knowledge in Part IV and in Part V.

- The last target group to be considered is experienced Python programmers. If working with Python is part of your everyday business, you can skim Part I, Part II, and, depending on your level of knowledge, Part III of the book. You'll be more interested in the two final parts, which serve as a helpful reference and provide further information and helpful advice on specific application topics.

1.5 Sample Programs

To supplement the printed examples, we provide additional examples that, for various reasons, are not included in this book. For example, this concerns more extensive programs, whose technical details we don't want to print for didactic reasons.

You can access this content through the online offering for this book at *www.rheinwerk-computing.com/5566*.

1.6 Preface To the First English Edition (2022)

This book is based on its German counterpart first published in 2008. Since then, the German version has been released in six editions, each of which has distinguished itself by its large scope and topicality. In the following, we provide an overview of how the German book has evolved since its initial publication. The most recent sixth edition served as the basis for the first English edition, which you are reading right now.

A lot has happened in the Python world since the first edition of this book was published in spring 2008. The 2.5 language version discussed at the time underwent a fundamental overhaul shortly afterward with the introduction of Python 3.0, in which the language was fundamentally modernized. To ease the transition, Python developers have also actively maintained and developed versions of Python 2 for years.

The transition period between Python generations was a tour de force: due to the intended breach of backward compatibility, important libraries of the Python ecosystem only gradually became compatible with Python 3. As of January 1, 2020, more than eleven years after the release of Python 3.0, support for Python 2 has officially ended, drawing a line under this chapter of Python's history.

The transition from Python 2 to Python 3 has also accompanied this book and sometimes presented the authors with great challenges. Keeping up with the rapid development of programming language, libraries, and operating systems wasn't always easy.

Nevertheless, we can sum up that the developments of the last few years have made the world of Python programming easier and more accessible. Installation instructions and explanations of the specifics of certain operating systems, which caused us great headaches in the first editions, have become almost superfluous due to the prevalence of package managers for Python today.

The book itself has also evolved technologically in the process: we have moved from an enclosed CD to an enclosed DVD and finally to online resources accompanying the book. What has remained is our constant ambition to further improve the book didactically and in terms of content and to keep it up-to-date. In particular, we also take into account the great feedback from our readers, for which we'd like to express our sincere thanks.

With this new English edition, we have thoroughly revised the entire book, polishing up dusty chapters and acknowledging current developments with new chapters. We have also carried out some restructuring with the aim of further improving comprehensibility and ease of reading. In addition to a number of smaller sections on various topics, this edition also includes a description of *Structural Pattern Matching* introduced in Python 3.10.

1.7 Acknowledgments

Now that we've presented the book to you and hopefully made it palatable, we'd like to thank those who accompanied us, supported us, and pushed us to write again and again during the preparation of the manuscript.

Our special thanks go to Dr. Ulrich Kaiser, whose constructive criticism and countless hours of proofreading significantly improved the quality of the book. Moreover, it's thanks to his initiative that we came to write a book at all. We're very happy that we could benefit from his expertise and experience.

In addition to technical correctness, the language used also contributes significantly to the quality of the book. For the German edition, we want to express our gratitude to Angelika Kaiser, who was able to transform even the most complicatedly convoluted sentence structures into clear, easily understandable formulations.

We also want to thank Herbert Ernesti for taking another look at the finished work as a whole and making many useful suggestions for improvement.

The beginner-friendliness of the explanations was experimentally tested by Anne Kaiser and found to be good; many thanks for this.

We'd like to thank Dr. Daniel Weiß, who designed an introductory lecture on Python based on this book for the first time in the winter term of 2015 at Karlsruhe Institute of Technology (KIT). His comments were able to significantly increase the quality of the book in some places.

Since 2016, the lecture has been offered every year and continues to be very popular. The didactic quality of the book in particular has benefited from the numerous discussions with Mr. Weiß and the students. Mr. Weiß himself writes about his experiences with Python:

Time and again, the idea of leveraging the benefits of Python in the context of teaching and scholarship was formulated by my colleagues. I was hesitant because I had no experience with Python at that time [2015]. After Johannes Ernesti agreed to support a lecture, Introduction to Python, I started to look into Python. This book was an ideal introduction. Interesting topics are also clearly presented in depth there. So learning Python was very easy.

Since 2016, we have offered the event at Karlsruhe Institute of Technology every summer term. There is tremendous interest among students, even beyond the Faculty of Mathematics. In spring 2020, the KIT Faculty of Mathematics awarded the course with the prize for particularly good teaching. Both the well-thought-out structure of this book and Johannes's collaboration in the conceptualization of the lecture have contributed decisively to this success. Having several years of experience with the Python programming language now, I continue to enjoy using the book.

We'd also like to thank all the staff at Rheinwerk Publishing who were involved in the creation of this book. We'd like to mention our German editors, Judith Stevens-Lemoine and Anne Scheibe, who helped us to find our way through the author jungle and gave us all the freedom we needed for our own ideas. For this English edition, we were supported by Rachel Gibson and Hareem Shafi, whom we would like to thank deeply.

Finally, we'd like to thank all readers of the previous German-language editions, whose countless emails with hints, comments, criticisms, and error corrections have been incorporated into this new edition.

Cologne and Dinslaken, August 2022

—**Johannes Ernesti**, *ernesti@python-book.com*
—**Peter Kaiser**, *kaiser@python-book.com*

Chapter 2
The Python Programming Language

In the previous chapter, we gave you an overview of this book and discussed the ways in which you should read it. Now we turn to the Python programming language, starting with an introduction to its history and basic concepts. The last two sections of this chapter cover the uses and applications of Python. You can think of this chapter as a narrative introduction to the topic that prepares for the technical entries that follow.

2.1 History, Concepts, and Areas of Application

In the following sections, we'll cover the history, concepts, and application of the Python programming language.

2.1.1 History and Origin

The Python programming language was developed in the early 1990s by *Guido van Rossum* at *the Centrum voor Wiskunde en Informatica* (CWI) in Amsterdam. It was originally intended as a scripting language for the Amoeba distributed operating system. The name Python doesn't refer to the snake family, but is a tribute to the British comedy group Monty Python.

Prior to Python, van Rossum had participated in the development of the ABC programming language, which was developed with the goal of being simple enough to be easily taught to an interested layperson with no programming experience. Van Rossum used the experience gained from positive and negative criticism of ABC to develop Python. He thus created a programming language that is powerful and at the same time easy to learn.

With version 3.0, which was released in December 2008, the language was revised from the ground up. The primary goal was to modernize the language while eliminating early design flaws that had to be kept in previous versions due to backward compatibility. With the official end of Python 2 support at the beginning of 2020, the long transition phase between language versions 2 and 3 has ended.

Meanwhile, Python has become one of the most popular programming languages and regularly takes top positions in popularity indexes of programming languages.[1]

---

1 For example, TIOBE, RedMonk, or PYPL.

In 2001, the nonprofit Python Software Foundation came into existence, which owns the rights to the Python code and promotes Python. For example, the Python Software Foundation organizes the PyCon conference, which is held annually in the US. Larger and smaller Python conferences are also held regularly in Europe.

2.1.2   Basic Concepts

Basically, Python is an imperative programming language, which combines other *programming paradigms* in it. For example, Python allows you to perform object-oriented and functional programming. If you can't make sense of these terms at the moment, don't worry; after all, you're supposed to learn programming with Python and thus the application of the different paradigms in this book.

Python is an interpreted programming language. Similar to Java or C#, Python has a *compiler* that reads the *source code* and generates a compilation, the so-called *byte code*. This byte code is then executed in a virtual machine, the *Python interpreter*.

Another concept Python has in common with Java, for example, is *platform independence*. A Python program is usually executable unmodified on all operating systems that are supported by the Python interpreter. This includes in particular the three major desktop operating systems: Windows, Linux, and macOS.

In addition to the interpreter and compiler, Python comes with an extensive *standard library*. This standard library allows the programmer to write concise programs in a short time that can perform very complex tasks. For example, Python provides extensive options for network communication or data storage. Because the standard library significantly enriches the programming options in Python, we'll give special attention to it in Part III and, to some extent, also in Part IV of this book.

A drawback of the ABC programming language, which van Rossum wanted to eliminate in the development of Python, was its lack of flexibility. A fundamental concept of Python is therefore to make it as easy as possible for the programmer to extend the standard library as desired. Python, as an interpreted programming language, itself offers only limited possibilities for low-level programming. However, program parts that are time-critical or require direct hardware access, can be implemented as *extensions* in C without any problem. This is made possible by the Python API.

Figure 2.1 contains an overview of the interacting concepts of Python described so far: A Python program is executed by the Python interpreter, which provides an extensive standard library that can be used by the program. In addition, the Python API allows an external C program to use or extend the interpreter.

As a last basic concept of Python, it should be mentioned that Python is subject to the PSF License.[2] This is a license for open-source software developed by the Python Software Foundation that is much less restrictive than the GNU General Public License, for

---

2 The license agreement is found at *https://docs.python.org/3/license.html*.

example. For instance, the PSF License allows the Python interpreter to be embedded in and shipped with applications at no license cost, without having to disclose the code or incur license fees. This policy also makes Python attractive for commercial applications.

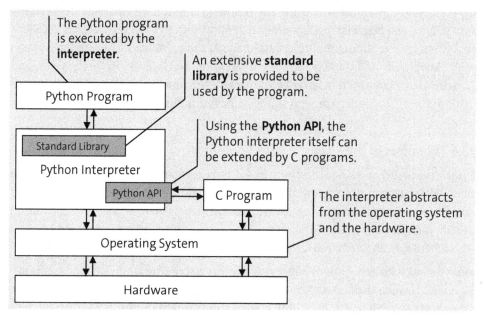

Figure 2.1 Overview of the Basic Concepts of Python

2.1.3   Possible Areas of Use and Strengths

Python's greatest strength is its *flexibility*. For example, Python can be used as a programming language for small and large applications, as a server-side programming language on the internet, or as a scripting language for a larger C or C++ application. Python is also spreading outside the traditional market, such as in the embedded sector. For example, Python interpreters exist for various smartphone or tablet systems or the Raspberry Pi.

Python is easy to learn and read due to its *simple syntax*. In addition, the automatic memory management and the extensive standard library allow programmers to tackle very complex problems with lean programs. For this reason, Python is also suitable for *rapid prototyping*. This type of development involves creating an executable prototype in the shortest possible time as a kind of feasibility study of a larger software program, which is then to be implemented later in another programming language. With the help of such a prototype, problems and design errors can be discovered even before the actual development of the software is started.

Another strength of Python is its *extensibility*, mentioned in the previous section. Because of this extensibility, Python developers can draw from a rich pool of third-party libraries. For example, there are connections to the most common graphical user interface (GUI) toolkits that enable the creation of Python programs with GUIs.

In recent years, Python has become the central programming language in emerging data science and artificial intelligence (AI) applications. Python provides an excellent ecosystem for scientific computing, data analysis, and visualization due to the NumPy, SciPy, Matplotlib, and pandas libraries. In addition, scikit-learn, PyTorch, Keras, and TensorFlow are large Python libraries for machine learning and deep learning that have made Python the standard programming language in this area.

2.1.4   Examples of Use

Python is widely known and used both by software companies and among scientists, as well as in the open-source community. Products written at least in part in Python range from web applications (e.g., Gmail, Google Maps, YouTube, Dropbox, Reddit) to development tools (e.g., Mercurial, SCons) to scientific platforms for machine learning (e.g., scikit-learn, PyTorch, TensorFlow) and human language processing (e.g., NLTK).

Many established applications support Python as a scripting language for extensions. Examples include the LibreOffice office suite as well as the Maya, Blender, ParaView, Cinema 4D, PaintShop Pro, and GIMP graphics and visualization applications.

A Python interface is provided for the Raspberry Pi single-board computer, and Python is recommended as a programming language.

In addition to those mentioned, there are countless other well-known applications that were written in Python or in whose environment Python is used. From the examples presented so far, you can see that Python is a popular, widely used, and modern programming language that's well worth learning.

2.2   Installing Python

You can download and install the latest version of Python from the official Python website at *http://www.python.org* as an installation file for your operating system.

However, in many cases it's more convenient to use a *Python distribution*. In addition to Python itself, such a distribution includes a large number of frequently used extensions and also provides tools for convenient postinstallation of additional modules.

In this book, we'll use the Python distribution called Anaconda, by Continuum Analytics. Almost everything we need for the sample programs is already included in the default installation of that distribution.

You can download the most recent version of Anaconda at *https://www.anaconda.com* for Windows, macOS, or Linux. Be aware that Anaconda does usually not install the most recent Python version by default due to its independent release cycle. For the purposes of this book we'll refer to version 2022-05 which defaults to Python 3.9. More recent interpreter versions can be installed via the Anaconda package repository as explained in Chapter 39, Section 39.2.

> **Note**
>
> On Linux and macOS, a Python interpreter is usually already preinstalled, which allows you to try out most of the sample programs in this book. However, this is often a relatively old version of Python, so newer language elements are not yet available. Also, you need to take care of installing the extensions needed in some chapters yourself, which occasionally causes problems.
>
> For these reasons, we recommend you also use Anaconda on Linux and macOS.

2.2.1   Installing Anaconda on Windows

Anaconda for Windows comes as an installer that can simply be executed. To install Anaconda, just click the **Next** button several times in the installation program and finally click **Install**.

After installation, you'll see a new group in the **Start** menu: **Anaconda3**. This group includes a number of programs, and at this point we're interested in the **Anaconda Prompt** or **Anaconda Powershell Prompt** entry.[3] If you click on this entry, a window with a black background opens where you can now start the interactive mode of Python using the `python` command and the graphical interactive development environment (IDLE) via the `idle` command.

Whenever a *shell* or the *command prompt* is referred to in later chapters, the Anaconda prompt is meant throughout.

2.2.2   Installing Anaconda on Linux

For Linux, Anaconda provides an installation script that you can run in a shell. To do this, in the directory where the installation file is located, you must run the following command without the leading dollar sign to start the installation process:

```
$ bash Anaconda3-2022.05-Linux-x86_64.sh
```

---

3 The difference is that the Anaconda prompt runs in the context of the classic Windows command prompt, while the Anaconda PowerShell prompt runs in the context of the modern Windows PowerShell. The use of Python is the same in both cases, so it's up to your personal preferences which of the two you want to use.

During the installation process, you can confirm almost all prompts with ⎡Enter⎤. At one point during the process, you need to confirm that you accept Anaconda's terms of use by answering "yes" to the corresponding question:

```
Do you approve the license terms? [yes|no]
>>> yes
```

At the end of the installation process, you'll be asked if you want to use the version of Python from the Anaconda distribution as your default Python. If this is the case, you should answer the question with "yes".

```
Do you wish the installer to prepend the Anaconda3 install location
to PATH in your /home/your_user/.bashrc ? [yes|no]
[no] >>> yes
```

If you don't enter "yes" here, you'll always have to make sure that the version of Anaconda gets started before you start Python in a shell:

```
$ export PATH=/home/your_user/anaconda3/bin:$PATH
```

After installing Anaconda, you should start interactive mode or IDLE from a shell using the python or idle3 commands.

> **Note**
>
> If you use the Python version included in your Linux distribution, you should be aware that many distributions require you to start Python 3.x via a different command than python, such as python3, because often Python 2.x and 3.x are installed in parallel.

2.2.3   Installing Anaconda on macOS

On macOS, you can choose between a graphical installer and installation via the command line. If you decide to use the command line, you can perform all the steps in the same way as described in the previous section for Linux, entering the respective commands in a terminal.

In both cases, once the installation is complete, you can use Python in a terminal via python and idle3.

> **Note**
>
> If you forget the 3 at the end of idle3, the IDLE version that is preinstalled on macOS will be started. For this reason, you should check if IDLE outputs Anaconda directly in the first line.

2.3   Installing Third-Party Modules

Python comes with many modules for various use cases in the default installation. This collection is complemented by a large number of available third-party modules, which you must postinstall before they can be used. The easiest way to do that is usually via the pip or conda package manager. For example, you can use

```
$ pip install pandas
```

or

```
$ conda install pandas
```

to install the pandas module, which allows you to process tabular data, as you'll see in Chapter 43, Section 43.4.

Details on how to use conda and pip can be found in Chapter 38, Section 38.4.

2.4   Using Python

Every installation of Python includes two important components besides the Python interpreter itself—namely, the interactive mode and IDLE.

In the *interactive mode*, also referred to as the *Python shell*, individual program lines can be entered and the results viewed directly. The interactive mode is thus interesting for learning the Python language, among other things, and is therefore used frequently in this book.

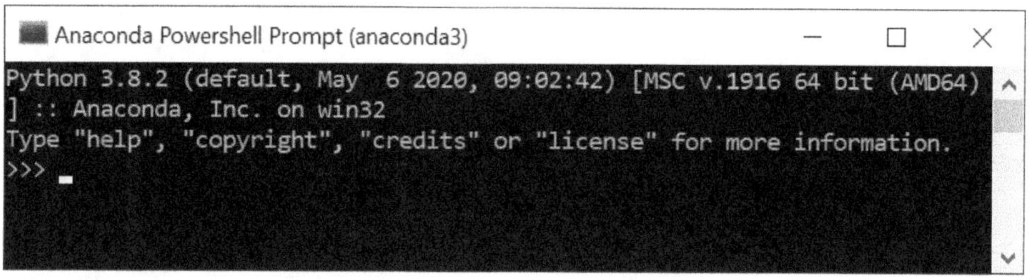

Figure 2.2 Python in Interactive Mode (Python Shell)

IDLE is a rudimentary Python development environment with a graphical user interface. When IDLE is started, initially only a window containing a Python shell opens. In addition, a new Python program file can be created and edited via the **File · New Window** menu item. After the program file has been saved, it can be executed via the **Run · Run Module** menu item in the Python shell of IDLE. Aside from that, IDLE provides the programmer with a couple of comfort functions, such as the colored highlighting of code elements (*syntax highlighting*) and automatic code completion.

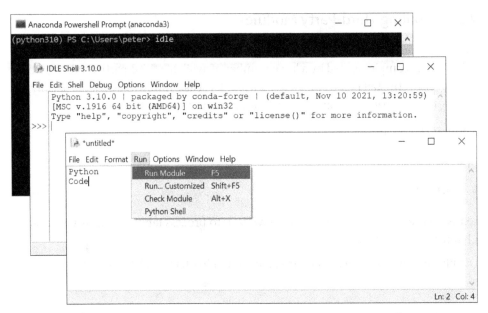

Figure 2.3 Python IDLE

If you aren't satisfied with IDLE, refer to the appendix of this book for an overview of the most common Python development environments.

PART I
Getting Started with Python

In the first part of this book, we'll provide an overview of elementary concepts of Python, which are also important for experienced Python developers. In many cases throughout these chapters, we give high-level application examples that don't go into detail so that we can cover a wider range of topics.

Chapter 3
Getting Started with the Interactive Mode

When you start the Python interpreter without any arguments, you enter the so-called *interactive mode*. This mode enables programmers to send commands directly to the interpreter without having to create a program first. The interactive mode is often used to quickly try out or test something. However, it's not suitable for writing real programs. Nevertheless, we would like to start here with the interactive mode, as it allows you to get started with the Python language quickly and easily.

This section is intended to familiarize you with some basics that are important for understanding the subsequent chapters. It's best to implement the examples in this chapter on your computer in parallel with your reading.

As a greeting, the interpreter outputs a few lines that you should now have in front of you in a form similar to the following:

```
Python 3.11.0b1 (main, Jun 20 2022, 21:48:01) [Clang 13.1.6 (clang-1316.0.21.2.5)]
on darwin
Type "help", "copyright", "credits" or "license" for more information.
>>>
```

Next to the prompt (>>>), you can enter any Python code.

As for the operation of the interactive mode, it should be mentioned that it has a history function. This means that you can use the [Up] and [Down] arrow keys to retrieve old inputs and don't need to reenter them. It's also possible to edit the inputs selected via the history.

Let's start by introducing some basic data types. For the time being, we'll restrict ourselves to integers, floats, character strings, lists, and dictionaries. There are certain rules according to which you have to write instances of these data types—for example, a numeric value or a character string—so that they can be recognized by the interpreter. Such a notation is referred to as a *literal*.

3.1 Integers

As a first and very simple example, we'll generate an integer in interactive mode. The interpreter responds by outputting its value:

```
>>> -9
-9
>>> 1139
1139
>>> +12
12
```

The literal for an integer consists of the digits 0 to 9. In addition, you can prefix a positive or negative sign. An unsigned number is always assumed to be positive.

It is possible to combine several integers into one arithmetic expression using arithmetic operators such as +, -, *, or /. In this case, the interpreter responds with the value of the expression:

```
>>> 5 + 9
14
```

As you can see, Python can be used quite intuitively as a kind of calculator. The next example is a bit more complex and includes several interlinked arithmetic operations:

```
>>> (21 - 3) * 9 + 6
168
```

Here you can see that the interpreter applies the usual mathematical calculation laws and outputs the expected result. The division result of two integers is not necessarily an integer again, which is why the division operator always returns the result as a float:

```
>>> 3/2
1.5
>>> 2/3
0.6666666666666666
>>> 4/4
1.0
```

> **Note**
>
> This feature distinguishes Python from many other programming languages that perform an integer division and return an integer as the result when two integers are divided. This is also the default behavior in Python 2.
>
> Integer division may well be a desired behavior, but it often causes confusion, especially for programming beginners, and was therefore dropped in Python 3. If you want to perform integer division in Python 3, you must use the // operator:
>
> ```
> >>> 3//2
> 1
> >>> 2//3
> 0
> ```

3.2 Floats

The literal for a float consists of a integer part, a decimal point, and a fractional part. As with integers, it's possible to specify a sign:

```
>>> 0.5
0.5
>>> -123.456
-123.456
>>> +1.337
1.337
```

Note that the decimal separator must be a period. A notation with a comma is not permitted. Floats can be used in terms just as intuitively as integers:

```
>>> 1.5 / 2.1
0.7142857142857143
```

It's also possible to specify a float in scientific notation:

```
>>> 12.345e3
12345.0
>>> 12.345E3
12345.0
```

An expression like XeY represents the number $X \cdot 10^Y$. In the preceeding example it evaluates to $12.345 \cdot 10^3$.

In Part II of the book, we'll return to these basic data types and cover them in greater detail. Next we'll look at another important data type: character strings.

3.3 Character Strings

In addition to numbers, *character strings*, also referred to as *strings*, are extremely important in almost every real-world program. Strings allow text to be read, saved, edited, or output by the user.

To create a string, the associated text is written in double quotation marks:

```
>>> "Hello World"
'Hello World'
>>> "abc123"
'abc123'
```

The single quotes that the interpreter uses to output the value of a string are an equivalent notation to the double quotes that we use and that you may also use:

```
>>> 'Hello World'
'Hello World'
```

Similar to integers and floats, you can also use operators for strings. For example, the + operator joins two strings:

```
>>> "Hello" + " " + "World"
'Hello World'
```

The two different notations for strings are useful, for example, when single or double quotation marks are to be included as characters in a string:

```
>>> 'He says "Hello"'
'He says "Hello"'
>>> "He says 'Hello'"
"He says 'Hello'"
```

3.4   Lists

Let's now turn to lists. A list is an ordered collection of elements of any data type. To create a list, the literals of the values it should contain are written in square brackets separated by commas:

```
>>> [1,2,3]
[1, 2, 3]
>>> ["This", "is", "a", "list"]
['This', 'is', 'a', 'list']
```

In addition, list elements may be defined in form of expressions:

```
>>> [-7 / 4, 5 * 3]
[-1.75, 15]
```

The elements of a list do not all have to be of the same type and in particular can be lists themselves, as the following example shows:

```
>>> ["Python", 1, 2, -7 / 4, [1,2,3]]
['Python', 1, 2, -1.75, [1, 2, 3]]
```

Similar to strings, lists can be extended by elements with the + operator; + forms the concatenation of two lists.

```
>>> [1,2,3] + ["Python", "is", "great"]
[1, 2, 3, 'Python', 'is', 'great']
```

List elements are numbered consecutively starting from 0 and may be accessed using the [] operator.

```
>>> x = ["Python", "is", "great"]
>>> x[0]
'Python'
>>> x[1]
'is'
>>> x[2]
'great'
```

3.5 Dictionaries

The fifth and last data type we want to introduce at this point is the *dictionary*. A dictionary stores mappings of keys to values. To create a dictionary, the key-value pairs are written in curly brackets separated by commas. There's a colon between a key and the corresponding value:

```
>>> d = {"key1": "value1", "key2": "value2"}
```

You can access an underlying value via a key. For this purpose, square brackets are used as in lists:

```
>>> d["key1"]
'value1'
>>> d["key2"]
'value2'
```

You can also use this access operation to modify values or enter new key-value pairs into the dictionary:

```
>>> d["key2"] = "value2.1"
>>> d["key2"]
'value2.1'
>>> d["key3"] = "value3"
>>> d["key3"]
'value3'
>>> d
{'key1': 'value1', 'key2': 'value2.1', 'key3': 'value3'}
```

Both keys and values can have different data types than the strings used at this point. We'll come back to that in due course.

We'll base our subsequent descriptions on the basic presentation of the five data types presented in the previous sections—integer, float, string, list, and dictionary—until we reach Part II of the book, where we'll go into greater detail about all the data types built into Python.

3.6 Variables

In Python, you can assign a name to a value like a number or a string. For this purpose, the name is written on the left and the corresponding literal on the right of an equal sign. Such an operation is referred to as an *assignment*.

```
>>> name = 0.5
>>> var123 = 12
>>> string = "Hello World!"
>>> list = [1,2,3]
```

The values associated with the names can be output later or used in calculations by entering the name instead of the respective value:

```
>>> name
0.5
>>> 2 * name
1.0
>>> (var123 + var123) / 3
8.0
>>> var123 + name
12.5
```

It's also possible to assign a name to the value of any expression, for example to the result of a calculation:

```
>>> a = 1 + 2
>>> b = var123 / 4
```

The part to the right of the equal sign is always evaluated first. For example, the instruction a = 1 + 2 always determines the result of 1 + 2 before assigning a name to the resulting value.

3.6.1 The Special Meaning of the Underscore

In interactive mode, the underscore (_) can always be used to access the last value output. In this way, for example, a previously output intermediate result can be picked up and used in a further calculation:

```
>>> 1 + 7
8
>>> _
8
>>> _ * 3
24
```

Note that the underscore takes on this special role exclusively in interactive mode and not in regular Python programs, as we'll describe later.

3.6.2   Identifiers

A *variable name*, also called an *identifier*, may consist of almost any letters and the underscore. After at least one leading letter or underscore, digits may also be used.[1]

> **Note**
>
> When using variables, note that Python is *case-sensitive*. This means that a distinction is made between upper and lower case. In practice, this means that the identifiers otto and Otto are not identical and thus can be associated with two different values.

Also note that umlauts and characters of international alphabets are allowed, as the following example shows:

```
>>> äöüßéè = 123
>>> äöüßéè
123
```

Certain keywords[2] are reserved in Python for the language itself and may not be used as identifiers. The appendix of this book provides an overview of all reserved words in Python.

3.7   Logical Expressions

In addition to arithmetic operators, there's a second set of operators that allow comparing values such as numbers:

```
>>> 3 < 4
True
```

Here we test if 3 is smaller than 4. The interpreter responds to such comparisons with a *truth value*—that is, True or False. A comparison is performed using a so-called relational operator—in this case, <.

Table 3.1 contains a list of the relational operators.

---

1 Frequently, variables that have only local and short-term significance are given a short, often one-letter name. You should note that the letters *o, O, I*, and *l* look like numbers in some fonts and are therefore unsuitable for a variable name.

2 In programming, a *keyword* is a word that carries a certain meaning; for example, it controls the program flow. In Python, for example, the if and for keywords can be used to initiate a conditional statement and a loop, respectively.

Comparison	Meaning
3 == 4	Is 3 equal to 4? Note the double equal sign that distinguishes the comparison from an assignment.
3 != 4	Is 3 different from 4?
3 < 4	Is 3 less than 4?
3 > 4	Is 3 greater than 4?
3 <= 4	Is 3 less than or equal to 4?
3 >= 4	Is 3 greater than or equal to 4?

Table 3.1 Comparisons in Python

In general, any arithmetic expression can be used for 3 and 4. When you combine two arithmetic expressions using one of the operators just described, you create a logical expression:

```
(a - 7) < (b * b + 6.5)
```

In addition to the arithmetic operators already introduced, there are three logical operators you can use to change the result of a logical expression or to link two logical expressions.

The not operator inverts the result of a comparison, thus turning True into False and False into True. Consequently, the expression not (3 < 4) is the same as 3 >= 4:

```
>>> not (3 < 4)
False
>>> 3 >= 4
False
>>> not (4 < 3)
True
>>> 4 >= 3
True
```

The and operator gets two logical expressions as operands and evaluates to True if and only if both the first and the second expression have evaluated to True. It thus corresponds to the word *and* in natural language that links two parts of a sentence. In the example, this may look as follows:

```
>>> (3 < 4) and (5 < 6)
True
>>> (3 < 4) and (4 < 3)
False
```

The or operator gets two logical expressions as operands and evaluates to False only if both the first expression and the second one evaluated to False. Thus, the operator returns True if at least one of its operands has returned True:

```
>>> (3 < 4) or (5 < 6)
True
>>> (3 < 4) or (4 < 3)
True
>>> (5 > 6) or (4 < 3)
False
```

For the sake of simplicity, we have only compared figures here. Of course, such a comparison only makes sense when more complex arithmetic expressions are compared. With the relational operators and the three Boolean operators, not, and, and or, you can already create very complex comparisons.

> **Note**
>
> Note that brackets have been added to all examples only for the purpose of clarity as priority rules among the operators make brackets superfluous. This means that every example presented here would work as expected even without brackets. Nevertheless, it makes sense, especially at the beginning, to make the affiliations visually unambiguous by placing brackets around them. A table with the priority rules for operators, the so-called operator ranking, can be found in Chapter 10, Section 10.2.

3.8 Functions and Methods

In this section, we'll provide a basic overview of functions and some concepts of object-oriented programming. In this regard, we'll restrict ourselves to the aspects needed in the following chapters. Both topics will again be dealt with in detail in Chapter 17 and in Chapter 19, respectively.

3.8.1 Functions

In Python, parts of a program can be encapsulated in functions and then executed by means of a function call. The goal of this approach is to avoid redundancy in the source code. Functionality that is needed frequently should always be implemented only once as a function and then used as such in the remaining program. In addition, using functions can improve the readability and maintainability of the source code as code parts that belong together are encapsulated into units.

Python provides a set of *built-in functions* a programmer can use at any time. As an example, this section uses the max built-in function, which determines the largest element of a list:

```
>>> max([1,5,2,7,9,3])
9
```

A function is called by writing the function name followed by the function parameters in parentheses. In the example, the max function expects exactly one parameter—namely, a list of values to be considered. The result of the calculation is returned as the return value of the function. You can imagine that the function call in the source code is replaced by the return value.

There is a variant of the max function that determines the largest parameter passed to it instead of the largest element of a list. To pass multiple parameters to a function, they are written in the parentheses and separated by commas when the function is called:

```
>>> max(1,5,3)
5
```

Of course, you can define your own functions in Python, but at this point it's sufficient to know how to use already existing functions. In Chapter 17, we'll talk about functions again in detail.

3.8.2   Methods

Creating a value of a particular data type, such as creating an integer via its literal, is referred to as *instantiating* and the resulting value is called an *instance*. For example, 2 is an instance of the integer data type, while [4,5,6] is an instance of the list data type. The data type of an instance determines which data is stored as well as a set of operations that can be performed on this data. Some of these operations are represented by operators; for example, the float data type provides the + operator for adding two floats. For the simple numeric data types, a few operators are sufficient to work with them. With more complex data types, such as lists, a whole series of operations is conceivable that cannot be represented by operators alone. For such cases, data types can define *methods*. These are functions executed in the context of a specific instance.

The list data type, for example, provides a sort method, which can be used to sort a list. To call a method, an instance is specified, either by a literal or a reference, followed by a period and the method call, which is structured like a function call:

```
>>> list = [2,7,3,2,7,8,4,2,5]
>>> list.sort()
>>> list
[2, 2, 2, 3, 4, 5, 7, 7, 8]
```

Another example is provided by the count method of the string data type, which counts how often a character occurs in a string:

```
>>> "Hello World".count("l")
3
```

The knowledge of functions and methods acquired here will be further deepened in the course of this book. In the following sections, we'll discuss for starters what is probably the most important function built into Python: print.

3.9   Screen Outputs

Although we'll often draw on the interactive mode, our goal is to write real Python programs as quickly as possible. It's a special feature of the interactive mode that the value of an entered expression is automatically output. In a normal program, on the other hand, screen outputs must be generated by the programmer explicitly. To output the value of a variable, Python uses the print function:

```
>>> print(1.2)
1.2
```

Note that while print outputs *values*, the automatic output of the interactive mode outputs *representations*, i.e. predominantly literals. For example, automatic output writes the value of a string in quotation marks while print doesn't:

```
>>> "Hello World"
'Hello World'
>>> print("Hello World")
Hello World
```

Here too, it's possible to use a variable name instead of a constant value without any problem:

```
>>> var = 9
>>> print(var)
9
```

Alternatively, you can output the result of an expression directly:

```
>>> print(-3 * 4)
-12
```

Using print also allows for outputting multiple variables or constants on one line. For this purpose, the values are separated by commas. Each comma is replaced by a space character in the output:

```
>>> print(-3, 12, "Python rocks")
-3 12 Python rocks
```

This is especially helpful if you want to output not only individual values, but also a short explanatory text about them. You can achieve something like this in the following way:

```
>>> var = 9
>>> print("The magic number is:", var)
The magic number is: 9
```

Finally, print prints a line feed after each output, so consecutive print calls result in multiple output lines.

Note

In Python 2, screen output was generated using the print keyword rather than the print function:

```
>>> print "This", "is", "Python", 2
This is Python 2
```

In most cases, the missing parentheses are the only difference. You can find more information about the differences between Python 2 and 3 in Chapter 45.

3.10   Modules

A decisive advantage of Python besides the simple and flexible programming language itself is the large amount of shipped *modules*, which in their entirety form the *standard library*.

Such modules often serve as a purposeful collection of additional functionality. There is, for example, the pprint module (for *pretty print*), which provides the pprint function. This function enables you to output instances of complex data types clearly formatted on the screen. It's thus an alternative to the built-in print function when only a single instance is to be output. Before you can use a module, you must include it using the import keyword:

```
>>> import pprint
```

Now the functions and constants available in pprint can be used in the subsequent program. In this case, we call the function pprint.pprint to clearly output a more extensive dictionary:

```
>>> d = {"Python is": ["awesome", "brilliant", "mega cool", "simple and
exciting"], "Python has": ["lots of modules", "always the right argument", "a
nicely formatted screen output"]}
>>> pprint.pprint(d)
{'Python has': ['lots of modules',
                'always the right argument',
                'a nicely formatted screen output'],
 'Python is': ['awesome', 'brilliant', 'mega cool', 'simple and exciting']}
```

For comparison, here is the unformatted output using the built-in print function:

```
>>> print(d)
{'Python is': ['awesome', 'brilliant', 'mega cool', 'simple and exciting'],
'Python has': ['lots of modules', 'always the right argument', 'a nicely
formatted screen output']}
```

For more information about the pprint module, see Chapter 27, Section 27.1. In Chapter 18, where we'll look more closely at the way the import keyword works. Much of the book is also devoted to the standard library, as well as third-party modules and libraries that usefully augment the Python language scope.

Chapter 4
The Path to the First Program

Now that we've covered some basic elements of the Python language in interactive mode, we want to transfer this knowledge to an actual program. In contrast to the interactive mode, which allows mutual interaction between the programmer and interpreter, the source code of a program is written into a file. This is read in and executed in its entirety by the interpreter.

In the following sections, you'll learn about the basic structures of a Python program and write your first simple sample program.

4.1 Typing, Compiling, and Testing

This section describes the workflows required to create and run a Python program. More generally, in much of the book we'll only write console applications, so we'll prepare you for that. A *console application* has a purely text-based interface to the user and runs in the *console* (or *shell*) of the respective operating system. For most examples and also for many real-world use cases, such a text-based interface is sufficient.[1]

Basically, a Python program consists of one or multiple program files. These program files use the *.py* file extension and contain the Python source code. The files are simple text files. Consequently, program files can be edited with a regular text editor.

Once a program file has been written, the next step is to execute it. If you use IDLE, the program file can be conveniently run via the **Run • Run Module** menu item. If you use an editor that doesn't support a comparable function, you must switch to the directory of the program file in a command line and—depending on your operating system—execute various commands.

4.1.1 Windows

On Windows, you must go to the directory where the program file is located and start the Python interpreter, using the `python` command followed by the name of the program file to be run.[2]

---

1 Of course, Python also allows for programming GUIs. This will be described in Chapter 41.
2 In older Windows versions, you can find the console via **Start • Programs • Accessories • Command Prompt**. In more recent versions of Windows, you must launch PowerShell.

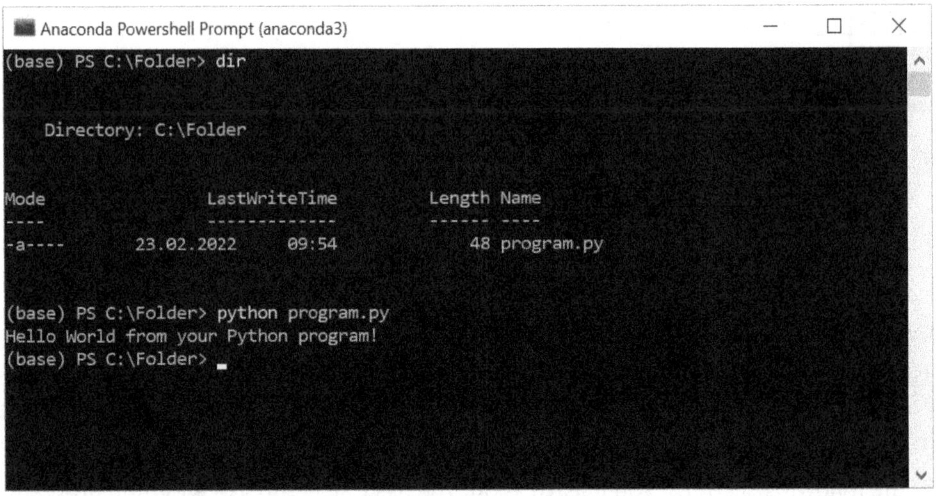

Figure 4.1 Running a Python Program in Windows

"Hello World from your python program!" is an output of the Python program in the *program.py* file, which proves that the Python program was actually executed.

> **Note**
>
> In Windows, it's also possible to execute a Python program by double-clicking on the respective program file. But the drawback of this is that the console window closes immediately after the program is terminated and you can't see the output of the program.

4.1.2   Linux and macOS

On Unix-like operating systems such as Linux or macOS, you also go to the directory where the program file is located and then start the Python interpreter, using the `python` command followed by the name of the program file to be run. In the following example, the program file program.py is run on Linux, which is located in the */home/user/folder* directory:

```
user@HOST ~ $ cd folder
user@HOST ~/folder $ python program.py
This is what your Python program writes to you
```

Please read the note in Chapter 2, Section 2.2, which states that the command you use to start Python may differ from the `python` command shown here, depending on the distribution.

4.1.3 Shebang

On a Unix-like operating system such as Linux, Python program files can be made directly executable using a *shebang* (#!), also referred to as a *magic line*. For this purpose, the first line of the program file must usually read as follows:

```
#!/usr/bin/python
```

In this case, the operating system is encouraged to always run this program file using the Python interpreter. On other operating systems, such as Windows, the shebang line is ignored.

Note that the Python interpreter might be installed on your system in a different directory than the one specified here. In general, therefore, the following shebang line is better as it's independent of the actual installation location of Python:

```
#!/usr/bin/env python
```

Further information on the interplay between Anaconda virtual environments and the shebang is provided in Chapter 39, Section 39.2. Also note that the executable flag of the program file must be set before the file is actually executable. This can be done using the following command:

```
chmod +x filename
```

To keep a high degree of clarity, the examples shown in this book don't include a shebang line. However, this doesn't explicitly mean that using a shebang line should be avoided.

4.1.4 Internal Processes

Up to this point, you should have a rough idea of what Python is all about and where the strengths of this programming language can be found. We have also provided the basic knowledge of creating and running a Python program file. But in the previous sections, terms like *compiler* or *interpreter* have been used without any further explanation. In this section, therefore, we'll look at the internal operations that occur when a Python program file is executed. Figure 4.2 illustrates what happens when a program file named *program.py* is executed.

When the program.py program file is executed, as described at the beginning of the chapter, it first passes through the *compiler*, a program that translates from one formal language to another. In the case of Python, the compiler translates from the Python language to *byte code*. The compiler is free to keep the generated byte code in memory or to save it as *program.pyc* on the hard drive.

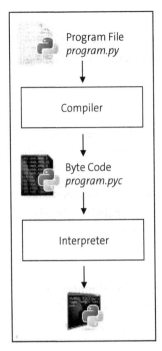

Figure 4.2 Compiling and Interpreting a Program File

Note that the byte code generated by the compiler can't be executed directly on the processor, unlike C or C++ compilations, for example. To run the byte code, another abstraction layer, the *interpreter*, is needed. The interpreter—often referred to as a *virtual machine*—reads the byte code generated by the compiler and executes it.

This principle of an interpreted programming language has several advantages. For example, the same Python code can be run unmodified on all platforms for which a Python interpreter is available. However, programs of interpreted programming languages usually run slower than a comparable C program executed directly on the processor because of the intermediary interpreter.[3]

4.2   Basic Structure of a Python Program

To give you a feel for the Python language, we'll first provide an overview of its syntax. The word *syntax* comes from the Greek and means "sentence structure." The syntax of a programming language is the complete description of permitted and forbidden constructions. The syntax is defined by a grammar that must be adhered to by the programmer. If he or she doesn't do that, the well-known *syntax error* will be triggered.

---

3 This statement does not necessarily hold true if the interpreter performs runtime optimization such as *just-in-time compilation*. Recent versions of CPython and the alternative interpreter *PyPy* (Chapter 38, Section 38.1) perform runtime optimization to accelerate program execution.

Python gives a programmer very precise instructions on how to structure the source code. Although experienced programmers may see this as a limitation, this feature benefits novice programmers in particular, because unstructured and cluttered code is one of the biggest sources of errors in programming.

Basically, a Python program consists of individual *statements*, which in the simplest case take up exactly one line in the source code. For example, the following statement prints text on the screen:

```
print("Hello World")
```

Some statements can be divided into a *statement header* and a *statement body*, where the body can contain further statements:

```
Statement header:
    Statement
    ...
    Statement
```

In a real Python program, this may look something like this:

```
if x > 10:
    print("x is greater than 10")
    print("Second line!")
```

The affiliation of the body to the header is specified in Python by a colon at the end of the statement header and by a deeper indentation of the statement body. Indentation can be done using both tabs and spaces, though you are well advised not to mix the two. We recommend an indentation depth of four spaces each.

Python differs here from many common programming languages, where the mapping of the statement header and statement body is achieved by curly brackets or keywords like *begin* and *end*.

Note

A program in which both spaces and tabs have been used can be compiled by the Python compiler without difficulty as each tab is internally replaced by eight spaces. However, this can cause hard-to-find errors because many editors use a tab width of four spaces by default. This makes certain sections of source code appear to be equally indented when in fact they are not.

Please set your editor to automatically replace each tab with spaces, or use only spaces to indent your code.

You may wonder now how statements that run over several lines are compatible with the interactive mode, in which only one line can be edited at a time. Well, in general, we'll try to avoid the interactive mode when a code sample is several lines long. Nevertheless, the question is justified. The answer is that the statements are entered quite intuitively line by line. When the interpreter detects that an instruction isn't yet complete, it changes the prompt from >>> to .... Let's enter the previous example into the interactive mode:

```
>>> x = 123
>>> if x > 10:
...     print("The interpreter is doing a good job")
...     print("Second line!")
...
The interpreter is doing a good job
Second line!
>>>
```

Note that you have to consider the current indentation depth, even if a line starts with .... Furthermore, the interpreter can't automatically detect the end of the statement body as it can contain any number of statements. For this reason, a statement body in interactive mode must be terminated by pressing the ⌷Enter⌷ key.

4.2.1   Wrapping Long Lines

Basically, source code lines can have any length. However, many programmers limit the length of their source code lines so that, for example, several source code files fit side by side on the screen or the code can be read comfortably on devices with a fixed line width. Common maximum line lengths are 80 or 120 characters. Within parentheses, you may wrap source code any way you like:

```
>>> var = (
... 10
... +
... 10
... )
>>> var
20
```

However, in many other places where parentheses are not permitted you are bound by Python's strict syntactic rules. By using the backslash notation, it's possible to break source code into a new line at almost any position:

```
>>> var \
... = \
... 10
>>> var
10
```

In general, a backslash can be placed anywhere a space could have been. Therefore, a backslash within a string is also possible:

```
>>> "Hello \
... World"
'Hello World'
```

Note, however, that indenting the wrapped part of the string will write spaces into the string. For this reason, you should prefer the following variant of writing a string across multiple lines:

```
>>> "Hello " \
... "World"
'Hello World'
```

4.2.2   Joining Multiple Lines

Just as you wrap a single-line statement to multiple lines using the backslash, you can combine multiple single-line statements into one line. For this purpose, the statements are separated from each other by a semicolon:

```
>>> print("Hello"); print("World")
Hello
World
```

Statements consisting of a statement header and a statement body can also be put on one line without using a semicolon, provided that the statement body itself doesn't consist of more than one line:

```
>>> x = True
>>> if x: print("Hello World")
...
Hello World
```

If the statement body is several lines long, they can be combined by a semicolon:

```
>>> x = True
>>> if x: print("Hello"); print("World")
...
Hello
World
```

All statements joined by a semicolon are treated as if they were equally indented. A colon alone increases the indentation depth. For this reason, in the preceding example, there's no way to write a statement on the same line that's no longer in the body of the if statement.

> **Note**
>
> Using the backslash and especially the semicolon quickly results in unreadable code. Therefore, you should use both notations only if you think it's conducive to readability and clarity.

4.3   The First Program

As an introduction to programming with Python, we'll now create a small sample program—the Guessing Numbers game. The idea of the game is as follows: The player should guess a number specified in the program. For this purpose, they can make as many attempts as they like. After each attempt, the program informs them whether the guessed number was too big, too small, or exactly right. Once the player guesses the number, the program outputs the number of attempts and exits. From the player's point of view, the whole thing should look like this:

```
Guess: 42
Too small
Guess: 10000
Too big
Guess: 999
Too small
Guess: 1337
Great, it took you only 4 attempts!
```

Let's now switch from the flow protocol to the actual implementation in Python.

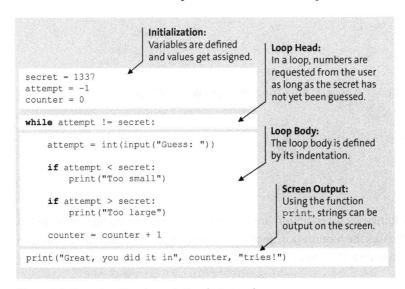

Figure 4.3 Guessing Numbers: A Simple Example

The highlighted areas of the program are discussed again in detail ahead.

4.3.1   Initialization

During initialization, the variables needed for the game are created. Python distinguishes among different data types, such as strings, integers, or floats. The type of a variable is determined at program runtime based on the value assigned to it, so it's not necessary to specify a data type explicitly. A variable can change its type in the course of the program.

In our game, variables for the searched number (secret), the user input (attempt), and the attempt counter (counter) are created and given initial values. The fact that attempt and secret have different values at the beginning of the program ensures that the loop will actually start.

4.3.2   Loop Header

A while loop is initiated. A while loop runs as long as the condition named in the loop header (attempt != secret) is met—in this case, until the attempt and secret variables have the same value. From the user's perspective, this means that the loop runs until the user input matches the number to be guessed.

The loop body belonging to the loop header can be recognized by the fact that the following lines have been indented one step further. As soon as the indentation moves one step to the left again, the loop body ends.

4.3.3   Loop Body

In the first line of the loop body, a number entered by the player is read and stored in the attempt variable. The user's input is read using input("Guess: ") and converted to an integer with int. This conversion is important because user input is generally read as a string. In our case, however, we want to continue using the input as a number. The string "Guess: " is output before the input and is used to prompt the user to enter the number.

After reading, it's checked individually whether the entered number attempt is larger or smaller than the searched number secret, and a corresponding message is output via print. Finally, the attempt counter counter is increased by one.

After the attempt counter is incremented, the loop body ends because the next line is no longer indented below the loop header.

4.3.4   Screen Output

The last program line is not part of the loop body. This means that it's not executed until the loop is completely run—that is, until the game is won. In this case, a success message and the number of attempts required are output. The game is finished.

Now create your first Python program by writing the program code to a file called *game.py* and running it. Change the start value of secret, and play the game.

4.4   Comments

You can certainly imagine that the goal is not to write programs that would fit on a postcard. Over time, the source code of your programs will become more extensive and complex. At some point, the time is reached when mere memory training is no longer sufficient to keep track of things. That's the point when comments come into play, at the latest.

A *comment* is a small piece of text that explains a certain part of the source code to point out problems, open tasks, or similar things. A comment is ignored by the interpreter, so it doesn't change the flow of the program.

The easiest way to write a comment is to use the *line comment*. This type of comment starts with the # character and ends with the end of the line:

```
# An example with comments
print("Hello world!") # Simple hello world output
```

For longer comments, a *block comment* is a good choice. A block comment begins and ends with three consecutive quotation marks:[4]

```
""" This is a block comment,
it can extend over several lines. """
```

Comments should only be used if they contribute to the understanding of the source code or contain valuable information. Commenting on every line, no matter how unimportant, leads to not seeing the forest for the trees.

4.5   In Case of Error

Perhaps you've already played with the sample program from Section 4.3 and come across the following or similar output from the interpreter:

---

4 As a matter of fact, this notation doesn't generate a block comment, but a multiline string—but such a string is also suitable for "commenting out" larger sections of source code.

```
File "hello_world.py", line 10
  if attempt < secret
                     ^
SyntaxError: expected ':'
```

This is an error message that indicates a syntax error in the program. Can you tell what exactly the error is in this case? Correct: the colon at the end of the line is missing.

Python provides important information when outputting an error message, which is helpful in troubleshooting:

- The first line of the error message indicates in which line and within which file the error occurred. In this case, it's line 8 in the *hello_world.py* file.

- The middle part shows the affected section of the source code, with the exact location to which the message refers marked with a small arrow. It's important that this is the place where the interpreter could first detect the error. This is not necessarily the same as where the mistake was made.

- The last line specifies the type of the error message—in this case, a SyntaxError. These are the most common error messages. They indicate that the compiler wasn't able to compile the program further due to a formal error.

In addition to the syntax error, there are a number of other error types, which can't all be discussed in detail here.[5] However, we'd like to highlight the IndentationError because it's often encountered by Python beginners. To demonstrate this, try running the following program:

```
i = 10
if i == 10:
print("Incorrectly indented")
```

You can see that the last line should actually be indented one step further. The way the program is written now, the if statement has no statement body. This isn't allowed, and an IndentationError occurs:

```
File "indent.py", line 3
  print("Incorrectly indented")
  ^
IndentationError: expected an indented block after 'if' statement on line 2
```

Now that we've familiarized ourselves with these basics, we can turn to the control structures that allow a programmer to control the flow of the program.

---

5 You find an overview of all error types in the appendix (Section A.4).

Note

With Python 3.10 and 3.11, many common error messages as well as their general formatting has been revised. Therefore, if you use an older version of Python, the actual outputs you see might differ from the ones printed in this book.

Chapter 5
Control Structures

A *control structure* is a construct for controlling the program flow. There are two types of control structures in Python: loops and conditionals. *Loops* are used to execute a block of code multiple times. *Conditionals*, on the other hand, tie a block of code to a condition. Python knows two subtypes each of loops and conditionals, which will be described in the following sections.

Control structures can be nested within each other in any way. The indentation depth grows continuously in the process.

5.1   Conditionals

In Python, there are two types of conditionals: the classic if statement,[1] and conditional expressions as an additional way of conditionally executing code. We'll discuss both types of conditionals in detail ahead and explain them with the help of examples. Let's start with the if statement.

5.1.1   The if Statement

The simplest type of a conditional is the if statement. An if statement consists of a statement header containing a condition and a code block as the statement body (see Chapter 4, Section 4.2).

The code block is executed only if the condition turns out to be true. The condition of an if statement must be an expression that can be interpreted as a truth value (True or False). Typically, the logical expressions introduced in Chapter 3, Section 3.7 are applied here:

```
if condition:
    Statement
    ...
    Statement
```

---

1 A *statement* is a standalone syntactic element in the source code. There are single-line statements, such as assignments, but also multiline statements that can contain further statements. An example of a multiline statement is the if statement mentioned here. Note that there is a difference between the terms *statement* and *expression*. Unlike a statement, an expression always has a value.

As an example, you can consider an if statement that outputs corresponding text only if the variable x has the value 1:[2]

```
if x == 1:
    print("x has value 1")
```

Of course, you can also use other comparative operators or a more complex logical expression and write more than one statement in the body:

```
if x < 1 or x > 5:
    print("x is less than 1 ...")
    print("... or greater than 5")
```

In many cases, a single if statement is not sufficient and you need a whole chain of mutually exclusive conditionals. In the following example, we want to output two different strings depending on whether x == 1 or x == 2. For this purpose, we can use two consecutive if statements:

```
if x == 1:
    print("x has value 1")
if x == 2:
    print("x has value 2")
```

This is an inefficient way to achieve the goal from the interpreter's point of view, however, because both conditions are evaluated and checked in any case. But the second conditional would no longer have to be considered if the condition of the first one had already yielded True. The variable x cannot have both values 1 and 2 under any circumstances. To make such cases more efficient from the perspective of the interpreter and clearer from the programmer's point of view, an if statement can be extended by one or more elif branches.[3] The condition of such a branch is evaluated only if all preceding if or elif conditions have been evaluated as False.

You can write the preceding example using elif as follows:

```
if x == 1:
    print("x has value 1")
elif x == 2:
    print("x has value 2")
```

An if statement can be extended by any number of elif branches:

---

2 Note that for this and the following examples, a variable x must already exist. If that's not the case, you'll get a NameError.

3 The term *elif* is an abbreviation for *else if*.

```
if condition:
    Statement
    ...
    Statement
elif condition:
    Statement
    ...
    Statement
elif condition:
    Statement
    ...
    Statement
```

In the source code, this could look as follows:

```
if x == 1:
    print("x has value 1")
elif x == 2:
    print("x has value 2")
elif x == 3:
    print("x has value 3")
```

As a final extension of the if statement, it's possible to intercept all previously unhandled cases at once. For example, imagine that we want to output not only a corresponding string if x == 1 or x == 2 applies, but also an error message in all other cases, such as if x == 35 applies. For this purpose, an if statement can be extended by an else branch. If this branch is to be used, it must be written at the end of the if statement:

```
if condition:
    Statement
    ...
    Statement
else:
    Statement
    ...
    Statement
```

In the source code, this can look as follows:

```
if x == 1:
    print("x has value 1")
elif x == 2:
    print("x has value 2")
else:
    print("Error: The value of x is neither 1 nor 2")
```

The code block subordinate to the else branch is run only if all previous conditions haven't been met. An if statement can have only one else branch. In the example, else was used in combination with elif, which is possible but not mandatory.

The following example provides an overview of the structure of an if statement including the possible branch types:

```
if condition:
    Statement
    Statement
elif condition:
    Statement
    Statement
else:
    Statement
    Statement
```

> **Note**
>
> If you already know a programming language such as C or Java, you might be interested to know that since Python 3.10 there is a counterpart to the switch/case control structure of these languages—namely, the match/case control structure, which we'll describe in Chapter 25. In Python versions prior to 3.10, you can mimic the behavior of this control structure by using a cascade of if/elif/else branches.

5.1.2 Conditional Expressions

Based on the previous section, consider the following code:

```
if x == 1:
    var = 20
else:
    var = 30
```

Considering that this is just a conditional assignment, the example is remarkably long at four lines. We'll now show you that this code fits on one line using a *conditional expression*.

Such a conditional expression can have two different values depending on a condition. For example, you can set var in the same assignment to either 20 or 30 depending on the value of x:

```
var = (20 if x == 1 else 30)
```

The parentheses enclose the conditional expression in this case. They aren't necessary, but they increase the level of clarity. The structure of a conditional expression is based on the English language and is as follows:

```
A if condition else B
```

It takes either the value A if the condition is fulfilled or, otherwise, the value *B*. So you could imagine that the conditional expression after the equal sign is replaced by either A or B—that is, 20 or 30 in the preceding example. Thus, after evaluating the conditional expression, the result is again a valid assignment.

This form of linking a statement to a condition can, of course, be applied to more than just assignments. In the following example, the same print statement outputs a different string depending on the value of x:

```
print("x has value 1" if x == 1 else "x is unequal to 1")
```

Note that condition can be a logical expression and A and B can be any two arithmetic expressions. Consequently, a complex conditional expression can also look like this:

```
xyz = (a * 2 if (a > 10 and b < 5) else b * 2)
```

It should be noted that the evaluation order of conditional expressions is different from the normal evaluation rules of Python code. The condition is always evaluated first and only then, depending on the result, follows either the left-hand or the right-hand part of the expression. Such an evaluation procedure is referred to as *lazy evaluation* because not all components of the statement are evaluated.

The conditional expressions presented here can be used in practice to elegantly shorten complex and long code. However, this is at the expense of readability and clarity. We'll therefore make use of it in this book only in exceptional cases. However, you're free to use conditional expressions in your own projects in any way that suits you.

5.2   Loops

A *loop* allows you to execute a block of code, the *loop body*, several times in a row. Python distinguishes between two types of loops: the while loop as a simple loop structure and the for loop for running through more complex data types.

5.2.1   The while Loop

We already used the while loop in the number-guessing game. It's used to execute a block of code as long as a certain condition is met. In our first program in Chapter 4,

Section 4.3, a while loop was used to read a new number from the player until the number entered matched the number we were looking for.

Basically, a while loop consists of a loop header containing the condition and a loop body corresponding to the code block to be executed (note that the loop runs *as long as* the condition is met, not *until* it is met):

```
while condition:
    Statement
    ...
    Statement
```

The following example is a somewhat abbreviated variant of the number-guessing game and is intended to illustrate the use of the while loop:

```
secret = 1337
attempt = -1
while attempt != secret:
    attempt = int(input("Guess: "))
print("You did it!")
```

The while keyword introduces the loop header, followed by the desired condition and a colon. In the subsequent lines, the loop body follows, indented one step further. There, a number is read by the user and given the name attempt. This process runs until the condition named in the loop header is met—that is, until the user's input (attempt) matches the secret number (secret).

5.2.2 Termination of a Loop

Because the variant of the number guessing game introduced in the previous section doesn't provide any clues as to which areas contain the number being searched for, a game can take quite a long time. Therefore, in this section, we want to enable the user to prematurely cancel the game by entering 0. This can be achieved by modifying the loop condition to the following:

```
attempt != secret and attempt != 0
```

This is an acceptable solution in this case, but if the loop condition is complex in itself and several termination conditions are added on top of it, the readability of the source code will suffer significantly.

An alternative solution is provided by the break keyword , which can be placed anywhere in the loop body and breaks the loop:

```
secret = 1337
attempt = -1
while attempt != secret:
    attempt = int(input("Guess: "))
    if attempt == 0:
        print("Game will be finished")
        break
print("You did it!")
```

Immediately after the user input, an if statement is used to check whether the input is 0. If this is the case, a corresponding message is output and the while loop is terminated via the break statement.

5.2.3   Detecting a Loop Break

In the previous section, the user was given the option to end the number-guessing game prematurely by entering 0. Unfortunately, the success message, which is supposed to signal to the player that he has guessed the number he had searched for, is displayed in any case after the loop has ended, even after the user has canceled the game:

```
Guess: 10
Guess: 20
Guess: 30
Guess: 0
Game will be finished
You did it!
```

So at this point, we're looking for a way to tell if the loop ended because of the loop condition or because of a break statement. For this purpose, similar to an if statement, a while loop can be extended by an else branch. The code block belonging to this branch is executed exactly once: when the loop has been completely processed—that is, when the condition returns False for the first time. In particular, the else branch doesn't get executed if the loop was terminated prematurely by a break statement:

```
while condition:
    Statement
    ...
    Statement
else condition:
    Statement
    ...
    Statement
```

Let's take look at a concrete example:

```
secret = 1337
attempt = -1
while attempt != secret:
    attempt = int(input("Guess: "))
    if attempt == 0:
        print("Game will be finished")
        break
else:
    print("You did it!")
```

From the user's point of view, this means the success message is output when the correct number has been guessed:

```
Guess: 10
Guess: 1337
You did it!
```

Conversely, if the user enters 0 to cancel the game, the else branch won't be executed, and thus no success message will be output:

```
Guess: 10
Guess: 0
Game will be finished
```

5.2.4 Aborting the Current Iteration

We have already presented a way to influence the flow of a loop using break. A second option is provided by the continue statement, which, in contrast to break, doesn't terminate the entire loop but only the current iteration. To illustrate this, let's consider the following example, which so far doesn't use a continue statement:

```
while True:
    number = int(input("Enter a number: "))
    result = 1
    while number > 0:
        result = result * number
        number = number - 1
    print("Result: ", result)
```

In an infinite loop—that is, a while loop whose condition is fulfilled under all circumstances—a number is read and the result variable is initialized with the value 1. In a subsequent while loop, result is multiplied by number until the condition number > 0 is met. In addition, in each pass of the inner loop, the value of number is decreased by 1.

After the inner loop has been passed through, the `result` variable is output. You'll probably have already recognized that the sample program calculates the factorial[4] of any
number entered:

```
Enter a number: 4
Result:   24
Enter a number: 5
Result:   120
Enter a number: 6
Result:   720
```

However, the preceding code also allows the following input:

```
Enter a number: -10
Result:   1
```

By entering a negative number, the condition of the inner loop is `False` right from the
start, so the loop won't be executed at all. For this reason, the value of `result` is output
immediately, which in this case is 1.

This is not what you would expect in this case. A negative number is an invalid entry.
Ideally, the program should abort the calculation when an invalid number is entered
and not display any result. This behavior can be implemented via a `continue` statement:

```
while True:
    number = int(input("Enter a number: "))
    if number < 0:
        print("Negative numbers are not allowed")
        continue
    result = 1
    while number > 0:
        result = result * number
        number = number - 1
    print("Result: ", result)
```

Immediately after the user's input has been read, an `if` statement checks whether it's a
negative number. If so, a corresponding error message is output and the current iteration is aborted. This means the program immediately jumps to the next iteration; that
is, the loop condition is checked and then the next number is read in by the user. From
the user's point of view, this means that after entering a negative number, no result is
output but an error message and the user is prompted to enter the next number:

---

4 The factorial $n!$ of a natural number n is the product of all natural numbers less than or equal to n:
$n! = 1 \cdot 2 \cdot \ldots \cdot (n-1) \cdot n$.

```
Enter a number: 4
Result:   24
Enter a number: 5
Result:   120
Enter a number: -10
Negative numbers are not allowed
Enter a number: -100
Negative numbers are not allowed
Enter a number: 6
Result:   720
```

In retrospect, we want to elaborate here once again on the difference between break and continue. While break terminates the loop completely, continue only terminates the current iteration; the loop itself continues to run:

```
while condition:
    ...
    if condition:
        continue      # jump back to while condition:

    ...
    if condition:
        break         # jump to First statement after loop

    ...
First statement after loop
```

5.2.5 The for Loop

In addition to the while loop described in the previous section, there is another loop available in Python—the for loop. A for loop is used to pass through an iterable object.[5] For this purpose, the for keyword is written, followed by an identifier, the in keyword, and the iterable object. Then the loop body follows, which is indented one level further:

```
for variable in object:
    Statement
    ...
    Statement
```

The current element of the iterable object can be accessed in the loop body via the selected identifier. Specifically, a for loop can iterate lists or strings—for example:

---

5 An *iterable object* is an instance of a data type that implements the iterator protocol. Apart from the already known lists and strings iterable data types, you'll get to know many more data types that can be iterated through via a for loop. For more information on iterable objects, see Chapter 21, Section 21.2.

```
>>> for x in [1,2,3]:
...     print(x)
...
1
2
3
>>> for c in "Python":
...     print(c)
...
P
y
t
h
o
n
```

In the course of this book, you'll get to know a few more data types that can be passed through in this way via a for loop.

> **Note**
>
> The for loop as it exists in Python is not a counterpart of the loop construct of the same name in C or Java. It's comparable to the foreach loop in PHP or Perl or to the range-based for loop in C++.

The break and continue keywords discussed in connection with the while loop for canceling a whole loop or a single iteration (Section 5.2.2 and Section 5.2.4) can also be used with the for loop and have the same meaning there. In addition, a for loop can have an else branch similar to the while loop, which is executed exactly when the loop has run through completely and hasn't been terminated prematurely via break:

```
for variable in object:
    Statement
    ...
    Statement
else:
    Statement
    ...
    Statement
```

5.2.6   The for Loop as a Counting Loop

In connection with the for loop, the built-in range function is of particular interest. It creates an iterable object that yields all the integers in a given range:

```
range(stop)
range(start, stop)
range(start, stop, step)
```

The *start* placeholder represents the number to start with. The loop is terminated as soon as *stop* has been reached. You should know that the loop counter itself never reaches the value *stop*, as it always remains smaller. In each iteration the loop counter is incremented by *step*. Both *start* and *stop* as well as *step* must be integers. Once all values have been specified, the for loop looks like this:

```
for i in range(1, 10, 2):
    print(i)
```

The count variable i now starts with the value 1; the loop is executed as long as i is less than 10, and in each iteration i is incremented by 2. Thus the loop outputs the values 1, 3, 5, 7, and 9 on the screen.

A for loop can be used not only in a positive direction; it's also possible to count down:

```
for i in range(10, 1, -2):
    print(i)
```

In this case, i is set to the value 10 at the beginning of the loop and is decreased by 2 in each pass. The loop runs as long as i is greater than 1, and outputs the values 10, 8, 6, 4, and 2 onto the screen.

This makes the for loop an ideal way to revise the example in the last section for calculating the factorial of a number. It's also an example of how while and for loops can be nested within each other:

```
while True:
    number = int(input("Enter a number: "))
    if number < 0:
        print("Negative numbers are not allowed")
        continue
    result = 1
    for i in range(2, number+1):
        result = result * i
    print("Result: ", result)
```

After an input is made by the user and checked for its sign, a for loop is initiated. The loop counter i of the loop starts with the value 2. The loop runs as long as i is less than number+1; the highest possible value of i is therefore number. In each iteration, the result variable is then multiplied by i.

5.3 The pass Statement

During the development of a program, it can happen that at a certain point in time, a control structure is only partially implemented. The programmer creates a statement header but doesn't add a statement body because they may want to take care of other, more important things first. However, a statement header hanging in the air without a corresponding body is a syntax error.

For this purpose, you can use the pass statement—a statement that does nothing at all. It can be applied as follows:

```
if x == 1:
    pass
elif x == 2:
    print("x has value 2")
```

In this case, only pass is found in the body of the if statement. Thus, if x has the value 1, nothing's going to happen.

The purpose of the pass statement is to avoid syntax errors in preliminary program versions. Finished programs usually don't contain any pass statements.

5.4 Assignment Expressions

In Python 3.8, *assignment expressions* were introduced. These are understood to be hybrids between an assignment and an expression that evaluates to the assignment value. In the following example, we'll determine the square of an integer y in terms of a simple arithmetic expression:

```
>>> y = 10
>>> y*y
100
```

Here, the interactive mode helps us capture the value of the expression y*y. For example, such an expression can be used in the context of a conditional statement, where its value becomes part of a larger logical expression:

```
>>> if y*y >= 100:
...     print("Yeah!")
...
Yeah!
```

An *assignment* assigns a name to the value of an expression, which can be used to reference it later in the program. Unlike an expression, an assignment itself has no value and therefore can't be used in the context of an arithmetic or logical expression:

```
>>> z = y*y
>>>
```

An assignment expression is a combination of an assignment and an expression implemented by the := operator:

```
>>> (z := y*y)
100
```

An assignment expression can therefore be used, for example, within the condition of an if statement to access an intermediate result of the condition later in the program:

```
>>> if (z := y*y) >= 100:
...      print("Yeah!")
...
Yeah!
>>> z
100
```

> **Note**
>
> The := operator is the weakest binding operator (see Section A.2 in the appendix), which is why assignment expressions within more complex expressions must usually be enclosed in parentheses.

For motivation, let's imagine a sample scenario in which we process a list of a variable size but limited by a maximum of 1000 elements. Furthermore, let's assume that if the maximum size is exceeded, we want to output an error message specifying the exact size of the list under consideration.

Checking for the maximum size in combination with the required error message can be done as follows:

```
if len(lst) > 1000:
    print("List too large:", len(lst), "elements")
```

The drawback of this compact solution is that the length len(lst) of the list has to be calculated twice, first to check if the list is too long and then again to compile the error message.[6] An alternative approach that avoids the double call of len is to determine the list length up front:

```
length = len(lst)
if length > 1000:
    print("List too large:", length, "elements")
```

---

6 In this concrete example, that's not too tragic as the length of a list can be determined efficiently. We consider len here as a placeholder for a more complex calculation.

This is also a valid solution, and it avoids the problem of double calculation by adding an extra line of code. Critics usually complain that such constructs make Python programs unnecessarily large and harder to grasp visually.

An assignment expression, using the := operator introduced in Python 3.8, allows the preceding example to be expressed in a compact manner and at the same time without multiple calculations:

```
if (length := len(lst)) > 1000:
    print("List too large:", length, "elements")
```

Note that assignment expressions can make a program more compact, but at the same time they limit its readability. For this reason, you should always use assignment expressions with moderation and caution.

> **Note**
>
> In addition to the terminology used here, other names for assignment expressions are also commonly used. These include the term *named expressions* due to the fact that the value of an expression can be assigned a name at the same time, and the ironic term *walrus operator* due to the appearance of the operator: :=.

5.4.1 The Guessing Numbers Game with Assignment Expressions

In Chapter 4, Section 4.3, we considered a program that successively reads input from the user and checks the input for a certain condition. This program can be adapted by combining reading the input and the check into the loop header using an assignment expression:

```
secret = 1337
counter = 1
while (attempt := int(input("Guess: "))) != secret:
    if attempt < secret:
        print("Too small")
    if attempt > secret:
        print("Too large")
    counter = counter + 1
print("Great, you did it in", counter, "tries!")
```

Using the := operator in combination with control structures such as loops or conditionals is a common use case often leading to more compact and less redundant code.

Chapter 6
Files

So far, we've discussed how to create and work with instances of various data types. In addition, you already know how the program flow can be affected by control structures. Now it's time to put this knowledge to good use and enable you to write more complex programs. This chapter is dedicated to the various options you have for the input or output of data. This refers in particular to reading and writing files, which is part of the standard repertoire of a programmer.

Before we turn specifically to reading and writing files in Python, the following section will introduce you to the necessary basics that enable you to do so.

6.1 Data Streams

A *data stream* is a continuous sequence of data. We distinguish between two types of data streams: data can be read from *incoming* data streams (*downstream*) and written to *outgoing* data streams (*upstream*). Screen output, keyboard input, and files and network connections are considered data streams.

Figure 6.1 illustrates the concept of data streams based on an example in which a program receives data from an incoming stream, calculates a result from it, and outputs the result to an outgoing stream. For example, you can imagine that the program reads a file and prints every other word contained in the file on the screen.

There are two standard data streams you have already used without knowing it: both the output of a string to the screen and a user input are nothing but operations on the standard input and output streams, stdin and stdout, respectively. The stdout output stream can be written to by using the built-in print function and read from the stdin input stream using input.

All major operating systems allow you to open data streams in text or binary mode. While there is usually no technical difference between text streams and binary streams, opening a stream using the appropriate mode is important. In text mode certain control characters such as e.g., newline characters or the *end-of-file (EOF) character* may be interpreted according to their respective semantics. In addition, Python automatically attempts to decode[1] the contents of text streams into str instances.

---

1 We will discuss the encoding and decoding of text in detail in Chapter 12, Section 12.5.4.

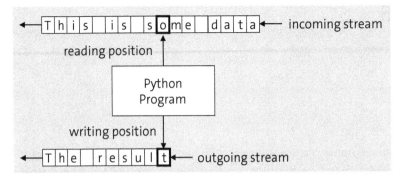

Figure 6.1 Program Reads Data from an Incoming Stream and Writes to an Outgoing Stream

As a final distinction, there are data streams in which you can position yourself at will, and those in which you can't. For example, a file represents a data stream in which the read/write position can be specified as desired. Examples of a stream in which this doesn't work include the standard input stream (stdin) and a network connection.

6.2   Reading Data from a File

First, we'll describe how you can read data from a file. To do this, we need to access that file in read-only mode. The test file we'll use in this example is a dictionary that contains in each line an English word and, separated from it by a space, its German translation. The file should be named *dictionary.txt*:

```
Spain Spanien
Germany Deutschland
Sweden Schweden
France Frankreich
Italy Italien
```

In the program, we want to prepare the data in this file so that we can conveniently access it later in a dictionary.[2] As a little extra, we'll extend the program to allow the user to ask the program for the translation of an English term.

6.2.1   Opening and Closing a File

First, the file must be opened for reading. For this purpose, we use the built-in open function. This function returns a so-called file object:

```
fobj = open("dictionary.txt", "r")
```

---

2 See Chapter 3, Section 3.5.

As the first parameter of open, we pass a string containing the path to the respective file. Note that both relative and absolute paths are allowed here.[3] The second parameter is also a character string and specifies the mode in which the file is to be opened, where "r" stands for *read* and means that the file is opened for reading. We associate the file object returned by the function with the fobj reference. If the file doesn't exist, a File-NotFoundError is generated:

```
Traceback (most recent call last):
  File "dictionary.py", line 1, in <module>
    fobj = open("dictionary.txt", "r")
FileNotFoundError: [Errno 2] No such file or directory: 'dictionary.txt'
```

Once open is called, the file object can be used to read data from the file. When the file has been read, it must be closed explicitly by calling the close method:

```
fobj.close()
```

After calling this method, no more data can be read from the file object.

6.2.2   The with Statement

In the previous section, you saw how you can open a file using the built-in open function and close it after using the close method of the opened file object:

```
fobj = open("dictionary.txt", "r")
# Do something with fobj
fobj.close()
```

The interplay of open and close is a typical pattern you will encounter again and again in various situations. In addition to file operations, network connections, for example, also represent situations in which a connection must first be established, then used, and finally closed.

The explicit use of open and close, as shown in the preceding example, bears the risk that due to a programming error or due to the omittance of error handling, the close method is not called and thus the file object is not closed. To make sure such errors won't happen, you should use the with statement to open a file:

```
with open("dictionary.txt", "r") as fobj:
    # Do something with fobj
    pass
```

---

3 An *absolute path* identifies a file starting from the root in the file system tree. On Windows, an absolute path might look like this: *C:\Program Files\TestProgram\dictionary.txt*. A *relative path* refers to the current working directory of the program. Here the ".." shortcut can be used for the parent directory. In the example, we use a relative path, so the *dictionary.txt* file must be in the same directory as the program.

As soon as the control flow leaves the statement block indented below a with statement, the file object opened with the with statement is automatically closed. In particular, this also applies in the event of an error that hasn't been handled.

Objects such as the file object that can be used in conjunction with a with statement are also referred to as *context managers*. At this point, it's sufficient to know that the with statement ensures that the context manager is closed properly in every case. We'll explore this topic further in Chapter 22.

6.2.3   Reading the File Content

In the next step, we want to read the file line by line. This is relatively simple as the file object can be iterated line by line. So we can use the old familiar for loop:

```
with open("dictionary.txt", "r") as fobj:
    for line in fobj:
        print(line)
```

In the for loop, we iterate over the file object line by line, with line each time referencing the contents of the current line. Currently, each line in the loop body is merely output. However, we want to build a dictionary in the program that contains the English terms as keys and the respective German terms as values after reading the file.

To do this, we first create an empty dictionary:

```
words = {}
```

Then the *dictionary.txt* file is opened for reading and iterated in a loop over all lines of the file:

```
with open("dictionary.txt", "r") as fobj:
    for line in fobj:
        assignment = line.split(" ")
        if len(assignment) == 2:     # consider only valid lines
            words[assignment[0]] = assignment[1]
```

In the loop body, we now use the split method of a string to break the currently read line into two parts of a list: the part to the left of the space—that is, the English word— and the part to the right of the space—that is, the German word. In the next line of the loop body, a new entry is then created in the dictionary, with the assignment[0] key (the English word) and the assignment[1] value (the German word). Finally, we decide to tacitly skip a line if we could not extract exactly two components from it. We chose this type of error handling for didactic reasons to keep the program as simple as possible. In practice, you should ask yourself whether you should output the problematic lines or even terminate the program with an error message.

Now modify the preceding code once so that after closing the file object, the generated dictionary is output with print. The output will look like this:

```
{'Spain': 'Spanien\n', 'Germany': 'Deutschland\n', 'Sweden': 'Schweden\n',
'France': 'Frankreich\n', 'Italy': 'Italien\n'}
```

You can see that after each value there is a \n, which is the escape sequence for a line break. This is because a line break in Python is considered a character and thus part of the file contents. Thus, each line of a file is read entirely, including a possible line break at the end. Of course, the line break is only read if it really exists.

We don't want to find the line break again in the final dictionary. For this reason, we call the strip method of the line string in each iteration. This removes all white space characters,[4] including line breaks, at the beginning and end of the string:

```
words = {}
with open("dictionary.txt", "r") as fobj:
    for line in fobj:
        line = line.strip()
        assignment = line.split(" ")
        if len(assignment) == 2:    # consider only valid lines
            words[assignment[0]] = assignment[1]
```

Thus, the content of the file has been completely transferred to a dictionary. As a little extra, we now want to allow the user to send translation requests to the program. In the flow sequence, it should look like this:

```
Enter a word: Germany
The German word is: Deutschland
Enter a word: Italy
The German word is: Italien
Enter a word: Greece
The word is unknown
```

In the program, we read requests from the user in an infinite loop. The in operator enables us to check if the read word exists as a key in the dictionary. If so, the corresponding German translation is output. If the entered word doesn't exist, an error message will be displayed:

```
words = {}
with open("dictionary.txt", "r") as fobj:
    for line in fobj:
        line = line.strip()
```

---

4 *White spaces* are characters that are typically not displayed on the screen. Examples of white spaces are spaces, tab characters, and line breaks. For more information on white spaces, see Chapter 12, Section 12.5.2.

```
        assignment = line.split(" ")
        if len(assignment) == 2:     # consider only valid lines
            words[assignment[0]] = assignment[1]
while True:
    word = input("Enter a word: ")
    if word in words:
        print("The German word is:", words[word])
    else:
        print("The word is unknown")
```

The sample program presented here is far from perfect, but it shows very nicely how file objects and also dictionaries can be used in a meaningful way. Feel free to expand the program. For example, you could allow the user to exit the program properly, offer translations in both directions, or allow the use of multiple source files.

6.3   Writing Data to a File

In the previous section, we focused on reading files. The fact that it also works the other way around is the topic of this section. To open a file for writing, we also use the built-in open function. You'll remember that this function expects a mode as second parameter, which had to be "r" for *read* in the last section. Similarly, "w" (for *write*) must be specified if the file is to be opened for writing. If the desired file already exists, it will be emptied. A file that doesn't exist yet will be created:

```
fobj = open("output.txt", "w")
```

After all data has been written to the file, the file object must be closed by calling the close method:

```
fobj.close()
```

Also, when writing a file, you should use the with statement instead of explicitly using open and close:

```
with open("output.txt", "w") as fobj:
    # Do something with fobj
    pass
```

To write a string to the open file, you can call the write method of the file object. The following sample program is intended as a counterpart to the example from the last section. We assume that words references a dictionary containing English terms as keys and the German translations as values—for example:

```
words = {
    "Germany": "Deutschland",
```

```
    "Spain": "Spanien",
    "Greece": "Griechenland"
}
```

So it's a dictionary like that created by the sample program from the previous section:

```
with open("output.txt", "w") as fobj:
    for engl in words:
        fobj.write(f"{engl} {words[engl]}\n")
```

First, we open a file called *output.txt* for writing and then iterate over all keys of the words dictionary. In each iteration, a correspondingly formatted string is written to the file via `fobj.write`. Note that when writing a file, you must explicitly jump to a new line by outputting \n.

We'll take a closer look at the f-string syntax f"..." for formatting strings in Chapter 12, Section 12.5.3. At this point, it should be sufficient for us to know that an f-string supports the definition of placeholders in the string which are replaced by the values of the expressions given in curly braces.

The file written by this example can be read again by the sample program from the last section.

6.4   Generating the File Object

As you can see from the previous examples, a file object can be created using the built-in open function. To this function, you can pass other parameters besides the file name and the mode, which are worth looking at. Also, in addition to the "r" and "w" modes already described, there are a few others we'll discuss ahead. Finally, we'll provide an overview of the methods of the resulting file object.

> **Note**
>
> This section contains detailed information about file objects and serves predominantly as a reference. As a result, you may skip it during your first read.

6.4.1   The Built-In open Function

The built-in open function opens a file and returns the created file object. Using this file object, you can subsequently perform the required operations on the file.[5]

---

5 In this book, we use square brackets [ ] to indicate optional positional parameters. For more details about this notation, see Chapter 8, Section 8.1.

open(filename, [mode, buffering, encoding, errors, newline])

We've already discussed the first two parameters in the previous sections. Those are the file name or path to the file to be opened and the mode in which the file is to be opened. A string must be passed for the mode parameter. All valid values and their meanings are listed in Table 6.1.

Mode	Description
"r"	The file is opened for reading only.
"w"	The file is opened for writing only. Any existing file with the same name will be overwritten.
"a"	The file is opened for writing only. A possibly existing file with the same name won't be overwritten, but extended.
"x"	The file is opened for writing only, if it doesn't already exist. If a file with the same name already exists, a FileExist-sError exception is raised.
"r+", "w+", "a+", "x+"	The file is opened for reading and writing. Note that "w+" will empty any existing file with the same name.
"rb", "wb", "ab", "xb", "r+b", "w+b", "a+b", "x+b"	The file will be opened in binary mode. Note that in this case, bytes instances must be used instead of strings (see Chapter 12, Section 12.5).

Table 6.1 File Modes

The mode parameter is optional and is assumed to be "r" if omitted.

The four additional optional parameters, buffering, encoding, errors, and newline, are not usually needed, and we'll illustrate their use with a number of similar interfaces throughout the book. Nevertheless, we want to provide a brief summary of their meaning at this point.

The fourth optional parameter, encoding, can be used to specify the *encoding* in which the file is to be read or written. The encoding determines how special characters beyond the ASCII character set are stored. For more information about encodings in Python, you can refer to the description of strings in Chapter 12, Section 12.5.4. There you'll also find more detailed information about the encoding and errors parameters. Specifying an encoding makes no sense when opening a file in binary mode and should be omitted in this case.

The fifth parameter, errors, determines how to deal with errors in encoding characters in the specified encoding. If the "ignore" value is passed for errors, they'll be ignored. A ValueError exception is raised for a value of "strict", which also happens if you don't specify the parameter.

The buffering parameter controls the internal buffer size, and newline specifies the characters to be recognized or used as new line characters when reading or writing the file.

6.4.2   Attributes and Methods of a File Object

The parameters specified when opening can be read again via the name, encoding, errors, mode, and newlines attributes of the resulting file object.

Table 6.2 briefly summarizes the most important methods of a file object. We'll discuss the seek and tell methods in more detail in the following section.

Method	Description
close()	Closes an existing file object. Note that no read or write operations may be performed after that.
fileno()	Returns the descriptor* of the opened file as an integer.
flush()	Orders pending write operations to be executed immediately.**
isatty()	True if the file object was opened on a data stream that can't be written or read at any position.
next()	Reads the next line of the file and returns it as a string.
read([size])	Reads size bytes of the file. If size is not specified or the file is smaller than size bytes, the file will be read in its entirety. The data is returned as a string or bytes string depending on the reading mode.
readline([size])	Reads one line of the file. The number of bytes to be read can be limited by specifying size.
readlines([sizehint])	Reads all lines and returns them as a list of strings. If sizehint is specified, the read process runs until approximately sizehint bytes have been read.***
seek(offset, [whence])	Sets the current read/write position in the file to offset.
tell()	Returns the current read/write position in the file.
truncate([size])	Deletes all data in the file after the current read/write position, or—if specified—everything except the first size bytes.
write(str)	Writes the str string to the file.
writelines(iterable)	Writes several lines to the file. The iterable iterable object must pass through strings, such as a list of strings, for example.

Table 6.2 Methods of a File Object

Method	Description
* A *file descriptor* is an identification number assigned by the operating system for open files. The default stdin and stdout streams have descriptors 0 and 1, respectively.	
** The operating system can buffer pending file operations for efficiency and execute them at a later time. This is the reason, for example, that USB sticks shouldn't be pulled out without logging them out of the operating system.	
*** In this context, *approximately* means that the number of bytes to be read may be rounded up to an internal buffer size.	

Table 6.2 Methods of a File Object (Cont.)

6.4.3   Changing the Write/Read Position

The previous examples have shown how files can be read or written in a sequential manner. Due to the special nature of files, it's possible to change the write or read position at will. For this purpose, you can use the seek and tell methods of the file object.

seek(offset, [whence])

The seek method of a file object sets the read/write position within the file. It is the counterpart of the tell method, which returns the current read/write position.

> **Note**
>
> The seek method has no effect in "a" mode. In "a+" mode, the read/write position is changed so that it can be read at any point in the file, but it's reset before a write operation.

If the file has been opened in binary mode, the offset parameter is counted in bytes from the beginning of the file. This interpretation of offset can be influenced by the optional whence parameter (see Table 6.3).

Value of whence	Interpretation of offset
0	Number of bytes relative to the beginning of the file
1	Number of bytes relative to the current read/write position
2	Number of bytes relative to the end of the file

Table 6.3 The whence Parameter

You won't be able to use seek as freely if the file is opened in text mode. Here, only return values of the tell method should be used as offset. Deviating values can cause undefined behavior.

In the following example, the seek method is used to determine the width, height, and color depth of a bitmap graphic:[6]

```python
from struct import unpack
with open("coffee.bmp", "rb") as f:
    f.seek(18)
    width, height = unpack("ii", f.read(8))
    f.seek(2, 1)
    bpp = unpack("H", f.read(2))[0]
print("Width:", width, "px")
print("Height:", height, "px")
print("Color depth:", bpp, "bpp")
```

From the specification of the bitmap file format,[7] we can see that the information we're looking for is located at offsets 18, 22, and 28, in the form of two consecutive four-byte values and one two-byte value. We therefore open the *image.bmp* file to read in binary mode and skip the first 18 bytes using the seek method. At this point, we can use read to read the width and height of the graphic. The values read via read are returned as a bytes string (see Chapter 12, Section 12.5) and must therefore be converted for our purposes into numbers. To do that, we use the unpack function from the struct module of the standard library. The format statement "ii" required by unpack states that the bytes string passed should be interpreted as two consecutive signed 32-bit integers. More about struct can be found in Chapter 44, Section 44.2.

After reading the width and height, we skip two more bytes from the current read position (the whence parameter is set to 1 in the seek call) and then can read two bytes containing the color depth of the image.[8] Finally, we output the read information and can check it for correctness with a graphics program, for example:[9]

```
Width: 800 px
Height: 600 px
Color depth: 24 bpp
```

---

6 The Windows bitmap file format (extension .bmp) is a widely used raster graphics format.
7 This can be found, for example, in Wikipedia at *https://en.wikipedia.org/wiki/BMP_file_format*.
8 The color depth is specified in bits per pixel (BPP).
9 If you get a negative height, this is not a bug in the program, but a peculiarity of the bitmap file format. Negative height information means that the image data is stored from top to bottom and not, as usual, from bottom to top.

Chapter 7
The Data Model

This chapter describes how Python manages data at runtime. In particular, we will discuss what variables actually are in Python and explain the related terms *object*, *instance* and *reference*.

In computer science, variables are generally understood as named storage locations for data of different types such as numbers, lists, or other structures. As you already know, in Python a new variable named a can be created as follows:

```
>>> a = 1337
```

Subsequently, the variable a can be used like the numerical value 1337:

```
>>> 2674 / a
2.0
```

To understand what happens internally when we create a new variable, two concepts need to be distinguished: instance and reference. An *instance* is a concrete data object in the memory created according to the template of a certain data type—for example, the special number 1337 according to the template of the data type int.

In the following sections, we'll only look at integers and strings for reasons of simplicity, but the principle applies to any kind of data object.

In the simplest case, an instance of an integer can be created as follows:

```
>>> 12345
12345
```

For us as programmers, however, this instance is not very useful, because although it's output after its creation, it will then no longer be accessible and so we can't continue to use its value.

This is where *references* come into play. Only references enable us to use instances because they allow us to access the instances. A reference is often simply called a *name* in Python. You can use the assignment operator = to create a reference to an instance, with the reference to the left and the instance to the right of the operator:

```
>>> a = 12345
```

With this, we can describe our example as follows: We create a new instance of an integer with the value 1337. We also create a reference a to this instance. This can also be illustrated graphically (see Figure 7.1).

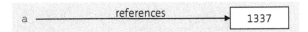

Figure 7.1 Schema of the Reference-Instance Relationship

It's also possible to provide previously referenced instances with additional references:

```
>>> reference1 = 1337
>>> reference2 = reference1
```

Graphically illustrated, the result looks like as shown in Figure 7.2.

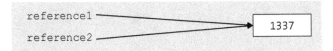

Figure 7.2 Two References to the Same Instance

It's particularly important to note that there is still only one instance with the value 1337 in the memory, although we can access it with two different names—reference1 and reference2. Thus, by assigning reference2 = reference1, the instance 1337 was not copied, but only referenced one more time.

Note that references to the same instance are independent of each other and the value referenced by the other references doesn't change when we assign a new instance to one of them:

```
>>> reference1 = 1337
>>> reference2 = reference1
>>> reference1
1337
>>> reference2
1337
>>> reference1 = 2674
>>> reference1
2674
>>> reference2
1337
```

Up to the first two outputs, the situation looks like the one shown in Figure 7.2: the two references, reference1 and reference2 point to the same instance 1337. We then create a new instance 2674 and assign it to reference1. The output shows that reference2 still points to 1337 and hasn't been changed. Thus, the situation after the third assignment is as shown in Figure 7.3.

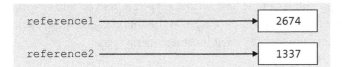

Figure 7.3 Two References Are Independent of Each Other

> **Note**
>
> As you've seen, the notion of a variable as a memory location in Python is only partially correct as variables in Python are references with symbolic names. For this reason, phrases frequently used in programming, such as *store in a variable*, are strictly speaking not applicable. Rather, it would be correct to speak of *referencing by a symbolic name*.
>
> In our experience, it's important to be aware of this correct view when working with Python. However, when the precise formulation is used consistently, other aspects are easily overshadowed by the more complicated form of expression. We have therefore decided to present you with the exact background in this chapter, but to use more imprecise formulations such as *storing in a variable* in the rest of the book if we think this will improve comprehensibility.

You now know that you must distinguish between two concepts: references to instances, and the instances themselves. In the following sections, we'll take a look at the properties of instances in more detail.

7.1 The Structure of Instances

Each instance in Python includes three components: its *data type*, its *value*, and its *identity*. Our initial example could be thought of as having three parts, as shown in Figure 7.4.

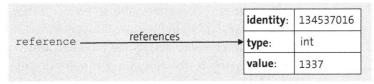

Figure 7.4 An Instance with Its Three Properties

7.1.1 Data Type

The data type serves as a blueprint when the instance is created and defines which values the instance may assume. For example, the int data type allows you to store an integer. Strings can be managed via the str data type. In the following example, you can see how to identify the data types of different instances using type:

```
>>> type(1337)
<class 'int'>
>>> type("Hello World")
<class 'str'>
>>> v1 = 2674
>>> type(v1)
<class 'int'>
```

The type function is useful, among other things, when you want to check whether two instances have the same type or whether an instance has a specific type:[1]

```
>>> v1 = 1337
>>> type(v1) == type(2674)
True
>>> type(v1) == int
True
>>> type(v1) == str
False
```

Note, however, that a type refers only to instances and has nothing to do with the linked references. A reference has no type and can reference instances of any type. The following is absolutely possible:

```
>>> first_a_string = "I am a string"
>>> type(first_a_string)
<class 'str'>
>>> first_a_string = 1789
>>> type(first_a_string)
<class 'int'>
```

So it's wrong to say "first_a_string has type str." The correct thing to say is "first_a_string currently references an instance of type str." However, since the former leads in many cases to much simpler and more comprehensible descriptions, this formulation is also often used in the context of Python. In this book we also simplify many descriptions in the interest of the readability in this way.

---

1 Experienced readers will be interested to know that isinstance (see Chapter 19, Section 19.9) can be used in the context of object-oriented programming to check whether an instance has a type derived from a given data type.

7.1.2   Value

What specifically constitutes the value of an instance depends on its type. Types can be, for example, numbers, strings, or data of other types, which you'll get to know later. In the preceding examples, they were 1337, 2674, 1798, "Hello world", and "I am a string".

You can use the == operator to compare instances with respect to their value:

```
>>> v1 = 1337
>>> v2 = 1337
>>> v1 == v2
True
>>> v1 == 2674
False
```

With the help of our graphical model (see Figure 7.5), the operation of the == operator can be well illustrated.

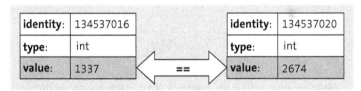

identity:	134537016		identity:	134537020
type:	int		type:	int
value:	1337	==	value:	2674

Figure 7.5 Value Comparison of Two Instances (in This Case, False)

The value comparison is only useful if it refers to structurally similar data types, such as integers and floats:

```
>>> number1 = 1987.0
>>> type(number1)
<class 'float'>
>>> number2 = 1987
>>> type(number2)
<class 'int'>
>>> number1 == number2
True
```

Although number1 and number2 have different types, comparing them via == returns the truth value True.

Structurally, numbers and strings have little in common as numbers are single values, while strings combine several letters into a single unit. For this reason, the == operator for the comparison between strings and numbers always returns False, even if the values look "the same" to a human:

```
>>> string = "1234"
>>> string == 1234
False
```

Whether the == operator is defined for two particular types depends on the data types themselves.[2] If it isn't present, the identity of the instances is used for comparison, which is explained in the following section.

7.1.3 Identity

The *identity* of an instance serves to distinguish it from all other instances. This can be compared to a person's individual fingerprint as it's unique for each instance within a program and cannot change. An identity is an integer and can be determined using the id function:

```
>>> id(1337)
134537016
>>> v1 = "Hello World"
>>> id(v1)
3082572528
```

Identities become important whenever you want to check if an instance is specific and not just one with the same type and value:

```
>>> v1 = [1,2,3]
>>> v2 = v1
>>> v3 = [1,2,3]
>>> type(v1) == type(v3)
True
>>> v1 == v3
True
>>> id(v1) == id(v3)
False
>>> id(v1) == id(v2)
True
```

In this example, Python has created two different instances with type list and value [1,2,3], where v1 and v2 reference the same instance. Figure 7.6 illustrates this graphically.

---

2 More precisely, it depends on the implementation of the *Magic Method* __eq__ of the data type (see Chapter 19, Section 19.11.2).

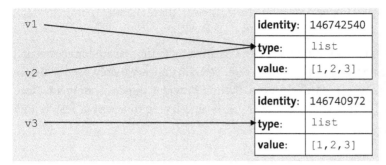

Figure 7.6 Three References, Two Instances

The comparison on identity equality is so important in Python that a separate operator has been defined for this purpose: is.

The expression id(reference1) == id(reference2) means the same as reference1 is reference2. Figure 7.7 illustrates this.

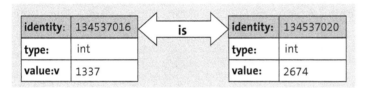

Figure 7.7 Identity Comparison of Two Instances

The comparison shown in Figure 7.7 yields the truth value False because the identities of the two instances differ.

7.2 Deleting References

During a program run, usually a lot of instances are created, but not all of them are needed all the time. Let's consider the following fictitious program start:

```
welcome = "Welcome to the sample program"
print(welcome)
# From this point on the rest of the program would continue
```

It's easy to see that the instance referenced by welcome is no longer needed after the welcome and thus wastes memory without any purpose during the rest of the program runtime. So what's preferable here is a way to remove instances on request that are no longer needed.

Python doesn't allow programmers to manage the memory directly; it instead does that for them. As a result, we can't manually delete existing instances but must rely on an automatism called *garbage collection*.[3] Nevertheless, there is a way to influence the process.

Instances that are no longer referenced are classified by Python as no longer needed and released accordingly. So if we want to remove an instance, we only need to delete all associated references. For this purpose, Python provides the del statement. Once it has been deleted, a reference no longer exists, and trying to access it results in a NameError:

```
>>> v1 = 1337
>>> v1
1337
>>> del v1
>>> v1
Traceback (most recent call last):
  File "<stdin>", line 1, in <module>
NameError: name 'v1' is not defined
```

If you want to delete multiple references at once, you can simply separate them using commas:

```
>>> v1 = 1337
>>> v2 = 2674
>>> v3 = 4011
>>> del v1, v2, v3
>>> v1
Traceback (most recent call last):
  File "<stdin>", line 1, in <module>
NameError: name 'v1' is not defined
```

To recognize when no more references exist for an instance, Python internally stores a counter for each instance, the so-called *reference count*. For newly created instances, the reference count has the value zero. Whenever a new reference to an instance is created, the instance's reference count increases by one, and whenever a reference is deleted, it decreases by one. Thus, the reference count of an instance always indicates the current number of references pointing to the instance. When the reference count of an instance reaches zero, there exists no reference pointing to this specific instance. Because instances are accessible to the programmer only by references, access to such an instance is no longer possible and it can therefore be deleted.

---

3 Garbage collection is a system that removes data objects that are no longer needed and releases the corresponding memory space. It works invisibly for the programmer in the background.

7.3   Mutable versus Immutable Data Types

Perhaps you've already come across the following seeming contradiction while trying out what we have just described:

```
>>> a = 1
>>> b = 1
>>> id(a)
9656320
>>> id(b)
9656320
>>> a is b
True
```

Why do a and b reference the same integer instance, as shown by the identity comparison, even though we explicitly created two instances with the value 1 in the first two lines?

To answer this question, you need to know that Python fundamentally distinguishes between two types of data types—namely, between *mutable* and *immutable* data types. As the names suggest, the difference between the two types is whether or not the value of an instance can change after its creation—that is, whether it is mutable. Instances of a mutable type are capable of taking on other values after they've been created, whereas this is not the case with immutable data types.

However, if the value of an instance can't change, it also makes no sense to manage several immutable instances of the same value in the memory; in an ideal world, exactly one instance is sufficient, to which all corresponding references point. Now, as you might imagine, integers are such an immutable data type, and Python has made the value 1 refer to the same instance twice for the purpose of optimization. Strings are also immutable.[4]

However, there's no guarantee that there'll always be exactly one instance of each required value of an immutable data type, although this would theoretically be possible. Each implementation of Python can choose its own variant here.

Things are different with regard to *mutable* data types: because Python must expect that the value of such an instance will subsequently change, the system of rereferencing already existing instances whenever possible isn't useful. So here you can rely on the fact that a new instance is always created.

This different behavior when dealing with *mutable* and *immutable* data types means that the same code can do fundamentally different things for different data types. The following examples are intended to make you aware of the specifics involved.

---

4 Of course, this doesn't mean that a programmer can't modify strings and integers. But what happens simply is that a new instance of the data type is created every time an immutable data type is manipulated, instead of modifying the old one.

First, we introduce the += operator, which can be used to append a string to an existing one:

```
>>> a = "water "
>>> a += "bottle"
>>> a
'water bottle'
```

So here, first a string with the value "water" is created, to which the string "bottle" is then appended.

In the same way, it's possible to append the elements of a list to an existing list using +=:

```
>>> a = [1,2]
>>> a += [3,4]
>>> a
[1, 2, 3, 4]
```

So everything indicates that the operator += does the same for strings and lists. In fact, however, there is a serious difference.

In the next example, we'll run the same code twice, once for a string and once for a list:

```
>>> a = "water "
>>> b = a
>>> a += "bottle"
>>> a
'water bottle'
>>> b
'water '
```

Again, we generate a string with the value "water". This time we let the reference b point to this string in addition to the reference a. Then we append the string "bottle" to the string referenced by a again and see in the output that b still references the string "water" while a points to the concatenation "water bottle".

If we do the same with instances of type list, things look different:

```
>>> a = [1,2]
>>> b = a
>>> a += [3,4]
>>> a
[1, 2, 3, 4]
>>> b
[1, 2, 3, 4]
```

This example is similar to the previous example with string instances: the list [1,2] corresponds to the string "water" and the list [3,4] to the string "bottle". Nevertheless, the list referenced by b has changed in this example, which was not the case with the string example.

To understand this difference, let's take a look at the operations of the two code sequences in detail.

In Figure 7.8, the sample code for strings and the resulting internal operations are contrasted.

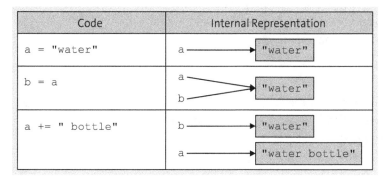

Code	Internal Representation
a = "water"	a ⟶ "water"
b = a	a ⟶ "water" b ⟶
a += " bottle"	b ⟶ "water" a ⟶ "water bottle"

Figure 7.8 The += Operator with str Instances

The sticking point can be found in the line a += "bottle". Because str is an immutable data type, it isn't possible to extend the existing str instance "water" by appending "bottle". Instead, a new str instance with the value "water bottle" is created at this point and then referenced by a. The instance still referenced by b with the value "water" is not affected.

The list example is different, as you can see in Figure 7.9.

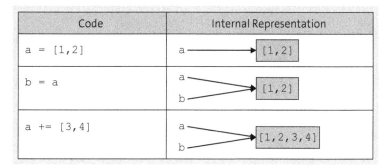

Code	Internal Representation
a = [1,2]	a ⟶ [1,2]
b = a	a ⟶ [1,2] b ⟶
a += [3,4]	a ⟶ [1,2,3,4] b ⟶

Figure 7.9 The += Operator for list Instances

Because list is a mutable data type, the list instance referenced jointly by a and b can be modified. For this reason, the line a += [3,4] doesn't cause a new list instance to be created but changes the already existing instance. Consequently, a and b continue to reference the same list and thus b is also affected by the manipulation on a.

This process, in which something is affected by processes in another place, is called a *side effect*.

Side effects generally occur exclusively with mutable data types and aren't restricted to the += operator. They come into play whenever the instance of a mutable data type is modified. For more information on side effects related to lists, see Chapter 12, Section 12.3.6. In Chapter 17, Section 17.10, we'll describe side effects in function calls.

As you continue reading this book, you'll become familiar with an entire range of mutable data types and operations that can be used to modify them. In doing so, you should keep in mind the behavior presented here.

Note

In this section, we considered the int and str data types as representatives of the immutable data types and list as a representative of the mutable data types. See Chapter 10 for a comprehensive list of Python's built-in data types, along with an indication of their mutability.

Chapter 8
Functions, Methods, and Attributes

In the previous chapters, we provided an example-based introduction to the Python language. This initially involved trying out simple examples in interactive mode and, building on this, writing a first sample program. After that, we discussed control structures, the runtime model, and input/output capabilities, three topics that should enable you to reproduce sample programs early on and experiment with Python yourself.

At this point, two other central topics are covered: passing parameters to functions or methods and dealing with instances. We'll restrict ourselves here to a generally understandable introduction with just as much detail as you need for the following chapters. A comprehensive discussion of the three topics follows in Chapter 17 and Chapter 19.

8.1   Parameters of Functions and Methods

A *function* is a named subroutine that encapsulates a commonly needed functionality and can be executed via a *function call*. An example of a function is the max *built-in function* for determining the largest element of a list:

```
>>> max([3,6,2,1,9])
9
```

The list whose largest element is to be determined is a *parameter* of the max function and is written into the parentheses when the function is called.

If a function call returns a result, this *return value* can be used as a normal instance:

```
>>> value = max([3,6,2,1,9])
>>> value/2
4.5
```

A *method* is a function that's executed in the context of a specific instance. For example, lists have a sort method that sorts the list for which it is called:

```
>>> list = [4,6,2,1,8,5,9]
>>> list.sort()
>>> list
[1, 2, 4, 5, 6, 8, 9]
```

The data type of an instance determines which methods are available to it.

Note

Below we will talk in a little more detail about the different possibilities for function parameters in Python. Note that the literature distinguishes between two terms, which are based on different views of a function call: *parameter* and *argument*.

While the term argument refers to a concrete value passed in a function call, the corresponding placeholder in the function definition is called a parameter.

It is important to be aware of this slight difference in meaning. However, to improve readability, we have decided against making a strict distinction between these meanings and use the terms parameter and argument almost synonymously in this book.

8.1.1   Positional Parameters

Many methods[1] need additional information besides the instance that the call references in order to work. For this purpose, so-called *parameters* are available, which are written, separated by commas, in the brackets at the end of the method call. Both references and literals can be specified as parameters:

```
var = 12
reference.method(var, "Hello World!")
```

The definition of a method determines how many and which parameters may be passed to it, which therefore varies from method to method.

Taken together, a method and the parameters it expects is referred to as an *interface*. Every time we describe a method in this book, we usually specify the associated interface in the following form:

method(parameter1, parameter2, parameter3)

In this case, the method expects three positional parameters named *parameter1*, *parameter2*, and *parameter3*. The term *positional* means that the instances passed in the method call are assigned to the parameters according to their position in the parameters list. In the case of the method call `reference.method(1, 45, -7)`, *parameter1* has the value 1, *parameter2* the value 45, and *parameter3* the value -7.

8.1.2   Keyword Arguments

You can also pass *keyword arguments* to a method. Keyword arguments are directly linked to the formal parameter name, and their order in the parameters list no longer matters. To pass a value as a keyword argument, you must assign the value to be passed

---

1 The explanations and examples in this section refer to methods, but they apply in a similar way to functions.

to the parameter name within the method call using the equal sign. Accordingly, the following two method calls are equivalent:

```
reference.method(1, 2, 3)
reference.method(parameter2=2, parameter1=1, parameter3=3)
```

You can also mix positional arguments and keyword arguments, but all keyword arguments must be located at the end of the argument list. Thus, the following call is equivalent to the previous two:

```
reference.method(1, parameter3=3, parameter2=2)
```

Only `parameter1` was passed as a positional argument, while `parameter2` and `parameter3` were passed as keyword arguments.

It's up to you which of the two transfer methods you want to use. Usually, however, parameters are passed as positional arguments because of the lower effort required for writing them.

8.1.3   Optional Parameters

There are *optional parameters* available, which must be passed only if needed. When we introduce methods with such parameters, they are indicated by square brackets in the interface description:

method(parameter1, [parameter2, parameter3])

In this example, `parameter1` is a required parameter, while `parameter2` and `parameter3` are two optional parameters. So the method can be called in different ways:

```
reference.method(1, 2, 3)
reference.method(1, 2)
reference.method(1)
```

8.1.4   Keyword-Only Parameters

A function or method can have *keyword-only parameters*. These are parameters that can only be passed in keyword notation. We'll indicate these parameters in a function or method interface by curly braces:

method(parameter1, parameter2, {parameter3})

Keyword-only parameters can be optional or nonoptional. The method can thus be called as follows:

```
reference.method(1, 2, parameter3=3)
reference.method(1, 2)
```

8.2 Attributes

In addition to methods, instances can also have *attributes*. An attribute constitutes a named part of the overall instance value. For example, every complex number has the attributes real and imag for accessing its real or imaginary part:

```
>>> number = 5 + 6j
>>> number.real
5.0
>>> number.imag
6.0
```

Because an expression of the form reference.attribute is itself a reference, it can be used like any other reference. For example, it can appear as an operand in calculations or be stored in a list:

```
>>> number.real*number.real + 5*number.imag
55.0
>>> [1, number.imag, number.real]
[1, 6.0, 5.0]
```

In particular, the instance referenced by reference.attribute may itself have an aaa attribute, which can then be accessed by reference.attribute.aaa. In the same way, accessing a method of the instance via reference.attribute.method(param1, param2) works.

In the example, the real attribute of a complex number points to a float, which in turn has an is_integer method to check whether it's an integer:

```
>>> number.real.is_integer()
True
```

Here the real part 5.0 of the complex number 5 + 6j was accessed via number.real and then the method is_integer of 5.0 was called.

In Python programs, such nested attribute and method accesses occur frequently.

Chapter 9
Sources of Information on Python

The goal of this book is to provide you with a comprehensive introduction to programming with Python. Unfortunately, the scope of this book is limited, so we'll have to omit details in some places and refer you to further documentation instead. But in everyday programming, it's sometimes these details that make the difference.

In this chapter, we'll briefly describe several sources of information about Python that are pretty useful. These sources are all available in English.

9.1 The Built-In Help Function

You can call the built-in help function to start the interactive help function of the Python interpreter. Via help(), introductory text is output, followed by a command prompt. This interactive help is useful if you need to look up terms.

Terms can include keywords (e.g., for), symbols (e.g., +), modules (e.g., pprint), or topics (e.g., DEBUGGING). A list of possible search terms in these categories can be displayed using the keywords, symbols, modules, and topics commands.

If a help page was found for a term you entered, it will be displayed in a read mode. Longer texts can be scrolled. This works on Linux with the Up and Down arrow keys and on Windows with the Space bar. The Q key takes you back from the read mode to the interactive mode, which you can exit using the quit() command or the Ctrl+D shortcut.

Python's interactive help is particularly useful for quickly finding answers to interface-related questions, such as, "What functions were included in the copy module again?" or "What was the default value of the indent parameter of the pprint.pprint function again?"

Instead of starting the interactive shell of the help function, an instance such as a module or a function can also be passed to the help function. Then the corresponding help page is displayed in read mode:

```
>>> import pprint
>>> help(pprint.pprint)
Help on function pprint in module pprint:
```

```
pprint(object, stream=None, indent=1, width=80, depth=None, *, compact=False)
    Pretty-print a Python object to a stream [default is sys.stdout].
```

Alternatively, a string can be passed that contains the search term:

```
>>> import copy
>>> help("copy.copy")
Help on function copy in copy:

copy.copy = copy(x)
    Shallow copy operation on arbitrary Python objects.

    See the module's __doc__ string for more info.
```

9.2   The Online Documentation

The texts displayed by Python's interactive help function are excerpts from the extensive online documentation. The latest version can be found at *https://docs.python.org*. There, you can switch to the documentation of an older Python version via a selection list in the upper-left-hand corner.

The online documentation is a great help for both beginners and experienced Python developers. It's worth looking up the topics covered in this book again in the documentation if you're interested because modules often provide a wealth of detailed functions that can't be described comprehensively here.

9.3   PEPs

The development processes for the Python language and the CPython reference interpreter are based on so-called *Python Enhancement Proposals (PEPs)*. These are short elaborations that identify a problem in the language or interpreter, summarize possible solutions and the discussion about them, and finally propose a solution. These PEPs are the basis for discussion among Python developers for possible innovations in future versions. PEPs can be accepted or rejected after discussion has taken place, with accepted PEPs then being implemented in a future version of Python.

Check out *https://www.python.org/dev/peps* for a list of all PEPs that have been proposed to this date. Especially if you have detailed questions about why a function was implemented in Python in a certain way, it makes sense to read through the associated PEP. It should be noted, however, that a PEP can sometimes be very technical and may be difficult to understand even for experienced Python developers.

PEP 435 is an example of an accepted and implemented PEP. It describes the Enum data type, which has been included in the language since Python 3.4.

Note

Rather interesting are PEPs 8 and 257, which describe conventions for formatting Python code and docstrings.[1] Although these PEPs are by no means binding, they are very popular in the community. It's therefore worth taking a look at them.

---

1 See *python.org/dev/peps/pep-0008* and *python.org/dev/peps/pep-0257*.

PART II
Data Types

In Part I of this book, you learned about and used some basic data types, such as integers, strings, and lists. As you probably already guessed, there is much more to learn about data types in Python beyond the introductory examples introduced in Part I. The second part of this book contains a comprehensive discussion of the basic data types defined in Python.

Chapter 10
Basic Data Types: An Overview

In Chapter 7, Section 7.1.1, we dealt with the notion of a *data type* as a blueprint for an instance. A data type thus specifies which values an instance can have. The data type of an instance can be identified via the built-in `type` function:

```
>>> x = "Hello"
>>> type(x)
<class 'str'>
```

In this chapter, we want to address some basic aspects of the topic of data types before we explore the central data types of Python one by one. We have already learned about many of the basic data types in Chapter 3 and tested them in practice.

From Chapter 7, Section 7.3, you also already know the basic concept of the mutability of instances. Instances of some data types, so-called mutable data types, can be modified. For other data types, referred to as *immutable data types*, new instances must be created when they're changed. See Table 10.1 for an overview of the built-in data types in Python, along with a note on their mutability.

Data Type	Stores	Mutability	Section
NoneType	Nothing	Immutable	Section 10.1
Numeric Data Types			
int	Integers	Immutable	Chapter 11, Section 11.4
float	Floats	Immutable	Chapter 11, Section 11.5
bool	Boolean values	Immutable	Chapter 11, Section 11.6
complex	Complex numbers	Immutable	Chapter 11, Section 11.7
Sequential Data Types			
list	Lists of any instances	Mutable	Chapter 12, Section 12.3
tuple	Lists of any instances	Immutable	Chapter 12, Section 12.4
str	Text as a sequence of letters	Immutable	Chapter 12, Section 12.5

Table 10.1 Overview of the Data Types in Python

Data Type	Stores	Mutability	Section
bytes	Binary data as a sequence of bytes	Immutable	Chapter 12, Section 12.5
bytearray	Binary data as a sequence of bytes	Mutable	Chapter 12, Section 12.5
Mappings and Sets			
dict	Key-value mappings	Mutable	Chapter 13, Section 13.1
set	Sets of hashable instances	Mutable	Chapter 13, Section 13.2.5
frozenset	Sets of hashable instances	Immutable	Chapter 13, Section 13.2.6

Table 10.1 Overview of the Data Types in Python (Cont.)

Beyond the data types listed in Table 10.1, this part of the book also describes other data types that can be imported via modules of the standard library.

10.1   Nothingness: NoneType

Let's start our journey through data types in Python with the simplest data type of all: the nothing. The corresponding basic data type is called NoneType. Of course, the question arises of why a data type is needed that is only there to represent nothing. Well, it's actually only logical. Let's imagine the following situation: You implement a method where any real number is a possible outcome. However, in some cases, the calculation may not be feasible. What value should be returned as the result? Correct: nothing.

There's only one instance of nothingness—namely, None. This is a constant you can use at any time in the source code:

```
>>> ref = None
>>> ref
>>> print(ref)
None
```

In the example, a reference named ref was created to None. In the second line, we notice that None actually corresponds to nothing: we try to output ref from the interpreter and actually get no result. To be able to output the value on the screen anyway, we have to use the print function.

It's already been mentioned that None is the only instance of nothingness. We can take advantage of this feature to check whether a reference points to None or not:

```
>>> if ref is None:
...     print("ref is None")
ref is None
```

The keyword is is used to check whether the instance referenced by ref is identical to None. This way of testing a value for None can be executed faster by the interpreter than the value-based comparison via the == operator, which is of course also possible. Note that these two operations are only superficially equivalent: With == two values and with is two identities are checked for equality.[1]

10.2 Operators

You know the term *operator* from math, where it denotes a formula character that stands for a certain arithmetic operation. In Python, for example, you can use operators to combine two numeric values into an arithmetic expression:

```
>>> 1 + 2
3
```

The values to which an operator is applied—in this case, 1 and 2—are called *operands*. There are also operators for other data types. For example, + can be used to join two strings:

```
>>> "A" + "B"
'AB'
```

So in Python, the meaning of an operator depends on which data type it is applied to.

10.2.1 Operator Precedence

We'll limit ourselves in this section to the operators +, -, *, and <, which are sufficient to explain the underlying principle. In the following examples, the three references a, b, and c occur again and again, and they are not created in the examples themselves. To run the examples, of course, the references must exist and reference, for example, an integer each.

Consider the following expressions:

```
(a * b) + c
a * (b + c)
```

Both are unambiguous in their meaning as the parentheses indicate which part of the expression is to be evaluated first. Let's write the preceding expression once without parentheses:

```
a * b + c
```

---

1 For more details, see Chapter 7.

Now it's no longer obvious which part of the expression should be evaluated first. A regulation is essential here, because depending on the evaluation sequence, different results can occur:

```
(2 * 3) + 4 = 10
2 * (3 + 4) = 14
```

To solve this problem, operators in Python, as in math, have a *precedence*, which is defined in such a way that * takes precedence over +. Table 10.2 shows the operator precedence for the operators defined in Python. In addition, the table provides a description of the usual meaning of an operator. Operators that are higher up in the table bind more strongly than operators located further down toward the bottom of the table. Operators that are in the same cell have an equally strong binding.

> **Note**
>
> Table 10.2 covers only a subset of the syntax elements that can be contained in a valid expression. The appendix of this book specifies the complete ranking of syntax elements in a valid expression.

Operator	Usual Meaning
x ** y	yth power of x
+x	Positive sign
-x	Negative sign
~x	Bitwise complement of x
x * y	Product of x and y
x / y	Quotient of x and y
x % y	Remainder for integer division of x by y
x // y	Integer division of x by y
x @ y	Matrix multiplication of x and y
x + y	Addition of x and y
x - y	Subtraction of x and y
x << n	Bitwise shift by n places to the left
x >> n	Bitwise shift by n places to the right
x & y	Bitwise AND between x and y
x ^ y	Bitwise exclusive OR between x and y
x | y	Bitwise nonexclusive OR between x and y

Table 10.2 Operator Precedence

Operator	Usual Meaning
x < y	Is x smaller than y?
x <= y	Is x less than or equal to y?
x > y	Is x greater than y?
x >= y	Is x greater than or equal to y?
x != y	Is x unequal to y?
x == y	Is x equal to y?
x is y	Are x and y identical?
x is not y	Are x and y not identical?
x in y	Is x located in y?
x not in y	Is x not located in y?
not x	Logical negation
x and y	Logical AND
x or y	Logical OR

Table 10.2 Operator Precedence (Cont.)

10.2.2 Evaluation Order

The operator precedence ensures the evaluation of an expression consisting of operators of different bindability. But what happens if the same operator appears several times in the expression? In that case, there can then no longer be any difference in the bindability. Let's consider the following expressions in this context:

```
a + b + c
a - b - c
```

In both cases, the evaluation order is not unambiguously clarified either by parentheses or by the operator precedence. You can see that this is not a problem for the evaluation of the first expression, but at least for the second expression a regulation is necessary, because depending on the evaluation order two different results are possible. In such a case, Python has the rule that expressions or subexpressions consisting only of operators with the same bindability are evaluated *from left to right*:

```
a + b + c == ((a + b) + c)
a - b - c == ((a - b) - c)
```

10.2.3 Concatenating Comparisons

With a few exceptions,[2] we've so far only described operators that return a value of the operand type as a result. Thus, the result of an addition of two integers is always an

---

2 An exception is the division operator /, whose result is a float even with integer operands.

integer. However, this is not the case for every operator. You already know the comparison operators, which, regardless of the data type of the operands, result in a truth value:

```
>>> 1 < 2.5
True
```

Think about the evaluation order of this expression:

```
a < b < c
```

Theoretically it's possible, and it's done this way in some programming languages, to proceed according to the schema discussed previously: the concatenated comparisons should be evaluated from left to right. In this case, a < b would be evaluated first, yielding True, for example. The next comparison would be True < c. Although such a form of evaluation is possible, it has no practical use—because what exactly is True < c supposed to mean?

In Python, certain operators are handled in a special way. The expression a < b < c is evaluated to be equivalent to the following:

```
a < b and b < c
```

This corresponds to the mathematical view because the expression actually means: "Is b between a and c?" This descriptive rule is applied in a similar way for more complex expressions. For example, the expression a < b <= c != d > e is evaluated as follows:

```
a < b and b <= c and c != d and d > e
```

This behavior applies to the following operators: <, <=, >, >=, ==, !=, is, is not, in, and not in.

Chapter 11
Numeric Data Types

In this chapter, we'll describe numeric data types, the first major group of data types in Python. Table 11.1 lists all the data types belonging to this group and describes their purpose.

Data Type	Description	Mutability*	Section
int	Integers	Immutable	Section 11.4
float	Floats	Immutable	Section 11.5
bool	Boolean values	Immutable	Section 11.6
complex	Complex numbers	Immutable	Section 11.7

* All numeric data types are immutable. This doesn't mean that there are no operators that change numbers, but rather that a new instance of the respective data type must be created after each change. So from the programmer's perspective, there is hardly any difference at first. For more details on the difference between mutable and immutable data types, see Chapter 7, Section 7.3.

Table 11.1 Numeric Data Types

The numeric data types form a group because they're related thematically. This relatedness is also reflected in the fact that the numeric data types have many operators in common. In the following sections, we'll cover these common operators, and then we'll discuss the int, float, bool, and complex numeric data types in detail.

11.1 Arithmetic Operators

An *arithmetic operator* is considered an operator that performs an arithmetic calculation—for example, addition or multiplication. For all numeric data types, the arithmetic operators listed in Table 11.2 are defined.

Operator	Result
x + y	Sum of x and y
x - y	Difference of x and y

Table 11.2 Common Operators of Numeric Data Types

Operator	Result
x * y	Product of x and y
x / y	Quotient of x and y
x % y	Remainder when dividing x by y*
+x	Positive sign
-x	Negative sign
x ** y	x to the power of y
x // y	Rounded quotient of x and y*

* The % and // operators have no mathematical meaning for complex numbers and are therefore not defined for the complex data type.

Table 11.2 Common Operators of Numeric Data Types (Cont.)

Note

Two notes for readers who are already familiar with C or a related programming language:

First, there are no equivalents in Python for the increment and decrement operators, ++ and --, from C.

Second, the % and // operators can be described as follows:

- x // y = round(x / y)
- x % y = x - y * round(x / y)

Python always rounds down, while C rounds up to zero. This difference occurs only if the operands have opposite signs.

Augmented Assignments

Besides these basic operators, there are a number of additional operators in Python. Often, for example, you want to calculate the total of x and y and store the result in x—that is, increase x by y. This requires the following statement with the operators shown previously:

```
x = x + y
```

For such cases, Python provides so-called *augmented assignments*, which can be regarded as an abbreviated form of the preceding statement. An overview of augmented assignments in Python in presented in Table 11.3.

Operator	Equivalent
x += y	x = x + y
x -= y	x = x - y
x *= y	x = x * y
x /= y	x = x / y
x %= y	x = x % y
x **= y	x = x ** y
x //= y	x = x // y

Table 11.3 Common Operators of Numeric Data Types

It's important to note that you can use any arithmetic expression for y here, while x must be an expression that could also be used as the target of a normal assignment such as a symbolic name or an item of a list or dictionary.

11.2   Comparison Operators

A *comparison operator* is an operator that computes a truth value from two instances. Table 11.4 lists the comparison operators defined for numeric data types.

Operator	Result
x == y	True if x and y are equal
x != y	True if x and y are different
x < y	True if x is less than y[*]
x <= y	True if x is less than or equal to y[*]
x > y	True if x is greater than y[*]
x >= y	True if x is greater than or equal to y[*]

[*] Because complex numbers can't be arranged in a meaningful way, the complex data type only allows for using the first two operators.

Table 11.4 Common Operators of Numeric Data Types

Each of these comparison operators returns a truth value as a result. Such a value is expected, for example, as a condition of an if statement. So the operators could be used as follows:

```
if x < 4:
    print("x is less than 4")
```

You can concatenate as many of the comparison operators as you like into a series. Strictly speaking, the preceding example is only a special case of this rule, as it has only two operands. The meaning of such a concatenation corresponds to the mathematical view and can be seen in the following example:

```
if 2 < x < 4:
    print("x is between 2 and 4")
```

We'll describe Boolean values in more detail in Section 11.6.

11.3   Conversion between Numeric Data Types

Numeric data types can be converted into each other using the int, float, bool, and complex built-in functions. Note that in the process, information can be lost depending on the transformation. As an example, let's consider some conversions in interactive mode:

```
>>> float(33)
33.0
>>> int(33.5)
33
>>> bool(12)
True
>>> complex(True)
(1+0j)
```

Instead of a concrete literal, a reference can also be used or a reference can be linked to the resulting value:

```
>>> var1 = 12.5
>>> int(var1)
12
>>> var2 = int(40.25)
>>> var2
40
```

Note

The complex data type assumes a special role in the conversions presented here as it can't be reduced to a single numerical value in a meaningful way. For this reason, a conversion such as int(1+2j) fails.

So much for the general introduction to numeric data types. The following sections will cover each data type in this group in more detail.

11.4   Integers: int

For working with integers, there is the data type int in Python. Unlike many other programming languages, this data type is not subject to any principal limits in its value range, which makes dealing with large integers in Python very convenient.[1]

We've already done a lot of work with integers, so using int doesn't really need any more demonstration. Nevertheless, for the sake of completeness, here is a small example:

```
>>> i = 1234
>>> i
1234
>>> p = int(5678)
>>> p
5678
```

Since the release of Python 3.6, an underscore can be used to group the digits of a literal:

```
>>> 1_000_000
1000000
>>> 1_0_0
100
```

Grouping doesn't change the numerical value of the literal, but it serves to increase the readability of numerical literals. Whether and how you group the digits is up to you.

11.4.1   Numeral Systems

Integers can be written in Python in multiple *numeral systems:*[2]

- Numbers written without a special prefix, as in the previous example, are interpreted in the *decimal system* (base 10). Note that such a number must not be preceded by leading zeros:

  ```
  v_dez = 1337
  ```

---

1 In Python 2, there were still two data types for integers: int for the limited number space of 32 bits or 64 bits, and long with an unlimited value range.
2 If you don't know what a numeral system is, you can easily skip this section.

- The prefix 0o ("zero-o") indicates a number written in the *octal system* (base 8). Note that only digits from 0 to 7 are allowed here:

```
v_oct = 0o2471
```

The lowercase *o* in the prefix can also be replaced with a capital *O*. However, we recommend that you always use a lowercase *o* because the uppercase *O* is almost indistinguishable from the zero in many fonts.

- The next and far more common variant is the *hexadecimal system* (base 16), which is identified by the prefix 0x or 0X ("zero-x"). The number itself may be formed from the digits 0–9 and the letters A–F or a–f:

```
v_hex = 0x5A3F
```

- In addition to the hexadecimal system, the *dual* system, also referred to as *binary system* (base 2), is of decisive importance in computer science. Numbers in the dual system are introduced by the prefix 0b, similar to the preceding literals:

```
v_bin = 0b1101
```

In the dual system, only the digits 0 and 1 may be used.

However, you may not want to limit yourself to these four numeral systems explicitly supported by Python; you may want to use a more exotic one. Of course, Python doesn't have a separate literal for every possible numeral system. Instead, you can use the following notation:

```
v_6 = int("54425", 6)
```

This is an alternative method of creating an instance of the int data type and providing it with an initial value. For this purpose, a string containing the desired initial value in the selected numeral system and the base of this numeral system as an integer are written in the brackets. Both values must be separated by a comma. In the example, a base 6 system was used.

Python supports numeral systems with a base from 2 to 36. If a numeral system requires more than 10 different digits to represent a number, the letters A to Z of the English alphabet are used in addition to the digits 0 to 9.

The v_6 variable now has the value 7505 in the decimal system.

For all numeral system literals, the use of a negative sign is possible:

```
>>> -1234
-1234
>>> -0o777
-511
>>> -0xFF
-255
>>> -0b1010101
-85
```

Note that the numeral systems are only alternate notations of the same values. The int data type, for example, doesn't switch to a kind of hexadecimal mode as soon as it contains such a value; the numeral system is only of importance for assignments or outputs. By default, all numbers are output in the decimal system:

```
>>> v1 = 0xFF
>>> v2 = 0o777
>>> v1
255
>>> v2
511
```

We'll return to how numbers can be output in other numeral systems later, in Chapter 12, Section 12.5.3 in the context of strings.

11.4.2 Bit Operations

As already mentioned, the dual system or binary system is of great importance in computer science. For the int data type, some additional operators are therefore defined that explicitly refer to the binary representation of the number. Table 11.5 summarizes these *bit operators*.

Operator	Augmented Assignment	Result
x & y	x &= y	Bitwise AND of x and y (AND)
x | y	x |= y	Bitwise nonexclusive OR of x and y (OR)
x ^ y	x ^= y	Bitwise exclusive OR of x and y (XOR)
~x		Bitwise complement of x
x << n	x <<= n	Bit shift by n places to the left
x >> n	x >>= n	Bit shift by n places to the right

Table 11.5 Bit Operators of the int Data Type

Because it may not be immediately clear what the individual operations do, we'll describe them in detail ahead.

Bitwise AND

The *bitwise AND* of two numbers is formed by linking both numbers in their binary representation bit by bit. The resulting number has a 1 in its binary representation exactly where both of the respective bits of the operands are 1, and a 0 in all other places. Figure 11.1 illustrates this.

Binary							Decimal
1	1	0	1	0	1	1	107
& 0	0	1	1	0	0	1	25
0	0	0	1	0	0	1	9

Figure 11.1 Bitwise AND

Let's now try out in the interactive mode of Python whether the bitwise AND with the operands selected in the graphic actually returns the expected result:

```
>>> 107 & 25
9
>>> 0b1101011 & 0b11001
9
>>> bin(0b1101011 & 0b11001)
'0b1001'
```

In the example we use the built-in function bin (see Chapter 17, Section 17.14.5) to represent the result of the bitwise AND in the binary system.

Bitwise OR

The *bitwise OR* of two numbers is formed by comparing both numbers in their binary representation bit by bit. The resulting number has a 1 in its binary representation exactly where at least one of the respective bits of the operands is 1. Figure 11.2 illustrates this.

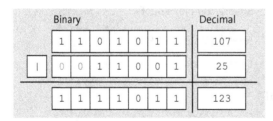

Binary							Decimal
1	1	0	1	0	1	1	107
| 0	0	1	1	0	0	1	25
1	1	1	1	0	1	1	123

Figure 11.2 Bitwise Nonexclusive OR

We'll now try out in the interactive mode of Python whether the bitwise OR with the operands selected in the graphic actually returns the expected result:

```
>>> 107 | 25
123
>>> 0b1101011 | 0b11001
123
```

```
>>> bin(0b1101011 | 0b11001)
'0b1111011'
```

In the example we use the built-in function bin (see Chapter 17, Section 17.14.5) to represent the result of the bitwise OR in the binary system.

Bitwise Exclusive OR

The *bitwise exclusive OR* (also *exclusive OR*) of two numbers is formed by comparing both numbers in their binary representation bit by bit. The resulting number has a 1 in its binary representation exactly where the respective bits of the operands differ from each other, and a 0 where they are the same. This is shown in Figure 11.3.

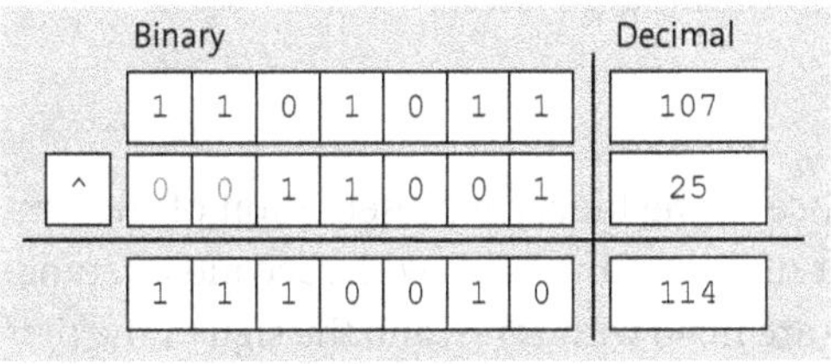

Binary							Decimal
1	1	0	1	0	1	1	107
0	0	1	1	0	0	1	25
1	1	1	0	0	1	0	114

Figure 11.3 Bitwise Exclusive OR

In the next step, we'll try out in the interactive mode of Python whether the bitwise exclusive OR with the operands selected in the graphic actually returns the expected result:

```
>>> 107 ^ 25
114
>>> 0b1101011 ^ 0b11001
114
>>> bin(0b1101011 ^ 0b11001)
'0b1110010'
```

In the example we use the built-in function bin (see Chapter 17, Section 17.14.5) to represent the result of the bitwise exclusive OR in the binary system.

Bitwise Complement

The *bitwise complement* forms the so-called one's complement of a dual number, which corresponds to the negation of all occurring bits. In Python, this isn't possible at the bit level because an integer is unlimited in length and the complement must always be formed in a closed number space. For this reason, the actual bit operation becomes an arithmetic operation and is defined as follows:[3]

---

3 This makes sense because the so-called *two's complement* is used to represent negative numbers in closed number spaces. This is obtained by adding 1 to the ones' complement.
So: $-x$ = two's complement of x = $\sim x + 1$. From this follows: $\sim x = -x - 1$.

$\sim x = -x - 1$

In the interactive mode, the functionality of the bitwise complement can be tested experimentally:

```
>>> ~9
-10
>>> ~0b1001
-10
>>> bin(~0b1001)
'-0b1010'
```

In the example we use the built-in function bin (see Chapter 17, Section 17.14.5) to represent the result of the bitwise complement in the binary system.

Bit Shift

The *bit shift* is used to shift the bit sequence in the binary representation of the first operand to the left or right by the number of places provided by the second operand. Any gaps that occur on the right-hand side are filled with zeros, and the sign of the first operand is retained. Figure 11.4 and Figure 11.5 illustrate a shift of two places to the left and to the right, respectively.

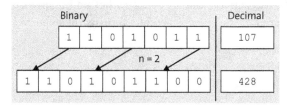

Figure 11.4 Bit Shift by Two Places to the Left

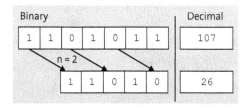

Figure 11.5 Bit Shift by Two Places to the Right

The gaps that occur in the bit representation on the right- or left-hand side are filled with zeros.

The bit shift is implemented arithmetically in Python, similar to the complement operator. A shift by x places to the right corresponds to an integer division by 2^x. A shift by x places to the left corresponds to a multiplication by 2^x.

For the bitwise shifts too, we can follow the examples shown in the graphics in the interactive mode:

```
>>> 107 << 2
428
>>> 107 >> 2
26
>>> bin(0b1101011 << 2)
'0b110101100'
>>> bin(0b1101011 >> 2)
'0b11010'
```

In the example we use the built-in function bin (see Chapter 17, Section 17.14.5) to represent the result of the bit shifts in the binary system.

11.4.3   Methods

The int data type has a method that refers to the binary representation of the integer. The bit_length method calculates the number of digits needed for the binary representation of the number:

```
>>> (36).bit_length()
6
>>> (4345).bit_length()
13
```

The binary representation of 36 is 100100, and that of 4345 is 1000011111001. Thus, the two numbers require 6 and 13 digits, respectively, for their binary representation.

> **Note**
>
> Note that the parentheses around the number literals are required for integers; otherwise there could be ambiguities with regard to the syntax for floats.

11.5   Floats: float

We mentioned floats briefly earlier. Now we'd like to describe in them in greater detail. To store a float with limited precision,[4] you can use the float data type.

As discussed previously, the literal for a float in the simplest case looks like this:

```
v = 3.141
```

---

4 See Section 11.5.2 for further remarks on the precision.

The parts before and after the period can be omitted if they have the value 0:

```
>>> -3.
-3.0
>>> .001
0.001
```

Note here that the period is an essential element of a float literal and as such must not be omitted.

Since Python 3.6, an underscore can also be used to group the digits of a float literal:

```
>>> 3.000_000_1
3.0000001
```

11.5.1 Exponential Notation

Python also supports a notation that allows you to use the exponential notation:

```
v = 3.141e-12
```

A lowercase or uppercase e separates the *mantissa* (3.141) from the *exponent* (-12). Translated into mathematical notation, this corresponds to the value $3.141 \cdot 10^{-12}$. Note that both the mantissa and the exponent must be specified in the decimal system. As no other numeral systems are supported, it's safe to use leading zeros:

```
v = 03.141e-0012
```

11.5.2 Precision

You may have just experimented a bit with floats and encountered a supposed error in the interpreter:

```
>>> 1.1 + 2.2
3.3000000000000003
```

Real numbers can't be stored with infinite precision in the float data type, but are instead approximated.

Technically savvy people and those switching from other programming languages will be interested to know that float instances in Python are IEEE-754 floats with double precision. The float data type in Python is thus comparable to the double data type in C, C++, and Java.

If you want to explicitly use single precision floats, you can draw on the float32 data type of the third-party NumPy library (see Chapter 43).

11.5.3 Infinite and Not a Number

The precision of float is limited. This also implies that there must be both an upper and lower limit for this data type. And indeed, floats that exceed a certain limit in size can no longer be represented in Python. If the limit is exceeded, the number is stored as inf[5] or as -inf if the number has fallen below the lower limit. So there is no error, and it's still possible to compare a number that's too high with others:

```
>>> 3.0e999
inf
>>> -3.0e999
-inf
>>> 3.0e999 < 12.0
False
>>> 3.0e999 > 12.0
True
>>> 3.0e999 == 3.0e999999999999
True
```

Although it's possible to compare two infinitely large floats with each other, you can only use them to a limited extent for calculations. Let's look at the following example:

```
>>> 3.0e999 + 1.5e999999
inf
>>> 3.0e999 - 1.5e999999
nan
>>> 3.0e999 * 1.5e999999
inf
>>> 3.0e999 / 1.5e999999
nan
>>> 5 / 1e9999
0.0
```

Two infinite floats can be easily added or multiplied. The result in both cases is again inf. However, there's a problem when trying to subtract or divide two such numbers. Because these arithmetic operations don't make sense, they result in nan. The nan status is comparable to inf, but it means "not a number"—that is, not calculable.

Note that neither inf nor nan is a constant you could use yourself in a Python program. Instead, you can create float instances with the values inf and nan as follows:

```
>>> float("inf")
inf
>>> float("nan")
nan
```

---

5 Here, *inf* stands for *infinity*.

```
>>> float("inf") / float("inf")
nan
```

11.6   Boolean Values: bool

An instance of the bool[6] data type can have only two different values: true or false—or, to stay within the Python syntax, True or False. For this reason, it's absurd to categorize bool as a numeric data type at first glance. As is common usage in many programming languages, in Python, True is regarded as similar to 1 and False as similar to 0, so that Boolean values can be calculated in the same way as, for example, integers. The names True and False are constants that can be used in the source code. Note especially that the constants start with an uppercase letter:

```
v1 = True
v2 = False
```

11.6.1   Logical Operators

One or more Boolean values can be combined into a Boolean expression using certain operators. When evaluated, such an expression results again in a Boolean value—that is, True or False. Before it gets too theoretical, Table 11.6 shows the so-called logical operators.[7] We'll follow that with further explanations and concrete examples.

Operator	Result
not x	Logical negation of x
x and y	Logical AND between x and y
x or y	Logical (nonexclusive) OR between x and y

Table 11.6 Logical Operators of the bool Data Type

Logical Negation

The *logical negation* of a Boolean value can be quickly explained: the corresponding not operator turns True into False and False into True. In a concrete example, this would look as follows:

```
if not x:
    print("x is False")
else:
    print("x is True")
```

---

6 The name bool goes back to the British mathematician and logician George Boole (1815–1864).

7 Note that there's a difference between logical operators, which refer to Boolean values, and binary operators, which refer to the binary representation of a number.

Logical AND

The *logical AND* between two truth values only returns True if both operands are already True. Table 11.7 lists all possible cases.

x	y	x and y
True	True	True
False	True	False
True	False	False
False	False	False

Table 11.7 Possible Cases of Logical AND

In a concrete example, the application of logical AND would look as follows:

```
if x and y:
    print("x and y are True")
```

Logical OR

The *logical OR* between two truth values results in a true statement if and only if at least one of the two operands is true. Accordingly, it's a nonexclusive OR. An operator for a logical exclusive OR doesn't exist in Python.[8] Table 11.8 lists all possible cases.

x	y	x or y
True	True	True
False	True	True
True	False	True
False	False	False

Table 11.8 Possible Cases of Logical OR

A logical OR could be implemented as follows:

```
if x or y:
    print("x or y is True")
```

Of course, you can combine all these operators and use them in a complex expression. This could look something like this:

```
if x and y or ((y and z) and not x):
    print("Holy cow")
```

---

8 A logical exclusive OR between x and y can be modeled using (x or y) and not (x and y).

At this point, we don't want to discuss this expression in further detail. Suffice to say that the use of parentheses has the expected effect—namely, that expressions in parentheses are evaluated first. Table 11.9 shows the truth value of the expression, as a function of the three parameters x, y, and z.

x	y	z	x and y or ((y and z) and not x)
True	True	True	True
False	True	True	True
True	False	True	False
True	True	False	True
False	False	True	False
False	True	False	False
True	False	False	False
False	False	False	False

Table 11.9 Possible Results of the Expression

The Combination of Logical Operators and Comparison Operators

At the beginning of the section on numeric data types, we introduced some comparison operators that yield a truth statement as a Boolean value. The following example shows that they can be used quite normally in combination with the logical operators:

```
if x > y or (y > z and x != 0):
    print("My goodness")
```

In this case, x, y, and z must be instances of comparable types, such as int, float, or bool.

11.6.2   Truth Values of Non-Boolean Data Types

Instances of any basic data type can be converted to a Boolean value using the built-in bool function:

```
>>> bool([1,2,3])
True
>>> bool("")
False
>>> bool(-7)
True
```

This is a useful property because an instance of the basic data types can often be in one of two stages: "empty" and "nonempty." For example, it often happens that you want to test whether a string contains letters or not. Because a string can be converted to a Boolean value, such a test is made very easy by logical operators:

```
>>> not ""
True
>>> not "abc"
False
```

By using a logical operator, the operand is automatically interpreted as a truth value.

For each basic data type, a specific value is defined as False. All other values are True. Table 11.10 lists the corresponding False value for each data type. Some of the data types haven't been introduced yet, but you shouldn't worry about that at this point.

Basic Data Type	False Value	Description
NoneType	None	The None value
Numeric Data Types		
int	0	The numeric value zero
float	0.0	The numeric value zero
bool	False	The boolean value False
complex	0 + 0j	The numeric value zero
Sequential Data Types		
str	""	An empty string
list	[]	An empty list
tuple	()	An empty tuple
Associative Data Types		
dict	{}	An empty dictionary
Quantities		
set	set()	An empty set
frozenset	frozenset()	An empty set

Table 11.10 Truth Values of the Basic Data Types

All other values result in True.

11.6.3   Evaluating Logical Operators

Python evaluates logical expressions basically from left to right—so in the following example, first a, then b:

```
if a or b:
    print("a or b are True")
```

However, it isn't guaranteed that every part of the expression will actually be evaluated. For optimization reasons, Python immediately terminates the evaluation of the expression when the result has been obtained. So, in the preceding example, if a already has the value True, the value of b is of no further concern; b would then no longer be evaluated. The following example demonstrates this behavior, which is referred to as *lazy evaluation*:

```
>>> a = True
>>> if a or print("Lazy "):
...     print("Evaluation")
...
Evaluation
```

Although the print function is called in the condition of the if statement, this screen output is never performed because the value of the condition is already certain after the evaluation of a. This detail seems unimportant, but it can lead to errors that are hard to find, especially in the context of functions with side effects.[9]

In Section 11.6.1, we mentioned that a Boolean expression always yields a Boolean value when evaluated. This is not quite correct because here too, the interpreter's way of working has been optimized in a way you should be aware of. This is clearly illustrated by the following example from the interactive mode:

```
>>> 0 or 1
1
```

From what we have discussed so far, the result of the expression should be True, which is not the case. Instead, Python returns the first operand here with the truth value True. In many cases this does not make a difference, because the returned value is automatically converted to the truth value True without any problem.

The evaluation of the two operators or and and works as follows: The logical OR (or) takes the value of the first operand that has the truth value True, or—if there is no such operand—the value of the last operand. The logical AND (and) takes the value of the first operand that has the truth value False, or—if there is no such value—the value of the last operand.

---

9 See Chapter 17, Section 17.10.

However, these details also have an entertaining value:

```
>>> "Python" or "Java"
'Python'
```

11.7   Complex Numbers: complex

Surprisingly, there is a data type for storing complex numbers among the basic data types of Python. In many programming languages, complex numbers would be more of a side note in the standard library or left out altogether. If you aren't familiar with complex numbers, you can safely skip this section. It doesn't cover anything that would be required for further learning Python.

Complex numbers consist of a real part and an imaginary part. The imaginary part is a real number multiplied by the imaginary unit j.[10] The imaginary unit j is defined as the solution of the following equation:

$$j^2 = -1$$

In the following example, we assign the name v to a complex number:

```
v = 4j
```

If you specify only an imaginary part, as in the example, the real part is automatically assumed to be 0. To determine the real part, it is added to the imaginary part. The following two notations are equivalent:

```
v1 = 3 + 4j
v2 = 4j + 3
```

Instead of a lowercase j, you can also use an uppercase J as a literal for the imaginary part of a complex number. It's entirely up to your preferences which of the two options you want to use.

Both the real and imaginary parts can be any real number. The following notation is therefore also correct:

```
v3 = 3.4 + 4e2j
```

At the beginning of the section on numeric data types, we already indicated that complex numbers differ from the other numeric data types. Since no mathematical ordering is defined for complex numbers, instances of the complex data type can only be checked for equality or inequality. The set of comparison operators is thus limited to == and !=.

---

10 The symbol of the imaginary unit, which is actually common in mathematics, is i. Python adheres to the notations of electrical engineering here.

Furthermore, both the % modulo operator and the // operator for integer division have no mathematical sense and are therefore not available in combination with complex numbers.

The complex data type has two attributes that make it easier to use it. For example, it can happen that you want to make calculations only with the real part or only with the imaginary part of the stored number. To isolate one of the two parts, a complex instance provides the attributes listed in Table 11.11.

Attribute	Description
x.real	Real part of x as a float
x.imag	Imaginary part of x as a float

Table 11.11 Attributes of the complex Data Type

These can be used as shown in the following example:

```
>>> c = 23 + 4j
>>> c.real
23.0
>>> c.imag
4.0
```

In addition to its two attributes, the complex data type has a method, which is explained in Table 11.12 as an example of a reference to a complex number called x.

Method	Description
x.conjugate()	Returns the complex number conjugated to x

Table 11.12 Methods of the complex Data Type

The following example demonstrates the use of the conjugate method:

```
>>> c = 23 + 4j
>>> c.conjugate()
(23-4j)
```

The result of conjugate is again a complex number and therefore also has the conjugate method:

```
>>> c = 23 + 4j
>>> c2 = c.conjugate()
>>> c2
(23-4j)
```

```
>>> c3 = c2.conjugate()
>>> c3
(23+4j)
```

Conjugating a complex number is a self-inverse operation. This means that the result of a double conjugation is again the initial number.

Chapter 12
Sequential Data Types

Sequential data types refers to a class of data types that manage sequences of similar or different *elements*. The elements stored in sequential data types have a defined order, and they can be accessed through unique indexes.

Python essentially provides the following five sequential types: str, bytes, bytearray, list, and tuple, see Table 12.1.

Data Type	Stores	Mutability	Section
list	Lists of any instances	Mutable	Section 12.3
tuple	Lists of any instances	Immutable	Section 12.4
str	Text as a sequence of letters	Immutable	Section 12.5
bytes	Binary data as a sequence of bytes	Immutable	Section 12.5
bytearray	Binary data as a sequence of bytes	Mutable	Section 12.5

Table 12.1 List of Sequential Data Types

12.1   The Difference between Text and Binary Data

The str data type is intended for storing and processing text. Therefore, a str instance consists of a sequence of letters, spaces, punctuation marks, and line feeds; these are exactly the components that make up text in human language. It's remarkable that this also works with regional special characters such as the German umlauts *ä*, *ü*, and *ö*.

In contrast, an instance of the bytes data type can store a binary data stream—that is, a sequence of bytes. The bytearray data type is also capable of storing binary data. However, bytearray instances are mutable, unlike bytes instances.

The structural separation of textual data and binary data is a feature that distinguishes Python from many other programming languages.

> **Note**
>
> The str and bytes data types represent one of the major differences between Python 2 and Python 3. In Python 2, there were the two data types, str and unicode, where str corresponded to the current bytes and unicode to the current str.

Because the old data type `str` often was used to store text strings, there were some stumbling blocks if you wanted to process special characters with Python programs.

Due to the `str` and `bytes` types in Python 3, the handling of strings is more clearly structured. However, you must pay attention to which data type functions of the standard library expect as parameters or return as return values and then make conversions if necessary.

For more information, see Section 12.5.4.

Instances of the `str` data type and of the `bytes` data type are immutable, so their value can't change after instantiation. Nevertheless, you can conveniently use and manipulate strings. When changes are made, the original string won't be changed because a new string is always created instead.

The `list` and `tuple` types can store sequences of any instances. The main difference between the two almost identical data types is that a list can be modified after it has been created, while a tuple does not allow the initial contents to be modified: `list` is a mutable, `tuple` an immutable data type.

Note

The distinction between mutable and immutable data types is very central in Python. Since the mutability is the essential difference between the data types `list` and `tuple`, the question arises why the tuple as an immutable variant of the list is actually needed.

One reason is that tuples, because of their immutability, can be used in situations for which lists are not suitable. For example, tuples can be used as keys in a dictionary, while lists are forbidden there. This is due to the concept of *hashability*, which is closely related to immutability.

For each instance of a sequential data type, there is a basic set of operators and methods that's always available. For the sake of simplicity, we'll introduce this using `list` and `str` instances as general examples for a mutable and an immutable sequential data type. Afterwards, we will dive deeper into specific aspects regarding the individual data types.

12.2 Operations on Instances of Sequential Data Types

The following operations are defined for all sequential data types (s and t are instances of the same sequential data type; i, j, k, and n are integers; and x is a reference to an instance; see Table 12.2).

Notation	Description	Section
x in s	Checks whether x is contained in s. The result is a truth value.	Section 12.2.1
x not in s	Checks if x is not contained in s. The result is a `bool` instance. Equivalent to not x in s.	Section 12.2.1
s + t	The result is a new sequence containing the concatenation of s and t.	Section 12.2.2
s += t	Creates the concatenation of s and t and assigns it to s.	Section 12.2.2
s * n or n * s	Returns a new sequence containing the concatenation of n copies of s.	Section 12.2.3
s *= n	Generates the product s * n and assigns it to s.	Section 12.2.3
s[i]	Returns the ith element of s.	Section 12.2.4
s[i:j]	Returns the section of s from i to j.	Section 12.2.5
s[i:j:k]	Returns the section of s from i to j, where only every kth element is considered.	Section 12.2.5
len(s)	Returns the number of elements of s.	Section 12.2.6
max(s)	Returns the largest element of s, provided that an ordering is defined for the elements.	Section 12.2.7
min(s)	Returns the smallest element of s, provided that an ordering is defined for the elements.	Section 12.2.7
s.index(x[, i[, j]])	Returns the index k of the first occurrence of x in the sequence s in the range $i \leq k < j$.	Section 12.2.8
s.count(x)	Counts how often x occurs in the sequence s.	Section 12.2.9

Table 12.2 Operations on Instances of Sequential Data Types

These operations are explained in detail ahead.

12.2.1   Checking for Elements

With the help of in, you can determine whether a certain element is contained in a sequence. For an instance of the list data type that contains both strings and numbers, it looks like this:

```
>>> lst = ["one", 2, 3.0, "four", 5, "six", "seven"]
>>> 3.0 in lst
True
>>> "four" in lst
True
>>> 10 in lst
False
```

Because the elements of a string are characters, we can use the operator to check whether a particular letter occurs in a string. The result is a truth value: True if the element is present and False if it isn't. In Python, you can represent characters using strings of the length 1:

```
>>> s = "This is our test string"
>>> "u" in s
True
>>> if "j" in s:
...     print("Yay, my favorite letter is included")
... else:
...     print("I don't like this string ...")
I don't like this string ...
```

You can also use the in operator to check whether a particular substring is contained in a string:

```
>>> s = "This is our test string"
>>> "is" in s
True
>>> "Hello" in s
False
```

This works only with strings—that is, instances of the types str, bytes, and bytearray. The in operator can't be used to check whether a sublist is contained in a list instance. The same applies to instances of the tuple type:

```
>>> [2,3] in [1,2,3,4]
False
```

To check the opposite—that is, whether an element is *not* contained in a sequence—you can use the not in operator. Its use is the same as that of the in operator, the only difference being that it produces the negated result of the in operator:

```
>>> "a" in "Dentist appointment"
True
>>> "a" not in "Dentist appointment"
False
```

At this point, you'll rightly ask yourself why a separate operator has been defined for this purpose when you can negate any Boolean value with not. The following checks are equivalent:

```
>>> "n" not in "Python is great"
False
>>> not "n" in "Python is great"
False
```

The reason for this seemingly superfluous definition is to make it easier to read. The expression x not in s reads exactly like an English sentence, unlike not x in s, which is more difficult to read.[1]

12.2.2   Concatenation

To concatenate sequences, the + operator is used. In the example, Mr. Miller's first and last name are concatenated along with a space character to form a new string:

```
>>> first_name = "Harold"
>>> last_name = "Miller"
>>> name = first_name + " " + last_name
>>> name
'Harold Miller'
```

Another way to concatenate strings is provided by the += operator for augmented assignments:

```
>>> s = "music "
>>> t = "loudspeaker"
>>> s += t
>>> s
'music loudspeaker'
```

Here, s += t for immutable data types is to be read in the same way as s = s + t because a new instance is actually created with the value of s + t, which is then referenced by s. So after the operation s += t, the three instances "music", "loudspeaker", and "music loudspeaker" exist in the memory, whereas there is no reference to "music" anymore.

This doesn't apply to mutable data types such as list. Here, no further instance with the value s + t is created, but the instance s is changed.

---

1 In addition, for the interpretation of not x in s, you need to know the precedence of the two operators, not and in, respectively. If the not operator binds more strongly, the expression would be evaluated like (not x) in s. If in has a higher priority, the expression would be treated as not (x in s). In fact, in binds stronger than not, making the latter interpretation the correct one.

In the following example, we investigate the effects of manipulating immutable data types based on the example of strings:

```
>>> s = "music "
>>> t = "loudspeaker"
>>> temp = s
>>> s += t
>>> s
'music loudspeaker'
>>> t
'loudspeaker'
>>> temp
'music '
```

Because a new str instance was created via the s += t statement, the str instance referenced by temp hasn't changed. This is different for the mutable list data type:

```
>>> s = [1,2]
>>> t = [3,4]
>>> temp = s
>>> s += t
>>> s
[1, 2, 3, 4]
>>> t
[3, 4]
>>> temp
[1, 2, 3, 4]
```

Here, s and temp refer to the same list instance even after the statement s += t because the existing list was modified and no new object was created. We say that operators exhibiting this behavior work *in place*. Incidentally, this also applies to the *= operator, which will be described in the following section.

12.2.3   Repetition

You can form the product of a sequence s with an integer n: n * s or s * n. The result is a new sequence containing n copies of s in succession:

```
>>> 3 * "abc"
'abcabcabc'
>>> "xyz" * 5
'xyzxyzxyzxyzxyz'
```

As is the case with concatenation, there is also an operator for the augmented assignment, *=:

```
>>> santa_claus = "ho"
>>> santa_claus *= 3
>>> santa_claus
'hohoho'
```

Lists of integers can be multiplied in the same way:

```
>>> [1,2] * 3
[1, 2, 1, 2, 1, 2]
```

Like += , the *= operator works also *in place*. We explained what exactly this means in the previous section using the operator +=.

Note that the objects located in the list are not copied when the list is multiplied, but the further list elements are only additional references to the same instances. This is especially relevant if the list elements themselves are mutable objects, in the following example single-element lists:

```
>>> x = [["nice"], ["list"]] * 3
>>> x
[['nice'], ['list'], ['nice'], ['list'], ['nice'], ['list']]
>>> x[1][0] = "what?"
>>> x
[['nice'], ['what?'], ['nice'], ['what?'], ['nice'], ['what?']]
```

By multiplying the initial list, x contains three references each to the lists ['nice'] and ['list']. As soon as we access and change the underlying instance via one of these references, we also change the other two associated entries of x via a side effect.

12.2.4   Indexing

As mentioned at the beginning of this chapter, sequences represent sequences of elements. Because these elements are stored in a specific order—for example, a string where the order of the letters is arbitrary would make little sense as a store for text—you can assign an *index* to each element of the sequence. For this purpose, all elements of the sequence are numbered consecutively from front to back, the first element getting the index 0.

The [] operator allows you to access a specific element of the sequence by writing the corresponding index in the square brackets:

```
>>> alphabet = "abcdefghijklmnopqrstuvwxyz"
>>> alphabet[9]
'j'
>>> alphabet[1]
'b'
```

```
>>> l = [1, 2, 3, 4, 5, 6]
>>> l[3]
4
```

To access the last or the xth element from the back, there is another indexing of the elements from the back to the front. The last element receives -1 as index, the penultimate one -2, and so on. Table 12.3 illustrates the two types of indexing.

Index from Front	0	1	2	3	4	5
Elements	P	y	t	h	o	n
Index from Back	−6	−5	−4	−3	−2	−1

Table 12.3 Indexing from Front and Back

In the following example, we use negative indexes to access the second to last character of a string or the last element of a list:

```
>>> name = "Python"
>>> name[-2]
'o'
>>> l = [1, 2, 3, 4, 5, 6]
>>> l[-1]
6
```

If you try to access a nonexisting element with an index, this will be acknowledged with an IndexError:

```
>>> too_short = "I'm too short"
>>> too_short[1337]
Traceback (most recent call last):
  File "<stdin>", line 1, in <module>
IndexError: string index out of range
```

12.2.5   Slicing

In addition to accessing individual elements of the sequence, you can also read entire subsequences using the [ ] operator. This is achieved by writing the beginning and the end of the relevant subsequence, separated by a colon, in the square brackets. The beginning is the index of the first element of the subsequence, and the end is the index of the first element that should no longer be included in the subsequence.

To extract the string "NEEDLE" from the string in the following example, we specify the index of the capital "N" and that of the first "h" after "NEEDLE":

```
>>> s = "haystackNEEDLEhaystack"
>>> s[8]
'N'
>>> s[14]
'h'
>>> s[8:14]
'NEEDLE'
```

Figure 12.1 illustrates the access to the subsequence.

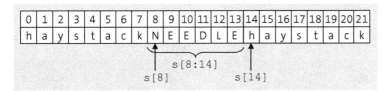

Figure 12.1 Extracting a Subsequence

You can extract parts of a list in a similar way:

```
>>> l = ["I", "am", "a", "list", "of", "strings"]
>>> l[2:5]
['a', 'list', 'of']
```

It's also possible to mix positive and negative indexes in this so-called *slicing* process. For example, the following code section determines a subsequence without the first and last elements of the original sequence:

```
>>> string = "python"
>>> string[1:-1]
'ytho'
>>> l = ["I", "am", "a", "list", "of", "strings"]
>>> l[1:-1]
['am', 'a', 'list', 'of']
```

The indexes can also be omitted, which results in the maximum or minimum possible value being assumed. If you omit the start index, the zeroth element is assumed to be the first element of the subsequence, and if you omit the end index, all letters are copied to the end. For example, if you want to determine the first five letters of a string or all of them starting from the fifth character,[2] this is how to do it:

```
>>> s = "abcdefghijklmnopqrstuvwxyz"
>>> s[:5]
'abcde'
```

---

2 Note here again that the indexing of the characters of a string starts at 0.

```
>>> s[5:]
'fghijklmnopqrstuvwxyz'
```

Slicing for Copying

If you omit both indexes (s[:]), you can also create a genuine copy of the sequence because then all elements are copied, from the first to the last. To see this, we first recall the behavior of the simple assignment:

```
>>> s1 = ["thesis"]
>>> s2 = s1
>>> s1 == s2
True
>>> s1 is s2
True
```

As expected, s1 and s2 reference the same instance, so they are identical. In the next example, we use slicing to create a real copy of the ["thesis"] list in the memory.[3] This can be seen in the identity comparison with is:

```
>>> s1 = ["thesis"]
>>> s2 = s1[:]
>>> s1 == s2
True
>>> s1 is s2
False
```

Note

If you use an immutable data type such as str instead of a mutable data type such as list in the preceding example, the expression s1 is s2 may evaluate to True in both cases. This is because for immutable data types, it makes no difference whether the instance is actually copied or the original instance is used: the value can't be changed anyway.

For this reason, an instance of an immutable data type isn't necessarily copied even when [:] is used, but is instead referenced one more time for efficiency.

If you use a string instead of a list, the differences to the previous example become clear:

```
>>> s1 = "Copy me"
>>> s2 = s1[:]
>>> s2 is s1
True
```

---

3 In real life, of course, you should never simply copy a PhD thesis!

Slicing with Steps

Slicing offers even more flexible options if you don't want to extract a whole subsequence, but only certain elements of this part. The *step* size allows you to specify how the indices are counted from the beginning to the end of a subsequence. The step size is specified after the trailing boundary, separated by another colon. For example, a step size of 2 ensures that only every other element is copied:

```
>>> digits = "0123456789"
>>> digits[1:10:2]
'13579'
```

The string containing every other element of digits starting from the first one—that is, the one with index zero—results in a new string with the odd digits. The boundary indexes can also be omitted in this extended notation. So the following code is equivalent to the previous example:

```
>>> digits = "0123456789"
>>> digits[1::2]
'13579'
```

A negative increment causes counting down from the start index to the end index, in which case the start index must reference an element of the sequence further back than the end index. With a step size of -1, for example, a sequence can be "flipped":

```
>>> name = "ytnoM Python"
>>> name[4::-1]
'Monty'
>>> name[::-1]
'nohtyP Monty'
```

With negative step sizes, the beginning and end of the sequence are swapped. Therefore, in the example name[4::-1], not everything from the fourth to the last character is read, but only the part from the fourth to the first character.

Important for the handling of slicing is the fact that indexes that are too large or too small don't cause an IndexError as is the case when accessing single elements. Too large indexes are internally replaced by the maximum possible index, those that are too small by the minimum possible index. If both indexes are outside the valid range or if the start index is larger than the end index when the step size is positive, an empty sequence is returned:

```
>>> s = "Much less than 1337 characters"
>>> s[5:1337]
'less than 1337 characters'
>>> s[-100:100]
'Much less than 1337 characters'
```

```
>>> s[1337:2674]
''
>>> s[10:4]
''
```

12.2.6   Length of a Sequence

The number of elements in a sequence defines the *length of the sequence*. The length of a sequence is a positive integer and can be determined via the built-in `len` function:

```
>>> string = "How long do you think I am?"
>>> len(string)
27
>>> len(["Hello", 5, 2, 3, "World"])
5
```

12.2.7   The Smallest and the Largest Element

To determine the smallest or largest element of a sequence, you can use the built-in `min` and `max` functions:

```
>>> l = [5, 1, 10, -9.5, 12, -5]
>>> max(l)
12
>>> min(l)
-9.5
```

However, these two functions are only useful if an *ordering* exists for the elements of the sequence. In Chapter 11, Section 11.7, on complex numbers, for example, the `complex` data type is described without an ordering. Likewise, it's not possible to compare entirely different data types, such as strings and numbers:

```
>>> l = [1,2, "world"]
>>> min(l)
Traceback (most recent call last):
  File "<stdin>", line 1, in <module>
TypeError: '<' not supported between instances of 'str' and 'int'
```

Nevertheless, `min` and `max` can be applied to strings in a meaningful way because for letters, their position in the alphabet[4] defines an ordering:

---

4 In fact, the alphabet represents only a part of this ordering. We will learn in Section 12.5.4 in connection with *encodings* that every character, also control characters, punctuation marks, foreign language characters and other symbols, has a unique index.

```
>>> max("who do you think will win")
'y'
>>> min("string")
'g'
```

12.2.8   Searching for an Element

You can use the index method of a sequence to determine the position of an element:

```
>>> digits = [1, 2, 3, 4, 5, 6, 7, 8, 9]
>>> digits.index(3)
2
>>> s = "Hello world"
>>> s.index("l")
2
```

To restrict the search to a subrange of the sequence, the method supports two optional parameters i and j, where i is the first index of the desired subsequence and j is the first index after the desired subsequence:

```
>>> sequence = [0, 11, 222, 3333, 44444, 3333, 222, 11, 0]
>>> sequence.index(222)
2
>>> sequence.index(222, 3)
6
>>> sequence.index(222, -5)
6
>>> "Hello World".index("l", 5, 100)
9
```

As with indexing elements of the sequence, negative values for i and j are counted from the end of the sequence. So in the preceding example, sequence.index(222, -5) was used to search in the $[44444, 3333, 222, 11, 0]$ subsequence, starting at the fifth element from the back.

If the element x isn't contained in s or in the specified subsequence, index results in a ValueError:

```
>>> s = [2.5, 2.6, 2.7, 2.8]
>>> s.index(2.4)
Traceback (most recent call last):
  File "<stdin>", line 1, in <module>
ValueError: 2.4 is not in list
```

12.2.9   Counting Elements

You can use `count` to determine how often a particular element `x` is contained in a sequence:

```
>>> s = [1, 2, 2, 3, 2]
>>> s.count(2)
3
>>> "Hello world".count("l")
3
```

The next section deals with operations that are only available for mutable sequences.

12.3   The list Data Type

In this section, you'll learn about the first mutable data type, *list*, in detail. Unlike the `str`, `bytes`, and `bytearray` sequential data types, which can only store elements (characters) of the same type, lists are suitable for managing any kind of instances of even different data types. A list can therefore contain numbers, strings, or even other lists as elements.

You can create a new list by writing an enumeration of its elements in square brackets `[]`:

```
>>> l = [1, 0.5, "String", 2]
```

The list l now contains two integers—a float and a string.

> **Note**
>
> A list can also be generated via *list comprehension*. In that case, not all elements of the list are explicitly listed but are generated via a formation rule similar to a `for` loop. For example, the following list comprehension generates a list of the squares of the numbers from 0 to 9:
>
> ```
> >>> [i*i for i in range(10)]
> [0, 1, 4, 9, 16, 25, 36, 49, 64, 81]
> ```
>
> Section 12.3.7 describes list comprehensions in greater detail.
>
> You can use unpacking when creating a list:
>
> ```
> >>> [1, 2, *[3, 4]]
> [1, 2, 3, 4]
> ```
>
> For more information on unpacking, see Section 12.4.1.

Because the list type named `list` within Python is a sequential data type, all the methods and procedures described in the last section can be applied to it. See Section 12.2 for a table of operations available for all sequential data types.

Unlike strings, the contents of a list can change even after it has been created, which is why a number of other operators and methods are available for it (see Table 12.4).

Operator	Effect	Section
s[i] = x	The element of s with index i is replaced by x.	Section 12.3.1
s[i:j] = t	The part s[i:j] is replaced by t. At the same time, t must be iterable.	Section 12.3.2
s[i:j:k] = t	The elements of s[i:j:k] are replaced by those of t.	Section 12.3.2
del s[i]	The ith element of s is removed.	Section 12.3.3
del s[i:j]	The part s[i:j] is removed from s. This is equivalent to s[i:j] = [].	Section 12.3.3
del s[i:j:k]	The elements of the subsequence s[i:j:k] are removed from s.	Section 12.3.3

Table 12.4 Operators for the list Data Type

We'll now explain these operators one by one with brief examples.

12.3.1 Changing a Value within the List: Assignment via []

You can replace elements of a list with others if you know their index:

```
>>> s = [1, 2, 3, 4, 5, 6, 7]
>>> s[3] = 1337
>>> s
[1, 2, 3, 1337, 5, 6, 7]
```

However, this method isn't suitable for inserting additional elements into the list. Only existing elements can be replaced, while the length of the list remains unchanged.

12.3.2 Replacing Sublists and Inserting New Elements: Assignment via []

It's possible to replace a whole sublist with other elements. To do this, you must write the part of the list to be replaced like you did in the slicing process, but it must be on the left-hand side of an assignment:

```
>>> shopping_list = ["bread", "eggs", "milk", "fish", "flour"]
>>> shopping_list[1:3] = ["water", "beef"]
>>> shopping_list
['bread', 'water', 'beef', 'fish', 'flour']
```

The list to be inserted may have more or fewer elements than the part to be replaced and may even be completely empty.

You can specify a step size, just like in slicing. In the following example, every third element of the s[2:11] subsequence is replaced by the corresponding element from ["A", "B", "C"]:

```
>>> s = [0, 1, 2, 3, 4, 5, 6, 7, 8, 9, 10]
>>> s[2:9:3] = ["A", "B", "C"]
>>> s
[0, 1, 'A', 3, 4, 'B', 6, 7, 'C', 9, 10]
```

If a step size is specified, the sequence on the right-hand side of the assignment must have as many elements as the subsequence on the left-hand side. If that's not the case, a ValueError will be generated.

12.3.3   Deleting Elements and Sublists: del in Combination with []

To remove a single value from a list, you can use the del operator:

```
>>> s = [26, 7, 1987]
>>> del s[0]
>>> s
[7, 1987]
```

In this way, entire sublists can also be removed:

```
>>> s = [9, 8, 7, 6, 5, 4, 3, 2, 1]
>>> del s[3:6]
>>> s
[9, 8, 7, 3, 2, 1]
```

For removing parts of a list, the step sequence of the slicing notation is also supported. In the following example, this removes all elements with an even index:

```
>>> s = ["a","b","c","d","e","f","g","h","i","j"]
>>> del s[::2]
>>> s
['b', 'd', 'f', 'h', 'j']
```

12.3.4 Methods of list Instances

Now that we've covered the operators for lists, let's turn to the methods of a list. In Table 12.5, s and t are lists, i, j, and k are integers, and x is an instance.[5]

Method	Effect
s.append(x)	Appends x to the end of list s.
s.extend(t)	Appends all elements of list t to the end of list s.
s.insert(i, x)	Inserts x at position i in list s. Then, s[i] has the value of x, with all subsequent elements moving up one place.
s.pop([i])	Returns the ith element of list s and removes it from s. If i isn't specified, the last element will be taken.
s.remove(x)	Removes the first occurrence of x from list s.
s.reverse()	Reverses the order of the elements in s.
s.sort([key, reverse])	Sorts list s.

Table 12.5 Methods of list Instances

Let's now take a more detailed look at the methods.

s.append(x)

The append method enables you to extend a list at the end by another element:

```
>>> s = ["There should be another string after me"]
>>> s.append("Here it is")
>>> s
['There should be another string after me', 'Here it is']
```

s.extend(t)

To append multiple elements to a list, you can use the extend method, which expects an iterable object—for example, another list—as the t parameter. As a result, all elements of t are appended to list s:

```
>>> s = [1, 2, 3]
>>> s.extend([4, 5, 6])
>>> s
[1, 2, 3, 4, 5, 6]
```

---

5 *Warning:* If parameters are bracketed with square brackets in the left-hand column, this still means that they are optional parameters. These square brackets have nothing to do with creating a new list.

s.insert(i, x)

With insert, you can insert a new element into a list at any position. The first parameter, i, specifies the desired index of the new element, the second, x, the element itself:

```
>>> first_with_gap = [1, 2, 3, 5, 6, 7, 8]
>>> first_with_gap.insert(3, 4)
>>> first_with_gap
[1, 2, 3, 4, 5, 6, 7, 8]
```

If the index i is too small, x is inserted at the beginning of s; if it's too large, it's appended at the end like with append.

s.pop([i])

The counterpart to append and insert is pop. This method allows you to remove any element from a list based on its index. If the optional parameter isn't specified, the last element of the list is removed. The removed element is returned by pop:

```
>>> s = ["H", "e", "l", "l", "o"]
>>> s.pop()
'o'
>>> s.pop(0)
'H'
>>> s
['e', 'l', 'l']
```

If you try to pass an invalid index or remove an element from an empty list, an IndexError will be generated.

s.remove(x)

If you want to remove an element with a certain value from a list, no matter what index it has, you can use the remove method. It removes the first element of the list which has the same value as x:

```
>>> s = ["W", "o", "o", "h", "o", "o"]
>>> s.remove("o")
>>> s
['W', 'o', 'h', 'o', 'o']
```

Attempting to remove an element that doesn't exist results in a ValueError.

s.reverse()

You can use reverse to reverse the order of elements in a list:

```
>>> s = [1, 2, 3]
>>> s.reverse()
>>> s
[3, 2, 1]
```

Unlike the s[::-1] slice notation, the reversal is done *in place*. Thus, no new list instance is created, while the old one is changed. This is particularly relevant if the list is very large and a copy would induce significant costs.

12.3.5   Sorting Lists: s.sort([key, reverse])

The sort method can be used to sort a list according to certain criteria. If you call the method without parameters, Python uses the normal comparison operators for sorting:

```
>>> l = [4, 2, 7, 3, 6, 1, 9, 5, 8]
>>> l.sort()
>>> l
[1, 2, 3, 4, 5, 6, 7, 8, 9]
```

If a list contains elements for which no ordering is defined, such as instances of the complex data type, calling sort without parameters will cause a TypeError:

```
>>> lst = [5 + 13j, 1 + 4j, 6 + 2j]
>>> lst.sort()
Traceback (most recent call last):
  File "<stdin>", line 1, in <module>
TypeError: '<' not supported between instances of 'complex' and 'complex'
```

To sort a list according to certain criteria, you can use the key parameter. The sort method expects a function in the key parameter, which is called before each comparison for both operands and therefore expects a parameter in its turn. In the result, not the operands are compared directly, but instead the corresponding return values of the passed function.

In the following example, we'll sort a list of names by length. For this purpose, we'll use the built-in function len, which assigns its length to each name. In practice, this looks as follows:

```
>>> l = ["Catherine", "Peter", "Bob", "Michael", "Emily", "Ben"]
>>> l.sort(key=len)
>>> l
['Bob', 'Ben', 'Peter', 'Emily', 'Michael', 'Catherine']
```

Whenever the sorting algorithm compares two elements of the list, such as "Michael" and "Bob", not the elements themselves are compared, but the corresponding return values of the key function. In our example, len("Michael") and len("Bob")—that is, the numbers 7 and 3—are thus compared. Consequently, the string "Bob" is to be placed before the string "Michael" in this example. Graphically, this example can be illustrated as shown in Figure 12.2.

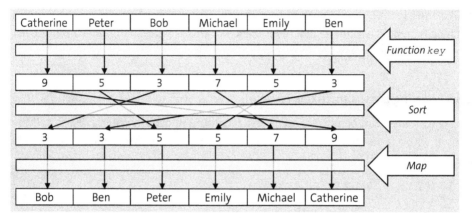

Figure 12.2 Sorting with Key

Of course, you can also pass more complex functions than the built-in len function. To learn how to define your own functions—for example, to use them with sort—see Chapter 17.

The last parameter, reverse, expects a Boolean value to be passed, indicating whether the sort order should be reversed:

```
>>> l = [4, 2, 7, 3, 6, 1, 9, 5, 8]
>>> l.sort(reverse=True)
>>> l
[9, 8, 7, 6, 5, 4, 3, 2, 1]
```

Note

It should be noted here that sort is a function that accepts only keyword arguments. If you try to pass positional arguments, this will cause an error. In the following example, we'll again try to sort the name list by length. However, this time we'll use a positional argument to pass len:

```
>>> l = ["Catherine", "Peter", "Bob", "Michael", "Emily"]
>>> l.sort(len)
Traceback (most recent call last):
  File "<stdin>", line 1, in <module>
TypeError: sort() takes no positional arguments
```

You may wonder how sort handles such values that are in the same place in the sort order. In the example shown previously, "Bob" and "Ben" with length 3 and "Peter" and "Emily" with length 5 each had the same value. In the next section, you'll learn what is meant by a *stable sorting method* and what that means for these values.

Stable Sorting Methods

An important property of sort is that it is a *stable sorting method*. Stable sorting methods are characterized by the fact that they don't swap the relative position of equivalent elements during sorting. Let's suppose you have the list of names shown in Table 12.6.

First Name	Last Name
Natalie	Smith
Matthew	Taylor
Felix	Crowe
Robert	Smith
Howard	Smith
Peter	Anderson

Table 12.6 List of Example Names

Now it's your job to sort this list alphabetically by last name. Groups with the same last name should be sorted by their respective first names. To solve this problem, you can sort the list by the first names in the first step, which results in the following arrangement (see Table 12.7).

First Name	Last Name
Felix	Crowe
Howard	Smith
Matthew	Taylor
Natalie	Smith
Peter	Anderson
Robert	Smith

Table 12.7 List of Names Sorted by First Name

As a result, we are now only interested in the positions of the three people whose last name is Smith. If you simply deleted all other names, the Smiths would be sorted correctly because their relative position was correctly established by the first sort run. Now the stability of the sort method comes into play, because when sorting by the last names again, this relative order is not affected. The end result would look as follows (see Table 12.8).

First Name	Last Name
Peter	Anderson
Felix	Crowe
Howard	Smith
Natalie	Smith
Robert	Smith
Matthew	Taylor

Table 12.8 Fully Sorted List of Names

If sort were not stable, there would be no guarantee that Howard would be ranked above Natalie and Robert.

12.3.6   Side Effects

In connection with the list data type in Python, there are a few peculiarities that aren't immediately obvious.[6]

You'll certainly remember the peculiarity of the += operator, which was explained in Section 12.2.2 in connection with the term *in place*. Let's take another look at this behavior to provide some more comprehensive explanations.

First, list is a mutable data type; therefore, changes to a list instance always affect all references that point to it. Let's consider the following example, in which the str immutable data type is compared with list:

```
>>> a = "Hello "
>>> b = a
>>> b += "world"
>>> b
'Hello world'
>>> a
'Hello '
```

---

6 These special features basically apply to all mutable data types.

This example simply creates a str instance with the value "Hello" and has the two references a and b point to it. Then, the += operator is used to append "world" to the string referenced by b. As you can see in the output—and as we expected—a new instance with the value "Hello world" is created and assigned to b, while a remains unaffected.

If we apply this example to lists, an important difference will emerge:

```
>>> a = [1337]
>>> b = a
>>> b += [2674]
>>> b
[1337, 2674]
>>> a
[1337, 2674]
```

Structurally, the code is similar to the str example, only this time the data type used is not str, but list. The interesting part is the output at the end, according to which a and b have the same value, although the operation was performed only on b. In fact, a and b refer to the same instance, which you can convince yourself of using the is operator:

```
>>> a is b
True
```

You should keep these so-called side effects[7] in mind when working with lists and other mutable data types. If you want to make sure that the original list is not modified, you should create a genuine copy using slicing:

```
>>> a = [1337]
>>> b = a[:]
>>> b += [2674]
>>> b
[1337, 2674]
>>> a
[1337]
```

In this example, the list referenced by a has been copied, protecting it from indirect manipulation via b. In such cases, you must weigh resource consumption against protection against side effects as copies of the lists must be created in the memory. This consumes computing time and memory, especially with long lists, and can therefore slow down the program.

In the context of side effects, the elements of a list are also worth looking at: a list doesn't store instances per se, but only references to them. On the one hand, this makes lists more flexible and increases their performance, but on the other hand, it

---

7 Side effects will play an important role in the context of functions in Chapter 17, Section 17.10.

also makes them susceptible to side effects. Let's take a look at the following example, which may seem weird at first sight:

```
>>> a = [[]]
>>> a = 4 * a
>>> a
[[], [], [], []]
>>> a[0].append(10)
>>> a
[[10], [10], [10], [10]]
```

Initially, a references a list that contains another, empty list. During the subsequent multiplication by the factor 4, the inner empty list is not copied, but only referenced three more times. So in the output we see the same list four times. Once this is understood, it is obvious why the 10 appended to the first element of a is also added to the other three lists: it is simply the same list. Figure 12.3 illustrates this.

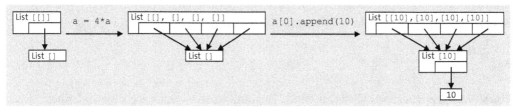

Figure 12.3 Side Effect when Multiple Elements Reference the Same List

It's also possible for a list to contain itself as an element:

```
>>> a = []
>>> a.append(a)
```

The result is an infinitely deep nesting as each list in turn contains itself as an element. Because only references need to be stored, this infinite nesting consumes very little memory and not, as one might initially assume, infinitely much. Nevertheless, such nestings bear the risk of endless loops if you want to process the contained data. For example, let's suppose you wanted to output such a list on the screen. This would result in an infinite number of opening and closing brackets. Nevertheless, it's possible to output such lists via print. Python checks whether a list contains itself, and then outputs three dots (...) instead of further nesting:

```
>>> a = []
>>> a.append(a)
>>> print(a)
[[...]]
```

Note that the notation with the three dots is not valid Python code for creating lists nested within themselves.

If you use lists yourself that might be recursive, you should equip your programs with queries to detect nesting of lists with themselves so that the program won't get stuck in an endless loop during processing.

12.3.7   List Comprehensions

It's a common problem for developers to want to create a new list from the elements of an existing list according to a certain calculation rule. Until now, you would have to do this awkwardly in a for loop. In the following example, we use this approach to generate a result list of the respective squares from a list of integers:

```
>>> lst = [1,2,3,4,5,6,7,8,9]
>>> result_lst = []
>>> for x in lst:
...     result_lst.append(x**2)
...
>>> result_lst
[1, 4, 9, 16, 25, 36, 49, 64, 81]
```

Python supports a more flexible syntax created specifically for this purpose: so-called *list comprehensions*. From a list of integers, the following list comprehension generates a new list containing the squares of these numbers:

```
>>> lst = [1,2,3,4,5,6,7,8,9]
>>> [x**2 for x in lst]
[1, 4, 9, 16, 25, 36, 49, 64, 81]
```

A list comprehension is enclosed in square brackets and consists of an expression followed by any number of for/in sections. A for/in section draws on the syntax of the for loop and specifies which identifier is used to iterate over which list—in this case, the identifier x over the list lst. The specified identifier can be used in the expression at the beginning of the list comprehension. The result of a list comprehension is a new list that contains as elements the results of the expression in each iteration step. The functionality of list comprehension presented previously can be summarized as follows: for each x element of lst list, take the square of x and insert the result into the result list.

This is the simplest form of list comprehension. The for/in section can be extended by a condition so that only certain elements are taken over into the new list. For example, we could extend the preceding list comprehension to form only the squares of even numbers:

```
>>> lst = [1,2,3,4,5,6,7,8,9]
>>> [x**2 for x in lst if x%2 == 0]
[4, 16, 36, 64]
```

For this purpose, the for/in section is extended by the if keyword, which is followed by a condition. Only if this condition returns True will the calculated element be included in the result list. This form of list comprehension can thus be described as follows: for each x element of list lst—if x is an even number—take the square of x and insert the result into the result list.

The next example is supposed to use a list comprehension to add two three-dimensional vectors represented as lists. Vectors are added coordinate by coordinate—in this case, element by element:

```
>>> v1 = [1, 7, -5]
>>> v2 = [-9, 3, 12]
>>> [v1[i] + v2[i] for i in range(3)]
[-8, 10, 7]
```

For this purpose, a list of indexes generated by range is iterated in the list comprehension. In each run, the respective coordinates are added and appended to the result list.

We already mentioned that a list comprehension can have any number of for/in sections. These can be considered similar to nested for loops. In the following sections, we'll describe an example in which this property is useful. First, we define two lists:

```
>>> lst1 = ["A", "B", "C"]
>>> lst2 = ["D", "E", "F"]
```

Now, a list comprehension is supposed to create a list containing all possible letter combinations that can be formed by first choosing a letter from lst1 and then choosing one from lst2. The combinations should appear as tuples in the list:

```
>>> [(a,b) for a in lst1 for b in lst2]
[('A', 'D'), ('A', 'E'), ('A', 'F'), ('B', 'D'), ('B', 'E'), ('B', 'F'),
('C', 'D'), ('C', 'E'), ('C', 'F')]
```

This list comprehension can be described as follows: for each a element of list lst1, go over all b elements of lst2 and insert the (a,b) tuple into the result list in each case.

List comprehensions provide an interesting and elegant way to write complex operations in a space-saving manner. Many problems for which list comprehensions are used could also be solved by the built-in map or filter functions (see Chapter 17, Section 17.14) or by a combination of the two, but list comprehensions are often more readable and lead to clearer source code.

12.4   Immutable Lists: tuple

The list is a very flexible sequential data type that can accommodate arbitrarily long sequence of elements. This section describes the *tuple*, a data type closely related to the list.

Unlike the list, the tuple is immutable, which opens the possibility of calculating *hash values* for tuples. This property is important for the use of tuples in combination with data types like the dictionary or the set (see Chapter 13), which are based on hash tables. Based on the condition that hash values can also be calculated for all elements of a tuple, it may therefore be used as a key in a dictionary or as an element in a set, which differentiates it from a list.

The concept of a tuple is related to that of the list, but due to its immutability, only the basic set of operations for sequential data types is available for tuple instances, as described in Section 12.2.

To create new tuple instances, you must use the parentheses, which—like lists—contain the elements of the tuple, separated by commas:

```
>>> a = (1, 2, 3, 4, 5)
>>> a[3]
4
```

An empty tuple is defined by two parentheses () without content. A special case involves tuples with only one element. If you try to create a tuple with only one element in the way described previously, the program will behave differently than intended:

```
>>> no_tuple = (2)
>>> type(no_tuple)
<class 'int'>
```

With (2), no new tuple instance is created because the parentheses are already used in this context for arithmetic operations with integers. Hence tuple literals containing only a single element are written with an additional comma after the element:

```
>>> a_tuple = (2,)
>>> type(a_tuple)
<class 'tuple'>
```

12.4.1   Packing and Unpacking

You can omit the enclosing parentheses in a tuple definition. Nevertheless, the references separated by commas are combined into a tuple, which is referred to as *tuple packing* or, more simply, *packing*:

```
>>> date = 7, 26, 1987
>>> date
(7, 26, 1987)
```

Conversely, it's also possible to *unpack* the values of a tuple:

```
>>> date = 7, 26, 1987
>>> (month, day, year) = date
>>> month
7
>>> day
26
>>> year
1987
```

This process is referred to as *tuple unpacking* or simply *unpacking*, and again the parentheses can be omitted. By combining packing and unpacking, you can very elegantly swap the values of two variables without a helper variable or combine several assignments in one line:

```
>>> a, b = 10, 20
>>> a, b = b, a
>>> a
20
>>> b
10
```

Unpacking is not limited to the tuple data type, but works for sequential data types in general. In this case, the term *sequence unpacking* is also commonly used:

```
>>> a, b, c = "abc"
>>> a
'a'
```

If applied properly, the use of this feature can contribute to the readability of programs as the technical detail of caching data moves to the background of the actual intent of swapping values.

Unpacking can also be used to read values at the beginning and end of a sequence. Let's consider the following example:

```
>>> numbers = [11, 18, 12, 15, 10]
>>> eleven, *others, ten = numbers
>>> eleven
11
>>> ten
10
```

```
>>> others
[18, 12, 15]
```

If an asterisk (*) is prefixed to a reference when unpacking, all other values of the sequence are stored in it. In the preceding example, the first value of numbers is stored in eleven and the last value in ten. The numbers in between are collected into others.

Any number of other references may precede and follow the asterisked entry. In particular, the first or last entry can have an asterisk:

```
>>> numbers = [11, 17, 17, 19, 10]
>>> *something, nineteen, ten = numbers
>>> nineteen
19
>>> ten
10
>>> eleven, *blah_blah_blah = numbers
>>> eleven
11
>>> blah_blah_blah
[17, 17, 19, 10]
```

There can always only be exactly one reference with an asterisk in an assignment with unpacking. This makes sense, as otherwise ambiguities can arise.

Note

In general, you should be careful when using unpacking for unordered data types. In the following example, the order of the elements 1, 2, and 3 depends on the order in which the set {3,1,2} is iterated over:

```
>>> a, b, c = {3, 1, 2}
>>> a, b, c
(1, 2, 3)
```

Because this order is an implementation detail, it may differ between different versions of Python, or even between different runs of the same program. For more details on sets, see Chapter 13, Section 13.2.

12.4.2   Immutable Doesn't Necessarily Mean Unchangeable!

Although tuple instances are immutable, the values of the elements contained during their generation may change. When a new tuple is created, the references it is to store are specified. If such a reference points to an instance of a mutable data type, such as a list, its value can still change:

```
>>> a = ([],)
>>> a[0].append("And yet it moves!")
>>> a
(['And yet it moves!'],)
```

The immutability of a tuple thus refers only to the references it contains and explicitly not to the instances behind it.

Thus, the fact that tuples are immutable is no guarantee that elements won't change once the tuple has been created.

12.5   Strings: str, bytes, bytearray

This section describes the handling of strings in Python, and in particular the properties of the str, bytes, and bytearray data types provided for this.

As you have already learned, strings are sequences of characters. This means that all operations for sequential types are available to them.[8]

The characters an instance of the str data type can store are letters, punctuation, spaces, German umlauts and other special characters. In contrast, the bytes and bytearray data types are intended for storing binary data. For this reason, instances of the bytes and bytearray data types consist of a sequence of individual bytes—that is, integers from 0 to 255.

For the time being, we'll deal only with str instances as dealing with str is not much different from dealing with bytes. Only when you convert str to bytes and vice versa are there some stumbling blocks, which are described in Section 12.5.4 about character sets and special characters.

To create new str instances, the following literals are available:

```
>>> string1 = "I was defined with double quotation marks"
>>> string2 = 'I was defined with single quotes'
```

The desired content of the string is written between the quotation marks, but mustn't contain any line feeds (in the following example, Enter was pressed at the end of the first line):

---

8 Because bytearray is a mutable data type, unlike str and bytes, many of the methods of the list data type are supported in addition to the basic set of operations for sequential data types presented in this chapter. For a listing of the methods provided by bytearray as a mutable sequential data type, see Chapter 19, Section 19.11.13.

```
>>> s = "First line
  File "<stdin>", line 1
    s = "First line
          ^
SyntaxError: unterminated string literal (detected at line 1)
```

String constants that can also extend over several lines are enclosed by """ or ''':[9]

```
>>> string3 = """First line!
... Ooops, another line"""
```

If two string literals are immediately following each other or separated by spaces, Python joins them to form a string:

```
>>> string = "First part" "Second part"
>>> string
'First partSecond part'
```

As you can see in the example, the spaces between the literals are no longer present when concatenating.

This type of concatenation is very suitable for splitting long or unwieldy strings into several program lines without storing the line feeds and spaces in the result, as would be the case with strings containing """ or '''. To achieve this separation, you must write the string parts in parentheses:

```
>>> a = ("Imagine a terribly "
...      "complicated string that "
...      "in no case can be written in one "
...      "line.")
>>> a
'Imagine a terribly complicated string that in no case can be written in one
line.'
```

As you can see, the string was stored as if it had been defined in a single line.

The creation of bytes instances works the same way as the creation of str instances described previously. The only difference is that you have to prepend a lowercase b to the string literal to obtain a bytes string:

---

9 You'll often come across strings in Python code that describe classes, functions, or modules. For these docstrings, the literal with three quotes is usually used. For more information on docstrings, see Chapter 37, Section 37.1.

```
>>> string1 = b"I am bytes!"
>>> string1
b'I am bytes!'
>>> type(string1)
<class 'bytes'>
```

The other types of string creation work in a similar way for bytes. Note, however, that you may only use ASCII characters within bytes literals (Section 12.5.4).

To create a new instance of the bytearray type, you can use the built-in bytearray function:

```
>>> string1 = b"Hello world"
>>> string2 = bytearray(string1)
>>> string2
bytearray(b'Hello world')
```

This way, a bytearray instance can be created that adopts its value from an existing bytes instance.

If you pass an integer *k* as a parameter to the built-in bytearray function, a new bytearray of the length *k* is created, where each of the bytes is assigned the value zero:

```
>>> bytearray(7)
bytearray(b'\x00\x00\x00\x00\x00\x00\x00')
```

In the next section, you'll learn what the \x00 representation of these characters is all about. This topic will be discussed again in Section 12.5.4 in the context of string encoding.

The relationship between the bytes and bytearray data types is similar to the relationship between the tuple and list data types. While the bytes data type represents an immutable sequence of byte values, a bytearray may be modified with the same operations you already know from lists:

```
>>> b = bytearray(b"Hello world")
>>> b[:5] = b"Bye"
>>> b
bytearray(b'Bye world')
>>> b.append(ord(b"!"))
>>> b
bytearray(b'Bye world!')
>>> b.extend(b"!!!")
>>> b
bytearray(b'Bye world!!!!')
```

12.5.1 Control Characters

There are special text elements that control the text flow and can't be displayed on the screen as individual characters. These so-called *control characters* include the line feed, the tabulator, and the backspace. The representation of such characters within string literals is done by means of special strings: *escape sequences*. Escape sequences are introduced by a backslash (\), followed by the identifier of the desired special character. For example, the "\n" escape sequence represents a line break:

```
>>> a = "First line\nSecond line"
>>> a
'First line\nSecond line'
>>> print(a)
First line
Second line
```

Note the difference between the output with print and without print in the interactive mode: the print statement converts the control characters to their screen representation (for example, "\n" starts a new line), while the output without the print statement displays a string literal with the escape sequences of the special characters on the screen.

For control characters, Python has the escape sequences listed in Table 12.9.

Escape Sequence	Meaning
\a	Bell (BEL) generates a signal tone.
\b	Backspace (BS) resets the output position by one character.
\f	Formfeed (FF) creates a form feed.
\n	Linefeed (LF) sets the output position to the next line.
\r	Carriage return (CR) sets the output position to the beginning of the next line.
\t	Horizontal tab (TAB) has the same meaning as the ⸢Tab⸥ key.
\v	The vertical tab (VT) is used for vertical indentation.
\"	Double quote.
\'	Single quote.
\\	Backslash that should really appear as such within the string.

Table 12.9 Escape Sequences for Control Characters

Control characters date from the time when output was mainly processed via printers. For this reason, some of these characters have little practical significance today.

The escape sequences for single and double quotes are necessary because Python uses these characters as delimiters for string literals. If the type of quote used to delimit a string is to occur as a character within that string, the corresponding quote must be specified there as an escape sequence:

```
>>> a = "The following single quote does not need to be encoded ' "
>>> b = "This double quote does \" "
>>> c = 'This is also true in strings with single quotes " '
>>> d = 'Here an escape sequence must be used \' '
```

In Section 12.5.4, we'll return to escape sequences and use them to encode special characters such as umlauts or the euro sign.

The automatic replacement of escape sequences is sometimes annoying, especially if a large number of backslashes are to occur in a string. For this purpose, Python provides the prefixes r and R, which can be prepended to a string literal. These prefixes mark the literal as a so-called *raw string*, which results in all backslashes being transferred one by one into the result string:

```
>>> "A \tstring with \\ many \nescape sequences\t"
'A \tstring with \\ many \nescape sequences\t'
>>> r"A \tstring with \\ many \nescape sequences\t"
'A \\tstring with \\\\ many \\nescape sequences\\t'
>>> print(r"A \tstring with \\ many \nescape sequences\t")
A \tstring with \\ many \nescape sequences\t
```

As you can see from the double backslashes in the literal of the result and the output via print, the escape sequences were not interpreted as masked special characters.

By using the rb or br prefix, you can create raw strings of the bytes type.

> **Note**
>
> To facilitate the migration from Python 2 to Python 3, you can optionally create str instances with or without a prefixed u. These u literals were used in Python 2 to create unicode instances, the counterpart of the str data type in Python 3:
>
> ```
> >>> u"The goshawk is the bird of the year 2015"
> 'The goshawk is the bird of the year 2015'
> ```

When we talk about *white spaces* in the following, we'll refer to all kinds of characters between words that are not displayed as separate characters. White spaces are characters listed in Table 12.10.

String literal	Name
" "	Blank character
"\n"	New line
"\v"	Vertical tab
"\t"	Horizontal tab
"\f"	Formfeed
"\r"	Carriage return

Table 12.10 List of White Space Characters

12.5.2 String Methods

In addition to the methods for sequential data types, string instances contain other methods that simplify the handling of strings. In the following sections, we'll discuss methods that are thematically related in each of the following categories:

- Splitting strings
- Searching substrings
- Replacing substrings
- Removing certain characters at the beginning or at the end of a string
- Aligning strings
- String tests
- Concatenating elements in sequential data types
- String formatting

Splitting Strings

To split strings into several parts according to certain rules, the following methods are available (see Table 12.11).

Method	Description
s.split([sep, maxsplit])	Splits s on occurrence of sep. The search starts at the beginning of the string.
s.rsplit([sep, maxsplit])	Splits s on occurrence of sep. The search starts at the end of the string.
s.splitlines([keepends])	Splits s on occurrence of new lines.

Table 12.11 String Methods for Separating Strings

Method	Description
s.partition(sep)	Splits s into two parts at the first occurrence of sep.
	In addition to the products of this separation, the resulting tuple contains the separator sep, if it occurs in s.
s.rpartition(sep)	Splits s into two parts at the last occurrence of sep.
	In addition to the products of this separation, the resulting tuple contains the separator sep, if it occurs in s.

Table 12.11 String Methods for Separating Strings (Cont.)

The split and rsplit methods split a string into its words and return them as a list. Here, the sep parameter specifies the string that separates the words, and maxsplit enables you to restrict the number of splits. If you don't specify maxsplit, the string will be split as many times as sep occurs in it. Any remainder is inserted as a string into the resulting list. Note that split starts splitting at the beginning of the string, while rsplit starts at the end:

```
>>> s = "1-2-3-4-5-6-7-8-9-10"
>>> s.split("-")
['1', '2', '3', '4', '5', '6', '7', '8', '9', '10']
>>> s.split("-", 5)
['1', '2', '3', '4', '5', '6-7-8-9-10']
>>> s.rsplit("-", 5)
['1-2-3-4-5', '6', '7', '8', '9', '10']
```

If several separators follow each other, they won't be combined, but separated again each time:

```
>>> s = "1---2-3"
>>> s.split("-")
['1', '', '', '2', '3']
```

If sep isn't specified, the two methods behave differently. First, all white spaces at the beginning and end of the string are removed, and then the string is split based on white spaces, this time combining consecutive separators into one:

```
>>> s = "  Any \t\t sentence with \n\r\t whitespaces"
>>> s.split()
['Any', 'sentence', 'with', 'whitespaces']
```

Calling split entirely without parameters is very useful to split a text string into its words, even if they aren't separated only by white spaces.

The splitlines method splits a string into its individual lines and returns a list containing the lines. Unix line feeds "\n", Windows line feeds "\r\n", and Mac line feeds "\r" are interpreted as separators:

```
>>> s = "Unix\nWindows\r\nMac\rLast line"
>>> s.splitlines()
['Unix', 'Windows', 'Mac', 'Last line']
```

If the separating line feeds at the ends of the lines are to be retained, the value True must be passed for the optional keepends parameter.

The partition method splits a string at the first place where the passed separator string sep occurs, and returns a tuple consisting of the part before the separator string, the separator string itself, and the part after. The rpartition method works the same way, except that it uses the last occurrence of sep in the source string as the separator:

```
>>> s = "www.python-book.com"
>>> s.partition(".")
('www', '.', 'python-book.com')
>>> s.rpartition(".")
('www.python-book', '.', 'com')
```

Searching for Substrings

To determine the position and the number of occurrences of a string in another string or to replace parts of a string, the methods listed in Table 12.12 are available.

Method	Description
s.find(sub, [start, end])	Searches for the sub string in the string s. The search starts at the beginning of the string.
s.rfind(sub, [start, end])	Searches for the sub string in the string s. The search starts at the end of the string.
s.index(sub, [start, end])	Searches for the sub string in the string s. The search starts at the beginning of the string. If sub is not present in s, an exception gets raised.
s.rindex(sub, [start, end])	Searches for the sub string in the string s. The search starts at the end of the string. If sub is not present in s, an exception gets raised.
s.count(sub, [start, end])	Counts the occurrences of sub in s.

Table 12.12 String Methods for Searching in Strings

The optional start and end parameters of the five methods are used to narrow the search range. If you specify start or end, only the substring s[start:end] will be considered.

> **Note**
>
> *Remember:* When slicing a string s using s[start:end], a substring is created that starts at s[start] and no longer contains the element s[end].

To find out whether and, if so, at what position a particular string occurs in another, Python provides the find and index methods, with their counterparts, rfind and rindex. The find method returns the index of the first occurrence of sub in s, while rfind correspondingly returns the index of the last occurrence. If sub isn't contained in s, find and rfind will return -1:

```
>>> s = "Let's see where the 'e' occurs in this string"
>>> s.find("e")
1
>>> s.rfind("e")
21
```

The index and rindex methods work in the same way, but generate a ValueError if sub is not contained in s:

```
>>> s = "This string is about to be searched"
>>> s.index("is")
2
>>> s.index("not available")
Traceback (most recent call last):
  File "<stdin>", line 1, in <module>
ValueError: substring not found
```

The reason for these almost identical methods is that error messages may be handled more elegantly than invalid return values.[10]

The number of occurrences of one substring within another can be determined via count:

```
>>> "Peter Piper picked a peck of pickled peppers".count("p")
7
```

Replacing Substrings

The methods listed in Table 12.13 can be used to replace certain parts or letters of strings with others.

---

10 You can find a more detailed description of this in Chapter 20.

Method	Description
s.replace(old, new, [count])	Replaces the occurrences of old in the string s with new.
s.lower()	Replaces all uppercase letters in s with corresponding lowercase letters.
s.upper()	Replaces all lowercase letters in s with corresponding uppercase letters.
s.swapcase()	Replaces all uppercase letters in s with corresponding lowercase letters and, vice versa, all lowercase letters with corresponding uppercase letters.
s.capitalize()	Replaces the first letter of s with the corresponding uppercase letter and all following uppercase letters with corresponding lowercase letters.
s.casefold()	Works similar to s.lower() and additionally substitutes special characters. One such example is the German letter ß which is substituted by ss. The behavior of casefold is defined in the Unicode standard and it is intended for comparisons between strings where case is not important.
s.title()	Changes the case of s so that words are all lowercase, except for the respective initial letter.
s.expandtabs([tabsize])	Indents s by replacing tabs ("\t") with white spaces.

Table 12.13 String Methods for Replacing Substrings

The replace method returns a string in which all occurrences of old have been replaced by new:

```
>>> false = "Python is not great!"
>>> true = false.replace("not", "really")
>>> true
'Python is really great!'
```

The count parameter can be used to limit the number of replacements:

```
>>> s = "Please replace only the first four e's"
>>> s.replace("e", "E", 4)
"PlEasE rEplacE only the first four e's"
```

An interesting special case arises when the empty string "" is passed as the first argument old. Then the string passed as new is inserted between all characters and at the beginning and end:

```
>>> s = "abcdefg"
>>> s.replace("", "--")
'--a--b--c--d--e--f--g--'
```

The `lower` method replaces all uppercase letters of a string with the corresponding lowercase letters and returns the result string:

```
>>> s = "FIRST ALL BIG AND THEN ALL SMALL!"
>>> s.lower()
'first all big and then all small!'
```

With `upper`, you can achieve exactly the opposite effect.

The `swapcase` method changes the case of all letters in a string by replacing all uppercase letters with the corresponding lowercase letters and vice versa:

```
>>> s = "iF ALL eNGLISH WORDS WERE WRITTEN LIKE THIS ..."
>>> s.swapcase()
'If all English words were written like this ...'
```

The `capitalize` method returns a copy of the source string with the first character converted to an uppercase letter, if that's possible:

```
>>> s = "everything small ... yet ;)"
>>> s.capitalize()
'Everything small ... yet ;)'
```

The `title` method creates a string where the first letter of each word is uppercase and the remaining letters are lowercase, as is common in English for titles:

```
>>> s = "i Am nOt rEAlly a tITLe yET"
>>> s.title()
'I Am Not Really A Title Yet'
```

Using `expandtabs`, you can have all tab characters ("\t") of a string replaced by spaces. The optional `tabsize` parameter specifies how many spaces should be inserted for a tab. If `tabsize` is not specified, eight spaces will be used:

```
>>> s = ("\tThis could be source code\n" +
...      "\t\tOne level further down")
>>> print(s.expandtabs(4))
    This could be source code
        One level further down
```

Removing Certain Characters at the Beginning or at the End of Strings

The `strip` methods allow you to remove unwanted characters at the beginning or end of a string (see Table 12.14).

Method	Description
s.strip([chars])	Removes certain characters at the beginning and end of the string s
s.lstrip([chars])	Removes certain characters at the beginning of the string s
s.rstrip([chars])	Removes certain characters at the end of the string s
s.removeprefix(prefix)	Removes a prefix string at the beginning of the string s
s.removesuffix(suffix)	Removes a suffix string at the end of the string s

Table 12.14 String Methods for Removing Certain Characters at the Beginning or End

The strip method removes unwanted characters at both sides of the string. The lstrip method removes only the characters on the left and rstrip only the characters on the right.

For the optional chars parameter, you can pass a string containing the characters to be removed. If you don't specify chars, all white spaces will be deleted:

```
>>> s = "    \t\n  \rSurrounded by whitespaces    \t\t\r"
>>> s.strip()
'Surrounded by whitespaces'
>>> s.lstrip()
'Surrounded by whitespaces    \t\t\r'
>>> s.rstrip()
'    \t\n  \rSurrounded by whitespaces'
```

For example, to remove all surrounding digits, you could proceed as follows:

```
>>> digits = "0123456789"
>>> s = "3674784673546Hidden between numbers3425923935"
>>> s.strip(digits)
'Hidden between numbers'
```

The removeprefix and removesuffix methods were added to the language scope with Python 3.9 and are thus only available in more recent language versions. You can remove a specified prefix or suffix from a string if it occurs:

```
>>> s = "PREFIX: This is my message (SUFFIX)"
>>> s.removeprefix("PREFIX: ")
'This is my message (SUFFIX)'
>>> s.removesuffix(" (SUFFIX)")
'PREFIX: This is my message'
>>> s.removesuffix("DOESNOTOCCUR")
'PREFIX: This is my message (SUFFIX)'
```

Aligning Strings

The methods listed in Table 12.15 create a string of a given length and align the source string in it in a particular way.

Method	Description
s.center(width, [fillchar])	Centers s in the resulting string
s.ljust(width, [fillchar])	Left-aligns s in the resulting string
s.rjust(width, [fillchar])	Right-aligns s in the resulting string
s.zfill(width)	Right-aligns s by filling in zeros on the left

Table 12.15 String Methods for Alignment

You can use the width parameter to specify the desired length of the new string. The optional fillchar parameter of the first three methods must be a string of length 1 and specifies the character to be used for filling up to the passed length. By default, spaces are used for filling:

```
>>> s = "Align me"
>>> s.center(50)
'                     Align me                     '
>>> s.ljust(50)
'Align me                                          '
>>> s.rjust(50, "-")
'------------------------------------------Align me'
```

If the length of s is greater than the value of the width parameter, a copy of s is returned because, in this case, there is not enough space for alignment.

The zfill method is a special case of rjust and is intended for strings that contain numeric values. Calling the zfill method creates a string of length width in which the source string is right-aligned and the left-hand side is filled with zeros:

```
>>> "13.37".zfill(20)
'00000000000000013.37'
```

String Tests

The methods listed in Table 12.16 return a truth value that states whether the contents of the string have a particular property. For example, via islower, you can check if all letters in s are lowercase.

Method	Description
s.isalnum()	True if all characters in s are letters or digits
s.isalpha()	True if all characters in s are letters
s.isascii()	True if s contains only characters from the ASCII character set*
s.isdigit()	True if all characters in s are digits
s.islower()	True if all letters in s are lowercase
s.isupper()	True if all letters in s are uppercase
s.isspace()	True if all characters in s are white spaces
s.istitle()	True if all words in s are capitalized
s.startswith(prefix, [start, end])	True if s starts with the string prefix
s.endswith(suffix, [start, end])	False if s ends with the string suffix

*In Section 12.5.4, you'll learn more about character sets and their meaning for special characters in strings.

Table 12.16 Methods for String Tests

Because the first seven methods in the table are very similar, one example should suffice at this point:

```
>>> s = "1234abcd"
>>> s.isdigit()
False
>>> s.isalpha()
False
>>> s.isalnum()
True
```

To check whether a string begins or ends with a certain string, you can use the startswith or endswith methods. The optional start and end parameters limit the query to the range s[start:end]—as was already the case with the search-and-replace methods:

```
>>> s = "www.python-book.com"
>>> s.startswith("www.")
True
>>> s.endswith(".com")
True
```

```
>>> s.startswith("python", 4)
True
```

Concatenating Elements in Sequential Data Types

A common task is to concatenate a list of strings using a separator. For this purpose, Python provides the join method (see Table 12.17).

Method	Description
s.join(seq)	Concatenates the elements of the seq sequence into a new string, where s is the separator

Table 12.17 String Method for Concatenating Multiple Elements with a Separator String

The seq parameter can be any iterable object, but all its elements must be strings. The elements of seq are concatenated with s as a separator. In the following example, several names are concatenated, separated by commas:

```
>>> contact_list = ["Mickey", "Minnie", "Donald", "Daisy"]
>>> ", ".join(contact_list)
'Mickey, Minnie, Donald, Daisy'
```

If a string is passed for seq, the result will be the concatenation of all letters, each separated by s:

```
>>> sentence = "Unintelligible sentence"
>>> "...um...".join(sentence)
'U...um...n...um...i...um...n...um...t...um...e...um...l...um...l...um...i...um.
..g...um...i...um...b...um...l...um...e...um... ...um...s...um...e...um...n...um
...t...um...e...um...n...um...c...um...e'
```

The join method is often used to concatenate the elements of a sequence without a separator. In this case, you call the join method of the empty string:

```
>>> "".join(["www", ".", "python-book", ".", "com"])
'www.python-book.com'
```

The following section deals with the topic of string formatting.

12.5.3   Formatting Strings

It often happens that you want to customize your screen outputs in a certain way. For example, to display a three-column table of numbers you must insert spaces—depending on the length of the numbers—so that the individual columns are displayed underneath each other. Customizing the output is also necessary if you want to output an amount of money stored in a float instance that has more than two decimal places.

To solve these kinds of problems, you can use the `format` method of the `str` data type. Using `format`, you can replace placeholders in a string with specific values. These placeholders are enclosed by curly brackets and can be both numbers and names. In the following example, we'll replace the placeholders {0} and {1} with two numbers:

```
>>> "It's {0}.{1}".format(13, 37)
"It's 13.37"
```

If numbers are used as placeholders, they must be numbered consecutively, starting at 0. Then they are replaced in order by the parameters passed to the `format` method—the first parameter replaces {0}, the second parameter replaces {1}, and so on.

It's also possible to have this numbering done implicitly by not writing anything between the curly brackets. Python then numbers the placeholders automatically, starting at 0:

```
>>> "It's {}.{}".format(13, 37)
"It's 13.37"
```

Names can also be used as placeholders. In this case, you must pass the values as keyword parameters to the `format` method:

```
>>> "It's {hour}.{minute}".format(hour=13, minute=37)
"It's 13.37"
```

All character strings that can also be used as variable names in Python can be used as names for the placeholders. In particular, your placeholder names shouldn't start with digits; otherwise, Python will try to interpret them as integers.

You can also mix numbered placeholders with symbolic placeholders:

```
>>> "It's {hour}.{0}".format(37, hour=13)
"It's 13.37"
```

This mixing of symbolic and numbered placeholders also works together with implicit numbering. In that case, Python numbers the placeholders automatically, starting at 0:

```
>>> "{h}oz. yeast, {}oz. flour, {w}fl.oz. water, {}oz. salt".format(
...       2, 15, h=0.2, w=3)
'0.2oz. yeast, 2oz. flour, 3fl.oz. water, 15oz. salt'
```

Instead of the numerical values used in the previous examples, you can generally use any objects as values, as long as they can be converted to a string.[11] In the following code snippet, different types of data are passed to the `format` method:

---

[11] For more details on how this conversion works internally and how it can be influenced, see Chapter 19, Section 19.11.

```
>>> "List: {0}, String: {string}, Complex number: {1}".format(
...      [1,2], 13 + 37j, string="Hello world")
'List: [1, 2], String: Hello world, Complex number: (13+37j)'
```

To insert the same value multiple times in a string, you can use a placeholder multiple times:

```
>>> "{h}{um} yeast, {}{um} flour, {w}{uv} water, {}{um} salt".format(
...      2, 15, h=0.2, w=3, um='oz.', uv='fl.oz.')
'0.2oz. yeast, 2oz. flour, 3fl.oz. water, 15oz. salt'
```

Here um and uv stand for "unit for mass" and "unit for volume."

If you want to prevent a curly bracket from being interpreted as a delimiter of a place-holder, you must use two brackets in a row. As a result, these double brackets are replaced by single ones:

```
>>> "Unformatted: {{NoPlaceholder}}. Formatted: {v}.".format(
...      v="only a test")
'Unformatted: {NoPlaceholder}. Formatted: only a test.'
```

> **Note**
>
> The format method has been the standard for string formatting since Python 3, replacing the % formatting operator that had been in use until then. Although the % operator still works for downward compatibility reasons, its use is not recommended; the format method should be used instead.
>
> For more details on how the % operator works, you can refer to Python's online documentation.

f-Strings

In Python 3.6, a special string literal was introduced that further simplifies the formatting of strings. As an example, let's define a time by creating the hour and minute variables:

```
>>> hour = 13
>>> minute = 37
```

You already know two ways to format the time as a string using the format string method:

```
>>> "It's {}.{}".format(hour, minute)
"It's 13.37"
>>> "It's {hour}.{minute}".format(hour=hour, minute=minute)
"It's 13.37"
```

In the first variant, the values are inserted into the string based on their position in the parameter list of the `format` call. This implicit assignment of placeholders to values results in compact code, but it can become confusing in more complex cases, especially when you insert new placeholders later. The second variant establishes an explicit assignment between placeholders and variables via a temporary identifier, which we also called `hour` or `minute` in the preceding example. This results in unambiguous, but also inconveniently redundant code.

Using *f-strings*, you can formulate the example unambiguously and compactly at the same time. An f-string is considered to be the special string literal `f""`, which automatically replaces placeholders with instances of the same name:

```
>>> f"It's {hour}:{minute}"
"It's 13:37"
```

Another important property of f-strings is that any expressions may be placed inside the placeholders, and their value is then inserted into the string at this point:

```
>>> f"It's soon {hour + 1}:{minute + 1}"
"It's soon 14:38"
>>> f"{60 * hour + minute} minutes of the day have allready passed"
'817 minutes of the day have allready passed'
>>> f"It's around {hour if minute < 30 else hour + 1}:00"
"It's around 14:00"
>>> f"It's {bin(hour)}:{bin(minute)}"
"It's 0b1101:0b100101"
```

In the following sections, we'll describe more details about string formatting, basically using the `format` method. Note, however, that the examples can be applied in a similar way to f-strings.

> **Note**
>
> With the exception of Chapter 31, we consistently use the established `format` method for string formatting in most of the the sample programs in this book. This is explicitly not meant to be an argument against the use of f-strings. You can decide according to your preferences or according to your application scenario which option suits you better.
>
> See Chapter 31 for examples of string formatting with f-strings in the application context of parallel programming.

Accessing Attributes and Methods

Besides simply replacing placeholders, you can also access attributes of the passed value in the format string. To do this, you must write the respective attribute, separated by a period, after the placeholder name, just as it works with the normal attribute access in Python.

The following example outputs the imaginary and real parts of a complex number in this way:

```
>>> c = 15 + 20j
>>> "Real part: {0.real}, Imaginary part: {0.imag}".format(c)
'Real part: 15.0, Imaginary part: 20.0'
```

As you can see, attribute access also works with numbered placeholders.

In addition to accessing attributes of the value to be formatted, the [ ] operator can also be used. For example, it enables you to output specific elements of a list:

```
>>> l = ["I'm first!", "No, I'm first!"]
>>> "{list[1]}. {list[0]}".format(list=l)
"No, I'm first!. I'm first!"
```

Even if you haven't learned about other data types that support the [ ] operator at this point, its use in format strings is not limited to sequential data types. In particular, this type of access is interesting in the case of dictionaries, which we'll describe in Chapter 13, Section 13.1.[12]

Both attribute access and the [ ] operator can also be used for the implicit numbering of placeholders:

```
>>> "Attribute: {.imag}, list element: {[1]}".format(
...     1+4j, [1,2,3])
'Attribute: 4.0, list element: 2'
```

The following sections describe how you can influence the replacement itself.

Formatting the Output

Up to this point, we've only used format to replace placeholders with specific values, without specifying the rules according to which the replacement is to be made. To do that, you can specify *format specifiers* separated from the placeholder name by a colon. For example, to output a float rounded to two decimal places, you would use the format specification .2f:

```
>>> "Amount: {:.2f} Euro".format(13.37690)
'Amount: 13.38 Euro'
```

---

12   Note that the dictionary keys are not enclosed in quotation marks, even if they should be strings. This results in the fact that, for example, the ":-]" key can't be used in a format string.

The effect of the format specifications depends on the data type that is passed as the value for the respective placeholder. We'll take a closer look at the formatting options for Python's built-in data types ahead.

Note that all formatting specifications are optional and independent of each other. For this reason, they can also occur individually.

Before we look at the formatting options in detail, we'd like to briefly show you the basic structure of a format specification:

```
[[fill]align][sign][#][0][minimumwidth][,][.precision][type]
```

The square brackets indicate that their content is optional. All of these fields will be described individually in the following sections.

Setting the Minimum Width: minimumwidth

If a simple integer is used as format specification, it specifies the minimum width the replaced value should have. For example, if you want to output a table of names and make sure that everything is flush underneath, you can achieve this as follows:

```
f = "{:15}|{:15}"
print(f.format("First name", "Last name"))
print(f.format("Daniel", "Rodriguez"))
print(f.format("Linda", "Moore"))
print(f.format("Steve", "Bishop"))
print(f.format("Kaylee", "Harris"))
```

In this tiny program, we format the two placeholders 0 and 1 with a width of 15 characters each. The output thus looks as follows:

```
First name     |Last name
Daniel         |Rodriguez
Linda          |Moore
Steve          |Bishop
Kaylee         |Harris
```

If a value is longer than the minimum width, the width of the inserted value is adjusted to the value and not cut off:

```
>>> "{long:2}".format(long="I'm longer than two characters!")
"I'm longer than two characters!"
```

Determining the Alignment: align

When you specify the minimum width of a field, you can determine the alignment of the value in case it doesn't fill the entire width—as was the case in the first of the previous two examples.

For example, to align an amount of money to the right as usual, you must place a > sign in front of the minimum width:

```
>>> "Final price: {sum:>5} Euro".format(sum=443)
'Final price:   443 Euro'
```

Table 12.18 contains a list of four alignment types.

Sign	Meaning
<	The value is inserted left-justified in the reserved space. This is the default behavior unless an alignment is specified.
>	The value is inserted right-justified in the reserved space.
=	Makes sure that for numeric values the sign is always at the beginning of the inserted value; only after that does an alignment to the right take place (see the example below).
	This specification is only useful for numeric values and causes a ValueError for other data types.
^	The value is inserted centered in the reserved space.

Table 12.18 Alignment Types

An example should clarify the not quite intuitive effect of the = alignment type. The position of the sign is interesting here:

```
>>> "Temperature: {:10}".format(-12.5)
'Temperature:       -12.5'
>>> "Temperature: {:=10}".format(-12.5)
'Temperature: -      12.5'
```

Note that an alignment specification has no effect if the inserted value is as long as or longer than the relevant minimum width.

Fill Characters: fill

Before you specify the alignment, you can specify the character you want to use for filling the excess characters during the alignment process. By default, the space character is used for this purpose. However, you can use any character you like:

```
>>> "{text:-^25}".format(text="Hello world")
'-------Hello world-------'
```

Here, the string "Hello World" was inserted centered and surrounded by minus signs.

Treating Signs: sign

Between the minimum width specification and the alignment specification, you can specify how to deal with the sign of a numeric value. The three possible formatting characters are shown in Table 12.19.

Sign	Meaning
+	A sign must be indicated for both positive and negative numerical values.
-	Only for negative numbers is this sign indicated. This is the default behavior.
Blank character	Using the blank character, you can ensure that a space is inserted instead of a sign for positive numerical values. Negative numbers get a minus as the sign with this setting.

Table 12.19 Different Types of Treating Signs

Let's demonstrate the handling of signs with a few simple examples:

```
>>> "Cost: {:+}".format(135)
'Cost: +135'
>>> "Cost: {:+}".format(-135)
'Cost: -135'
>>> "Cost: {:-}".format(135)
'Cost: 135'
>>> "Cost: {: }".format(135)
'Cost:  135'
>>> "Cost: {: }".format(-135)
'Cost: -135'
```

As already mentioned, the alignment specification = only makes sense when used with a sign:

```
>>> "Cost: {:=+10}".format(-135)
'Cost: -       135'
```

As you can see, in the preceding example, the minus sign is inserted at the beginning of the reserved space; only after that is the number 135 aligned to the right.

Types of Number Representation: type

To be able to further customize the output for numerical values, there are various output types that are inserted at the very end of the format specification. For example, the b type specification outputs integers in binary notation:

```
>>> "Funny Bits: {:b}".format(109)
'Funny Bits: 1101101'
```

Python provides a total of eight possible type specifications for integers, which are listed in Table 12.20.

Sign	Meaning
b	The number is output in binary notation.
c	The number is interpreted as a Unicode character.
	For more information on Unicode, see Section 12.5.4.
d	The number is output in decimal notation. This is the default behavior.
o	The number is output in octal notation.
x	The number is output in hexadecimal notation, using lowercase letters for the digits a to f.
X	Like x, but with uppercase letters for the digits from A to F.
n	Like d, but it tries to use the usual character for the region to separate numbers (e.g., a dot versus a comma as a thousands separator).

Table 12.20 Integer Output Types

There's another alternative mode for the output of integers, which you can activate by writing a hash (#) between the minimum width and the sign. In this mode, outputs in numeral systems with bases other than 10 are identified by appropriate prefixes:

```
>>> "{:#b} vs. {:b}".format(109, 109)
'0b1101101 vs. 1101101'
>>> "{:#o} vs. {:o}".format(109, 109)
'0o155 vs. 155'
>>> "{:#x} vs. {:x}".format(109, 109)
'0x6d vs. 6d'
```

There are also various output types for floats, which are listed in Table 12.21.

Sign	Meaning
e	The number is output in scientific notation, using a lowercase e to separate the mantissa and exponent.
E	Like e, but with a capital E as separator.
f	The number is output as a decimal number with a decimal point.

Table 12.21 Output Types for Floats

Sign	Meaning
g	The number is output as for f if it isn't too long. For numbers that are too long, the e type is automatically used.
G	Like g, except that the E type is used for numbers that are too long
n	Like g, but it tries to use a separator adapted to the region.
%	The numerical value is first multiplied by one hundred and then output, followed by a percent sign.
Not specified	Like g, but at least one decimal place is specified.

Table 12.21 Output Types for Floats (Cont.)

The following example illustrates the formatting for floats:

```
>>> "{number:e}".format(number=123.456)
'1.234560e+02'
>>> "{number:f}".format(number=123.456)
'123.456000'
>>> "{number:n}".format(number=123.456)
'123.456'
>>> "{number:%}".format(number=0.75)
'75.000000%'
```

Precision with Floats: precision

It's possible to specify the number of decimal places when outputting floats. To do this, you write the relevant number, separated by a period, between the minimum length and the output type, as we did in our introductory example:

```
>>> "Amount: {:.2f} Euro".format(13.37690)
'Amount: 13.38 Euro'
```

The excess decimal places won't be truncated during formatting, but rounded.

Note that in this example the minimum length hasn't been specified, and therefore the format specification starts with a period.

As a final formatting option, 0 can be inserted just before the minimum width. This zero causes the excess space to be filled with zeros and the sign to be inserted at the beginning of the reserved space. Thus, this mode is equivalent to the alignment type = and the fill character 0:

```
>>> "The following holds true: {z1:05} == {z2:0=5}.".format(z1=23, z2=23)
'The following holds true: 00023 == 00023.'
```

Thousands Separation: The , and _ Options

If the , option is set, blocks of thousands are separated by a comma. Meanwhile, _ allows you to set the underscore as a thousands separator:

```
>>> "A lot of money: {:,d}".format(12345678900)
'A lot of money: 12,345,678,900'
>>> "A lot of money: {:_d}".format(12345678900)
'A lot of money: 12_345_678_900'
```

Self-Documenting Expressions in f-Strings

Python 3.8 introduced *self-documenting expressions* in f-strings, which are used to easily format debug outputs. Such outputs are inserted when testing programs to observe the values of certain variables. A typical debug output that includes an f-string could look like the following:

```
>>> variable_1 = 12
>>> variable_2 = 17
>>> print(f"variable_1={variable_1}, variable_2={variable_2}")
variable_1=12, variable_2=17
```

Such outputs are often inserted into the program code for a short time during debugging and removed later. For this reason, it can be very annoying to have to write the variable names twice for a clean debug output: once for the output of the variable name itself and once for the output of the value of the variable.

A self-documenting expression provides help in this context. It makes it possible to formulate the preceding example in a compact way:

```
>>> print(f"{variable_1=}, {variable_2=}")
variable_1=12, variable_2=17
```

Note the equal sign, which indicates a self-documenting expression, instead of the usual colon in the placeholder. In the formatted result, in addition to the values of the variables, their identifiers are automatically inserted so that it's always clear how the output values are to be assigned.

As with regular placeholders in f-strings, self-documenting expressions don't necessarily have to consist of only one identifier, as the following example shows:

```
>>> import math
>>> f"{math.cos(math.pi)=}"
'math.cos(math.pi)=-1.0'
```

12.5.4   Character Sets and Special Characters

In the previous sections, we learned about the str for text and bytes for byte sequences data types. These two data types are very similar, not least because both can be interpreted as a string and instantiated via a corresponding literal:

```
>>> "Python"
'Python'
>>> b"Python"
b'Python'
```

In this case, we have instantiated the Python string once as text and once as a byte sequence, which at first seems to make no difference. Internally, however, very different representations of the string are generated in the two cases, which we notice in particular if our string is to contain special characters:

```
>>> "Püthøn"
'Püthøn'
>>> b"Püthøn"
  File "<stdin>", line 1
    b"Püthøn"
            ^
SyntaxError: bytes can only contain ASCII literal characters
```

While str literals may contain any special characters without a problem, this is apparently not possible for bytes literals without further ado. Also, the conversion between str and bytes instances isn't possible automatically, which is why, for example, a bytes string can't be appended to a str string:

```
>>> "P" + b"ython"
Traceback (most recent call last):
  File "<stdin>", line 1, in <module>
TypeError: can only concatenate str (not "bytes") to str
```

In general, text data in Python programs should be represented by str instances whenever possible as these can represent any special character without a problem. Nevertheless, it's often necessary to represent strings explicitly as byte sequences. This is especially the case when text data is read or output via binary interfaces. Such binary interfaces can be enforced, for example, by file operations, direct memory access, network connections, databases, or external libraries.

In Figure 12.4, this principle is illustrated using two Python programs that exchange strings via a byte-oriented communication channel, such as a network connection. Internally, both programs use str instances and can thus process any special characters. For communication, the sender must *encode* its strings into byte sequences, while the receiver *decodes* the received byte sequences back into str instances. For this process, both sides agree on the "utf8" encoding.

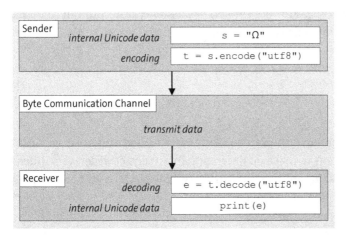

Figure 12.4 Encoding and Decoding of Character Strings for Transmission Purposes in a Byte-Oriented Communication Channel

In this section, we'll take a look at how the str and bytes data types represent strings internally, and finally discuss how a conversion between the two worlds is possible.

Character Encoding

First, we want to develop an idea of how a computer handles strings internally. To start, it can be said that a computer actually doesn't know any characters at all as only bits and numerical values based on them can be represented in its memory. To still produce screen output or perform other operations with characters, defined translation tables are available, so-called *codepages*, which assign a certain number to each letter. This assignment means that, in addition to letters and digits, punctuation marks and special characters are also mapped. There are also nonprintable *control characters*, such as the tabulator or the line feed (see Table 12.9).

The best-known and most important character set is the *ASCII character* set,[13] which implements a seven-bit character encoding. This means that each character utilizes seven bits of memory, so a total of 2^7 (128) different characters can be mapped. The definition of the ASCII character set is based on the alphabet of the English language, which in particular doesn't contain special characters such as *ä*, *ø*, or *ü*. To be able to represent such special characters, the ASCII code was extended by increasing the storage space for a character by one bit, so that 2^8 (256) different characters can be stored.

This extension of the ASCII character set results in space for 128 additional special characters. The codepage used determines which interpretation these further places have

---

13   ASCII is an abbreviation for American Standard Code for Information Interchange.

in concrete terms. Which codepage is to be used depends on the configuration of the respective computer. In particular, operating system and regional settings affect the selection of the codepage.

Encoding and Decoding

The `bytes` data type represents a sequence of bytes that, depending on the codepage used, can represent a character string in particular. Python allows the programmer to instantiate `bytes` strings directly via a special literal, provided that the characters contained in the literal are limited to the ASCII character set as the lowest common denominator of all character sets. This explains the behavior we observed at the beginning when instantiating `bytes` strings with and without special characters:

```
>>> b"Python"
b'Python'
>>> b"Püthøn"
  File "<stdin>", line 1
SyntaxError: bytes can only contain ASCII literal characters
```

If we still want to represent the string Püthøn as a `bytes` string, such as to output it as part of a binary I/O operation, we must first create a `str` string and then *encode* it. This can be done using the `encode` method of the `str` data type, which requires the character set to be used for encoding to be specified when it's called:

```
>>> str_string = "Püthøn"
>>> bytes_string = str_string.encode("iso-8859-15")
>>> bytes_string
b'P\xfcth\xf8n'
```

In the iso-8859-15 encoded `bytes` string, all characters not included in the ASCII character set are represented as escape sequences. These are introduced by the \x prefix followed by a two-digit hexadecimal number indicating the numeric value of the encoded character. In the example, the special characters ü and ø are represented with the escape sequences \xfc and \xf8, which stand for the numeric decimal values 252 and 248.

In the process of *decoding*, a `bytes` string is transformed into a `str` string using the `decode` method. Also in this case, the character set to be used must be specified:

```
>>> bytes_string.decode("iso-8859-15")
'Püthøn'
```

Figure 12.5 summarizes the processes of encoding and decoding and the corresponding conversions between `str` and `bytes`.

The iso-8859-15 codepage (also referred to as *Latin-9*) used in this case covers all important characters for Western Europe, such as umlauts, accents, and the euro sign. In addition to iso-8859-15, there is a plethora of codepages with different objectives and widely varying degrees of dissemination. Modern operating systems are usually based on Unicode and the associated codepage UTF-8, which we'll look at in more detail in the following sections.

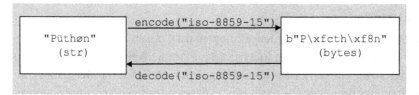

Figure 12.5 Encoding and Decoding of a Character String

The Universal Character Set Unicode

A major drawback of the character-encoding approach described so far is the limitation on the number of characters. Imagine a string containing an elaboration on authors from different language areas with original citations: they would quickly reach the limit of eight-bit encoding due to the many different alphabets and wouldn't be able to digitize the work. Or imagine you wanted to encode a text in Chinese, which would become impossible due to the more than 100,000 characters in that language.

An obvious solution to this problem is to increase the memory space per character, but this introduces new drawbacks. For example, if you use 16 bits for each character, the number of characters is still limited to 65,536. It can be assumed that languages will continue to develop and that this number will therefore no longer be sufficient in the long run.[14] Furthermore, in the 16-bit example, the memory requirements for a string would double because twice as many bits would be used for each character as with extended ASCII encoding, and this despite the fact that a large part of all texts consists mainly of a small subset of all available characters.

A long-term solution to the encoding problem was finally devised by the Unicode standard, which provides variable encoding lengths for individual characters. In principle, Unicode is a huge table that assigns a number, called a *code point*, to each known character. This table is maintained and constantly expanded by the Unicode Consortium, a nonprofit institution. Code points are usually written as "U+x", where x is the hexadecimal representation of the code point.

What's really new about Unicode is the Unicode Transformation Format (UTF) procedure, which can represent code points by byte sequences of different lengths. There are several of these transformation formats, but the most important and widely used one is UTF-8. UTF-8 uses up to seven bytes to encode a single character, with the actual length depending on the frequency of the character in texts. For example, all characters

---

14 It is indeed the case that 16 bits are already insufficient to encode all the characters of written language.

of the ASCII standard can be encoded with one byte each, which has the same numerical value as the corresponding ASCII encoding of the character. This procedure ensures that every string encoded with ASCII is also a valid UTF-8 code: UTF-8 is compatible with ASCII. At this point, we aren't interested further in the technical implementation of Unicode, but rather in how we can use Unicode in Python.

Unicode in Python

In Python, there's a clear separation between binary data (bytes data type) and text data (str data type) at the level of data types for strings. So long as you work with text data, with the str data type, you usually don't need to bother about character encoding. An exception is the explicit use of a special character within a string literal via its Unicode code point.

As you've already seen in the example at the beginning of this section, you can encode special characters in string literals using escape sequences. We used escape sequences that start with \x. However, these sequences are only suitable for characters that use one of the first 256 code points. For any Unicode character, such as the euro symbol (€; code point 8364, hexadecimal 0x20ac), there are escape sequences that are introduced with \u:

```
>>> s = "\u20ac"
>>> print(s)
€
```

In addition to the code point, a Unicode character has a unique name by which it can be identified. The \N escape sequence allows you to use special characters by their Unicode name in string literals:

```
>>> "\N{euro sign}"
'€'
```

In the example, the \N escape sequence was used to insert the euro sign based on its Unicode name, *euro sign*, within a string literal.

> **Note**
>
> The popular emojis in chat applications are also defined in the Unicode standard and can be used in Python programs via their respective code points or via their unique names.
>
> The following code enables you to decorate your program outputs with a beautiful Python emoji, for example:
>
> ```
> >>> "\N{Snake}"
> '🐍'
> ```

> Note that the specific appearance of an emoji is not standardized and depends on the system font used in each case.

The built-in chr and ord functions enable you to convert Unicode code points and the corresponding characters into each other:

```
>>> chr(8364)
'€'
>>> ord("€")
8364
```

For encoding or decoding with UTF-8, the "utf-8" character set is specified when calling the encode and decode methods:

```
>>> str_string ="Püthøn"
>>> bytes_string = str_string.encode("utf-8")
>>> bytes_string
b'P\xc3\xbcth\xc3\xb8n'
>>> bytes_string.decode("utf-8")
'Püthøn'
```

Other Character Sets

So far, we've only dealt with the two encoding methods: "iso-8859-15" and "UTF-8". There are quite a few other methods besides these two, many of which are natively supported by Python. Each of these encodings has a name in Python that you can pass to the encode method. Table 12.22 shows a few of these names as examples.

Name in Python	Properties
"ascii"	Encoding using the ASCII table; English alphabet, English digits, punctuation marks and control characters; one byte per character
"utf-8" or "utf8"	Encoding for all Unicode code points; downward compatible with ASCII; variable number of bytes per character
"iso-8859-15"	Encoding of the characters for Western Europe as standardized by the International Organization for Standardization (ISO) in 1999
"cp1252"	Encoding for Western Europe used by older Windows versions; in addition to ASCII characters, support for European special characters, especially the euro sign; downward compatible with ASCII; one byte per character

Table 12.22 Four of the Encodings Supported by Python

Note that Unicode and UTF-8 have now become the standard in many places and have displaced other character encodings. Thanks to this, developers have to worry less and less about adequate character encoding than they had to in the past.

If you try to decode a `bytes` string with the wrong character set, the result depends on whether or not the code points used in the string are also defined in the character set used for decoding. If they are, nonsense will be decoded; if not, a `UnicodeDecodeError` will be generated:

```
>>> bytes_string.decode("utf-8")
'Püthøn'
>>> bytes_string.decode("iso-8859-15")
'PÃŒthÃžn'
>>> bytes_string.decode("ascii")
Traceback (most recent call last):
  File "<stdin>", line 1, in <module>
UnicodeDecodeError: 'ascii' codec can't decode byte 0xc3 in position 1: ordinal
not in range(128)
```

The `encode` and `decode` methods provide an optional `errors` parameter that defines the procedure to follow in such error cases. The most important values for `errors` are summarized in Table 12.23.

Value	Meaning
`"strict"`	Default setting. Any character that can't be encoded will cause an error.
`"ignore"`	Characters that can't be encoded are ignored.
`"replace"`	Characters that can't be encoded are replaced by a placeholder: during encoding by the question mark `"?"`, during decoding by the Unicode character U+FFFD.
`"xmlcharrefreplace"`	Nonencodable characters are replaced by their XML entity.[*] (Only possible with `encode`.)
`"backslashreplace"`	Nonencodable characters are replaced by a backslashed `\x` escape sequence.

[*]   This is a special way of formatting for displaying special characters in XML files. For more information about XML files, please refer to Chapter 32.

Table 12.23 Values for the errors Parameter of Encode and Decode

Let's look again at the decoding of the `bytes` string `bytes_string` from the last example with different values for `errors`:

```
>>> bytes_string.decode("ascii", "ignore")
'Pthn'
>>> bytes_string.decode("ascii", "replace")
'P??th??n'
>>> bytes_string.decode("ascii", "backslashreplace")
'P\\xc3\\xbcth\\xc3\\xb8n'
```

To avoid having to work around encoding problems with these tools up front, you should always use universal encoding schemes such as UTF-8 whenever possible.

Encoding Declaration for Python Source Code

By default, Python assumes that program files are stored in UTF-8 encoding, which is especially relevant when special characters are used in string literals, identifiers, or comments. The UTF-8 encoded storage of Python program files is also the default behavior of established Python editors and development environments.

If you want to deviate from this default behavior, you can insert an *encoding declaration* in the header of a Python program file. This is a line that identifies the encoding in which the program file was saved. An encoding declaration is usually located directly below the shebang line[15] or in the first line of the program file and looks like this:

```
# -*- coding: cp1252 -*-
```

In this case, the obsolete cp1252 Windows character set was used.

> **Note**
>
> In Python 3, encoding declarations are needed only in the rare cases where you don't want to use the common default encoding, UTF-8.
>
> Note, however, that Python 2 assumes ASCII encoding of program files by default. Without an encoding declaration, no special characters can be used in string literals or comments here.

---

15   The meaning of a shebang line is explained in Chapter 4, Section 4.1.1.

Chapter 13
Mappings and Sets

In this chapter, we'll take a look at two more categories of data types: mappings and sets. The *mappings* category contains data types that establish a mapping between different objects. The only basic data type that falls into this category is the *dictionary*.

A *set* is a unordered collection of elements in which each element may be contained only once. In Python, there are two basic data types for representing sets: set for a mutable set and frozenset for an immutable set. Thus, set is mutable and frozenset is immutable.

Data type	Stores	Mutability	Section
dict	Key-value mappings	Mutable	Section 13.1
set	Sets of any instances	Mutable	Section 13.2
frozenset	Sets of any instances	Immutable	Section 13.2

Table 13.1 List of Data Types for Mappings and Sets

13.1 Dictionary: dict

The name of the dict data type already provides a good indication of what is hidden behind it: a *dictionary* contains any number of *key/value pairs*, where the key doesn't necessarily have to be an integer like in a list. You may already be familiar with this data type from another programming language, where it's referred to as an *associative array* (in PHP, among others), *map* (in C++, among others), or *hash* (in Perl, among others). The dict data type is mutable; that is, it can be modified.

13.1.1 Creating a Dictionary

The following example explains how to create a dict with multiple key-value pairs inside curly brackets. In addition, the association with a dictionary becomes apparent:

```
translations = {"Germany": "Deutschland", "Spain": "Spanien"}
```

In this case, a dict is created with two entries separated by a comma. The first entry assigns the value "Germany" to the key "Deutschland". Key and value are separated from each other by a colon. All pairs do not necessarily have to be written in one line. Inside the curly brackets, the source code can be formatted as you wish:

```
translations = {
    "Germany": "Deutschland",
    "Spain": "Spanien",
    "France": "Frankreich"
}
```

There can be another comma after the last key-value pair, but it's not needed.

In addition to the approach via the literal, a dictionary can also be created using the built-in dict function. To do this, either an iterable object containing the key/value pairs is passed, or the pairs are passed as keyword parameters to the function:

```
>>> dict([("Germany", "Deutschland"), ("Spain", "Spanien")])
{'Germany': 'Deutschland', 'Spain': 'Spanien'}
>>> dict(Germany="Deutschland", Spain="Spanien")
{'Germany': 'Deutschland', 'Spain': 'Spanien'}
```

If you decide to specify keyword parameters, you must keep in mind that in this case the dictionary keys can only be strings that comply with the naming rules of an identifier.

Note

A dictionary can also be created using *dict comprehension*. Here, not all key-value pairs of the dictionary are explicitly listed, but are generated via a formation rule similar to a for loop. The following dict comprehension creates a dictionary that assigns the respective squares to the numbers from 0 to 4:

```
>>> {i: i*i for i in range(5)}
{0: 0, 1: 1, 2: 4, 3: 9, 4: 16}
```

Section 13.1.6 contains more information about dict comprehension.

In addition, unpacking can be used when creating a dictionary:

```
>>> {"a": 1, **{"b": 2, "c": 3}}
{'a': 1, 'b': 2, 'c': 3}
```

For more information on unpacking, see Chapter 12, Section 12.4.1.

13.1.2   Keys and Values

Each key must be unique in the dictionary, so no second key with the same name may exist. Although formally, the following is possible, only the second key-value pair gets transferred to the dictionary:

```
d = {
    "Germany": "Deutschland",
    "Germany": "Bayern"
}
```

In contrast to that, the values of a dictionary don't have to be unique; that is, they may occur more than once:

```
d = {
    "Germany": "Deutschland",
    "Allemagne": "Deutschland"
}
```

In the previous examples, in all pairs, both the key and the value were a string. But it doesn't have to be that way:

```
mapping = {
    0: 1,
    "abc": 0.5,
    1.2e22: [1,2,3,4],
    (1,3,3,7): "def"
}
```

In a dictionary, any instances, whether mutable or immutable, can be used as values. However, only instances of immutable data types may be used for the key. These are all the data types discussed so far, with the exception of lists and the dictionaries themselves. For example, if you try to create a dictionary in which a list is used as a key, the interpreter reports a corresponding error:

```
>>> d = {[1,2,3]: "abc"}
Traceback (most recent call last):
  File "<stdin>", line 1, in <module>
TypeError: unhashable type: 'list'
```

This limitation results from the fact that the keys of a dictionary are managed using a *hash value* calculated from their value. Basically, a hash value can be calculated from any object; however, this makes little sense for mutable objects as the hash value would also change when the object changes. Such a change would then interfere with the key management of a dictionary. For this reason, mutable objects are "unhashable," as stated in the error message shown above.[1]

---

1 In Chapter 19, Section 19.11.1, you'll learn how to implement hash calculation for custom data types.

13.1.3 Iteration

A dictionary is an iterable object that iterates through all the keys it contains. In the following example, we iterate through the keys of the translations dictionary and output them with print:

```
for key in translations:
    print(key)
```

As expected, the output of the code looks like this:

```
Germany
Spain
France
```

Using the "values" and "items" methods, the values of the dictionary can also be iterated alone or in combination with their respective keys:

```
>>> for value in translations.values():
...     print(value)
...
Deutschland
Spanien
Frankreich
>>> for key, value in translations.items():
...     print(key, "->", value)
...
Germany -> Deutschland
Spain -> Spanien
France -> Frankreich
```

The keys of a dictionary are always iterated in the order in which they were added to the dictionary.

> **Note**
> Prior to Python 3.7, a dictionary used to be an *unordered* data type. This meant that the keys were not necessarily iterated over in the order in which they were added to the dictionary. Since Python 3.7, the insertion order is guaranteed to be preserved during iteration.

Note that you must not resize the dictionary while iterating it. For example, the size of the dictionary would be affected by the addition or deletion of a key-value pair. If you try to do that nevertheless, you'll get the following error message:

```
Traceback (most recent call last):
  File "<stdin>", line 1, in <module>
RuntimeError: dictionary changed size during iteration
```

This restriction applies only to operations that affect the size of the dictionary, such as adding and removing entries. If you only change the associated value of a key in a loop, no error will occur.

13.1.4 Operators

Up until this point, you have learned what a dictionary is and how it is created. In addition, we have gone into a few specifics. Now we'll discuss the operators available for dictionaries which are listed in Table 13.2.

Operator	Description
len(d)	Returns the number of all key-value pairs contained in dictionary d
d[k]	Access to the value with key k
del d[k]	Deletes key k and its value
k in d	True if key k is located in d
k not in d	True if key k is not located in d
d1 | d2	Combines two dictionaries: d1 and d2 (new in Python 3.9)

Table 13.2 Operators of a Dictionary

In the following sections, the operators of a dictionary will be described in greater detail. Most of the operators are explained using the translations dictionary, which is defined as follows:

```
translations = {
    "Germany": "Deutschland",
    "Spain": "Spanien",
    "France": "Frankreich"
}
```

Length of a Dictionary

To determine the length of a dictionary, you can use the built-in len function. The length corresponds to the number of key-value pairs:

```
>>> len(translations)
3
```

Accessing a Value

The operator [ ] can be used to access a value of a dictionary. To do that, you must write the corresponding key in square brackets after the name of the dictionary. In the case of the sample dictionary, such access could look like this:

```
>>> translations["Germany"]
'Deutschland'
```

The operator [ ] can be used not only for read accesses, but also to reinsert or replace an entry in a dictionary. In the following example, the value assigned to the "Germany" key in the translations dictionary is set to "Bayern":

```
>>> translations["Germany"] = "Bayern"
```

A subsequent read access to the key "Germany" shows that the previous value "Deutschland" has actually been replaced by "Bayern":

```
>>> translations["Germany"]
'Bayern'
```

If a key that doesn't yet exist in the dictionary is accessed in write mode, the dictionary is extended by the key-value pair specified in the access. If, on the other hand, a nonexistent key is accessed in read mode, the interpreter responds with a KeyError:

```
>>> translations["Greece"]
Traceback (most recent call last):
  File "<stdin>", line 1, in <module>
KeyError: 'Greece'
```

> **Note**
>
> The keys of a dictionary are compared with each other on the basis of their values when they are accessed, not on the basis of their identities. This is because the keys are internally represented by their hash value, which is formed solely based on the value of an instance.
>
> In practice, this means that, for example, the accesses d[1] and d[1.0] are equivalent.

Deleting a Key-Value Pair

To delete an entry in a dictionary, the keyword del can be used in combination with the access operator. In the following example, the entry "Germany": "Deutschland" will be removed from the dictionary:

```
del translations["Germany"]
```

The dictionary itself still exists even if it has become empty by deleting the last entry.

Testing for Specific Keys

Similar to lists, the operators in and not in exist for dictionaries and are used to test whether or not a key exists in a dictionary. They return the corresponding result as a truth value:

```
>>> "France" in translations
True
>>> "Spain" not in translations
False
```

Combining Two Dictionaries

As of Python 3.9, the | operator is defined for dictionaries, which merges the key-value pairs of two dictionaries d1 and d2 into a new dictionary:

```
>>> {"France": "Frankreich"} | {"Spain": "Spanien"}
{'France': 'Frankreich', 'Spain': 'Spanien'}
```

The | operator can also be used as an augmented assignment |= to add key-value pairs from another dictionary to an existing dictionary d:

```
>>> d = {}
>>> d |= {"France": "Frankreich"}
>>> d |= {"Spain": "Spanien"}
>>> d
{'France': 'Frankreich', 'Spain': 'Spanien'}
```

If a key occurs in both dictionaries to be combined, the corresponding key-value pair of the right operand is always included in the result.

> **Note**
> Note that the | and |= operators for combining two dictionaries were added to the language scope as of Python 3.9, making them a fairly new language feature. In older Python versions, the update method can be used instead.

13.1.5 Methods

In addition to the operators, some methods are defined to facilitate working with dictionaries (see Table 13.3).

Method	Description
d.clear()	Empties dictionary d.
d.copy()	Creates a copy of d.

Table 13.3 Methods of a Dictionary

Method	Description
d.get(k, [x])	Returns d[k] if key k is present, otherwise x.
d.items()	Returns an iterable object that yields all key-value pairs of d.
d.keys()	Returns an iterable object that yields all keys of d.
d.pop(k)	Returns the value associated with key k and deletes the key-value pair from dictionary d.
d.popitem()	Returns an arbitrary key-value pair of d and removes it from the dictionary.
d.setdefault(k, [x])	The opposite of get. Sets d[k] = x if key k isn't present.
d.update(d2)	Adds a dictionary d2 to d and overwrites the values of already existing keys if necessary.
d.values()	Returns an iterable object that yields all values of d.

Table 13.3 Methods of a Dictionary (Cont.)

Aside from these methods, the dict data type also provides a static method. This is a method that can be called even without a concrete dictionary instance (see Table 13.4).

Method	Description
dict.fromkeys(seq, [value])	Creates a new dictionary with the values of the seq list as key and sets each value initially to value

Table 13.4 Static Method of a Dictionary

Now we'll explain the mentioned methods in detail and provide a short example for each of them in the interactive mode. All examples are to be understood in the following context:

```
>>> d = {"k1": "v1", "k2": "v2", "k3": "v3"}
>>> d
{'k1': 'v1', 'k2': 'v2', 'k3': 'v3'}
```

So there is a dictionary d with three key-value pairs in each example. In the examples, we'll modify the dictionary and let the interpreter output its value.

d.clear()

The clear method deletes all key-value pairs from d. It doesn't have the same effect as del d because the dictionary itself isn't deleted, but only emptied:

```
>>> d = {"k1": "v1", "k2": "v2", "k3": "v3"}
>>> d.clear()
>>> d
{}
```

d.copy()

The copy method creates a copy of the dictionary d:

```
>>> d = {"k1": "v1", "k2": "v2", "k3": "v3"}
>>> e = d.copy()
>>> e
{'k1': 'v1', 'k2': 'v2', 'k3': 'v3'}
```

Note that although the dictionary itself is copied, the values are still references to the same objects. This is illustrated by the following example:

```
>>> d1 = {"key": [1,2,3]}
>>> d2 = d1.copy()
>>> d2["key"].append(4)
>>> d2
{'key': [1, 2, 3, 4]}
>>> d1
{'key': [1, 2, 3, 4]}
```

A dictionary d1 is created containing a single key-value pair with a list as its value. The dictionary d1 is copied by calling the copy method, and then the list referenced as the value in the d2 copy is extended by one element. Because the copy method performs only a shallow copy, both dictionaries d1 and d2 contain a reference to the same list:

```
>>> d1["key"] is d2["key"]
True
```

Changing this list causes both dictionaries to change accordingly. A deep copy, which also copies the values of a dictionary, can be created with the copy module of the standard library (see Chapter 44, Section 44.7).

d.get(k, [x])

The get method provides access to a value of the dictionary. Unlike the access operator, however, no exception is generated if the key doesn't exist. Instead, the optional parameter x is returned in this case. If x hasn't been specified, it is assumed to be None. The following line, value = d.get(k,x), can therefore be regarded as a replacement for the following code:

```
if k in d:
    value = d[k]
else:
    value = x
```

The get method can be used as follows:

```
>>> d = {"k1": "v1", "k2": "v2", "k3": "v3"}
>>> d.get("k2", 1337)
'v2'
>>> d.get("k5", 1337)
1337
```

d.items()

The items method returns an iterable object across all key-value pairs in the dictionary. This can be iterated with a for loop as follows:

```
>>> d = {"k1": "v1", "k2": "v2", "k3": "v3"}
>>> for pair in d.items():
...     print(pair)
('k1', 'v1')
('k2', 'v2')
('k3', 'v3')
```

In each iteration, the pair variable contains the respective key-value pair as a tuple.

d.keys()

The keys method returns an iterable object across all keys in the dictionary. In the following example, all keys present in dictionary d are output via print:

```
>>> d = {"k1": "v1", "k2": "v2", "k3": "v3"}
>>> for key in d.keys():
...     print(key)
k1
k2
k3
```

We mentioned at the beginning that no special method is needed to iterate over all the keys of a dictionary. The keys method can be therefore be avoided using the following code:

```
>>> for key in d:
...     print(key)
k1
```

```
k2
k3
```

d.pop(k)

The pop method deletes the key-value pair with key k from the dictionary and returns the value of this pair:

```
>>> d = {"k1": "v1", "k2": "v2", "k3": "v3"}
>>> d.pop("k1")
'v1'
>>> d.pop("k3")
'v3'
>>> d
{'k2': 'v2'}
```

d.popitem()

The popitem method returns an arbitrary key-value pair as a tuple and removes it from the dictionary. Note that the returned pair is arbitrary, but not random:[2]

```
>>> d = {"k1": "v1", "k2": "v2", "k3": "v3"}
>>> d.popitem()
('k3', 'v3')
>>> d
{'k1': 'v1', 'k2': 'v2'}
```

If d is empty, a corresponding exception is generated:

```
Traceback (most recent call last):
  File "<stdin>", line 1, in <module>
KeyError: 'popitem(): dictionary is empty'
```

d.setdefault(k, [x])

The setdefault method adds the key-value pair {k: x} to dictionary d if key k doesn't exist. The x parameter is optional and defaults to None.

```
>>> d = {"k1": "v1", "k2": "v2", "k3": "v3"}
>>> d.setdefault("k2", 1337)
'v2'
>>> d.setdefault("k5", 1337)
1337
```

---

2 This means the key-value pairs are returned by the popitem method in an order that depends on the implementation. However, this order is not random; for example, the last inserted key-value pair could always be returned.

```
>>> d
{'k1': 'v1', 'k2': 'v2', 'k3': 'v3', 'k5': 1337}
```

Regardless of whether or not the key-value pair has been written to the dictionary, the setdefault method returns the value d[k].

d.update(d2)

The update method extends dictionary d by the keys and values of dictionary d2, which is passed to the method as a parameter:

```
>>> d = {"k1": "v1", "k2": "v2", "k3": "v3"}
>>> d.update({"k4": "v4"})
>>> d
{'k1': 'v1', 'k2': 'v2', 'k3': 'v3', 'k4': 'v4'}
```

If both dictionaries have the same key, the value in d associated with that key is over-written with the one from d2:

```
>>> d.update({"k1": "python rulez"})
>>> d
{'k1': 'python rulez', 'k2': 'v2', 'k3': 'v3', 'k4': 'v4'}
```

d.values()

The values method behaves similarly to keys, the difference being that all values are iterated:

```
>>> d = {"k1": "v1", "k2": "v2", "k3": "v3"}
>>> for value in d.values():
...     print(value)
v1
v2
v3
```

dict.fromkeys(seq, [value])

The static fromkeys method creates a new dictionary using the entries of the seq iterable object as keys. The value parameter is optional. However, should it be specified, it will be used as the value of any key-value pair:

```
>>> dict.fromkeys([1,2,3], "python")
{1: 'python', 2: 'python', 3: 'python'}
```

If the value parameter is omitted, None is always entered as the value:

```
>>> dict.fromkeys([1,2,3])
{1: None, 2: None, 3: None}
```

13.1.6   Dict Comprehensions

To generate a dictionary, Python provides a process analogous to list comprehensions, which is referred to as *dictionary comprehension* or *dict comprehension* for short.

The structure of a dict comprehension is similar to that of a list comprehension (see Chapter 12, Section 12.3.7), so let's start directly with an example:

```
>>> names = ["Donald", "Scrooge", "Daisy", "Gilbert"]
>>> {k: len(k) for k in names}
{'Donald': 6, 'Scrooge': 7, 'Daisy': 5, 'Gilbert': 7}
>>> {k: len(k) for k in names if k[0] == "D"}
{'Donald': 6, 'Daisy': 5}
```

Here, a dict comprehension was used to create a dictionary containing a given list of strings as keys and the lengths of the respective key strings as values.

Looking at the example, two differences from list comprehensions immediately stand out:

- Unlike a list comprehension, a dict comprehension is enclosed in curly brackets.
- In a dict comprehension, a key-value pair must be added to the dictionary in each run of the loop. This is at the beginning of the comprehension, where the key and value are separated by a colon.

Apart from that, you can use a dict comprehension as you already know it from list comprehensions. Both types can also be used together. Here's another example:

```
>>> lst1 = ["A", "B", "C"]
>>> lst2 = [2, 4, 6]
>>> {k:[k*i for i in lst2] for k in lst1}
{'A': ['AA', 'AAAA', 'AAAAAA'], 'B': ['BB', 'BBBB', 'BBBBBB'],
'C': ['CC', 'CCCC', 'CCCCCC']}
```

This code creates a dictionary that uses a list comprehension to generate a list as a value for each key, containing two, four, and six times the key, respectively.

13.2   Sets: set and frozenset

A *set* is a unordered collection of elements in which each element may be contained only once. In Python, there are two basic data types for representing sets: set for a mutable set and frozenset for an immutable set.

13.2.1   Creating a Set

Note that whether a mutable or an immutable set is instantiated, a set can contain only immutable elements. Table 13.1 provides an overview of the basic data types and their mutability. For example, if you try to create a set that should contain a list as an element, the interpreter reports a corresponding error:

```
>>> set([1, 2, list()])
Traceback (most recent call last):
  File "<stdin>", line 1, in <module>
TypeError: unhashable type: 'list'
```

Similar to dictionaries, the rationale for this behavior is that the elements of a set are managed internally using a persistent hash value that can be determined only for instances of immutable data types.

An empty instance of the data types set and frozenset can be created as follows:

```
>>> set()
set()
>>> frozenset()
frozenset()
```

If the set already contains elements at the time of instantiation, these can be passed to the constructors as elements of an iterable object—for example, a tuple:

```
>>> set(("A", "B", "C"))
{'C', 'B', 'A'}
>>> frozenset([True, 47, (1,2,3)])
frozenset({True, (1, 2, 3), 47})
```

In addition, there is a special literal for creating variable sets. As in math, the elements the set is supposed to contain are written in curly brackets separated by commas:

```
>>> s = {1, 2, 3, 99, -7}
>>> s
{1, 2, 99, 3, -7}
```

This kind of notation bears a problem: because the curly brackets are already used for dictionaries, it isn't possible to create an empty set with this literal; {} always instantiates an empty dictionary. Thus, as shown previously, empty sets must be instantiated via set(). There is no literal for the frozenset data type; it must always be instantiated via the frozenset() constructor.

> **Note**
>
> With a *set comprehension*, a set can be created by specifying a formation rule for the elements, similar to a for loop.

The following set comprehension creates a set with the squares of the numbers from 0 to 9:

```
>>> {i*i for i in range(10)}
{0, 1, 64, 4, 36, 9, 16, 49, 81, 25}
```

Apart from the brackets, a set comprehension works like a list comprehension (see Chapter 12, Section 12.3.7). So no further examples are needed for you to use them successfully.

When creating a set, you can use unpacking:

```
>>> {1, 2, *[3, 4]}
{1, 2, 3, 4}
```

For more information on unpacking, please refer to Chapter 12, Section 12.4.1.

13

13.2.2   Iteration

A *set* is an iterable object that can be iterated in a `for` loop. Let's take a look at the following example:

```
set = {1, 100, "a", 0.5}
for element in set:
    print(element)
```

This code generates the following output:

```
a
1
100
0.5
```

Unlike the keys of a dictionary, the elements of a set are not iterated in the order in which they were inserted into the set. In fact, they are iterated in an arbitrary but always the same order for the current program run, which results from the arrangement of the elements in the hash table underlying the set.

Note

An important detail to be mentioned in this context is that the order of elements of a set differs between program runs:

```
>>> {"A", "B", "C"}
{'A', 'C', 'B'}
... (Restart interpreter) ...
>>> {"A", "B", "C"}
{'C', 'A', 'B'}
```

The reason for this behavior is *hash randomization.* To prevent malicious denial-of-service attacks on hash tables, hash values aren't formed completely deterministically in Python. Instead, they contain a *salt* randomly determined at the start of the interpreter.

If you need a consistent iteration sequence across program runs, such as in the context of a reproducible test, you can enforce a constant salt via the PYTHONHASHSEED environment variable.

13.2.3   Operators

The set and frozenset data types have a common interface, which will be explained in more detail in the following sections. Let's start by covering all the common operators. For the sake of simplicity, we'll refer exclusively to the set data type when describing the operators. Nevertheless, they and the methods described later can be used in the same way for frozenset.

Operator	Description
len(s)	Returns the number of all elements contained in set s.
x in s	True if x is contained in set s, otherwise False.
x not in s	True if x isn't contained in set s, otherwise False.
s <= t	True if set s is a subset of set t, otherwise False.
s < t	True if set s is a proper subset[*] of set t, otherwise False.
s >= t	True if set t is a subset of set s, otherwise False.
s > t	True if set t is a proper subset of set s, otherwise False.
s | t	Creates a new set containing all elements of s and t. Thus, this operation forms the union of two sets.
s & t	Creates a new set containing the objects that are both elements of set s and elements of set t. So this operation forms the intersection of two sets.
s - t	Creates a new set with all elements of s except those also contained in t. So this operation creates the difference of two sets.
s ^ t	Creates a new set containing all objects that occur in either s or t, but not both. Thus, this operation forms the symmetric difference[**] of two sets.

Table 13.5 Operators of the set and frozenset Data Types

Operator	Description
*	A set *T* is referred to as a *proper subset* of a second set *M* if *T* is a subset of *M* and there's at least one element that is contained in *M* but not in *T*.
**	The *symmetric difference* of two sets A and B contains all elements of A and B that are contained in exactly one of the two sets only. Thus, the ^ operator can be modeled as follows: A ^ B = (A | B) - (A & B).

Table 13.5 Operators of the set and frozenset Data Types (Cont.)

Augmented assignments also exist for some of these operators (see Table 13.6).

Operator	Corresponding expression
s |= t	s = s | t
s &= t	s = s & t
s -= t	s = s - t
s ^= t	s = s ^ t

Table 13.6 Operators of the set Data Type

These operators also exist for the frozenset data type. However, they don't change the set itself, but instead create a new frozenset instance that contains the result of the operation and is referenced by s from now on.

In the following sections, we'll describe all operators clearly on the basis of examples. The examples should be regarded in the following context:

```
>>> s = {0,1,2,3,4,5,6,7,8,9}
>>> t = {6,7,8,9,10,11,12,13,14,15}
```

Thus, there are two sets named s and t, each of which has only numeric elements for reasons of clarity. The sets overlap in a certain range. Graphically, the initial situation can be illustrated as shown in Figure 13.1. The dark gray area corresponds to the intersection of s and t.

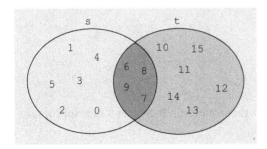

Figure 13.1 Initial Situation

Number of Elements

To determine the number of elements contained in a set, we use the built-in len function—as with the sequential data types and the dictionary:

```
>>> len(s)
10
```

Does the Set Contain an Element?

To test whether a set contains an element, you can use the in operator. Likewise, its
counterpart, not in, can be used to check the opposite:

```
>>> 10 in s
False
>>> 10 not in t
False
```

Is It a Subset?

To test whether a set is a subset of another set, the <= and >= operators as well as < and >
are used for proper subsets:

```
>>> u = {4,5,6}
>>> u <= s
True
>>> u < s
True
>>> u >= s
False
>>> u <= t
False
```

Note the difference between *subset* (<=, >=) and *proper subset* (<, >) in the following
example:

```
>>> m = {1,2,3}
>>> n = {1,2,3}
>>> m <= n
True
>>> m < n
False
```

Union of Two Sets

For the union of two sets, Python provides the | operator. It creates a new set contain-
ing all the elements contained in s or in t:

```
>>> s | t
{0, 1, 2, 3, 4, 5, 6, 7, 8, 9, 10, 11, 12, 13, 14, 15}
```

Figure 13.2 illustrates this.

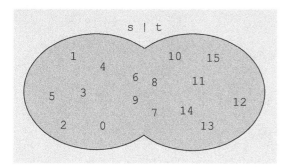

Figure 13.2 Union of the Sets s and t

The unification operator uses the same symbol as the bitwise OR of two integers. This is because the union of the sets s and t contains all the elements that are contained in s OR in t. Note that, as with the bitwise operator, this is a nonexclusive OR, so the union set also contains the elements that occur in both s and t.

Intersection

To determine the intersection of two sets, we use the & operator. This operator creates a new set that contains all the elements included in both the first and second operands:

```
>>> s & t
{8, 9, 6, 7}
```

Let's also take a look at the effects of this operator (see Figure 13.3).

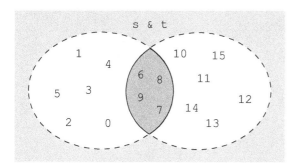

Figure 13.3 Intersection of the Sets s and t

The intersection of two sets s and t contains all elements that occur in s AND t. This explains the choice of the operator symbol &, which is also used for the bitwise AND.

Difference of Two Sets

To determine the difference of two sets, we use the - operator. As a result, a new set is formed that contains all elements of the first operand that aren't contained in the second operand at the same time:

```
>>> s - t
{0, 1, 2, 3, 4, 5}
>>> t - s
{10, 11, 12, 13, 14, 15}
```

Figure 13.4 illustrates this.

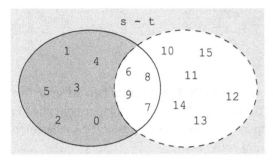

Figure 13.4 Difference of the Sets s and t

Symmetric Difference of Two Sets

To determine the symmetric difference of two sets, we use the ^ operator, which creates a new set containing all elements that occur in either the first or the second operand, but not in both at the same time:

```
>>> s ^ t
{0, 1, 2, 3, 4, 5, 10, 11, 12, 13, 14, 15}
```

Let's take a look at the diagram in Figure 13.5.

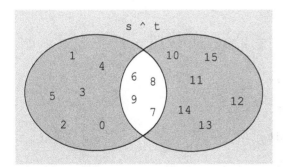

Figure 13.5 Symmetric Difference of the Sets s and t

234

The symmetric difference set of two sets s and t contains those elements that are contained either in s or in t (but not in both sets). This explains the choice of the operator symbol ^, which is also used for the bitwise excluding OR (XOR).

13.2.4 Methods

The set and frozenset data types provide a small number of methods, most of which are equivalent to one of the operators already described (see Table 13.7).

Method	Description
s.issubset(t)	Equivalent to s <= t
s.issuperset(t)	Equivalent to s >= t
s.isdisjoint(t)	Checks whether the sets s and t are *disjoint*—that is, whether they have an empty intersection
s.union(t)	Equivalent to s | t
s.intersection(t)	Equivalent to s & t
s.difference(t)	Equivalent to s - t
s.symmetric_difference(t)	Equivalent to s ^ t
s.copy()	Creates a copy of set s

Table 13.7 Methods of the set and frozenset Data Types

The difference between the <=, >=, |, &, -, and ^ operators and the issubset, issuperset, union, intersection, difference, and symmetric_difference methods, each with the same meaning, is that when using the operators both operands must be set or frozenset instances, whereas the methods accept any sequential data type for parameter t:

```
>>> {1,2,3} | frozenset([4,5,6])
{1, 2, 3, 4, 5, 6}
>>> {1,2,3} | "ABC"
Traceback (most recent call last):
  File "<stdin>", line 1, in <module>
TypeError: unsupported operand type(s) for |: 'set' and 'str'
>>> {1,2,3}.union("ABC")
{1, 2, 3, 'A', 'C', 'B'}
```

Aside from this difference, the methods behave like the associated operators.

You can create a copy of a set using the copy method:

```
>>> m = s.copy()
>>> m
```

```
{0, 1, 2, 3, 4, 5, 6, 7, 8, 9}
>>> m is s
False
>>> m == s
True
```

It's important that you copy only the set itself. The elements it contains are references to the same objects in both the original set and the copy. You already know this from Chapter 12, Section 12.3.6.

13.2.5   Mutable Sets: set

As a data type for mutable sets, set provides some methods (see Table 13.8) that go beyond the basic ones just described. Note that all methods introduced here are not available for frozenset.

Method	Description
s.add(e)	Inserts object e as an element into set s.
s.clear()	Deletes all elements of set s, but not the set itself.
s.difference_update(t)	Equivalent to s -= t.
s.discard(e)	Deletes element e from set s. If e is not present, this will be ignored.
s.intersection_update(t)	Equivalent to s &= t.
s.remove(e)	Deletes element e from set s. If e is not present, an exception will be generated.
s.symmetric_difference_update(t)	equivalent to s ^= t.
s.update(t)	equivalent to s |= t.

Table 13.8 Methods of set Data Type

In the following sections, we'll explain these methods based on some examples.

s.add(e)

The add method inserts an element e into set s:

```
>>> s = {1,2,3,4,5}
>>> s.add(6)
>>> s
{1, 2, 3, 4, 5, 6}
```

If e is already contained in the set, the set won't change.

s.clear()

The clear method removes all elements from set s. The set itself is still preserved after clear has been called:

```
>>> s = {1,2,3,4,5}
>>> s.clear()
>>> s
set()
```

s.discard(e)

The discard method deletes an element e from set s. The only difference from the remove method is that no error message is generated if e is not contained in s:

```
>>> s = {1,2,3,4,5}
>>> s.discard(5)
>>> s
{1, 2, 3, 4}
>>> s.discard(17)
>>> s
{1, 2, 3, 4}
```

s.remove(e)

The remove method deletes the element e from set s:

```
>>> s = {1,2,3,4,5}
>>> s.remove(5)
>>> s
{1, 2, 3, 4}
```

If the element to be deleted isn't contained in the set, an error message will be generated:

```
>>> s.remove(17)
Traceback (most recent call last):
  File "<stdin>", line 1, in <module>
KeyError: 17
```

13.2.6 Immutable Sets: frozenset

Because a frozenset is just a version of the set type that may not be changed once it has been created, all operators and methods have already been explained as part of the basic functionality at the beginning of the section.

Note, however, that a frozenset can't be instantiated like a set using curly brackets. The instantiation of a frozenset always happens as follows:

```
>>> fs_empty = frozenset()
>>> fs_full = frozenset([1,2,3,4])
>>> fs_empty
frozenset()
>>> fs_full
frozenset({1, 2, 3, 4})
```

When frozenset is called, an iterable object, such as a set, can be passed, whose elements are to be entered into frozenset.

Note that a frozenset is not only immutable by itself, but may also contain only immutable elements:

```
>>> frozenset([1, 2, 3, 4])
frozenset({1, 2, 3, 4})
>>> frozenset([[1, 2], [3, 4]])
Traceback (most recent call last):
  File "<stdin>", line 1, in <module>
TypeError: unhashable type: 'list'
```

So what are the advantages of explicitly treating a set as immutable? Well, remember that only an immutable object can be used as the key of a dictionary.[3] Thus, within a dictionary, a frozenset can also be used as a key, as opposed to a set. Let's try to illustrate this with the following example:

```
>>> d = {frozenset([1,2,3,4]): "Hello World"}
>>> d
{frozenset({1, 2, 3, 4}): 'Hello World'}
```

In contrast, here's what happens when you try to use a set as a key:

```
>>> d = {{1,2,3,4}: "Hello World"}
Traceback (most recent call last):
  File "<stdin>", line 1, in <module>
TypeError: unhashable type: 'set'
```

With the set and frozenset data types, we've discussed the last basic data types. In the following chapters, we'll cover other interesting data types from the standard library.

---

3 Again, due to the hash value to be calculated. See Chapter 19, Section 19.11.1 to learn how to implement hash calculation for custom data types.

Chapter 14
Collections

The `collections` module in the standard library contains advanced *container data types*. This term refers to data types that represent collections of objects in the broadest sense. While the generic container types `list`, `tuple`, `dict` and `set` belong to the basic data types, some more specific container types can be found in the `collections` module.

Function or Data Type	Description	Section
ChainMap	A concatenation of dictionaries	Section 14.1
Counter	A dictionary for recording frequencies	Section 14.2
defaultdict	A dictionary that supports a default value for not included keys	Section 14.3
deque	A doubly linked list	Section 14.4
namedtuple	A function to create named tuples	Section 14.5

Table 14.1 Contents of the Collections Module

To be able to use the `collections` module, it must first be imported:

```
>>> import collections
```

14.1   Chained Dictionaries

The `ChainMap` data type allows you to access multiple dictionaries simultaneously as if their contents were combined in one dictionary. In the process, the dictionaries are chained. This means that when accessed, the assigned value of the first dictionary containing the specified key is always returned.

A `ChainMap` can be used when data is split between different dictionaries. In the following example, we have the results of the group stage of the 2014 World Cup in individual dictionaries. To keep the example short, we limit ourselves to the groups A and G:

```
>>> group_a = {
...     "Brazil": 7,
...     "Mexico": 7,
```

```
...        "Croatia": 3,
...        "Cameroon": 0
... }
>>> group_g = {
...        "Germany": 7,
...        "USA": 4,
...        "Portugal": 4,
...        "Ghana": 1
... }
```

Using a `ChainMap`, the score of a team can be found in a single query, regardless of which group it played in:

```
>>> groups = collections.ChainMap(group_a, group_g)
>>> groups["Brazil"]
7
>>> groups["Germany"]
7
```

You can imagine that when the `ChainMap` is accessed, the dictionaries it contains are queried in the order in which they were passed to the `ChainMap` constructor. Thus, if a key appears in several dictionaries of the `ChainMap`, the dictionary that was first named when the `ChainMap` was created and that contains the key determines the value that the `ChainMap` returns when accessing this key.

14.2   Counting Frequencies

It often happens that you're interested in the frequency distribution of the elements of an iterable object—for example, how often individual letters occur in a string.[1] This problem can be elegantly solved with a dictionary:

```
>>> t = "This is the text"
>>> d = {}
>>> for c in t:
...        if c in d:
...            d[c] += 1
...        else:
...            d[c] = 1
...
```

---

[1] Such a frequency analysis can be used, for example, to break the Caesar encryption method. This takes advantage of the fact that the letters in natural language text are not evenly distributed. For example, the e is the most common letter in the English language.

```
>>> d
{'T': 1, 'h': 2, 'i': 2, 's': 2, ' ': 3, 't': 3, 'e': 2, 'x': 1}
```

The counter data type of the collections module is a dictionary that automatically adds a key-value pair {k: 0} to the dictionary when accessed with an unknown key k. This data type can be used to simplify the code shown previously:

```
>>> t = "This is the text"
>>> d = collections.Counter()
>>> for c in t:
...     d[c] += 1
...
>>> d
Counter({' ': 3, 't': 3, 'h': 2, 'i': 2, 's': 2, 'e': 2, 'T': 1, 'x': 1})
```

In the example, the data already has the form of an iterable object. In such a case, this object can be passed when counter is instantiated. This turns the example into a one-liner:

```
>>> collections.Counter("This is the text")
Counter({' ': 3, 't': 3, 'h': 2, 'i': 2, 's': 2, 'e': 2, 'T': 1, 'x': 1})
```

The counter data type provides some methods in addition to the functionality of a dictionary, which are discussed ahead. The examples are to be understood in the context of the counter instance d created in the previous example.

d.elements()

This method returns an iterator over the elements of a counter instance. Each element is considered as often as its current counter value.

```
>>> list(d.elements())
['T', 'h', 'h', 'i', 'i', 's', 's', ' ', ' ', ' ', 't', 't', 't', 'e', 'e', 'x']
```

d.most_common([n])

This method returns a list of the n most frequent elements. The list consists of tuples containing the respective element and its frequency:

```
>>> d.most_common(3)
[(' ', 3), ('t', 3), ('h', 2)]
```

If the parameter n is not specified, the returned list contains all elements.

d.subtract([iterable])

This method subtracts the frequencies of the elements of iterable from the frequencies in d. For example, it's possible to find the characters by whose frequencies German and English texts can best be distinguished from each other:

```
>>> import collections
>>> with open("german.txt", "r") as f_de:
...     ger = collections.Counter(f_de.read().lower())
>>> with open("english.txt", "r") as f_en:
...     eng = collections.Counter(f_en.read().lower())
>>> eng.most_common(5)
[('e', 6357), ('a', 4188), ('n', 4154), ('t', 4150), ('r', 3822)]
>>> ger.most_common(5)
[('e', 8030), ('n', 4953), ('i', 3819), ('r', 3581), ('s', 3276)]
>>> eng.subtract(ger)
>>> eng.most_common(5)
[('o', 2030), ('a', 1494), ('t', 938), ('y', 758), ('p', 531)]
```

First, the contents of two files of equal size, each containing a German and an English text, are read and a frequency analysis is performed using the counter data type. Apart from umlauts and ß, the texts don't contain any special characters. Using the subtract method, the German letter frequencies are subtracted from the English ones. The result shows that an English text can obviously be distinguished from a German text by the absolute frequencies of the letters *o* and *a*.[2]

d.update([iterable])

The update function behaves like subtract, the only difference being that the frequencies contained in iterable aren't subtracted, but added to the frequencies of d.

14.3   Dictionaries with Default Values

The defaultdict data type is a generalization of the counter data type described in the previous section. For a counter instance, when a nonexistent key k is accessed, the key-value pair {k: 0} is automatically added to the dictionary. A defaultdict instance in this case adds the key-value pair {k: x()}, where x represents any data type.

The value data type is passed during the instantiation process. The defaultdict can then be used like a normal dictionary.

---

2 More interesting than the absolute frequency distribution is actually the relative frequency, where the letter *y* is very significant. This letter represents only 0.04% of the characters in German, while in English it is 1.974%. Based on this difference, the two languages can be distinguished from each other with a high degree of certainty.

For example, if you want to group the words of a text according to their length, you can do this using the basic dict data type as follows:

```
>>> t = "if for else while elif with not and or try except"
>>> d = {}
>>> for word in t.split(" "):
...         if len(word) in d:
...             d[len(word)].append(word)
...         else:
...             d[len(word)] = [word]
...
>>> d
{2: ['if', 'or'], 3: ['for', 'not', 'and', 'try'], 4: ['else', 'elif', 'with'],
5: ['while'], 6: ['except']}
```

This can be solved more easily with defaultdict:

```
>>> import collections
>>> t = "if for else while elif with not and or try except"
>>> d = collections.defaultdict(list)
>>> for word in t.split(" "):
...         d[len(word)].append(word)
...
>>> d
defaultdict(<class 'list'>, {2: ['if', 'or'], 3: ['for', 'not', 'and', 'try'],
4: ['else', 'elif', 'with'], 5: ['while'], 6: ['except']})
```

14.4   Doubly Linked Lists

Let's consider the following two variants of filling a list with the numbers from 0 to 9999. In the first version, the numbers are added one by one at the end of the list:

```
l = []
for x in range(10000):
    l.append(x)
```

In the second variant, the numbers are inserted at the beginning of each list:

```
l = []
for x in range(9999, -1, -1):
    l.insert(0, x)
```

Both examples generate the same list, but it turns out that the first variant runs much faster than the second one. This is due to the fact that the basic list data type has been optimized in terms of access via indexes and appending new elements to the end of the list. When inserting a value at the beginning of a list, all elements contained in the list must be recopied; that is, they must actually be moved one place to the right.

The deque (for *double-ended queue*) data type of the collections module implements a *doubly linked list* that supports the efficient insertion of elements at the beginning or end. If a deque instance were used instead of a list in the preceding examples, no difference in runtime would be noticeable.

In addition to the append, copy, count, extend, index, insert, pop, remove, and reverse methods, as well as the + and * operators, which are known from the basic list data type, the deque data type contains the additional methods listed in Table 14.2.

Method	Description
appendleft(x)	Inserts the element x at the beginning of the list.
clear()	Empties the list.
extendleft(iterable)	Inserts the elements from iterable at the beginning of the list.
popleft()	Returns the first element and removes it from the list.
rotate(n)	Rotates the list by n elements. This means that the last n elements of the list are deleted and inserted at the beginning.

Table 14.2 Methods of the deque Data Type

The following example shows the use of deque instances:

```
>>> d = collections.deque([1,2,3,4])
>>> d.appendleft(0)
>>> d.append(5)
>>> d
deque([0, 1, 2, 3, 4, 5])
>>> d.extendleft([-2, -1])
>>> d
deque([-1, -2, 0, 1, 2, 3, 4, 5])
>>> d.rotate(4)
>>> d
deque([2, 3, 4, 5, -1, -2, 0, 1])
```

In addition, it's possible to specify a maximum length when instantiating a doubly linked list. When an element is added on one side in a list of maximum length, the last element on the other side is removed:

```
>>> d = collections.deque([1,2,3,4], 4)
>>> d
deque([1, 2, 3, 4], maxlen=4)
```

```
>>> d.append(5)
>>> d
deque([2, 3, 4, 5], maxlen=4)
>>> d.appendleft(1)
>>> d
deque([1, 2, 3, 4], maxlen=4)
```

The maximum length of a deque instance can be accessed via the maxlen attribute.

> **Note**
>
> The flexibility deque provides with regard to adding and removing elements comes at a price. Although the deque data type supports element access via indexes, this is generally slow compared to the basic data type, list.

14.5   Named Tuples

Many functions in the standard library return their result as a *named tuple*. This is a tuple for which each of its fields has a name. The values of the tuple can be accessed via the field names, which is why named tuples lead to more readable code. An example of a named tuple is version_info in the sys module of the standard library, which specifies the version of the Python interpreter:

```
>>> import sys
>>> sys.version_info
sys.version_info(major=3, minor=11, micro=0, releaselevel='beta', serial=1)
```

The fields of a named tuple can be accessed like attributes:

```
>>> sys.version_info.major
3
```

A named tuple can be created using the namedtuple function of the collections module. The namedtuple function creates a new data type derived from the basic tuple data type with the name typename. Instances of this data type allow you to access the individual elements of the underlying tuple via fixed names.

The field_names parameter is used to specify the names of the elements of the tuple. Here, either a list of strings can be passed or a single string in which the names are separated by spaces or commas. The names must follow the rules of a Python identifier and also must not start with an underscore. Once the data type has been created, the field names are stored in the _fields class attribute:

```
>>> Book = collections.namedtuple("Book",
...                      ["title", "author", "number_of_pages", "ISBN"])
>>> py = Book("The Art of Computer Programming", "Donald E. Knuth",
...           3168, "978-0321751041")
>>> py.author
'Donald E. Knuth'
>>> py[1]
'Donald E. Knuth'
>>> Book._fields
('title', 'author', 'number_of_pages', 'ISBN')
```

When instantiating a named tuple—in this case, of the book data type—values must be specified for all fields of the tuple. After that, a field can be accessed by an index as well as by the assigned name.

If the value True is passed for the rename parameter, invalid field names are accepted. Such fields can then only be accessed via their index. The rename parameter defaults to False, which raises a ValueError exception in case of invalid field names.

The verbose parameter, which is preset to False, controls whether the class definition of the data type is output after it has been created.

Chapter 15
Date and Time

In this chapter, you'll get to know the Python modules that help you work with time and date information. Python provides two modules for this purpose: time and datetime.

The time module is oriented toward the functions implemented by the underlying C library, while datetime provides an object-oriented interface for working with points in time and time spans.

> **Note**
>
> This chapter is basically intended as a reference. We therefore encourage you to skim it first if you are generally interested and to look into the relevant details in each case if you have specific questions.

In the following sections, we'll take a closer look at both modules and their functions. To be able to use the time and datetime modules, you must first import them:

```
>>> import time
>>> import datetime
```

15.1 Elementary Time Functions—time

Before we get into the functions of the time module in more detail, we'll introduce some terms that are necessary for understanding how time is managed.

The time module is directly based on the time functions of the C library of the operating system and therefore stores all time data as Unix time stamps. A *Unix time stamp* describes a point in time by the number of seconds that have elapsed since 0:00 on January 1, 1970.[1]

For example, the Unix time stamp with the value 1190132696.0 marks 6:24 p.m. and 56 seconds on September 18, 2007, as exactly 1,190,132,696.0 seconds have elapsed since the beginning of the Unix epoch up to this point.

---

1 The time of 0:00 on January 1, 1970, is regarded as the start of the so-called Unix epoch. It was introduced for the uniform description of times.

When dealing with time stamps, it's necessary to distinguish between two different indications: *local time* and *Coordinated Universal Time*.

Local time depends on the location of the clock being checked and refers to what the clocks at that location must indicate to be correct. Coordinated Universal Time is understood to be the local time on the original meridian, which runs through the UK, among other places. Coordinated Universal Time is abbreviated as UTC.[2] All local times can be specified relative to UTC based on the deviation in hours. For example, Central Europe has local time UTC+1, which means that Central European clocks are ahead by one hour compared to those in the UK.

The actual local time is influenced by one more factor: daylight saving time (DST). This time shift depends on the legal regulations of the respective region and usually has a different value depending on the season. The time module finds out for the programmer which DST value is the correct one on the currently used platform at the current location, so you don't have to worry about that.

15.1.1   The struct_time Data Type

Besides the already mentioned time representation by Unix time stamps, there is another representation of times via the struct_time data type. The instances of the struct_time type have nine attributes that can be addressed either via an index or their name. Table 15.1 shows the exact structure of the data type.

Index	Attribute	Meaning	Value Range
0	tm_year	The year	
1	tm_mon	The month	1-12
2	tm_mday	The day in the month	1-31
3	tm_hour	The hour	0-23
4	tm_min	The minute	0-59
5	tm_sec	The second*	0-61
6	tm_wday	The weekday (0 corresponds to Monday)	0-6
7	tm_yday	The day in the year	0-366

Table 15.1 Structure of the struct_time Data Type

---

2 No, the abbreviation UTC for Coordinated Universal Time is not incorrect. It derives from an attempt to find a compromise between the English variant, *Coordinated Universal Time*, and the French designation, *Temps Universel Coordonné*.

Index	Attribute	Meaning	Value Range
8	tm_isdst	Indicates whether the time stamp has been adjusted for DST	0: No 1: Yes -1: Unknown

* It's actually the range from 0 to 61 to compensate for so-called *leap seconds*. Leap seconds are used to compensate for the inaccuracies of the earth's rotation in time indications. As a rule, you won't have to bother about that.

Table 15.1 Structure of the struct_time Data Type (Cont.)

You can create new instances of the struct_time data type by passing a sequence of the nine elements from Table 15.1 to the constructor:

```
>>> t = time.struct_time((2007, 9, 18, 18, 24, 56, 0, 0, 0))
>>> t.tm_year
2007
```

To all functions that expect struct_time instances as parameters, you can alternately pass a tuple with nine elements that contains the desired values for the corresponding indexes.

Let's now move on to the description of module functions and attributes.

15.1.2 Constants

The time module contains the attributes listed in Table 15.2.

Attribute	Description
altzone	Shift of local time including DST against UTC in seconds
daylight	Indicates whether the local time zone uses DST
timezone	Shift of local time without DST against UTC in seconds
tzname	Time zone description

Table 15.2 Attributes of the Time Module

Daylight Saving Time: daylight and altzone

The daylight constant has a value different from 0 if the local time zone uses DST. If DST is not used in the local time zone, daylight has the value 0. The shift caused by DST can be determined using the altzone constant, which specifies the shift of local time from UTC in seconds, taking into account any DST change that may be applicable. If the current time zone is east of the original meridian, the value of altzone is positive; if the local time zone is west of it, it is negative.

The altzone constant should only be used if daylight doesn't have the value 0.

Time Zones: tzname and timezone

The tzname constant contains a tuple with two strings. The first string is the name of the local time zone, while the second one is that of the local time zone with DST. If the local time doesn't use DST, you shouldn't use the second element of the tuple.

```
>>> time.tzname
('CET', 'CEST')
```

The timezone constant stores the shift of the local time relative to UTC in seconds, whereby a possibly existing DST is not considered.

15.1.3   Functions

Table 15.3 provides an overview of the functions of the time module.

Function	Description
asctime([t])	Converts the passed struct_time instance to a string.
perf_counter() perf_counter_ns()	Provides points in time suitable for measuring the performance of programs.
ctime([secs])	Converts the passed Unix time stamp to a string. If no time stamp was passed, the current system time is used.
gmtime([secs])	Converts a Unix time stamp to a struct_time instance. This is based on UTC.
localtime([secs])	Converts a Unix time stamp to a struct_time instance. The local time is used as a basis.
mktime(t)	Converts a struct_time instance to a Unix time stamp. The local time is used as a basis.
sleep(secs)	Interrupts the program flow for the passed time span in seconds.
strftime(format, [t])	Converts a struct_time instance to a string according to the passed rules.
strptime(string, [format])	Interprets a string as time according to the passed rules and returns a matching struct_time instance.
time() time_ns()	Returns the current Unix time stamp. This is based on UTC.

Table 15.3 Functions of the time Module

asctime([t])

This function converts a `struct_time` instance or tuple with nine elements into a string. The structure of the resulting string is shown in the following example:

```
>>> time.asctime((1987, 7, 26, 10, 40, 0, 0, 0, 0))
'Mon Jul 26 10:40:00 1987'
```

If the optional parameter t isn't passed, `asctime` returns a string for the current system time.

The `ctime` function does the same as `asctime`, but for Unix time stamps.

> **Note**
>
> The `asctime` function always returns a string consisting of 24 characters formatted as shown in the example.
>
> If you need to get more control over the appearance of the resulting string, the `strftime` method is the better option.

perf_counter(), perf_counter_ns()

The `perf_counter` function returns a time counter that's well suited for measuring run-times within programs. In this context, the clock with the highest resolution provided by the operating system is used:

```
>>> start = time.perf_counter()
>>> compute_intensive_function()
>>> end = time.perf_counter()
>>> print("The function ran for "
...       "{:1.2f} seconds".format(end - start))
The function ran for 7.46 seconds
```

The `perf_counter_ns` variant differs from `perf_counter` in that the result is returned as an integer in nanoseconds rather than as a float in seconds. By using `perf_counter_ns`, you can avoid inaccuracies in the nanosecond range that are due to the lossy representation of floats.

gmtime([secs])

This function converts a Unix time stamp into a `struct_time` object. UTC is always used, and the `tm_isdst` attribute of the resulting object always has the value 0.

If the secs parameter isn't passed or has the value `None`, the current time stamp is used as returned by the `time` function:

```
>>> time.gmtime()
time.struct_time(tm_year=2022, tm_mon=7, tm_mday=1, tm_hour=22, tm_min=21,
tm_sec=13, tm_wday=4, tm_yday=182, tm_isdst=0)
```

So the preceding example was executed according to UTC on July 1, 2022, at 22:21 (10:21p.m.).

localtime([secs])

This is just like gmtime, but this function converts the passed time stamp into a specification of the local time zone.

mktime(t)

This function converts a struct_time instance to a Unix time stamp of the local time. The return value is a float.

The localtime and mktime functions are inverse functions of each other:

```
>>> t1 = time.localtime()
>>> t2 = time.localtime(time.mktime(t1))
>>> t1 == t2
True
```

sleep(secs)

The sleep function interrupts the program execution for the passed period of time. The secs parameter must be a float that specifies the duration of the interruption in seconds.

If you interrupt a program via sleep, it will go into idle mode and won't utilize the processor.

strftime(format, [t])

This function converts the struct_time instance t or a nine-element tuple t into a string. Here, the first parameter named format is passed a string containing the desired format of the output string.

Similar to the format operator for strings, the format string contains a number of placeholders that are replaced by the corresponding values in the result. Each placeholder consists of a percentage sign and an identification letter. Table 15.4 shows all supported placeholders.

Characters	Meaning
%a	Local abbreviation for the name of the day of the week.
%A	Complete name of the day of the week in the local language.
%b	Local abbreviation for the name of the month.
%B	Complete name of the month in the local language.
%c	Format for appropriate date and time representation on the local platform.
%d	Number of the day in the current month. Results in a string of length 2 in the range [01,31].
%H	Hour in 24-hour format. The result always has two digits and is in the range [00,23].
%I	Hour in 12-hour format. The result always has two digits and is in the range [01,12].
%j	Number of the day in the year. The result always has three digits and is in the range [001, 366].
%m	Number of the month, consisting of two digits in the range [01,12].
%M	Minute as a number consisting of two digits. Is always in the range [00,59].
%p	Local equivalent for a.m. or p.m.[*]
%S	Seconds as a number consisting of two digits. Is always in the range [00,61].
%U	Number of the current week in the year, with Sunday being considered the first day of the week. The result always has two digits and is in the range [01,53]. The period at the beginning of a year before the first Sunday is defined as week 0.
%w	Number of the current day in the week. Sunday is considered day 0. The result is in the range [0,6].
%W	like %U, except that instead of Sunday, Monday is considered day 0 of the week.
%x	Date format of the local platform.
%X	Time format of the local platform.
%y	Year without century indication. The result always consists of two digits and is in the range [00,99].
%Y	Complete year with century indication.

Table 15.4 Overview of All Placeholders of the strftime Function

Characters	Meaning
%Z	Name of the local time zone or an empty string if no local time zone has been set.
%%	Results in a percentage sign % in the result string.
•	From Latin *ante meridiem* ("before noon") or Latin *post meridiem* ("after noon")

Table 15.4 Overview of All Placeholders of the strftime Function (Cont.)

For example, the following expression enables you to generate an output of the current time in a format common for Germany:

```
>>> time.strftime("%d.%m.%Y um %H:%M:%S Uhr")
'02.07.2022 um 00:27:38 Uhr'
```

strptime(string, [format])

You can use strptime to convert a time string back to a time.struct_time instance. The format parameter specifies the format in which the string contains the time. The structure of such format strings is the same as for strftime:

```
>>> time_string = '19.09.2007 at 00:21:17'
>>> time.strptime(time_string, "%d.%m.%Y at %H:%M:%S")
time.struct_time(tm_year=2007, tm_mon=9, tm_mday=19, tm_hour=0, tm_min=21,
tm_sec=17, tm_wday=2, tm_yday=262, tm_isdst=-1)
```

If you don't specify the optional format parameter, the default "%a %b %d %H:%M:%S %Y" value is used. This corresponds to the output format of ctime and asctime.

time(), time_ns()

This returns the current Unix time stamp in UTC as a float.

Note that not all systems support a higher resolution than one second, so the fractional part isn't necessarily reliable.

The time_ns variant differs from time in such a way that the result isn't returned as a float in seconds, but as an integer in nanoseconds. By using time_ns, inaccuracies in the nanosecond range, which are due to the lossy representation of floats, can be avoided.

15.2   Object-Oriented Date Management: datetime

The datetime module is more abstract compared to the time module and also more convenient to use due to its own time and date types.

Four data types are provided (see Table 15.5), which we'll describe individually in the following sections.

Data Types of datetime		Section
date	A data type for storing dates.	Section 15.2.1
time	Saves points in time for a specific day.	Section 15.2.2
datetime	The combination of datetime.date and datetime.time to store times that include both a date and a time.	Section 15.2.3
timedelta	It's possible to create differences between datetime.date and also datetime.datetime instances. The results of such subtractions are datetime.timedelta objects.	Section 15.2.4

Table 15.5 The Data Types of the datetime Module

15.2.1   datetime.date

A datetime.date instance describes a day on the timeline by storing the year, month, and day in its attributes.

In the simplest case, you create a datetime.date instance by specifying these three values, as in the following example for March 28, 1995:

```
>>> d = datetime.date(1995, 3, 28)
>>> d
datetime.date(1995, 3, 28)
```

The constructor checks if the passed date is valid and raises a ValueError if the data is invalid. For example, unlike 1995, 1996 was a leap year:

```
>>> datetime.date(1996, 2, 29)
datetime.date(1996, 2, 29)
>>> datetime.date(1995, 2, 29)
Traceback (most recent call last):
  File "<stdin>", line 1, in <module>
ValueError: day is out of range for month
```

You can use datetime.date.today() to create a datetime.date instance representing the current day, whereas to create a datetime.date instance from a Unix time stamp, you can use the datetime.date.fromtimestamp class method:

```
>>> datetime.date.today()
datetime.date(2020, 3, 9)
>>> datetime.date.fromtimestamp(0)
datetime.date(1970, 1, 1)
```

Table 15.6 lists the most important methods for handling `datetime.date` instances.

Method	Description
`ctime()`	Generates a string specifying the day described by the `datetime.date` instance in the format `'Tue Oct 23 00:00:00 1989'`.
`fromisoformat(date_string)`	Creates a `datetime.date` instance from a string of the form `"YYYY-MM-DD"`.
`isoformat()`	Converts the `datetime.date` instance to a string of the form `"YYYY-MM-DD"`.
`replace({year, month, day})`	Creates a new `datetime.date` instance from an existing one by replacing individual elements.
`strftime(format)`	Converts the `datetime.date` instance to a string according to a format description (see `time.strftime` in Section 15.1.3).
`timetuple()`	Creates a `time.struct_time` instance corresponding to the date of the `datetime.date` instance.
`weekday()`	Returns the day within the week. In this context, 0 corresponds to Monday and 6 to Sunday.

Table 15.6 Important Methods of the datetime.date Data Type

15.2.2 datetime.time

Objects of the `datetime.time` type are used to manage times of day based on the hour, minute, second, and also microsecond.

A `datetime.time` instance has the attributes `hour`, `minute`, `second`, and `microsecond` for the hours, minutes, seconds, and microseconds since the start of the day. Each of these attributes can be passed to the constructor, the default value being 0 in each case:

```
>>> datetime.time(2, 30, 25)
datetime.time(2, 30, 25)
>>> datetime.time(minute=10)
datetime.time(0, 10)
>>> datetime.time(hour=12, second=36, microsecond=123456)
datetime.time(12, 0, 36, 123456)
```

Table 15.7 provides an overview of the most important methods of the `time` data type.

Method	Description
`fromisoformat(time_string)`	Creates a `datetime.time` instance from a string of the form `"HH:MM:SS.mmmmmm"`.
`isoformat()`	Creates a string in the format `"HH:MM:SS.mmmmmm"`, which describes the time. If the `microsecond` attribute has the value 0, the string has the format `"HH:MM:SS"`.
`replace([hour, minute, second, microsecond])`	Creates a new `time` instance from an existing one by replacing the passed information.
`strftime(format)`	Converts a `time` instance into a string according to the passed format description. See `time.strftime` in Section 15.1.3.

Table 15.7 Important Methods of the datetime.time Data Type

15.2.3   datetime.datetime

To describe a complete point in time, the individual capabilities of the `datetime.date` and `datetime.time` data types aren't sufficient because time specifications usually consist of a date and the time on the respective day.

The `datetime.datetime` data type is exactly what its name suggests: a type for storing a combination of date and time information. It combines the capabilities of `datetime.date` and `datetime.time` in one data type.

datetime(year, month, day, [hour, minute, second, microsecond])

As with `datetime.date` and `datetime.time`, new `datetime.datetime` instances are created by specifying the respective components of the time. The parameters have the same meaning as the identically named elements of the constructors of `date` and `time` in Section 15.2.1 and in Section 15.2.2, where the optional parameters default to 0:

```
>>> gifts = datetime.datetime(1989, 12, 25, 18, 30)
>>> gifts
datetime.datetime(1989, 12, 25, 18, 30)
```

A `datetime` instance has an attribute for each of these parameters. So for example, the minute and month can be read as follows:

```
>>> gifts.minute
30
>>> gifts.month
12
```

There are other class methods to conveniently create specific `datetime.datetime` instances.

now() and utcnow()

The `now()` method creates a `datetime` instance that stores the current local time, while `utcnow()` uses the current UTC time:

```
>>> datetime.datetime.now()
datetime.datetime(2020, 4, 6, 17, 54, 46, 638458)
>>> datetime.datetime.utcnow()
datetime.datetime(2020, 4, 6, 15, 54, 50, 309061)
```

fromtimestamp(timestamp) and utcfromtimestamp(timestamp)

The `fromtimestamp` method creates a `datetime.datetime` instance that represents the same time as the Unix time stamp passed for `timestamp` in the system's local time. For `utcfromtimestamp`, the result contains the UTC time of the time stamp.

combine(date, time)

This creates a `datetime.datetime` object that stems from the combination of `date` and `time`. The `date` parameter must contain a `datetime.date` instance, and the `time` parameter must refer to a `datetime.time` object.

Alternatively, you can pass a `datetime.datetime` object for `date`. In this case, the time contained in `date` is ignored and only the date is considered.

strptime(date_string, format)

Interprets the string passed as `date_string` parameter as time information according to the format description from `format` and returns a corresponding `datetime` object.

For the format description, the same rules apply as for `time.strftime` in Section 15.1.3.

The most important methods of a `datetime.datetime` instance are listed in Table 15.8.

Method	Description
`ctime()`	Converts a datetime instance to a string in the format `'Tue Oct 23 16:03:12 1989'`.
`date()`	Returns a `datetime.date` object corresponding to the day of the datetime instance.
`fromisoformat(date_string)`	Creates a `datetime.datetime` instance from a string of the form `"YYYY-MM-DDTHH:MM:SS.mmmmmm"`.

Table 15.8 Important Methods of the datetime.datetime Data Type

Method	Description
isoformat([sep])	Converts the datetime instance to a string in the format "YYYY-MM-DDTHH:MM:SS.mmmmmm", where sep can be used to specify a string that acts as a separator between date and time information.
replace([year, month, day, hour, minute, second, microsecond])	Creates a new datetime instance from the existing one by replacing the passed values.
strftime(format)	Converts a datetime object to a string according to a format description. The format is identical to the time.strftime function (Section 15.1.3).
time()	Returns a datetime.time object corresponding to the time of day of the datetime instance.
timetuple()	Creates a time.struct_time instance that describes the same time as the datetime instance (Section 15.1.3).
weekday()	Returns the day of the week as a number, where Monday is 0 and Sunday is 6.

Table 15.8 Important Methods of the datetime.datetime Data Type (Cont.)

15.2.4   datetime.timedelta

Instances of the datetime.timedelta data type can be used to describe time spans, such as those that occur when you create the difference between two datetime.datetime instances:

```
>>> d1 = datetime.datetime(1989, 1, 9, 12, 0, 0)
>>> d2 = datetime.datetime(1989, 2, 10, 20, 15, 0)
>>> delta1 = d2 - d1
>>> delta1
datetime.timedelta(days=32, seconds=29700)
```

Here, a datetime.timedelta instance stores the number of days, seconds, and microseconds of the time span separately. In the example, therefore, there are 32 days and 29,700 seconds between the two points in time. The days, seconds, and microseconds attributes can be used to access the respective portion of the time span.

```
>>> delta1.days, delta1.seconds, delta1.microseconds
(32, 29700, 0)
```

A time span has a sign that indicates whether the time span points in the direction of the future or the past. In the preceding example, 32 days and 29,700 seconds must pass from time d1 into the future to arrive at d2. If the difference is reversed, the sign changes:

```
>>> delta2 = d1 - d2
>>> delta2
datetime.timedelta(days=-33, seconds=56700)
```

This indication is to be understood in such a way that starting from d2, you must first go 33 days in the direction of the past and then go 56,700 seconds in the direction of the future to arrive at d1.

Even if it's not obvious at first glance, delta1 and delta2 each describe the same duration, once with a negative and once with a positive sign. This becomes clear when you calculate the sum of the two:

```
>>> delta1 + delta2
datetime.timedelta(0)
```

This behavior is due to the fact that seconds and microseconds are always positive for datetime.timedelta instances. Only the indication of the day can have a negative sign.

A day has 24 × 60 × 60 (86,400) seconds. So if you want to go 32 days and 29700 seconds into the past, you might as well first go 33 days toward the past and then make up for the amount you have gone too far as a result. This surplus amounts to 86,400 seconds.

So that you don't have to do this simple but impractical calculation yourself, the constructor of datetime.timedelta does this job for you. It converts the time span, which is calculated as the total of the passed values, into a datetime.timedelta instance.

For example, to create a datetime.timedelta instance that points 32 days and 29,700 seconds into the past, as we just described, you can use the following call:

```
>>> datetime.timedelta(days=-32, seconds=-29700)
datetime.timedelta(days=-33, seconds=56700)
```

All parameters are optional and have the default value 0, and floats can be passed in addition to integers. In this case, all fractional parts of days are combined and the value rounded to the nearest timedelta instance:

```
>>> datetime.timedelta(days=0.5)
datetime.timedelta(seconds=43200)
```

The only method of a timedelta.timedelta instance is total_seconds(), which converts a time span to an indication in seconds. The return value is a float so that the microsecond portions can also be represented:

```
>>> delta1 = datetime.timedelta(days=32, seconds=29700)
>>> delta1.total_seconds()
2794500.0
>>> delta2 = datetime.timedelta(days=32, seconds=29700, milliseconds=123)
>>> delta2.total_seconds()
2794500.123
```

This representation in seconds can be reversed so that we can get the original datetime.timedelta instance again from 2794500.123:

```
>>> delta2
datetime.timedelta(days=32, seconds=29700, microseconds=123000)
>>> delta3 = datetime.timedelta(seconds=2794500.123)
>>> delta3
datetime.timedelta(days=32, seconds=29700, microseconds=123000)
```

Consequently, a datetime.timedelta instance can be viewed as a simple number—namely, its equivalent in seconds. It's therefore not surprising that datetime.timedelta instances can be computed like numbers:

```
>>> week = datetime.timedelta(days=7)
>>> day = week/7
>>> day
datetime.timedelta(days=1)
>>> year = 52*week + day
>>> year
datetime.timedelta(days=365)
>>> year/week
52.142857142857146
```

Table 15.9 provides an overview of the available arithmetic operations for datetime.timedelta instances.

Operations (t1,t2 timedelta Instances, i int Instance, f float Instance)	
t1 + t2	Calculates the sum of two timedelta instances.
t1 – t2	Calculates the difference of two timedelta instances.
t1 * i t1 * f	Creates a timedelta instance that's i or f times as long as t1. If the sign of i or f is negative, the direction on the time axis is also reversed.
t1 / t2 t1 / i t1 / f	Forms the quotient of two timedelta instances or one timedelta instance and an integer or float.

Table 15.9 Calculating with datetime.timedelta Instances

Operations (t1,t2 timedelta Instances, i int Instance, f float Instance)	
t1 // t2 t1 // i	Like the / operator, except that it's additionally rounded off to the nearest integer.
t1 % t2	Returns the division remainder when dividing two timedelta instances as a timedelta instance.
<, <=, >, >=	Compares two timedelta instances.
q,r = divmod(t1,t2)	Generates a tuple of q = t1//t2 and r = t1%t2—that is, the rounded quotient and the division remainder.
abs(t1)	Creates a timedelta instance describing the same duration as t1, but pointing in the direction of the positive time axis.

Table 15.9 Calculating with datetime.timedelta Instances (Cont.)

15.2.5   Operations for datetime.datetime and datetime.date

As shown in previous examples, datetime.date and datetime.datetime instances can also be used for calculations. Differences between two datetime.date or two datetime.datetime instances are possible:

```
>>> p = datetime.date(1987, 1, 9)
>>> j = datetime.date(1987, 7, 26)
>>> delta1 = j-p
>>> delta1
datetime.timedelta(days=198)
>>> s = datetime.datetime(1995, 1, 1)
>>> o = datetime.datetime(1995, 5, 4, 12, 00)
>>> delta2 = o-s
>>> delta2
datetime.timedelta(days=123, seconds=43200)
```

The result of such a difference is a datetime.timedelta instance. Time spans can in turn be added to or subtracted from times and dates:

```
>>> p + delta1
datetime.date(1987, 7, 26)
>>> o - 2*delta2
datetime.datetime(1994, 8, 30, 12, 0)
```

If a datetime.timedelta instance is added to or subtracted from a datetime.date instance, only the days attribute is taken into consideration:

```
>>> p + datetime.timedelta(days=5)
datetime.date(1987, 1, 14)
```

> **Note**
>
> Because the sign of a `datetime.timedelta` instance is only stored in the `days` attribute, every started day in the direction of the past is reflected there. For this reason, you must be careful when computing with negative `datetime.timedelta` instances when you use `datetime.date`:
>
> ```
> >>> date = datetime.date(1995, 3, 15)
> >>> three_quarter_day = datetime.timedelta(days=0.75)
> >>> three_quarter_day
> datetime.timedelta(seconds=64800)
> >>> m_three_quarter_day = -three_quarter_day
> >>> m_three_quarter_day
> datetime.timedelta(days=-1, seconds=21600)
> >>> date - three_quarter_day
> datetime.date(1995, 3, 15)
> >>> date + m_three_quarter_day
> datetime.date(1995, 3, 14)
> ```
>
> Although `three_quarter_day` and `m_three_quarter_day` describe time spans with the same duration, only the addition of `m_three_quarter_day` changes the date. This is because `m_three_quarter_day.days==-1`, while `three_quarter_day.days==0`.

Furthermore, `datetime.date` instances or `datetime.datetime` instances can be compared to the comparison operators `<` and `>` as well as `<=` and `>=`. In this case, the date that is further in time toward the past is considered "smaller":

```
>>> datetime.date(1987, 7, 26) < datetime.date(1987, 11, 3)
True
```

15.3   Time Zones: zoneinfo

Python also provides support for dealing with local time zones in addition to the functions described here. For this purpose, instances of the `datetime.time` and `datetime.datetime` types can be provided with information about the time zone to which they refer. In the following sections, we'll introduce the `zoneinfo` module of the standard library, which is intended for the representation of time zone information, referring mainly to the `datetime.datetime` data type.

15.3.1   The IANA Time Zone Database

To work with time data in local time zones, we first need a data basis because there is an abundance of different time zones worldwide, each with its own special features—for example, regarding the change between DST and standard time or the regulation of leap seconds. In addition, time zones and their characteristics have been changed frequently throughout history, so a historical time in a local time zone may be understood under different conditions than a current one. Time zones are also expected to be subject to constant change in the future.

The Internet Assigned Numbers Authority (IANA) standardization organization regularly publishes a time zone database, often referred to as *tz database* or *zoneinfo*. In it, you can find two ways to divide the world into time zones, as described ahead.

Administrative Time Zones

Classically, the world is divided into *administrative time zones* with a fixed offset from UTC. An example of an administrative time zone is Central European Time (CET), with a fixed offset of one hour from UTC (UTC+1). During the year, Central Europe switches between the administrative time zones of CET and Central European Summer Time (CEST; UTC+2).

Time Zones by Geographical Area

The prevailing alternative is the division into *geographical areas* that have historically had a single definition of time. The advantage of this subdivision is that, for example, the change between DST and standard time and even its historical introduction or suspension can be specified unambiguously by indicating a geographical area. These areas are named after large or well-known cities—for example, Europe/Berlin or Europe/Paris. These examples show the advantage of specifying time zones according to geographical areas: although Berlin and Paris nowadays always follow the same time, historically this wasn't always the case.

Downloading the Database

The IANA time zone database is already installed on many systems and is maintained and kept up-to-date by the respective provider. For this reason, Python always uses the system's default database, if such is available.

Some operating systems, including Microsoft Windows, use other sources for defining time zones instead that are incompatible with the zoneinfo module. For this reason, the Python package index (PyPI) contains the tzdata package, which can be installed via pip or conda:

```
$ pip install tzdata
$ conda install -c conda-forge tzdata
```

If the time zone database isn't available in the system, Python draws on the tzdata package. If that isn't installed either, operations with time zones will raise a ZoneInfo-NotFoundError exception.

15.3.2 Specifying the Time in Local Time Zones

To specify a time with reference to a local time zone, the `tzinfo` parameter can be used when instantiating `datetime.time` or `datetime.datetime`. For this purpose, an instance of the `ZoneInfo` class from the `zoneinfo` module of the standard library can be passed, which is used to describe a time zone:

```
>>> from datetime import datetime, timedelta
>>> from zoneinfo import ZoneInfo
>>> d = datetime(2022, 3, 26, 12, tzinfo=ZoneInfo("Europe/Berlin"))
```

When we output the `datetime` instance via `print`, we can see that the date and time information has been augmented by its difference from the coordinated universal time:

```
>>> print(d)
2022-03-26 12:00:00+01:00
```

So in this case, we're looking at a time indication that is shifted by one hour with respect to UTC. With the `astimezone` method, we can convert the date and time to any other time zone:

```
>>> print(d.astimezone(ZoneInfo("UTC")))
2022-03-26 11:00:00+00:00
>>> print(d.astimezone(ZoneInfo("America/New_York")))
2022-03-26 07:00:00-04:00
```

The result of such a conversion is a new `datetime` instance describing the same point in time, but with respect to a different time zone.

15.3.3 Calculating with Time Indications in Local Time Zones

Using `datetime` in combination with `zoneinfo` allows the programmer to conveniently compare and account for time data in local time zones. However, there is an important feature to consider, which we'd like to discuss on the basis of an example.

Let's assume the `datetime` instance d, which describes a point in time just before the change from standard time to DST, in the Europe/Berlin local time zone:

```
>>> d1 = datetime(2022, 3, 26, 12, tzinfo=ZoneInfo("Europe/Berlin"))
```

Now we want to increment the time described by d by one day:

```
>>> d2 = d1 + timedelta(days=1)
```

As a result, the resulting time is in DST and the operation can be seen from two different perspectives:

- In the *time interval perspective*, we expect there to be exactly one day, or 24 hours, between d1 and d2. We'd expect the result to be March 27, 2022, at 1 p.m. due to the change to DST. This view is particularly relevant when time differences are considered—for example, in the context of a runtime measurement.

- In the *calendrical perspective*, we expect there to be exactly one calendrical day between d1 and d2. In this case, we'd expect the result to be March 27, 2022, at 12 (noon), regardless of any change to DST. This view is particularly relevant when calendar time differences are considered—for example, in the context of regularly recurring events or notifications at a specific time of day. These shouldn't be delayed by one hour due to a change to DST.

Both views are justifiable and have useful applications. Thus, the behavior of arithmetic operations on time specifications in local time zones must be specified by means of conventions. In the case of datetime and zoneinfo, the behavior of an arithmetic operation depends on whether arithmetic is performed within the same time zone or between two different time zones.

Calculating with Time Data of the Same Local Time Zone

In the case of the example mentioned above, we calculate a time incremented by one day starting from a given time d1 in the Europe/Berlin local time zone:

```
>>> d1 = datetime(2022, 3, 26, 12, tzinfo=ZoneInfo("Europe/Berlin"))
>>> d2 = d + timedelta(days=1)
```

This operation takes place exclusively within the Europe/Berlin local time zone, and accordingly the result is also understood in this time zone. In such operations, the calendar view is always used, so that d2 indicates the same time as d1 despite the change to DST:

```
>>> print(d2)
2022-03-27 12:00:00+02:00
```

We can recognize the change between DST and standard time by the tzname, utcoffset, and dst methods, each of which expresses different aspects:

```
>>> d1.tzname()
'CET'
>>> d2.tzname()
'CEST'
```

The tzname method specifies the administrative time zone in effect at the times of d1 and d2 respectively. We see that at the time of d1, CET is in effect, while at the time of d2, CEST is in effect:

```
>>> d1.utcoffset()
datetime.timedelta(seconds=3600)
>>> d2.utcoffset()
datetime.timedelta(seconds=7200)
```

The utcoffset method specifies the offset from UTC valid at the respective times of d1 and d2 as a timedelta instance. Here, too, the case of d2 shows an additional shift of one hour due to the applicable DST:

```
>>> d1.dst()
datetime.timedelta(0)
>>> d2.dst()
datetime.timedelta(seconds=3600)
```

The dst method specifies the shift between the d1 and d2 times and the respective standard time of the region.

Calculating with Time Data of Different Local Time Zones

Unlike calculations within a local time zone, calculations across different time zones don't use the calendar view. Instead, the result is understood as an absolute time span. As an example, consider times d1 and d2 in the New York local time zone:

```
>>> d3 = datetime(2022, 3, 26, 12, tzinfo=ZoneInfo("America/New_York"))
>>> d4 = d3 + timedelta(days=1)
>>> d3.tzname()
'EDT'
>>> d4.tzname()
'EDT'
```

Calling tzname confirms that there's no change between DST and standard time at these times in the local time zone of New York.[3] If we now calculate the difference between the German d1 and d2 times and the corresponding d3 and d4 times in New York, we see that DST starting in Germany is reflected in the result, and the results are thus to be understood as absolute time spans:

```
>>> d3 - d1
datetime.timedelta(seconds=18000)
>>> d4 - d2
datetime.timedelta(seconds=21600)
```

For comparison purposes, here's the analogous calculation within the German time zone, which results in exactly one day's difference due to the calendrical view, despite the beginning of DST:

---

3 This takes place somewhat earlier than in Germany. At the time under consideration, Eastern Daylight Time (EDT) and thus local DST is in effect in New York.

```
>>> d2 - d1
datetime.timedelta(days=1)
```

Should you wish to force the time span view for calculations within the same time zone, you can achieve this by switching to UTC (or another administrative time zone) in the interim:

```
>>> UTC = ZoneInfo("UTC")
>>> Berlin = ZoneInfo("Europe/Berlin")
>>> print(d2.astimezone(UTC) - d1.astimezone(UTC))
23:00:00
>>> print((d1.astimezone(UTC) + timedelta(days=1)).astimezone(Berlin))
2022-03-27 13:00:00+02:00
```

Chapter 16
Enumerations and Flags

In this chapter, we'll describe *enumerations*, another interesting data type that Python makes available to the developer as part of the standard library.

This is not a fixed, defined data type, but rather an approach to defining your own task-specific data types.

In the context of object-oriented programming in Chapter 19, we'll discuss in depth how to create custom data types with any functionality. At this point, we'll jump ahead a bit and tackle creating our own enumeration types.

> **Note**
>
> In this chapter, we use the terminology and also the syntax of object-oriented programming, which you'll get to know in its entirety in Chapter 19. At this point, it suffices to know that a data type is defined by a *class*. The class basically determines which attributes and methods instances of this data type have and how they behave. In Python, classes can be defined using the `class` keyword.

16.1 Enumeration Types: enum

An enumeration type is a data type whose value range is a set of symbolic constants. An example of this is the (still imaginary) data type weekday, whose instances each represent one day of the week. With the means described up to this point, this data type can be implemented as an integer or a string, for example. Both variants assume an implicitly defined assignment of numbers or character strings to the abstract "day of the week" concept. But this kind of assignment poses some problems:

- The operators of the `int` and `str` data types are still available, but they lose their meaning. For example, it's not clear what "Monday divided by Tuesday" should mean.

- There's no check of whether the value assigned to a weekday variable is valid.

- The value of a weekday variable can be compared to other `int` or `str` instances without a weekday meaning. Possibly worse, day of the week variables can be compared to values representing instances of other enumerations, such as traffic light colors.

- For screen outputs, the day of the week isn't output, but the internally assigned value—in the worst case, a number without any reference to the parent concept. This makes it difficult to understand debug output, for example.

The enum module from the standard library provides the basic enum class for immutable enumeration types. In the following example, the already mentioned weekday data type is implemented as an enumeration type:

```
>>> import enum
>>> class Weekday(enum.Enum):
...       Monday = 1
...       Tuesday = 2
...       Wednesday = 3
...       Thursday = 4
...       Friday = 5
...       Saturday = 6
...       Sunday = 7
...
```

For each day of the week, a symbolic constant is created in the weekday class derived from enum. Each constant is assigned an internal value. This value is an integer in this case, but it doesn't have to be.

A concrete day of the week can now be created using the defined constant, the assigned internal value, or its name:

```
>>> Weekday.Saturday
<Weekday.Saturday: 6>
>>> Weekday(6)
<Weekday.Saturday: 6>
>>> Weekday["Saturday"]
<Weekday.Saturday: 6>
```

You can also see from these examples that the screen output of an enumeration value contains its symbolic name. This name can be accessed via the name attribute:

```
>>> Weekday.Saturday.name
'Saturday'
```

Enumeration values can only be compared with each other. In particular, comparison with the internal value evaluates to False:

```
>>> Weekday.Monday != Weekday.Tuesday
True
>>> Weekday.Monday == 1
False
```

Enumeration types allow for running through their values. Any aliases will be skipped (*aliases* are enumeration values that are assigned the same internal value as a previously defined enumeration value):

```
>>> for day in Weekday:
...     print(day)
...
Weekday.Monday
Weekday.Tuesday
Weekday.Wednesday
Weekday.Thursday
Weekday.Friday
Weekday.Saturday
Weekday.Sunday
```

Since Python 3.6, the auto function is available, which can be used to define an enumeration type without assigning concrete internal values:

```
>>> class Weekday(enum.Enum):
...     Monday = enum.auto()
...     Tuesday = enum.auto()
...     Wednesday = enum.auto()
...     Thursday = enum.auto()
...     Friday = enum.auto()
...     Saturday = enum.auto()
...     Sunday = enum.auto()
...
>>> Weekday.Monday
<Weekday.Monday: 1>
```

16.2   Enumeration Types for Bit Patterns: flag

Python 3.6 introduced the flag enumeration type, which defines the internal values so that the symbolic constants can be combined using bitwise operators. This is illustrated by the following example, in which the state of a traffic light system is represented by a combination of symbolic constants:

```
>>> class TrafficLight(enum.Flag):
...     Red = enum.auto()
...     Amber = enum.auto()
...     Green = enum.auto()
...
```

16

With the help of the bitwise OR, two symbolic constants, also referred to as *flags*, can be combined:

```
>>> combined_state = TrafficLight.Red | TrafficLight.Amber
```

In our example, `combined_state` would describe a traffic light where the red and amber lights are currently on together.

The bitwise AND can be used to check whether a symbolic constant is included in a combination:

```
>>> combined_state & TrafficLight.Red
<TrafficLight.Red: 1>
>>> combined_state & TrafficLight.Green
<TrafficLight: 0>
```

The result of the bitwise AND can be interpreted as a truth value:

```
>>> bool(combined_state & TrafficLight.Red)
True
>>> bool(combined_state & TrafficLight.Green)
False
```

16.3   Integer Enumeration Types: IntEnum

One advantage of the `enum` enumeration type is that the symbolic enumeration values are strictly separated from their internal representations. For this reason, the comparison between the symbolic value `Weekday.Monday` and the numeric value 1 always evaluates to `False`, even though the value 1 is the internal representation of `Weekday.Monday` in the enumeration.

Occasionally, however, this kind of comparability is explicitly desired. For this purpose, the `enum` module contains the `IntEnum` data type, which can be used in a similar way to `enum`. Enumeration values of an enumeration type that inherits from `IntEnum` can be used as if they were integers:

```
>>> class Weekday(enum.IntEnum):
...     Monday = 1
...     Tuesday = 2
...     Wednesday = 3
...     Thursday = 4
...     Friday = 5
...     Saturday = 6
...     Sunday = 7
...
```

```
>>> Weekday.Monday < 10
True
>>> Weekday.Monday * 2
2
>>> Weekday.Monday + Weekday.Tuesday
3
```

In particular, comparisons and operations with values of different IntEnum enumerations are also permitted.

PART III

Advanced Programming Techniques

The third part of this book covers essential programming concepts and their implementation in Python. You will find a comprehensive introduction to each topic and to its application in Python. First, we discuss writing functions, and then we cover the use of modules and packages. We'll also explore object-oriented programming. Based on this, we'll deal with handling exceptions in Python as well as more advanced topics such as iterators or generators and context objects.

Chapter 17
Functions

From mathematics, you know the term *function*, which designates an assignment rule. For example, the function $f(x) = x^2$ assigns the parameter x its square. In the mathematical sense, a function consists of a name, a list of parameters, and a calculation rule for the function value.

In programming, you can also find the mathematical concept of a function. For example, we have already discussed the built-in `len` function, which calculates the length of an iterable object. To do this, it's passed as an argument to the corresponding object and returns the result as a return value:

```
>>> len("This string is an argument")
26
```

Obviously, there is some analogy here to the mathematical concept of a function. A function in programming consists of a *function name*, a list of *function parameters*, and a code block—the *function body*. When a function is called, the function body is executed, taking into account the arguments passed. A function in Python, such as `len`, may or may not have a *return value*.[1]

Functions are used in programming to avoid redundancies in the source code. This means that pieces of code that are needed repeatedly in the same or a similar form in the program aren't rewritten each time, but encapsulated in a function. This function can then be called at the points where it's needed. In addition, functions are an elegant tool for dividing long source code into subroutines in a meaningful way. This increases the readability and maintainability of the code.

In the following sections, we'll explain the handling of an existing function using the example of `range`. You already know much of what is being described here from Chapter 8; nevertheless, we'd like to review it once more.

The built-in `range` function was introduced in Chapter 5, Section 5.2.6, and it creates an iterable object across a finite number of consecutive integers:

```
result = range(0, 10, 2)
```

---

1 In Python—unlike in Pascal, for example—no distinction is made between the terms *function* and *procedure*. A procedure is a function that has no return value.

In the preceding example, range was called; this is referred to as the *function call*. For this purpose, a (possibly empty) pair of parentheses is written after the name of the function. Inside these parentheses are the *parameters* of the function, separated by commas. The number and type of parameters a function expects depends on the definition of the function and can vary considerably. In this case, range needs three parameters to obtain sufficient information. The set of parameters is called the *function interface*. Concrete instances passed through an interface are called *arguments*. A *parameter*, on the other hand, denotes a placeholder for arguments.[2]

Once the function has been processed, its result is returned. You can figuratively imagine that the function call as it appears in the source code is replaced by the return value. In the preceding example, we directly assigned a name to the return value of range and can henceforth access it via result. For example, we can iterate over the result of the range call in a for loop:

```
>>> result = range(0, 10, 2)
>>> for i in result:
...     print(i)
...
0
2
4
6
8
```

You can also transfer the result of the range call to a list:

```
>>> lst = list(result)
>>> lst
[0, 2, 4, 6, 8]
>>> lst[3]
6
```

So much for the use of predefined functions for now. Python allows you to write your own functions that you can use according to the same scheme as described here. In the following section, we'll take a look at how you can create your own function.

17.1   Defining a Function

Before we venture into actual source code, we'd like to recapitulate what constitutes a function—that is, what has to be specified when defining a function:

---

2 It is important to be aware of this slight difference in meaning. However, to improve readability, we have decided against making a strict distinction between these meanings and use the terms parameter and argument almost synonymously in this book.

- A function must have a *name* by which it can be called in other parts of the program. The composition of the function name follows the same rules as the naming of an identifier.[3]

- A function must have an *interface* through which information is transferred from the calling program part to the context of the function. An interface can consist of any number of parameters (possibly none). Within the function, each of these parameters is given a name. They can then be used like references in the function body.

- A function must return a *value*. Each function automatically returns None if the return value is not explicitly specified.

To define a function in Python, you can use the def keyword. The syntax of the definition looks like this:

```
def function_name(parameter_1, …, parameter_n):
    Statement_1
    Statement_2
    …
```

The def keyword is followed by the selected function name. After that, the names of all parameters are listed in parentheses. The definition of the interface is followed by a colon and, indented by one step, the function body. The function body can be any code block in which the parameter names may be used as references. Within the function body, you can also call functions.

Let's consider the actual implementation of a function that calculates the factorial of an integer and prints the result on the screen:

```
def fac(number):
    result = 1
    for i in range(2, number+1):
        result *= i
    print(result)
```

With this example you can easily understand how the number parameter is processed in the function body. After the calculation is done, the result is output via print. The number reference is defined only inside the function body and has nothing to do with other references outside the function.

When you save and run the preceding example now, you'll notice that no error message is displayed, but nothing else happens either. Well, that's because we've only defined one function so far. To see it in action, we need to call them at least once. The

---

3 This means the function name must be composed of uppercase and lowercase letters, numbers, and the underscore (_), but it mustn't start with a number. You may also use letters that are not in the English alphabet, but we generally advise against this.

following program reads numbers from the user in a loop and calculates their factorial using the function just defined:

```python
def fac(number):
    result = 1
    for i in range(2, number+1):
        result *= i
    print(result)


while True:
    user_input = int(input("Enter a number: "))
    fac(user_input)
```

You can see that the source code has been split into two components: first, the function definition at the top, and second, the main program to be executed at the bottom. The main program consists of an infinite loop in which the fac function is called with the entered number as parameter.

17.2 Return Values

Consider again the two components of the program. It would be desirable, in the spirit of encapsulating functionality, to modify the program so that the main program alone takes care of interacting with the user and initiating the calculation, while the fac subroutine actually performs the calculation. The main goal of this approach is to allow the fac function to be called in other parts of the program to calculate another factorial. It should be possible to use the calculation result for further operations, e.g., screen outputs or additional calculations. For this purpose, it's essential that fac deals exclusively with the calculation. It doesn't fit into this concept that fac outputs the result of the calculation itself.

Ideally, our fac function should complete the calculation and return the result to the main program so that the output can be done there. This is achieved by using the return keyword, which immediately terminates the execution of the function and returns any specified return value:

```python
def fac(number):
    result = 1
    for i in range(2, number+1):
        result *= i
    return result


while True:
    user_input = int(input("Enter a number: "))
    print(fac(user_input))
```

A function can be terminated via return at any time in the function flow. The following version of the function checks if the passed parameter is a negative number before calculating. If that's the case, the handling of the function is aborted:

```python
def fac(number):
    if number < 0:
        return None
    result = 1
    for i in range(2, number+1):
        result *= i
    return result

while True:
    user_input = int(input("Enter a number: "))
    result = fac(user_input)
    if result is None:
        print("Error during calculation")
    else:
        print(result)
```

In the second line of the function body, the value None was explicitly returned via return None, which is not absolutely necessary. The following code is equivalent:

```python
if number < 0:
    return
```

From the point of view of the program flow, it doesn't matter whether you return None explicitly or implicitly. For reasons of readability, return None is nevertheless useful in this case because it's an explicitly desired return value. It's part of the function logic and not merely a by-product of the function termination.

The fac function, as seen in this example, can be called at any time to calculate a factorial, regardless of the context in which that factorial is needed.

Of course, you can define and call several custom functions in your source code. The following example is not intended to output an error message when a negative number is entered, but to output the factorial of its absolute value:

```python
def absolute(number):
    if number < 0:
        return -number
    else:
        return number

def fac(number):
    result = 1
    for i in range(2, number+1):
```

```
        result *= i
    return result

while True:
    user_input = int(input("Enter a number: "))
    print(fac(absolute(user_input)))
```

For calculating the absolute value of a number, Python also provides the built-in abs function. You'll learn about it later in this chapter.

17.3   Function Objects

One more term should be introduced before we turn to the function parameters. A function not only can be called by its name, but also can be treated like an instance. For example, it's possible to query the type of a function. The following examples assume that the fac function is available in interactive mode:

```
>>> type(fac)
<class 'function'>
>>> p = fac
>>> p(5)
120
>>> fac(5)
120
```

By defining a function, a so-called *function object* is created, which is referenced by the function name. In Python, functions are instances just like numbers or strings, for example.

17.4   Optional Parameters

At the beginning of this chapter, we introduced the concept of functions in Python using the built-in range function. You'll certainly remember from Chapter 5, Section 5.2.6 about the for loop that the last of the three parameters of the range function is optional, which means that it can be omitted when you call the function. An optional parameter must be preassigned with a value internally in the function, usually a default value, which is sufficient in a majority of function calls. In the range function, the third parameter controls the step size and is preset to 1. The following calls of range are therefore equivalent:

```
range(2, 10, 1)
range(2, 10)
```

This is interesting because it often occurs that a function has a default behavior, which should be adaptable to special conditions by additional parameters. However, in most cases where the default behavior is sufficient, it would be cumbersome to still specify the parameters that aren't needed for this call. Therefore, predefined parameter values are often a useful addition to a function interface.

To preset a function parameter with a default value, this value is written after the parameter name in the function definition, together with an equal sign. The following function is to calculate the sum of two, three, or four integers depending on the application and return the result. The programmer should only have to specify as many numbers as required when calling the function:

```
>>> def my_sum(a, b, c=0, d=0):
...     return a + b + c + d
```

To perform an addition, at least two parameters must have been passed. The other two are preset with 0. If they aren't explicitly specified in the function call, they won't be included in the addition. The function can be called as follows:

```
>>> my_sum(1, 2)
3
>>> my_sum(1, 2, 3)
6
>>> my_sum(1, 2, 3, 4)
10
```

Note that optional parameters may only be placed at the end of a function interface. This means that an optional parameter mustn't be followed by a nonoptional parameter. This restriction is important so that all specified parameters can be uniquely assigned when calling the function.

17.5   Keyword Arguments

Besides the *positional arguments* used so far, there is another way to pass arguments in Python. Such arguments are called *keyword arguments*. This is an alternative technique of passing arguments when calling a function. Nothing changes in the function definition. To do this, let's consider the sum function that we wrote in the previous section:

```
>>> def my_sum(a, b, c=0, d=0):
...     return a + b + c + d
```

This function can also be called as follows:

```
>>> my_sum(d=1, b=3, c=2, a=1)
7
```

For this purpose, the parameters are set to the desired value in the function call, as with an assignment. Because the respective parameter name must be specified in the function call, the assignment is unique under all circumstances. This allows the programmer to specify keyword arguments in any order.

It's possible to combine both forms of argument passing. Note that no positional arguments may follow keyword arguments, so the latter must always be at the end of the function call:

```
>>> my_sum(1, 2, c=10, d=11)
24
```

Also note that only those parameters may be passed as keyword arguments that haven't already been passed as positional arguments in the same function call.

17.6 Arbitrarily Many Parameters

Let's recall again the use of the built-in print function:

```
>>> print("P")
P
>>> print("P", "y", "t", "h", "o", "n")
P y t h o n
>>> print("P", "y", "t", "h", "o", "n", " ", "i", "s", " ",
... "g", "r", "e", "a", "t")
P y t h o n   i s   g r e a t
```

Obviously, it's possible to pass any number of arguments to the print function. This property isn't exclusive to the print function: you can also define your own functions that can be passed any number of arguments.

For both forms of argument passing (positional and keyword) there is a notation that allows a function to accept any number of arguments. Let's continue to look at positional arguments for now. Consider the following function definition:

```
>>> def function(a, b, *other):
...     print("Fixed parameters:", a, b)
...     print("Other parameters:", other)
...
```

First, two parameters, a and b, are defined in the classical way, plus a third one, called other. The asterisk in front of its name is important. If this function was called, a and b would reference the first two passed instances, as you already know. Interestingly, other henceforth references a tuple that contains all the additional passed instances. This becomes clear if we consider the following function calls:

```
>>> function(1, 2)
Fixed parameters: 1 2
Other parameters: ()
>>> function(1, 2, "Hello World", 42, [1,2,3,4])
Fixed parameters: 1 2
Other parameters: ('Hello World', 42, [1, 2, 3, 4])
```

Thus, the other parameter references an empty tuple on the first call and a tuple containing all instances beyond a and b in the order in which they were passed on the second call.

At this point, we'd like to extend the my_sum function defined in the previous example so that it can calculate the sum of mulltiple parameters specified by the user:

```
>>> def my_sum(*parameters):
...     s = 0
...     for p in parameters:
...         s += p
...     return s
```

The following example demonstrates the use of the extended my_sum function in interactive mode:

```
>>> my_sum(1, 2, 3, 4, 5)
15
>>> my_sum(1, 2, 3, 4, 5, 6, 7, 8, 9, 10, 11, 12)
78
```

This way of allowing a function to receive any number of parameters also works for keyword parameters. The difference is that the parameter that should contain all other instances passed as keyword arguments must be written with two asterisks in the function definition. Furthermore, it doesn't reference a tuple later, but a dictionary. This dictionary contains the respective parameter name as key and the passed instance as value. Consider the following function definition:

```
>>> def function(a, b, **other):
...     print("Fixed parameters:", a, b)
...     print("Other parameters:", other)
```

And these two matching function calls:

```
>>> function(1, 2)
Fixed parameters: 1 2
Other parameters: {}
>>> function(1, 2, johannes="ernesti", peter="kaiser")
Fixed parameters: 1 2
Other parameters: {'johannes': 'ernesti', 'peter': 'kaiser'}
```

So the other parameter references a dictionary that contains all passed keyword parameters with values.

Both techniques for receiving any number of parameters can be used together, as the following function definition shows:

```
>>> def function(*positional, **keyword):
...     print("Positional:", positional)
...     print("Keyword:", keyword)
>>> function(1, 2, 3, 4, hello="world", key="word")
Positional: (1, 2, 3, 4)
Keyword: {'hello': 'world', 'key': 'word'}
```

You can see that positional references a tuple with all positional parameters, while keyword references a dictionary with all keyword parameters.

17.7 Keyword-Only Parameters

You can also define parameters that may be passed exclusively as keyword parameters. Such *keyword-only parameters* are written after the parameter in the function definition, which receives any number of positional arguments:

```
>>> def f(a, b, *c, d, e):
...     print(a, b, c, d, e)
```

In this case, the function interface consists of the two positional parameters a and b, the option for other positional arguments *c, and the two keyword-only parameters d and e. There is no way to pass the d and e parameters except as keyword arguments:

```
>>> f(1, 2, 3, 4, 5)
Traceback (most recent call last):
  File "<stdin>", line 1, in <module>
TypeError: f() missing 2 required keyword-only arguments: 'd' and 'e'
>>> f(1, 2, 3, 4, 5, d=4, e=5)
1 2 (3, 4, 5) 4 5
```

As with positional parameters, keyword-only parameters must be specified unless they are assigned a default value:

```
>>> def f(a, b, *c, d=4, e=5):
...     print(a, b, c, d, e)
...
>>> f(1, 2, 3)
1 2 (3,) 4 5
```

If in addition the passing of any number of keyword parameters is to be made possible, the ** notation necessary for this follows after the keyword-only parameters at the end of the function definition:

```
>>> def f(a, b, *args, d, e, **kwargs):
...     print(a, b, args, d, e, kwargs)
```

It's also possible to define keyword-only parameters without allowing any number of positional parameters at the same time. For this purpose, the keyword-only parameters in the function interface are separated from the positional parameters by an asterisk (*):

```
>>> def f(a, b, *, c, d):
...     print(a, b, c, d)
...
>>> f(1, 2, 3, 4)
Traceback (most recent call last):
  File "<stdin>", line 1, in <module>
TypeError: f() takes 2 positional arguments but 4 were given
>>> f(1, 2, c=3, d=4)
1 2 3 4
```

17.8   Positional-Only Parameters

In addition to keyword-only parameters, you can also mark *positional-only parameters*. This refers to function parameters that may only be passed as a positional argument and not as a keyword argument.

Positional-only parameters must be placed at the very beginning of the parameter list of a function and are separated from the remaining parameters by a forward slash (/):

```
>>> def f(a, b, /, c, d):
...     print(a, b, c, d)
...
>>> f(1, b=2, c=3, d=4)
Traceback (most recent call last):
  File "<stdin>", line 1, in <module>
TypeError: f() got some positional-
only arguments passed as keyword arguments: 'b'
>>> f(1, 2, c=3, d=4)
1 2 3 4
```

The syntax for defining positional-only parameters can be combined here with the previously discussed types of parameters in function interfaces. Positional-only parameters are always at the beginning of the parameter list and can be optional.

Possible application scenarios for positional-only parameters include the following:

- In preliminary interfaces, function parameters can be provisionally named and then declared to be positional-only parameters. In this way, a downward compatible subsequent renaming can be performed.

- The names of positional-only parameters can be reused when passing any number of keyword arguments via **kwargs. In this way, they simplify the definition of functions that must receive any kind of keyword arguments while having a positional parameter.

> **Note**
>
> Note that the syntax for marking positional-only parameters is valid only from Python 3.8 onward and will cause a SyntaxError in earlier language versions.

17.9   Unpacking When Calling a Function

In this section, you'll learn another way of passing parameters to a function. To do this, let's suppose we wanted to determine the sum of all entries in a tuple using the extended version of the my_sum function defined in Chapter 17, Section 17.6. This currently requires the following notation:

```
>>> t = (1, 4, 3, 7, 9, 2)
>>> my_sum(t[0], t[1], t[2], t[3], t[4], t[5])
26
```

This is very cumbersome. Furthermore, we run counter to the general nature of the my_sum function, because the number of elements of the t tuple must always be known. It would thus be much better to have a way of passing a list of arguments stored in an iterable object directly to a function. This process is called *unpacking* and works similarly to unpacking for sequential data types (see Chapter 12, Section 12.4.1).

Unpacking an iterable object is done by passing the object to the function preceded by an asterisk (*). In the following example, the iterable object created by the built-in range function is used to calculate the my_sum of the first 100 natural numbers using the my_sum function:[4]

```
>>> my_sum(*range(101))
5050
```

---

4 As a reminder: The iterable object returned by the function call of range(n) iterates through all integers from 0 up to and including *n*-1. For this reason, 101 must be passed instead of 100 in the example.

When the function is called, each element of the iterable object—in this case, the numbers from 0 to 100—is passed to the function as a separate parameter. Not only does unpacking a parameter list work in the context of a function that expects any number of parameters, it can also be used with the original my_sum function that determines the sum of a maximum of four parameters:

```
>>> def my_sum(a, b, c=0, d=0):
...     return a + b + c + d
```

Note that the iterable object to be unpacked also provides a maximum of four (and a minimum of two) elements:

```
>>> t = (6, 3, 9, 12)
>>> my_sum(*t)
30
>>> my_sum(*[4, 6, 12, 7, 9])
Traceback (most recent call last):
  File "<stdin>", line 1, in <module>
TypeError: my_sum() takes from 2 to 4 positional arguments but 5 were given
```

Analogous to unpacking a tuple to a list of positional parameters, a dictionary can be unpacked to a list of keyword parameters. The difference in notation is that to unpack a dictionary, two asterisks must be prepended:

```
>>> d = {"a": 7, "b": 3, "c": 4}
>>> my_sum(**d)
14
```

It's also worth mentioning that the techniques for unpacking parameter lists can be combined, as shown in the following example:

```
>>> my_sum(1, *(2,3), **{"d": 4})
10
```

Furthermore, it's possible to unpack multiple sequences or dictionaries in the same function call:

```
>>> my_sum(*(1,2), *(3,4))
10
>>> my_sum(*(1,2), **{"c": 3}, **{"d": 4})
10
```

Keyword arguments must not be passed more than once.

In addition, you can also use packing or unpacking when creating sequential data types, sets, and dictionaries:

```
>>> A = [1,2,3]
>>> B = [3,4,5]
>>> [1, *A, *B]
[1, 1, 2, 3, 3, 4, 5]
>>> {1, *A, *B}
{1, 2, 3, 4, 5}
>>> (1, *A, *B)
(1, 1, 2, 3, 3, 4, 5)
>>> {"a": 10, **{"b": 11, "c": 12}, "d": 13}
{'a': 10, 'b': 11, 'c': 12, 'd': 13}
>>> {"a": 10, **{"b": 11, "c": 12}, "d": 13, **{"e": 14}}
{'a': 10, 'b': 11, 'c': 12, 'd': 13, 'e': 14}
```

If the same key is passed multiple times in a dictionary, later occurrences overwrite previous occurrences:

```
>>> {"a": 10, **{"a": 11, "b": 12}, "a": 13, **{"b": 14}}
{'a': 13, 'b': 14}
```

Note

In general, you should be careful when using unpacking for unordered data types. In the following example, the order of elements 1, 2, 3, 4, and 5 depends on the order in which the set {3,4,1,2,5} is iterated over:

```
>>> [0, *{3, 4, 1, 2, 5}]
[0, 1, 2, 3, 4, 5]
```

Because this order is an implementation detail, it may differ between different Python versions and – in case of sets – even between different program runs using the same Python version.

17.10   Side Effects

So far, we have skillfully avoided this issue, but you should always keep in mind that so-called side effects can always occur when an instance of a mutable data type, such as a list or a dictionary, is passed as a function parameter.

In Python, a function call doesn't create any copies of the instances passed as arguments, but works internally in the function with references to the arguments. This method of parameter passing is called *call by reference*. This is in contrast to the *call by value* principle, which works on copies of the arguments within the function. The latter variant, which is supported by many other programming languages, is free of side effects, but slower due to the copy process.

Let's consider the following example:

```
>>> def f(a, b):
...     print(id(a))
...     print(id(b))
...
>>> p = 1
>>> q = [1,2,3]
>>> id(p)
134537016
>>> id(q)
134537004
>>> f(p, q)
134537016
134537004
```

In interactive mode, we first define a function f that expects two parameters a and b and outputs their respective identities. Then, references p and q are created, referencing an integer and a list, respectively. Then we output the identities of the two references and call the created function f. You can see that the output identities are the same. Thus, both p and q and a and b in the function body are references to the same instances. You can imagine this as implicit assignments of the passed arguments to the respective parameter names at the beginning of the function header. This implementation of the call by reference principle is often referred to as *call by sharing*.

The following code illustrates this model of thought using the previous function f as an example, although of course you shouldn't employ this way of programming in practice:

```
>>> def f():
...     a = p
...     b = q
...     print(id(a))
...     print(id(b))
```

As with assignments in the same namespace, a and p now reference the same object, as do b and q.

It makes no difference whether the referenced objects are instances of a mutable or immutable data type. Nevertheless, the use of immutable data types is basically free of side effects as they're automatically copied when changed and other existing references aren't affected. For example, if we increased a in the function body by one, a and p would reference different instances afterward. This results in the fact that no side effects occur when using immutable data types in function interfaces.[5]

---

5 Note that this doesn't apply to immutable instances that contain mutable instances. Thus, when passing parameters to a tuple containing a list, side effects may occur.

Mutable data types, such as lists or dictionaries, can't give us this security. Let's look at the following example:

```
>>> def f(lst):
...     lst[0] = 42
...     lst += [5,6,7,8,9]
>>> numbers = [1,2,3,4]
>>> f(numbers)
>>> numbers
[42, 2, 3, 4, 5, 6, 7, 8, 9]
```

First, a function is defined that expects a list as a parameter and modifies it in the function body. Then a list of integers is created, which is passed to the function as a parameter and finally output. The output shows that the changes to the list are not limited to the context of the function alone, but also have an effect within the main program. This phenomenon is referred to as a *side effect*. If a function needs to access an instance of a mutable data type in a way other than read-only, and side effects are not explicitly desired, you should create a copy of the instance within the function or when passing parameters. Based on the preceding example, this may look as follows:[6]

```
>>> numbers = [1,2,3,4]
>>> f(numbers[:])
>>> numbers
[1, 2, 3, 4]
```

There is another, rarer form of side effect that occurs when a mutable data type is used as the default value of a parameter:

```
>>> def f(a=[1,2,3]):
...     a += [4,5]
...     print(a)
...
>>> f()
[1, 2, 3, 4, 5]
>>> f()
[1, 2, 3, 4, 5, 4, 5]
>>> f()
[1, 2, 3, 4, 5, 4, 5, 4, 5]
>>> f()
[1, 2, 3, 4, 5, 4, 5, 4, 5, 4, 5]
```

We'll define a function in interactive mode that expects a single parameter prepopulated with a list. In the function body, this list is extended by two elements and then

---

6 You'll remember that slicing a list always creates a copy of it. In the example, slicing without specifying start and end indexes was used to create a complete copy of the list.

output. After calling the function several times, it can be seen that the default value was apparently always the same instance and that a new list with the value [1, 2, 3] was not generated with each call.

This is because an instance that's used as a default value is created only once and not anew with each function call. In general, you should therefore refrain from using instances of mutable data types as default values. Instead, you can make use of the following pattern:

```
>>> def f(a=None):
...     if a is None:
...         a = [1,2,3]
```

Of course, you can use an instance of any other immutable data type instead of None without side effects.

17.11 Namespaces

Up to this point, a function body has been considered as an encapsulated section that can exchange information with the main program only via parameters or the return value. At first, this isn't a bad way of looking at things because it keeps your interface "clean." In some situations, however, it makes sense to let a function act beyond its local namespace, which will be described in this chapter.

17.11.1 Accessing Global Variables: global

First, we must distinguish between two concepts. If we are in the context of a function—that is, in the function body—then we can of course create and use references and instances there. However, these are only accessible inside the function body during a function call. They exist in the *local namespace*. In contrast, references of the main program exist in the *global namespace*. Likewise, a distinction is also made between *global references* and *local references*. Let's look at the following example:

```
def f():
    a = "local string"
b = "global string"
```

The distinction between the global and local namespace becomes clear with the following example:

```
>>> def f(a):
...     print(a)
>>> a = 10
>>> f(100)
100
```

In this example, a reference named a exists in both the global and local namespaces. In the global namespace, it references the integer 10; in the local namespace of the function, it references the passed parameter—in this case, the integer 100. It's important to understand that these two references – although having the same name – have nothing to do with each other as they exist in different namespaces. Figure 17.1 summarizes the concept of namespaces.

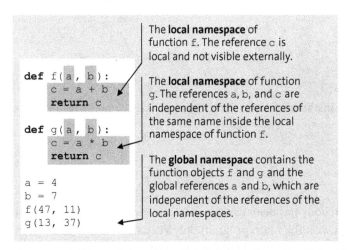

Figure 17.1 Differentiation of Local Namespaces from the Global Namespace Using an Example

17.11.2 Accessing the Global Namespace

In the local namespace of a function body, read access to a global reference is possible at any time as long as no local reference of the same name exists:

```
>>> def f():
...     print(s)
...
>>> s = "global string"
>>> f()
global string
```

As soon as an attempt is made to assign a new instance to a global reference, a corresponding local reference is created instead:

```
>>> def f():
...     s = "local string"
...     t = "other local string"
...     print(s, "/", t)
...
>>> s = "global string"
>>> f()
```

```
local string / other local string
>>> s
'global string'
>>> t
Traceback (most recent call last):
  File "<stdin>", line 1, in <module>
NameError: name 't' is not defined
```

A function can still assign instances to global references using the global statement. To do that, the global keyword must be written in the function body, followed by one or more names that should be treated as global references:

```
>>> def f():
...     global s, t
...     s = "local string"
...     t = "other local string"
...     print(s, "/", t)
...
>>> s = "global string"
>>> f()
local string / other local string
>>> s
'local string'
>>> t
'other local string'
```

In the function body of f, s and t are explicitly marked as a global reference and can henceforth be used as such.

17.11.3 Local Functions

You can also define *local functions*. These are functions created in the local namespace of another function and are only valid there like any other reference in the local namespace. The following example shows such a function:

```
>>> def global_function(n):
...     def local_function(n):
...         return n**2
...     return local_function(n)
...
>>> global_function(2)
4
```

Inside the global function called global_function, a local function named local_function has been defined. Note that the respective parameter n doesn't necessarily reference the same value, although it has the same name. The local function can be called in the namespace of the global function completely like any other function.

Because it has its own namespace, the local function doesn't have access to local references of the global function. To still pass some selected references to the local function, we use a trick with preassigned function parameters:

```
>>> def global_function(n):
...     def local_function(n=n):
...         return n**2
...     return local_function()
...
>>> global_function(2)
4
```

As you can see, the local function no longer needs to be explicitly passed the parameter n when it's called. Instead, it's passed implicitly in the form of a preassigned parameter.

17.11.4 Accessing Parent Namespaces: nonlocal

In the previous section, we talked about the two existing namespaces, the global and local namespaces. This subdivision is correct, but it undercuts an interesting case: according to Chapter 17, Section 17.11.3, local functions may also be defined within functions. Local functions, of course, again bring their own local namespace inside the local namespace of the parent function. That means that the nested function can access variables in its own namespace, variables defined in the parent function and global variables. Thus, with nested function definitions, you can't divide the world of namespaces into a local and a global level. Nevertheless, the question also arises here of how a local function can access references that are located in the local namespace of the parent function.

The global keyword can't help us here because it only provides access to the outermost, global namespace. But for this purpose, there is the nonlocal keyword. Let's take a look at the following example:

```
>>> def function1():
...     def function2():
...         nonlocal res
...         res += 1
...     res = 1
...     function2()
...     print(res)
...
>>> function1()
2
```

Inside the function1 function, a local function2 function has been defined to increment the res reference from the local namespace of function1. To do that, res must be marked as nonlocal within function2. The notation is based on accessing references from the global namespace via global.

After function2 is defined, res is defined in the local namespace of function1 and associated with the value 1. Finally, the function2 local function is called and the value of res is output. In the example, function1 outputs the value 2.

The nonlocal keyword can also be used with multiple, nested functions, as the following extension to the previous example shows:

```
>>> def function1():
...     def function2():
...         def function3():
...             nonlocal res
...             res += 1
...         nonlocal res
...         function3()
...         res += 1
...     res = 1
...     function2()
...     print(res)
...
>>> function1()
3
```

Now an additional local function function3 has been defined in the local namespace of function2. The res variable can also be incremented from the local namespace of function3 using nonlocal. The function1 function outputs the value 3 in this example.

In general, the way nonlocal works for deeper function nesting is that it moves up the hierarchy of namespaces and binds the first reference with the specified name into the namespace of the nonlocal keyword.

17.11.5   Unbound Local Variables: A Stumbling Block

In this section, we'll describe a stumbling block when using local and global variables with the same name. In the following example, we first define a global variable called name and then a function called hello that outputs a friendly greeting to the person defined by name:

```
>>> name = "Peter"
>>> def hello():
...     print("Hello,", name)
>>> hello()
Hello, Peter
```

As we have discussed before, the global variable can be accessed via the name identifier within the function. Creating a local variable of the same name in the namespace of the hello function is also possible and works as expected:

```
>>> name = "Peter"
>>> def hello():
...     name = "Johannes"
...     print("Hello,", name)
>>> hello()
Hello, Johannes
```

Now we'll try to combine both variants by first outputting the value of the global variable, but then creating and outputting a local variable with the same name:

```
>>> name = "Peter"
>>> def hello():
...     print("Hello,", name)
...     name = "Johannes"
...     print("Hello,", name)
...
>>> hello()
Traceback (most recent call last):
    ...
UnboundLocalError: cannot access local variable 'name' where it is not associate
d with a value
```

You can see that the first access to the name variable in this case fails with an UnboundLocalError. The reason is that the name identifier in the local namespace of the hello function is already reserved for a local variable at the time of compiling the function. This reservation won't change during the runtime of the function. So even though we haven't created the local variable name yet, its name is already reserved for a local variable at the time of the first print call.

A similar effect can be achieved if we remove the local variable name from the local namespace in the course of the function execution using del:

```
>>> name = "Peter"
>>> def hello():
...     name = "Johannes"
...     print("Hello,", name)
```

```
...       del name
...       print("Hello,", name)
>>> hello()
Hello, Johannes
Traceback (most recent call last):
  ...
UnboundLocalError: cannot access local variable 'name' where it is not
associated with a value
```

Note in this case that the UnboundLocalError only occurs on the second access to name—
that is, after the output of "Hello, Johannes".

17.12   Anonymous Functions

When sorting a list using the built-in sorted function, a function can be passed that
describes the ordering of the elements. In this way, the elements can be sorted according to self-defined criteria:

```
>>> def s(x):
...       return -x
...
>>> sorted([1,4,7,3,5], key=s)
[7, 5, 4, 3, 1]
```

In this case, the function s has been defined to negate a passed value, thus sorting the
list in descending order. Functions like s used in such or similar contexts are usually
very simple and are defined, used, and then forgotten.

Using the lambda keyword, a small anonymous function can be created instead:

```
>>> s = lambda x: -x
```

The lambda keyword is followed by a parameter list and a colon. The colon must be followed by any arithmetic or logical expression whose result is returned by the anonymous function. Note that the restriction to an arithmetic expression precludes the use
of control structures, but not the use of a conditional expression.

A lambda expression results in a function object and can be called as usual: s(10). The
return value in this case would be -10. However, as the name implies, anonymous functions are often used without assigning them a name. An example of this is provided by
the sorting problem described at the beginning:

```
>>> sorted([1,4,7,3,5], key=lambda x: -x)
[7, 5, 4, 3, 1]
```

Let's look at a slightly more complex example of an anonymous function with three parameters:

```
>>> f = lambda x, y, z: (x - y) * z
```

Anonymous functions can be called without referencing them previously. To do this, the lambda expression must be enclosed in parentheses:

```
>>> (lambda x, y, z: (x - y) * z)(1, 2, 3)
-3
```

17.13   Recursion

Python allows the programmer to write so-called *recursive* functions. These are functions that call themselves. The called function calls itself until a termination condition ends this otherwise endless recursion. The number of nested function calls is referred to as *recursion depth* and is limited to a certain value by the runtime environment.

In the following example, a recursive function has been written for calculating the factorial of an integer:

```
def fac(n):
    if n > 1:
        return fac(n - 1) * n
    else:
        return 1
```

It's not the purpose of this section to fully introduce the subject of recursion. Instead, we'd like to give you just a brief overview here. If you don't understand the example right away, don't feel discouraged, because you can program in Python very well without using recursion. Nevertheless, you shouldn't neglect recursion altogether as it's an interesting way to write very elegant programs.[7]

17.14   Built-In Functions

In the course of the book, we've often referred to *built-in functions*. These are predefined functions that are available to the programmer at any time. For example, you already know the built-in len and range functions. In this section, we'll describe a selection of built-in functions in detail (see Table 17.1). Note that there are other built-in functions that cannot be discussed here because they require object-oriented program-

---

7 Any recursive function can be transformed into an iterative one—sometimes with a lot of effort. An iterative function doesn't call itself, but solves the problem solely by using control structures—specifically, loops. A recursive function is often more elegant and shorter than its iterative counterpart, but usually slower as well.

ming concepts. A complete overview of all Python built-in functions can be found in the appendix of this book.

Built-in function	Description	Section
`abs(x)`	Calculates the amount of the number x.	Section 17.14.1
`all(iterable)`	Checks whether all elements of the iterable object return the value `True`.	Section 17.14.2
`any(iterable)`	Checks whether at least one element of the iterable object returns the value `True`.	Section 17.14.3
`ascii(object)`	Creates a printable string describing the `object` object. Special characters are masked so that the output contains only ASCII characters.	Section 17.14.4
`bin(x)`	Returns a string representing the integer x as a binary number.	Section 17.14.5
`bool([x])`	Converts x into a Boolean value.	Section 17.14.6
`breakpoint()`	Stops the program flow and starts the integrated command line debugger PDB (see Chapter 36, Section 36.1) at the position of the function call.	–
`bytearray([source, encoding, errors])`	Creates a new `bytearray` instance.	Section 17.14.7
`bytes([source, encoding, errors])`	Creates a new `bytes` instance.	Section 17.14.8
`chr(i)`	Returns the character with the Unicode code point i.	Section 17.14.9
`complex([real, imag])`	Creates a complex number.	Section 17.14.10
`dict([arg])`	Creates a dictionary.	Section 17.14.11

Table 17.1 Built-In Functions Described in This Section

Built-in function	Description	Section
divmod(a, b)	Returns a tuple with the result of an integer division and the remainder. divmod(a, b) is equivalent to (a // b, a % b).	Section 17.14.12
enumerate(iterable, [start])	Returns an enumeration iterator for the passed iterable object.	Section 17.14.13
eval(expression, [globals, locals])	Evaluates the expression Python expression.	Section 17.14.14
exec(object, [globals, locals])	Executes Python code.	Section 17.14.15
filter(function, iterable)	Allows you to filter specific elements out of an iterable object.	Section 17.14.16
float([x])	Converts x into a float.	Section 17.14.17
format(value, [format_spec])	Formats a value value with the format_spec format specification.	Section 17.14.18
frozenset([iterable])	Creates an immutable set.	Section 17.14.19
globals()	Returns a dictionary with all references of the global namespace.	Section 17.14.20
hash(object)	Returns the hash value of the object instance.	Section 17.14.21
help([object])	Launches the built-in interactive help of Python.	Section 17.14.22
hex(x)	Returns the hexadecimal value of the integer x as a string.	Section 17.14.23
id(object)	Returns the identity of the object instance.	Section 17.14.24
input([prompt])	Reads a string from the keyboard.	Section 17.14.25
int(x, [base])	Converts x into an integer.	Section 17.14.26

Table 17.1 Built-In Functions Described in This Section (Cont.)

Built-in function	Description	Section
len(s)	Returns the length of an s instance.	Section 17.14.27
list([iterable])	Creates a list.	Section 17.14.28
locals()	Returns a dictionary containing all references of the local namespace.	Section 17.14.29
map(function, [*iterables])	Applies the function function to each element of the passed iterable objects.	Section 17.14.30
max(iterable, {default, key}) max(arg1, arg2, [*args], {key})	Returns the largest element of iterable.	Section 17.14.31
min(iterable, {default, key}) min(arg1, arg2, [*args], {key})	Returns the smallest element of iterable.	Section 17.14.32
oct(x)	Returns the octal value of the integer x as a string.	Section 17.14.33
open(file, [mode, buffering, encoding, errors, newline, closefd])	Creates a file object.	Chapter 6, Section 6.4.1
ord(c)	Returns the Unicode code point of the character c.	Section 17.14.34
pow(x, y, [z])	Performs an exponentiation.	Section 17.14.35
print([*objects], {sep, end, file})	Outputs the passed objects to the screen or to other output streams.	Section 17.14.36
range([start], stop, [step])	Creates an iterator over a sequence of numbers from start to stop.	Section 17.14.37
repr(object)	Returns a string representation of the object instance.	Section 17.14.38

Table 17.1 Built-In Functions Described in This Section (Cont.)

17

Built-in function	Description	Section
reversed(seq)	Creates an iterator that iterates backward through the seq iterable object.	Section 17.14.39
round(x, [n])	Rounds the number x to n decimal places.	Section 17.14.40
set([iterable])	Creates a set.	Section 17.14.41
sorted(iterable, [key, reverse])	Sorts the iterable object.	Section 17.14.42
str([object, encoding, errors])	Creates a string.	Section 17.14.43
sum(iterable, [start])	Returns the sum of all elements of the iterable object.	Section 17.14.44
tuple([iterable])	Creates a tuple.	Section 17.14.45
type(object)	Returns the data type of an instance.	Section 17.14.46
zip([*iterables])	Combines several sequences into tuples—for example, to iterate them with a for loop.	Section 17.14.47

Table 17.1 Built-In Functions Described in This Section (Cont.)

17.14.1   abs(x)

The abs function calculates the absolute value of x. The x parameter must be a numeric value—e.g., an instance of the int, float, bool, or complex data type:

```
>>> abs(1)
1
>>> abs(-12.34)
12.34
>>> abs(3 + 4j)
5.0
```

17.14.2   all(iterable)

The all function always returns True if all elements of the iterable object passed as a parameter—for example, a list or a tuple—yield the truth value True. It's used as follows:

```
>>> all([True, True, False])
False
>>> all([True, True, True])
True
```

The passed iterable object doesn't necessarily have to pass through `bool` instances only. Instances of other data types are converted to truth values according to the rules described in Chapter 11, Section 11.6.2.

17.14.3 any(iterable)

The `any` function works in a similar way to `all`. It always returns `True` if at least one element of the iterable object passed as a parameter—for example, a list or a tuple—returns the truth value `True`. It's used as follows:

```
>>> any([True, False, False])
True
>>> any([False, False, False])
False
```

The passed iterable object doesn't necessarily have to pass through `bool` instances only. Instances of other data types are converted to truth values according to the rules described in Chapter 11, Section 11.6.2.

17.14.4 ascii(object)

The `ascii` function returns a readable equivalent, e.g. a literal, of the `object` instance as a string. Unlike the built-in `repr` function, which exists for the same purpose, the string returned by `ascii` contains only characters of the ASCII character set:

```
>>> ascii(range(0, 10))
'range(0, 10)'
>>> ascii("Püthon")
"'P\\xfcthon'"
>>> repr("Püthon")
"'Püthon'"
```

17.14.5 bin(x)

The `bin` function returns a string containing the integer passed for x in its binary representation:

```
>>> bin(123)
'0b1111011'
```

```
>>> bin(-12)
'-0b1100'
>>> bin(0)
'0b0'
```

17.14.6 bool([x])

This function creates an instance of the data type bool with the truth value of the instance x. The truth value of x is determined according to the rules specified in Chapter 11, Section 11.6.2.

If no parameter is passed, the bool function returns the Boolean value False.

17.14.7 bytearray([source, encoding, errors])

The bytearray function creates an instance of the bytearray data type,[8] which represents a sequence of byte values—that is, integers in the number range from 0 to 255. Note that unlike bytes, bytearray is a mutable data type.

The source parameter is used to initialize the byte array and can have different meanings.

If a string is passed for source, it's encoded into a byte sequence using the encoding and errors parameters and then used to initialize the byte array. Here, the encoding and errors parameters have the same meaning as in the built-in str function.

If an integer is passed for source, a byte array of length source is created and filled with zeros.

If an iterable object, such as a list, is passed for source, the byte array is filled with the elements over which source iterates. Note that these must be integers in the number range from 0 to 255.

In addition, any instance of a data type that supports the so-called buffer protocol can be passed for source. These include, for example, the bytes and bytearray data types themselves:

```
>>> bytearray("äöü", "utf-8")
bytearray(b'\xc3\xa4\xc3\xb6\xc3\xbc')
>>> bytearray([1,2,3,4])
bytearray(b'\x01\x02\x03\x04')
>>> bytearray(10)
bytearray(b'\x00\x00\x00\x00\x00\x00\x00\x00\x00\x00')
```

---

8 For more details on the bytearray data type, see Chapter 12, Section 12.5.

> **Note**
>
> In Windows, there may be problems with entering special characters in the command prompt. If you come across this type of problem, you can use IDLE to run the affected examples.
>
> For more information on this, please refer to Chapter 12, Section 12.5.4.

17.14.8 bytes([source, encoding, errors])

This function creates an instance of the bytes[9] data type, which, like the bytearray data type, stores a sequence of byte values. In contrast to bytearray, however, it's an immutable data type, which is why we also refer to it as a bytes string.

The source, encoding, and errors parameters are used to initialize the byte sequence as in the built-in bytearray function:

```
>>> bytes(10)
b'\x00\x00\x00\x00\x00\x00\x00\x00\x00\x00'
>>> bytes([1,2,3])
b'\x01\x02\x03'
>>> bytes("äöü", "utf-8")
b'\xc3\xa4\xc3\xb6\xc3\xbc'
```

17.14.9 chr(i)

The chr function returns a string of length 1 containing the character with the Unicode code point i:

```
>>> chr(65)
'A'
>>> chr(33)
'!'
>>> chr(8364)
'€'
```

For more information on character encodings, see Chapter 12, Section 12.5.4.

17.14.10 complex([real, imag])

This function creates an instance of the data type complex[10] for storing a complex number. The generated instance has the complex value *real* + *imag* · *j*. Missing parameters are assumed to be 0.

---

9   See Chapter 12, Section 12.5.

10 See Chapter 11, Section 11.7.

It's also possible to pass a string containing the literal of a complex number to the complex function. In this case, however, no further parameter may be specified:

```
>>> complex(1, 3)
(1+3j)
>>> complex(1.2, 3.5)
(1.2+3.5j)
>>> complex("3+4j")
(3+4j)
>>> complex("3")
(3+0j)
```

Note that any passed string mustn't contain any spaces around the + operator:

```
>>> complex("3 + 4j")
Traceback (most recent call last):
  File "<stdin>", line 1, in <module>
ValueError: complex() arg is a malformed string
```

However, spaces at the beginning or end of the string are not a problem.

17.14.11   dict([source])

This function creates an instance of the dict data type.[11] If no parameter is passed, it creates an empty dictionary. Using one of the following calls, you can fill the dictionary with values when creating it:

- If source is a dictionary, the keys and values of this dictionary are copied to the new one. Note that this doesn't create copies of the values, but the values continue to reference the same instances:

  ```
  >>> dict({"a": 1, "b": 2})
  {'a': 1, 'b': 2}
  ```

- Alternatively, source can be an object iterating over tuples, where each tuple must contain two elements: the key and the value associated with it.

  ```
  >>> dict([("a", 1), ("b", 2)])
  {'a': 1, 'b': 2}
  ```

- In addition, dict allows you to pass keys and values as keyword arguments. The parameter names are used as keys. Note that this subjects you to the constraints of an identifier when assigning names:

  ```
  >>> dict(a=1, b=2)
  {'a': 1, 'b': 2}
  ```

---

11   See Chapter 13, Section 13.1.

17.14.12 divmod(a, b)

The divmod function returns the following tuple: (a//b, a%b). With the exception of complex, instances of any numeric data types can be passed for a and b:

```
>>> divmod(2.5, 1.3)
(1.0, 1.2)
>>> divmod(11, 4)
(2, 3)
```

17.14.13 enumerate(iterable, [start])

The enumerate function creates an iterable object that yields tuples of the form (i, iterable[i]) rather than over the elements of iterable alone. In this context, i is a loop counter that starts at start (0 by default). These tuple structures become apparent when the result of an enumerate call is converted to a list:

```
>>> list(enumerate(["a", "b", "c", "d"]))
[(0, 'a'), (1, 'b'), (2, 'c'), (3, 'd')]
```

This makes enumerate particularly suitable for for loops in which a numeric loop counter is supposed to be included. Within a for loop, enumerate can be used as follows:

```
>>> for i, value in enumerate([1,2,3,4,5]):
...     print("The value of iterable in position", i, "is:", value)
The value of iterable in position 0 is: 1
The value of iterable in position 1 is: 2
The value of iterable in position 2 is: 3
The value of iterable in position 3 is: 4
The value of iterable in position 4 is: 5
```

17.14.14 eval(expression, [globals, locals])

The function eval evaluates the expression Python expression as a string and returns its result:

```
>>> eval("1+1")
2
```

When calling eval, the desired global and local namespace in which the expression is to be evaluated can be specified via the globals and locals parameters. If these parameters aren't specified, expression is evaluated in the environment where eval was called:

```
>>> x = 12
>>> eval("x**2")
144
```

> **Note**
>
> Sometimes eval is used to interpret user input as Python code:
>
> ```
> >>> eval(input("Enter Python code: "))
> Enter Python code: 2**4
> 16
> ```
>
> Note that this use of eval is potentially risky if user input isn't carefully checked. A malicious user or an untrusted data source can manipulate the program execution here.

17.14.15 exec(object, [globals, locals])

The exec function executes Python code that's available as a string:

```
>>> code = """
... x = 12
... print(x**2)
... """
>>> exec(code)
144
```

When you call exec, the desired global and local namespace in which to execute the code can be specified via the globals and locals parameters. If these parameters aren't specified, the code will be executed in the environment where exec was called.

> **Note**
>
> The same safety warning applies to exec as to eval from the previous section: check user input carefully before passing it to exec!

17.14.16 filter(function, iterable)

The filter function expects a function object as its first parameter and an iterable object as its second parameter. The function object passed for function must expect a parameter and return a Boolean value.

The filter function calls the passed function for each element of the iterable iterable object and creates an iterable object that iterates through all elements of list for which function returned True. This will be explained by the following example, where filter is used to filter out the odd numbers from a list of integers:

```
>>> filterobj = filter(lambda x: x%2 == 0, range(21))
>>> print(list(filterobj))
[0, 2, 4, 6, 8, 10, 12, 14, 16, 18, 20]
```

17.14.17   float([x])

This creates an instance of the `float` data type.[12] If the parameter x hasn't been specified, the value of the instance will be initialized with `0.0`, otherwise with the passed
value. With the exception of `complex`, instances can be passed all numeric data types for
x:

```
>>> float()
0.0
>>> float(5)
5.0
```

It's also possible to pass a string for x that contains a float:

```
>>> float("1e30")
1e+30
>>> float("0.5")
0.5
>>> float("inf")
inf
```

17.14.18   format(value, [format_spec])

The `format` function returns the `value` value according to the `format_spec` format specification. For example, a monetary amount can be rounded to two decimal places in the
output as follows:

```
>>> format(1.23456, ".2f") + "€"
'1.23€'
```

For detailed information on format specifications, see Chapter 12, Section 12.5.3 on
string formatting.

17.14.19   frozenset([iterable])

This function creates an instance of the `frozenset`[13] data type for storing an immutable
set. If the `iterable` parameter is specified, the elements of the generated set are taken
from this iterable object. If the `iterable` parameter is not specified, `frozenset` generates
an empty set.

Note that a `frozenset` mustn't contain any mutable elements; furthermore, each element can occur only once in a set:

---

12   See Chapter 11, Section 11.5.
13   See Chapter 13, Section 13.2.

```
>>> frozenset()
frozenset()
>>> frozenset({1,2,3,4,5})
frozenset({1, 2, 3, 4, 5})
>>> frozenset("Pyyyyyyython")
frozenset({'t', 'P', 'n', 'y', 'h', 'o'})
```

17.14.20 globals()

The built-in globals function returns a dictionary with all global references of the current namespace. The keys correspond to the reference names as strings and the values to the respective instances:

```
>>> a = 1
>>> b = {}
>>> c = [1,2,3]
>>> globals()
{..., 'a': 1, 'b': {}, 'c': [1, 2, 3]}
```

The returned dictionary contains other references that exist in the global namespace besides those created in the example, which was indicated in the example with the three dots.

17.14.21 hash(object)

The hash function calculates the *hash value* of the object instance and returns it. A hash value is an integer generated from the type and value of the instance. Such a value can be used to effectively check two more complex instances for equality. For example, the keys of a dictionary are managed internally by their hash values:

```
>>> hash(12345)
12345
>>> hash("Hello World")
-1324507931790039535
>>> hash((1,2,3,4))
485696759010151909
```

Note the difference between mutable and immutable instances. Although a hash value can also be formally calculated from mutable instances, this value would only be valid as long as the instance wasn't changed. For this reason, it isn't useful to compute hash values of mutable instances; mutable instances are "unhashable":

```
>>> hash([1,2,3,4])
Traceback (most recent call last):
  File "<stdin>", line 1, in <module>
TypeError: unhashable type: 'list'
```

> **Note**
>
> Hash values of str, bytes, and datetime instances are randomized for security reasons. This means that hash values of these data types differ in two different interpreter processes. Within the same process, however, they don't change.

17.14.22   help([object])

The help function starts the interactive help of Python. If the object parameter is a string, it will be looked up in the help system. If it's a different instance, a dynamic help page will be generated for it. See Chapter 37, Section 37.1 for further details.

17.14.23   hex(x)

The hex function generates a string containing the integer passed as parameter x in hexadecimal notation. The number, as it appears in the string, corresponds to the Python literal for hexadecimal numbers.

```
>>> hex(12)
'0xc'
>>> hex(0xFF)
'0xff'
>>> hex(-33)
'-0x21'
```

17.14.24   id(object)

The id function returns the identity of any instance. The identity of an instance is an integer that uniquely identifies the instance.

```
>>> id(1)
134537016
>>> id([1,2,3])
4328840000
>>> id("test")
4326941040
```

For more information on identities, see Chapter 7, Section 7.1.3.

17.14.25   input([prompt])

The input function reads an input from the user and returns it in the form of a string. The prompt parameter is optional. Here you can specify a string to be output before the prompt:

```
>>> s = input("Enter a text: ")
Enter a text: Python is good
>>> s
'Python is good'
```

> **Note**
>
> The behavior of the built-in input function was changed in Python 3. In Python 2, the user's input was evaluated by the interpreter as a Python expression and the result of this evaluation was returned as a string. So the "old" input function corresponded to the following code:
>
> ```
> >>> eval(input("Prompt: "))
> Prompt: 2+2
> 4
> ```
>
> The input function as it exists in current versions of Python was called raw_input in Python 2.

17.14.26   int([x, base])

This function creates an instance of the int data type.[14] The instance can be initialized by specifying x with a value. If no parameter is specified, the created instance receives the value 0.

If a string is passed for x, the int function expects this string to contain the desired integer value. The optional base parameter can be used to specify the base of the numeral system in which the number was written:

```
>>> int(5)
5
>>> int("FF", 16)
255
>>> int(hex(12), 16)
12
```

---

14   See Chapter 11, Section 11.4.

17.14.27 len(s)

The len function returns the length or the number of elements of s. For s, sequences, mappings, or sets can be passed:

```
>>> len("Hello World")
11
>>> len([1,2,3,4,5])
5
>>> len({"a": 1, "b": 2})
2
```

17.14.28 list([sequence])

This function creates an instance of the list data type[15] from the elements of sequence. The sequence parameter must be an iterable object. If it's omitted, an empty list will be generated:

```
>>> list()
[]
>>> list((1,2,3,4))
[1, 2, 3, 4]
>>> list({"a": 1, "b": 2})
['a', 'b']
```

The list function can be used to transform any iterable object into a list:

```
>>> list(range(0, 10, 2))
[0, 2, 4, 6, 8]
```

17.14.29 locals()

The built-in locals function returns a dictionary with all local references of the current namespace. The keys correspond to the reference names as strings and the values to the respective instances. This is illustrated by the following example:

```
>>> def f(a, b, c):
...     d = a + b + c
...     print(locals())
...
>>> f(1, 2, 3)
{'a': 1, 'b': 2, 'c': 3, 'd': 6}
```

Calling locals in the namespace of the main program is equivalent to calling globals.

---

15 See Chapter 12, Section 12.3.

17.14.30   map(function, [*iterable])

This function expects a function object as first parameter and an iterable object as second parameter. Optionally, further iterable objects can be passed, but they must have the same length as the first one. The passed function must expect as many parameters as iterable objects have been passed.

The map function calls function for each element of iterable and returns an iterable object that iterates through the respective return values of function. If several iterable objects are passed, the nth elements of these objects are passed to function in each case.

In the following example, the function object is created as an anonymous function using lambda. It's also possible to define a function via def and pass its name.

In the first example, we use map to generate a list of squares of the elements of an initial list:

```
>>> f = lambda x: x**2
>>> result = map(f, [1,2,3,4])
>>> list(result)
[1, 4, 9, 16]
```

In the second example, we use map to create from two lists one that contains the sums of the respective elements of the initial lists:

```
>>> f = lambda x, y: x+y
>>> result = map(f, [1,2,3,4], [1,2,3,4])
>>> list(result)
[2, 4, 6, 8]
```

Figure 17.2 illustrates this example. The incoming and outgoing iterable objects are each shown vertically.

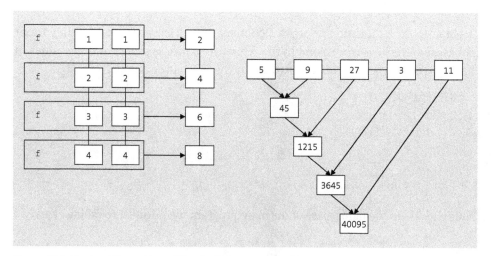

Figure 17.2 Mode of Operation of the Built-In map Function

In both examples, lists were used that contained only numeric elements. This doesn't necessarily have to be the case. The elements an iterable object passed to map may yield depends on which types function expects as arguments.

17.14.31   max(iterable, {default, key}), max(arg1, arg2, [*args], {key})

If no additional parameters are passed, max expects an iterable object and returns its largest element:

```
>>> max([2,4,1,9,5])
9
>>> max("Hello World")
'r'
```

If multiple parameters are passed, max behaves in such a way that the largest passed parameter will be returned:

```
>>> max(3, 5, 1, 99, 123, 45)
123
>>> max("Hello", "World", "!")
'World'
```

The max function can optionally be passed a function object via the key keyword parameter. The maximum is then determined by comparing the return values of this function. Thus, the key parameter can be used to specify a custom ordering. In the following example, key is to be used to make the max function *case insensitive* for strings. For this purpose, let's first take a look at the normal call without key:

```
>>> max("a", "P", "q", "X")
'q'
```

Without a custom key function, the largest parameter is determined by including uppercase and lowercase letters. The following key function converts all letters to lowercase up front:

```
>>> f = lambda x: x.lower()
>>> max("a", "P", "q", "X", key=f)
'X'
```

The map function determines the largest of its arguments based on the values modified by f, but returns it unmodified.

The last keyword parameter, default, can be used to specify a value to be returned by max if iterable is empty.

17.14.32 min(iterable, {default, key}), min(arg1, arg2, [*args], {key})

The min function behaves like max, but determines the smallest element of a sequence or the smallest passed parameter.

17.14.33 oct(x)

The oct function generates a string containing the passed integer x in octal notation:

```
>>> oct(123)
'0o173'
>>> oct(0o777)
'0o777'
```

17.14.34 ord(c)

The ord function expects a string of length 1 and returns the Unicode code point of the contained character:

```
>>> ord("P")
80
>>> ord("€")
8364
```

For more information on Unicode and code points, see Chapter 12, Section 12.5.4.

17.14.35 pow(x, y, [z])

Calculates x ** y or, if z was specified, x ** y % z. Using the z parameter, pow uses a more efficient implementation than the expressions pow(x, y) % z or x ** y % z:

```
>>> 7 ** 5 % 4
3
>>> pow(7, 5, 4)
3
```

17.14.36 print([*objects], {sep, end, file, flush})

The print function writes the text equivalents of the instances passed for objects to the file data stream. So far, we've used print only to write to the screen or standard output. But here you can see that print allows you to write to any file object open for writing via the file keyword parameter:

```
>>> with open("datei.txt", "w") as f:
...     print("Hello World", file=f)
```

The sep keyword parameter, which is preassigned with a space, is used to specify the separator to be placed between two values to be output:

```
>>> print("Hello", "World")
Hello World
>>> print("Hello", "you", "beautiful", "world", sep="-")
Hello-you-beautiful-world
```

The second keyword parameter, end, is used to determine which character print should output last—that is, after all passed instances have been output. This parameter is preassigned with a new line character:

```
>>> print("Hello", end=" World\n")
Hello World
>>> print("Hello", "World", end="AAAA")
Hello WorldAAAA>>>
```

In the last example, the prompt of the interpreter is located directly after the output generated by print because, in contrast to the default behavior of print, no new line character was output at the end.

Using the last parameter, flush, you can force an emptying of the data stream buffer after the output.

17.14.37   range([start], stop, [step])

The range function creates an iterable object over consecutive numeric values. The generated sequence begins with start, ends before stop, and increments the previous value by step in each step. Both start and step are optional and preset with 0 and 1 respectively.

Note that stop indicates a limit that isn't reached. So the numbering starts at 0 and ends one step before stop would be reached.

The iterable object returned by range is a range object. This is displayed in the interactive mode output as follows:

```
>>> range(10)
range(0, 10)
```

To illustrate which numbers the range object iterates over, it was converted to a list using list in the following examples:

```
>>> list(range(10))
[0, 1, 2, 3, 4, 5, 6, 7, 8, 9]
>>> list(range(5, 10))
```

```
[5, 6, 7, 8, 9]
>>> list(range(2, 10, 2))
[2, 4, 6, 8]
```

It's also possible to specify a negative step size:

```
>>> list(range(10, 0, -1))
[10, 9, 8, 7, 6, 5, 4, 3, 2, 1]
>>> list(range(10, 0, -2))
[10, 8, 6, 4, 2]
```

> **Note**
>
> In Python 2, the built-in range and xrange functions existed. The old range function returns the result as a list, while the xrange function works like the range function in current versions of Python.

17.14.38   repr(object)

The repr function returns a string containing a printable representation of the object instance, e.g. a literal. For many instances, repr tries to write the Python code in the string that would create the corresponding instance. However, for some instances this isn't possible or practical. In such a case, repr at least outputs a short description of the instance including its data type and a selection of attribute values.

```
>>> repr([1,2,3,4])
'[1, 2, 3, 4]'
>>> repr(0x34)
'52'
>>> repr(set([1,2,3,4]))
'{1, 2, 3, 4}'
>>> with open("file.txt", "w") as file:
...     repr(file)
"<_io.TextIOWrapper name='file.txt' mode='w' encoding='UTF-8'>"
```

17.14.39   reversed(sequence)

With reversed, a sequence instance of a sequential data type can be iterated backward:

```
>>> for i in reversed([1, 2, 3, 4, 5, 6]):
...     print(i)
6
5
4
```

```
3
2
1
```

17.14.40   round(x, [n])

The round function rounds the float x to n decimal places. The n parameter is optional and preset with 0:

```
>>> round(-0.5)
0
>>> round(0.5234234234234, 5)
0.52342
>>> round(0.5, 4)
0.5
```

17.14.41   set([iterable])

This function creates an instance of the set data type.[16] If specified, all elements of the iterable object are included in the set. Note that a set mustn't contain any duplicates, so each element occurring multiple times in iterable is entered only once:

```
>>> set()
set()
>>> set("Hello World")
{'d', 'r', 'e', 'l', ' ', 'W', 'H', 'o'}
>>> set({1,2,3,4})
{1, 2, 3, 4}
```

17.14.42   sorted(iterable, [key, reverse])

The sorted function generates a sorted list from the elements of iterable:

```
>>> sorted([3,1,6,2,9,1,8])
[1, 1, 2, 3, 6, 8, 9]
>>> sorted("Hello World")
[' ', 'H', 'W', 'd', 'e', 'l', 'l', 'l', 'o', 'o', 'r']
```

The way sorted operates is identical to that of the sort method of the sequential data types we described in Chapter 12, Section 12.3.4.

---

16   See Chapter 13, Section 13.2.

17.14.43   str([object, encoding, errors])

The str method creates a string,[17] which contains a readable description of the instance passed as object. If object isn't passed, str generates an empty string:

```
>>> str(None)
'None'
>>> str()
''
>>> str(12345)
'12345'
>>> str(str)
"<class 'str'>"
```

The str function can be used to convert a bytes string or a bytearray instance into a string. This process is referred to as *decoding*, and at least the encoding parameter must have been specified:

```
>>> b = bytearray([1,2,3])
>>> str(b, "utf-8")
'\x01\x02\x03'
>>> b = bytes("Hellö Wörld", "utf-8", "strict")
>>> str(b)
"b'Hell\\xc3\\xb6 W\\xc3\\xb6rld'"
>>> str(b, "utf-8")
'Hellö Wörld'
```

For the encoding parameter, a string must be passed that contains the encoding with which the bytes string was encoded—in this case, utf-8. The errors parameter wasn't specified in the preceding example; it determines how to deal with decoding errors. Table 17.2 lists the possible values for errors and their meaning.

Errors	Description
"strict"	In case of a decoding error, a ValueError exception is raised.
"ignore"	Errors during decoding are ignored.
"replace"	A character that couldn't be decoded is replaced by the U+FFFD Unicode character (?), also referred to as the *replacement character*.

Table 17.2 Possible Values of the errors Parameter

---

17   See Chapter 12, Section 12.5.

> **Note**
>
> Note that the `str` data type has undergone a revision in Python 3. Unlike the `str` data type from Python 2, in Python 3 it's intended to store Unicode text. So it's comparable to the `unicode` data type from Python 2. The `str` data type in Python 2 can be compared to the `bytes` string in Python 3.
>
> For more information about the `str` and `bytes` data types and about Unicode, see Chapter 12, Section 12.5.4.

17.14.44   sum(iterable, [start])

The `sum` function calculates the sum of all elements of the iterable object and returns the result. If the optional `start` parameter is specified, it will also be included in the sum as the start value of the calculation:

```
>>> sum([1,2,3,4])
10
>>> sum({1,2,3,4}, 2)
12
```

17.14.45   tuple([iterable])

This function creates an instance of the `tuple` data type[18] from the elements of `iterable`:

```
>>> tuple()
()
>>> tuple([1,2,3,4])
(1, 2, 3, 4)
```

17.14.46   type(object)

The `type` function returns the data type of the passed `object`:

```
>>> type(1)
<class 'int'>
>>> type("Hello World") == str
True
>>> type(sum)
<class 'builtin_function_or_method'>
```

---

18   See Chapter 12, Section 12.4.

17.14.47 zip([*iterables], {strict})

The zip function takes any number of iterable objects as parameters. If not all of them have the same length, the longer ones will be considered only up to the length of the shortest of these objects.

The return value is an iterable object that iterates over tuples containing the ith elements of the passed sequences in the ith iteration step:

```
>>> result = zip([1,2,3,4], [5,6,7,8], [9,10,11,12])
>>> list(result)
[(1, 5, 9), (2, 6, 10), (3, 7, 11), (4, 8, 12)]
>>> result = zip("Hello World", "HeWo")
>>> list(result)
[('H', 'H'), ('e', 'e'), ('l', 'W'), ('l', 'o')]
```

The enumerate function described in Chapter 17, Section 17.14.13 is a special case of the zip function:

```
>>> s = "Python"
>>> list(zip(range(len(s)), s))
[(0, 'P'), (1, 'y'), (2, 't'), (3, 'h'), (4, 'o'), (5, 'n')]
```

In Python 3.10, the keyword-only strict parameter was added, whose default value is False. If strict=True is passed, zip raises an exception if the passed iterable objects have different lengths:

```
>>> s = "strict check"
>>> list(zip(s, "Hello", strict=True))
Traceback (most recent call last):
  File "<stdin>", line 1, in <module>
ValueError: zip() argument 2 is shorter than argument 1
```

Among other things, this mode ensures that data isn't ignored unnoticed because one of the iterable objects provides fewer elements than another.

This chapter provided information about the first selection of built-in functions. Chapter 19, Section 19.9 contains descriptions of the built-in functions with an object-oriented background.

Chapter 18
Modules and Packages

So-called *modules* allow the source code to be structured into independent units. A module usually provides data types and functions that serve a specific purpose, such as working with files of a particular file format. Modules can be *imported* into a program and then provide the programmer with the included functionality. Basically, there are three types of modules:

- Modules of the *standard library* are present in every Python installation and can therefore be expected by every Python program. Some of the standard library modules can be found in the *lib/python3.11* subdirectory of the Python installation. Some other standard library modules, for example sys, are implemented directly in the Python interpreter and are called *built-in modules*.

- In addition, any Python program can import *global* modules, also referred to as *libraries*. Global modules are installed systemwide in the *site-packages* subdirectory of the Python installation and are equally available to all Python programs. It's possible to write your own global modules or install a third-party global module.

- The last variant is a *local module*. This is the encapsulation of individual program parts in their own program files. These files can be imported like libraries, but aren't available in any other Python program. This form of modularization is useful in programming because it allows the programmer to divide long program code into different program files in a manageable way.

In Python, the most important difference between local and global modules is the location where they are stored. While local modules are usually located in the program directory or one of its subdirectories, global modules are stored in several specified directories of the Python installation.

The directories where the Python interpreter looks for local and global modules are listed in the sys.path list:

```
>>> import sys
>>> sys.path
['', '/python/installation/lib/python311.zip', '/python/installation/lib/
python3.11', '/python/installation/lib/python3.11/lib-dynload', '/python/
installation/lib/python3.11/site-packages']
```

The directories are searched in the order they appear in sys.path, with the empty string at the beginning of the list representing the local working directory. Additional directories can be specified using the PYTHONPATH environment variable. These are then entered in second place, after the local working directory, in sys.path. The sys.path list may be modified by the program.

18.1   Importing Global Modules

A global module—whether it's a part of the standard library or a self-written one—can be imported using the import statement. In the following examples, we'll primarily use the math module of the standard library. This is a module that provides mathematical functions like sin or cos as well as mathematical constants like pi. To take advantage of this functionality in a program, the import statement is used in the following form:

```
>>> import math
```

An import statement consists of the import keyword followed by a module name. You can import several modules at the same time by writing them after the keyword, separated by commas:

```
>>> import math, random
```

This is equivalent to the following:[1]

```
>>> import math
>>> import random
```

Although an import statement can basically be placed anywhere in the source code, it makes sense to import all modules at the beginning of the source code for the sake of clarity.

Once a module has been imported, a new namespace is created with its name. All functions, data types, and values of the module can be used in the program via this namespace. A namespace can be handled like an instance, while the functions of the module can be used like methods of the namespace. Thus, the following sample program imports the math module and calculates the sine of the number π:

```
>>> import math
>>> math.sin(math.pi)
1.2246467991473532e-16
```

---

1   For reasons of clarity, it's generally recommended to import each module in a separate line.

It's possible to specify the namespace name using an `import/as` statement:

```
>>> import math as mathematics
>>> mathematics.sin(mathematics.pi)
1.2246467991473532e-16
```

This new name is not an additional option. The `math` module is now accessible exclusively through the name `mathematics`.

Furthermore, the `import` statement can be used in such a way that no separate namespace will be created for the imported module, but all elements of the module are imported in the global namespace of the program:

```
>>> from math import *
>>> sin(pi)
1.2246467991473532e-16
```

Note that names starting with an underscore will not be imported in this way. These elements of a module are considered implementation details and therefore internal to the module.

18

Note

The purpose of namespaces is to encapsulate sections with different topics, such as the contents of a module, and to address them via a common name. If you import the complete contents of a module in the global namespace of a program, the library may interfere with any references that may exist. In such a case, the already existing references are overwritten without a comment, as shown in the following example:

```
>>> pi = 1234
>>> from math import *
>>> pi
3.141592653589793
```

For this reason, it makes sense to encapsulate a module in its own namespace when it's fully imported, thus keeping the number of elements imported into the global namespace to a minimum.

In the preceding note box, we mentioned that you should minimize the number of objects to be imported into the global namespace. For this reason, the `from/import` statement with asterisk is not recommended. However, it's possible to specify a list of elements of the module to be imported instead:

```
>>> from math import sin, pi
>>> sin(pi)
1.2246467991473532e-16
```

In this case, only the sin function and the pi constant will be imported into the global namespace. Here too, you can specify your own name by placing as after the name:

```
>>> from math import sin as hello, pi as world
>>> hello(world)
1.2246467991473532e-16
```

So much for importing global modules. You're going to learn more about Python's standard library in Part III of this book.

> **Note**
>
> The enumeration of objects to be imported with a from/import statement can become quite long under certain circumstances. In such cases, it may be enclosed in parentheses. The advantage of this notation is that expressions in parentheses can be formatted in any way, including wrapping them across multiple lines:
>
> ```
> >>> from math import (
> ...     sin, cos, tan,
> ...     sinh, cosh, tanh
> ... )
> ```
>
> Note that as opposed to the from/import statement, parentheses mustn't be used in a normal import statement.

18.2   Local Modules

Now that you have learned about the import statement, let's look at how you can create and import local modules by yourself. Note that this isn't a global module that is available in every Python program, but a module that can only be used locally in your own Python program. In terms of usage, there's hardly any difference between local and global modules. In this section, we'll create a program that reads an integer, calculates its factorial and reciprocal, and outputs the results. The mathematical calculations are supposed to be encapsulated not only in functions, but also in a separate module. For this purpose, we first write them in a file called *mathshelper.py*:

```
def fac(n):
    result = 1
    for i in range(2, n+1):
        result *= i
    return result

def recipr(n):
    return 1 / n
```

The functions should be self-explanatory. The *mathshelper.py* file creates only the fac and recipr functions, which can be called from other modules.

Now we'll create a program file named *program.py*, which should contain the main program. Both files must be located in the same directory. In the main program, we first import the local mathshelper module. The module name of a local module corresponds to the file name of the associated program file without the file extension. The module name must follow the rules of naming an identifier. This means in particular that no dot is allowed in the file name, except for the dot before the file extension:

```
>>> import mathshelper
>>> print("factorial:", mathshelper.fac(5))
factorial: 120
>>> print("reciprocal:", mathshelper.recipr(5))
reciprocal: 0.2
```

As you can see, you can import and use the local module in the main program like a global module.

> **Note**
>
> When importing a module, Python distinguishes between uppercase and lowercase also on Windows. This means you can't import a module file named *XYZ.py* via the xyz statement. Instead, you must write import XYZ.

18.2.1   Name Conflicts

Creating custom modules can easily cause name conflicts with global modules. For example, we could have named our program file used previously as *math.py*, resulting in the module name math. But this module would conflict with the math module of the standard library. In this case, it's no longer obvious whether import math imports the local or the global module math. For this purpose, the interpreter follows a defined order of locations to search when a module is to be imported:

- First, the interpreter checks if a built-in module of the specified name exists.
- If no built-in module of the specified name was found, the local program folder is searched for a file with the corresponding name. In the conflict case described, it would be determined in the first step that a local module named math already exists. If such a local module does exist, it will be imported and no further search performed.
- If no local module of the specified name was found, the search will be extended to global modules.

- If no global module with the specified name was found either, a `ModuleNotFoundError` will be generated:

```
Traceback (most recent call last):
  File "<stdin>", line 1, in <module>
ModuleNotFoundError: No module named 'bla'
```

18.2.2   Module-Internal References

In each module, there are references containing information about the module itself. These are summarized in Table 18.1. Note that there are two underscores both before and after the name of the reference.

Reference	Description
__builtins__	A dictionary containing the names of all built-in types and functions as keys and the instances associated with the names as values
__file__	A string containing the name of the module's program file and path; not available for modules of the standard library
__name__	A string containing the name of the module

Table 18.1 Global Variables in a Module

18.2.3   Executing Modules

If the module is imported via an `import` statement, the code it contains is executed. This affects, for example, definitions of functions or classes that will subsequently be contained in the resulting namespace. However, a module is basically no different from a normal Python program. In particular, it isn't limited to function or class declarations; it can contain any code. This code is also executed when the module is imported. Conversely, a module doesn't necessarily have to be imported, but can also be executed directly via the Python interpreter. In a nutshell: the difference between a program and a module consists only of how it's executed.

You can tell whether a program file is running as a program or as a module by the value of `__name__`. For an imported module, `__name__` references the module name; for an executed program, it references the `"__main__"` string. This makes it possible to react when a module is executed directly:

```
if __name__ == "__main__":
    print("This is a module and should be imported.")
```

18.3   Packages

Python allows you to encapsulate multiple modules in one *package*. This is advantageous if these modules belong together thematically. In contrast to a single module, a package can contain any number of other packages, which in turn can contain modules or packages.

To create a package, a subfolder must be created in the program directory. The name of the folder must correspond to the name of the package. Additionally,[2] this folder can contain a program file named *__init__.py* (note the two underscores both before and after *init* here). This file contains initialization code that's executed once when the package is imported.

> **Note**
>
> If a package and a module with the same name exist in the same directory, this will cause a name conflict. Basically, if the names are identical, a package takes precedence over a module, so there'll no longer be a direct way to import the module.

A program with multiple packages and subpackages has a directory structure similar to that shown in Figure 18.1.

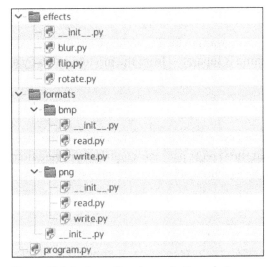

Figure 18.1 Package Structure of a Sample Program

This is the directory structure of a fictitious image-editing program. The main program is located in the *program.py* file. Besides the main program, two packages exist in the program directory:

---

2 In this context, namespace packages that don't contain an *__init__.py* file are an exception. For more information about namespace packages, see Section 18.3.2.

- The `effects` package is supposed to apply certain effects to a previously loaded image. For this purpose, the package contains three modules in addition to the __init__.py file, each of which provides a basic effect. These modules are `blur` (for blurring the image), `flip` (for flipping the image), and `rotate` (for rotating the image).

- The `formats` package is supposed to be able to read and write certain graphic formats. For this purpose, we assume that two functions named `read_image` and `write_image` are defined in its __init__.py file. At this point, we won't go into further detail about functional interfaces. To allow reading and writing graphics of various formats, the `formats` package contains two subpackages named `bmp` and `png`, each comprising two modules for reading and writing the corresponding format, respectively.

In the main program, the `effects` and `formats` packages are first imported and used:

```
>>> import effects
>>> import formats
```

The `import` statement executes the __init__.py program file of the package to be imported and makes the contents of this file available as a module in its own namespace. Thus, after the import statements just presented, you could access the `read_image` and `write_image` functions as follows:

```
>>> formats.read_image()
>>> formats.write_image()
```

To be able to modify the now loaded image, we want to load a module from the `effects` package. For this purpose, the package name is separated from the module name by a dot in the `import` statement:

```
>>> import effects.blur
```

In this case, the `effects` package was previously imported. If that hadn't been the case, importing `effects.blur` would ensure that the `effects` package would be imported first and the associated __init__.py file would be executed. After that, the `blur` submodule is imported and can be used:

```
>>> effects.blur.blur_image()
```

> **Note**
>
> A program file that's inside a package structure can be executed as follows:
>
> ```
> $ python -m formats.png.read
> ```
>
> This way, the entire package structure is loaded so that relative `import` statements (Section 18.3.3) will retain their validity.

18.3.1 Importing All Modules of a Package

When importing a module, `from xyz import *` can be used to import the entire module contents into the current namespace. This doesn't work for packages, as this could take a long time in case of large packages, and blindly importing the entire package contents could have undesirable side effects.

For this reason, the preceding statement doesn't import all the modules contained in the package into the current namespace, but only the package itself, and it executes the initialization code in *__init__.py*. All references created in this file are introduced into the current namespace.

There are two ways to achieve the desired behavior of the statement. Both must be implemented by the author of the package:

- First, all modules of the package can be imported within the *__init__.py* file via the `import` statement. This has the effect that they would be imported when the package is imported and thus after the code of the *__init__.py* file has been executed.
- Second, this can be done by creating a reference called `__all__`, which must reference a list of strings with the module names to be imported:

    ```
    __all__ = ["blur", "flip", "rotate"]
    ```

It's up to the programmer's discretion to decide how `from xyz import *` should handle the packages. Note, however, that importing the complete module or package contents into the current namespace can cause undesirable name conflicts. For this reason, you should always keep imported modules in their own namespace.

18.3.2 Namespace Packages

A *namespace package* is a package that can consist of several parts stored in different locations. This can be useful, for example, when several components of a related library are to be distributed independently of each other. When importing such a package, the individual components are assigned to the same namespace.

Because multiple folders can belong to a namespace package, there is no longer a unique *__init__.py* file. On the contrary: the presence or absence of the *__init__.py* file determines whether a package is imported as a regular package or as a namespace package.

Let's suppose two folders named *package* existed in different locations in the file system where Python looks for modules and packages. Both folders have the same name, but contain different modules: *directory1/package/module1.py* and *directory2/package/module2.py*.

Both modules can then be imported via the package name `package` as if they were imported in a regular package in the same folder. Assuming that both modules output their names on being imported, we see the following behavior:

```
>>> import package.module1
module1
>>> import package.module2
module2
```

Any regular package can be made a namespace package by removing the *__init__.py* file. Note, however, that importing namespace packages takes longer than importing regular packages because all known directories must be searched for components of the package.

18.3.3   Relative Import Statements

Large libraries often consist not only of a single module or package, but contain various subpackages, thus defining an arbitrarily complex *package structure*. Within such a package structure, a *relative* variant of the import statement is required, which imports a subpackage based on a relative path specification. In this way, a package can import a second package that is, for example, two levels above the importing package in the package structure. A relative import statement is written as follows:

```
from . import xyz
```

This statement imports the package (or module) xyz from the directory specified between from and import. A dot represents the current directory. Each additional dot symbolizes the directory located one level higher.

In the context of the fictitious image editor from Figure 18.1, the following statement in the read module of the png package would import the corresponding module for bitmaps:

```
from ..bmp import read
```

The read module is imported from the bmp package, which is located one level above the importing package in the package structure.

A relative import statement fails if it's executed outside a package structure.

The classic import statement, as discussed in the previous sections, is also referred to as the *absolute* import statement and can be used within a package structure to only import global modules. In all other cases, you must use a relative import statement.

The options discussed at the beginning for renaming an imported package or module also apply to relative import statements:

```
from ..bmp import read as read_bmp
```

18.4   The importlib Package

The importlib package of the standard library implements the import behavior under-lying the import statement. There are three basic uses for this package:

- It contains the import_module function, which can be used to import a module or package without using the import statement. This is useful, for example, if the name of the module to be imported is available as a string.

- It defines so-called importers. Using these importers, it's possible to intervene in the import process and thus modify the default behavior of the import statement.

- The implementation of the import process is thus written in the Python language itself. In particular, this means that alternative Python interpreters don't need to provide their own implementation; they can also use importlib.

18.4.1   Importing Modules and Packages

The importlib package defines the import_module function, which can be used to import a module without using the import statement. The import_module function is passed the name of the module or package to be imported as a string:

```
>>> import importlib
>>> math = importlib.import_module("math")
>>> math.cos(0)
1.0
```

The imported module gets returned by import_module.

If a relative import is to be performed, a string containing the path to the basic package referenced by the relative import must be passed for the optional second parameter.

In the context of the package structure from Figure 18.1, the relative import statement from the previous examples, from ..bmp import read, is roughly equivalent to all of the following calls of import_module:

```
read = importlib.import_module("..bmp.read", __package__)
read = importlib.import_module("..bmp.read", "formats.png")
read = importlib.import_module(".bmp.read", "formats")
```

18.4.2   Changing the Import Behavior

Note

This section is intended for advanced readers and covers a rarely needed topic. It assumes basic knowledge in the areas of object orientation (see Chapter 19) and excep-tion handling (see Chapter 20).

From the user's point of view, the essential aspect of the `importlib` package is certainly the definition of the `import_module` function; however, the package also offers useful options for intervening in the interpreter's import process. For example, these methods enable you to load modules from compressed archives or from the internet. In addition, it's also possible to create modules dynamically when embedding them. For this reason, at this point we'll provide a brief overview of how the import of modules and packages works internally and how you can implement a self-defined behavior.

The import behavior is determined by a combination of so-called finders and loaders. A finder locates the module to be imported by its name and instantiates a matching loader to import it. The `sys.path_hooks` list contains the finders registered in the entire system. Because there are different types of places where finders can look for modules, for each entry in `sys.path` the registered finders are asked one after the other whether they are suitable for this path. The first finder in `sys.path_hooks` that declares itself suitable for one of the paths is responsible for finding modules in that path.

When processing an `import` statement, the paths entered in `sys.path` are iterated in sequence, and the associated finder is instructed to find the module to be imported. If one of the finders finds the module, the loader it instantiates must import the module. The following principle applies here: after the first finder has found the module, the search is aborted.

The Finder

A *finder* is a class containing a `find_module` method in addition to its constructor. This method is called when a module is searched in a path assigned to the finder. Via the constructor, the finder indicates for which paths it is suitable. In the following sections, we'll develop a sample finder that identifies text files as modules:

```python
import os
class TextFinder:
    def __init__(self, path):
        if path != "#":
            raise ImportError
    def find_module(self, fullname, path=None):
        if os.path.exists(fullname + ".txt"):
            return TextLoader(path)
        else:
            return None
```

For each entry in `sys.path` that doesn't yet have an associated finder, the registered finders are instantiated one after the other. When instantiating, the respective path is passed to the constructor. If a finder doesn't want to be responsible for the specified path, it must raise an `ImportError` exception. In the example, we write a finder that is only responsible for the "#" path. This is an artificial entry we'll add to sys.path later so as not to interfere with the rest of the import behavior.

The find_module method is called when the finder is instructed to find a module named fullname. To do this, it checks whether the *fullname.txt* file exists and, if so, instantiates a matching loader—in this case, TextLoader for importing a text file.

The Loader

A *loader* essentially implements the load_module method, to which the module name is passed. It's responsible for importing the module and returning the resulting module instance. In addition, the module must be entered in the sys.modules module index, and various attributes of the module must be initialized.

If the module already exists in sys.modules, which means it's imported a second time, a loader should return the instance contained in sys.modules. If loading a module fails, load_module raises an ImportError exception.

To create a new module instance, the new_module function of the imp module from the standard library can be used:

```python
import types
class TextLoader:
    def __init__(self, path):
        pass
    def load_module(self, fullname):
        if fullname in sys.modules:
            return sys.modules[fullname]
        module = types.ModuleType(fullname, "Docstring")
        module.__file__ = fullname + ".txt"
        module.__package__ = None
        module.__loader__ = self
        try:
            with open(fullname + ".txt") as f:
                module.text = f.read()
            sys.modules[fullname] = module
            return module
        except FileNotFoundError:
            raise ImportError
```

In the sample implementation, we try to read the text file matching the module name and, if successful, insert the contained text into the module as the text attribute.

To test the import of text files, TextFinder must be registered as the finder, and the "#" virtual path must be added to sys.path:

```
import sys
sys.path_hooks.append(TextFinder)
sys.path.append("#")
```

Both the finder class and the virtual path can be inserted further up the respective lists to give them a higher priority.

If a module is now imported, the paths contained in sys.path will be processed as usual. Because the "#" virtual path was added to the end of the list, the default finders with the default paths are checked first. If none of the standard finders can find the module, TextFinder will try to load the module as a text file:

```
>>> import testfile
>>> testfile
<module 'testfile' (<__main__.TextLoader object at 0x7f089dcce880>)>
>>> testfile.text
'This is the content of the test file\n'
```

Finders and loaders can be separate classes, as shown in the example, but they can also be the same class. In this case, the find_module method may return its own instance: self.

18.5   Planned Language Elements

The Python language is in constant development, and each new version brings new language elements that may render old Python code incompatible with the latest version of the interpreter. While developers do their best to maintain maximum compatibility, simply adding a keyword, for example, has already made code incompatible that uses the new keyword as a normal identifier.

The interpreter contains a mode that allows you to use some selected language elements of the upcoming Python version with the current version. This is to simplify the change from one version to the next as tests can be run against some new features of the next version before it's published.

To import a scheduled feature, you can use an import statement:

```
from __future__ import language_element
```

The language elements can be used as if they were encapsulated in a module called __future__. Note, however, that you can't handle the __future__ module quite as freely as you are used to from other modules. For example, you may import it only at the beginning of a program file. Only comments, empty lines, or other future imports may precede such an import statement.

An example of a future import is print_function, which was introduced in Python 2.6, where it imports the print function. At the same time, the print keyword is removed from the language when importing print_function. In this way, the behavior of Python 3 can be emulated:

```
>>> from __future__ import print_function
>>> print "Test"
  File "<stdin>", line 1
    print "Test"
               ^
SyntaxError: invalid syntax
>>> print("Test")
Test
```

This particular future import comes in handy when preparing legacy Python 2 code for being ported to Python 3.

18

Chapter 19
Object-Oriented Programming

So far, as users, we've worked with various objects, such as strings, lists, dictionaries, file objects, and many more. In this chapter, we'll show you how we can define our own objects that are customized according to our personal requirements. The term *object orientation* describes a programming paradigm that can be used to ensure the consistency of data objects and improve the reusability of source code. These advantages are achieved by combining data structures and the associated operations into one *object* and allowing access to these structures only via specific interfaces.

We'll illustrate this approach with an example by first developing a solution in the previous way and then implementing it a second time, but this time using Python's object-oriented mechanisms.

19.1 Example: A Non-Object-Oriented Account

Let's suppose you were to develop an account-management system for a bank that governs the creation of new accounts, transfers, and deposits and withdrawals. One possible approach would be to create a dictionary for each bank account, storing all the information about the customer and their financial status. To support the desired operations, you must define functions for manipulating the dictionary. A dictionary for a simplified account then looks as follows:[1]

```
account = {
    "owner": "Steve Miller",
    "account_number": 567123,
    "account_balance": 12350.0,
    "max_daily_turnover": 1500,
    "turnover_today": 10.0
}
```

---

1 We use float instances here to store monetary amounts to keep the examples simple. With this data type, information can be lost when it comes to very large amounts. For this reason, you should choose a more suitable representation of the amounts in banking applications—for example, using the decimal.Decimal type. See Chapter 26, Section 26.3.

For the model, we assume that each account has an "owner" identified by a string containing the relevant name. The account has an "account_number" which is a unique integer to distinguish the account from all other accounts. The float associated with the "account_balance" key is used to store the current balance in USD. The "max_daily_turnover" and "turnover_today" keys are used to limit each customer's daily turnover to a certain amount for their own protection. The value stored using the key "max_daily_turnover" specifies the maximum amount of money that can be moved from or to the account per day. With "turnover_today", the system "remembers" how much has already been turned over today. At the beginning of a new day, this value is reset to zero.

19.1.1   Creating a New Account

Based on this data structure, we'll now define the required operations as functions. First, we need a function that creates a new account according to certain specifications:

```python
def new_account(owner, account_number, account_balance,
                max_daily_turnover=1500):
    return {
        "owner": owner,
        "account_number": account_number,
        "account_balance": account_balance,
        "max_daily_turnover": max_daily_turnover,
        "turnover_today": 0
    }
```

19.1.2   Transferring Money

A transfer of funds always involves a sender (the source account) and a receiver (the destination account). In addition, to carry out the transfer, the respective amount of money must be known. So the function will expect three parameters: source, destination, and amount. According to our requirements, a transfer is possible only if the daily turnover of the two accounts doesn't exceed its limit. The transfer function is supposed to return a truth value indicating whether the transfer could be executed or not. This allows it to be implemented as follows:

```python
def money_transfer(source, destination, amount):
    # Here we test whether the transfer is possible
    if (amount < 0 or
        source["turnover_today"] + amount > source["max_daily_turnover"] or
        destination["turnover_today"] + amount >
            destination["max_daily_turnover"]):
```

```
        # Transfer impossible
        return False
    else:
        # Everything's OK - Let's go
        source["account_balance"] -= amount
        source["turnover_today"] += amount
        destination["account_balance"] += amount
        destination["turnover_today"] += amount
        return True
```

The function first checks whether the transfer is feasible and terminates the function call early with the return value False if it isn't. If a valid value was passed for the amount and no daily turnover limit is exceeded, the function updates account balances and daily turnover according to the transfer and returns True.

19.1.3   Depositing and Withdrawing Money

The remaining operations for our model accounts involve the deposit or withdrawal of money at an ATM or bank counter. Both functions require the relevant account and the respective amount of money as parameters:

```
def deposit(account, amount):
    if amount < 0 or \
        account["turnover_today"] + amount > account["max_daily_turnover"]:
        # Daily limit exceeded or invalid amount
        return False
    else:
        account["account_balance"] += amount
        account["turnover_today"] += amount
        return True


def withdraw(account, amount):
    if (amount < 0 or \
        account["turnover_today"] + amount > account["max_daily_turnover"]):
        # Daily limit exceeded or invalid amount
        return False
    else:
        account["account_balance"] -= amount
        account["turnover_today"] += amount
        return True
```

These functions also return a truth value, depending on their success.

343

19.1.4   Viewing the Account Balance

To get an overview of the current status of our accounts, we must define a simple output function:

```
def show_account(account):
    print("Account of {}".format(account["owner"]))
    print("Current account balance: {:.2f} USD".format(
        account["account_balance"]))
    print("(Today already {:.2f} of {} USD turned over)".format(
        account["turnover_today"], account["max_daily_turnover"]))
```

Using these definitions, we could simulate, for example, the following banking operations:

```
>>> a1 = new_account("Steve Miller", 567123, 12350.0)
>>> a2 = new_account("John Smith", 396754, 15000.0)
>>> money_transfer(a1, a2, 160)
True
>>> money_transfer(a2, a1, 1000)
True
>>> money_transfer(a2, a1, 500)
False
>>> deposit(a2, 500)
False
>>> show_account(a1)
Account of Steve Miller
Current account balance: 13190.00 USD
(Today already 1160.00 of 1500 USD turned over)
>>> show_account(a2)
Account of John Smith
Current account balance: 14160.00 USD
(Today already 1160.00 of 1500 USD turned over)
```

First, Steve Miller opens a new account a1 with account number 567123 and with an initial balance of 12,350 USD. John Smith deposits 15,000 USD in his new account a2 with account number 396754. Both have chosen the default maximum daily turnover of 1,500 USD. Now the two start doing business with each other: Mr. Miller buys a used smartphone from Mr. Smith for 160 USD and pays for it via wire transfer. On the same day, Mr. Miller buys Mr. Smith's used laptop computer for 1,000 USD. When Mr. Smith shows a strong interest in Mr. Miller's home theater system in the evening and wants to transfer 500 USD to him for it, he is disappointed because the transfer fails. Completely surprised, Mr. Smith comes to the premature conclusion that he doesn't have money in his account. For this reason, he wants to deposit the amount into his account and then initiate the transfer again. But when the deposit is also rejected, he calls a bank clerk who takes a look at the information for the accounts involved. In doing so, the bank clerk can see that the requested transfer exceeds the daily limit of Mr. Smith's account and therefore can't be executed.

As you can see, our bank simulation works as expected and allows us to handle account data with relative ease. However, it has an unattractive peculiarity, which we'll describe in the following sections.

In the example, the data structure and the functions for processing it are defined separately, which means that the account dictionary must be passed as a parameter for each function call.

However, it's possible to take the position that an account can only be used meaningfully with the associated management functions and, conversely, that the management functions of an account are only useful in connection with the account.

Object orientation satisfies precisely this position by combining data and processing functions into *objects*. In this context, the data of such an object are referred to as *attributes*, while the processing functions are called *methods*. Attributes and methods are summarized as the *members* of a class. The object of an account can thus be represented in a schema as follows (see Table 19.1).

Account	
Attributes	Methods
owner account_balance max_daily_turnover turnover_today	new_account() money_transfer() deposit() withdraw() show()

Table 19.1 Schema of an Account Object

You're already familiar with the terms *attribute* and *method* from previous chapters on basic data types because each instance of a basic data type represents an object—even though you may not have known it at the time. Moreover, you already know that you can access the attributes and methods of an object by writing the reference to the object and its member separated by a period.

Let's assume a1 and a2 are account objects as shown in the preceding schema, with the data for Mr. Miller and Mr. Smith. Then we can formulate the preceding example as follows:[2]

---

2 Of course, the code isn't yet executable because the definition for the account objects is missing. We'll develop that in the following sections.

```
>>> a1.money_transfer(a2, 160)
True
>>> a2.money_transfer(a1, 1000)
True
>>> a2.money_transfer(a1, 500)
False
>>> a2.deposit(500)
False
>>> a1.show()
Account of Steve Miller
Current account balance: 13190.00 USD
(Today already 1160.00 of 1500 USD turned over)
>>> a2.show()
Account of John Smith
Current account balance: 14160.00 USD
(Today already 1160.00 of 1500 USD turned over)
```

The money_transfer and show methods now have one parameter less when called because the account they each reference is now at the beginning of the call. Because the show method now automatically references an account, we have shortened the name of the method accordingly.

From the introduction to basic data types, you're already familiar with the handling of objects and the use of their attributes and methods. In this chapter, you'll learn how to create your own objects using classes.

19.2   Classes

Objects are created via *classes*. A class is a formal description of the structure of an object, which states what attributes and methods it has.

But using a class alone doesn't make much sense: it only represents the description of an object type but is not an object itself.[3] You can compare the relationship between class and object with that between a baking recipe and a cake. The recipe defines the ingredients and the manufacturing process of a cake and thus its characteristics. Nevertheless, a recipe alone is not enough to invite relatives to share a delicious cake on a Sunday afternoon. Only during the baking process does the abstract description become a finished cake.

Another name for an object is an *instance*. Object-oriented baking is therefore called *instantiation*. Just as there can be multiple cakes for a single recipe, there can be multiple instances of a class (see Figure 19.1).

---

3 Strictly speaking, classes in Python are also instances of so-called *metaclasses*. However, this shouldn't play a role here.

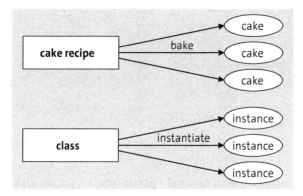

Figure 19.1 Analogy of Recipe/Cake and Class/Object

To define a new class in Python, you can use the class keyword followed by the name of the new class. The simplest class has neither methods nor attributes and is defined as follows:

```
class Account:
    pass
```

As mentioned earlier, you can't use a class on its own because it's only an abstract description. For this reason, we now want to create an instance of the still-empty account sample class. To instantiate a class, you call the class like a function without parameters by following the class name with a pair of parentheses. The return value of this call is a new instance of the class:

```
>>> Account()
<__main__.Account object at 0x7f118556de10>
```

The output tells us that the return value of Account() is an instance of the Account class in the __main__ namespace and stored at a certain memory address; it's sufficient for us to know that a new instance of the Account class has been created.

19.2.1   Defining Methods

Basically, a method differs from a function only in two aspects: First, it's defined within a block introduced by class, and second, it always receives as its first parameter a reference to the instance through which it is invoked. This first parameter only needs to be explicitly written in the definition and is automatically linked to the corresponding instance when the method is called. Because the reference is to the object itself, the first parameter is named self. Just like functions, methods have their own namespace, can access global variables, and return values to the calling level.

This allows us to add the missing methods to our account class, initially writing down only the method headers without the included code:

```
class Account:
    def money_transfer(self, destination, amount):
        pass
    def deposit(self, amount):
        pass
    def withdraw(self, amount):
        pass
    def show(self):
        pass
```

Note the self parameter at the beginning of each method's parameter list, for which a reference to the instance is automatically passed to the left of the dot when it's called:

```
>>> a = Account()
>>> a.deposit(500)
```

Here, a reference to the account a is passed to the deposit method, which can then be accessed within deposit via the self parameter.

In the next section, you'll learn how you can manipulate the creation process for new objects and create new attributes.

19.2.2   The Constructor

The lifecycle of each instance is always the same: it is created, used, and then eliminated. The class—that is, the blueprint—is responsible for ensuring that the instance is in a well-defined state at all times. For this purpose, a special method is available that's automatically called when an object is instantiated to put the object in a valid initial state. This method is referred to as the *constructor* of a class.

To give a class a constructor, you must define a method called __init__:[4]

```
class SampleClass:
    def __init__(self):
        print("This is the constructor speaking")
```

If we now create an instance of SampleClass, the __init__ method is implicitly called, and the text "This is the constructor speaking" appears on the screen:

```
>>> SampleClass()
This is the constructor speaking
<__main__.SampleClass object at 0x7f118556dfd0>
```

---

4 The word init is surrounded by two underscores (_) each on its left and right sides. Methods built according to the __WORD__ schema have a special meaning in Python. We'll discuss this in more detail later in Section 19.11.

It makes sense that constructors don't have any return values as they aren't called directly and a reference to the new instance is already returned when a new instance is created.

> **Note**
>
> If you already know other object-oriented programming languages and are wondering how to implement a destructor in Python, you should note at this point that there is no destructor in Python that's guaranteed to be called at the end of an instance's lifetime.
>
> A similar behavior can be implemented using the __del__ method (Section 19.11.1) or by implementing a context manager (Chapter 22).

19.2.3 Attributes

Because the main task of a constructor is to establish a consistent initial state of the instance, all attributes of a class should be defined there.[5] The definition of new attributes can be done by a value assignment as you know it from normal variables. This allows us to replace the new_account function with the constructor of the Account class, which can then be implemented as follows:

```python
class Account:
    def __init__(self, owner, account_number, account_balance,
                       max_daily_turnover=1500):
        self.owner = owner
        self.account_number = account_number
        self.account_balance = account_balance
        self.max_daily_turnover = max_daily_turnover
        self.turnover_today = 0
    # The remaining methods will be placed here
```

Because self contains a reference to the instance to be created, we can use it to create the new attributes, as shown in the example. On this basis, the other functions of the non-object-oriented variant based on dictionaries can also be transferred to the account class.

19.2.4 Example: An Object-Oriented Account

The following example contains the complete Account class:

```python
class Account:
    def __init__(self, owner, account_number, account_balance,
                       max_daily_turnover=1500):
```

---

5 There are few special cases in which it's necessary to deviate from this rule. As a rule, you should create all attributes of your classes in the constructor.

```python
        self.owner = owner
        self.account_number = account_number
        self.account_balance = account_balance
        self.max_daily_turnover = max_daily_turnover
        self.turnover_today = 0
    def money_transfer(self, destination, amount):
        # Here the test takes place whether the transfer is possible
        if (amount < 0 or
            self.turnover_today + amount > self.max_daily_turnover or
            destination.turnover_today + amount > destination.max_daily_turnover
            ):
            # Transfer impossible
            return False
        else:
            # Everything OK - Let's go
            self.account_balance -= amount
            self.turnover_today += amount
            destination.account_balance += amount
            destination.turnover_today += amount
            return True
    def deposit(self, amount):
        if (amount < 0 or
            self.turnover_today + amount > self.max_daily_turnover):
            # Daily limit exceeded or invalid amount
            return False
        else:
            self.account_balance += amount
            self.turnover_today += amount
            return True
    def withdraw(self, amount):
        if amount < 0 or self.turnover_today + amount > self.max_daily_turnover:
            # Daily limit exceeded or invalid amount
            return False
        else:
            self.account_balance -= amount
            self.turnover_today += amount
            return True
    def show(self):
        print("Account of {}".format(self.owner))
        print("Current account balance: {:.2f} USD".format(
            self.account_balance))
        print("(Today already {:.2f} of {} USD turned over)".format(
            self.turnover_today, self.max_daily_turnover))
```

At this point, we have achieved our goal of combining the account data and the associated processing functions into a single unit.

Using the new account class, we can replay Mr. Smith's and Mr. Miller's transactions from the beginning of the chapter:

```
>>> a1 = Account("Steve Miller", 567123, 12350.0)
>>> a2 = Account("John Smith", 396754, 15000.0)
>>> a1.money_transfer(a2, 160)
True
>>> a2.money_transfer(a1, 1000)
True
>>> a2.money_transfer(a1, 500)
False
>>> a2.deposit(500)
False
>>> a1.show()
Account of Steve Miller
Current account balance: 13190.00 USD
(Today already 1160.00 of 1500 USD turned over)
>>> a2.show()
Account of John Smith
Current account balance: 14160.00 USD
(Today already 1160.00 of 1500 USD turned over)
```

In the following section, we'll try to find out how we can structure our example so that it can be easily generalized for new problems.

19.3   Inheritance

In addition to the structural merging of data and the methods working on it into a single unit, the concept of object orientation aims to improve the reusability of program code. This means that a program can be adapted with little effort to problems similar to the one for which the program was originally developed.

In concrete terms, this means that new classes can be derived from existing classes in order to extend them with additional functionality. The derived class *inherits* all the capabilities from its *base class*, so initially it's a copy of that class. In this context, we say that the base class passes on its capabilities to a child class, which in turn inherits them. After this inheritance step, you can adapt the derived class to the new requirements.

Before we apply inheritance to our account class, we'll describe some abstract examples to show you how inheritance works in Python.

19.3.1 A Simple Example

To make one class inherit from another, you write the base class in parentheses after the class name when defining the child class. So in the following example, class B inherits from class A:

```
class A:
    pass
class B(A):
    pass
```

Classes A and B are still pretty boring because they contain no methods or attributes. For this reason, we'll extend our classes as follows:

```
class A:
    def __init__(self):
        print("Constructor of A")
        self.x = 1337
    def m(self):
        print("Method m of A. It's self.x =", self.x)
class B(A):
    def n(self):
        print("Method n of B")
b = B()
b.n()
b.m()
```

In this example, class A is extended with a constructor that creates an attribute x with the value 1337. In addition, class A receives a method m. Both the constructor and the m method each output a message to the screen. In addition, we provide class B with a method n, which also outputs a message. At the end of the small program, an instance of class B is created and its n and m methods are called.

The output shows that B has inherited both the constructor and method m from class A. The attribute x was also created properly:

```
Constructor of A
Method n of B
Method m of A. It's self.x = 1337
```

The constructor of a class has the task to bring the class into a well-defined initial state. As the output of the preceding program shows, when an instance of class B was created, the constructor of class A was called. Now, in practice, it often happens that a derived class requires a different constructor than its base class in order to perform its own initializations.

19.3.2 Overriding Methods

We therefore extend our class B with its own constructor, which creates an attribute y and also generates an output. In addition, we extend method n so that it outputs the value of attribute y:

```
class B(A):
    def __init__(self):
        print("Constructor of B")
        self.y = 10000
    def n(self):
        print("Method n of B. It's self.y =", self.y)
b = B()
b.n()
b.m()
```

The output of this example surprises us with an error message:

```
Constructor of B
Method n of B. It's self.y = 10000
Traceback (most recent call last):
    ...
AttributeError: 'B' object has no attribute 'x'
```

According to the screen output, the constructor of B and the methods n and m are called. However, method m complains that the instance has no attribute x.

This is not surprising as the constructor of A, which is responsible for creating the attribute x, isn't called at all. The rationale for this behavior is as follows: Class B initially inherited the __init__ method—that is, the constructor—from class A, but then *overwrote* it with its own constructor. As a result, when an instance of class B is created, only the new constructor defined by B will be called, while the constructor of A doesn't come into play.

In general, we speak of *overriding a method* when a class reimplements a method it has previously inherited from its base class.

Basically, however, it's necessary to call the overridden constructor of the base class to put the instance in a consistent state. Therefore, it's possible to explicitly call overridden methods of the base class:

```
class B(A):
    def __init__(self):
        print("Constructor of B")
        super().__init__()
        self.y = 10000
```

```
    def n(self):
        print("Method n of B. It's self.y =", self.y)
b = B()
b.n()
b.m()
```

The super().__init__() line explicitly calls the constructor of base class A within the constructor of class B. The built-in super function finds that A is the base class of B and that therefore the __init__ method of A should be called via super().__init__().

The output of the code shown previously shows that the constructor of A is now called as desired, and the call of method m also works fine:

```
Constructor of B
Constructor of A
Method n of B. It's self.y = 10000
Method m of A. It's self.x = 1337
```

The overriding of methods isn't limited to the constructor, and any method of the base class can also be called explicitly like the constructor in the preceding example above. To illustrate this, in the following example, we'll override method m of A in class B and use super to call m of A again:

```
class B(A):
    def __init__(self):
        print("Constructor of B")
        super().__init__()
        self.y = 10000
    def n(self):
        print("Method n of B. It's self.y =", self.y)
    def m(self):
        print("Method m of B.")
        super().m()
b = B()
b.m()
```

The output of this sample program is as follows:

```
Constructor of B
Constructor of A
Method m of B.
Method m of A. It's self.x = 1337
```

Thus, method m of base class A was called via super().m(), as desired.

> **Note**
>
> Methods of the base class can also be called explicitly without `super`. In the constructor of B, `super().__init__()` can be replaced by `A.__init__(self)` to call the constructor of A. However, this requires the explicit specification of the base class for each call, even though it's clear from the context.

Now we have the tool at hand to apply the concept of inheritance to our account example. In doing so, we'll decompose our program into several classes that inherit from each other.

19.3.3   Example: Checking Account with Daily Turnover

Object-oriented programming aims to reuse existing code or provide code that can be easily adapted to new requirements. As a result, when developing an object-oriented program, you should always make sure to keep your classes as universal as possible. Only then will it be possible to adopt parts of the program for solving new problems by intelligent inheritance.

As an example, we'll develop a `CheckingAccountWithDailyTurnover` class that functions in the same way as the `Account` class presented earlier. However, this time we'll make sure to structure our program code in such a way that it can be easily used for similar tasks.

The starting point of our program is the `Account` class from Section 19.2, whose attributes can initially be divided into two categories:

- Data related to the handling of money in the account (`account_balance`, `max_daily_turnover`, `turnover_today`)
- Data related to the customer (`owner`, `account_number`)

All methods except the `show` method use only attributes of the first category. For this reason, we'll now implement the first structural separation by splitting an account into two parts.

One part is supposed to take care of the account balance management, while the other part is to store the customer data.

The ManagedMoneyAmount Class

From an abstract point of view, a class that manages the balance of our account must support deposits, withdrawals, and transfers of funds to other accounts. It must be possible to link these operations to certain conditions—namely, whether or not the respective maximum daily turnovers are met.

In addition to accounts, however, there are other entities that manage an amount of money according to certain rules. For example, the money in a wallet can be interpreted as an account balance. The "deposit" and "withdraw" operations then describe the process of placing cash in the wallet and withdrawing cash from it, respectively. This situation is similar to a safe or the credit on a prepaid card.

Thus, it's useful to implement a class that allows for managing an amount of money according to certain rules. This ManagedMoneyAmount class will then serve as the basis for the CheckingAccountWithDailyTurnover class, but it will remain useful for other applications as well:

```python
class ManagedMoneyAmount:
    def __init__(self, initial_amount):
        self.amount = initial_amount
    def deposit_possible(self, amount):
        return True
    def withdraw_possible(self, amount):
        return True
    def deposit(self, amount):
        if amount < 0 or not self.deposit_possible(amount):
            return False
        else:
            self.amount += amount
            return True
    def withdraw(self, amount):
        if amount < 0 or not self.withdraw_possible(amount):
            return False
        else:
            self.amount -= amount
            return True
    def show(self):
        print("Amount: {:.2f}".format(self.amount))
```

In the constructor of the class, the amount attribute is created and set to the passed initial value. The deposit and withdraw methods can be used to change the amount, each returning True if the operation was successful and False if a problem occurred. The show method displays the currently available amount on the screen.

The key feature of the ManagedMoneyAmount class lies in the deposit_possible and withdraw_possible methods, which are used by the deposit and wihdraw methods respectively, to check whether the respective operation can be performed.

These are intended to be overridden by derived classes to set the desired conditions. Because they return True in the ManagedMoneyAmount class, deposits and withdrawals are possible without restrictions so long as these methods are not overridden.

The GeneralAccount Class

Among other things, our ManagedMoneyAmount class still lacks the ability to transfer money between different instances to mimic the functionality of our initial Account class. Because this is an operation that should be handled by all accounts, we'll now derive a GeneralAccount class from ManagedMoneyAmount and extend it with a money_transfer method.

In addition, an account always includes the customer data of the respective account owner. We'll store this data in the customer_data attribute, the value of which will set the first parameter of the constructor. We will deal with the definition of the class used to store the customer data at a later stage:

```python
class GeneralAccount(ManagedMoneyAmount):
    def __init__(self, customer_data, account_balance):
        super().__init__(account_balance)
        self.customer_data = customer_data
    def money_transfer(self, destination, amount):
        if (self.withdraw_possible(amount) and
            destination.deposit_possible(amount)):
            self.withdraw(amount)
            destination.deposit(amount)
            return True
        else:
            return False
    def show(self):
        self.customer_data.show()
        super().show()
```

The new money_transfer method accesses the withdraw_possible and deposit_possible methods to check the feasibility of the transfer. For the transfer itself, the withdraw and deposit methods are used.

To output an instance of the GeneralAccount class, the show method is overridden so that the customer data is output first and then the show method of the ManagedMoneyAmount base class is called. This assumes that the instance referenced by the customer_data attribute has a method called show.

The GeneralAccountWithDailyTurnover Class

Now it's time to extend the GeneralAccount class with the ability to limit the daily turnover. For this purpose, we derive the GeneralAccountWithDailyTurnover class from GeneralAccount and override some of the methods:

```python
class GeneralAccountWithDailyTurnover(GeneralAccount):
    def __init__(self, customer_data, account_balance, max_daily_turnover=1500):
        super().__init__(customer_data, account_balance)
```

19

```
        self.max_daily_turnover = max_daily_turnover
        self.turnover_today = 0.0
    def transfer_possible(self, amount):
        return (self.turnover_today + amount <= self.max_daily_turnover)
    def withdraw_possible(self, amount):
        return self.transfer_possible(amount)
    def deposit_possible(self, amount):
        return self.transfer_possible(amount)
    def deposit(self, amount):
        if super().deposit(amount):
            self.turnover_today += amount
            return True
        else:
            return False
    def withdraw(self, amount):
        if super().withdraw(amount):
            self.turnover_today += amount
            return True
        else:
            return False
    def show(self):
        super().show()
        print("Today already {:.2f} of {:.2f} USD turned over".format(
            self.turnover_today, self.max_daily_turnover))
```

The `deposit_possible` and `withdraw_possible` methods are overridden so that—depending on the daily turnover—they enable or block deposits and withdrawals. Both methods use the new `transfer_possible` method for this purpose.

The `deposit` and `withdraw` methods are adjusted to update the `turnover_today` attribute if necessary. Last but not least, the `show` method adds information about the daily turnover to the output of `GeneralAccount.show`.

Thus, the `GeneralAccountWithDailyTurnover` class has the same functionality to manage the account balance as that initial `Account` class. What's still missing is the management of customer data.

The Checking Account Data Class

The customer data associated with a checking account is stored in instances of the `CheckingAccountCustomerData` class. In addition to two attributes that store the name of the account owner and the account number, this class also has a `show` method to output the information onto the screen:

```
class CheckingAccountCustomerData:
    def __init__(self, owner, account_number):
        self.owner = owner
        self.account_number = account_number
    def show(self):
        print("Owner:", self.owner)
        print("Account number:", self.account_number)
```

Now we can define the CheckingAccountWithDailyTurnover class.

The CheckingAccountWithDailyTurnover Class

Finally, we derive the CheckingAccountWithDailyTurnover class from the GeneralAccount-WithDailyTurnover class and provide it with the relevant customer data by overriding the constructor:

```
class CheckingAccountWithDailyTurnover(GeneralAccountWithDailyTurnover):
    def __init__(self, owner, account_number, account_balance,
                       max_daily_turnover=1500):
        customer_data = CheckingAccountCustomerData(owner, account_number)
        super().__init__(customer_data, account_balance, max_daily_turnover)
```

This class maps the entire functionality of the Account class, so we can now run our opening example about Mr. Miller and Mr. Smith:

```
>>> a1 = CheckingAccountWithDailyTurnover("Steve Miller", 567123, 12350.0)
>>> a2 = CheckingAccountWithDailyTurnover("John Smith", 396754, 15000.0)
>>> a1.money_transfer(a2, 160)
True
>>> a2.money_transfer(a1, 1000)
True
>>> a2.money_transfer(a1, 500)
False
>>> a2.deposit(500)
False
>>> a1.show()
Owner: Steve Miller
Account number: 567123
Amount: 13190.00
Today already 1160.00 of 1500.00 USD turned over
>>> a2.show()
Owner: John Smith
Account number: 396754
Amount: 14160.00
Today already 1160.00 of 1500.00 USD turned over
```

In the following section, we'll demonstrate that due to this structure, our program can be extended easily.

Possible Extensions to the Account Class

Via piecemeal refinement using the principle of inheritance, we have now derived the CheckingAccountWithDailyTurnover class from our initial concept of a managed amount of money. This class now has the same functionality as the Account class. Figure 19.2 graphically illustrates the resulting class hierarchy.

The benefit of this structure becomes obvious when we introduce new classes that can draw on existing functionality. As an example, we'll use the Wallet, Safe, CheckingAccount, NumberedAccount, and NumberedAccountWithDailyTurnover classes.

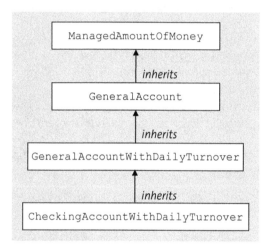

Figure 19.2 Class Hierarchy of the Account Example

Before we dive into describing and implementing these classes, let's first take a look at the emerging class hierarchy, shown in Figure 19.3.

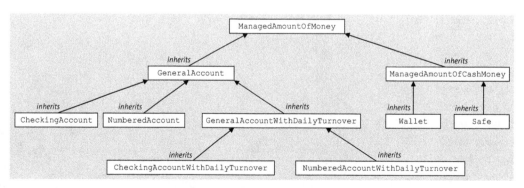

Figure 19.3 Extended Class Hierarchy of the Account Example

Both the Wallet and Safe classes manage a cash amount, which is why we first derive a ManagedCashAmount class from the ManagedMoneyAmount class. Unlike the general amount of money under management, a cash amount can't be negative. For this reason, the ManagedCashAmount class overrides the withdrawPossible method to avoid negative amounts.

In addition to the checking accounts for which transactions are limited by a maximum daily turnover, we now model checking accounts with no turnover limit through the CheckingAccount class. This class is derived directly from the GeneralAccount class and uses the same customer data as CheckingAccountWithDailyTurnover.

To be able to manage numbered accounts in addition to checking accounts, we'll create a new class that can be used to manage the customer data of a numbered account.[6] Thus, the NumberedAccount and NumberedAccountWithDailyTurnover classes can be derived from the GeneralAccount and GeneralAccountWithDailyTurnover classes, respectively.

Now let's look at how to implement the Wallet, Safe, CheckingAccount, NumberedAccount, and NumberedAccountWithDailyTurnover classes.

The ManagedCashAmount, Wallet, and Safe Classes

The ManagedCashAmount class adjusts the ManagedMoneyAmount class to avoid a negative value for the Amount attribute:

```python
class ManagedCashAmount(ManagedMoneyAmount):
    def __init__(self, cash_amount):
        if cash_amount < 0:
            cash_amount = 0
        super().__init__(cash_amount)
    def withdraw_possible(self, amount):
        return (self.amount >= amount)
```

In the constructor, we ensure that the amount cannot be initialized with a negative value, and the withdraw_possible method returns True exactly when the amount in the wallet is at least as large as the amount to be withdrawn.

The Wallet and Safe classes now inherit from the ManagedCashAmount class:

```python
class Wallet(ManagedCashAmount):
    # TODO: Special methods for a wallet
    pass
class Safe(ManagedCashAmount):
    # TODO: Special methods for a safe
    pass
```

---

6 This NumberedAccountCustomerData class, just like the CheckingAccountCustomerData class, isn't listed in Figure 19.3 because it doesn't inherit from ManagedMoneyAmount.

The two comments are intended to suggest that there are still methods missing at this point that turn a wallet and a safe into special managed money amounts. Because we aren't developing complete software at this point but simply demonstrating the basic extensibility of the program, we won't go into these details. As an exercise, you can consider for yourself what functionality makes sense in these two cases.

The CheckingAccount, NumberedAccount, and NumberedAccountWithDailyTurnover Classes

The CheckingAccount class inherits directly from the GeneralAccount class:

```
class CheckingAccount(GeneralAccount):
    def __init__(self, owner, account_number, account_balance):
        customer_data = CheckingAccountCustomerData(owner, account_number)
        super().__init__(customer_data, account_balance)
```

Similar to the CheckingAccountCustomerData class, we introduce the NumberedAccount CustomerData class to manage the customer data of a numbered account. In our model, a numbered account is described by an identification number:

```
class NumberedAccountCustomerData:
    def __init__(self, identification_number):
        self.identification_number = identification_number
    def show(self):
        print("Identification number:", self.identification_number)
```

Using this class, we can define the NumberedAccount and NumberedAccountWithDailyTurn over classes:

```
class NumberedAccount(GeneralAccount):
    def __init__(self, identification_number, account_balance):
        customer_data = NumberedAccountCustomerData(identification_number)
        super().__init__(customer_data, account_balance)
class NumberedAccountWithDailyTurnover(GeneralAccountWithDailyTurnover):
    def __init__(self, account_number, account_balance, max_daily_turnover):
        customer_data = NumberedAccountCustomerData(account_number)
        super().__init__(customer_data, account_balance, max_daily_turnover)
```

For demonstration purposes, we use the two classes in a small sample program:

```
>>> na1 = NumberedAccount(113427613185, 5000)
>>> na2 = NumberedAccountWithDailyTurnover(45657364234, 12000, 3000)
>>> na1.withdraw(1000)
True
>>> na2.deposit(1500)
True
>>> na1.money_transfer(na2, 2000)
False
```

```
>>> na1.show()
Identification number: 113427613185
Amount: 4000.00
>>> na2.show()
Identification number: 45657364234
Amount: 13500.00
Today already 1500.00 of 3000.00 USD turned over
```

Instances na1 and na2 of both the NumberedAccount class and the NumberedAccountWith DailyTurnover class are created. Then 1,000 USD is withdrawn from the first account and 1,500 USD is deposited into the second. Finally, we try to transfer 2,000 USD from account na1 to account na2. Because this would exceed the daily turnover of na2, the transfer fails.

As the output shows, the two classes work just like the other account classes.

19.3.4 Outlook

The great advantage of inheritance is that you can derive new classes from existing classes and then adapt them to the problem to be solved. In doing so, the derived class can draw on the entire functionality provided by the base class. Consequently, only the methods not suited for the new problem must be implemented or overridden.

For example, if we were to develop the CurrentAccount, NumberedAccount, Current AccountWithDailyTurnover, and NumberedAccountWithDailyTurnover classes based on the Account class, without resorting to inheritance, we'd have to reimplement the deposit and withdraw methods in each of these classes. This would have resulted in very similar code in several places in our program. This duplication of code unnecessarily inflates the size of a program, which makes maintenance and further development more diffi-cult as work or corrections always have to be carried out in several places at the same time.

Based on intelligent structuring using inheritance, you can develop programs that work with a minimum of functionality duplication.

In large software projects, we don't deal with just a handful of classes, as in our model example, but with hundreds or thousands of classes. In such an environment, the sav-ings made by means of inheritance are even more noticeable.

19.4 Multiple Inheritance

Up to this point, we've always let a subclass inherit from exactly one base class. How-ever, there are situations where a class should inherit the capabilities of two or even more base classes to achieve the desired result. This concept, where a class inherits from multiple base classes, is referred to as *multiple inheritance*.

19

If you want a class to inherit from multiple base classes, you can write the base classes separated by commas in the parentheses after the class name:

```
class NewClass(BaseClass1, BaseClass2, BaseClass3):
    # Definition of methods and attributes
    pass
```

In this example, the NewClass class inherits from three classes: BaseClass1, BaseClass2, and BaseClass3.

Multiple inheritance is a very complex topic, which is why we'll limit ourselves here to just one abstract example to help you understand the idea behind it.

Assume we have two classes to describe off-road vehicles and watercraft: Offroad Vehicle and Watercraft. Now, if we want to define an AmphibiousVehicle class, both the OffroadVehicle class and the Watercraft class are eligible as base classes because an amphibious vehicle fits into both categories.

It's therefore consistent to let the AmphibiousVehicle class inherit from both of these classes, as illustrated by Figure 19.4.

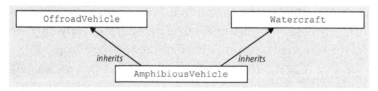

Figure 19.4 Multiple Inheritance Using the Example of an Amphibious Vehicle

As a result, the AmphibiousVehicle class inherits the methods of both the OffroadVehicle and Watercraft classes.

It's no coincidence that only a few languages support the concept of multiple inheritance, as there are a number of principle problems.

For example, say that several base classes implement a method with the same name. The inheriting class then inherits this method from whichever base class is furthest to the left in the list of base classes.

Now, two methods with the same name don't have to perform the same task at all. So in the worst case, the inheriting class may become unusable because it can inherit only one of the conflicting methods.

In practice, multiple inheritance usually can be circumvented, so we won't discuss it any further here.

19.5   Property Attributes

Sometimes it's useful to manipulate access to the attributes of a class according to certain rules. For example, there are attributes for which only certain values make sense. In our Account class (Section 19.2.2), for example, there is the daily_turnover attribute, whose values should always be positive; otherwise, they wouldn't make sense.

19.5.1   Setters and Getters

Setter and getter methods represent a concept of object-oriented programming for controlling access to attributes. Instead of accessing an attribute directly, access to it is controlled by special methods.

To keep the following example manageable, we'll introduce a new class A that has an attribute managed via setter and getter methods. The transfer to the account example is a simple exercise:

```python
class A:
    def __init__(self):
        self._x = 100
    def get_x(self):
        return self._x
    def set_x(self, value):
        if value < 0:
            return
        self._x = value
```

Using the get_x getter method and the set_x setter method, we can now work with the attribute _x of A, whereby negative assignments of _x are prevented by set_x:

```python
a = A()
print(a.get_x())
a.set_x(300)
print(a.get_x())
a.set_x(-20)
print(a.get_x())
```

The output of this example shows that the attempt to set _x to the value -20 fails:

```
100
300
300
```

> **Note**
>
> Python provides no enforced protection against attributes being used directly without using setter and getter methods. For this reason, it's still possible to access the _x attribute directly with a._x in the preceding example.
>
> It's a convention among Python developers not to use attributes and methods starting with an underscore from the outside if possible. Such attributes and methods are considered implementation details and don't belong to the interface of the class.
>
> This is why we chose the name _x for the attribute in our example.

19.5.2 Defining Property Attributes

The explicit management of attributes by means of setter and getter methods is messy because, when using a class, you now have to distinguish between attributes you are allowed to use directly and those whose access needs to be controlled by setter and getter methods.

The so-called *property attributes* solve this problem by implicitly calling setter and getter methods when writing or reading an attribute.

We can use them to adapt our class so that it can be used in the following way, and we can still guarantee for valid assignments of x:

```
a = A()
a.x = 300
print(a.x)
a.x = -20
print(a.x)
```

To achieve this, we need to create x as a property attribute using the built-in property function.

property([fget, fset, fdel, doc])

For the fget parameter, a reference to a getter method for the new attribute is expected. The fset parameter specifies the associated setter method. The fdel parameter can be used to additionally specify a method that is to be executed when the attribute is deleted via del. The attribute can be provided with a so-called docstring via the doc parameter. You can find more information on the docstring concept in Chapter 35, Section 35.1.

We now extend class A with a property attribute x that uses the get_x and set_x methods for access. Internally, the value of x is still stored in the _x attribute. We also add output to the get_x and set_x methods to see that they are actually called implicitly:

```
class A:
    def __init__(self):
        self.x = 100
    def get_x(self):
        print("Getter called")
        return self._x
    def set_x(self, value):
        print("Setter called")
        if value < 0:
            return
        self._x = value
    x = property(get_x, set_x)
a = A()
a.x = 300
print(a.x)
a.x = -20
print(a.x)
```

As you can see from the output, the setter and getter methods were implicitly called when the attribute was accessed. In particular, this was the case when the x attribute was initialized in the constructor. In addition, the invalid assignment of the -20 value was prevented:

```
Setter called
Setter called
Getter called
300
Setter called
Getter called
300
```

When using setter and getter methods, keep in mind that doing so causes a method to be called for every attribute access, which can slow a program down if there are many such accesses.

19.6 Static Methods

The methods and attributes we've defined for our classes so far have always referred to concrete instances. In particular, each instance of the Account class (Section 19.2.2) has its own values for its owner, account_number, account_balance, max_daily_turnover, and turnover_today attributes, and the money_transfer, deposit, withdraw, and show methods can be meaningfully called only in conjunction with an existing instance of the Account class.

Such methods and attributes, which always refer to concrete instances, are referred to as *nonstatic*. This is contrasted with the *static* methods and attributes that are shared by all instances of a class.

To define a static method, you can use the built-in staticmethod function. In the following example, a class A is defined that has a static method m:

```
>>> class A:
...     def m():
...         print("Hello static method!")
...     m = staticmethod(m)
>>> A.m()
Hello static method!
```

A static method is defined like a normal function and bound to a class as a static method by the staticmethod function.

Because a static method doesn't refer to an instance of the class, it doesn't require a self parameter. Moreover, it can be called directly from the class without the need to create an instance first.

In Python, static methods are often used to provide alternative constructors. For example, we can extend the Account class with a static method that creates a junior account. In this regard, a junior account is characterized by a preset low daily limit:

```
class Account:
    # The remaining methods will be placed here
    def junior_account(owner, account_number, account_balance):
        return Account(owner, account_number, account_balance, 20)
    junior_account = staticmethod(junior_account)
jr = Account.junior_account("Ethan Peters", 436574, 67)
jr.show()
```

The output of this program looks as follows:

```
Account of Ethan Peters
Current account balance: 67.00 USD
(Today already 0.00 of 20 USD turned over)
```

Thus, the junioraccount method in turn creates a new instance of the Account class, passing the fixed value 20 for the daily limit.

Such an alternative constructor is also referred to as a *factory function*.

19.7   Class Methods

Besides the static methods that can exist separately from an instance, there is another kind of method that doesn't refer to an instance of a class. These so-called *class methods* expect a reference to the class for which they are called as the first parameter. To define a class method, you can use the built-in classmethod function.

In the following example, the three A, B, and C classes are defined, where C and B inherit from A, respectively. Class A has a class method m that outputs the type of the instance that was used to call the method:

```
class A:
    def m(cls):
        print("I am", cls)
    m = classmethod(m)
class B(A):
    pass
class C(A):
    pass
A.m()
a = A()
b = B()
c = C()
a.m()
b.m()
c.m()
```

The output of the program looks as follows:

```
I am <class '__main__.A'>
I am <class '__main__.A'>
I am <class '__main__.B'>
I am <class '__main__.C'>
```

Using A.m(), we call the class method m of A without referring to an instance of the class. As the first line of the output shows, for the first parameter cls of m, class A itself was passed.

We then create instances of classes A, B, and C and call method m on these new instances. Again, for the cls parameter, each would pass the class of the instance it was called with. In an ordinary method, a reference to the instance itself would have been passed as the first parameter.

Note

Both staticmethod and classmethod are typically used as *function decorators*. You'll learn more about this topic in Chapter 23.

19.8 Class Attributes

In addition to class methods, there are also attributes that don't refer to instances of the class, but to the class itself. These attributes can be accessed both via the class itself and via its instances.

The following example defines a class D with a class attribute x:

```
class D:
    x = 10
print(D.x)
d = D()
print(d.x)
```

A class attribute thus can be created directly by an assignment within the body of the class statement. The example produces the following output:

```
10
10
```

So again, you can access class attributes both directly through the class and through instances of the class.

19.9 Built-in Functions for Object-Oriented Programming

From Chapter 17, Section 17.14, you already know many Built-in Functions, which are available to the programmer at any time. In the overview in Chapter 17, Section 17.14, we have intentionally left out Built-in Functions that relate to object-oriented programming in order to discuss them here. Table 19.2 lists those built-in functions that are specifically related to objects and classes.

Name	Description
getattr(object, name, [default])	Returns the value of the name attribute of the object instance.
setattr(object, name, value)	Sets the value of the name attribute of the object instance to the value value.
hasattr(object, name)	Checks whether the object instance has the name attribute. If the attribute is present, True will be returned, otherwise False.
delattr(object, name)	Removes the name attribute from the object instance.

Table 19.2 Built-In Functions for Object Orientation

Name	Description
isinstance(object, classinfo)	Checks if the object instance is an instance of the class(es) described by classinfo.
issubclass(class_, classinfo)	Checks whether the class_ class is a subclass of the class(es) described by classinfo.

Table 19.2 Built-In Functions for Object Orientation (Cont.)

19.9.1   Functions for Managing the Attributes of an Instance

To manage the attributes of an instance, you can use the setattr, getattr, and delattr functions. An attribute can be accessed by passing the name of the attribute as a string.

getattr(object, name, [default])

This function returns the attribute with the name name of the object instance, if this attribute exists. If default is passed, the value of default is returned if the name attribute isn't present.

The following example accesses an existing attribute and a nonexisting attribute using getattr. Here the getattr(a, "x") call is equivalent to a.x:

```
>>> class A:
...     def __init__(self):
...         self.x = 42
>>> a = A()
>>> getattr(a, "x")
42
>>> getattr(a, "y", 404)
404
```

If the attribute isn't present and no value is passed for default, getattr will raise an AttributeError exception:

```
>>> getattr(a, "y")
Traceback (most recent call last):
  File "<stdin>", line 1, in <module>
AttributeError: 'A' object has no attribute 'y'
```

setattr(object, name, value)

This function sets the value of the name attribute of the object instance to the value value.

The following example defines a class that creates 10 attributes in a loop:

```
>>> class B:
...     def __init__(self):
...         for i in range(10):
...             setattr(self, "x{}".format(i), i)
>>> b = B()
>>> b.x3
3
>>> b.x8
8
```

A call of the form setattr(a, "x", value) is equivalent to a.x = value.

delattr(object, name)

Using delattr, you can selectively delete attributes of an instance. Let's again use the B class from the preceding setattr example:

```
>>> b = B()
>>> b.x4
4
>>> delattr(b, "x4")
>>> b.x4
Traceback (most recent call last):
  File "<stdin>", line 1, in <module>
AttributeError: 'B' object has no attribute 'x4'
```

The delattr(b, "x4") call has the same effect as del b.x4.

19.9.2 Functions for Information about the Class Hierarchy

In this section, we'll use the following sample program as our starting point:

```
class A:
    pass
class B(A):
    pass
class C(B):
    pass
class D:
    pass
a = A()
b = B()
c = C()
d = D()
```

isinstance(object, classinfo)

This function checks whether object is an instance of the classinfo class(es) and returns either True or False accordingly. Either a single class or a tuple of multiple classes can be passed for the classinfo parameter:

```
>>> isinstance(a, A)
True
>>> isinstance(a, (B,C))
False
>>> isinstance(a, (A,B,C))
True
```

The return value of isinstance is True even if object is the instance of a class that inherits from one of the classes in classinfo:

```
>>> isinstance(c, A)
True
>>> isinstance(c, (B,D))
True
```

issubclass(class_, classinfo)

The issubclass function can be used to check whether the class_ class[7] was derived from one of the classes in classinfo. Just as with isinstance, either a single class or a tuple of multiple classes can be passed for classinfo:

```
>>> issubclass(B,A)
True
>>> issubclass(B,(D,A))
True
>>> issubclass(A,C)
False
>>> issubclass(D,(A,B,C))
False
```

19.10   Inheriting Built-In Data Types

Since data types and classes were unified in Python 2.3, Python is object-oriented from the ground up. This means that basically everything you come across when using Python is an instance of some class. From the simple number to the classes[8] themselves, each object has its own attributes and methods.

---

7 The underscore at the end of class_ was added so that the parameter doesn't collide with the class keyword used to define a class.

8 The data type of class instances are so-called *metaclasses*, whose use is not described in this book.

In particular, it's possible to inherit from built-in data types such as list or dict.

The following example implements a subclass of list that automatically sorts its elements after each change:

```python
class SortedList(list):
    def __init__(self, *args, **kwargs):
        super().__init__(*args, **kwargs)
        self.sort()
    def __setitem__(self, key, value):
        super().__setitem__(key, value)
        self.sort()
    def append(self, value):
        super().append(value)
        self.sort()
    def extend(self, sequence):
        super().extend(sequence)
        self.sort()
    def insert(self, index, value):
        super().insert(index, value)
        self.sort()
    def reverse(self):
        pass
    def __iadd__(self, s):
        res = super().__iadd__(s)
        self.sort()
        return res
    def __imul__(self, n):
        res = super().__imul__(n)
        self.sort()
        return res
```

To do this, all methods of list that insert elements into the list are overridden so that the list is sorted after the respective operation. Because the list is sorted, it shouldn't be possible to reverse its order, which is why the reverse method is deprived of its functionality.

For the realization of the methods, of course, the implementation of list is still used.

The following sample program illustrates the use of the new class:

```python
l = SortedList([6,4,3])
print(l)
l.append(2)
print(l)
```

```
l.extend([67,0,-56])
print(l)
l += [100,5]
print(l)
l *= 2
print(l)
```

As you can see, the new class can be used just like list.[9] Only the outputs clarify the difference in functionality:

```
[3, 4, 6]
[2, 3, 4, 6]
[-56, 0, 2, 3, 4, 6, 67]
[-56, 0, 2, 3, 4, 5, 6, 67, 100]
[-56, -56, 0, 0, 2, 2, 3, 3, 4, 4, 5, 5, 6, 6, 67, 67, 100, 100]
```

Although inserted in an arbitrary order, the elements of the list are sorted after each operation.

19.11   Magic Methods and Magic Attributes

There are a number of special methods and attributes in Python to provide classes with special capabilities. The names of these methods and attributes each begin and end with two underscores. In the course of the last sections, you already got to know one of these so-called magic methods or magic attributes—namely, the constructor named __init__.

The handling of these methods and attributes is "magical" in that they are usually not used directly by name, but are used implicitly in the background when needed. For example, the __init__ constructor is called whenever a new object of a class is created, even if there is no explicit call—for example, with classname.__init__() in the appropriate place.

Many magic methods allow you to customize the behavior of built-in functions and operators for your own classes—so that instances of your classes can be compared to the < and > comparison operators, for example.

19.11.1   General Magic Methods

Table 19.3 contains frequently used magic methods.

---

9 We assume that an ordering exists for the elements of the list. If you insert elements that can't be sorted, this will result in an error.

Name	Description
`__init__(self, ...)`	The constructor of a class. Called when a new instance is created. For more information, see Chapter 19, Section 19.2.2.
`__del__(self)`	The finalizer of a class. Called when an instance is destroyed.
`__repr__(self)`	The return value of `obj.__repr__` specifies what `repr(obj)` should return. If possible, this should be valid Python code that creates the `obj` instance when executed.
`__str__(self)`	The return value of `obj.__str__` specifies what `str(obj)` should return. If possible, this should be a human-readable representation of `obj` in the form of a `str` instance.
`__bytes__(self)`	The return value of `obj.__bytes__` specifies what `bytes(obj)` should return. This should be a `bytes` instance.
`__bool__(self)`	The `__bool__` method should return a truth value indicating how to convert the object to a `bool` instance. If `__bool__` isn't implemented, the return value of `__len__` is used instead. If both methods don't exist, all instances of the class in question are treated as `True`.
`__call__(self, ...)`	The `__call__` method makes sure that the instances of a class can be called like functions.
`__complex__(self)`	Specifies which value the built-in `complex` function should return for an instance of the class.
`__int__(self)`	Specifies which value the built-in `int` function should return for an instance of the class.
`__float__(self)`	Specifies which value the built-in `float` function should return for an instance of the class.
`__round__(self, [n])`	Specifies which value the built-in `round` function should return for an instance of the class. The n parameter specifies the number of decimal places to be rounded.
`__hash__(self)`	The `__hash__` method of an instance determines which value the built-in `hash` function should return for the instance.
`__index__(self)`	If a data type is to be used as an index, as required for slicing, for example, it must override the `__index__` parameterless method. The return value of `__index__` must be an integer (`int`).

Table 19.3 General Magic Methods

In the following sections, we'll describe some of these methods in greater detail.

__del__(self)

The __del__ (self) finalizer of an instance is called when no more references point to the instance and it is deleted by Python's memory management. In the following example, the finalizer of class A is therefore called only once:

```
>>> class A:
...      def __del__(self):
...           print("This is the finalizer speaking.")
>>> a = A()
>>> b = a
>>> del a
>>> del b
This is the finalizer speaking.
```

Thus, the del x statement doesn't immediately call x.__del__.

The following example shows two instances a and b that reference each other cyclically via the attribute x. This means that there are still references to the two instances even if they are no longer accessible to the rest of the program:

```
>>> class B:
...      def __init__(self, name):
...           self.Name = name
...      def __del__(self):
...           print("This is the finalizer of", self.Name)
>>> a = B("a")
>>> b = B("b")
>>> a.x = b
>>> b.x = a
>>> del a,b
>>>
```

Interestingly, no finalizer of the nonaccessible instances is called at this point. The calls of the __del__ method don't occur until the Python interpreter is terminated:

```
>>> exit()
This is the finalizer of a
This is the finalizer of b
```

So you can't rely on the finalizer being called promptly after the last accessible reference to an instance has been deleted.[10]

---

10 On the other hand, you can also not rely on the finalizer *not* being called immediately after deleting the last reference, as shown in the example. This is an implementation detail of the Python interpreter which might change in future Python versions.

Note

Because Python's memory management takes care of releasing memory, the finalizer is of less importance than the destructor in other languages with manual memory management, such as C++.

In particular, you should be aware there's no guarantee that Python calls the finalizer within a certain time after deleting the last reference to an instance. Finalizers in Python are therefore only suitable to a limited extent for cleanup tasks such as closing files or terminating network connections.

Classes that need to perform necessary cleanup tasks such as closing open file objects should instead be implemented as context managers (see Chapter 22).

__call__(self, ...)

The __call__ method makes sure the instances of a class can be called like functions.

The following example implements a Power class that's used to calculate powers. This information about which exponent is to be used is passed to the constructor as a parameter. Through the __call__ method, the instances of Power can be called like functions to calculate powers:

```python
class Power:
    def __init__(self, exponent):
        self.exponent = exponent

    def __call__(self, basis):
        return basis ** self.exponent
```

Now we can comfortably work with powers:

```python
>>> power_of_3 = Power(3)
>>> power_of_3(2)
8
>>> power_of_3(5)
125
```

__hash__(self)

The __hash__ method of an instance determines which value the built-in function hash should return for the instance. The hash values must be integers and are especially important for using instances as keys for dictionaries.

The condition for a valid hash value is that objects that are considered to be the same when compared via == also have the same hash value. Furthermore, the hash value of an instance mustn't change at runtime, which is why it can only be meaningfully defined for immutable data types.

> **Note**
>
> A class that implements __hash__ should also implement the __eq__ method. This makes it *hashable*. Only hashable instances can be used as keys for a dictionary or stored in sets.

Customizing Access to Attributes

The methods and attributes in Table 19.4 are used to specify what Python should do when the attributes of an instance are read or written.

Name	Description
__dict__	Each instance has an attribute called __dict__ that stores the members of the instance in a dictionary.
__getattr__(self, name)	Called when the attribute with the name name is read but doesn't exist. The __getattr__ method should either return a value to apply to the attribute or generate an AttributeError.
__getattribute__(self, name)	Called whenever the value of the attribute named name is read, even if the attribute already exists.
__setattr__(self, name, value)	The __setattr__ method is called whenever the value of an attribute is changed by assignment or a new attribute is created.
__delattr__(self, name)	Called when the attribute named name is deleted via del.
__slots__	Instructs Python to manage the attributes of a class in a way that saves memory.

Table 19.4 Methods and Attributes for Controlling Access to Attributes

In the following sections, we'll describe some of the table entries in greater detail.

__dict__

Each instance has an attribute called __dict__, which stores the members of the instance in a dictionary.

So the following two lines of code produce the same result, assuming obj is an instance of a class that defines an attribute a:

```
>>> obj.a
'The value of attribute a'
>>> obj.__dict__["a"]
'The value of attribute a'
```

__getattribute__(self, name)

Called whenever the value of the attribute named name is read, even if the attribute already exists.

If a class implements both __getattr__ and __getattribute__(self, name), only the latter function is called when reading attributes, unless __getattribute__ itself calls __getattr__.

> **Note**
>
> You should never access the attributes of the instance inside __getattribute__ with self.attribute because to do so would result in an endless recursion.
>
> Instead, you should always use ___getattribute__ of the base class—for example, object.__getattribute__(self, "attribute").

__setattr__(self, name, value)

The __setattr__ method is called whenever the value of an attribute is changed by assignment or a new attribute is created. The name parameter specifies a string containing the name of the attribute to be modified. With value, the new value is passed.

For example, __setattr__ can be used to specify which attributes an instance is allowed to have at all, by simply ignoring all other values or acknowledging them with error output.

> **Note**
>
> Never use an assignment of the form self.attribute = value inside __setattr__ to set the attributes to specific values as this would result in an endless recursion: __setattr__ would be called again for each assignment.
>
> To change attribute values in __setattr__, you should use the __setattr__ method of the base classes—for example, object.__setattr__(self, "attribute", value).

__slots__

Instances in Python are flexible and powerful, which makes working with Python pretty convenient. For example, you can add attributes dynamically at runtime:

```
>>> class A:
...     pass
>>> a = A()
>>> a.x = 10
>>> a.x
10
```

This flexibility comes at the cost of computation time and memory, since a `dict` instance is created for each instance to manage the attributes.

If you define a simple class with few attributes, of which there are a very large number of instances at runtime, this can unnecessarily waste memory.

To save memory in such a case, you can restrict the attributes of the instances of a class when defining the class. This loses the flexibility to be able to dynamically create new attributes, but the Python interpreter can then manage the attributes more efficiently, saving memory.

The following example defines a class B whose instances can only have the attributes x and y:

```
>>> class B:
...     __slots__ = ("x", "y")
...     def __init__(self):
...         self.x = 1
...         self.y = 2
>>> b = B()
>>> b.x
1
>>> b.y
2
>>> b.z = 3
Traceback (most recent call last):
  File "<stdin>", line 1, in <module>
AttributeError: 'B' object has no attribute 'z'
```

As you can see, it's not possible to create another attribute z. As a result, instances of class B consume less memory than those of a class without a `__slots__` definition.

> **Note**
>
> There are some peculiarities concerning the handling of `__slots__`. For example, a `__slots__` definition can't be inherited by subclasses.

19.11.2 Overloading Operators

An *operator* is a rule that calculates a new value from a set of *operands*. You've already encountered a lot of operators in this book—for example, in the form of arithmetic operators:

```
>>> 1 + 2
3
```

In this example, the + operator was used to calculate the sum of two int instances. However, the + operator can also be used to concatenate strings—for example:

```
>>> "Hello " + "world"
'Hello world'
```

This adjusted behavior of an operator is made possible by internally calling a special method that determines what the operator should do. In the case of the + operator, this is the __add__ method. Therefore, the following two expressions are equivalent:[11]

```
>>> 1 + 2
3
>>> (1).__add__(2)
3
```

So you can also define operators for your own classes by overriding the methods following them.

As an example, we'll implement a small class for managing lengths with units that supports the operators for addition and subtraction. The __sub__ method is used to implement the - operator.

The class will internally convert all measurements into meters for the calculations. Their definition is as follows:

```
class Length:
    conversion = {
        "m": 1, "dm": 0.1, "cm": 0.01,
        "mm": 0.001, "km": 1000,
        "ft": 0.3048,  # feet
        "in": 0.0254,  # inch
        "mi": 1609.344 # miles
    }
    def __init__(self, value, unit):
        self.value = value
        self.unit = unit
```

---

11 The parentheses around the 1 are necessary because a period directly following the 1 would be interpreted as a decimal point.

```
    def __str__(self):
        return "{:f} {}".format(self.value, self.unit)
    def __add__(self, other):
        z = self.value * self.conversion[self.unit]
        z += other.value * self.conversion[other.unit]
        z /= self.conversion[self.unit]
        return Length(z, self.unit)
    def __sub__(self, other):
        z = self.value * self.conversion[self.unit]
        z -= other.value * self.conversion [other.unit]
        z /= self.conversion[self.unit]
        return Length(z, self.unit)
```

The Length.conversion dictionary contains factors used to convert common measures of length into meters. The __add__ and __sub__ methods overload the operator for addition (+) and the operator for subtraction (-) respectively, by first converting the numerical values of both operands into meters according to their units, then offsetting them, and finally converting them back into the unit of the operand further to the left.

Let's take a look at the following application of the Length class:

```
>>> a1 = Length(5, "cm")
>>> a2 = Length(3, "dm")
>>> print(a1 + a2)
35.000000 cm
>>> print(a2 + a1)
3.500000 dm
```

As you can see, the calculations work as they should. It's remarkable that the unit in the output changes depending on the order of operands. This is due to the fact that the Length class here always uses the unit of the operand further to the left as the unit of the result.

> **Note**
>
> If an operation implemented in a binary operator is not performable due to the data type of other, you should return the NotImplemented constant. This way, the interpreter is encouraged to try alternative ways to compute the result, including the operator implementations with reversed operand order, which we will cover next.
>
> Note the difference between the NotImplemented constant and the NotImplementedError exception type.

In addition to the + and - operators, Python also contains a number of other operators. We distinguish among several types of operators, as shown in Table 19.5.

Category	Description	Examples
Comparison operators	Compare two instances with each other and return a `bool` instance as the result.	`<, >, ==`
Binary arithmetic operators	Operators that are applied to two operands. The return type depends on the operator and the operands.	`+, -, *, /, %, @`
Binary operators with reversed operand order	Operators that are applied to two operands. The return type depends on the operator and the operands.	`+, -, *, /, %, @`
Augmented assignments	Operators that combine an operation and an assignment.	`+=, -=, *=, /=, @=`
Unary operators	Operators with only one operand, such as a sign.	`+, -`

Table 19.5 Types of Operators

Note

The @ operator is a new addition in Python 3.5 and is used to provide an easy-to-read syntax for matrix multiplications.

Comparison Operators

The following magic methods are used to customize the behavior of the comparison operators for the class.

For example, to compare two instances of the Account class (see Chapter 19, Section 19.2.2), we can use the account number. This provides a reasonable interpretation for the comparison of accounts via ==. The method for comparisons using == is referred to as __eq__ (from *equals*, "is equal to") and expects an instance as parameter with which the object is to be compared and for which __eq__ was called.

The following sample code extends the Account class from the introduction to object orientation with the ability to be meaningfully compared via ==:

```python
class Account:
    def __init__(self, owner, account_number, account_balance,
                    max_daily_turnover=1500):
        self.owner = owner
        self.account_number = account_number
        self.account_balance = account_balance
        self.max_daily_turnover = max_daily_turnover
```

```
        self.turnover_today = 0

    def __eq__(self, a2):
        return self.account_number == a2.account_number
```

Now we create three accounts, two of which will have the same account number, and compare them with the == operator. Of course, this scenario will always remain a pipe dream for Donald Duck:

```
>>> account1 = Account("Scrooge McDuck", 1337, 9999999999999999)
>>> account2 = Account("Donald Duck", 1337, 1.5)
>>> account3 = Account("Gladstone Gander", 2674, 50000)
>>> account1 == account2
True
>>> account1 == account3
False
```

Python replaces the statement account1 == account2 internally with account1.__eq__ (account2) when executed.

In addition to the __eq__ method, there are a number of other comparison methods, each corresponding to a comparison operator. All these methods expect another parameter besides self, which must reference the instance with which self is to be compared.

Table 19.6 shows all comparison methods and their equivalents. The origin column can help you to better remember the method names and their meaning.

Operator	Method	Meaning
<	__lt__(self, other)	Less than
<=	__le__(self, other)	Less than or equal to
==	__eq__(self, other)	Equal
!=	__ne__(self, other)	Not equal
>	__gt__(self, other)	Greater than
>=	__ge__(self, other)	Greater than or equal to

Table 19.6 Magic Methods for Comparisons

Note

If a class doesn't implement any of the __eq__ or __ne__ methods, instances of the class are compared using == and != based on their identity.

If it isn't possible to compare the instance referenced by `self` with `other`, then the constant `NotImplemented` should be returned. In this case, Python tries to evaluate the expression using fallback mechanisms such as operator implementations with reversed operand order.

Binary Operators

A binary operator is an operator that processes two operands. Examples of binary operators are +, -, *, and /.

All methods for overloading binary operators expect a parameter that references the second operand. The first operand used is always the instance passed for the `self` parameter. Its return value must be a new instance containing the result of the calculation.

An example of using binary operators can be found at the beginning of Section 19.11.2.

Table 19.7 lists all binary operators[12] and their corresponding magic methods.

Operator	Magic Method	Operator	Magic Method
+	__add__(self, other)	%	__mod__(self, other)
-	__sub__(self, other)	>>	__lshift__(self, other)
*	__mul__(self, other)	<<	__rshift__(self, other)
/	__truediv__(self, other)	&	__and__(self, other)
//	__floordiv__(self, other)	|	__or__(self, other)
divmod()	__divmod__(self, other)	^	__xor__(self, other)
**	__pow__(self, other, [modulo])	@	__matmul__(self, other)

Table 19.7 Magic Methods for Binary Operators

If it isn't possible to perform the operation using the instances referenced by `self` with `other`, then the constant `NotImplemented` should be returned.

Binary Arithmetic Operators with Reversed Operand Order

When Python is to evaluate an expression of the form *operand1 operator operand2*, such as 2 * "abc", it first tries to use a matching method of the first operand. If that doesn't exist or returns `NotImplemented`, then an attempt is made to find a corresponding method for the second operand.

---

12 Of course, the comparison operators are also binary operators. However, for the sake of clarity, we've described them separately.

However, the second operand must implement a special method for swapped operands.[13] Table 19.8 lists all method names available for this and the corresponding operators, with an equivalent for each of the binary operators.

Operator	Magic Method	Operator	Magic Method
+	__radd__(self, other)	divmod()	__rdivmod__(self, other)
-	__rsub__(self, other)	>>	__rlshift__(self, other)
*	__rmul__(self, other)	<<	__rrshift__(self, other)
/	__rtruediv__(self, other)	&	__rand__(self, other)
//	__rfloordiv__(self, other)	|	__ror__(self, other)
**	__rpow__(self, other, [modulo])	^	__rxor__(self, other)
%	__rmod__(self, other)	@	__rmatmul__(self, other)

Table 19.8 Magic Methods for Binary Operators of the Right Operand

If it isn't possible to perform the operation using the instances referenced by self with other, then the constant NotImplemented should be returned.

Augmented Assignments

You can also overload the augmented assignments, which associate an arithmetic operation with an assignment. In case of an augmented assignment, the respective operator is followed by an equal sign:

```
>>> a = 10
>>> a += 5
>>> a
15
```

By default, Python uses the operator itself for such assignments, so a += 5 is internally executed like a = a + 5.

However, this procedure is not always desired, since in this case += always creates a new instance of the respective data type for the result. Particularly with mutable container types such as lists or dictionaries we would like to implement augmented assignments *in place*. In the case of lists += is equivalent to a call of the method extend.

Table 19.9 contains all operators for augmented assignments and the corresponding methods.

---

13 The fact that attention is paid to the order here is important because is it not true that all operations do not care about the order of the operands. For example, it makes a difference whether "x" + "y " or "y" + "x" is evaluated.

Operator	Magic Method	Operator	Magic Method
+=	__iadd__(self, other)	>>=	__ilshift__(self, other)
-=	__isub__(self, other)	<<=	__irshift__(self, other)
*=	__imul__(self, other)	&=	__iand__(self, other)
/=	__itruediv__(self, other)	|=	__ior__(self, other)
//=	__ifloordiv__(self, other)	^=	__ixor__(self, other)
**=	__ipow__(self, other, [modulo])	@=	__imatmul__(self, other)
%=	__imod__(self, other)		

Table 19.9 Methods for Augmented Assignment

Note

Even if the augmented assignment operators modify the self instance, they must return a reference to the result of the calculation—in this case, self.

Unary Operators

The methods in Table 19.10 are used to overload the unary operators. Unlike binary operators, unary operators expect only one operand. Unary operators include the + and - signs, the built-in abs function to determine the absolute value, and the tilde character (~) to calculate the complement of a value.

Operator	Magic method	Operator	Magic method
+	__pos__(self)	abs	__abs__(self)
-	__neg__(self)	~	__invert__(self)

Table 19.10 Magic Methods for the Unary Operators

The methods should return the result if the calculation is successful. If it isn't possible to process the other operand, then NotImplemented should be returned.

19.11.3   Emulating Data Types: Duck Typing

In Python, the methods a data type implements decide which category of data types it belongs to. For this reason, you can make your own data types "look" like numeric or sequential data types, for example, by implementing the appropriate interface.

This concept of judging the type of an instance based on the methods present rather than the class is referred to as *duck typing*. The name goes back to the popular *duck test*. As formulated by the US poet James Whitcomb Riley (1849-1916), it reads:

"When I see a bird that walks like a duck and swims like a duck and quacks like a duck, I call that bird a duck."

Transferred to the instances in a program, this means that, for example, all instances are treated as numbers that behave in the same way as other numbers. It doesn't matter whether the instances are of the int, float, or complex types. In particular, it's possible to define a separate class that also behaves like a number and is thus treated like one.

The principle is not to forcefully implement as many operators and methods as possible, but only those that make sense for the class. All other methods should either not be implemented at all or return the constant NotImplemented.

In the following sections, you'll get to know the methods a data type must implement to be a numeric data type according to duck typing. We'll also cover the interfaces of sequences and mappings.

Emulating Numeric Data Types

A numeric data type should implement as many arithmetic operators as possible. It can also define methods to convert it to other numeric data types, if that's possible.

Table 19.11 provides an overview of the possible methods.

Name or Short Description	Description
Arithmetic operators	Calculation operators for the sum, difference, quotient, and so on
__complex__	Conversion to complex
__int__	Conversion to int
__float__	Conversion to float
__round__	Rounding of the value
__index__	Use as index

Table 19.11 Special Methods a Numeric Data Type Should Define if Possible

Implementing a Context Manager

A *context manager* is an instance that can be used in conjunction with the with statement. You can find out more about with in Chapter 22.

To be used with `with` as a context manager, two methods must be implemented, which are listed in Table 19.12.

Name	Description
`__enter__(self)`	Builds the context and returns the object to be used.
`__exit__(self, ...)`	Clears up after leaving the body of the `with` statement.

Table 19.12 Methods for Context Managers

In contrast to `__del__`, the immediate call of the `__exit__` method of a context manager is guaranteed as soon as the control flow leaves the associated `with` context. For this reason, context managers are particularly suitable for ensuring that certain resources, such as file objects, are released as soon as they are no longer needed.

Emulating Containers

Using the following methods, you can create your own container data types. A *container* is an instance that can *contain* other instances. Examples include the list, the dictionary, and the set.

A basic distinction is made between *sequential containers*, whose elements can be addressed via integers,[14] and *mapping containers*, whose indexes can have any shape.

Methods for General Containers

First, there's a set of methods that both sequential and mapping containers should implement (see Table 19.13).

Method	Description
`__len__(self)`	Returns the number of elements in the container as an integer.
`__getitem__(self, key)`	Reads one or more elements from the container when the [ ] operator is used.
`__setitem__(self, key, value)`	Modifies the element of the container associated with the key key.
`__delitem__(self, key)`	Removes the element with the key index from the container.

Table 19.13 Methods That Can Implement All Container Data Types

---

14 The elements should be numbered consecutively, starting with 0.

Method	Description
`__iter__(self)`	Must return an iterator over the values of the sequential container or the keys of the mapping container.
	For more information about iterators, see Chapter 21, Section 21.2.
`__contains__(self, item)`	Checks whether `item` is contained in the container.

Table 19.13 Methods That Can Implement All Container Data Types (Cont.)

Now we'll introduce the methods that are specifically intended for sequential containers.

Methods for Sequential Containers

All sequential containers should implement the addition (concatenation) and multiplication (repetition) methods in addition to the general methods for containers (see Table 19.14).

Methods	Description
`__add__(self, other)` `__radd__(self, other)` `__iadd__(self, other)`	Concatenates the sequence with the `other` sequence. In the case of a mutable data type, `__iadd__` should modify the instance referenced by `self`; that is, it should work in place.
`__mul__(self, other)` `__rmul__(self, other)` `__imul__(self, other)`	Should produce a sequence that emerges from the instance referenced by `self` by repeating it `other` times. For strings, for example, this looks as follows: `>>> 5*"a"` `'aaaaa'`

Table 19.14 General Methods for Sequential Containers

Mutable sequences should additionally define the methods shown in Table 19.15. For examples of these methods, you can take a look at the `list` data type in Chapter 12, Section 12.3.

Methods	Description
`append(x)`	Appends `x` to the end of the sequence.
`count(x)`	Counts the occurrences of `x` in the sequence.

Table 19.15 Methods for Mutable Sequences

Methods	Description
index(x, [i, j])	Returns the index of the first occurrence of x in the sequence. The optional i and j parameters can be used to narrow down the search range.
extend(s)	Extends the sequence by the elements of the sequence s.
insert(i, x)	Inserts the element x at position i in the sequence.
pop([i])	Returns the ith element of the sequence and removes it from it. If i isn't specified, the last element will be returned and then removed.
remove(x)	Removes the first occurrence of x in the sequence from it.
__reversed__(self)	Returns an iterator for reverse traversal of the sequential data type. The sequence doesn't get changed in the process.
reverse()	Reverses the order of the sequence in place.
sort([key, reverse])	Sorts the sequence in place.

Table 19.15 Methods for Mutable Sequences (Cont.)

Methods for Mapping Containers

All mapping data types should implement methods in addition to the methods for general containers; these additional methods are listed in Table 19.16.[15]

Method	Meaning
m.keys()	Returns an iterator over the keys of m.
m.values()	Returns an iterator over the values of m.
m.items()	Returns an iterator over the key-value pairs of m.
m.has_key(k)	Checks if the k key exists in m.
m.get(k, [d])	If the k key exists in m, m[k] is returned; otherwise d.
m.clear()	Removes all elements from m.
m.setdefault(k, [x])	If the k key exists in m, m[k] is returned. If the k key doesn't exist in m, m[k] is set to the value x and x is returned.
m.pop(k, [d])	If the k key exists in m, m[k] is returned and then deleted via del. If the k key doesn't exist in m, d is returned.

Table 19.16 Methods for Mapping Types

---

15 If the descriptions given here are not detailed enough for you, refer back to Chapter 13, Section 13.1.

Method	Meaning
m.popitem()	Returns an arbitrarily selected key-value pair from m and then removes it from m.
m.copy()	Returns a copy of m.
m.update(b)	Accepts all key-value pairs from b into m. Existing entries will be overridden.

Table 19.16 Methods for Mapping Types (Cont.)

19.12 Data Classes

A *data class* is an aggregation of data into a structured unit.

It's a structured collection of data that shares common semantics in the context of a program.

As a first introduction, let's assume we need to write a program that processes addresses, and an address should consist of a street number, street name, state, zip code,[16] and city:

```
2 Heritage Dr.
Quincy, MA 02171
```

For ease of processing, we want to store addresses so that the individual components can be accessed at any time. That means that saving the full address as a string, for example, is not an option. The tools known to us so far allow the following approaches to the representation of addresses in our program.

19.12.1 Tuples and Lists

One option is to represent addresses as tuples or lists with a defined sequence of elements:

```
>>> address = (2, "Heritage Dr", "MA", "02171", "Quincy")
```

This way of representing an address is simple and can be implemented quickly. However, access to individual elements of the address, such as the street number, is done via indexes fixed by convention:

```
>>> print(address[0])
2
```

---

16 We'll represent the zip code by a string, since there is the possibility of leading zeros.

This type of element access, whose semantics aren't obvious, makes the code increasingly confusing and cryptic. It also leads to the need for error-prone index adjustments in the code for a subsequent extension of the address tuple. In addition, due to errors or user input, lists and tuples of completely different structures can be processed by the program, which can ultimately cause errors in the program execution that are difficult to understand.

For these reasons, tuples and lists should be used for storing structured data only in exceptional cases or for very simple data structures.

19.12.2   Dictionaries

Many Python developers would represent a record like our address as a dictionary:

```
>>> address = {
...     "street_number": 2,
...     "street": "Heritage Dr",
...     "state": "MA",
...     "zip": "02171",
...     "city": "Quincy",
... }
```

In this way, some of the shortcomings of tuples and lists for storing structured data can be circumvented. For example, the element access code is now self-explanatory:

```
>>> print(address["street_number"])
2
```

Even the subsequent extension of an address dictionary is no problem. However, there is also no inherent check for completeness of the data set in the dictionary, so that incomplete addresses are also processed by our program. This flexibility can be a major advantage or disadvantage depending on the application scenario.

19.12.3   Named Tuples

The named tuple we discussed in Chapter 14, Section 14.5 represents one approach to mitigating the limitations of tuples for representing structured data. In this case, we create a new data type, addr, via namedtuple; when instantiated, it interprets a tuple with four entries as an address record and offers the individual elements of the address via attributes:

```
>>> import collections
>>> Address = collections.namedtuple(
...     "Address",
...     ("street_number", "street", "state", "zip", "city")
... )
```

```
>>> address = Address(2, "Heritage Dr", "MA", "02171", "Quincy")
>>> address
Address(street_number=2, street='Heritage Dr', state='MA', zip='02171',
        city='Quincy')
```

With the named tuple, accesses to address elements become attribute accesses and thus semantically unique in the code:

```
>>> print(address.street_number)
2
```

This attribute access enables an integrated development environment, for example, to automatically provide context-sensitive help. Beyond that, however, similar to the dictionary, no check for the consistency of the dataset takes place. Meaningful default values for individual address elements can't be defined either.

Another drawback of the solutions mentioned so far is that they inherit all properties of their respective base data types, tuple or dictionary. This makes named tuples immutable and iterable, for example, which might not make any sense depending on the use case. The adaptation of such a data type to the circumstances of the use case isn't possible without further ado.

19.12.4 Mutable Data Classes

Python 3.7 introduced data classes to the language for a comprehensive representation of structured data. A *data class* is created like a class using the class keyword, preceded by the dataclass decorator[17] from the dataclasses module:

```
>>> import dataclasses
>>> @dataclasses.dataclass
... class Address:
...     pass
```

The elements of the dataset to be represented in our Address data class are defined via class attributes:

```
>>> @dataclasses.dataclass
... class Address:
...     street_number: int
...     street: str
...     state: str
...     zip: str
...     city: str
```

---

17 For more information on decorators, see Chapter 23. An understanding of how decorators work isn't required for an introduction to data classes, so we'll just use the @ syntax for now and return to it later.

For each attribute, in addition to its name, the expected data type is specified, separated by a colon. For more details on the syntax of these *annotations*, see Chapter 24, Section 24.1. It's important to note that despite the annotations, there are no standard type checks.[18]

When instantiating the new `address` data type, the individual elements of the address can be passed as positional parameters or as keyword parameters:

```
>>> address = Address(2, "Heritage Dr", "MA", "02171", "Quincy")
>>> address
Address(street_number=2, street='Heritage Dr', state='MA', zip='02171',
       city='Quincy')
```

By default, a data class is a mutable data type, so the elements of the address can be assigned new values. In addition, some *magic methods* (Section 19.11) are added automatically, so that addresses can be compared with each other, for example.

19.12.5   Immutable Data Classes

Using the `frozen` parameter of the `dataclass` decorator, we can also create a data type for immutable addresses:

```
>>> @dataclasses.dataclass(frozen=True)
... class FrozenAddress:
...     street_number: int
...     street: str
...     state: str
...     zip: str
...     city: str
```

In this case, `FrozenAddress` becomes an *immutable* and *hashable* data type whose instances may also be used, for example, as keys of a dictionary or as elements of a set.

19.12.6   Default Values in Data Classes

Data classes allow individual attributes to be assigned default values. In the example, we assign the `city` attribute the default value `None`, which it should always have if it hasn't been specified during instantiation. In this way, the specification of a city becomes optional when instantiating addresses:

```
>>> @dataclasses.dataclass()
... class Address:
...     street_number: int
```

---

18   You can still implement type checks if they are needed. More information on this topic can be found in Chapter 24.

```
...        street: str
...        state: str
...        zip: str
...        city: str = ""
```

By adding the __post_init__ method, which is called after executing the constructor automatically defined for the data class, we can revise the passed information when instantiating an address. This is useful, for example, to check it for consistency or, as in our case, to automatically replace optional information:

```
>>> @dataclasses.dataclass()
... class Address:
...        street_number: int
...        street: str
...        state: str
...        zip: str
...        city: str = ""
...        def __post_init__(self):
...          if not self.city and self.state == "MA" and self.zip == "02171":
...            self.city = "Quincy"
```

The revised Address data class can now automatically determine the city based on the specified state and zip code:[19]

```
>>> address = Address(2, "Heritage Dr", "MA", "02171")
>>> address
Address(street_number=2, street='Heritage Dr', state='MA', zip='02171',
        city='Quincy')
```

In conclusion, data classes are full-fledged classes. So, for example, we can add any functionality in the form of methods or implement an inheritance hierarchy of data classes.

---

19 At least, as long as it's Quincy, MA and the zip code is 02171. At this point, imagine a more complex process for mapping zip codes to city names.

Chapter 20
Exception Handling

Imagine a program that has a comparatively deep call hierarchy; that is, functions call other subfunctions, which in turn call functions again. It's often the case that the higher-level functions can't continue working correctly if an error has occurred in one of their subfunctions. The information that an error has occurred must therefore be passed up through the call hierarchy so that each higher-level function can react to the error and adapt to it.

20.1 Exceptions

Up to this point, we've been able to identify errors that occurred within a function solely on the basis of the function's return value. It takes a lot of effort to pass such a return value up through the function hierarchy, especially because they are exceptions to the regular program flow. So we'd spend a lot of code doing that to deal with rare cases.

Python supports a programming concept called *exception handling*. In the event of an error, a subfunction generates a so-called *exception* and raises it upward, figuratively speaking. The execution of the function is then finished. Each parent function now has three options:

- It handles the exception, executes the code intended to handle the error, and then continues normally. In such a case, other higher-level functions won't notice the exception.

- It handles the exception, executes the code intended for the error case, and raises the exception further up. In that case, the execution of this function will immediately be terminated, and the parent function is faced with the choice of handling the exception or not.

- It lets the exception pass without intercepting it. In this case, the execution of the function will immediately be terminated and the parent function is faced with the choice of handling the exception or not.

Consider the following output:

```
>>> abc
Traceback (most recent call last):
```

```
  File "<stdin>", line 1, in <module>
NameError: name 'abc' is not defined
```

So far, with such an output, we have quite generally spoken of an *error* or an *error message*, but that's not entirely correct: in the following sections, we'll refer to this output as *traceback*. The information contained in a traceback and how it can be interpreted has already been described in Chapter 4, Section 4.5. A traceback is displayed whenever an exception has been passed all the way to the top without being handled. But what exactly is an exception?

An *exception* is an object that contains attributes and methods for classifying and handling an error. Some of this information is displayed in the traceback, such as the description of the error (name 'abc' is not defined). An exception can be caught and handled in the program itself without the user being aware of it. You'll learn more about handling an exception later in this chapter. If an exception doesn't get handled, it will be output as a traceback and the program flow is terminated.

20.1.1 Built-In Exceptions

Python has a number of built-in exceptions—for example, the already known Syntax Error, NameError, and TypeError exceptions. Such exceptions are raised by functions of the standard library or by the interpreter itself. Because they are built in, they can be used at any time in the source code:

```
>>> NameError
<class 'NameError'>
>>> SyntaxError
<class 'SyntaxError'>
```

The built-in exceptions are organized hierarchically; that is, they inherit from common base classes. For this reason, they are largely identical in their attribute and method scope. The appendix contains a list of built-in exception types with brief explanations.

BaseException

The BaseException class is the base class for all exceptions and thus provides basic functionality that's available for all exception types. Let's describe it now.

The basic BaseException functionality consists of an essential attribute called args. This is a tuple in which all parameters are stored that were passed to the exception when it was instantiated. Using these parameters, it's then possible later when handling the exception to obtain detailed information about the error that occurred. The following example demonstrates the use of the args attribute:

```
>>> e = BaseException("Hello world")
>>> e.args
('Hello world',)
>>> e = BaseException("Hello world",1,2,3,4,5)
>>> e.args
('Hello world', 1, 2, 3, 4, 5)
```

So much for the direct use of exception classes.

20.1.2 Raising an Exception

So far, we've only looked at exceptions raised by the Python interpreter in an error case. However, you can also raise an exception yourself by using the raise statement:

```
>>> raise SyntaxError("Hello world")
Traceback (most recent call last):
  File "<stdin>", line 1, in <module>
SyntaxError: Hello world
```

This is done by writing the raise keyword followed by an instance. This may only be an instance of a class derived from BaseException. Furthermore, raising a class derived from BaseException is also possible without first creating an instance. An exception raised in this way will then not contain an error message:

```
>>> raise SyntaxError
Traceback (most recent call last):
  File "<stdin>", line 1, in <module>
SyntaxError: None
```

Raising instances of other data types, especially strings, is not possible:

```
>>> raise "Hello world"
Traceback (most recent call last):
  File "<stdin>", line 1, in <module>
TypeError: exceptions must derive from BaseException
```

In the following section, we'll describe how exceptions can be handled in the program so that they don't end in a traceback, but can be used for exception handling. We'll stick with built-in exceptions both in this section and the next. Custom exception types will be the topic of Chapter 20, Section 20.1.4.

20.1.3 Handling an Exception

This section is about how an exception raised in a subfunction can be handled in the call levels above it. *Handling* an exception is necessary to be able to respond to the error that occurred. Suppose you have a program that reads data from a file specified by the user. For this purpose, the program uses the following, still very simple get function, which returns the opened file object:

```
def get_file(name):
    return open(name)
```

If no file with the specified name exists, the built-in open function raises a FileNotFound Error exception. Because the get function doesn't respond to this exception, it's passed up the call hierarchy and eventually causes the program to terminate prematurely.

Now, incorrect user input constitutes a problem you should consider when writing an interactive program. The following variant of the get_file function handles a FileNotFoundError exception raised by open and in this case returns the value None instead of the opened file object:

```
def get_file(name):
    try:
        return open(name)
    except FileNotFoundError:
        return None
```

To handle an exception, a try/except statement is used. Initially, this type of statement consists of two parts:

- The try block is introduced by the try keyword, followed by a colon and any code block indented one step to the right. This code block is executed first. If an exception occurs in this code block, its execution is immediately terminated and the except branch of the statement is executed.

- The except branch is introduced by the except keyword, followed by an optional list of exception types for which this except branch should be executed. Note that multiple exception types can be specified as a tuple. You'll see an example of this later. The list of exception types can be followed, also optionally, by the as keyword, followed by a freely selectable identifier. Here you specify under which name you can access the handled exception instance in the except branch. For example, this way you can access the information stored in the args attribute of the exception instance. You'll also see examples of this in the course of this chapter.

  The except keyword is followed by a colon and any code block, indented one step further. This code block is only executed if one of the listed exceptions was raised within the try block.

Thus, a basic try/except statement has the following structure:

```
try:
    Statement
    Statement
```

```
except ExceptionType as name:
    Statement
    Statement
```

Let's return to our sample function, get_file. It's quite possible for a function call to mistakenly pass a list instead of a string for name, for example. In such a case, not a FileNotFoundError but a TypeError is raised, which at this moment won't be handled by the try/except statement:

```
>>> get_file([1,2,3])
Traceback (most recent call last):
  File "<stdin>", line 1, in <module>
  File "<stdin>", line 3, in get
TypeError: expected str, bytes or os.PathLike object, not list
```

The function is now to be extended so that a TypeError will also be handled and so that None will be returned afterward. There are three main ways available to do that. The first one consists of adding TypeError to the list of exception types to handlle in the existing except branch. Note that two or more exception types must be specified as tuples in the header of an except branch:

```
def get_file(name):
    try:
        return open(name)
    except (FileNotFoundError, TypeError):
        return None
```

This is simple and leads to the desired result in the selected example. However, imagine you want to execute different code depending on the exception type. To achieve such a behavior, a try/except statement can have more than one except branch:

```
def get_file(name):
    try:
        return open(name)
    except FileNotFoundError:
        return None
    except TypeError:
        return None
```

The third and less elegant option is to handle all kinds of exceptions at once. For this purpose, an except branch is written without specifying an exception type:

```
def get_file(name):
    try:
        return open(name)
```

```
except:
    return None
```

An exception is nothing more than an instance of a particular class. Consequently, the question arises whether and how to gain access to the raised exception instance within an except branch. This is possible by specifying the previously mentioned as identifier part in the header of the except branch. Under the name specified there, you can then access the raised exception instance within the code block:[1]

```
try:
    print([1,2,3][10])
except (IndexError, TypeError) as e:
    print("Error message:", e.args[0])
```

The output of this example is as follows:

```
Error message: list index out of range
```

In addition, a try/except statement may have an else branch and a finally branch, each of which may occur only once per statement. The code block associated with the else branch is executed if no exception has occurred, and the code block associated with the finally branch is executed in any case after all exceptions have been handled and the corresponding else branch has been executed, regardless of whether or which exceptions have occurred previously. The finally branch is therefore particularly suitable for actions that must be carried out in any case, such as closing a file object.

Both the else and finally branches must be written at the end of the try/except statement. If both branches occur, the else branch must precede the finally branch.

Figure 20.1 shows a complete try/except statement.

---

1 The possibly confusing print([1,2,3][10]) notation is equivalent to:
   lst = [1,2,3]
   print(lst[10]).

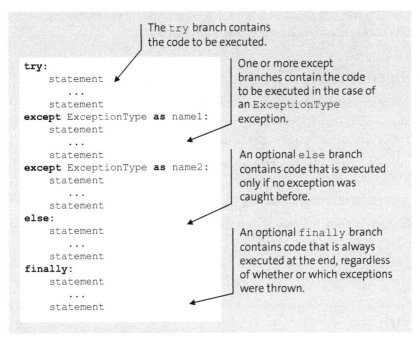

The `try` branch contains the code to be executed.

```
try:
    statement
    ...
    statement
except ExceptionType as name1:
    statement
    ...
    statement
except ExceptionType as name2:
    statement
    ...
    statement
else:
    statement
    ...
    statement
finally:
    statement
    ...
    statement
```

One or more except branches contain the code to be executed in the case of an ExceptionType exception.

An optional `else` branch contains code that is executed only if no exception was caught before.

An optional `finally` branch contains code that is always executed at the end, regardless of whether or which exceptions were thrown.

Figure 20.1 Complete Try/Except Statement

Finally, a few remarks about how a try/except statement is executed: First, the code associated with the try branch is executed. If an exception is raised within this code, the code associated with the corresponding except branch is executed. If there is no matching except branch, the exception is not handled and, if not handled elsewhere, ends up as a traceback on the screen. If no exception is raised in the try branch, none of the except branches are executed; the else branch is. The finally branch is executed at the end in any case.

Exceptions raised within an except, else, or finally branch can not be handled by subsequent except branches of the same statement. However, it's possible to nest try/except statements:

```
try:
    try:
        raise TypeError
    except IndexError:
        print("An IndexError has occurred")
except TypeError:
    print("A TypeError has occurred")
```

A TypeError is raised in the try branch of the inner try/except statement, which is not handled by the statement itself. Figuratively speaking, the exception then moves one level up and runs through the next try/except statement. In it, the raised TypeError is handled and a corresponding message is output. So the output of the example looks as follows: A TypeError has occurred. No traceback is displayed.

20.1.4   Custom Exceptions

When raising and handling exceptions, you aren't limited to the built-in set of exception types: you can also create new types yourself. Many third-party libraries use this possibility to offer special exception types tailored to the respective application.

To define your own exception type, all you need to do is create your own class that inherits from the Exception base class, and then add more attributes and methods to handle your exception entirely as required.

Now let's define a rudimentary account class that supports the withdrawal of a specific amount of money as its only operation:

```
class Account:
    def __init__(self, amount):
        self.account_balance = amount
    def withdraw(self, amount):
        self.account_balance -= amount
```

In this implementation of the class, it's possible to overdraw the account by any amount. In a somewhat more sophisticated variant, overdrawing the account is to be prevented and a self-defined exception is to be raised when attempting to withdraw more money than is available. To do this, we'll first define a class derived from the Exception base class and add attributes for the account balance and the amount to be withdrawn:

```
class AccountBalanceError(Exception):
    def __init__(self, account_balance, amount):
        super().__init__(account_balance, amount)
        self.account_balance = account_balance
        self.amount = amount
```

Then we'll modify the withdraw method of the Account class to raise an AccountBalanceError instance on an invalid withdrawal:

```
class Account:
    def __init__(self, amount):
        self.account_balance = amount
    def withdraw(self, amount):
        if amount > self.account_balance:
            raise AccountBalanceError(self.account_balance, amount)
        self.account_balance -= amount
```

The additional information passed to the constructor of the class is not displayed in the traceback:

```
>>> a = Account(1000)
>>> a.withdraw(2000)
Traceback (most recent call last):
  File "<stdin>", line 1, in <module>
  File "<stdin>", line 7, in withdraw
AccountBalanceError: (1000, 2000)
```

It only comes into effect when the exception is handled and processed:

```
try:
    a.withdraw(2000)
except AccountBalanceError as e:
    print("Account balance: {} USD".format(e.account_balance))
    print("Unable to withdraw {} USD".format(e.amount))
```

This code handles the resulting exception and then outputs an error message. Using the additional information provided by the class through the account-balance and amount attributes, the preceding withdrawal process can be reconstructed. The output of the example is as follows:

```
Account balance: 1000 USD
Unable to withdraw 2000 USD
```

For a self-defined exception with additional information to also contain an error message, it must implement the __str__ magic method:

```
class AccountBalanceError(Exception):
    def __init__(self, account_balance, amount):
        super().__init__(account_balance, amount)
        self.account_balance = account_balance
        self.amount = amount
    def __str__(self):
        return "Account balance too low (need {} USD more)".format(
                self.amount - self.account_balance)
```

A traceback caused by this exception looks as follows:

```
>>> a = Account(1000)
>>> a.withdraw(2000)
Traceback (most recent call last):
  File "<stdin>", line 1, in <module>
  File "<stdin>", line 7, in withdraw
AccountBalanceError: Account balance too low (need 1000 USD more)
```

20.1.5   Re-Raising an Exception

In some cases, especially with a deep function hierarchy, it makes sense to handle an exception, start the error handling provided for this case, and then raise the exception again. Let's look at the following example:

```python
def function3():
    raise TypeError
def function2():
    function3()
def function1():
    function2()
function1()
```

In the example, the function1 function is called, which in turn calls function2, in which function3 is called. Thus, there's a total of three nested function calls. In the innermost of these function calls, in function3, a TypeError exception gets raised. This exception isn't handled, so the associated traceback looks as follows:

```
Traceback (most recent call last):
  File "test.py", line 10, in <module>
    function1()
  File "test.py", line 8, in function1
    return function2()
  File "test.py", line 5, in function2
    return function3()
  File "test.py", line 2, in function3
    raise TypeError
TypeError
```

As expected, the traceback describes the function hierarchy at the time of the raise statement. This list is also referred to as a *callstack*.

The idea behind the exception principle is that an exception works its way up the call hierarchy and can be handled at any station. In our example, we want the function1 function to handle the TypeError exception so that it can perform special error handling tailored to the TypeError. After function1 has performed its function, internal error handling, the exception is to be passed up. To do that, it's raised again as in the following example:

```python
def function3():
    raise TypeError
def function2():
    function3()
def function1():
    try:
```

```
        function2()
    except TypeError:
        # Error handling
        raise TypeError
function1()
```

In contrast to the previous example, the traceback that occurs now looks as follows:

```
Traceback (most recent call last):
  File "test.py", line 14, in <module>
    function1()
  File "test.py", line 12, in function1
    raise TypeError
TypeError
```

You can see that this traceback contains information about the context of the second raise statement.[2] However, this isn't important at all, but rather a by-product of the error handling within function1. It would be ideal if, despite the temporary handling of the exception in function1, the resulting traceback described the context of the original raise statement. To achieve this, a raise statement can be written without specifying an exception type:

```
def function3():
    raise TypeError
def function2():
    function3()
def function1():
    try:
        function2()
    except TypeError as e:
        # Error handling
        raise
function1()
```

The traceback output in this example looks as follows:

```
Traceback (most recent call last):
  File "test.py", line 16, in <module>
    function1()
  File "test.py", line 11, in function1
    function2()
  File "test.py", line 7, in function2
```

---

2 In fact, due to *exception chaining* (see Chapter 20, Section 20.1.6), the traceback output also contains information about the original exception. However, this should not be of further interest to us at this point.

```
    function3()
  File "test.py", line 4, in function3
    raise TypeError
TypeError
```

You can see that this is the stack trace of the location where the exception was originally raised. The traceback thus contains the desired information about the location where the error actually occurred.

20.1.6   Exception Chaining

Occasionally it happens that within an except branch you need to raise another exception—either because another error occurred during the handling of the exception or in order to "rename" the exception that arose.

If another exception is raised within an except branch, Python automatically applies what is called *exception chaining*. The previous exception is appended as context for the newly raised exception so that maximum information is passed on. For example, let's take a look at the following code:

```
try:
    [1,2,3][128]
except IndexError:
    raise RuntimeError("Bad error")
```

The output is as follows:

```
Traceback (most recent call last):
  File "test.py", line 3, in <module>
    [1,2,3][128]
IndexError: list index out of range
The above exception was the direct cause of the following exception:
Traceback (most recent call last):
  File "test.py", line 5, in <module>
    raise RuntimeError("Bad error") from e
RuntimeError: Bad error
```

It accesses the 128th element of a three-element list, which provokes an IndexError exception. This exception is caught, and a RuntimeError exception is raised when it's handled. From the traceback output, you can see that the original IndexError exception was appended to the new RuntimeError exception.

The raise/from syntax can be used to control the exception chaining behavior. When raising an exception, a context can be specified, which is then taken into account in the resulting traceback. This context can be, for example, a second exception:

```
>>> raise IndexError from ValueError
ValueError
The above exception was the direct cause of the following exception:
Traceback (most recent call last):
  File "<stdin>", line 1, in <module>
IndexError
```

It turns out that we can use the raise/from syntax to trigger exception chaining. Alternatively, the raise/from syntax can be used to prevent the automatic appending of an exception:

```
try:
    [1,2,3][128]
except IndexError:
    raise RuntimeError("Bad error") from None
```

In this case, the resulting traceback contains only the newly created RuntimeError exception. The original IndexError exception is lost.

20.2 Assertions

20

The assert keyword enables you to integrate assertions into a Python program. By writing an assert statement, the programmer specifies a condition that is essential for the execution of the program and that must always hold True when the assert statement is reached. If the condition of an assert statement evaluates to False, an AssertionError exception is raised. In the following interactive mode session, several assert statements were entered:

```
>>> lst = [7, 1, 3, 5, -12]
>>> assert max(lst) == 7
>>> assert min(lst) == -12
>>> assert sum(lst) == 0
Traceback (most recent call last):
  File "<stdin>", line 1, in <module>
AssertionError
```

An error message can also be specified in the assert statement, which is inserted in the AssertionError exception in the event of a failure. This error message can be written after the condition separated by a comma:

```
>>> lst = [7, 1, 3, 5, -12]
>>> assert max(lst) == 7, "max is broken"
>>> assert min(lst) == -12, "min is broken"
>>> assert sum(lst) == 0, "sum is broken"
```

```
Traceback (most recent call last):
  File "<stdin>", line 1, in <module>
AssertionError: sum is broken
```

The assert statement is thus a practical tool for tracing errors and makes it possible to terminate the program flow if certain requirements aren't met. Often, assert is used to check at key points in the program whether all variables have the expected values.

Note that assert statements are usually only needed during the development of a program; they would be rather disruptive in a finished program. For this reason, assert statements are executed only if the global __debug__ constant references the value True. This constant is False only if the interpreter was started with the -O command line option. If the __debug__ constant references the value False, assert statements will be ignored and thus no longer affect the runtime of your program.

> **Note**
>
> Note that you mustn't change the value of __debug__ in the program itself; you can only use the -O command line option to determine whether assert statements should be executed or ignored.

20.3   Warnings

A *warning* is understood to be an exception that doesn't change the program flow, but only appears in the standard stderr error stream (see Chapter 29, Section 29.2.3) to inform the programmer of a questionable but not critical circumstance.

A typical example of a warning is the DeprecationWarning, which informs the developer or user that the running program uses functionality that will no longer be available in future Python versions or future versions of a library. This finding is not a problem for the current program flow, but it's important enough that it should be made known.

> **Note**
>
> The appendix lists the types of warnings defined by default in Python and explains their meaning.

The warnings module of the standard library allows you to control displaying or ignoring warnings of different content and different sources via complex filter rules. By default, Python suppresses some warnings, especially if they come from imported modules. However, these filter rules are often adapted to new circumstances by Python developers.

The warnings module contains the simplefilter function, which can override the preset filter rules with a general rule. In this way, warnings can be universally suppressed, for example:

```
>>> import warnings
>>> warnings.simplefilter("ignore")
```

Likewise, all warnings can be turned into exceptions that interrupt the program flow. In this case, warnings can also be handled:

```
>>> warnings.simplefilter("error")
```

Other possible arguments are "default" for suppressing reoccurring warnings from the same source, "always" for outputting all warnings, "module" for outputting only the first warning of a module, and "once" for suppressing reoccurring warning types.

Note

Warnings can also be turned into errors using the -W command line parameter of the Python interpreter. In this way, the behavior of a Python program with respect to warnings can be changed without modifying the code:

```
$ python -W error program.py
```

Similarly, the default, always, module, and once arguments also can be used.

20

Chapter 21
Generators and Iterators

In the previous chapters, we've frequently used terms such as *iterate* or *iterable object*. Without having defined this exactly, it's intuitively clear that this means the successive consideration of the individual elements of a corresponding instance. For example, a for loop can be used to iterate over a list:

```
>>> for x in [1,2,3,4]:
...     print(x)
...
1
2
3
4
```

In this chapter, we want to put the notion of iterating on a solid footing by introducing the central concepts of *generators* and *iterators*. Then we'll get to know itertools, a module of the standard library that provides a collection of generators for various interesting use cases.

21.1 Generators

In this section, we'll describe the concept of generators, which can be used to conveniently generate sequences of values. Because this still sounds very abstract, we'll start directly with an example. You'll certainly remember the built-in function range, which plays an important role in connection with for loops:

```
>>> for i in range(10):
...     print(i, end=" ")
0 1 2 3 4 5 6 7 8 9
```

As you already know, range(10) returns an iterable object that can be used to loop through the numbers 0 through 9. You have already learned that range doesn't create a list of these numbers for this purpose but generates them on demand. It often happens that you'll want to process a list of objects with a loop without the entire list as such having to be in the memory. For the preceding example, this means that though we process the numbers from 0 to 9, we don't need the list [0, 1, 2, 3, 4, 5, 6, 7, 8, 9] at any time.

This principle is now generalized to allow any sequence of objects that do not all have to be located together in the memory, to be iterated using loops—for example, if we want to iterate over the first n square numbers.

This is where so-called generators come into play. A generator is a function that, when called, creates an iterable object that returns the elements of a virtual[1] sequence one after the other. So for the square numbers example, we'd need a generator that returns the first n square numbers in sequence. The definition of these constructs, also referred to as *generator functions*, is similar to that of regular functions. The generator we need can be implemented as follows:

```
def square_generator(n):
    for i in range(1, n+1):
        yield i*i
```

This generator now allows us to elegantly output the first 10 square numbers on the screen:

```
>>> for i in square_generator(10):
...     print(i, end=" ")
1 4 9 16 25 36 49 64 81 100
```

The `square_generator(10)` function call returns an iterable object (the `generator` instance) that can be iterated with a `for` loop:

```
>>> square_generator(10)
<generator object square_generator at 0x7feb157ebbf8>
```

The crux of generators lies in the `yield` statement, which we use to return the individual values of the virtual sequence. The syntax of `yield` is very similar to the syntax of the `return` statement and therefore doesn't need to be explained any further. The decisive factor is how `yield` affects the control flow of the program compared to `return`.

If a `return` is reached in a normal function during a program run, the control flow is returned to the next higher level and the function call is terminated. As a result, the local namespace of the function call will be deleted. When calling the function again, Python would start once more at the beginning of the function and execute it in its entirety.

In contrast, when a `yield` statement is reached, the current position within the generator function and its local namespace are saved, and the control flow returns to the calling program by yielding the value specified after `yield`. At the next iteration step, Python then continues after the last executed `yield` and can access the old local vari-

---

1 *Virtual* here means that this sequence doesn't have to be stored completely in the memory at any time and can still be iterated.

ables, in this case i and n, again. Only when the end of the function is reached will the final cleanup begin.

Generator functions may well contain multiple yield statements:

```python
def generator_with_multiple_yields():
    a = 10
    yield a
    yield a*2
    b = 5
    yield a+b
```

This generator can also be iterated with a for loop:

```python
>>> for i in generator_with_multiple_yields():
...     print(i, end=" ")
10 20 15
```

In the first iteration step, the local variable a is created in the generator function and its value is then passed to the loop with yield a. The next iteration then continues at yield a*2, with the returned 20 showing that the value of a has indeed been preserved between calls. During the last iteration step, we also create the local variable b with the value 5 and pass the sum of a and b to the loop, which outputs 15. Because the end of the generator function has now been reached, the loop will terminate after three passes and finally release the local namespace.

It's also possible to leave a generator function early if necessary. To achieve this, you must use the return statement without a return value. The following generator creates a sequence of girls' names or girls' and boys' names depending on the value of the optional parameter also_boys:

```python
def names(also_boys=True):
    yield "Ella"
    yield "Linda"
    if not also_boys:
        return
    yield "Phillip"
    yield "Steve"
```

Using the built-in list function, we can create a list from the values of the generator, which contains either only "Ella" and "Linda" or additionally "Phillip" and "Steve":

```python
>>> list(names())
['Ella', 'Linda', 'Phillip', 'Steve']
>>> list(names(False))
['Ella', 'Linda']
```

> **Note**
>
> You have the option to exchange data with a generator. The send and throw methods used for this purpose are addressed in Chapter 44, Section 44.6.

21.1.1   Subgenerators

A generator can transfer control to another generator. This makes it possible to factorize out parts of a generator to separate generators. For example, we can split the name generator from the previous section into two subgenerators, boys and girls:

```python
def boys():
    yield "Phillip"
    yield "Steve"


def girls():
    yield "Ella"
    yield "Linda"


def names(also_boys=True):
    yield from girls()
    if also_boys:
        yield from boys()
```

The new name generator behaves exactly like the version without subgenerators:

```python
>>> list(names())
['Ella', 'Linda', 'Phillip', 'Steve']
>>> list(names(False))
['Ella', 'Linda']
```

Note that the values generated by a subgenerator are passed through directly to the calling level. The delegating generator doesn't have access to these values. In the example, the names Ella, Linda, Phillip, and Steve are written directly into the resulting list by the girls and boys generators, without the names generator seeing them. To return data to the delegating generator, we can use the return statement. The yield from statement obtains the returned value after passing through the subgenerator. As an example, let's extend the boys and girls subgenerators in such a way that they return the number of the respective names via return:

```python
def boys():
    yield "Phillip"
    yield "Steve"
```

```
    return 2

def girls():
    yield "Ella"
    yield "Linda"
    return 2

def names(also_boys=True):
    number_of_girls = (yield from girls())
    print("{} girls".format(number_of_girls))
    if also_boys:
        number_of_boys = (yield from boys())
        print("{} boys".format(number_of_boys))
```

Now the names generator outputs the respective numbers via print:

```
>>> list(names())
2 girls
2 boys
['Ella', 'Linda', 'Phillip', 'Steve']
```

We have explained the functionality of yield from here using subgenerators. It should be mentioned that yield from also works with arbitrary iterable objects:

```
>>> def names():
...     yield from ["Ella", "Linda", "Phillip", "Steve"]
>>> list(names())
['Ella', 'Linda', 'Phillip', 'Steve']
```

> **Note**
>
> If a generator passes the control to a subgenerator, the subgenerator takes care of all received values and exceptions. For more details on raising exceptions in a generator, see Chapter 44, Section 44.6.2.

Example: Traversing a Binary Tree with Subgenerators

A more practical example of subgenerators is the traversal of a binary tree. A *binary tree* is a data structure composed of a tree-like concatenation of nodes. Each node has a value and can have a left or right child, each of which is a node as well. An example of a binary tree is shown in Figure 21.1.

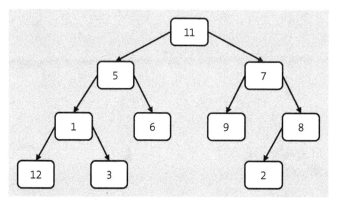

Figure 21.1 Binary Tree

When traversing the tree, all nodes are traversed in sequence. This can be achieved, for example, by so-called in-order traversing. At a node, the left subtree is traversed first, then the value of the node itself is output, and finally the right subtree is traversed. This can be realized by the following Node class, which contains a traverse method:

```
class Node:
    def __init__(self, value, left=None, right=None):
        self.left = left
        self.value = value
        self.right = right

    def traverse(self):
        if self.left:
            for k in self.left.traverse():
                yield k
        yield self.value
        if self.right:
            for k in self.right.traverse():
                yield k
```

The two for loops in the traverse generator method iterate the values of the left and right subtrees and recursively access the traverse generator method of the respective subtree for this purpose. Here, control can now be explicitly transferred via yield from, so that the traverse method can be rewritten as follows:

```
def traverse(self):
    if self.left:
        yield from self.left.traverse()
    yield self.value
    if self.right:
        yield from self.right.traverse()
```

We can now build and traverse the sample tree from Figure 21.1:

```
bl_ = Node(left=Node(12), value=1, right=Node(3))
bl = Node(left=bl_, value=5, right=Node(6))

br_ = Node(left=Node(2), value=8)
br = Node(left=Node(9), value=7, right=br_)

tree = Node(left=bl, value=11, right=br)
print(list(tree.traverse()))
```

The output we get is a list of all nodes of the tree:

```
[12, 1, 3, 5, 6, 11, 9, 7, 2, 8]
```

21.1.2   Generator Expressions

In Chapter 12, Section 12.3.7, you learned about list comprehensions, which allow you to create lists in a simple way. For example, the following list comprehension generates a list of the first 10 square numbers:

```
>>> [i*i for i in range(1, 11)]
[1, 4, 9, 16, 25, 36, 49, 64, 81, 100]
```

If you now want to determine the sum of these first 10 square numbers, you can do so using the built-in sum function:

```
>>> sum([i*i for i in range(1, 11)])
385
```

So far, so good. However, this creates an unneeded list instance containing all square numbers ahead of the summation.

To continue enjoying the comfort of list comprehensions in such cases, we can use *generator expressions*. Generator expressions look exactly like the corresponding list comprehensions, except that instead of square brackets ([ ]), we must use parentheses (()) as delimiters. This allows us to formulate the example shown previously in a memory-saving way using a generator expression:

```
>>> sum((i*i for i in range(1, 11)))
385
```

The enclosing parentheses can be omitted if the expression is already bracketed anyway. So in the sum example, we can remove a pair of parentheses:

```
>>> sum(i*i for i in range(1, 11))
385
```

21

Generators can help you improve your programs in terms of both readability and execution speed. Whenever you have to deal with a complicated and thus poorly readable while loop, you should check whether a generator can do the job more elegantly.

We've limited ourselves in this section to the definition of generators and their use in the for loop or with list. In the following section, you'll learn about their background and technical implementation: the underlying concepts behind generators and the for loop are those of iterators.

21.2   Iterators

You have often come across the term *iterable object* while reading this book, but so far you only know that you can iterate such instances with a for loop, for example, or pass them as parameters to certain functions, such as list. In this section, we'll now take a look at the background and functionality of these objects.

Data types that combine multiple elements in one instance, such as lists, sets, or dictionaries, are referred to as *containers*. An *iterator* is an abstraction layer that allows enumerating the elements of a container through a standardized interface.

This abstracts from the concrete peculiarities of the container to access its elements so that any iterable object can be traversed with the same code. It's then no longer important to know how the container stores the elements and how else they can be accessed.

21.2.1   The Iterator Protocol

The interface defined for this purpose is called *iterator protocol* and is defined as follows: Each iterable instance must implement a parameterless __iter__ method that returns an *iterator object*. The iterator object must also have an __iter__ method that simply returns a reference to the iterator object itself. It must also have a __next__ method that returns the next element of the container being traversed each time it's called. Once the end of the iteration is reached, the __next__ method must raise the StopIteration exception.

To be able to start the iteration, a reference to the iterator must be determined via the built-in iter function. The iter(object) statement calls the __iter__ method of the object instance and passes the result as a return value to the calling layer. From the returned iterator instance, the __next__ method can then be called until it raises the StopIteration exception.

21.2.2 Example: The Fibonacci Sequence

To shed more light on this abstract description, we'll develop a class that allows us to iterate over the Fibonacci sequence.[2] The Fibonacci sequence is a sequence of integers in which each element $f(n)$ can be calculated by the sum of its two predecessors, $f(n-2) + f(n-1)$. By definition, the first two elements are set to $f(1) = f(2) = 1$. The beginning of the infinite sequence is shown in Table 21.1.

n	1	2	3	4	5	6	7	8	9	10	11	12	13	14
f(n)	1	1	2	3	5	8	13	21	34	55	89	144	233	377

Table 21.1 First 14 Elements of the Fibonacci Sequence

The Fibonacci class, which we discuss below, uses the iterator protocol to implement an iterator that iterates over the Fibonacci sequence.

```python
class Fibonacci:
    def __init__(self, max_n):
        self.max_n = max_n
        self.n = 0
        self.a = 0
        self.b = 1
    def __iter__(self):
        return self
    def __next__(self):
        if self.n < self.max_n:
            self.n += 1
            self.a, self.b = self.b, self.a + self.b
            return self.a
        else:
            raise StopIteration
```

The Fibonacci class here expects the number of the element after which the iteration should stop as a parameter for its constructor. We store this number in the max_n attribute and then use the n attribute to count how many elements have already been returned. To remember the current position in the sequence between __next__ calls and to be able to calculate the next element, we store the last returned element and its successor in the a and b attributes of the Fibonacci class. We won't define a separate iterator class, so we'll have the __iter__ method return a reference to the Fibonacci

---

2 Many processes in nature, such as the number of seeds in a sunflower flower, can be described by Fibonacci numbers. Moreover, the quotient of consecutive elements converges to the golden ratio for large values of n ($\phi = 1.618...$), a ratio often associated with beauty.

instance itself—that is, self.[3] The __next__ method takes care of calculating the current element of the sequence and updates the caches and the counter. When the end of the desired subsequence is reached, StopIteration is raised.

The class can now be processed with all constructs that support the iterator protocol, such as the for loop and the built-in list and sum functions:

```
>>> for f in Fibonacci(14):
...     print(f, end=" ")
...
1 1 2 3 5 8 13 21 34 55 89 144 233 377
>>> list(Fibonacci(16))
[1, 1, 2, 3, 5, 8, 13, 21, 34, 55, 89, 144, 233, 377, 610, 987]
>>> sum(Fibonacci(60))
4052739537880
```

21.2.3   Example: The Golden Ratio

Using a small subclass of Fibonacci, we can also create an iterator that lets us iterate the ratios of two consecutive Fibonacci numbers. Here you can see that the quotients approach the golden ratio. The subclass only needs to override the __next__ method of the Fibonacci class and then return the quotients instead of the sequence elements. We benefit from the fact that in attribute b, we already calculate the value of the next element up front. The implementation then looks as follows:

```
class GoldenRatio(Fibonacci):
    def __next__(self):
        super().__next__()
        return self.b / self.a
```

Even the first fourteen elements of this sequence reveal the convergence. The golden ratio, rounded to six decimal places, is 1.618034:

```
>>> for g in GoldenRatio(14):
...     print("{:.6f}".format(g), end=" ")
...
1.000000 2.000000 1.500000 1.666667 1.600000 1.625000 1.615385
1.619048 1.617647 1.618182 1.617978 1.618056 1.618026 1.618037
```

21.2.4   A Generator for the Implementation of __iter__

It's possible to implement the __iter__ method of an iterable object as a generator. In the case of the Fibonacci sequence, this technique results in much more elegant code

---

3   As a result, there can be only one iterator for each instance of the Fibonacci class. You can read more about this ahead—in particular, in Chapter 21, Section 21.2.6.

because we now no longer need to remember the state of the iterator between __next__ calls, nor do we need to explicitly define __next__:

```python
class Fibonacci2:
    def __init__(self, max_n):
        self.max_n = max_n
    def __iter__(self):
        a, b = 0, 1
        for n in range(self.max_n):
            a, b = b, a + b
            yield a
```

Instances of the Fibonacci2 class behave exactly like the solution without a generator approach during iteration:

```python
>>> list(Fibonacci2(10))
[1, 1, 2, 3, 5, 8, 13, 21, 34, 55]
```

However, the GoldenRatio class can no longer be implemented as a subclass of Fibonacci2 in the same way as above because the caching of the values and also the __next__ method are now encapsulated in the generator.

21.2.5   Using Iterators

Now you've learned how to implement a valid iterator interface in your own classes. Next, we'll take a look at this topic from the opposite side and look at how we can use this iterator interface so that we can also write functions that can handle any iterable instance, rather than just lists or other sequences.

We'll consider a simple for loop for this purpose, and then go behind the scenes by programming an equivalent loop without for that explicitly uses the iterator protocol:

```python
>>> for i in range(10):
...     print(i, end=" ")
...
0 1 2 3 4 5 6 7 8 9
```

As you already know, to iterate a sequence we need the associated iterator object. This provides us with the built-in iter function, which, as explained in the previous section, calls the __iter__ method of the passed object:

```python
>>> iter(range(10))
<range_iterator object at 0x7f7ef190dab0>
```

Using the __next__ method of the iterator object, we now determine all elements in turn. Here we won't call the __next__ method directly but will use the built-in next function. The next(i) call is equivalent to i.__next__():

```
>>> i = iter(range(3))
>>> next(i)
0
>>> next(i)
1
>>> next(i)
2
>>> next(i)
Traceback (most recent call last):
  File "<stdin>", line 1, in <module>
StopIteration:
```

If i.__next__ is called again after returning the last element, the method raises the StopIteration exception as expected.

The built-in next function provides an optional second parameter, default. If a value is passed for default, the built-in next function handles the StopIteration exception and returns the value of default:

```
>>> i = iter(range(2))
>>> next(i, 111)
0
>>> next(i, 111)
1
>>> next(i, 111)
111
>>> next(i, 111)
111
```

If we handle the StopIteration exception ourselves with a try/except statement, we can recreate the for loop as follows:

```
>>> i = iter(range(10))
>>> while True:
...     try:
...         print(next(i), end=" ")
...     except StopIteration:
...         break
...
0 1 2 3 4 5 6 7 8 9
```

Of course, the for loop in Python is not implemented as in the example but is an optimized routine of the Python interpreter.

> **Note**
>
> If a generator function contains a `return` statement, the returned value is stored in `StopIteration` and can be read via its `value` attribute:
>
> ```
> >>> def test():
> ...     yield 10
> ...     yield 20
> ...     return 1337
> ...
> >>> i = test()
> >>> while True:
> ...     try:
> ...         print(next(i))
> ...     except StopIteration as e:
> ...         print("Return:", e.value)
> ...         break
> ...
> 10
> 20
> Return: 1337
> ```
>
> Here, `return value` in a generator is equivalent to `raise StopIteration(value)`.

The `for` loop can also iterate over an iterator itself and doesn't have to create one. The following two loops are therefore equivalent:

```
>>> for i in range(3):
...     print(i, end=" ")
...
0 1 2
>>> for i in iter(range(3)):
...     print(i, end=" ")
...
0 1 2
```

The fact that `for` itself calls `iter` once again, as illustrated in the alternative `while` loop, is not a problem insofar as the `__iter__` method of an iterator object must return a reference to the object itself. If a is an iterator object, then (a is iter(a)) always holds, as the following example illustrates:

```
>>> a = iter(range(10))  # create a range iterator
>>> a is iter(a)
True
```

In contrast, the `__iter__` method of an iterable object doesn't need to return a reference to itself, nor does it always need to return the same iterator instance:

```
>>> a = [1, 2, 3]  # an iterable object
>>> iter(a) is iter(a)
False
```

21.2.6   Multiple Iterators for the Same Instance

Conversely, this means that the built-in function `iter` can return different iterators when called for the same iterable object, which is also useful for traversing a list with two different iterators, for example:

```
>>> l = [1, 2, 3]
>>> for i in l:
...       for j in l:
...           print(i,j, end=", ")
...       print()
...
1 1, 1 2, 1 3,
2 1, 2 2, 2 3,
3 1, 3 2, 3 3,
```

In this example, each element of list l is combined with every other element of the list, and the resulting pairs are output. For this purpose, a for loop was used in each case.

If we try to run the same code with an instance of the `Fibonacci` class from the beginning of this section, we'll get a different result:

```
>>> l = Fibonacci(3)
>>> for i in l:
...       for j in l:
...           print(i,j, end=", ")
...       print()
...
1 1, 1 2,
```

Again, we expected to output each of the first three Fibonacci numbers, 1, 1, and 2, combined with each other, to obtain an output as follows:

```
1 1, 1 1, 1 2,
1 1, 1 1, 1 2,
2 1, 2 1, 2 2,
```

This deviant behavior is due to the fact that the `__iter__` method of the `Fibonacci` class doesn't create a new iterator but returns a reference to the respective object itself. Thus, there can be only one iterator at a time for an instance of the Fibonacci class, which must be shared by the two for loops in the example.

The exact procedure is as follows: First, an instance of the Fibonacci class is created, setting the attributes l.n and l.a to 0, and the attribute l.b to 1. Then, in the outer loop, the first Fibonacci number 1 is determined by calling the __next__ method and referenced with i. The first Fibonacci number 1 is determined by calling the __next__ method.

Now the inner loop starts, which in turn again calls the __iter__ method of instance l and receives a reference to the same iterator object as the outer loop. Subsequently, j iterates over the second and third Fibonacci numbers 1 and 2 in the inner loop and combines them with the value 1 of i.

Following this, the outer loop calls the __next__ method of l again, which still raises the StopIteration exception because the end of the common iterator was already reached in the inner loop. This ends the program at this point.

As you can see, unexpected behavior can occur when an iterator is implicitly shared across multiple loops. We can remedy this by modifying the Fibonacci class to return a new iterator object each time __iter__ is called:

```python
class Fibonacci3:
    class FibonacciIterator:
        def __init__(self, max_n):
            self.max_n = max_n
            self.n, self.a, self.b = 0, 0, 1
        def __iter__(self):
            return self
        def __next__(self):
            if self.n < self.max_n:
                self.n += 1
                self.a, self.b = self.b, self.a + self.b
                return self.a
            else:
                raise StopIteration
    def __init__(self, max_n):
        self.max_n = max_n
    def __iter__(self):
        return self.FibonacciIterator(self.max_n)
```

The new Fibonacci3 class defines another class, FibonacciIterator, which is responsible for the actual iterating and was defined in the same way as the Fibonacci class. Each time a new iterator is requested via an instance of the Fibonacci3 class, a new object of the FibonacciIterator class is created.

21

Thus, the two nested loops from before deliver the expected result:[4]

```
>>> l = Fibonacci3(3)
>>> for i in l:
...      for j in l:
...          print(i,j, end=", ")
...      print()
...
1 1, 1 1, 1 2,
1 1, 1 1, 1 2,
2 1, 2 1, 2 2,
```

Because of these potential problems, it's generally a good idea to create a new iterator each time __iter__ is called, if possible.

21.2.7   Disadvantages of Iterators Compared to Direct Access via Indexes

Iterators are well suited for iterating through all elements of a sequence and implementing this uniformly for all container data types. In contrast, indexes allow for read and write access to the elements of a container in any order, which isn't possible with the iterator approach.

In this respect, the indexes can't be completely replaced by iterators, but are supplemented by them for special cases.

21.2.8   Alternative Definition for Iterable Objects

In addition to the definition for iterable objects described previously, there's another way to make a class iterable. Because it's possible with many sequences and containers to number the elements consecutively and to address them via integer indexes, an object is already iterable if you can address its elements via integer indexes using the __getitem__ method—that is, with the [] operator. If you call the built-in iter function with such an instance as a parameter, Python takes care of creating the iterator. Each time the __next__ method of the generated iterator is called, the __getitem__ method of the iterable instance is called, always passing an integer as a parameter. The count of the passed indexes starts at 0 and doesn't end until the __getitem__ method produces an IndexError as soon as an invalid index has been passed.

For example, a class for iterating over the first max_n square numbers may look like this if it also supports determining their length using len:

```
class Squares:
    def __init__(self, max_n):
```

---

4 Try the same example with the Fibonacci2 class from Chapter 21, Section 21.2.4. Can you explain the result?

```
        self.max_n = max_n
    def __getitem__(self, index):
        index += 1   # 0*0 is not very interesting ...
        if index > len(self) or index < 1:
            raise IndexError
        return index*index
    def __len__(self):
        return self.max_n
```

To demonstrate this hidden iterator, let's output a list of the first 20 square numbers:

```
>>> list(Squares(20))
[1, 4, 9, 16, 25, 36, 49, 64, 81, 100, 121, 144, 169, 196, 225, 256, 289, 324,
361, 400]
```

21.2.9   Function Iterators

The last option for iterators in Python are so-called function iterators. These are objects that call a particular function until it returns a special value—the *terminator* of the sequence. You can create a function iterator using the built-in iter function, passing a reference to the function you want to iterate over as the first parameter and the value of the terminator as the second parameter.

iter(function, terminator)

A useful example is the readline method of the file object, which returns the value of the next line until the end of the file has been reached. If there is no more data after the current reading position of the file instance, readline returns an empty string. If there was a file named *friends.txt* in the current working directory, which contained four names, "Luke", "Michael", "Leo", and "John", each on a separate line, we could iterate over it as follows:

```
>>> with open("friends.txt") as file:
...     for line in iter(file.readline, ""):
...         print(line.strip(), end=" ")
Luke Michael Leo John
```

> **Note**
> This example is only intended to illustrate function iterators. You can also directly iterate over the lines of a file this way:
>
> ```
> >>> with open("friends.txt") as file:
> ...     for line in file:
> ...         print(line.strip(), end=" ")
> ```

21

21.3 Special Generators: itertools

At this point, we want to introduce the itertools module of the standard library, which contains generator functions that are often useful in everyday programming. For example, itertools allows you to iterate over all combinations or permutations of elements in a given list.

Table 21.2 lists the generators contained in the itertools module and explains them briefly. Detailed descriptions follow in the subsequent sections.

Function	Description
accumulate(iterable, [func])	Iterates the partial sums of the elements of iterable
chain([*iterables])	Iterates the concatenation of the passed iterable objects
combinations(iterable, r)	Iterates all r-element combinations of iterable
combinations_with_replacement(iterable, r)	Traverses all r-element combinations from iterable (with replacement)
compress(data, selectors)	Traverses the elements of data for which the corresponding element of selectors returns True
count(start, step)	Counts, starting with start, numbers in the distance of step
cycle(iterable)	Iterates the elements of iterable in an infinite loop
dropwhile(predicate, iterable)	Traverses all elements of iterable starting from the element for which predicate returns False for the first time
filterfalse(predicate, iterable)	Traverses all elements of iterable for which predicate returns False
groupby(iterable, key)	Traverses the elements of iterable, grouped by the key function key
islice(iterable, [start], stop, [step])	Enables slicing of iterable objects
permutations(iterable, r)	Iterates all r-element permutations of iterable
product([*iterables], repeat)	Traverses the Cartesian product of the passed iterable objects
repeat(object, [times])	Repeats the object times times

Table 21.2 Functions of the itertools Module

Function	Description
starmap(function, iterable)	Calls the function function with the elements of iterable as parameters and iterates the results
takewhile(predicate, iterable)	Traverses all elements of iterable up to the element for which predicate returns False for the first time
tee(iterable, [n])	Creates n independent iterators for iterable
zip_longest([*iterables], fillvalue)	Like the built-in function zip, but doesn't truncate the iterable objects based on the length of the shortest one

Table 21.2 Functions of the itertools Module (Cont.)

For illustration purposes, the following examples transfer the iterators returned by the generator functions into lists and output them. To be able to follow the examples, you must have previously imported the itertools module:

```
>>> import itertools
```

21.3.1 accumulate(iterable, [func])

The accumulate function creates an iterator that yields the partial sums of the elements of iterable. This is illustrated by the following example:

```
>>> list(itertools.accumulate([1,2,3,4]))
[1, 3, 6, 10]
```

The generated iterator yields the elements 1, 1 + 2, 1 + 2 + 3, and 1 + 2 + 3 + 4.

For the optional func parameter, you can pass a self-defined operator that should be used instead of the addition operator. This must be a function object that expects two parameters and calculates a return value from them.

21.3.2 chain([*iterables])

The chain function creates an iterator, which iterates all elements of the passed iterable objects in sequence:

```
>>> list(itertools.chain("ABC", "DEF"))
['A', 'B', 'C', 'D', 'E', 'F']
```

You can see that first the elements of the first string are traversed, followed by the elements of the second passed string.

In some cases, it's inconvenient to pass iterable objects individually as parameters. For this purpose, you can use the chain.from_iterable function, which expects a sequence of iterable objects as the only parameter:

```
>>> list(itertools.chain.from_iterable(["ABC", "DEF", "GHI"]))
['A', 'B', 'C', 'D', 'E', 'F', 'G', 'H', 'I']
```

The two functions only differ in the way their arguments are passed to them.

21.3.3   combinations(iterable, r)

The combinations function yields all combinations with r elements of iterable. In the case of a combination, no attention is paid to the order of the elements put together. Consequently, swapping elements of a combination won't result in a new combination. In the following example, all three-digit combinations of the numbers from 0 to 3 are iterated:

```
>>> list(itertools.combinations(range(4), 3))
[(0, 1, 2), (0, 1, 3), (0, 2, 3), (1, 2, 3)]
```

For example, you can see that the arrangement (1, 0, 2) isn't listed because it's only obtained by swapping the elements from the combination (0, 1, 2).

In the next example, you can see that the generated combinations depend on the order of the elements in iterable:

```
>>> list(itertools.combinations("ABC", 2))
[('A', 'B'), ('A', 'C'), ('B', 'C')]
>>> list(itertools.combinations("CBA", 2))
[('C', 'B'), ('C', 'A'), ('B', 'A')]
```

If you're interested in a generator that pays attention to the order of the elements, you'll want to iterate all the permutations. In this case, the permutations function is the better choice.

21.3.4   combinations_with_replacement(iterable, r)

The combinations_with_replacement function yields all combinations with r elements of iterable, just like combinations, but with repeated elements. This means that an element from iterable may occur multiple times in a combination:

```
>>> list(itertools.combinations_with_replacement(range(4), 3))
[
(0, 0, 0), (0, 0, 1), (0, 0, 2), (0, 0, 3), (0, 1, 1), (0, 1, 2), (0, 1, 3), (0,
 2, 2), (0, 2, 3), (0, 3, 3), (1, 1, 1), (1, 1, 2), (1, 1, 3), (1, 2, 2), (1, 2,
 3), (1, 3, 3), (2, 2, 2), (2, 2, 3), (2, 3, 3), (3, 3, 3)]
```

As is the case with combinations, the order of the elements is not important.

21.3.5 compress(data, selectors)

The compress function creates an iterator that yields those elements of the data iterable object whose corresponding element in selectors has the value True. This is illustrated by the following example:

```
>>> list(itertools.compress("ABCDEFGH", [1,1,1,0,0,1,0,1]))
['A', 'B', 'C', 'F', 'H']
```

The list passed for selectors specifies that the first three and the sixth and eighth elements of data are to be traversed.

21.3.6 count([start, step])

The count function creates an iterator that yields the values *start* + *n* · *step* for all $n \geq 0$. Floats can be passed for both start and step. By default, it starts at 0 and the step size is set to 1. Note that this iterator doesn't stop counting by itself:

```
>>> for i in itertools.count(-5):
...     print(i)
...     if i >= 0:
...         break
...
-5
-4
-3
-2
-1
0
```

The function count is also useful in combination with the built-in map function (see Chapter 17, Section 17.14.30). This is demonstrated by the following example, which outputs square numbers between 0 and 30:

```
>>> m = map(lambda x: x**2, itertools.count())
>>> for i in m:
...     if i > 30:
...         break
...     print(i)
...
0
1
4
```

9
16
25

21.3.7 cycle(iterable)

The cycle function iterates all elements of the iterable object and then starts over again. The iterator generated by cycle runs in an infinite loop. Note that the cycle function internally makes a copy of each element of iterable and uses it when iterating again. This might result in significant memory consumption, depending on the length of iterable.

21.3.8 dropwhile(predicate, iterable)

The dropwhile function is passed an iterable iterable object and a predicate function. It first calls the predicate function for all elements of iterable and ignores any element for which predicate returned True. When predicate returns False for the first time, each subsequent element of iterable is traversed, regardless of what value predicate returns for those elements. So you can think of the predicate function as a start signal:

```
>>> p = lambda x: x.islower()
>>> list(itertools.dropwhile(p, "abcdefgHIJKLMnopQRStuvWXYz"))
[
'H', 'I', 'J', 'K', 'L', 'M', 'n', 'o', 'p', 'Q', 'R', 'S', 't', 'u', 'v', 'W',
'X', 'Y', 'z']
```

In this example, all letters after the lowercase letters at the beginning are included in the result list. You can see that lowercase letters are also included in the result after the p predicate function returns True for the first time.

21.3.9 filterfalse(predicate, iterable)

The filterfalse function yields all elements of iterable for which the predicate function returns False. Calling filterfalse is thus equivalent to the following generator expression:

```
(x for x in iterable if not predicate(x))
```

In the following example, only the uppercase letters of a string are traversed:

```
>>> p = lambda x: x.islower()
>>> list(itertools.filterfalse(p, "abcDEFghiJKLmnoP"))
['D', 'E', 'F', 'J', 'K', 'L', 'P']
>>> list((x for x in "abcDEFghiJKLmnoP" if not p(x)))
['D', 'E', 'F', 'J', 'K', 'L', 'P']
```

21.3.10   groupby(iterable, [key])

The groupby function creates an iterator that yields the elements of iterable in a grouped manner. The grouping is performed using the key function passed for key. If the key parameter isn't specified, the elements are grouped based on their value.

The iterator generated by groupby yields tuples containing the respective group key and an iterator over the group elements. The following example demonstrates how groupby works:

```
>>> for l in list(itertools.groupby("AAABBBCCC")):
...     print(list(l))
...
['A', <itertools._grouper object at 0x7f4784b6c310>]
['B', <itertools._grouper object at 0x7f4784b6c5d0>]
['C', <itertools._grouper object at 0x7f4784b6c390>]
>>> [list(g) for k, g in itertools.groupby('AAABBBCCC')]
[['A', 'A', 'A'], ['B', 'B', 'B'], ['C', 'C', 'C']]
```

With the help of a separate key function, the elements can be grouped according to other aspects. In the following example, a key function is used to perform grouping by word length:

```
>>> def f(x):
...     return len(x)
...
>>> words = ["for", "while", "and", "or", "if", "elif", "else"]
>>> [list(g) for k, g in itertools.groupby(words, f)]
[['for'], ['while'], ['and'], ['or', 'if'], ['elif', 'else']]
```

This reveals an important requirement for the order of elements in iterable. Although the words *for* and *and* are the same length, they weren't grouped together. For grouping via groupby to work, the objects contained in iterable must be presorted with respect to the key function used.

21.3.11   islice(iterable, [start], stop, [step])

The islice function transfers the functionality of slicing, which you know about from sequential data types, to any iterable object. The function creates an iterator that starts at the element with the sequence number start, stops before the element with the number stop, and advances by step elements in each step:

```
>>> list(itertools.islice("ABCDEFGHIJKL", 2, 8, 2))
['C', 'E', 'G']
>>> "ABCDEFGHIJKL"[2:8:2]
'CEG'
```

21

21.3.12 permutations(iterable, [r])

The permutations function creates an iterator over all permutations with r elements of the iterable object:

```
>>> list(itertools.permutations(range(3), 2))
[(0, 1), (0, 2), (1, 0), (1, 2), (2, 0), (2, 1)]
```

As you can see, the arrangements (0,1) and (1,0) are both included in the result list. Unlike combinations, permutations depend on the order in which they are arranged:

```
>>> list(itertools.permutations("ABC", 2))
[('A', 'B'), ('A', 'C'), ('B', 'A'), ('B', 'C'), ('C', 'A'), ('C', 'B')]
>>> list(itertools.permutations("CBA", 2))
[('C', 'B'), ('C', 'A'), ('B', 'C'), ('B', 'A'), ('A', 'C'), ('A', 'B')]
```

This example shows that, again, the order of permutations in the result list depends on the order of the elements to be permuted in iterable.

21.3.13 product([*iterables], [repeat])

The product function creates an iterator that yields the Cartesian product of the passed iterable objects. The result consists of all the tuples that can be formed from one element of each passed iterable object. In this case, an element is located in the tuple at exactly the same position as the iterable object in the parameter list from which it originates. This is illustrated by the following example:

```
>>> list(itertools.product("ABC", [1,2]))
[('A', 1), ('A', 2), ('B', 1), ('B', 2), ('C', 1), ('C', 2)]
```

Here, each character contained in the "ABC" string was associated once with all elements of the [1,2] list.

Using the optional repeat keyword parameter, for example, an iterable object can be "multiplied" by itself multiple times without having to pass it to the function multiple times:

```
>>> list(itertools.product("AB", "AB", "AB"))
[
('A', 'A', 'A'), ('A', 'A', 'B'), ('A', 'B', 'A'), ('A', 'B', 'B'), ('B', 'A', '
A'), ('B', 'A', 'B'), ('B', 'B', 'A'), ('B', 'B', 'B')]
>>> list(itertools.product("AB", repeat=3))
[
('A', 'A', 'A'), ('A', 'A', 'B'), ('A', 'B', 'A'), ('A', 'B', 'B'), ('B', 'A', '
A'), ('B', 'A', 'B'), ('B', 'B', 'A'), ('B', 'B', 'B')]
```

21.3.14   repeat(object, [times])

The `repeat` function creates an iterator, which returns `object` over and over again. Optionally, you can use the `times` parameter to specify how many iteration steps should be performed:

```
>>> list(itertools.repeat("A", 10))
['A', 'A', 'A', 'A', 'A', 'A', 'A', 'A', 'A', 'A']
```

If the `times` parameter isn't specified, the iterator returned by `repeat` runs endlessly.

21.3.15   starmap(function, iterable)

The `starmap` function works similarly to the built-in `map` function. The `function` function is called for each parameter list contained in `iterable`. The iterator generated by `starmap` yields the results of these function calls:

```
>>> list(itertools.starmap(max, [(1,2), (4,4,3,6), [2,3,9]]))
[2, 6, 9]
```

In this example, the `starmap` function was used together with the built-in `max` function to traverse the largest elements of each tuple.

21.3.16   takewhile(predicate, iterable)

The `takewhile` function is the counterpart to `dropwhile`. It creates an iterator that yields the elements of `iterable` as long as the `predicate` function returns `True` for the elements. As soon as a predicate call has returned the value `False`, the iterator terminates:

```
>>> p = lambda x: x.islower()
>>> list(itertools.takewhile(p, "abcdefGHIjklMNOp"))
['a', 'b', 'c', 'd', 'e', 'f']
```

In this case, `takewhile` was used to obtain only the lowercase letters at the beginning of the passed string.

21.3.17   tee(iterable, [n])

The `tee` function creates n independent iterators over the elements of `iterable`. By default, n=2 iterators are generated.

```
>>> list(itertools.tee([1,2,3,4]))
[<itertools._tee object at 0x7f26a9e69e48>, <itertools._
tee object at 0x7f26a9e69f08>]
>>> [list(x) for x in itertools.tee([1,2,3,4])]
[[1, 2, 3, 4], [1, 2, 3, 4]]
```

After calling tee, only the iterators returned by tee should be used and not the one passed as a parameter.

21.3.18   zip_longest([*iterables], {fillvalue})

The zip_longest function works similarly to the built-in zip function. The difference is that with zip_longest, the longest of the passed iterable objects is always decisive, and missing elements with the other objects are filled with fillvalue:

```
>>> list(zip("ABC", "abcde"))
[('A', 'a'), ('B', 'b'), ('C', 'c')]
>>> list(itertools.zip_longest("ABC", "abcde"))
[('A', 'a'), ('B', 'b'), ('C', 'c'), (None, 'd'), (None, 'e')]
>>> list(itertools.zip_longest("ABC", "abcde", fillvalue="-"))
[('A', 'a'), ('B', 'b'), ('C', 'c'), ('-', 'd'), ('-', 'e')
```

Chapter 22
Context Manager

There are operations that must be executed in a certain context and for which it must be ensured that the context is correctly deinitialized at all times—for example, even if an exception occurs. An example of such a context is an open file object: it must be ensured that the close method of the file object is called even if an exception was raised between the call of open and that of the close method of the file object.

For these purposes, Python defines so-called *context objects*. These are objects that have the magic __enter__ and __exit__ members to enter and exit the context, respectively. For the use of context objects, there is the with statement, which you'll get to know in the following section.

22.1 The with Statement

If you want to perform an operation in the context of an open file object, the following try/finally statement is necessary with the conventional language elements of Python:

```python
f = open("file.txt", "r")
try:
    print(f.read())
finally:
    f.close()
```

First, a file named *file.txt* is opened for reading. The subsequent try/finally statement makes sure that f.close is called in any case. The drawback of this notation is that the programmer must make sure the file object gets deinitialized correctly. The with statement transfers this responsibility to the object itself and allows for a short and elegant alternative to the code shown previously:

```python
with open("program.py", "r") as f:
    print(f.read())
```

The with statement consists of the with keyword followed by an instance. Optionally, the instance can be followed by the as keyword and an identifier. This identifier is referred to as the *target*, and its meaning depends on the instance used. In the preceding example, f references the open file object.

Instead of nesting several with statements, the respective instances and identifiers can also be written in a with statement, separated by commas. Thus the following code:

```
with open("file1.txt", "r") as f1, open("file2.txt", "r") as f2:
    print(f1.read())
    print(f2.read())
```

Is equivalent to the following:

```
with open("file1.txt") as f1:
    with open("file2.txt", "r") as f2:
        print(f1.read())
        print(f2.read())
```

If multiple instances are used in the same with statement, this often results in very long lines. In such cases, it's a good idea to use the backslash (\) to split them across several lines, as described in Chapter 4, Section 4.2.1. Since Python 3.10, you can also position the list in parentheses behind with and thus allow any number of line breaks:

```
with (
    open("file1.txt", "r") as f1,
    open("file2.txt", "r") as f2
):
    print(f1.read())
    print(f2.read())
```

To understand what exactly happens when we use a with statement, in the following example we'll define a class that can be used with the with statement. Such a class is referred to as a *context manager*.

The MyLogging class is intended to keep a rudimentary log file. To do this, it implements the entry function, which writes a new line to the log file. The class definition looks as follows:

```
class MyLogging:
    def __init__(self, filename):
        self.filename = filename
        self.f = None
    def entry(self, text):
        self.f.write("==>{}\n".format(text))
    def __enter__(self):
        self.f = open(self.filename, "w")
```

```
        return self
    def __exit__(self, exc_type, exc_value, traceback):
        self.f.close()
```

There isn't much to be said about the first two methods of the class. The `__init__` constructor is passed the file name of the log file, which is stored internally in the `self.filename` attribute. In addition, the `self.f` attribute is created, which will later reference the opened file object.

The `entry` method is supposed to write the passed text into the log file. To do that, it calls the `write` method of the file object. Note that the `entry` method can be called only inside a `with` statement because the file object is opened and closed only in the following magic methods.

The mentioned `__enter__` and `__exit__` magic methods represent the core of the class and must be implemented if the class is to be used in conjunction with `with`. The `__enter__` method is called when the context is established—that is, before the body of the `with` statement gets executed. The method receives no parameters, but returns a value. The return value of `__enter__` is later referenced by the target identifier, if one was specified. In the case of the sample class, the `self.filename` file is opened for writing, and a reference to the `MyLogging` instance itself is returned with `return self`.

The second magic method, `__exit__`, is called when the context is exited—that is, after the body of the `with` statement has been either fully executed or terminated prematurely by an exception. In the case of the sample class, the open `self.f` file object is closed. More details about the three parameters of the `__exit__` method follow ahead.

The `MyLogging` class we just created can be used with `with` as follows:

```
with MyLogging("logfile.txt") as log:
    log.entry("Hello world")
    log.entry("How are you doing?")
```

First, an instance of the `MyLogging` class is created, passing the file name `logfile.txt`. The `with` statement first causes the `__enter__` method of the instance to be executed and its return value to be referenced by `log`. Then the body of the `with` statement is executed, in which the `entry` method is called twice in total and thus text is written to the log file. After the statement body has been executed, the `__exit__` method of the `log` instance is called once.

22.1.1   __enter__(self)

This magic method is called once to open the context before the body of the `with` statement is executed. The return value of this method is referenced by the target identifier in the body of the `with` statement.

22.1.2   __exit__(self, exc_type, exc_value, traceback)

The __exit__ magic method is called once to close the context after the body of the with statement has been executed. The exc_type, exc_value, and traceback parameters specify the type, value, and traceback object of any exception raised within the with statement body. If no exception was raised, all three parameters reference None. The return value controls how you can proceed with a raised exception: If the method returns True, the exception will be suppressed. If the return value is False, the exception will be re-raised.

22.2   Helper Functions for with Contexts: contextlib

The contextlib module of the standard library contains functions and decorators for handling with contexts. For example, objects can be extended to become context managers that were not actually created for this purpose. Other functions in contextlib allow you to suppress certain exceptions or redirect screen output.

To run the examples in this section, the contextlib module must first be imported:

```
>>> import contextlib
```

22.2.1   Dynamically Assembled Context Combinations - ExitStack

The with statement provides a simple and elegant syntax for executing program parts within a defined context—for example, in the context of an open file object. Moreover, you know that multiple with statements can be nested, so we can easily execute program parts in the context of multiple open file objects:

```
>>> with open("file1.txt") as file1:
...     with open("file2.txt") as file2:
...         with open("file3.txt") as file3:
...             pass # Do something with three files
```

Alternatively, the three files could be opened in a with statement. But no matter in which variant, it must be determined up front how many file objects are to be opened when entering the context.

Using the ExitStack context manager from the contextlib module, dynamically assembled combinations of context managers can be combined into a common context manager and then used in their entirety with the with statement:

```
>>> num = 10
>>> with contextlib.ExitStack() as s:
...     names = [f"file_{i}.txt" for i in range(num)]
```

```
...        files = [s.enter_context(open(name, "w")) for name in names]
...        for file in files:
...            file.write("Test!")
```

In the example, an ExitStack context named s is entered using the with statement. Within this context, we first prepare the file names and then successively open the associated file objects. Each of these file objects is then attached to the ExitStack by calling the enter_context method. Of course, not only file objects but any context manager could be associated with ExitStack at this point.

When leaving the context defined by ExitStack, the __exit__ methods of the context managers belonging to ExitStack are called in reverse order. In the example, this means the last opened file will be closed first.

22.2.2   Suppressing Certain Exception Types

The contextlib module contains the suppress context manager, which suppresses exceptions of certain types when they are raised in the with context:

```
>>> x = ["I appear"]
>>> with contextlib.suppress(IndexError):
...     print(x[0])
...     print(x[1])
...
I appear
```

This code is equivalent to the following try/except statement, which is slightly less readable:

```
>>> x = ["I appear"]
>>> try:
...     print(x[0])
...     print(x[1])
... except IndexError:
...     pass
...
I appear
```

The suppress function can be passed any number of exception types as parameters.

22.2.3   Redirecting the Standard Output Stream

The redirect_stdout context manager from the contextlib module enables you to redirect the standard output stream used for screen output using print, for example:

```
>>> with open("out.txt", "w") as f_out:
...     with contextlib.redirect_stdout(f_out):
...         print("Screen")
...         print("output")
```

In the sample program shown here, redirect_stdout was used to redirect all screen output to the *out.txt* file. Except for the error handling, the code is equivalent to the following:

```
>>> import sys
>>> with open("out.txt", "w") as f_out:
...     sys.stdout = f_out
...     print("Screen")
...     print("output")
...     sys.stdout = sys.__stdout__
```

Furthermore, the redirect_stdout function overrides the global sys.stdout reference. You should therefore pay attention to possible side effects.

> **Note**
>
> Like redirect_stdout, the redirect_stderr context manager is available here, which redirects the standard stderr error stream.

22.2.4   Optional Contexts

In certain situations, you may want to optionally execute code that was implemented using a context manager without that context manager. As an example, let's consider the redirect_stdout context manager discussed in the previous section for redirecting the standard output stream.

In the following, we'll use the nullcontext context manager from the contextlib module to redirect the standard output stream, or not, depending on a dynamically configurable setting:

```
>>> stdout_redirect = False
>>> with open("out.txt", "w") as f_out:
...     if stdout_redirect:
...         context = contextlib.redirect_stdout(f_out)
...     else:
...         context = contextlib.nullcontext()
...     with context:
...         print("Screen")
```

```
...        print("output")
Screen
output
```

Depending on the setting in stdout_redirect, the screen outputs within the second with statement are either executed in the context of redirect_stdout or in the context of nullcontext. The nullcontext context manager does nothing at all when it's entered and exited and is therefore well suited as an alternative in situations like the one shown in the example, when the redirection of the output stream is to be switched off.

22.2.5   Simple Functions as Context Manager

A classic context manager that can be used in a with statement is a class that implements the __enter__ and __exit__ methods. The contextmanager decorator from the contextlib module allows you to write much simpler context managers based on a function.

> **Note**
>
> The contextmanager function presented here is a *decorator*. This is a special function whose task is to manipulate other functions and thereby add functionality, for example. Python supports the convenient use of decorators by means of a special syntax. You can find out more about the topic of decorators in Chapter 23.

A function decorated with contextmanager must return a generator object[1] via exactly one element:

```
import time
@contextlib.contextmanager
def runtime():
    start = time.perf_counter()
    try:
        yield
    finally:
        print("Runtime: {:.2f} s".format(time.perf_counter() - start))
```

In the example, the parameterless runtime function was decorated with contextmanager. Technically, it must now return a generator that generates a single element. This is realized by the yield statement in the function body. The function body can be divided mentally into two areas: the part before yield and the part after. When using runtime in a with context, you can think of the part before yield as the implementation of __enter__, and the part after yield as the implementation of __exit__.

---

1 For more information on generators, see Chapter 21, Section 21.1.

The runtime function, which has been expanded to a context manager, can now be used to measure the runtime of program sections:

```
>>> with runtime():
...     x = 0
...     for i in range(10000000):
...         x += (-1)**i * i  # A time-consuming calculation
...
Runtime: 5.09 s
```

Chapter 23
Decorators

In this chapter, we'll explore how behavior implemented in functions and classes can be customized and augmented by wrapper functions. This is especially interesting when the wrapper function performs a generic customization that can be applied in the same way to many different functions or classes. Encapsulation in such a wrapper function then avoids multiple implementations of the same behavior in different functions.

In the following sections, we'll first develop our own wrapper function using a simple example and then use *decorators* to introduce an elegant syntax for the function's use. We'll then develop a generic cache for function calls in a more complex example and transfer the concept of wrappers and decorators to classes. Finally, we'll discuss the functools module of the standard library, which contains, among other things, a collection of useful decorators.

23.1 Function Decorators

As a simple example, let's assume a set of functions, each of which puts the program to sleep for a certain amount of time in its own way using time.sleep:

```
>>> import time
>>> import random
>>> def small_nap():
...     time.sleep(random.randint(1, 3))
>>> def precise_nap(n):
...     time.sleep(n)
>>> def power_nap(stay_awake=False):
...     if not stay_awake:
...         time.sleep(0.1)
```

Now we're interested in how long the calls of these functions actually take. To avoid having to implement time measurement in each of the three functions independently, we'll write a generic wrapper function that receives a function object and adds time measurement to it:

```
>>> def with_timing(fn):
...     def wrapper(*args, **kwargs):
...         t = time.perf_counter()
...         try:
...             return fn(*args, **kwargs)
...         finally:
...             e = time.perf_counter()
...             print(f"Runtime of {fn.__name__}: {e - t}s")
...     return wrapper
```

The with_timing function is supposed to define a suitable wrapper function for a given function object fn, which extends fn by a time measurement. For this purpose, the wrapper function wrapper is defined locally inside of with_timing. This function takes any number of positional and keyword parameters, which is important as it will later replace the actual small_nap, precise_nap, and power_nap functions with their individual interfaces. The interface of the wrapper does not necessarily have to consist of the generic parameters *args and **kwargs as in the example but may be more specific. It is important that it matches the interfaces of the functions to which the wrapper is to be applied.

The wrapper itself behaves essentially like the fn function object it's supposed to extend: it calls fn with the parameters passed to it and returns its return value. It also measures start and end time and outputs its runtime after calling fn.

We can now add time measurement to the existing functions using with_timing:

```
>>> small_nap = with_timing(small_nap)
>>> precise_nap = with_timing(precise_nap)
>>> power_nap = with_timing(power_nap)
```

The functions manipulated in this way can be used on the basis of their original definition, but they now automatically have a time measurement run along with them:

```
>>> small_nap()
Runtime of small_nap: 2.001250743865967s
>>> precise_nap(1)
Runtime of precise_nap: 1.004967212677002s
>>> power_nap(stay_awake=True)
Runtime of power_nap: 3.0994415283203125e-06s
```

This principle of adding functionality to functions using generic wrappers is widely used. An example you are already familiar with is the built-in staticmethod function, which was introduced in Chapter 19, Section 19.6:

```
class MyClass:
    def method():
        pass
    method = staticmethod(method)
```

In addition, a wealth of other applications of this principle can be found in the standard library.

23.1.1 Decorating Functions and Methods

In the previous section, we applied a generic wrapper to various function objects, e.g.:

```
>>> small_nap = with_timing(small_nap)
```

Python provides a special syntax to perform such manipulations of function objects via wrapper functions directly during the function definition. To do this, we'll write a *function decorator* before the function definition:

```
>>> @with_timing
... def small_nap():
...     time.sleep(random.randint(1, 3))
```

A decorator is applied to a function by writing the name of the decorator with the @ character immediately preceding the function definition. The application of static-method can also be formulated using a function decorator:

```
class MyClass:
    @staticmethod
    def method():
        pass
```

23.1.2 Name and Docstring after Applying a Decorator

You may have already noticed that the function object that was manipulated using a wrapper function has lost its original name and docstring:

```
>>> small_nap.__name__
'wrapper'
```

This is because it's been replaced by a wrapper function called wrapper, and the __name__ and __doc__ attributes thus refer to the name and docstring of this wrapper function.

By applying the wraps decorator from the functools module to the wrapper function, this information can be automatically transferred so that the application of a decorator is transparent with respect to the __name__ and __doc__ attributes:

```
>>> def with_timing(fn):
...     @functools.wraps(fn)
...     def wrapper(*args, **kwargs):
...         t = time.perf_counter()
...         try:
...             return fn(*args, **kwargs)
...         finally:
...             e = time.perf_counter()
...             print(f"Runtime of {fn.__name__}: {e - t}s")
...     return wrapper
```

23.1.3   Nested Decorators

Function decorators can be nested within each other, as the following example shows:

```
@dec1
@dec2
def function():
    pass
```

This function definition is equivalent to the following code:

```
def function():
    pass
function = dec1(dec2(function))
```

Needless to say, both dec1 and dec2 must be implemented before the examples are executable.

23.1.4   Example: A Cache Decorator

The following example shows an interesting approach to *caching* function calls, where the results of complex calculations are automatically saved. These can then be replayed with the same parameters in the next function call without having to perform the calculations again. Caching a function is done just by specifying a function decorator—that is, without interfering with the function itself—and also works with all function calls where only hashable instances are passed. To do this, let's first look at the definition of the calculation function, which in this case calculates the factorial of an integer, including the decorator:

```
@CacheDecorator()
def fac(n):
    result = 1
```

```
    for i in range(2, n+1):
        result *= i
    return result
```

The function decorator is interesting here because it's not a function, but a class called CacheDecorator that is instantiated in the decorator. You surely remember that a class can be made callable by implementing the __call__ magic method and thus making it behave like a function object. We have to make this workaround because we need to store the results of the calculations so that they are still available in later calls of the decorator. This isn't possible with a function, but it is with a class. The definition of the decorator class looks as follows:

```
class CacheDecorator:
    def __init__(self):
        self.cache = {}
        self.func = None
    def cached_func(self, *args):
        if args not in self.cache:
            self.cache[args] = self.func(*args)
            print("Result calculated")
        else:
            print("Result loaded")
        return self.cache[args]
    def __call__(self, func):
        self.func = func
        return self.cached_func
```

In the constructor of the CacheDecorator class, an empty dictionary is created for the cached values. In addition to the constructor, the __call__ method is implemented, among others. This method makes instances of the class callable so that they can be used like a function object.[1] To be used as a function decorator, the __call__ method must accept a function object as a parameter and return a function object. The returned function object is then associated with the originally passed function as a modified version of it. In the example, __call__ returns the function object of the cached_func method.

So the cached_func method now should be called instead of the originally created function. For it to do its job, it has access to the function object of the actual function, which is referenced by the self.func attribute. The cached_func method accepts any number of positional arguments as it should later work for as many function interfaces as possible.[2] These arguments are available within the method as tuples.

---

1 For more details on this, please refer to Chapter 19, Section 19.11.1.
2 Because the parameters passed in a function call are used as keys for the internal cache dictionary, only instances of hashable data types may be passed.

Now a check must be carried out as to whether the tuple with the passed arguments already exists as a key in the self.cache dictionary. If so, the function has already been called with exactly the same arguments, and the cached return value can be returned directly. If the key doesn't exist, the self.func calculation function is called with the passed arguments and the result is cached. After that, it will be returned.

In real applications, we would omit the print outputs when calculating or loading the results, but they help us verify the operation of our cache at this point:

```
>>> fac(10)
Result calculated
3628800
>>> fac(20)
Result calculated
2432902008176640000
>>> fac(20)
Result loaded
2432902008176640000
>>> fac(10)
Result loaded
3628800
```

As you can see, the first two results were calculated, while the last two were loaded from the internal cache. This kind of caching provides significant speed advantages depending on the application area and the complexity of the calculation.

In Chapter 17, Section 17.13 we developed a recursive implementation of the factorial function fac. What happens if you run it in combination with the CacheDecorator? Can you explain the result?

> **Note**
>
> Be aware that there is no logic for clearing cache entries implemented in CacheDecorator. The cache will therefore continue to grow as it is used. Thus, think of CacheDecorator solely as an example of how to use decorators, and not as a ready-to-use implementation for caching function calls. In Chapter 23, Section 23.3.3, we discuss the lru_cache decorator from the functools module as a ready-to-use alternative to CacheDecorator.

23.2 Class Decorators

The principle of function decorators can be applied in a similar way as *class decorators*, with the only difference being that the object to be manipulated is not a function but a class.

From Chapter 19, Section 19.12, you already know about the data classes that are defined using a class decorator:

```
>>> import dataclasses
>>> @dataclasses.dataclass
... class SomeDataClass:
...     python: str
...     works: int
...     well: list
>>> SomeDataClass("Test", 123, ["A", "B", "C"])
SomeDataClass(python='Test', works=123, well=['A', 'B', 'C'])
```

Much like the previous examples on function decorators, this definition of a data class can also be formulated as follows:

```
>>> class AnotherDataClass:
...     python: str
...     works: int
...     well: list
>>> AnotherDataClass = dataclasses.dataclass(AnotherDataClass)
>>> AnotherDataClass("Test", 123, ["A", "B", "C"])
AnotherDataClass(python='Test', works=123, well=['A', 'B', 'C'])
```

23.3   The functools Module

The functools module of the standard library contains functions and decorators that can be used to modify callable objects, such as functions or methods, at an abstract level. This section describes how you can simplify interfaces, add a cache, and complete an ordering of custom classes.

23.3.1   Simplifying Function Interfaces

The functools module contains the partial function, which can be used to simplify function interfaces. To do this, let's take a look at the following function:

```
def f(a, b, c, d):
    print("{} {} {} {}".format(a,b,c,d))
```

The f function expects many parameters—four, to be precise. Now let's imagine we have to call the f function very often in the program and always pass the same values for the b, c, and d parameters. The partial function can be used to change the interface of f so that only the a parameter, which is actually of interest, needs to be passed.

partial(func, [*args], {kwargs})**

The partial function is passed a function object whose interface is to be simplified. In addition, the positional and keyword parameters to be fixed are also passed.

The partial function returns a new function object with the same interface as func, but simplified by the parameters specified in args (arguments) and kwargs (keyword arguments). When the returned function object is called, these fixed parameters will automatically be added.

This is demonstrated in the following example, using the f function defined previously:

```
>>> import functools
>>> f_new = functools.partial(f, b="you", c="beautiful", d="world")
>>> f_new("Hello,")
Hello, you beautiful world
>>> f_new("Bye,")
Bye, you beautiful world
```

First, the f function is defined, which accepts four parameters and outputs them one after the other on the screen. Because the last three parameters of this interface are always the same in this program, we don't want to repeat them every time and can simplify the interface using partial.

To do this, we call the partial function and pass the function object of f as the first parameter. This is followed by the three fixed values for parameters b, c, and d in the form of keyword parameters. The partial function returns a function object corresponding to the f function with a simplified interface. This function object can be called with a single parameter, as shown in the example. The f function is passed this parameter together with the three fixed parameters.

Apart from keyword parameters, you can also pass positional parameters[3] to the partial function, which are then also passed as such to the function to be simplified. Note that the fixed parameters must then be located at the beginning of the function interface. Let's look at the following example:

```
>>> f_new = functools.partial(f, "Hello", "you", "beautiful")
>>> f_new("world")
Hello you beautiful world
>>> f_new("woman")
Hello you beautiful woman
```

The first three parameters of the f function are always the same and are to be set as positional parameters using the partial function. The resulting f_new function object

---

3 A mixture of positional and keyword parameters may also be specified.

can be called with a parameter that's passed as a fourth parameter in addition to the three fixed parameters when the resulting function call of f is made.

23.3.2   Simplifying Method Interfaces

Analogous to the partial function just discussed for simplifying function interfaces, the partialmethod function exists for simplifying method interfaces. Using partial method, you can create variants of a method with certain parameters predefined. Let's look at the following example:

```
>>> import functools
>>> class Quote:
...     def __init__(self):
...         self.source = "Unknown"
...     def quote(self, text):
...         print("{}: '{}'".format(self.source, text))
...     def set_source(self, source):
...         self.source = source
...     set_donald = functools.partialmethod(set_source, "Donald Duck")
...     set_goofy = functools.partialmethod(set_source, "Goofy")
...
>>> quote = Quote()
>>> quote.set_donald()
>>> quote.quote("Quack")
Donald Duck: 'Quack'
```

In the example, two simplifications of the set_source method have been added to the Quote class, each specifying a particular author. The partialmethod function has the same interface as partial, and setting parameters works according to the same principle.

23.3.3   Caches

Using the lru_cache decorator, which is included in the functtools module, you can provide a function with a cache. A *cache* is memory that saves past function calls. If a parameter assignment has already occurred during the function call, the result can be read from the cache and the function doesn't have to be executed again. This principle can provide a great runtime advantage, especially for CPU-intensive and frequently called functions.

> **Note**
>
> When a function result is read from the cache, the function is not executed. Thus, caching only makes sense if the function is free of side effects and deterministic; that is, the result is always the same with the same parameter assignment.

lru_cache([maxsize, typed])

The lru_cache decorator provides a function with a least recently used (LRU) cache with maxsize entries. In an LRU cache, a new entry always displaces the entry that hasn't occurred for the longest time, provided the cache is completely full. If the value None is passed for maxsize, the cache has no maximum size and can grow indefinitely. The typed parameter, which defaults to False, specifies whether equivalent instances of different data types, such as 2 and 2.0, should be considered equal (False) or not equal (True).

In the following example, the fac function for calculating the factorial of an integer is defined and cached:

```
>>> import functools
>>> @functools.lru_cache(20)
... def fac(n):
...     res = 1
...     for i in range(2, n+1):
...         res *= i
...     return res
...
>>> [fac(x) for x in [7, 5, 12, 3, 5, 7, 3]]
[5040, 120, 479001600, 6, 120, 5040, 6]
```

Using the cache_info method, which the lru_cache decorator adds to the decorated function object, you can get information about the current state of the cache:

```
>>> fac.cache_info()
CacheInfo(hits=3, misses=4, maxsize=20, currsize=4)
```

The result is a named tuple with the following entries (see Table 23.1).

Entry	Description
hits	The number of function calls whose results were read from the cache
misses	The number of function calls whose results were not read from the cache

Table 23.1 Entries in the CacheInfo Tuple

Entry	Description
maxsize	The maximum size of the cache
currsize	The current size of the cache

Table 23.1 Entries in the CacheInfo Tuple (Cont.)

In addition to cache_info, a function object decorated with lru_cache has a parameter-less method called cache_clear that clears the cache.

> **Note**
>
> Internally, the cache is implemented as a dictionary in which the parameter assignment of a function call is used as the key. For this reason, only instances of hashable data types may be passed to a function object that uses the LRU cache presented here.

23.3.4 Completing Orderings of Custom Classes

A class that defines an *ordering*—that is, for which the <, <=, >, and >= comparison operators work—must implement each of the corresponding __lt__, __le__, __gt__, and __ge__ magic methods. However, one of these methods would already suffice to describe the order.

The total_ordering decorator that's included in the functtools module extends a class that provides only one of these magic methods, plus the __eq__ method by the respective other comparison methods.

23.3.5 Overloading Functions

There are operations that are defined for instances of different data types but must be implemented differently depending on the data type. An example of such an operation is the built-in print function, which selects an output variant based on the data types passed.

The functtools module contains the singledispatch decorator, which allows the overloading of functions. *Overloading* adds implementation variants of a function under the same name. When the function is called, the interpreter selects which concrete variant is executed based on the data type of the passed parameters. In the case of singledispatch, the variant to be executed is selected based on the data type of the first passed parameter—hence the name.

The following example defines the mult function, which ignores the data types passed to it and therefore shows a different behavior regarding numbers and strings:

```
>>> def mult(x):
...         return x*2
...
>>> mult(5)
10
>>> mult("5")
'55'
```

The singledispatch decorator can be used to overload the function for strings so that in this case, a multiplication is performed on the numerical value contained in the string:

```
>>> import functools
>>> @functools.singledispatch
... def mult(x):
...         return x*2
...
>>> @mult.register(str)
... def _(x):
...         return str(int(x)*2)
...
```

The mult output function is defined as in the previous example and also provided with the singledispatch decorator. This decorator extends the function with the register method, which can be used to overload it.

In the second part of the example, a variant of the mult method is implemented for strings. This variant, which has the temporary name _, is registered as a variant of mult via the mult decorator. Depending on the parameters, one of the two variants of mult will now be executed:

```
>>> mult(5)
10
>>> mult("5")
'10'
```

In this way, a function can be overloaded as often as needed. If a variant is to be available for multiple data types, the register decorators can be chained:

```
>>> @mult.register(float)
... @mult.register(str)
... def _(x):
...         return str(int(x)*2)
...
>>> mult(5.0)
'10'
>>> mult("5")
'10'
```

Note

This type of function overloading is not a fundamental concept of Python, but was introduced so that basic functions of the standard library, including `print` or `len`, could be conveniently implemented in Python. Function overloading in Python is therefore associated with major limitations:

- It isn't possible to overload any kind of function, but only those that have been decorated with `singledispatch`.
- An overloadable function may have only one nonoptional parameter.
- Other languages, such as C++, for example, offer extensive freedom in overloading functions. The approach presented here significantly differs from that.

23

Chapter 24
Annotations for Static Type Checking

Python is a *dynamically typed* language. This means that the data type assigned to an instance isn't determined before the program is actually executed. Interfaces are also often implicitly defined by the capabilities of an instance, rather than by the data type; this principle is referred to as *duck typing* (see Chapter 19, Section 19.11.3). For example, there are many functions and methods in the standard library that expect a *file-like object*, an object that provides an interface for writing and reading data. However, two file-like objects can have completely different data types.

This flexibility is one of Python's great strengths, but it also leads to the fact that it's never formally specified for function and method interfaces which data types fulfill the requirements of the function and are thus eligible as parameters. Even integrated development environments sometimes don't provide any reliable help here, which results in major problems, especially in large software projects.

Due to this problem, a more or less standardized syntax for type comments has been established during the course of many years, which can be understood and processed by a developer as well as by development environments and tools for static code analysis:

```python
def repeat(s, n):
    # type: (str, int) -> str
    return s*n
```

A *type comment* is therefore a pure annotation of the function interface that gives a human developer and an automatic code tool alike a hint as to which data types are possible for the interface. In particular, the type comment is optional by nature and doesn't affect the execution of the program. The data types annotated within a type comment, and later also within annotations, are also referred to as *type hints*.

To be able to provide a formal syntax for this use case of *type annotations*, so-called function annotations were introduced with Python 3.0 and extended in Python 3.8 by the possibility of annotating variables and attributes:

```python
def repeat(s: str, n: int) -> str:
    return s*n
```

Similar to type comments, annotations don't affect the program flow in any way, but represent optional additional information intended to support the developer and their automated tools. In particular, no type checking takes place even if annotations do exist, and there are no plans to depart from the principle of duck typing despite the existence of annotations.

In the following sections, we'll describe the syntax of annotations and the closely related typing module of the standard library. Many integrated development environments (IDEs) for Python are able to understand annotations and use the information they contain for context help or warnings about potential errors. Figure 24.1 and Figure 24.2 show two examples in which the *PyCharm* IDE uses annotations to provide context help to the developer.

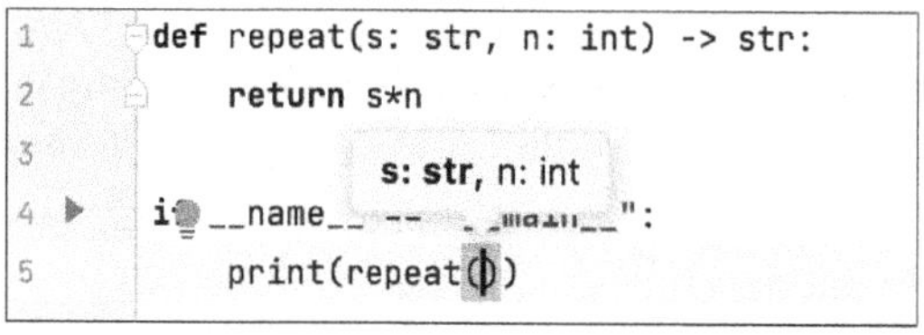

```
1    def repeat(s: str, n: int) -> str:
2        return s*n
3                         s: str, n: int
4  ▶   if __name__ == "__main__":
5        print(repeat())
```

Figure 24.1 PyCharm IDE Displays Context Help Based on Annotations

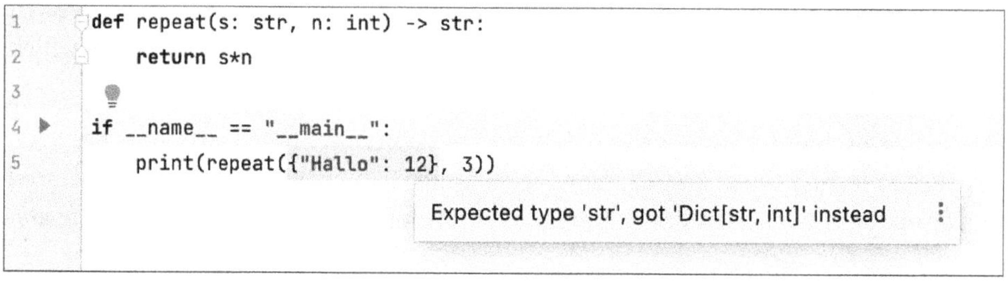

```
1    def repeat(s: str, n: int) -> str:
2        return s*n
3       💡
4  ▶   if __name__ == "__main__":
5        print(repeat({"Hallo": 12}, 3))
                         Expected type 'str', got 'Dict[str, int]' instead   ⋮
```

Figure 24.2 PyCharm IDE Flags Potential Errors in the Code Based on Annotations

> **Note**
>
> In this chapter, we'll deal exclusively with annotations as a modern variant of type comments. Note, however, that many Python codebases continue to use type comments. This particularly affects code that must be executable in both Python 3 and Python 2 as annotations were only introduced with Python 3.

24.1   Annotations

In Chapter 19, Section 19.12, we mentioned *annotations* for the first time because their specification is required when defining data classes. At this point, we'd like to shed some light on what annotations actually are and what purpose they serve in the context of typing.

Using annotations, the programmer can specify additional information when defining variables and attributes and within function and method interfaces. This information is optional and can consist of any Python expression. They don't change anything in the program execution at first, and you could say that the Python interpreter doesn't care about annotations. Nevertheless, annotations can indeed contain useful additional information that can be accessed via two mechanisms:

- The `typing` module of the standard library provides access to the annotations made by the programmer at program runtime. In this way, the annotations made in a function interface can be used, for example, during function execution. Whether and how annotations are read and used for program execution is always decided by the developer of the program.

- By convention, annotations can contain additional information that isn't considered for the program flow itself, but on which external tools for code analysis are based—supporting features of an IDE, for example.

As described at the beginning of this chapter, annotations provide a way to add additional information to certain definitions within the Python syntax. At first, the concept of annotations doesn't define what this additional information should look like.

However, annotations were introduced against the background of an essential area of use and are also primarily used in this context in practice: the typing of Python code.

> **Note**
>
> We consider annotations in this chapter exclusively in the context of typing, which is the principal area of use for this concept. However, you should keep in mind that the syntax of annotations is not fundamentally limited to type information.

24.1.1 Annotating Functions and Methods

The elements of a function or method interface—that is, parameters and return values—can be provided with annotations, which in this context are also referred to as *function annotations*:

```python
def function(p1: Annotation1, p2: Annotation2) -> Annotation3:
    Function body
```

When defining a function, a colon can be written after each parameter, followed by an annotation. An annotation may be any Python expression. The specification of an annotation is optional. The parameter list can be followed by an optional annotation for the return value of the function. This annotation is introduced by an arrow (->). Only after this annotation does a colon follow, which introduces the function body.

In the following example, we'll define the repeat function, whose task is to return a string consisting of the n-fold repetition of the input string s:

```
>>> def repeat(s: str, n: int) -> str:
...        return s*n
```

In doing so, we use annotations to mark the expected data types of the s and n function parameters, as well as the data type of the return value. As already mentioned, we haven't changed the behavior of the repeat function in any way compared to a variant without annotations. In particular, repeat can also be called with arguments that contradict the annotations of the function interface:

```
>>> repeat("P", 3)
'PPP'
>>> repeat(["P"], 3)
['P', 'P', 'P']
```

Nevertheless, the annotation of the function interface provides clarity by hinting to the developer in an unambiguous way about which data types the original developer of the function intended for its interface. This information is especially important in large, collaborative software projects.

Modern IDEs[1] are capable of reading type information from annotations and can therefore provide informative context help for the repeat function and even warn against an incorrect use of the function.

The interfaces of methods can be annotated with type information in a similar way. For this purpose, we extend the previous example of the repeat function with an (admittedly pointless) StringTools class, within which repeat is again defined as a method:

```
>>> class StringTools:
...        def repeat(self, s: str, n: int) -> str:
...            return s*n
...
>>> st = StringTools()
>>> st.repeat("P", 3)
'PPP'
```

24.1.2   Annotating Variables and Attributes

Similar to the annotation of parameters occurring in the context of a function or method interface, since Python 3.6, annotations can also be specified when defining variables and attributes. The essential motivation is the same: even though annotations of variables and attributes can basically consist of any Python expression, they

---

1 For an overview of development environments for Python, see Section A.5 in the appendix.

are intended for specifying data type information and are usually used in that way in practice.

Variables can always be annotated where values are assigned to them. In particular, the annotation assigned to an identifier can therefore change during the program run if new values are assigned to the same name several times and different annotations are specified there in each case.

Like annotations of function parameters, annotations of variables are written after the identifier, separated by a colon, but before the equal sign of the assignment:

```
>>> s: str = "Hello world"
>>> n: int = 12
>>> l: list = [1, 2, 3]
```

This works for global variables at the module level as well as for local variables within functions or methods.[2] In the following example, this becomes clear by means of a variant of the repeat function extended by an intermediate variable, result:

```
>>> def repeat(s: str, n: int) -> str:
...     result: str = s*n
...     return result
```

Even when defining attributes at the class or instance level, annotations can be specified using the usual syntax:

```
>>> class Class:
...     class attribute: int = 1
...     def __init__(self):
...         self.instanceattribute: str = "Hello world"
```

Like other annotations, annotations of variables and attributes are essentially ignored by the Python interpreter, so they don't directly affect the program flow.

> **Note**
>
> One difference between annotations for global and local variables is that the Python expression behind an annotation is evaluated for global variables, class attributes, and within function and method interfaces to provide its value at runtime:
>
> ```
> >>> x: blahblah = 12
> Traceback (most recent call last):
>   File "<stdin>", line 1, in <module>
> NameError: name 'blahblah' is not defined
> ```

---

2 In fact, even arbitrary assignments can be annotated in this way:
```
>>> lst = [1, 2, 3, 4]
>>> lst[1]: str = "test"
```

In contrast, the Python expressions behind the annotations of local variables and instance attributes are not evaluated. In Section 24.1.3, we'll see that those expressions can't be accessed at program runtime either:

```
>>> def function():
...     x: blahblah = 12
...     return x
...
>>> function()
12
```

See also Section 24.1.4 for more information on when exactly the evaluation of an annotation takes place.

It's possible to perform a standalone variable annotation, independent of a concurrent assignment. The following syntax creates only the annotation required for the identifier k and doesn't define k itself:

```
>>> k: str
>>> k
Traceback (most recent call last):
  File "<stdin>", line 1, in <module>
NameError: name 'k' is not defined
```

This syntax is convenient, for example, to have to annotate variable definitions in conditionals only once:

```
>>> k: str
>>> if True:
...     k = "Hello"
... else:
...     k = "world"
```

Another use case is the annotation of a loop variable or the variables of a with context as the syntax of both constructs doesn't permit embedded annotations:

```
>>> city: str
>>> for city in ["Chicago", "Boston", "Atlanta", "Seattle"]:
...     print(city)
```

24.1.3   Accessing Annotations at Runtime

Annotations have been introduced in Python as a syntax extension that supports external utilities simply and syntactically unambiguously with type information about variables, attributes, and function and method interfaces. Such external utilities can, for example, display context help as part of an IDE or point out potential errors in the code.

Annotations in themselves do not fundamentally change the runtime behavior of a Python code, with the limitation that an exception can be raised if the annotation consists of an invalid expression.

Basically, annotations are intended for type information, and it's generally recommended to use them exclusively in this context. Nevertheless, their syntax is of a general nature that permits any Python expression as an annotation and thus could also be used in other areas. In this section, we'll describe how you can access annotations at program runtime. Let's take another look at the repeat function from the previous section:

```
>>> def repeat(s: str, n: int) -> str:
...     result: str = s*n
...     return result
```

If you need to access the annotations of the repeat function at runtime, you can do so using the get_type_hints function of the typing module of the standard library, which returns the annotations as a dictionary. This dictionary contains the parameter names or "return" for the return value annotation as keys and the respective annotation expressions as values:

```
>>> import typing
>>> typing.get_type_hints(repeat)
{'s': <class 'str'>, 'n': <class 'int'>, 'return': <class 'str'>}
```

Likewise, the type information of an annotated method interface can be accessed at runtime—for example, that of the repeat method of the StringTools class we defined in the previous section:

```
>>> typing.get_type_hints(StringTools.repeat)
{'s': <class 'str'>, 'n': <class 'int'>, 'return': <class 'str'>}
```

The get_type_hints function is also capable of returning the annotations for the global variables of a module or the class attributes of a class. Annotations for local variables within functions and instance attributes can't be determined at runtime. These are intended for the sole purpose of informing external utilities.

Note

Internally, the interpreter stores the annotations in the __annotations__ attribute of the annotated object. This dictionary has the same form as the dictionary returned by get_type_hints:

```
>>> repeat.__annotations__
{'s': <class 'str'>, 'n': <class 'int'>, 'return': <class 'str'>}
```

However, __annotations__ is an implementation detail of the Python interpreter whose name and organization may change in future Python versions. For this reason, accessing annotations via get_type_hints is the recommended choice.

24.1.4   When are Annotations Evaluated?

As mentioned in the previous sections, annotations can be full-featured, sometimes complex expressions that are evaluated in the interpreter's default behavior at the time the annotation is defined.[3] This leads to the fact that, for example, when importing a module, all annotations contained in it must be evaluated and their values entered into the __annotations__ dictionary. Because annotations are primarily used to inform an external system for type checking, their values are usually of no interest at runtime and are therefore unnecessarily paid for by a lengthy import.

Another problem with the immediate evaluation of annotations is forward references, such as the annotation of a function interface with data types that aren't fully defined at the position of the annotation. For example, the following attempt at a type annotation for the __add__ magic method on a self-defined class will fail:

```
>>> class Test:
...     def __add__(self, other: Test):
...         pass
Traceback (most recent call last):
  File "<stdin>", line 1, in <module>
  File "<stdin>", line 2, in Test
NameError: name 'Test' is not defined
```

At this point, the problem is that the Test class isn't yet completely defined at the time of definition of the __add__ method and thus also at the time of evaluation of its annotations. Annotations of methods can therefore not refer to the respective classes in which they are defined. In such cases, you can help yourself by wrapping the annotation in a string:

```
>>> class Test:
...     def __add__(self, other: "Test"):
...         pass
```

---

3 An exception are annotations of local variables, which are never evaluated. We discussed this in Section 24.1.2.

Alternatively, you can use the future import `annotations`, which delays the evaluation time of annotations and thus allows the previous example to be executed without string wrapping:

```
>>> from __future__ import annotations
>>> class Test:
...     def __add__(self, other: Test):
...         pass
```

The future import makes sure that annotations aren't evaluated at the time of their definition, but are stored as strings instead:

```
>>> Test.__add__.__annotations__
{'other': 'Test'}
```

The evaluation is done only when the annotations are actually used and is done implicitly by calling `get_type_hints`:

```
>>> import typing
>>> typing.get_type_hints(Test.__add__)
{'other': <class '__main__.Test'>}
```

It's planned to make the delayed evaluation of annotations the standard behavior in future versions of Python. But as this change would be potentially incompatible with existing code, the future import is necessary for its activation until further notice.

24.2 Type Hints: The typing Module

In the previous section, we looked at annotations as a syntax that allows the developer to add additional information to the definition of functions, methods, variables, and attributes. Basically, this additional information can be any Python expression, but in practice we usually restrict ourselves to type information—so-called type hints. These annotations can be read by external utilities that support the programmer on this basis, for example, with context help.

So far, we've looked at annotations with simple data types such as `int` or `str` and used these examples to clarify the basic syntactic form of an annotation. In this section, we'll take advantage of the fact that type hints can also be more complex expressions, which, in combination with the `typing` module of the standard library, allows us to cleanly annotate even complex function interfaces, for example.

The `typing` module defines standardized placeholders for common data types in Python and allows their combination to specify more complex data structures. In the following sections, we'll describe some important use cases for annotations using typing, but you should note that these are only a selection of the possibilities typing provides.

The examples in the following sections refer to simple function interfaces, but they also can be applied to other use cases in the annotation of methods, variables, and attributes.

24.2.1   Valid Type Hints

As part of the introduction of annotations to the Python programming language, conventions were established[4] describing what a valid type hint may consist of. Accordingly, a type hint may consist of any built-in and user-defined classes, including modules from the standard library or external third-party modules and packages. In addition, the types contained in the typing module of the standard library in particular are permitted, in which generic placeholder types are defined for various application purposes—for example, nested data structures.

24.2.2   Container Types

When using container types, for example lists or dictionaries, in combination with type annotations, the following problem arises: container types contain instances of other data types. Therefore, the type hint *list*, for example, is not very informative. Instead, type hints are needed that can also specify the data types of instances contained in container objects.

For this purpose, Type Hints for container types can be supplemented with Type Hints for the contained instances as follows:

```
>>> v1: list[int] = [1, 2, 3, 4, 5]
>>> v2: tuple[int, str, int] = (1, "test", 2)
>>> v3: tuple[int, ...] = (1, 2, 3, 4, 5)
>>> v4: dict[int, str] = {1: "test_1", 2: "test_2"}
>>> v5: set[int] = {1, 2, 3}
>>> v6: frozenset[int] = {1, 2, 3}
```

These type hints are also called *generics*. Special attention should be paid to the difference between tuple and list. While list[int] denotes a list with any number of elements of type int, the data types specified for tuple correspond directly to the elements of the tuple. If you want to denote a tuple with any number of integers, as with the variable v3 in the example, you must additionally append the ellipse.

In the following example we annotate a function interface with container data types:

---

4 This has been done with PEP-484.

```
def function(p1: list[str], p2: dict[int, list[str]]):
    pass
```

In the definition of function the parameter p1 is annotated with the type hint *list of strings*, while the parameter p2 gets the type hint *dictionary, which maps from integers to lists of strings*. Within square brackets the data types of the instances contained in the respective container type are specified, whereby these in turn may be generics.

Note

The use of built-in data types as generics in the context of annotations was introduced with Python 3.9. In older language versions, special generics from the typing module can be used instead:

```
>>> from typing import List, Dict
>>> v1: List[int] = [1, 2, 3, 4]
>>> v2: Dict[int, str] = {1: "test_1", 2: "test_2"}
```

In addition, the modern behavior can also be activated in older language versions via a future import (see Chapter 18, Section 18.5):

```
>>> from __future__ import annotations
>>> x: dict[str, str]
```

24.2.3 Abstract Container Types

The generics discussed in the previous section can be used to define annotations for complex container types. Especially in function interfaces, however, the concrete data type of a container object is not relevant in many cases, but rather its properties in the sense of duck typing. Functions, for example, can often process arbitrary iterable objects instead of just lists.

In such cases it is advised to use the *abstract base classes* (ABC) from the collections. abc module for annotations. In the following example we define some variables annotated with a selection of the abstract base classes from collections.abc:

```
>>> import collections.abc
>>> v1: collections.abc.Iterable[int]
>>> v2: collections.abc.Iterator[int]
>>> v3: collections.abc.Sequence[int]
>>> v4: collections.abc.MutableSequence[int]
>>> v5: collections.abc.Mapping[int]
>>> v6: collections.abc.MutableMapping[int]
>>> v7: collections.abc.Set[int]
>>> v8: collections.abc.MutableSet[int]
```

We will not delve further into the topic of abstract base classes in Python here, but refer you to the online documentation for more information.

24.2.4   Type Aliases

Complex type hints can quickly become confusing and may therefore be assigned to a new name, the so-called type alias:

```
>>> from typing import Dict, List
>>> MyType = Dict[int, List[str]]
>>> def function(p: MyType):
...     pass
```

In this case, the MyType type alias was defined as a dictionary that maps from integers to lists of strings. From now on, this alias can be used in interface definitions without any problem.

24.2.5   Type Unions and Optional Values

If in a function interface for a parameter a set of possible data types becomes eligible, a union set of data types, a so-called type union, can be formed via the union type from the typing module:

```
>>> from typing import Union
>>> def function(p: Union[int, float]):
...     pass
```

In the example, the type hint of the p function parameter states that instances of the int and float data types may be passed equally.

> **Note**
> Since Python 3.10, the | operator, which you know from the bitwise OR, can be used to write type unions more easily. The preceding example can then also be written as follows:
>
> ```
> >>> def function(p: int | float):
> ...     pass
> ```

A special case of using type unions, which plays a major role in practice, are optional values: often the value None is accepted at function interfaces in addition to instances of the data type actually intended for a parameter. For this frequently used special case, the typing module provides the Optional type, which allows for the following two equivalent notations:

```
>>> from typing import Union, Optional
>>> def function1(p: Union[int, None]):
...     pass
>>> def function2(p: Optional[int]):
...     pass
```

The second variant, function2, is only a shorthand notation for the first variant: for the p parameter, int instances are generally expected, with the exception of the additionally allowed value None.

Note

Like other annotations, the Optional type hint contains no semantics for the function interface. In particular, the type hint remains, regardless of whether or not the p parameter is optional. A combination of an optional parameter p and the Optional type hint can look like this:

```
>>> def function3(p: Optional[int] = None):
...     pass
```

Another special case of type unions is the union of all possible types, e.g. a function parameter for which any data type may be passed. For this case, the typing module contains the Any type:

```
>>> from typing import Any
>>> def function(p: Any):
...     pass
```

Implicitly, all missing type hints are assumed to be Any.

24.2.6   Type Variables

It often occurs that there are dependencies between the data types of a function interface. For example, we can think of a function that uses lists of instances of any type and always returns an instance of the same data type as contained in list. This kind of dependency between data types of a function interface can be specified via *type variables*:

```
>>> from typing import List, TypeVar
>>> T = TypeVar("T")
>>> def function(p: List[T]) -> T:
...     return p.pop()
```

In this case, a type variable T was created. It was further specified in the type hints of the p parameter and the return value of function that a list with instances of the arbitrary data type T may be passed, and at the same time an instance of the same data type is returned.

Type variables may be restricted to certain data types:

```
>>> P = TypeVar("P", str, bytes)
```

In the example, type variable P is defined, which can be either a string or a bytes string. The strings "T" and "P", which were specified in the examples when instantiating TypeVar, correspond to the names of the type variables. These occur in error messages, for example.

24.3   Static Type Checking in Python: mypy

In the previous two sections, we've looked at ways to annotate interfaces and definitions with type hints. These annotations are a particularly important source of information for static type checking tools.

Such static type checking is performed by an external tool—not by the Python interpreter itself, in that it analyzes the source code of a Python program and checks for possible errors in the use of data types in interfaces. In this case, the analysis is performed *statically*; that is, the program is not executed.

Such code analysis is often performed implicitly by modern IDEs. Many of them aren't limited to errors in handling data types, but also recognize other types of errors and error-prone program patterns. Type hints support these processes and enable more in-depth analyses. For an overview of Python development environments and their capabilities, see Section A.5 in the appendix.

If you want to perform static type checking independently of an integrated development environment, you can use the *mypy* tool, which has become a standard in this field.

24.3.1   Installation

Because mypy is a third-party package, it must be installed before you can use it. This can be done conveniently via the Anaconda package manager if it isn't already installed by default:

```
$ conda install mypy
```

If you don't use Anaconda, mypy can alternatively be installed via the Python package manager *pip*:

```
$ pip install mypy
```

If you use Linux, an installation may also be possible via the package manager of your Linux distribution.

24.3.2   Example

At this point, we'd like to use a simple example to illustrate how mypy works. To do this, we'll first write two functions that summarize in a descriptive way our upcoming travel destinations and the chosen means of transportation:

```
from typing import List
def fly(destinations):
    print("We are flying to:", ", ".join(destinations))
def walk(destinations: List[str]):
    print("We are walking to:", ", ".join(destinations))
```

The functions basically work the same on an input list of strings. For the walk function, however, we've annotated type hints, thus giving the mypy analysis tool the opportunity to perform type checking. The fly function was defined entirely without annotations.

In the rest of the program, we'll call the fly and walk functions in different ways—both correctly and wrongly:

```
if __name__ == "__main__":
    fly(["Rome", "Paris", "New York"])
    fly([0, 1, 2])
    fly(4)
    walk(["Rome", "Paris", "New York"])
    walk([0, 1, 2])
    walk(4)
```

Here, it's obvious that calling fly or walk with arguments [0, 1, 2] and 4 will cause an error in the program execution. At this point, however, we aren't interested in the program execution itself, but in whether mypy can warn us about these supposed programming errors.

For this purpose, we run mypy in a shell, passing the test.py Python program file to be examined as a parameter:

```
$ mypy test.py
test.py:15: error: List item 0 has incompatible type "int"; expected "str"
test.py:15: error: List item 1 has incompatible type "int"; expected "str"
test.py:15: error: List item 2 has incompatible type "int"; expected "str"
test.py:16: error: Argument 1 to "walk" has incompatible type "int"; expected
"List[str]"
Found 4 errors in 1 file (checked 1 source file)
```

From the output, we can see that mypy has correctly detected the wrong calls of the walk function and is able to issue appropriate warnings. IDEs such as PyCharm would also flag a potential error at this point. But the fly function defined without type hints is not detected by mypy and will surprise us with an error only at the time of execution.

Chapter 25
Structural Pattern Matching

Using conditional statements, which we discussed in detail in Chapter 5, Section 5.1, you can adapt the control flow of your programs—for example, to specific events or data read in whatever way. In Python 3.10, *structural pattern matching* was introduced. This is another control structure for special types of conditionals, which we'll take a closer look at in this section.

25.1 The match Statement

We'll start with a small example by imagining that our program should respond to a series of commands—for example, those entered by the user or read from a file. Such behavior can be implemented using the if-elif-else statement, as shown in the following abstract example:

```python
command = "version"    # from the user or other data source
if command == "time":
    show_time()
elif command == "memory":
    show_memory()
elif command == "version":
    show_program_version()
elif command == "end":
    program_end()
else:
    print(f"Unknown command: {command}")
```

You may have noticed that in each of the conditions of the statement, it must be written again explicitly that a comparison is carried out with the command variable, which makes the program text relatively long. Structural pattern matching allows you to specify once at the beginning of the statement that different *cases* are to be distinguished for the same value without having to specify this value again in each of the conditions:

```python
command = "version"    # from the user or other data source
match command:
    case "time":
```

```
        show_time()
    case "memory":
        show_memory()
    case "version":
        show_program_version()
    case "end":
        program_end()
    case _:
        print(f"Unknown command: {command}")
```

The match statement specifies for which object the different cases are to be distinguished. Each of the cases is specified by case followed by the corresponding pattern. In the simplest case, a *pattern* consists of a literal, such as a string literal or a literal for a number, as in the previous example. Just as with a conditional statement with if-elif-else, the different cases are checked in the order of their definition, and in case of a match, the program code is executed below the first matching pattern. The last case statement in our example doesn't contain a concrete value at all, but only an identifier—namely, _—which results in the pattern matching any possible value. For more details about this special pattern, you can refer to Chapter 25, Section 25.2.6.

In general, a match-case statement has the following structure:

```
match expression:
    case pattern:
        Statement
        ...
        Statement
    case pattern:
        Statement
        ...
        Statement
    ...
```

Just as there can be any number of elif branches in the if statement, any number of case statements is allowed within a match block.

25.2   Pattern Types in the case Statement

The structural pattern matching of Python provides wide-ranging options to define patterns. We'll highlight several of these in this section.

25.2.1   Literal and Value Patterns

The simplest case of a pattern is to explicitly write the matching value as a literal, as we did in the introductory example for strings. The following literals are allowed:

- string literals
- literals for signed and unsigned numbers
- None, True, and False

In addition, it's possible not to specify values explicitly by their literal, but to use a reference to the desired value instead. To avoid ambiguities with the capture patterns we'll describe later (see Chapter 25, Section 25.2.6), there is a restriction here that references must be specified including the namespace they are contained in. Local or global variables, on the other hand, can't be used. In the following example, we'll use the StatusCodes enumeration type derived from Enum (see Chapter 16, Section 16.1) to create a namespace for the comparison values:

```python
from enum import Enum

class StatusCodes(Enum):
    OK = 0
    NETWORK_ERROR = 1
    SYSTEM_ERROR = 2

status = StatusCodes.SYSTEM_ERROR
match status:
    case StatusCodes.OK:
        print("Operation completed successfully")
    case StatusCodes.NETWORK_ERROR:
        print("A network error has occurred")
    case StatusCodes.SYSTEM_ERROR:
        print("A system error has occurred")
    case _:
        print(f"Unknown status: {status}")
```

In this example, the system error pattern fits, which gives the corresponding output: A system error has occurred.

25.2.2   OR Pattern

It often isn't necessary to implement separate, special treatment for each of the possible values because a group of similar values can be handled in the same way. You can do this in the case statement by listing the related values separated by the OR operator (|):

```
match status:
    case StatusCodes.OK:
        print("Operation completed successfully")
    case StatusCodes.NETWORK_ERROR | StatusCodes.SYSTEM_ERROR:
        print("An error has occurred")
    case _:
        print(f"Unknown status: {status}")
```

Unlike the previous example, here network and system errors are handled by the same case block. The use of the | operator is not limited to literal or value patterns; it can also be combined with the pattern types described in the following sections.

25.2.3   Patterns with Type Checking

Patterns can check not only the value itself, but also the data type of a value. For this purpose, you must write a reference to the desired data type followed by a pair of parentheses:

```
class A:
    pass

value = 3.14
match value:
    case str():
        print(f"The string is: {value}")
    case int() | float() | complex():
        print(f"Here we have the number {value}.")
    case list():
        print(f"A list: {value}")
    case A():
        print("My class A :-)")
    case _:
        print(f"{type(value)}: {value}")
```

As you can see, you can use the built-in data types as well as self-defined classes.

Note

For classes, there is an additional option to check for specific attribute values in the pattern. We'll describe this mechanism in Section 25.2.9.

25.2.4   Specifying Conditions for Matches

The question whether the program code within a case block should be executed in case of a match can be linked to a condition. This is especially useful if a pattern such as the type patterns from the previous example matches not only one specific value, but a large number of different values. For this purpose, you can use the following extended variant of the case statement:

```
case pattern if condition:
```

You can use any expression for the condition, as you already know from the if statement.

The following program is based on the previous example and distinguishes between finite and infinite numbers:

```
import math
class Constants:
    inf = math.inf
    minf = -math.inf


value = 12345
match value:
    case int() | float() | complex() if abs(value) < Constants.inf:
        print(f"Here we have the finite number {value}.")
    case math.inf | Constants.minf:
        print("This is infinite!")
    case _:
        print(f"{type(value)}: {value}")
```

Because no expressions and no local or global references may be used within patterns, we use class attributes inf and minf of the custom class Constants in the second case statement instead of the invalid math.inf | -math.inf pattern.

25.2.5   Grouping Subpatterns

Similar to arithmetic expressions, you can group parts of patterns via parentheses. For example, the following three patterns are identical in meaning:

```
int() | float() | complex()
(int() | float()) | complex()
(int() | (float() | complex()))
```

First, the use of parentheses allows us to structure our patterns more clearly; second, it enables us to split long patterns over several lines:

```
case (
    int() | float() | complex()
) if abs(value) < math.inf:
```

Later in this chapter, you'll see how useful pattern grouping is in interaction with other pattern types—for example, to avoid ambiguity.

25.2.6 Capture and Wildcard Patterns

It's possible to bind a value matched by a pattern to a new name using the case statement in order to continue using it in the further program run. The following example uses this mechanism to determine the last string and the last finite number from a sequence of values. To do this, we must write the as keyword followed by the desired name after the pattern:

```
values = ["Hello", [], -5, 6, 3, float("-inf"), "world", {4, 6}]
last_finite_number, last_string = None, None
for value in values:
    match value:
        case (
            int() | float() | complex() as number
        ) if abs(value) < float("inf"):
            last_finite_number = number
        case str() as string:
            last_string = string
print(f"Last finite number: {last_finite_number}")
print(f"Last string:        {last_string}")
```

As you'll probably already expect, the output of this program is as follows:

```
Last finite number: 3
Last string:        world
```

You can also assign names to entire or partial patterns. This is particularly useful in conjunction with sequence and mapping patterns, but can also be used to define a pattern that matches any value, as we did in the in the opening example of this chapter using the name _:

```
a = "Test"
match "something":
    case a:
        print(f"It is {a}!")
print(a)
```

The output is as follows:

```
It is something!
something
```

As you can see, the pattern matched the value "something", which would have happened in the same way with any other value. In addition, this has caused the previous value of a, "test", to be overridden by the matched value, "something".

The names assigned within the case statement are set in the current local namespace in case of a match, similar to what happens with an assignment. This can have unwanted side effects if it binds an existing name to a new value. To prevent this from happening, you can use the name _, which is intended as a wildcard. The existence and value of _ isn't changed by a match statement:

```
_ = "Test2"
match "something":
    case _:
        print(f"It is {_}!")
print(_)
```

In contrast to the previous output, this program provides the following:

```
It is Test2!
Test2
```

As you can see, the value of _ wasn't changed by the match. Also within the case block, _ contained the Test2 string regardless of the matched value "something". Due to its semantics, the wildcard _ is suitable for patterns or subpatterns whose values you don't want to reuse in your program.

Combining Capture Patterns with Type Checking

In section Section 25.2.3, we implemented a type check using patterns like int() as x and, in the case of a match, bound the value to the name x.

Another option is to write the desired name in the parentheses after the type name. For example, the int(x) pattern matches an integer and binds the value directly to the name x.

More generally, the syntax Class(a, b, c) performs position-based matching of attributes, which we will discuss in Section 25.2.9.

Combining Capture Patterns with OR Patterns

Names can also be assigned within OR patterns. However, you must make sure that the same names are assigned in all alternatives of the OR pattern. For example, the following three patterns are valid and equivalent with regard to their meaning because the name number is assigned the same value in each of the cases:

```
int() | float() | complex() as number
(int() as number) | (float() as number) | (complex() as number)
int(number) | (float() as number) | complex(number)
```

Note that when you use as in combination with OR patterns for naming purposes, parentheses may need to be used to avoid ambiguity.

25.2.7   Sequence Patterns

In the previous examples, our patterns have been limited to a concrete value or values of specific data types. However, you can also define sequence patterns that match sequences of a specific structure. The syntax is based on that of unpacking; see Chapter 12, Section 12.4.1.

A Simple Example

In the following example, we'll use sequence patterns to generate a compact output depending on the number of elements in a list. Here, we use capture patterns to assign names to specific elements and parts of the list:

```
def print_list(x):
    match x:
      case []:
          print("(empty)")
      case [a]:
          print(f"[{a}]")
      case [a, b]:
          print(f"[{a}, {b}]")
      case [a, b, *rest]:
          print(f"[{a}, ..., {rest[-1]}]")
print_list([1])
print_list([1, 2])
print_list(list(range(100)))
```

The output of this program is as follows:

```
[1]
[1, 2]
[0, ..., 99]
```

For example, as with unpacking, this involves binding the names a and b to the first two elements of the matched sequence in the pattern, [a, b, *rest]. Then rest enables us to access all other elements starting from the third entry of the sequence.

A More Complex Example

The generator defined in the following example (see Chapter 21, Section 21.1), range_plus_plus, is a modification of the built-in range function to define number sequences using the ellipsis literal, ...[1] For example, range_plus_plus(1, ..., 4, 10, ..., 14) returns an iterator over the sequence of numbers 1, 2, 3, 4, 10, 11, 12, 13, 14. The implementation uses value patterns, sequence patterns, patterns with type checking, conditions on patterns, the wildcard _, and capture patterns, all of which have been described in previous sections. In addition, range_plus_plus calls itself recursively as a subgenerator via yield from:

```python
import math
import itertools
def range_plus_plus(*args):
    match args:
        case []:
            return
        case [e, int(a), *rest] if e is ...:
            yield from range(a + 1)
            yield from range_plus_plus(*rest)
        case [int(a), e, int(b), *rest] if e is ...:
            yield from range(a, b + 1)
            yield from range_plus_plus(*rest)
        case [int(a), e, math.inf] if e is ...:
            yield from itertools.count(start=a)
        case [int(a), *rest]:
            yield a
            yield from range_plus_plus(*rest)
        case _:
            raise ValueError(f"Invalid range: {args}")
```

For a range definition like 4, ..., math.inf, range_plus_plus returns a generator over all integers starting from the number 4.

> **Note**
>
> Just as with unpacking, you can choose between parentheses and square brackets in sequence patterns without affecting the semantics of the pattern—for example, (e, int(a), *rest) instead of [e, int(a), *rest].
>
> A special case is the pattern for sequences with one element: to avoid ambiguity with grouping subpatterns, you must write (x,) instead of [x] in this case.

---

1 The ellipsis literal, ..., is used to create a reference to the only instance of the ellipsis data type. This data type was introduced for special index notations for arrays in the numpy context and is generally used very rarely. We've chosen it here because it's very useful for this specific example.

25.2.8 Mapping Patterns

Similar to how sequence patterns can be used to match sequences of certain structure, mappings structured in certain ways, such as `dict` instances, can be described using *mapping patterns*. The syntax is similar to that of the `dict` literal and can be interpreted as a transference of unpacking (Chapter 12, Section 12.4.1) to mapping data types.

The Syntax of Mapping Patterns

To define an mapping pattern, you must use the curly brackets, { and }. Within the brackets, you define which keys must be included in the mapping. In addition, requirements can be formulated for each value via a pattern by writing the pattern separated by a colon after the key. For example, the pattern `{"statement": str(), "timestamp": (int() | float())}` can be used for all d mapping containing the `"statement"` and `"timestamp"` keys if in addition `d["statement"]` is a string and `d["timestamp"]` is an integer or a float. For each of the following examples, a note is added about whether or not they fit this pattern:

```
{"statement": "SHUTDOWN"}                                    # does not fit
{"statement": 123, "timestamp": "sometime"}                 # does not fit
{"statement": "SHUTDOWN", "timestamp": 554256000.0}         # fits
{"statement": "SHUTDOWN", "timestamp": 554256000, "a": 3}   # fits
```

If you are also interested in the keys that aren't specified by the pattern, you can use the double asterisk operator to assign a name that references the rest of the mapping. Consider the following example:

```
value = {"statement": "SHUTDOWN", "timestamp": 554256000, "a": 3}
match value:
    case {"statement": str(), "timestamp": (int() | float()), **rest}:
        print(f"Rest: {rest}")
```

This example generates the following output:

```
Rest: {'a': 3}
```

Within the subpatterns for the values of the mapping, we can draw on the full range of pattern types from this chapter. For example, we can bind the values to self-selected names with capture patterns:

```
value = {"statement": "SHUTDOWN", "timestamp": 554256000, "a": 3}
match value:
    case {
        "statement": str(statement),
        "timestamp": (int() | float() as timestamp)
    }:
        print(f"statement: {statement}, timestamp: {timestamp}")
```

The output of this program reads accordingly:

```
statement: SHUTDOWN, timestamp: 554256000
```

To require only that a particular key exists, regardless of what value it maps to, a capture pattern with the wildcard _ is appropriate. You can use the wildcard more than once:

```
value = {"statement": "SHUTDOWN", "timestamp": 554256000, "a": 3}
match value:
    case {"a": _, "timestamp": _}:
        print("The keys 'a' and 'timestamp' exist!")
```

This is confirmed by the following output: The keys 'a' and 'timestamp' exist!.

A More Complex Example

As a somewhat more practical example, we'd like to use mapping patterns to output addresses stored in dictionaries for printing on an envelope. Our program should be able to cope with addresses as they are used in Germany and the US. Because both the appropriate data formats for addresses in the two countries and the common notation on a letter differ, we use structural pattern matching with mapping patterns to handle the cases separately:

```
addresses = [
    {"type": "DE", "name": "DeepL SE", "street": "Maarweg 165",
     "city": "Cologne", "ZIP": 50825},
    {"type": "US", "name": "Linux Foundation", "street": "548 Market St",
     "city": "San Francisco", "state": "CA", "ZIP": "94104"},
    {"something": "something else"},
]

def print_address(address):
    match address:
        case {
            "type": ("DE" | "Deutschland" | "Germany"),
            "name": str(name),
            "street": str(street),
            "city": str(city),
            "ZIP": (str() | int()) as zip_code
        }:
            print(name)
            print(street)
            print(f"{zip_code} {city}")
            print("Germany")
```

```
    case {
        "type": ("US" | "USA" | "United States"),
        "name": str(name), "street": str(street),
        "city": str(city),
        "state": str(state),
        "ZIP": (str() | int()) as zip_code
    }:
        print(name)
        print(street)
        print(f"{city} {state} {zip_code}")
        print("US")
    case x:
        print(f"Unknown data format: {x}")


for address in addresses:
    print_address(address)
    print("---")
```

This program uses capture patterns, or patterns and type checking patterns, to produce the following output:

```
DeepL SE
Maarweg 165
50825 Cologne
Germany
---
Linux Foundation
548 Market St
San Francisco CA 94104
US
---
Unknown data format: {'something': 'something else'}
---
```

Mapping patterns are well suited to handle complex structured instances.

25.2.9   Patterns for Objects and Their Attribute Values

In Section 25.2.3, you learned about patterns we can use to check whether a value is an instance of a particular data type. The following program uses this mechanism to recognize complex numbers:

```
value = 1 + 5j
match value:
    case complex():
        print("A complex number!")
```

Python supports more advanced ways for this pattern type to also refer to the attributes of the value.

Checking Attribute Values by their Name

As you saw in Chapter 11, Section 11.7, instances of the complex data type have the real and imag attributes for the real and imaginary parts of the complex number, respectively. We can define patterns that check the presence and value of these attributes in addition to the data type:

```
    case complex(real=realpart, imag=0):
        print(f"Real number {realpart}")
```

The complex(imag=0, real=realpart) pattern checks three aspects here:

- The matched value is an instance of the complex data type.
- The matched value has the imag and real attributes.
- The imag attribute of the matched value matches the literal pattern 0.

As with sequence or mapping patterns, it's possible to assign names to attribute values in the case of a match, as was applied to the real part of the complex number in the preceding example.

This mechanism isn't limited to built-in data types; it can also be applied to user-defined classes. The match constructions in the following example use this pattern type to evaluate and display simple arithmetic operations for integers:

```
class Task:
    def __init__(self, operand1, operator, operand2):
        self.op1 = operand1
        self.operator = operator
        self.op2 = operand2

    def evaluate(self):
        match self:
            case Task(operator=op, op1=int(op1), op2=int(op2)):
                match op:
                    case "+": return op1 + op2
                    case "-": return op1 - op2
                    case "*": return op1 * op2
                    case "/": return op1 // op2
                    case _: raise ValueError(f"Unknown operator: {op}")
```

25

```
        case Task(operator=op, op1=Task() as op1, op2=op2):
            return Task(op1.evaluate(), op, op2).evaluate()
        case Task(operator=op, op1=op1, op2=Task() as op2):
            return Task(op1, op, op2.evaluate()).evaluate()
        case _:
            print("Invalid task:", self)

    def __str__(self):
        match (self.operator, self.op1, self.op2):
            case (op, Task() as op1, Task() as op2):
                return f"({op1}) {op} ({op2})"
            case (op, Task() as op1, int(op2)):
                return f"({op1}) {op} {op2}"
            case (op, int(op1), Task() as op2):
                return f"{op1} {op} ({op2})"
            case (op, op1, op2):
                return f"{op1} {op} {op2}"

task = Task(Task(Task(23,"-",3), "/", 5), "+", Task(2,"*",3))
print(f"{task} = {task.evaluate()}")
```

The output of the example shows that the calculation works:

```
((23 - 3) / 5) + (2 * 3) = 10
```

As you can see in the evaluate method, it's absolutely possible to nest multiple match constructs within each other. The strategy for evaluating Task is to recursively evaluate the first and second operands, respectively, until both are integers. For this case, the evaluate method then draws on the arithmetic operations provided by Python. The __str__ magic method (Chapter 19, Section 19.11.1) distinguishes among different cases for the types of operands in order to output parentheses only when needed.

Matching Attribute Values via the Position in the Pattern

In many use cases, there is a natural ordering of attributes, so addressing each attribute by name is not helpful for the comprehensibility of the pattern. In the previous example for the evaluation of computational tasks, you can assume that the order Operand1 Operator Operator2 is so natural that you don't want to repeat the names of the attributes in every pattern as, for example, in the following pattern:

```
Task(operator=op, op1=int(op1), op2=int(op2))
```

Python provides the __match_args__ magic attribute for this purpose, which can be used to define for which of the attributes a natural order exists and what it looks like. The following example uses this option to provide an order to the attributes of the Task class. Notice how this adjustment simplifies the patterns used in the evaluate method. Because this has no effect on the patterns in the __str__ method, we have omitted the corresponding code from the example:

```python
class Task:
    __match_args__ = ("op1", "operator", "op2")
    def __init__(self, operand1, operator, operand2):
        self.op1 = operand1
        self.operator = operator
        self.op2 = operand2

    def evaluate(self):
        match self:
            case Task(int(op1), op, int(op2)):
                match op:
                    case "+": return op1 + op2
                    case "-": return op1 - op2
                    case "*": return op1 * op2
                    case "/": return op1 // op2
                    case _: raise ValueError(f"Unknown operator: {op}")
            case Task(Task() as op1, op, op2):
                return Task(op1.evaluate(), op, op2).evaluate()
            case Task(op1, op, op2=Task() as op2):
                return Task(op1, op, op2.evaluate()).evaluate()
            case _:
                print("Invalid task:", self)
    # remaining code as in the previous example
```

Try to check for yourself that the program works flawlessly even after this simplification.

Mixed Matching of Attributes via Position and Name

You can also mix both options by specifying a part of the attributes by their position and another part by their name:

```python
class A:
    __match_args__ = ("x", "z")
    def __init__(self, x, y, z, a):
        self.x = x
        self.y = y
        self.z = z
        self.a = a
```

25

```
a = A(1, 2, 3, 4)
match a:
    case A(1, 3, y=2):
        print("Match!")
```

Here, literal patterns 1 and 3 reference the x and z attributes of class A. Similar to calling methods and functions (Chapter 17, Section 17.5), there is the restriction that the attributes referenced by their names must be located at the end of the pattern.

PART IV

The Standard Library

The fourth part of this book deals with Python's standard library. The standard library consists of modules and packages that you can import and use at any time to address specific problems. In the following chapters, we'll discuss selected contents of the standard library, sticking to a project-oriented approach, except for a few particularly important modules that will be described using reference style.

For example, the standard library contains modules and packages for mathematical functions, regular expressions, access to operating system or file system information, parallel programming, data storage, and network communication and for debugging or quality assurance.

Chapter 26
Mathematics

We'll start with those modules of the standard library that can be used to perform mathematical calculations in the broadest sense. Table 26.1 lists the modules that will be described in this chapter.

Module	Description	Section
math	Mathematical functions	Section 26.1
cmath	Mathematical functions for complex numbers	Section 26.1
random	Generate random numbers or random selections from given collections	Section 26.2
statistics	Functions for statistical calculations	Section 26.3
decimal	Precise representation of decimal numbers	Section 26.4
hashlib	Hash functions	Section 26.5

Table 26.1 Mathematical Modules of the Standard Library

Note that at this point, we'll discuss the functionality included in the standard library, which is sufficient for many use cases. In addition, the numpy, scipy, and matplotlib libraries have established themselves in the Python universe as a comprehensive basis for efficient scientific calculations and visualizations. For an introduction to this subject, see Chapter 43.

26.1 Mathematical Functions: math, cmath

The math module is part of the standard library and provides mathematical functions and constants.

> **Note**
>
> The math module doesn't offer operations for complex numbers. Most importantly, this means that a function contained in math will never accept a complex parameter or return a complex result.

> If a complex result is explicitly required, the cmath module can be used instead of math, which contains those functions of math that have a reasonable extension on the complex numbers.

In the following sections, the functions contained in math or cmath are presented in groups according to different topics. In the respective tables, the cmath column indicates whether a function is also contained in the cmath module.

Apart from a wealth of functions, the math and cmath modules define six constants (see Table 26.2).

Constant	Description	cmath
e	The Euler number *e*	Yes
pi	The number pi (π)	Yes
inf	The value "infinite," equivalent to float("inf")	Yes
nan	The value "not a number," equivalent to float("nan")	Yes
infj	The complex value "infinity," equivalent to float("infj")	Exclusively
nanj	The complex value "not a number," equivalent to float("nanj")	Exclusively

Table 26.2 Constants of the math and cmath Modules

Before you can use the following examples in the interactive mode, you must import math or cmath:

```
>>> import math
>>> import cmath
```

26.1.1   General Mathematical Functions

The math and cmath modules respectively define the general mathematical functions listed in Table 26.3.

Function	Description	cmath
ceil(x)	Returns the smallest integer greater than or equal to x.	No
copysign(x, y)	Transfers the sign from y to x and returns the result.	No
fabs(x)	Returns the amount of x. The result is always a float.	No
factorial(x)	Calculates the factorial of the integer x.	No

Table 26.3 Number Theoretic Functions in math and cmath

Function	Description	cmath
floor(x)	Returns the largest integer less than or equal to x.	No
fmod(x, y)	Calculates x modulo y.	No
frexp(x)	Extracts mantissa and exponent of x.	No
fsum(iterable)	Calculates the sum of the floats contained in iterable.	No
gcd(*integers)	Returns the greatest common divisor of the passed numbers. (Since Python 3.9, more than two parameters are possible.)	No
isclose(a, b, {rel_tol, abs_tol})	Returns True exactly when a and b are sufficiently close. The permissible tolerances can be defined as relative and/or absolute values via rel_tol and abs_tol.	Yes
isfinite(x)	Returns True exactly when x doesn't reference any of the values inf, -inf, or nan.*	Yes
isinf(x)	Returns True exactly when x is positive or negative infinite.	Yes
isnan(x)	Returns true exactly when x has the value nan.	Yes
lcm(*integers)	Returns the least common multiple of the passed numbers. (New in Python 3.9.)	No
ldexp(m, e)	Determines a float from mantissa m and exponent e.	No
modf(x)	Returns a tuple with the integer part and the fractional part of the float x.	No
nextafter(x, y)	Returns the next exactly representable float starting from x in the direction of y. (New in Python 3.9.)	No
prod(iterable, {start})	Calculates the product of the values contained in iterable, where start can be used to specify the initial product value.	No
trunc(x)	Returns the integer part of x as an integer. Behaves like floor for positive values of x and like ceil for negative values of x.	No

Table 26.3 Number Theoretic Functions in math and cmath (Cont.)

26

Function	Description	cmath
ulp(x)	Returns the value of the float that results when all bits except the least significant bit in the binary representation of the mantissa of x are set to zero. For example, ulp(1.0) returns the relative machine precision. (New in Python 3.9.)	No
*	These values represent positive and negative infinity and not a number, respectively. For more details, see Chapter 11, Section 11.5.	

Table 26.3 Number Theoretic Functions in math and cmath (Cont.)

The following sections provide detailed explanations of a selection of the functions presented in Table 26.3.

fmod(x, y)

The fmod function calculates x modulo y. Note that this function doesn't always calculate the same result as x % y. Thus, fmod returns the result with the sign of x, while x % y returns the result with the sign of y. In general, fmod should be preferred for modulo operations with floats and the modulo operator % for operations with integers.

```
>>> math.fmod(7.5, 3.5)
0.5
```

frexp(x)

The frexp function extracts the mantissa and exponent of the passed number x. The result is a tuple of the form (m, e), where m is the mantissa and e is the exponent. The mantissa and exponent are to be understood in the context of the formula $x = m \cdot 2^e$:

```
>>> math.frexp(2.5)
(0.625, 2)
```

fsum(iterable)

The fsum function calculates the sum of the floats contained in iterable:

```
>>> math.fsum([1.5, 7.34, 2, 4.78])
15.620000000000001
```

The advantage of fsum over the built-in sum function, which can basically be used for the same purpose, is that fsum tries to keep the errors caused by the summation in floating-point arithmetic as small as possible. Thus, the result of fsum is more accurate than the result of sum.

26.1.2 Exponential and Logarithm Functions

The math or cmath modules define the functions listed in Table 26.4, which refer to the exponential or logarithm function.

Function	Description	cmath
exp(x)	Calculates e^x.	Yes
log(x, [base])	Calculates the logarithm of x to base base. If base hasn't been specified, the natural logarithm (base e) is calculated.	Yes
log10(x)	Calculates the logarithm of x to base 10.	Yes
log2(x)	Calculates the logarithm of x to base 2.	No
pow(x, y)	Calculates x^y.	No
sqrt(x)	Calculates the square root of x.	Yes

Table 26.4 Exponential and Logarithm Functions in math and cmath

26.1.3 Trigonometric and Hyperbolic Functions

The math and cmath modules, respectively, define the trigonometric functions listed in Table 26.5.

Function	Description	cmath
sin(x)	Calculates the sine of x.	Yes
cos(x)	Calculates the cosine of x.	Yes
tan(x)	Calculates the tangent of x.	Yes
asin(x)	Calculates the arcsine of x.	Yes
acos(x)	Calculates the arccosine of x.	Yes
atan(x)	Calculates the arctangent of x.	Yes
sinh(x)	Calculates the hyperbolic sine of x.	Yes
cosh(x)	Calculates the hyperbolic cosine of x.	Yes
tanh(x)	Calculates the hyperbolic tangent of x.	Yes
asinh(x)	Calculates the inverse hyperbolic sine of x.	Yes
acosh(x)	Calculates the inverse hyperbolic cosine of x.	Yes

Table 26.5 Trigonometric and Hyperbolic Functions of the math and cmath Modules

26

Function	Description	cmath
atanh(x)	Calculates the inverse hyperbolic tangent of x.	Yes
atan2(y, x)	Calculates atan(x / y).	No

Table 26.5 Trigonometric and Hyperbolic Functions of the math and cmath Modules (Cont.)

26.1.4   Distances and Norms

To calculate the length of a two-dimensional vector (x,y), you can use the hypot function (for *hypotenuse*) of the math module:

```
>>> math.hypot(1,1)
1.4142135623730951
```

Alternatively, if the distance between two vectors p and q of any dimension is required, you can use the dist function, where p and q must each be iterable objects of the same length:

```
>>> math.dist((1,1), (2,2))
1.4142135623730951
```

26.1.5   Converting Angles

To convert angles between radians and degrees, the math module contains the degrees and radians functions:

```
>>> math.degrees(math.pi/2)
90.0
>>> math.radians(90)
1.5707963267948966
```

26.1.6   Representations of Complex Numbers

The phase, polar, and rect functions contained in cmath can be used for converting different representations of complex numbers into each other. For this purpose, a complex number a + bj is taken as a point (a,b) in two-dimensional space. This space is referred to as the *complex plane*. The complex number can be expressed either in *Cartesian coordinates* using the values a and b or in *polar coordinates* using the angle ? and the radius r. Figure 26.1 shows the two forms of representation of complex numbers using an example.

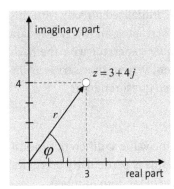

Figure 26.1 Cartesian and Polar Representations of the Complex Number 3+4j

The phase, polar, and rect functions allow you to represent a complex number in Cartesian coordinates or in polar coordinates:

```
>>> cmath.phase(3+4j)
0.9272952180016122
>>> cmath.polar(3+4j)
(5.0, 0.9272952180016122)
>>> cmath.rect(5.0, 0.9272952180016122)
(3.0000000000000004+3.9999999999999996j)
```

26.2   Random Number Generator: random

The random module of the standard library generates pseudorandom numbers and provides additional functions for applying random operations to basic data types.

> **Note**
>
> The random module doesn't generate true random numbers, but so-called pseudorandom numbers. True random numbers are not computable by a computer. A pseudorandom number generator is initialized with an integer and generates a deterministic but apparently random sequence of pseudorandom numbers. This sequence of numbers repeats itself after a certain number of generated random numbers. In the case of the algorithm used by default in Python, this period is $2^{19937} - 1$ numbers.

The pseudorandom number generator implemented in random can be initialized using the seed function:

```
>>> import random
>>> random.seed(12)
```

If the seed is an integer, the random number generator is initialized directly with this number. Alternatively, an instance of the NoneType, float, str, bytes, and bytearray data types can be passed, which initializes the random number generator with the hash value of this instance. If no parameter is passed, the current system time serves as the seed. In this way, the generated numbers can be considered quasi-random:

```
>>> random.seed()
```

If the random number generator is initialized with the same value at different times, it will generate the same sequence of numbers each time. This is particularly useful for achieving reproducible program execution despite the use of random numbers.

26.2.1   Saving and Loading the Random State

The getstate function returns a tuple describing the current state of the random number generator. With the help of the setstate function, the status of the generator can be saved and restored at a later time—for example, after a reinitialization in the meantime:

```
>>> state = random.getstate()
>>> random.setstate(state)
```

The generator then continues to run as if the interruption had not occurred.

26.2.2   Generating Random Integers

To generate a (pseudo)random integer, you can use the randint function, to which the required interval boundaries can be passed:

```
>>> random.randint(0, 10)
4
```

In this case, integers between 0 and 10 are randomly generated, and the interval limits 0 and 10 can also be valid results.

A little more control over the possible results is provided by the randrange function. It returns a randomly chosen element from the number space that a call of the built-in range function with the same parameters would produce:

```
>>> random.randrange(0, 50, 2)
40
```

In this case, a random even number between 0 and 49 was generated.

Another way to generate random numbers is to use the getrandbits function, which generates a random bit sequence of fixed length and returns it as an integer:

```
>>> random.getrandbits(8)
156
```

In this case, the getrandbits function was used to generate a random byte (8 bits).

26.2.3   Generating Random Floats

The random module contains some functions to generate a random float according to a chosen probability distribution. The simplest of these functions is random, which is used to generate an uniformly distributed random number between 0 and 1:

```
>>> random.random()
0.6018018690250143
```

The related uniform function produces a uniformly distributed random number within the specified interval limits:

```
>>> random.uniform(0, 10)
5.044950881560962
```

In addition, the random module contains further functions that generate random numbers according to other probability distributions. The best known of these distributions is the *normal* or *Gaussian distribution*. You can generate a normally distributed random number as follows:

```
>>> random.gauss(0, 1)
1.4999823501567913
```

The expected value (μ) and standard deviation (σ) are passed as parameters.

26.2.4   Random Operations on Sequences

The random module contains several functions that perform random operations on sequences, including the choice function, which returns a random element of the passed nonempty sequence:

```
>>> random.choice([1,2,3,4,5])
5
>>> random.choice([1,2,3,4,5])
2
>>> random.choice(["A", "B", "C"])
'B'
```

Similar to choice, the function choices can be used to get k randomly chosen elements from the passed sequence. The elements are chosen *with replacements* which means that individual elements may be chosen multiple times.

```
>>> random.choices(range(100), k=4)
[76, 41, 39, 5]
```

The `sample` function is passed a `population` sequence and an integer k as parameters. The result is a new list with k randomly chosen elements from `population`. The elements are chosen *without replacements* which means that individual elements may be chosen at most once. In this way, for example, a certain number of winners could be drawn from a list of lottery participants. Note that the order of the generated list is also random and that values occurring multiple times in `population` can also be drawn multiple times:

```
>>> pop = [1,2,3,4,5,6,7,8,9,10]
>>> random.sample(pop, 3)
[7, 8, 5]
>>> random.sample(pop, 3)
[5, 9, 7]
```

The `sample` function can also be used in combination with the built-in `range` function:

```
>>> random.sample(range(10000000), 3)
[4571575, 2648561, 2009814]
```

The `shuffle` function puts the elements of sequence x in a random order. Note that this function is not without side effects as the passed sequence gets modified. For this reason, only instances of mutable sequential data types may be passed for x:

```
>>> l = [1,2,3,"A","B"]
>>> random.shuffle(l)
>>> l
[1, 'B', 2, 'A', 3]
```

In Python 3.9, the `randbytes` function was introduced, which generates a random byte sequence of a given length as a `bytes` string:

```
>>> random.randbytes(4)
b'\x86\x0f\xa3\xbe'
>>> random.randbytes(4)
b'A\x12u\xa3'
```

In this case, a sequence of four random bytes was generated. In the output representation of the result, these bytes are output as escape sequences if they do not correspond to printable ASCII characters.

26.2.5   SystemRandom([seed])

In addition to the functions described previously, the random module contains a class called SystemRandom that allows you to use the operating system's random number generator instead of Python's own. This class doesn't exist on all operating systems, but on the most common ones.[1]

When instantiating the class, a number or instance can be passed to initialize the random number generator. After that, the SystemRandom class can be used like the random module as it implements most of the functions contained in the module as methods.

Note, however, that not all the functionality of random is available in SystemRandom. Thus, a call of the seed method is ignored, while calls of the getstate and setstate methods raise a NotImplementedError exception:

```
>>> sr = random.SystemRandom()
>>> sr.randint(1, 10)
9
```

26.3   Statistical Calculations: statistics

The statistics module of the standard library contains a number of useful functions that perform simple statistical calculations.

The functions contained in the statistics module usually operate on a *sample*, an iterable object that iterates through numeric values. An example of a sample consisting of 10 floats could look as follows:

```
>>> data = [1.0, 2.0, 2.0, 5.7, 7.0, 1.1, 4.0, 2.0, 6.5, 1.5]
```

Basically, a sample for use with the statistics module can contain integers, floats, and the decimal and fraction data types from the decimal and fractions modules.

> **Note**
> A sample should always consist of instances of a single data type; otherwise, the functions implemented in statistics might show undefined behavior.

Now, for example, the mean and median of the data sample can be determined using the mean and median functions:

26

---

1 Including Windows, Linux and macOS

```
>>> import statistics
>>> statistics.mean(data)
3.477777777777778
>>> statistics.median(data)
2.0
```

Table 26.6 provides an overview of the most important functions included in statistics.

Function	Description
mean(data)	Calculates the arithmetic mean or average of the data sample.
geometric_mean(data)	Calculates the geometric mean of the data sample.
harmonic_mean(data)	Calculates the harmonic mean of the data sample.
median(data)	Calculates the median of the data sample.
median_low(data)	Calculates the lower median of the data sample.
median_high(data)	Calculates the upper median of the data sample.
mode(data)	Determines the mode or modal value of the data sample—that is, the most frequently occurring element.
multimode(data)	Similar to mode, but determines a list of modal values when several elements of the sample occur with equal frequency.
stdev(data)	Calculates the standard deviation of the data sample.
variance(data)	Calculates the variance of the data sample.
pstdev(data)	Calculates the standard deviation of the data population.
pvariance(data)	Calculates the variance of the data population.

Table 26.6 Functions for Statistical Calculations in the statistics Module

The statistics module contains two functions each for calculating standard deviation and variance: stdev and pstdev as well as variance and pvariance. The difference is that stdev and variance assume that the data passed to them represents a sample of the total population. With pstdev and pvariance, it is assumed that the data passed to them represents the total population. The stdev and variance functions include a correction for the fact that standard deviation and variance on samples are systematically underestimated.

26.4   Intuitive Decimal Numbers: decimal

You'll certainly remember the following example, which shows that calculation errors occur when using the built-in `float` data type:

```
>>> 1.1 + 2.2
3.3000000000000003
```

This is because not every decimal number can be represented by the internal memory model of `float`, but only approximated to a certain accuracy.[2] These calculation errors are usually accepted for reasons of efficiency. In some cases, however, for example when calculating with monetary amounts, it is particularly inconvenient that even simple floating point numbers such as 1.1 and 2.2 cannot be represented exactly and calculations with currency amounts therefore quickly become error-prone.

The `decimal` module contains the `Decimal` data type, which can store and process decimal numbers with a user-chosen finite precision:

```
>>> from decimal import Decimal
```

> **Note**
>
> The functionality of the `decimal` module described here is based on the General Decimal Arithmetic Specification by IBM. For this reason, it's possible that you already know a similar module from another programming language.
>
> For example, there are libraries that implement the `decimal` module in the same or modified form for C, C++, Java, and Perl.

26

26.4.1   Using the Data Type

There is no literal that enables you to create instances of the `Decimal` data type directly, as is the case with `float`, for example. To create a `Decimal` instance with a specific value, you must explicitly instantiate the data type. You can pass the value to the constructor as a string:

```
>>> Decimal("0.9")
Decimal('0.9')
>>> Decimal("1.33e7")
Decimal('1.33E+7')
```

This is the most common way to instantiate `Decimal`. You can also pass an integer or a tuple to the constructor:

---

2   This is not a Python-specific problem, but a fundamental limitation of floating-point representation in computers.

```
>>> Decimal(123)
Decimal('123')
>>> Decimal((0, (3, 1, 4, 1), -3))
Decimal('3.141')
```

In the case of a tuple, the first element determines the sign, where 0 represents a positive number and 1 represents a negative number. The second element must be another tuple containing all digits of the number. The third element of the tuple is the shift of the decimal point in the number specified in the previous element.

> **Note**
>
> It's possible to pass a float directly to the constructor of the Decimal class:
>
> ```
> >>> Decimal(0.7)
> Decimal('0.6999999999999999555910790149937383830547332763671875')
> ```
>
> You should always keep in mind that the inaccuracy of float is transferred to the Decimal instance during the initialization process.

Once a Decimal instance has been created, it can be used like an instance of a numeric data type. This means in particular that all operators known from these data types are also defined for Decimal. You can also use Decimal in operations with other numeric data types. In a nutshell, Decimal fits well into the existing world of numeric data types:

```
>>> Decimal("0.9") * 5
Decimal('4.5')
>>> Decimal("0.9") / 10
Decimal('0.09')
>>> Decimal("0.9") % Decimal("1.0")
Decimal('0.9')
```

A special feature of the data type is the retention of trailing zeros in the fractional part of a decimal number, although they are actually superfluous. This is useful, for example, when calculating with monetary amounts:

```
>>> Decimal("2.50") + Decimal("4.20")
Decimal('6.70')
```

Instances of the Decimal type can be compared with each other or with instances of other numeric data types:

```
>>> Decimal("0.7") < Decimal("0.8")
True
>>> Decimal(0.7) == 0.7
True
```

```
>>> Decimal("0.7") == 0.7
False
```

A `Decimal` value can be converted to a value of any other numeric data type. Note that these conversions are usually lossy, so the value loses accuracy:

```
>>> float(Decimal("1.337"))
1.337
>>> float(Decimal("0.9"))
0.9
>>> int(Decimal("1.337"))
1
```

This property enables you to pass `Decimal` instances as parameters of built-in functions or functions of the `math` library as a matter of course:

```
>>> import math
>>> math.sqrt(Decimal("2"))
1.4142135623730951
```

> **Note**
>
> Although `Decimal` instances can be passed to functions of the `math` module, these functions never return a `Decimal` instance, so you run the risk of losing accuracy due to the `float` return value.

For some mathematical functions, a `Decimal` instance provides special methods. Each of these methods allows you to pass a `context` object in addition to its specific parameters. Such a `context` object describes the context in which the calculations are to be performed—for example, to how many decimal places exactly rounding is to be performed. You'll learn more about the `context` object later in this section.

The most important methods of a `Decimal` instance `d` are listed in Table 26.7.

Method	Meaning
`d.exp([context])`	e^d
`d.fma(other, third[, context])`	$d \cdot other + third^*$
`d.ln([context])`	$log_e(d)$
`d.log10([context])`	$log_{10}(d)$
`d.logb([context])`	$log_b(d)$

Table 26.7 Mathematical Methods of the Decimal Data Type

Method	Meaning
`d.sqrt([context])`	$\sqrt{d}$
`d.as_integer_ratio()`	Returns numerator and denominator of d as tuples.

* The advantage of this method is that it performs the calculation in one shot; that is, it doesn't continue with a rounded intermediate result of the multiplication.

Table 26.7 Mathematical Methods of the Decimal Data Type (Cont.)

The use of these methods is demonstrated in the following example:

```
>>> d = Decimal("9")
>>> d.sqrt()
Decimal('3')
>>> d.ln()
Decimal('2.197224577336219382790490474')
>>> d.fma(2, -7)
Decimal('11')
```

> **Tip**
>
> Programming with the `Decimal` data type involves a lot of typing as no literal exists for this data type. Many Python programmers make do by giving the data type a shorter name:
>
> ```
> >>> from decimal import Decimal as D
> >>> D("1.5e-7")
> Decimal('1.5E-7')
> ```

26.4.2 Nonnumeric Values

From Chapter 11, Section 11.5, you already know about the `nan` and `inf` values of the `float` data type, which always occur when a calculation isn't possible or a number exceeds the number space of `float`. The `Decimal` data type is based on this approach and allows you to initialize `Decimal` instances with such a state. The values listed in Table 26.8 are possible.

Value	Meaning
`Infinity, Inf`	Positive infinite
`-Infinity, -Inf`	Negative infinite

Table 26.8 Nonnumeric Values of the Decimal Data Type

Value	Meaning
NaN	Invalid value (not a number)
sNaN	Invalid value (signaling not a number)[*]

[*]   The difference between this and NaN is that an exception is raised as soon as an attempt is made to continue computing with sNaN. Arithmetic operations with NaN are performed, but always result in NaN.

Table 26.8 Nonnumeric Values of the Decimal Data Type (Cont.)

These nonnumeric values can be used like numbers:

```
>>> Decimal("NaN") + Decimal("42.42")
Decimal('NaN')
>>> Decimal("Infinity") + Decimal("Infinity")
Decimal('Infinity')
>>> Decimal("sNaN") + Decimal("42.42")
Traceback (most recent call last):
  File "<stdin>", line 1, in <module>
InvalidOperation: [<class 'decimal.InvalidOperation'>]
>>> Decimal("Inf") - Decimal("Inf")
Traceback (most recent call last):
  File "<stdin>", line 1, in <module>
InvalidOperation: [<class 'decimal.InvalidOperation'>]
```

26.4.3   The Context Object

The Decimal data type allows you to store decimal numbers with arbitrary finite precision. The precision—that is, the number of decimal places—is one of several global settings encapsulated within a context object.

For accessing the current context of arithmetic operations, the getcontext and setcontext functions exist within the decimal module.

At this point, we'd like to discuss three attributes of the Context object that can affect the calculations.

prec

The prec attribute (for *precision*) determines the precision of the Decimal instances of the current context. The value is the number of decimal places to be calculated and is preset to 28:

```
>>> import decimal
>>> c = decimal.getcontext()
>>> c.prec = 3
```

26

```
>>> Decimal("1.23456789") * Decimal("2.3456789")
Decimal('2.90')
```

Emin and Emax

The Emin and Emax attributes define the maximum and minimum size of the exponent, respectively. Both must reference an integer. If the result of a calculation exceeds this limit, an exception is raised:

```
>>> import decimal
>>> c = decimal.getcontext()
>>> c.Emax = 9
>>> Decimal("1e100") * Decimal("1e100")
Traceback (most recent call last):
  File "<stdin>", line 1, in <module>
Overflow: [<class 'decimal.Overflow'>]
```

This section was intended as a basic introduction to the decimal module. This module provides many more options to make calculations or to adapt results of these calculations to your own needs. If your interest in this module has been piqued, we encourage you to research its other uses, especially in the Python documentation.

Note, however, that there's usually no need for such precise calculations as the Decimal data type provides. The speed advantage of float usually outweighs the accuracy gain of Decimal.

26.5   Hash Functions: hashlib

The hashlib module of the standard library implements the most common *hash functions*. A hash function is a complex algorithm that calculates a *hash value* from a parameter, usually a string. What can such a hash value be used for? In the following, we describe a practical example that has been simplified[3] for presentation purposes.

Imagine you are developing forum software that will later be used for a community on the internet. Before users may post to the forum, they must log in with a user name and the relevant password. Of course, it's in the interest of the forum operator and especially the users themselves that the password doesn't fall into the wrong hands. So the question is how to make the login procedure as secure as possible.

The most intuitive way would be to submit the user name and password to the forum software. There, these two pieces of information are compared with the credentials of all users, and if a match is found, access to the forum is granted.

---

3 In real-world software, correct handling of user data such as passwords is non-trivial and error prone. To prevent security issues, you should either know exactly what you are doing or use well-established standard methods.

If such software actually performed the login procedure this way, the user name and password would have to be stored in plain text in the internal database of the forum. This wouldn't be a big problem in regard to the user name as that's generally public information. But storing the password in plain text in such a database would be grossly negligent. An attacker who gains access to the database via a security gap in another part of the software would immediately be in possession of all passwords of the logged-in users. This becomes especially explosive when you consider that many people still use the same password for multiple user accounts.

It would therefore be desirable to be able to determine the correctness of a password with a probability close to certainty without having to store reference passwords in plain text. And this is where hash functions come into play. A hash function is passed a parameter and calculates the so-called hash value from it. Now, when a new user logs into the forum software and chooses his password, it won't be entered into the database in plain text; the hash value of the password will be stored instead.

When logging in, the user sends the password to the server. The server then calculates the hash value of the transmitted password and compares it with the stored hash values.[4]

For such a login procedure to work and for a potential attacker not to be able to calculate passwords even with access to the database, hash functions have to meet some requirements:

- A hash function represents *one-way coding*. This means that the calculation of the hash value is not reversible, so you can't infer the original parameter from a hash value with reasonable effort.

- With hash functions, so-called collisions occur as a matter of principle, meaning that two different parameters result in the same hash value. An essential step to cracking a hash function is to be able to calculate such collisions. A hash function should therefore make the calculation of collisions so difficult that they can only be determined with an extremely high investment of resources.

- A hash function should be as arbitrary as possible so that you can't conclude that you are close to the password you're looking for based on a similar hash value. As soon as the parameter of the hash function is changed minimally, a completely different hash value should be calculated.

- Last but not least, a hash function should be quick to compute. In addition, it must be possible to efficiently compare the resulting hash values with each other.

The field of application for hash functions is wide. Beyond the password example, they're also used for comparing large files, among other things. Instead of comparing

---

4 Because hash functions are deterministic, it's still possible for an attacker to try probable passwords and compare the hash values with those stored in the database. Such a *dictionary attack* is made more difficult by means of a *salt*, a random number appended to a password before its hash value is determined.

these files with each other byte by byte, their hash values are calculated and compared. The hash values can be used to tell whether the files are different with certainty or identical with high probability. This is especially interesting when it isn't possible to compare the files directly due to limited bandwidth. For example, comparing hash values is the most efficient way to verify the authenticity of a file downloaded from the internet. Another interesting application of hash functions is *blockchain technology*, which can be used, for example, to implement decentralized data storage with traceable modification history.

Note that the probability of a collision is very low for the procedures implemented in the hashlib module, but it's still theoretically present.

26.5.1 Using the Module

First, the hashlib module contains a set of classes, each implementing a hash algorithm (see Table 26.9).

Class	Algorithm	Hash size	Description
blake2s blake2b	BLAKE2	variable	–
md5	MD5	128-bit	Message-Digest Algorithm 5
sha1	SHA-1	160-bit	Secure Hash Algorithm 1
sha224 sha256 sha384 sha512	SHA	224-bit 256-bit 384-bit 512-bit	Secure Hash Algorithm
sha3_224 sha3_256 sha3_384 sha3_512	SHA-3	224-bit 256-bit 384-bit 512-bit	Secure Hash Algorithm 3

Table 26.9 Supported Hash Functions

> **Note**
> Note that the MD5 and SHA-1 algorithms have already been broken to some extent. They should therefore no longer be used in safety-relevant applications.

The use of these classes is identical. Therefore, we describe it here using the md5 class as an example. During the instantiation of the md5 class, a bytes instance is passed whose hash value is to be calculated:

```
>>> import hashlib
>>> m = hashlib.md5(b"Hello world")
```

By calling the digest method, the calculated hash value is returned as a byte sequence. Note that the returned bytes instance may well contain nonprintable characters:

```
>>> m.digest()
b'>%\x96\ny\xdb\xc6\x9bgL\xd4\xecg\xa7,b'
```

By calling the hexdigest method, the calculated hash value is returned as a string containing a sequence of two-digit hexadecimal numbers. These hexadecimal numbers each represent one byte of the hash value. The returned string contains only printable characters:

```
>>> m.hexdigest()
'3e25960a79dbc69b674cd4ec67a72c62'
```

26.5.2   Other Hash Algorithms

In addition to the hash algorithms listed previously, which are guaranteed to be present in hashlib, the module provides a number of other algorithms whose availability depends on the operating system. These additional algorithms can be instantiated using the new function. Note that you must pass the name of the algorithm to it:

```
>>> m = hashlib.new("md4", b"Hello world")
>>> m.hexdigest()
'2f34e7edc8180b87578159ff58e87c1a'
```

The set of total available algorithms is provided via algorithms_available:

```
>>> hashlib.algorithms_available
{'sha3_512', 'blake2s', 'md5', 'ripemd160', 'sha512_256', 'sha224', 'sha3_384',
'sha512_224', 'sha3_224', 'sm3', 'shake_256', 'whirlpool', 'sha384', 'sha512',
'md4', 'md5-sha1', 'shake_128', 'sha3_256', 'blake2b', 'mdc2', 'sha1', 'sha256'}
```

26.5.3   Comparing Large Files

Hash functions calculate a short hash value from a basically unlimited amount of data. Due to the properties of a hash function, the probability of finding two different sets of data that result in the same hash value is very low. This makes hash functions suitable for comparing large files with each other without the files having to be in a common location. This makes it possible, for example, to determine whether a file stored on a server needs to be reuploaded because it has changed on the user's computer.

The following sample program reads two files and compares them based on their hash values:

```
import hashlib
with open("file1.txt", "rb") as f1, open("file2.txt", "rb") as f2:
    if hashlib.md5(f1.read()).digest() == hashlib.md5(f2.read()).digest():
        print("The files are identical")
    else:
        print("The files are different")
```

In this case, the widely used md5 hash function was used, but the other functions included in hashlib can also be used.

For working with data streams, the hash classes contain the update method, which can be used to extend the amount of data specified during its creation:

```
>>> h1 = hashlib.md5(b"First.")
>>> h1.update(b"Second.")
>>> h1.update(b"Third.")
>>>
>>> h2 = hashlib.md5(b"First.Second.Third.")
>>> h1.digest() == h2.digest()
True
```

The above example program for comparing two files is implemented inefficiently since the contents of the files are read completely into the RAM and only after that the respective hash values are calculated. With very large files this requires unnecessarily much RAM or cannot be accomplished at all, if the available RAM is smaller than the files. Using the update method, you can read the files sequentially in small parts and update the hash value for each part:

```
def my_file_hash(filename, buffer_size=1024):
    with open(filename, "rb") as f:
        h = hashlib.md5(f.read(buffer_size))
        while data := f.read(buffer_size):
            h.update(data)
    return h
```

The function my_file_hash reads blocks with buffer_size bytes from the file at a time and updates the hash value with this data. For large files, this procedure significantly reduces memory consumption.

26.5.4 Passwords

The following sample program uses the hashlib module to implement password protection. The password should not be stored as plain text in the source code, but as a hash value. This ensures that the passwords can't be viewed, even if someone comes into possession of the hash values. Internet portals that require registration, such as forums, also store user passwords as hash values:

```python
import hashlib
pwhash = "329670c3265b6ccd392e622733e9772f"
m = hashlib.md5(input("Your password, please: ").encode("utf-8"))
if pwhash == m.hexdigest():
    print("Access allowed")
else:
    print("Access denied")
```

The program reads a password from a user, calculates the MD5 hash value of this password, and compares it with the stored hash value. In this case, the previously calculated pwhash hash value is predefined in the program. Under normal circumstances, it would be in a database with other hash values or stored in a file. If both values match, "Access allowed" is output symbolically. The password for this program is "My password".

Using a hash value to store passwords is common practice. However, the hash functions discussed so far, including in particular the md5 function used in the previous example, are only suitable for this purpose to a limited extent as they're vulnerable to brute force attacks. To store passwords securely, you should follow two basic principles:

- You should use a *salt*. This is a string appended to the password before the hash value is calculated. This way, different hash values can be stored for two users, even if they use the same password. This prevents passwords from being cracked using precalculated plain text tables, so-called *rainbow tables*.

- You should apply the hash function repeatedly in a certain number of rounds to set the calculation time of the hash function. This makes it difficult to try out a large number of possible passwords.

Especially for storing passwords, the hashlib module contains the pbkdf2_hmac[5] function:

```
pbkdf2_hmac(name, password, salt, rounds)
```

It calculates a password hash for the password password with the salt using round rounds of the algorithm. The algorithm implemented here is based on one of the basic hash functions discussed at the beginning of the section. The name parameter can be used to specify which of the hash functions should be used:

```
>>> hashlib.pbkdf2_hmac("sha256", b"password", b"salt", 100000)
b'\x03\x94\xa2\xed\xe32\xc9\xa1>\xb8.\x9b$c\x16\x04\xc3\x1d\xf9x\xb4\xe2\xf0
\xfb\xd2\xc5I\x940\x9dy\xa5'
```

---

5 The name of this function comes from *Password-Based Key Derivation Function 2*.

Chapter 27
Screen Outputs and Logging

At this point, we'd like to look at modules of the standard library that usefully supplement the possibilities of screen output. These are the pprint module for clearly formatted output of complex instances, which we also used briefly in Chapter 3, Section 3.10, and the logging module for formatted output of log messages on the screen or in log files.

The modules discussed in this chapter are intended to complement the built-in print function that's usually used and which has been described in detail in Chapter 17, Section 17.14.36.

27.1 Formatted Output of Complex Objects: pprint

The standard library contains the pprint module (for *pretty print*), which can be used for a neatly formatted representation of a Python data type on the screen. The module makes especially the output of complex data types such as long lists more readable. Before examples can be executed, the module must be imported:

```
>>> import pprint
```

The pprint module essentially contains a function of the same name that can be called to output an instance.

pprint(object, [stream, indent, width, depth], {compact})

The pprint function prints the object instance formatted on the stream stream. If you don't pass the stream parameter, pprint writes to the standard output stream sys. stdout. The indent, width, and depth parameters can be used to control the formatting of the output. The number of spaces to be used for indentation can be passed for indent. The indent parameter is preset with 1.

The optional width parameter can be used to specify the maximum number of characters for the width of the output. This parameter is preset with 80 characters.

In the following example, we first create a list of strings using a method of our choice and output it formatted via pprint:

```
>>> strings = [f"The value of {i}**2 is {i**2}" for i in range(10)]
>>> pprint.pprint(strings)
['The value of 0**2 is 0',
 'The value of 1**2 is 1',
 'The value of 2**2 is 4',
 'The value of 3**2 is 9',
 'The value of 4**2 is 16',
 'The value of 5**2 is 25',
 'The value of 6**2 is 36',
 'The value of 7**2 is 49',
 'The value of 8**2 is 64',
 'The value of 9**2 is 81']
```

To perform a comparison, we output strings once again unformatted via print:

```
>>> print(strings)
['The value of 0**2 is 0', 'The value of 1**2 is 1', 'The value of 2**2 is 4',
'The value of 3**2 is 9', 'The value of 4**2 is 16', 'The value of 5**2 is 25',
'The value of 6**2 is 36', 'The value of 7**2 is 49', 'The value of 8**2 is 64',
'The value of 9**2 is 81']
```

The depth parameter is an integer and determines the depth to which subinstances, such as nested lists, are to be output. If a value other than None is passed for depth, pprint omits deeper nested elements indicating these by three dots (...).

The compact keyword parameter can be used to control how compactly extensive structures (e.g., long lists) are displayed. If True is passed here, for example, each element of strings is not written to a separate line.

Should you wish to further process the output of pprint, you can use the pformat function, which returns the formatted representation as a string:

```
>>> s = pprint.pformat(strings)
>>> print(s)
['The value of 0**2 is 0',
 'The value of 1**2 is 1',
 'The value of 2**2 is 4',
 'The value of 3**2 is 9',
 'The value of 4**2 is 16',
 'The value of 5**2 is 25',
 'The value of 6**2 is 36',
 'The value of 7**2 is 49',
 'The value of 8**2 is 64',
 'The value of 9**2 is 81']
```

The pformat function has the same interface as pprint, the only difference being that the stream parameter is missing.

27.2   Log Files: logging

The `logging` module provides a flexible interface for logging the program flow. The program sequence is logged by sending messages to the `logging` module at various points in the program. These messages can have different levels of urgency. For example, there are error messages, warnings, and debug information. The `logging` module can process these messages in many ways. It's common to add a timestamp to the message and either output it to the screen or write it to a file.

In this section, the use of the `logging` module is shown on the basis of several examples in interactive mode. To be able to execute the sample programs correctly, the `logging` module must first be imported:

```
>>> import logging
```

Before messages can be sent to the logger, it must be initialized by calling the `basicConfig` function. The following example sets up a logger that writes all incoming messages to the `program.log` log file:

```
>>> logging.basicConfig(filename="program.log")
```

Using the `log` function included in the module, messages can now be passed to the logger. The `log` function gets the urgency level of the message as its first parameter and the message itself in form of a string as its second parameter:

```
>>> logging.log(logging.ERROR, "An error has occurred")
>>> logging.log(logging.INFO, "This is information")
```

By calling the `shutdown` function, the logger is correctly deinitialized and any pending write operations are performed:

```
>>> logging.shutdown()
```

Of course, the `ERROR` and `INFO` urgency levels are not the only ones available. Table 27.1 lists all the predefined levels you can choose from. The table is ordered by urgency, with the most urgent level listed last.

Level	Description
NOTSET	No urgency level
DEBUG	A message that's only relevant to the programmer for debugging purposes
INFO	An information message about the program status
WARNING	A warning message indicating a possible error

Table 27.1 Predefined Urgency Levels

27

Level	Description
ERROR	An error message after which the program can continue to run
CRITICAL	A message about a critical error that results in the immediate termination of the program or the currently performed operation

Table 27.1 Predefined Urgency Levels (Cont.)

For convenience, a separate function exists for each urgency level. Thus, the two function calls of log from the last example are equivalent to the following:

```
logging.error("An error has occurred")
logging.info("This is information")
```

If you look at the log file after calling these two functions, you'll notice that there is only one entry:

```
ERROR:root:An error has occurred
```

This is due to the fact that in its basic configuration, the logger only logs messages whose urgency is greater than or equal to that of a warning. To log debug and info messages as well, you must pass a suitable value in the level keyword parameter when calling the basicConfig function:

```
logging.basicConfig(
    filename="program.log",
    level=logging.DEBUG)
logging.error("An error has occurred")
logging.info("This is information")
```

In this example, the minimum urgency was set to DEBUG. This means that all messages that have at least an urgency of DEBUG will be logged. Consequently, both messages also appear in the log file:

```
ERROR:root:An error has occurred
INFO:root:This is information
```

Table 27.2 lists the most important keyword parameters that can be passed to the basicConfig function.

Parameter	Description
datefmt	Specifies the date format, which will be described in the following section.
filemode	Specifies the mode* in which the log file is to be opened (default value: "a").

Table 27.2 Keyword Parameters of the basicConfig Function

Parameter	Description
filename	Specifies the file name of the log file.
format	Specifies the message format, which will be described in the following section.
handlers	Specifies a list of handlers to be registered. For more details, see Section 27.2.2.
level	Sets the minimum urgency for messages to be included in the log file.
stream	Specifies a stream to which the log messages are to be written. If the stream and filename parameters are both specified, stream will be ignored.
style	Determines the formatting syntax for the message. The default value of "%" imposes the old % syntax from Python 2, while a value of "{" imposes the new string formatting syntax.**

*   The different modes in which files can be opened are listed in Chapter 6, Section 6.4.

** For more details on string formatting, see Chapter 12, Section 12.5.3.

Table 27.2 Keyword Parameters of the basicConfig Function (Cont.)

27.2.1   Customizing the Message Format

As you can see from the previous examples, a log file entry doesn't have a timestamp by default. However, you can customize the format of the logged message. To do that, you must pass the format keyword parameter when calling the basicConfig function:

```
logging.basicConfig(
    filename="program.log",
    level=logging.DEBUG,
    style="{",
    format="{asctime} [{levelname:8}] {message}")
logging.error("An error has occurred")
logging.info("This is information")
logging.error("And another error")
```

You can see that a format string has been passed that contains the template for a message as it should later appear in the log file. The asctime, levelname, and message identifiers stand for the timestamp, the urgency level, and the message. The messages generated by this example look as follows:

```
2020-02-05 14:28:55,811 [ERROR   ] An error has occurred
2020-02-05 14:29:00,690 [INFO    ] This is information
2020-02-05 14:29:12,686 [ERROR   ] And another error
```

Table 27.3 lists the most important identifiers that may be used within the format string. Depending on the context in which the message is generated, some of the identifiers have no meaning.

Identifiers	Description
asctime	Time of reporting. The date and time format can be specified via the datefmt parameter when calling the basicConfig function. More details follow after this table.
filename	The filename of the program file in which the message was sent.
funcName	The name of the function in which the message was sent.
levelname	The urgency level of the message.
lineno	The source code line where the message was placed.
message	The text of the message.
module	The name of the module in which the message was sent. The module name corresponds to the filename without the file extension.
pathname	The path to the program file where the message was placed.
process	The ID of the process in which the message was sent.
thread	The ID of the thread in which the message was sent.

Table 27.3 Identifiers in the format String

It is possible to customize the format used to output timestamps. For example, we can set a date format common in Germany and, in addition, disable the output of the millisecond parts. The format of the timestamp can be specified by the datefmt keyword parameter when calling basicConfig:

```
logging.basicConfig(
    filename="program.log",
    level=logging.DEBUG,
    style="{",
    format="{asctime} [{levelname:8}] {message}",
    datefmt="%d.%m.%Y %H:%M:%S")
logging.error("An error has occurred")
```

The placeholders used in the date format template were introduced in Chapter 15, Section 15.1. The message generated by this example looks as follows:

```
05.02.2020 14:38:49 [ERROR   ] An error has occurred
```

27.2.2 Logging Handlers

So far, we've exclusively described how the logging module can be used to write all incoming messages to a file. In fact, the module is very flexible in this respect and allows writing not only to files, but also to streams, for example, or sending the messages over a network connection. For this purpose, you can use *logging handlers*. Strictly speaking, we've already used an implicit handler in the previous sections without being aware of it.

To set up a specific handler, you must create an instance of the handler class. This instance can then be used by the logger. In the following example, all messages are to be written to a stream—namely, sys.stdout. For this purpose, the logging.StreamHandler handler class is used:

```python
import logging
import sys
handler = logging.StreamHandler(sys.stdout)
frm = logging.Formatter("{asctime} {levelname}: {message}",
                        "%d.%m.%Y %H:%M:%S", style="{")
handler.setFormatter(frm)
logger = logging.getLogger()
logger.addHandler(handler)
logger.setLevel(logging.DEBUG)
logger.critical("A really critical error")
logger.warning("And a subsequent warning")
logger.info("This, on the other hand, is just for your information")
```

First, the handler—in this case, a StreamHandler—is instantiated. The next step is to create an instance of the Formatter class. This class encapsulates the formatting statements we passed in the previous examples when calling the basicConfig function. Using the setFormatter method, the formatting statements are made known to the handler.

To register the handler with the logger, we obtain access to the logger instance that was previously used implicitly via the getLogger function. Then addHandler is used to add the handler and setLevel is used to set the relevant urgency level.

After that, the messages are not sent via functions of the logging module, but via the critical, warning, and info methods of the Logger instance logger. The sample program outputs the following text on the screen:

```
05.02.2020 17:21:46 CRITICAL: A really critical error
05.02.2020 17:21:46 WARNING: And a subsequent warning
05.02.2020 17:21:46 INFO: This, on the other hand, is just for your information
```

The following sections describe the most important additional handler classes included in the logging or logging.handlers package.

27

logging.FileHandler(filename, [mode, encoding, delay])

This handler writes the log entries to the `filename` file. The file will be opened in the `mode` mode. The `FileHandler` handler can also be used implicitly by specifying the `filename` and `filemode` keyword parameters when calling the `basicConfig` function.

The `encoding` parameter can be used to specify the encoding used to write the file. If you pass `True` for the `delay` parameter, the file will wait to be opened until data is actually to be written.

logging.StreamHandler([stream])

This handler writes the log entries to the `stream` stream. Note that the `StreamHandler` handler can also be used implicitly by specifying the `stream` keyword parameter when calling the `basicConfig` function.

logging.handlers.SocketHandler(host, port)
logging.handlers.DatagramHandler(host, port)

These handlers send the log entries through a TCP interface (`SocketHandler`) or through a UDP network interface (`DatagramHandler`) to the hostname `host` using the port `port`.

logging.handlers.SMTPHandler(mailhost, from, to, subject, [credentials])

This handler sends the log entries as an email to the `to` address. In this process, `subject` is entered as the subject and `from` as the sender address. You can use the `mailhost` parameter to specify the SMTP server to be used. If this server requires authentication, you can pass a tuple containing a user name and password for the optional last parameter, `credentials`.

Chapter 28
Regular Expressions

The `re` module of the standard library provides extensive options for using regular expressions. In a *regular expression*, a text pattern is described by a special syntax, which can then be applied to different texts or text fragments. Basically, there are two major areas of use for regular expressions:

- *Matching* checks whether or not a text section matches the regular expression pattern. An example of matching is a test that checks whether an entered email address is syntactically valid.

- The second possible use of regular expressions is *searching*, which searches for text fragments within a larger text that match a regular expression.

Searching is a discipline in its own right as this behavior can't be efficiently implemented by the programmer himself via matching. An example of use is the syntax highlighter of your Python environment, which searches for special sections of code like keywords or strings to highlight them graphically.

A regular expression in Python can be specified using a string that contains the corresponding rules. Contrary to other programming languages, Python doesn't provide a separate literal for this purpose.

In the following sections, we want to introduce you to the syntax of regular expressions. Entire books have already been published on this topic alone, which is why the description here is comparatively brief and basic. There are several notations available for describing regular expressions. Python follows the syntax used in the Perl programming language.

28.1 Syntax of Regular Expressions

Basically, the string `"python"` is already a regular expression, which exactly matches the string `"python"`. Directly specified individual letters are called *character literals*. Character literals within regular expressions are *case-sensitive*, meaning that the preceding expression wouldn't match the string `"Python"`.

You can use a number of control characters in regular expressions, making the expression more flexible and powerful. These will be described in the following sections.

> **Note**
>
> If you're already familiar with regular expressions, you may have just become aware of a problem. The backslash is an important character for describing regular expressions, and of all things, this character already carries meaning within a string: normally, a backslash introduces an escape sequence. You can now either always use the escape sequence for a backslash ("\\") or draw on the raw strings of Python, which are prefixed with an r:
>
> r"\Hello world"

28.1.1   Any Character

The simplest generalization that can be used within a regular expression is to mark any character with a period.[1] Thus, the expression r".ython" matches "python" and "Python" as well as "Jython", but not "blython" or "ython" because of exactly one single arbitrary character.

28.1.2   Character Classes

Apart from explicitly marking a character as arbitrary, you can also specify a class of characters that may occur at that position. For this purpose, the valid characters are written in square brackets at the corresponding position:

r"[jp]ython"

This regular expression works similarly to the one in the last section, but only allows the letters j and p as the first character of the word. Thus, the expression matches both "jython" and "python", but not "Python", "jpython", or "ython". To allow the respective uppercase letters in the word as well, you can expand the expression in the following way:

r"[jJpP]ython"

Within a character class, it's possible to allow entire ranges of characters. This causes the following syntax to be used:

r"[A-Z]ython"

---

[1] Here you can see that a period within a regular expression has a special meaning. To describe the actual . character, it must be preceded by a backslash in the regular expression: r"P\.thon" only matches the string "P.thon". This applies in a similar way to other characters with special semantics when used in regular expressions, such as brackets.

This regular expression allows any uppercase letter as the initial letter of the word, but no lowercase letter or number, for example. To allow for multiple ranges, you can simply write them one after the other:

`r"[A-Ra-r]ython"`

For example, this regular expression matches both `"Qython"` and `"qython"`, but not `"Sython"` or `"3ython"`.

You can also use digit ranges as a character class:

`r"[0-9]ython"`

As a last option provided by a character group, characters or character ranges can be excluded. For this purpose, a circumflex (^) is written at the beginning of the character group. Thus, the regular expression `r"[^pP]ython"` allows you to use any character, except for an uppercase or lowercase *P*. Consequently, both `"Sython"` and `"wython"` work, while `"Python"` and `"python"` are excluded.

Note that within a character class, except for the hyphen and the circumflex, there are no characters that have a special meaning. In particular, this means that a period in a character class actually describes the . character and not just any character.

28.1.3   Quantifiers

So far, we can set up certain rules for individual characters in a regular expression. However, we'll face a problem if we want to allow a certain number or even any number of these characters to be located at a certain position in the word. For this purpose, you can use *quantifiers*. These are special characters that are written after a single character literal or class and indicate how often the character literal or class may occur. Table 28.1 lists all quantifiers and briefly explains their meaning. After that, we'll demonstrate the use of quantifiers with a few examples.

Quantifier	Meaning
?	The preceding character or character class may occur either once or not at all.
*	The preceding character or character class may occur any number of times in succession, which means, among other things, that it may also be omitted.
+	The preceding character or character class may occur any number of times in succession, but at least once. Consequently, it mustn't be omitted.

Table 28.1 Quantifiers in Regular Expressions

The following three examples show a regular expression with one quantifier each:

- `r"P[Yy]?thon"`

  This regular expression expects at most one occurrence of the uppercase or lower-case *Y* in the second position of the word. Thus, for example, the expression matches the words `"Python"` and `"Pthon"`, but not `"Pyython"`.

- `r"P[Yy]*thon"`

  This regular expression expects an arbitrarily frequent occurrence of the uppercase or lowercase *Y* in the second position of the word. Thus, for example, the expression matches the words `"Python"`, `"Pthon"`, and `"PyyYYYthon"`, but not `"Pzthon"`.

- `r"P[Yy]+thon"`

  This regular expression expects at least one occurrence of the uppercase or lower-case *Y* in the second position of the word. Thus, for example, the expression matches the words `"Python"`, `"PYthon"`, and `"PyyYYYthon"`, but not `"Pthon"`.

In addition to quantifiers, there's a syntax that enables you to specify exactly how many repetitions of a character group are allowed. Here, the lower and upper limits for repetitions are written in curly brackets after the corresponding character or group of characters. Table 28.2 lists the range of possibilities for this notation.

Syntax	Meaning
`{num}`	The preceding character or character class must occur exactly num times.
`{min,}`	The preceding character or character class must occur at least min times.
`{,max}`	The preceding character or character class may occur at most max times.
`{min,max}`	The preceding character or character class must occur at least min times and may occur at most max times.

Table 28.2 Repetitions in Regular Expressions

Let's now modify the previous example for these quantifiers too and take a look at their effects:

- `r"P[Yy]{2}thon"`

  This regular expression expects exactly two uppercase or lowercase *Y*s in the second position of the word. Thus, for example, the expression matches the words `"Pyython"` or `"PYython"`, but not `"Pyyython"`.

- `r"P[Yy]{2,}thon"`

  This regular expression expects at least two uppercase or lowercase *Y*s in the second position of the word. Thus, for example, the expression matches the words `"Pyython"`, `"PYython"`, and `"PyyYYYthon"`, but not `"Python"`.

- `r"P[Yy]{,2}thon"`

  This regular expression expects a maximum of two uppercase or lowercase *Y*s in the second position of the word. Thus, for example, the expression matches the words `"Python"`, `"Pthon"`, and `"PYYthon"`, but not `"Pyyython"`.

- `r"P[Yy]{1,2}thon"`

  This regular expression expects at least one and at most two uppercase or lowercase *Y*s in the second position of the word. Thus, for example, the expression matches the words `"Python"` or `"PYython"`, but not `"Pthon"` or `"PYYYthon"`.

28.1.4   Predefined Character Classes

So that you don't have to reinvent the wheel for every regular expression, there is a set of predefined character classes that include, for example, all digits or all alphanumeric characters. These character classes are often needed when working with regular expressions and can therefore be abbreviated by a special code. Each of these codes starts with a backslash. Table 28.3 lists the most important predefined character classes with their meanings.

Character Class	Meaning
`\d`	Matches all digits of the decimal system. Is equivalent to `[0-9]`.
`\D`	Matches all characters that are not digits of the decimal system. Is equivalent to `[^0-9]`.
`\s`	Matches all white space characters. Is equivalent to `[ \t\n\r\f\v]`.
`\S`	Matches all characters that are not white space. Is equivalent to `[^ \t\n\r\f\v]`.
`\w`	Matches all alphanumeric characters and the underscore. Is equivalent to `[a-zA-Z0-9_]`.
`\W`	Matches all characters that are not alphanumeric and not underscores. Is equivalent to `[^a-zA-Z0-9_]`.

Table 28.3 Predefined Character Classes in Regular Expressions

> **Note**
>
> Regular expression operations can be performed in two modes, which can be distinguished by the regular expression type:[2]
>
> - If the regular expression is a bytes string, the operations are performed in the ASCII character space.
> - If the regular expression is a string, the operations are performed in the Unicode character space.
>
> The character classes provided in Table 28.3 are extended analogously in the case of a Unicode expression. For example, German umlauts count as alphanumeric characters in this case.

The predefined character classes can be used like normal characters in regular expressions. Thus, the expression r"P\w*th\dn" matches the words "Pyth0n" or "P_th1n", but not "Python", for example.

Note that the usual escape sequences that can be used inside a string also retain their meaning inside a regular expression—even if written in a raw string—and don't interfere with the character classes presented here. In this context, the most common ones are \n, \t, \r, and \\, but especially also \x.[3]

Furthermore, the backslash allows you to use characters with special meaning as regular characters within a regular expression. This way, you can use the * or + characters, for example, without them being considered quantifiers. Thus, the regular expression r"*Py\.\.\.on*" only matches the string "*Py...on*".

28.1.5 Other Special Characters

Sometimes rules need to be established that go beyond the mere character level. For example, it can be useful to create a regular expression that matches only if the word is located at the beginning or end of a line of text. For such and similar cases, there is a set of special characters that are applied in the same way as the predefined character classes. Table 28.4 lists all additional special characters and provides a brief explanation for each.

Special Characters	Meaning
\A	Matches only at the beginning of a string.
\b	Matches only at the beginning or end of a word. A word can consist of all characters of class \w and is delimited by a character of class \W.

Table 28.4 Special Characters in Regular Expressions

---

2 An alternative option is provided by the ASCII flag, which can be found in Section 28.2.7.
3 For explanations of escape sequences, see Chapter 12, Section 12.5.1 and Section 12.5.4.

Special Characters	Meaning
\B	Matches only if it's not the beginning or end of a word.
\Z	Matches only at the end of a string.
^	Matches only at the beginning of a string. If the MULTILINE flag has been set, ^ will also fit directly after each newline character within the string.[*]
$	Matches only at the end of a string. If the MULTILINE flag is set, $ will also fit directly before each newline character within the string.

[*]   For more details on the MULTILINE flag, see Section 28.2.7.

Table 28.4 Special Characters in Regular Expressions (Cont.)

In the actual example, the regular expression r"Python\Z" only matches the string "Python", but not "Python rocks". Beyond the special characters listed in Table 28.4, the escape sequences known for string literals can also be used within regular expressions.

28.1.6   Nongreedy Quantifiers

We have already discussed the ?, *, and + quantifiers. These are referred to as *greedy* in the terminology of regular expressions. This classification is especially important for searching. Consider the following regular expression:

```
r"Py.*on"
```

This expression matches any substring that starts with Py and ends with on. In between the two, there can be any number of unspecified characters. When performing a search, the expression is to be used to isolate various substrings from a longer string that match the regular expression.

Let's now mentally apply the regular expression to the following string:

```
"Python Python Python"
```

Would you say that three results are found? That's wrong. It's exactly one result, namely the substring "**Py**thon Python Py**thon**". Here's why: the greedy quantifier * was used. Such a greedy quantifier has the ambition to "devour" the maximum possible number of characters. Thus, during searching, if greedy quantifiers are used, the largest possible matching string is always found.

This behavior can be reversed so that the smallest possible matching string is always found. To do this, you can append a question mark to each quantifier. This turns the

28

quantifier into a *nongreedy* one. Let's suppose searching on the above string was performed with the regular expression r"Py.*?on". If so, the partial string "Python" would actually have been found three times as a result. This works for the quantifiers ?, *, +, and {}.

28.1.7   Groups

A part of a regular expression can be combined to a *group* by means of parentheses. This way of grouping has three main advantages:

- A group can be considered as a unit and as such can be assigned a quantifier. This way, for example, multiple occurrences of a certain string can be allowed:

  r"(?Python)+ is good"

  In this expression, there is a group around the subexpression r" ?Python". This subexpression matches the string "Python" with an optional space at the beginning. The entire group can now occur any number of times, making the above regular expression match both "Python is good" and "Python Python Python is good". But the group must occur at least once, and the expression doesn't match the string " is good".

  Note the space at the beginning of the group to understand how the expression works.

- The second advantage of a group is that you can access it after the searching or matching has been done. This means, for example, you could check whether an entered URL is valid and filter out subdomain, domain, and top level domain at the same time.

  For more details on how accessing groups works, see Section 28.2.

- There are groups that are used more frequently in a regular expression. To avoid having to write them each time, groups are numbered consecutively, starting with 1, and can then be referenced by their index. Such a reference consists of a backslash followed by the index of the respective group and matches the same substring that the group matched. Thus, the regular expression r"(Python) \1" matches "Python Python".

28.1.8   Alternatives

Another option provided by the syntax of regular expressions is *alternatives*. Basically, this is an OR operation of two characters or groups of characters, as you already know from Python's or operator. This association is implemented by the vertical line character, |, also called the *pipe*.

r"P(ython|eter)"

This regular expression matches both the "Python" and "Peter" strings. Later, the group enables you to read which of the two alternatives occurred.

28.1.9 Extensions

At this point, we have covered the most important aspects of the syntax of regular expressions. In addition to this more or less standardized syntax, Python allows the use of so-called extensions. An extension is structured as follows:

```
(?...)
```

The three dots are replaced by an identifier of the required extension and further extension-specific information. This syntax was chosen because an opening parenthesis followed by a question mark has no syntactical meaning and therefore was "free." Note, however, that an extension doesn't necessarily create a new group, even if the parentheses suggest it. In the following sections, we'll go into more detail about the extensions that can be used in the regular expressions of Python.

(?aiLmsux)

This extension allows you to set one or more flags for the whole regular expression. Each of the *a*, *i*, *L*, *m*, *s*, *u*, and *x* characters denotes a specific flag. The term *flag* has already been used to describe a setting that can be either enabled or disabled. A flag can be set either in the regular expression itself, just by this extension, or by a parameter of the `re.compile` function (Section 28.2.6). In connection with this function, we'll go into more detail about the meaning of each flag. For example, the i flag makes the regular expression *case-insensitive*:

```
r"(?i)P"
```

This expression matches both "P" and "p". Since Python 3.6, flags can be set or removed for parts of the regular expression. The following two regular expressions each change the case sensitivity for the two central letters of the word *Python*:

```
r"Py(?i:th)on"
r"(?i)Py(?-i:th)on"
```

For example, the first expression matches the string "PyThon", while the second one matches "pYthON", for instance.

(?:...)

This extension is used like normal parentheses but doesn't create a group. This means you can't access a partial expression bracketed by this extension at a later time. Otherwise, this syntax is equivalent to parentheses:

```
r"(?:abc|def)"
```

28

With the help of this construct, a regular expression can be structured without incurring overhead due to the formation of groups. This extension is also useful for applying quantifiers to parts of a regular expression.

(?P<name>...)

This extension creates a group with the specified name. The special feature of such a named group is that it can be referenced not only by its index, but also by its name, see *(?P=name)* below. The name must be a valid identifier:

```
r"(?P<helloworld>abc|def)"
```

(?P=name)

This extension matches everything the already defined group named name matched as well. So this extension allows you to reference a named group:

```
r"(?P<py>[Pp]ython) is as (?P=py) should be"
```

This regular expression matches the string "Python is as Python should be", for example.

(?#...)

This extension represents a comment. The content of the parentheses is simply ignored:

```
r"Py(?#blahblahblah)thon"
```

(?=...)

This extension only matches if the regular expression ... will match next. Thus, the extension anticipates without actually advancing in the evaluation of the expression.

For example, the regular expression r"\w+(?= Miller)" can be used to search for the first names of all people with the last name Miller appearing in the text. The obvious alternative r"\w+ Miller" would include not only the first names, but always the last name Miller in the result. You can easily apply this example to the following three extensions, so we won't provide any examples there.

(?!...)

This extension matches only if the regular expression ... *won't* match next. This extension is the counterpart to the previous one.

(?<=...)

This extension only matches if the regular expression ... has matched before. It thus accesses parts of the string that have already been evaluated, without returning the evaluation itself.

(?<!...)

This extension matches only if the regular expression ... hasn't matched before. It is thus the counterpart to the previous one.

(?(id/name)yes-pattern|no-pattern)

This complicated looking extension can be used as a conditional in a regular expression. Depending on whether a group with the specified index or name matched a substring, either (in the positive case) the *yes-pattern* or (in the negative case) the *no-pattern* gets tested. The *no-pattern* is separated from the *yes-pattern* by a vertical line, but it can also be omitted:

```
r"(?P<parenthesis>\()?Python(?(parenthesis)\))"
```

In this expression, a group called `parenthesis` is first created, which may occur not more than once and consists of an opening parenthesis. This is followed by the string `Python`, and finally a closing parenthesis is required by the extension if an opening one occurred previously—that is, if the group `parenthesis` matched before.

Thus, the regular expression matches the strings `"Python"` and `"(Python)"`, for example, but not `"(Python"`.

This should be enough theory about the syntax of regular expressions. Although this section may have been a bit dry and theoretical, it's quite important to deal with regular expressions because in many cases their use is particularly elegant.

In the following sections, we'll talk about the practical use of regular expressions in Python. First of all, this includes the use of the `re` module. After that, we'll describe a small sample project for matching or searching.

28

28.2 Using the re Module

Having described the syntax of regular expressions in greater detail, we'll now take a look at their actual usage in Python. The examples in the following sections will be implemented in the interactive mode and are based on the assumption that the `re` module has already been imported:

```
>>> import re
```

> **Note**
>
> The functions presented in the following sections allow you to pass a set of settings via the optional last `flags` parameter, which enables you to influence the evaluation of the regular expressions. For more information on flags, see Section 28.2.7.

28.2.1 Searching

The search function is passed a pattern regular expression and a string string.

search(pattern, string, [flags])

It then returns the first substring of string matching pattern as a match object:[4]

```
>>> re.search(r"P[Yy]thon", "Python or PYthon and Python")
<re.Match object; span=(0, 6), match='Python'>
```

The findall function has the same interface as search and searches string for matches to the pattern regular expression. All nonoverlapping matches found are returned as a list of strings:

```
>>> re.findall(r"P[Yy]thon", "Python or PYthon and Python")
['Python', 'PYthon', 'Python']
```

If pattern contains one or more groups, only the parts matched by the groups will be written to the result list instead of the complete matching substring:

```
>>> re.findall(r"P([Yy])thon", "Python or PYthon and Python")
['y', 'Y', 'y']
>>> re.findall(r"P([Yy])th(.)n", "Python or PYthon and Python")
[('y', 'o'), ('Y', 'o'), ('y', 'o')]
```

If there are several groups, then that's a list of tuples. The alternative finditer function works like findall, but returns the result as an iterator over match objects.

28.2.2 Matching

The match function is passed a pattern regular expression and a string string and checks if pattern matches a part at the beginning of string.

match(pattern, string, [flags])

In particular, string doesn't have to match entirely with pattern. If matching is successful, the result is returned as a match object:

```
>>> re.match(r"P.th", "python")
>>> re.match(r"P.th", "Python")
<re.Match object; span=(0, 4), match='Pyth'>
```

If there is no match at the beginning of the string, None will be returned

The fullmatch function has the same interface as match and, unlike match, checks whether pattern matches the entire string string:

---

4 For more information on match objects, see Section 28.2.8.

```
>>> re.fullmatch(r"P.th", "Python")
>>> re.fullmatch(r"P.thon", "Python")
<re.Match object; span=(0, 6), match='Python'>
```

28.2.3   Splitting a String

The split function is passed a pattern regular expression and a string and searches string for matches with pattern. All matching substrings are considered separators, and the parts in between are returned as a list of strings:

```
>>> re.split(r"\s", "Python Python Python")
['Python', 'Python', 'Python']
```

Any groups that occur within the regular expression are also returned as elements of this list:

```
>>> re.split(r"(,)\s", "Python, Python, Python")
['Python', ',', 'Python', ',', 'Python']
```

In this regular expression, any comma followed by a white space is treated as a separator.

If the optional last maxsplit parameter is specified and is not 0, the string will be split for a maximum of maxsplit times. The remainder string is returned as the last element of the list:

```
>>> re.split(r"\s", "Python Python Python", 1)
['Python', 'Python Python']
```

28.2.4   Replacing Parts of a String

The sub function has the following interface:

sub(pattern, repl, string, [count, flags])

It searches string for nonoverlapping matches with the pattern regular expression. A copy of string is returned in which all matching substrings have been replaced by the repl string:

```
>>> re.sub(r"[Jj]a[Vv]a","Python", "Java or java and jaVa")
'Python or Python and Python'
```

Instead of a string, a function object can also be passed for repl. This is called for each match found and is passed the respective match object as the only parameter. The matching substring is replaced by the return value of the function.

In the following example, a function object is passed for the repl parameter to censor naughty words in a text:

```
>>> def f(m):
...     return "x" * len(m.group(0))
...
>>> re.sub(r"\b(\w*?sex\w*?)\b", f,
...     "Essex isn't Middlesex")
'xxxxx isn't xxxxxxxxx'
```

The sub function searches the specified text for words containing the sex subword. These words are then replaced by as many xs as the corresponding word is long using the function f.

It's possible to reference regular expression groups by using the \g<name> or \g<index> notations:

```
>>> re.sub(r"([Jj]ava)", r"Python instead of \g<1>", "Take Java")
'Take Python instead of Java'
```

The optional count parameter can be used to specify the maximum number of substitutions that may be performed.

The alternative subn function works in a similar way to sub, but returns the number of substitutions made in addition to the result string:

```
>>> re.subn(r"[Jj]a[Vv]a","Python", "Java or java and jaVa")
('Python or Python and Python', 3)
```

28.2.5   Replacing Problem Characters

The escape function converts all nonalphanumeric characters of the passed string into their corresponding escape sequence and returns the result as a string. This function is useful if you want to embed a string in a regular expression but can't be sure if special characters like periods or question marks are included:

```
>>> re.escape("Does this really work? ... (yes!)")
'Does\\ this\\ really\\ work\\?\\ \\.\\.\\.\\ \\(yes!\\)'
```

Note that the escape sequences in the string literal are each preceded by a double backslash. This is because the result is printed using a regular string literal instead of a raw string literal.

28.2.6   Compiling a Regular Expression

The compile function compiles a regular expression to a *regular expression object* (*RE object*). The returned object provides essentially the same functionality as the re module, but operations performed on it are usually faster:

```
>>> regexp = re.compile(r"P[Yy]thon")
>>> regexp.findall("Python or PYthon and Python")
['Python', 'PYthon', 'Python']
```

Especially programs that evaluate a large number of different regular expressions with high frequency should compile the regular expressions. Due to an internal caching mechanism of the re module, frequent evaluation of the same regular expression isn't critical.

28.2.7   Flags

In the previous sections, so-called *flags* were mentioned several times. These are settings that affect the evaluation of a regular expression. Flags can be specified either in the expression itself by an extension or as a parameter of one of the functions available in the re module. They only influence the expression that's currently being processed and don't remain active afterward. Each flag is contained as a constant in the re module and can be addressed via a long or a short version of its name. Table 28.5 lists all flags and explains their meaning.

Alias	Name	Meaning
re.A	re.ASCII	If this flag is set, the character classes \w, \W, \b, \B, \s, and \S are restricted to the ASCII character set.
re.I	re.IGNORECASE	If this flag is set, the regular expression evaluation becomes *case-insensitive*, which means, for example, that the character group [A-Z] would match both uppercase and lowercase letters.
re.L	re.LOCALE	If this flag is set, certain predefined character classes are made dependent on the current localization. This concerns the groups \w, \W, \b, \B, \s, and \S.
re.M	re.MULTILINE	If this flag is set, ^ will match at the beginning of the string as well as after each newline character, and $ before each newline character. Normally ^ and $ only match at the beginning and end of the string respectively.
re.S	re.DOTALL	If this flag is set, the special character . actually matches any character. Normally the dot matches any character except the newline character, \n.

Table 28.5 Flags

28

Alias	Name	Meaning
re.X	re.VERBOSE	If this flag is set, white space characters such as spaces, tabs, or newline characters are ignored in the regular expression as long as they aren't preceded by a backslash. In addition, a # sign introduces a comment. This means that everything after this character up to a newline character is ignored.
		Because this flag adds a lot of value to the readability of regular expressions, it will be discussed separately in Section 28.5.

Table 28.5 Flags (Cont.)

Most of the previously presented functions of the re module have an optional flags parameter, which can be used to specify a combination of flags:

```
>>> print(re.match(r"python", "Python"))
None
>>> print(re.match(r"python", "Python", re.I))
<re.Match object; span=(0, 6), match='Python'>
```

As you can see in the example, the behavior of the match function adapts to the passed flags. In this case, the matching was first case-sensitive and then case-insensitive. Flags can be combined using the binary OR (|), for example:

```
re.I | re.S | re.M
```

28.2.8   The Match Object

The results of match or search operations are returned as match objects by the previously introduced functions—for example, match and search. The match object contains more details about the match that is currently under consideration. For this purpose, a match object defines the attributes listed in Table 28.6.

Attribute	Description
pos, endpos	Start or end index of the substring that was considered by the search or match call
re	The original regular expression as a string
string	The string referenced by this match object

Table 28.6 Attributes of a Match Object

The group method provides convenient access to the substring that matched the different groups of the regular expression. If only one argument was passed, the return value is a string; otherwise, it's a tuple of strings. If a group doesn't match any substring, then None is returned for it:

```
>>> m1 = re.match(r"(P[Yy])(th.n)", "Python")
>>> m1.group(1)
'Py'
>>> m1.group(1, 2)
('Py', 'thon')
```

An index of 0 returns the entire matching string:

```
>>> m1.group(0)
'Python'
```

The groups method returns a list of all substrings matching the groups contained in the regular expression:

```
>>> m1.groups()
('Py', 'thon')
```

The start and end or span methods can be used to obtain the substring matching a group via its start or end index in the input string:

```
>>> m1.start(2)
2
>>> m1.end(2)
6
>>> m1.span(2)
(2, 6)
```

Especially for named groups, there is the groupdict function, which maps the names of the groups to the substrings matching them:

```
>>> m2 = re.match(r"(?P<group1>P[Yy])(?P<group2>th.n)", "Python")
>>> m2.groupdict()
{'group1': 'Py', 'group2': 'thon'}
```

Since Python 3.6, match objects allow for index-based access, equivalent to calling groups:

```
>>> m1[1]
'Py'
>>> m2["group2"]
'thon'
```

28

28.3   A Simple Sample Program: Searching

So far, the syntax of regular expressions and their use by the re module of the standard library have been discussed. At this point, we would like to present two more small sample projects that focus on the use of regular expressions. First, we'll explain searching in this simple example; matching will be dealt with in the subsequent, more complex example.

Searching is used to find and filter out patterns within a longer text. In our sample program, searching is intended to retrieve all links from any HTML file along with their description. To do this, we must first visualize the structure of an HTML link:

```
<a href="URL">description</a>
```

Because HTML is not case-sensitive, we should use the regular expression with the IGNORECASE flag. Furthermore, the example just shown is the simplest form of an HTML link; in addition to the URL and description, other information can be provided.

The following regular expression matches both the previous and other, more complex HTML links:

```
r"<a .*href=[\"\'](.*?)[\"\'].*>(.*?)</a>"
```

The regular expression contains two groups, one for the URL and one for the description, so that these two pieces of information can be read later. Within these groups, nongreedy quantifiers are used; otherwise, several links could be erroneously combined into one.

So let's turn to the sample program:

```
import re
with open("rheinwerk-publishing.html", "r") as f:
    html = f.read()
it = re.finditer(r"<a .*?href=[\"\'](.*?)[\"\'].*?>(.*?)</a>", html, re.I)
for n, m in enumerate(it):
    print("#{} Name: {}, Link: {}".format(n, m.group(2), m.group(1)))
```

First, an HTML file—in this case, *rheinwerk-publishing.html*—is opened and read using the read method of the file object. Then the finditer function of the re module is called to find all matches to the regular expression discussed earlier in the HTML code. The result is returned as an iterator and referenced by it.

Finally, it is iterated over, with the current match available as a match object m in each iteration step. Now, the partial strings that fit the two groups of the regular expression are output.

You can test the program with any HTML pages. To do this, just visit a website on the internet that is as complex as possible, such as that of a news magazine, and save it as an HTML file. You'll see that the sample program finds the included links here as well.

> **Note**
>
> Parsing HTML content is a non-trivial task for which regular expressions are only partially suitable. If you want to delve deeper into this topic, we recommend using third-party libraries specifically designed for this purpose, such as beautifulsoup, which we do not cover further in this book, however, due to space limitations.

28.4   A More Complex Sample Program: Matching

It's a common problem, especially on the web, to validate entered form data and to filter out the important information from the input. Of course, this is also possible with normal string operations, but this problem can be solved elegantly and with relatively little code using regular expressions.

Our sample program is supposed to read all relevant information from a kind of electronic business card and prepare it in a machine-readable form. The business card is saved in a text file in the following format:

```
Name: John Doe
Addr: Samplestreet 123
      12345 Sampletown
P:    +1 781 228 5070
```

The program should now read this text file, extract the information it contains, and prepare it to form a dictionary like the following:

```
{
    'Name': ('John', 'Doe'),
    'Addr': ('Samplestreet', '123', '12345', 'Sampletown'),
    'P': ('+1', '781', '228', '5070')
}
```

We assume that the text file always contains only one data record.

Let's first go into more detail about how the sample program works. The business card consists of various pieces of information, always provided with a heading or category ("Name", "Addr", and "P"). Separating the category from the information isn't a complicated matter as the colon doesn't occur within the category names and thus the first occurrence of a colon in a line always marks the transition between category and information. The third line is a problem because no explicit heading is given here. In such a

547

case, the line is appended to the information of the previous heading. In this way, a dictionary can be created that maps the headings to the relevant information.

Let's now move on to the implementation. To do this, we first write a function that reads the data line by line and formats it into a dictionary:

```python
def read_file(filename):
    d = {}
    with open(filename) as f:
        for line in f:
            if ":" in line:
                key, d[key] = (s.strip() for s in line.split(":",1))
            elif "key" in locals():
                d[key] += "\n{}".format(line.strip())
    return d
```

The read_file function is passed the filename string with a path specification. Within the function, the file is read line by line. Each line is divided into two parts, category and information, on the basis of the first colon, and by using the strip method, they're stripped of superfluous blanks. Then the heading and information are written to dictionary d, and the current heading is additionally referenced by key.

Wherever there was no colon in a line, the information was wrapped to several lines. For us, this means that we first also apply the strip method to the complete line contents and then append it to the already existing value in the dictionary under the key heading. For this purpose, the key reference must exist, of course. Because it's only created within the if statement, it's assumed that a line with a colon must come before a line without a colon. Although there is no meaningful file in which this assumption doesn't hold, we explicitly check the elif branch to see if the key reference does exist.

The result of this function is a dictionary with the headings as keys and the associated information (in the form of strings) as values. The second function in the example parses the data using regular expressions and then stores it as a tuple in the dictionary. To do this, we first create a dictionary called regexp that provides a regular expression for each heading that can be used to validate the information:

```python
regexp = {
    "Name": r"([A-Za-z]+)\s([A-Za-z]+)",
    "Addr": r"([A-Za-z]+)\s(\d+)\s*(\d{5})\s([A-Za-z]+)",
    "P": r"(\+\d{1,3})\s(\d{3})\s(\d{3})\s(\d{4,})"
}
```

These regular expressions have several groups to make it easier to split the information into the different individual pieces of information.

The function used to analyze the data looks as follows:

```python
def analyze_data(data, regexp):
    for key in data:
        if key not in regexp:
            return False
        m = re.match(regexp[key], data[key])
        if not m:
            return False
        data[key] = m.groups()
    return True
```

The analyze_data function is passed two dictionaries as parameters: first the regexp dictionary that was just created, and second, the dictionary created by the read_file function, which contains the read data.

The function iterates over the data dictionary in a for loop and applies the regular expression to the read string using the re.match function, matching the current heading. The returned match object is referenced by m.

Then, we test whether re.match returned the value None. If so, the analyze_data function will return False. Otherwise, the current value of the data dictionary is overwritten with the substring that matched each regular expression group. The group method of the match object returns a tuple of strings. After running through the analyze_data function, the dictionary contains the required data in formatted form.

Last but not least, the code that triggers the reading and preparation of the data is still missing:

```python
data = read_file("id.txt")
if analyze_data(data, regexp):
    print(data)
else:
    print("The data is incorrect")
```

Depending on the truth value returned by the analyze_data function, either the prepared data or an error message will be output.

Hopefully, these two examples have helped you get a hands-on introduction to the world of regular expressions. Note that the presented program actually works, but it's far from perfect. Feel free to expand or adapt it as you wish. For example, the regular expressions don't yet allow umlauts or punctuation marks in the street name. And you could also add an email address to the business card and program.

28.5   Comments in Regular Expressions

Depending on the application, regular expressions can become so complex in practice that their meaning isn't readily apparent to the reader of the program. In such cases, it's useful to use the VERBOSE flag of the re module. As described in Table 28.5, this flag ensures that all white space characters within the regular expression are ignored unless they are preceded by a backslash. This can be used to visually structure a regular expression by selectively inserting spaces and line breaks. As an example, let's consider the regular expression for finding links in HTML pages, as introduced in Section 28.3:

```
r"<a .*href=[\"\'](.*?)[\"\'].*>(.*?)</a>"
```

This expression can be used reformatted using the VERBOSE flag as follows:

```
import re
with open("rheinwerk-publishing.html", "r") as f:
    html = f.read()
    it = re.finditer(r"""
        <a\ .*?
            href=[\"\']
                    (.*?)
                [\"\']
        .*?>
            (.*?)
        </a>
    """, html, re.I | re.VERBOSE)
for n, m in enumerate(it):
    print("|{} Name: {}, Link: {}".format(n, m.group(2), m.group(1)))
```

While the above program behaves exactly like the one from Section 28.3, there are three major differences:

1. The string containing the regular expression was split into several lines using triple quotes, and its structure was highlighted by spaces at the line beginnings.

2. For the flags parameter of the finditer function, the re.VERBOSE flag also was passed.

3. The space character after the a at the beginning of the expression has been prefixed with a backslash so that it's taken into account despite the VERBOSE flag.

In addition to the pure structuring of regular expressions, the VERBOSE flag also provides the option to insert comments—for example, to explain parts of the expression or to highlight special features. To use a comment in a regular expression, the # symbol is used. The hash ensures that it itself and everything else that follows in the same line is ignored when interpreting the regular expression. We can use this to comment on the preceding regular expression, for example:

```
it = re.finditer(r"""
    <a\ .*?              # Warning: Space after a requires backslash
        href=[\"\']      # Double or single quotes
                         # enclose the target of the link
              (.*?)      # We allow any characters in the link target ...
          [\"\']
    .*?>
        (.*?)            # ... just like in the link text
    </a>
""", html, re.I | re.VERBOSE)
```

As with the program code itself, it's an art and a matter of personal taste to decide how much and what exactly you want to comment on or leave uncommented.

28

Chapter 29

Interface to Operating System and Runtime Environment

To make your programs interact with the operating system on which they run, you need access to the operating system's functions. One problem here is that the various operating systems sometimes differ greatly in their range of functionality and in the way the available operations are used. However, Python was designed from the ground up to be a cross-platform language. To be able to run programs that need to draw on operating system functionality on as many platforms as possible without any modification, an interface has been created that provides uniform access to operating system functionality. Plainly speaking, this means that by using this uniform interface, you can write programs that remain platform-independent, even if they are based on operating system functionality.

This interface is implemented by the os and sys modules, which we'll describe in greater detail in the following sections. After that, we'll take a look at the argparse module of the standard library, which provides convenient access to command line parameters.

29.1 Operating System Functionality: os

You can use the os module to access functionality and information provided by the operating system. Because the os module serves in large parts very specific and rarely needed use-cases, we'll limit ourselves to a selected subset here.

The os module contains some functions associated with the file system, as well as the os.path submodule for path name manipulation and processing. This will be the topic of Chapter 30, Section 30.1 and Section 30.2.

The os module has its own exception type, called os.error. An alternative name for the error class is OSError.

> **Note**
>
> All methods and functions provided by os that accept str instances as parameters can also be called with bytes instance instead. However, this also changes the return value.
>
> In short: str in—str out; bytes in—bytes out.

To run the following sample programs, the os module must first be imported:

```
>>> import os
```

29.1.1   environ

The os module contains a dictionary environ that can be used to access the environment variables provided for your program by the operating system. For example, you can use os.environ['HOME'] on many platforms to determine the active user's home directory. The following examples show the value of os.environ['HOME'] on a Windows and a Linux machine:

```
>>> print(os.environ['HOME'])
C:\Documents and Settings\username
>>> print(os.environ['HOME'])
/home/username
```

You can also change the values of os.environ, but this can cause problems on certain platforms—e.g., FreeBSD and macOS—and should therefore be used with caution.

29.1.2   getpid()

The Python process that executes the currently running program has a unique identification number. It can be determined via os.getpid():

```
>>> os.getpid()
1360
```

29.1.3   cpu_count()

The cpu_count() module returns the number of processors of the computer. Virtual cores are counted as separate processors:

```
>>> os.cpu_count()
8
```

For example, the system on which this line was executed has a processor with four cores, each of which has two virtual cores.

29.1.4   system(cmd)

The os.system module enables you to execute any commands of the operating system as if they were issued it in a system console. The following example creates a new folder named test_folder using the mkdir command:

```
>>> os.system("mkdir test_folder")
0
```

The return value of os.system is the status code that the called program returned—in this case, 0, which means success.

One problem with the os.system function is that the output of the called program can't be retrieved offhand. For this purpose, you can use the os.popen function.

29.1.5   popen(command, [mode, buffering])

The os.popen function executes any command as if on an operating system command line. The function returns a *file-like object*[1] that can be used to access the output of the executed program. As with the built-in open function, the mode parameter specifies whether the file object is to be opened in read ("r") or write ("w") mode. With write access, data can be transferred to the running program.

In the following example, we'll use the dir Windows command to create a list of files and folders under the *C:* directory:[2]

```
>>> output = os.popen("dir /B C:\\")
>>> files = [line.strip() for line in output]
>>> files
['AUTOEXEC.BAT', 'CONFIG.SYS', 'Documents and Settings', 'Programs', 'WINDOWS']
```

You can read more about the exact meaning of mode and buffering in Chapter 6, Section 6.4.1 about file handling.

29.2   Accessing the Runtime Environment: sys

29

The sys module of the standard library provides predefined variables and functions related or closely related to the Python interpreter. For example, you can use the sys module to query the version number of the interpreter or the operating system. The module provides the programmer with a range of information that can sometimes be very useful.

To run the examples in this section, the sys module must first be imported:

```
>>> import sys
```

---

1 A *file-like object* provides the same interface as a file object. However, the data doesn't need to be read from a file; it can also be located in the memory or read via a network connection, for example.

2 The /B parameter of the dir command ensures that only a list of files and directories is generated without any additional information.

29.2.1   Command Line Parameters

The sys.argv list contains the command line parameters with which the Python program was called. argv[0] is the name of the program itself. Consider the exemplary program call $ program.py -blah 0 -bubble abc. Here, argv references the following list:

```
['program.py', '-blah', '0', '-bubble', 'abc']
```

In the interactive mode, argv is empty. You should use the argparse module if you want to manage command line parameters conveniently (Section 29.3).

29.2.2   Default Paths

The path list contains paths that are searched in the order of their appearance by the interpreter when a module is imported. The first found module with the searched name will be imported.

The programmer is free to modify the list so that the import of a module is done according to his requirements. For more details about module imports in Python, see Chapter 18.

29.2.3   Standard Input/Output Streams

The sys module contains references to the standard input/output streams of the system. These are the file objects used for input and output of the interpreter. Here, sys.stdin (for *standard input*) denotes the file object from which user input is read when input is called. To the sys.stdout (standard output) file object, all outputs of the Python program are written, while outputs of the interpreter, such as tracebacks, are written to sys.stderr (standard error).

Replacing these file objects with your own file objects allows you to redirect input and output to other streams. The original streams of sys.stdin, sys.stdout, and sys.stderr are stored in sys.__stdin__, sys.__stdout__, and sys.__stderr__ so that they can always be restored.

29.2.4   Exiting the Program

The exit function of the sys module raises a SystemExit exception. If not handled, this will cause the program to terminate without traceback output:

```
>>> sys.exit()
```

Optionally, you can pass an integer, which will be passed to the operating system as an *exit code*. An exit code of 0 generally represents a successful termination of the program, while an exit code not equal to 0 represents a program termination due to an error:

```
>>> sys.exit(1)
```

If you have passed another instance, such as a string, it will be output to stderr before the program is terminated with exit code 0:

```
>>> sys.exit("Error")
Error
```

29.2.5   Details of the Python Version

The sys.implementation named tuple provides information about the running Python interpreter. In addition to the also individually provided hexversion and version_info entries, the tuple with the entry name contains the name of the interpreter—for example, "cpython" for the default implementation:

```
>>> sys.implementation
namespace(name='cpython', cache_tag='cpython-311', version=sys.version_
info(major=3, minor=11, micro=0, releaselevel='beta', serial=1), hexversion=
51052721, _multiarch='darwin')
```

The two version and hexversion components of sys.implementation can also be retrieved separately via sys.version_info and sys.hexversion respectively:

```
>>> sys.version_info
sys.version_info(major=3, minor=11, micro=0, releaselevel='beta', serial=1)
>>> hex(sys.hexversion)
'0x30b00b1'
```

The sys.hexversion constant contains the version number of the Python interpreter as an integer. If it's written as a hexadecimal number by calling the built-in hex function, as in the preceding example, executed under Python 3.11.0 (Beta 1), the structure of the number becomes clear. It's guaranteed that hexversion will increase with each Python version, so you can use the < and > operators to test whether the version of the interpreter you're using is older or more recent than a particular reference version number.

Finally, you can use the sys.executable string to determine the full path to the currently running Python interpreter.

29

29.2.6   Operating System Details

The sys.platform string contains an identifier of the running operating system. The identifiers of the three most popular operating systems are listed in Table 29.1.

System	ID
Linux	"linux"
macOS	"darwin"
Windows	"win32"

Table 29.1 Identifiers of Different Operating Systems

> **Note**
>
> Until Python 3.2, the value of platform on Linux was "linux2" or "linux3", depending on the Linux kernel version. As of Python 3.3, the value on Linux is consistently "linux".
>
> For this reason, it's advisable to use sys.platform.startswith("linux") to check if the program is running on a Linux system.

On Windows systems, you can use the sys.getwindowsversion function, which returns details about the version of the Windows operating system currently in use:

```
>>> sys.getwindowsversion()
sys.getwindowsversion(major=10, minor=0, build= 14393, platform=2,
service_pack='')
```

The function returns a named tuple whose first three elements are integers and describe the version number. The fourth element is also an integer and represents the platform used. The values listed in Table 29.2 are valid.

Platform	Meaning
0	Windows 3.1 (32-bit)
1	Windows 95/98/ME
2	Windows NT/2000/XP/Server 2003/Vista/Server 2008/7/8/10/11
3	Windows CE

Table 29.2 Windows Platforms

The last element of the tuple is a string that contains further information.

To distinguish between the individual Windows versions grouped under platform 2, you can refer to the version number (consisting of the major and minor fields of the tuple; see Table 29.3).

Name	major	minor
Windows 2000	5	0
Windows XP	5	1
Windows Server 2003	5	2
Windows Vista or Windows Server 2008	6	0
Windows 7	6	1
Windows 8	6	2
Windows 10	10	0

Table 29.3 Windows Versions

On operating systems other than Microsoft Windows, the getwindowsversion function is not available.

The sys.byteorder constant specifies the byte order[3] of the current system. The value is either "big" for a *big-endian* system, where the most significant byte is stored first, or "little" for a *little-endian* system, where the least significant byte is stored first.

29.2.7 Hooks

The sys module provides access to so-called *hooks*. These are functions that are called when the Python interpreter performs certain actions. By overwriting these functions, the programmer can "hook" into the interpreter and thus change the way the interpreter works.

displayhook(value)

The displayhook function is called whenever the result of an expression is to be output in interactive mode—for example, in the following situation:

```
>>> 42
42
```

By overwriting displayhook with a custom function, this behavior can be changed. In the following example, we output the identity for an entered expression instead of its value:

---

3 The byte order specifies the order in which the individual bytes of a value that occupies more than one byte are stored in the memory. The byte order is relevant when binary data is exchanged between different platforms. An x86 PC is a little-endian system.

```
>>> def f(value):
...     print(id(value))
...
>>> sys.displayhook = f
>>> 42
139716935035616
>>> 97 + 32
139716935038400
>>> "Hello world"
139716901939824
```

Note that displayhook isn't called when output is done via print:[4]

```
>>> print("Hello world")
Hello world
```

You can access the original function object of displayhook via sys.__displayhook__ and thus restore the original functionality:

```
>>> sys.displayhook = sys.__displayhook__
```

excepthook(type, value, traceback)

The excepthook function is called whenever an uncaught exception occurs. It's responsible for outputting the traceback. By overwriting this function with a custom function object, for example, errors can be logged or the output of a traceback can be changed.

The excepthook function is passed the exception type, the exception value (usually the error message), and a so-called traceback object, which contains information about the location where the exception was raised.

In the following example, we'll set up a hook that enriches the drab traceback by a sardonic comment:

```
>>> def f(type, value, traceback):
...     print('gnahahaha: "{}"'.format(value))
...
>>> sys.excepthook = f
>>> abc
gnahahaha: "name 'abc' is not defined"
```

You can access the original function object of excepthook via sys.__excepthook__ and thus restore the original functionality:

```
>>> sys.excepthook = sys.__excepthook__
```

---

4 That would be very inconvenient as we're doing a print output in the hook itself. If a print output called the hook again, we'd find ourselves in an endless recursion.

29.3 Command Line Parameters: argparse

In the previous section on the sys module of the standard library, we discussed the global sys.argv list, which you can use to access the command line parameters passed when calling a Python program. However, this rudimentary access to command line parameters is often not sufficient. The argparse module described in this section allows you to handle command line parameters more conveniently.

So far, this book has dealt exclusively with console programs—that is, programs that have a purely text-based interface to the user. Such programs are usually started from a *console*, also referred to as *shell*—such as, for example, the command prompt in Windows.[5]

On Windows, a Python program is started from the command prompt by changing to the program directory and then entering the name of the program file, e.g. program.py. For Unix-like systems such as Linux or macOS, you can use python program.py or make the Python file executable itself by adding a shebang header line, see Chapter 4, Section 4.1.1. In Addition, you need to set the executable flag of the file using the chmod command or the file manager. After that, the program can directly be executed from within the program directory by entering ./program.py on these systems. The program call can be followed by options and arguments:

- An *argument* is written after the name of the program file. To draw a comparison to function parameters, we could speak of *positional arguments*. This means, above all, that the arguments are assigned on the basis of their order. For example, a program call with three arguments might look as follows:

```
$ program.py dylan 1337 james
```

- In addition to arguments, you can pass *options* that are similar to keyword arguments. This means that each option has a name and is addressed via this name. When calling the program, options must be written in front of the arguments, and each must be preceded by a hyphen. This is followed by the option name, a space, and the desired value. A program call with options and arguments can thus look as follows:

```
$ program.py -a dylan -b james -c 1337 hello world
```

In this case there are three options named a, b, and c, with the values "dylan", "james", and 1337. In addition, two arguments are given: the "hello" and "world" strings.

In addition to these parameterized options, there are parameterless options, which are comparable to a flag. This means they are either present (enabled) or absent (disabled):

---

5 In more recent Windows versions, *PowerShell* replaces the command prompt.

```
$ programm.py -a -b 1 hello world
```

In this case, a is a parameterless option.

In the remainder of this chapter, we'll discuss the use of the argparse module using two examples.

29.3.1   Calculator: A Simple Example

The first example is a simple calculator program in which both the arithmetic operation and the operands are specified via command line parameters.

The program should be called as follows:

```
$ calc.py -o add 7 5
$ calc.py -o sub 13 29
$ calc.py -o mult 4 11
$ calc.py -o div by 3 2
```

The -o option specifies an arithmetic operation that is applied to the subsequent two arguments. If the -o option is missing, the arguments are to be added.

At the beginning of the program, the ArgumentParser class of the argparse module must be imported and instantiated:

```
from argparse import ArgumentParser
parser = ArgumentParser()
```

Then you can add permitted options to the ArgumentParser instance using the add_argument method. In our case, that's just one:

```
parser.add_argument("-o", "--operation", default="add")
```

The first parameter of the method specifies the short name of the option. Each option can also be used with a written-out version of the name, provided that this alternative is specified using the second parameter. In this case, the -o and --operation options are equivalent. The last parameter sets a default value for this option, which will be used if the option isn't specified.

Note

On Windows, the slash is also commonly used as a prefix character for optional command line arguments. This convention isn't supported by argparse by default, but it can be implemented via the optional prefix_chars parameter:

```
parser = ArgumentParser(prefix_chars="/")
parser.add_argument("/operation", default="add")
```

Next to the -o option, the arguments for the two operands must be added. At the same time, the name and the allowed data type of the arguments are specified:

```
parser.add_argument("op1", type=float)
parser.add_argument("op2", type=float)
```

Once all options and arguments have been added, the `parse_args` method is called, which reads the command line parameters and processes them in the desired form:

```
args = parser.parse_args()
```

Next, we create a dictionary that contains all possible arithmetic operations as keys and the corresponding calculation function as the respective value. The keys are the same as those that can be specified via the -o option, so we can directly infer the calculation function to use based on the string passed in the option:

```
calc = {
    "add": lambda a, b: a + b,
    "sub": lambda a, b: a - b,
    "mult": lambda a, b: a * b,
    "div": lambda a, b: a / b
}
```

Basically, only the value that was passed with the -o option must now be read. Accessing an option is straightforward using the `args` instance returned by `parse_args` as each option is available under its chosen name as an attribute of that instance. The name we chose for the -o option was `operation`. Arguments can be accessed in the same way:

```
op = args.operation
if op in calc:
    print("Result:", calc[op](args.op1, args.op2))
else:
    parser.error("{} is not an operation".format(op))
```

For errors that occur due to wrong or missing command line parameters, you can use the `error` method of the `ArgumentParser` instance, which outputs a corresponding error message and terminates the program.

Before we move on to a more complex sample program, let's discuss the constructor of the `ArgumentParser` class and its `add_argument` method in detail.

ArgumentParser([description, epilog, prog, usage, add_help, argument_default])

The constructor of the `ArgumentParser` class can be passed a number of keyword parameters, the most important of which are briefly explained in Table 29.4. Many of the

29

parameters refer to the dynamically generated help page provided by the `argparse` module. See the next section for an example of how to use this help page.

Parameter	Meaning
description	A string that's displayed on the help page before the explanation of the options and arguments.
epilog	A string that's displayed on the help page after the explanation of the options and arguments.
prog	The program name as displayed on the help page. By default, the name of the program file is used here.
usage	A string that summarizes the use of the program with its command line parameters. By default, this string is generated automatically.
add_help	Specifies whether a help page should be provided via the -h or --help options. The default value is True.
argument_default	Sets a global default value for unspecified options or arguments. The argparse.SUPPRESS value causes unspecified options or arguments to be ignored. The default value is None.

Table 29.4 Keyword Parameters of the ArgumentParser Constructor

add_argument([*name_or_flags, action, nargs, const, default, type, choices, required, help, metavar, dest, version])

The `add_argument` method adds an argument or option to the program interface. A number of parameters can be specified, the most important of which are described in Table 29.5.

Parameter	Meaning
*name_or_flags	For an argument, a single string specifying the argument name. For an option, a series of strings specifying the alternative names of the option. A leading hyphen is used to distinguish between an argument and an option.

Table 29.5 Parameters of the add_argument Method

Parameter	Meaning
action	Specifies how the internal value of the parameter is to be derived from the value specified by the user. Possible values are as follows: ■ "store" stores the value unmodified. ■ "store_const" stores a constant value. This constant is specified by the const keyword parameter. ■ "store_true" is like store_const, with const=True. ■ "store_false" is like store_const, with const=False. ■ "append" stores the value as an element of a list. This is useful if an option may be used multiple times. ■ "append_const" is like append, with the constant value specified by the const keyword parameter. ■ "version" outputs version information and exits the program. The version keyword parameter must be specified. The default value is "store".
nargs	Allows you to control how often an argument or option may or must be specified. The passed values are then made available internally in the program as elements of a list. Possible values for nargs are an integer N for exactly N times, "?" for once or not at all, "*" for any number of times, and "+" for any number of times but at least once.
default	Specifies the value that an option should take if no corresponding value has been passed by the user. The default value is None.
type	Normally, the user specifications are interpreted as strings. With the help of the type parameter, the information can be converted automatically into another data type.
choices	An iterable object that contains the values from which the user can choose for an option or argument.
required	Determines whether an option must be specified by the user.
help	A string describing the argument or option. This description is displayed on the automatically generated help page.
metavar	The help page defaults to the actual internal names of the arguments and options specified for dest. This name can be changed using the metavar parameter.
dest	A string that specifies the internal name of an argument or option. By default, this name is determined automatically.

Table 29.5 Parameters of the add_argument Method (Cont.)

29

29.3.2   A More Complex Example

In the previous section, we showed you a minimal example of how to use `argparse`. That sample program will be extended in this section to introduce further options provided by the `argparse` module. Here you can first see the source code of the modified sample program:

```python
from argparse import ArgumentParser
parser = ArgumentParser(description = "A calculator")
parser.add_argument("-o", "--operation", default="plus",
                    help="arithmetic operation")
parser.add_argument("operands", metavar="operand", type=float,
                    nargs="+", help="operands")
parser.add_argument("-i", "--integer", dest="type",
                    action="store_const", const=int, default=float,
                    help="integer calculation")
args = parser.parse_args()
calc = {
    "add": lambda a, b: a + b,
    "sub": lambda a, b: a - b,
    "mult": lambda a, b: a * b,
    "div": lambda a, b: a / b
}
op = args.operation
if op in calc:
    result = args.type(args.operands[0])
    for z in args.operands[1:]:
        result = calc[op](result, args.type(z))
    print("Result:", result)
else:
    parser.error("{} is not a valid operation".format(op))
```

First, the `help` keyword parameter is passed consistently when adding new arguments. Here you can specify a description of the argument as a string, which the `argparse` module will use to provide a dynamically generated help page. This help page is displayed when the program is invoked with the -h or --help option. For the example, the help page looks as follows:

```
usage: calculator2.py [-h] [-o OPERATION] [-i] operand [operand ...]
A calculator
positional arguments:
  operand               operands
optional arguments:
  -h, --help            show this help message and exit
```

```
-o OPERATION, --operation OPERATION
                        arithmetic operation
-i, --integer           integer calculation
```

The help page shows another change in the sample program: no longer are two arguments, op1 and op2, expected, but a list of any number of arguments (but at least one argument). You can achieve this by setting the nargs parameter to the value "+" in the add_argument call. In addition, metavar is used to specify a name under which the argument will appear on the help page. The calculation of the result from the args.operands operand list is done from left to right, which is especially important for the - and / operators, where the evaluation order is important.[6] The exemplary call $ python calculator2.py -o minus 1 2 3 performs the calculation 1 - 2 - 3 and computes the result -4.

29

---

6 Such operators are also referred to as *nonassociative*. For example, the following is generally true
   for subtraction:$(a - b) - c \neq a - (b - c)$.

Chapter 30
File System

This chapter describes modules that provide functions for accessing the file system. These include the os.path module for working with file paths, and os and shutil for basic file system operations. Finally, we'll describe the tempfile module, through which temporary files can be created.

First, you'll learn about the functions the os module provides for working with the file system.

30.1   Accessing the File System: os

The functions described in the following sections allow you to navigate through the file system, find information about files and folders, and rename, delete, or create them, just like if you were using a shell or file manager. To be able to execute the examples listed ahead, the os module must first be imported:

```
>>> import os
```

You'll often be able to pass a path as a parameter to the functions described. In this context, we distinguish between *absolute* and *relative paths*, with the latter referring to the current working directory of the running program.

Unless otherwise noted, paths are passed as str or bytes instances (see Table 30.1).

Name	Description
access(path, mode)	Checks the access rights the program has on the passed path.
chdir(path)	Sets the current working directory to path.
getcwd()	Returns the path of the current working directory.
chmod(path, mode)	Changes the access rights of path.
listdir([path])	Creates a list of all files and directories located under path.
mkdir(path, [mode])	Creates a new directory at path.

Table 30.1 Methods for Accessing the File System.

Name	Description
makedirs(path, [mode])	Creates a new directory at path. If necessary, parent directories are also created.
remove(path)	Removes the file specified with path from the file system.
removedirs(path)	Deletes an entire folder structure. In doing so, it deletes all folders one after the other from the lowest to the highest level, provided that they are empty.
rename(src, dst)	Renames the file or folder specified with src to dst.
renames(src, dst)	Like rename, but creates the directory structure of the destination path if needed. Also, after the renaming process, it tries to clean the src path from empty folders using removedirs.
replace(src, dst)	Replaces the dst file or directory with src.
rmdir(path)	Removes the passed directory from the file system or raises os.error exception if the directory doesn't exist. This works only with empty directories.
walk(top, [topdown, onerror])	Recursively traverses the directory tree under top.

Table 30.1 Methods for Accessing the File System. (Cont.)

30.1.1   access(path, mode)

The access method allows you to check which permissions the running Python program has for accessing path. The mode parameter specifies a bit mask containing the permissions to be checked.

The values listed in Table 30.2 can be passed individually or combined using bitwise OR.

Constant	Meaning
F_OK	Checks whether the path exists at all
R_OK	Checks whether the path may be read
W_OK	Checks whether the path may be written
X_OK	Checks whether the path is executable

Table 30.2 Value for the mode Parameter of os.access

The return value of access is True if all values passed for mode apply to the path and False if at least one access right doesn't apply to the program:

```
>>> os.access("python.exe", os.F_OK | os.X_OK)
True
```

Calling os.access in the preceding example shows that the local *python.exe* file exists and that it can be executed.

30.1.2   chmod(path, mode)

This function sets the access rights of the file or folder referenced by the passed path. The mode parameter is a three-digit octal number, where each digit specifies the access rights for a class of users. The first digit represents the *owner* of the file, the second stands for the relevant *group*, and the third for all *other users*.

The individual digits are sums of the three values listed in Table 30.3.

Value	Description
1	Execute
2	Write
4	Read

Table 30.3 Access Flags for os.chmod

For example, if you now make the following chmod call, you grant the owner full read and write access:

```
>>> os.chmod("a_file", 0o640)
```

However, they still can't execute the file. All other users in the group are allowed to read the file, but not to modify it, and for all others outside the group the content of the file is hidden due to the lack of a read permission.

Note the leading 0o in the access rights, which constitutes the literal of an octal number.

30.1.3   listdir([path])

This function returns a list specifying all files and subfolders of the folder passed with path. This list doesn't contain the special entries for the directory itself (".") and for the parent directory ("..").

The elements of the list have the same type as the passed path parameter—that is, either str or bytes. Any special characters that occur are encoded using UTF-8.

30

30.1.4   mkdir(path, [mode]) and makedirs(path, [mode])

These functions creates a new folder in the path passed with path. The optional mode parameter specifies a bit mask that defines the access rights for the new folder. By default, the octal number 0o777 is used for mode (see also chmod).

If the specified folder already exists, an os.error exception will be raised.

Note that mkdir can only create the new folder if all parent directories already exist:

```
>>> os.mkdir(r"C:\This\specific\path\does\not\yet\exist")
[...]
FileNotFoundError: [WinError 3] The system cannot find the specified path: 'C:\\
This\\specific\\path\\does\\not\\yet\\exist'
```

If you want the complete folder structure to be created when needed, you should use makedirs:

```
>>> os.makedirs(r"C:\This\specific\path\does\not\yet\exist")
>>>
```

If the passed folder already exists, an os.error exception will be raised.

30.1.5   remove(path)

This function removes the file specified with path from the file system. If you pass a path to a folder instead of a path to a file, remove will raise an os.error exception.

> **Note**
> Note that on Windows systems, it isn't possible to delete a file that's currently in use. In this case, an exception will also be raised.

30.1.6   removedirs(path)

This function deletes an entire folder structure recursively provided all the folders are empty. If the folder on the lowest level can't be deleted, an os.error exception will be raised. Errors that occur when removing directories on higher levels are ignored.

Consider the following call of removedirs:

```
>>> os.removedirs(r"C:\Any\sample\path")
```

Then the system will first try to delete the folder at *C:\Any\sample\path*. If successful, *C:\Any\sample* will be removed, and if that's successful too, *C:\Any* will be removed afterward.

To delete nested, nonempty directories, you can use the shutil.rmtree function.

30.1.7   rename(src, dst) and renames(old, new)

These functions rename the file or folder specified with src to dst. If a file or folder already exists under the dst path, then os.error will be raised.

> **Note**
> On Unix systems, a file already accessible under the dst path is overwritten without any message when you call rename. However, an exception still will be generated for folders that already exist.

The os.rename method works only if all parent directories of dst already exist. If you want to create the necessary directory structure, you must use os.renames instead.

30.1.8   walk(top, [topdown, onerror])

A convenient way to completely traverse a directory tree is provided by the walk function. The top parameter specifies a path to the root of the subtree to be traversed. The iteration is done in such a way that walk returns a tuple with three elements for the top folder and for each of its subfolders. For example, such a tuple may look as follows:

```
('a\path', ['folder1'], ['file1', 'file2'])
```

The first element is the relative path from top to the subfolder, the second element contains a list of all folders the current subfolder itself contains, and the last element contains the names of all files of the subfolder.

To understand this in detail, let's look at a sample directory tree (see Figure 30.1).

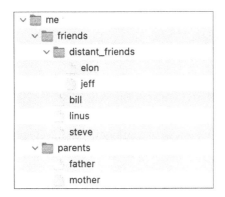

Figure 30.1 Sample Directory Tree

Assume that the current working directory is the folder that is the direct parent of the me folder.

Then we look at the output of walk for the me directory:

```
>>> for t in os.walk("me"):
...     print(t)
...
('me', ['parents', 'friends'], [])
('me/parents', [], ['father', 'mother'])
('me/friends', ['distant_friends'], ['bill', 'linus', 'steve'])
('me/friends/distant_friends', [], ['elon', 'jeff'])
```

As you can see, for each folder a tuple is created that contains the described information. The double backslashes (\\) occur because the example was executed on a Windows machine and backslashes within string literals must be written as escape sequences.

You can also customize the lists stored in the tuple as per your requirements—for example, to change the order in which the subdirectories of the current directory should be visited, or if you have made changes such as adding or deleting files and folders.

Using the optional topdown parameter, whose default value is True, you can specify where the walk should start. The default setting is to start in the directory closest to the root in the directory tree; in the example, that's me. If topdown is set to False, then os.walk will do exactly the opposite and start with the deepest nested folder. In the sample tree, that's me/friends/distant_friends:

```
>>> for t in os.walk("me", False):
...     print(t)
...
('me/parents', [], ['father', 'mother'])
('me/friends/distant_friends', [], ['elon', 'jeff'])
('me/friends', ['distant_friends'], ['bill', 'linus', 'steve'])
('me', ['parents', 'friends'], [])
```

Last but not least, you can use the last parameter onerror to specify how the function should behave if an error occurs while retrieving the contents of a directory. To this end, you can pass a reference to a function that expects a single parameter. In the event of an error, this function is then called with an os.error instance describing the error as a parameter.

Note

If you use an operating system that supports symbolic links to directories, these won't be included when traversing the structure to avoid infinite loops.

30.2   File Paths: os.path

Different platforms have different conventions for file system paths. For example, while Windows operating systems expect the drive to which the path refers at the beginning of an absolute path name, Unix prefixes the path with a slash. In addition, the separators for individual folders within the path differ; Microsoft has opted for the backslash, in contrast to the Unix world, where the slash is common.

As a programmer for cross-platform software, you're now faced with the problem that your programs have to cope with these different conventions and also those of other operating systems.

To allow handling file system paths conveniently, the `os.path` module was developed.

You can use this module in two different ways:

- You can first import os and then access it via `os.path`.
- You can import `os.path` directly.

Table 30.4 provides an overview of the most important functions of the `os.path` module.

Name	Description
abspath(path)	Returns the corresponding absolute and normalized path (see os.normpath) for a relative path.
basename(path)	Returns the base name of the path.
commonprefix(list)	Returns the longest common base path of the path list list.
dirname(path)	Returns the path to the directory where path is located, e.g., to determine the parent directory of a file.
exists(path)	Returns True if the path exists in the file system, otherwise False.
getatime(path)	Returns the time of the last access to path as a Unix timestamp.*
getmtime(path)	Returns the time of the last change of path as a Unix timestamp.

Table 30.4 Most Important Functions of the os.path Module

30

Name	Description
getsize(path)	Returns the size in bytes of the file to be found under path. The return value is always an int instance.
isabs(path)	The return value is True if path is an absolute path specification, otherwise False.
isfile(path)	Returns True if path refers to a file, otherwise False. The function may follow symbolic links.
isdir(path)	If the passed path refers to a folder, True will be returned, otherwise False.
islink(path)	Returns True if path refers to a symbolic link, otherwise False.
join(path, *paths)	Concatenates the passed paths to an overall path.
normcase(path)	Converts a Unix path to a Windows path.
realpath(path)	Returns an equivalent path that doesn't contain symbolic links.
split(path)	Splits path into the directory and the file. Both elements are returned in a tuple.
splitdrive(path)	Splits path into the drive letter and the path on the drive. Both elements are returned in a tuple.
splitext(path)	Splits the path into the path to the file and the file extension. Both elements are returned in a tuple.

*   *Unix timestamps* are integers that indicate the seconds since the beginning of the *Unix epoch*—that is, since January 1, 1970.

Table 30.4 Most Important Functions of the os.path Module (Cont.)

30.2.1   abspath(path)

This function returns the corresponding absolute and normalized path (see os.norm-path) for a relative path. The following example illustrates how this works:

```
>>> os.path.abspath(".")
'Z:\\examples\\os'
```

In this case, using the "." relative path to the current directory, we found out that our script is stored at 'Z:\\examples\\os'.

30.2.2   basename(path)

This function returns the so-called base name of the path. The base name of a path is the part after the last folder separator, such as \ or /. This function is very good for extracting the filename from a full path:

```
>>> os.path.basename(r"C:\Games\StrategyGames\Civilization.exe")
'Civilization.exe'
```

Note

This function differs from the basename Unix command in that it returns an empty string if the string ends with a folder separator:

```
>>> os.path.basename(r"/usr/include/")
''
```

In contrast, the output of the Unix command of the same name looks as follows:

```
$ basename /usr/include/
include
```

30.2.3   commonprefix(list)

This function returns a string that contains the longest common prefix of all paths in list:

```
>>> os.path.commonprefix([
...     r"C:\Games\StrategyGames\Civilization.exe",
...     r"C:\Games\ShooterGames\Counterstrike.exe",
...     r"C:\Games\StrategyGames\TheSettlers.exe"])
'C:\\Games\\S'
```

It isn't guaranteed that the resulting string is also a valid and existing path as the paths are considered simple strings.

30.2.4   dirname(path)

This function returns the parent folder of path:

```
>>> os.path.dirname(r"C:\Games\StrategyGames\Civilization.exe")
'C:\\Games\\StrategyGames'
```

Just as with os.path.basename, the behavior of dirname is different for paths that end with a folder separator:

```
>>> os.path.dirname(r"/usr/include")
'/usr'
```

30

```
>>> os.path.dirname(r"/usr/include/")
'/usr/include'
```

30.2.5   join(path, *paths)

This function merges the passed path specifications into a single path by concatenating them. Here, the usual separator of the operating system is used:

```
>>> os.path.join(r"C:\Games", r"StrategyGames\Civilization.exe")
'C:\\Games\\StrategyGames\\Civilization.exe'
```

If an absolute path is passed as a second or later argument, os.path.join will ignore all previously passed paths:

```
>>> os.path.join(r"This\gets\ignored", r"C:\Games", r"StrategyGames\
Civilization.exe")
'C:\\Games\\StrategyGames\\Civilization.exe'
```

30.2.6   normcase(path)

On operating systems that aren't case-sensitive for paths (e.g., Windows), all uppercase letters are replaced by their lowercase equivalents. In addition, all slashes are replaced with backslashes on Windows:

```
>>> os.path.normcase(r"C:\Games/StrategyGames/Civilization.exe")
'c:\\games\\strategygames\\civilization.exe'
```

On Unix, the passed path is returned without any modification.

30.2.7   split(path)

This function splits the passed path into the name of the folder or file it describes and the path to the parent directory, and it returns a tuple containing the two parts:

```
>>> os.path.split(r"C:\Games\StrategyGames\Civilization.exe")
('C:\\Games\\StrategyGames', 'Civilization.exe')
```

> **Note**
>
> If the path ends with a slash or backslash, the second element of the tuple is an empty string:
>
> ```
> >>> os.path.split("/home/username/")
> ('/home/username', '')
> ```

30.2.8   splitdrive(path)

This function splits the passed path into the drive specification and the rest of the path if the platform supports drive specifications:

```
>>> os.path.splitdrive(r"C:\Games/StrategyGames/Civilization.exe")
('C:', '\\Games/StrategyGames/Civilization.exe')
```

On operating systems that don't support drive letters, the first string of the tuple is an empty string:

```
>>> os.path.splitdrive("/usr/share/bin")
('', '/usr/share/bin')
```

30.2.9   splitext(path)

This function splits path into the path to the file and the file extension. Both elements are returned in a tuple:

```
>>> os.path.splitext(r"C:\Games\StrategyGames\Civilization.exe")
('C:\\Games\\StrategyGames\\Civilization', '.exe')
```

30.3   Accessing the File System: shutil

The shutil module can be regarded as a supplement to os and os.path and contains functions that relate in particular to copying and removing files. It abstracts from platform-specific commands such as copy on Windows or cp on Unix. In addition, shutil includes functions for creating and unpacking archive files, such as ZIP or TAR archives.

The functions listed in Table 30.5 are implemented by shutil, where the src and dst parameters are strings containing the path of the source and destination files, respectively.

Name	Description
Directory and File Operations	
chown(path, [user, group])	Sets the owner and group of path to the passed values user and group, respectively.
copy(src, dst, [follow_symlinks])	Copies the file under src to dst. Unlike copyfile, dst can also refer to a directory to which the file is to be copied.

Table 30.5 Functions of the shutil Module

Name	Description
copyfile(src, dst, [follow_symlinks])	Copies the file under src to dst. If the file already exists under dst, it will be overwritten without prompting. For this purpose, the dst path must be writable. Otherwise a PermissionError exception will be raised.
copyfileobj(fsrc, fdst, [length])	Copies the contents of the fsrc file object opened for reading to the fdst object opened for writing.
copymode(src, dst, [follow_symlinks])	Copies the access rights from the src path to the dst path. In this process, the content of dst as well as the owner and the group remain untouched. Both paths must already exist in the file system.
copystat(src, dst, [follow_symlinks])	Like copymode, but in addition, the time of the last access and the time the last modification are also copied.
copy2(src, dst, [follow_symlinks])	Like copy, but the time of the last access and the time of the last change also are copied.
copytree(src, dst, [symlinks, ignore, copy_function, ignore_dangling_symlinks])	Copies the entire directory structure under src to dst.
disk_usage(path)	Returns information about the memory capacity, utilization, and free memory under path as tuples.
ignore_patterns([*patterns])	Creates a function that can be passed for the ignore parameter in the copytree function to exclude certain files from being copied.
move(src, dst)	Moves the file or folder from src to dst.
rmtree(src, [ignore_errors, onerror])	Deletes the entire directory structure under src.
which(cmd, [mode, path])	Returns the path of the executable file associated with the cmd command.

Table 30.5 Functions of the shutil Module (Cont.)

Name	Description
Archive Operations	
`make_archive(base_name, format, [root_dir])`	Creates an archive file containing files in the `root_dir` directory and returns the name of the archive.
`get_archive_formats()`	Returns a list of available formats for creating archives.
`get_unpack_formats()`	Returns a list of available formats for unpacking archives.
`unpack_archive(filename, [extract_dir, format])`	Unpacks the archive under `filename` into the `extract_dir` directory.

Table 30.5 Functions of the shutil Module (Cont.)

In the following sections, we'll describe first the functions for directories and files and then the archive operations in greater detail. To be able to execute the listed examples, the shutil module must first be imported:

```
>>> import shutil
```

30.3.1   Directory and File Operations

copy(src, dst [follow_symlinks])

This operation copies the file under the src path to dst. The dst parameter can contain a path to a file that will either be created or overwritten. If dst points to a folder, a new file with the filename of src will be created in the dst folder or overwritten if necessary. This is the main difference from the copyfile function, which doesn't accept any folder as its destination.

The access rights are copied as well.

If the follow_symlinks parameter has the value False, symbolic links themselves will be copied, while the default value True ensures that instead of a symbolic link the file referenced by it is copied.

copytree(src, dst, [symlinks, ignore, copy_function, ignore_dangling_symlinks])

This operation copies the entire directory structure under src to dst. The dst path mustn't refer to an already existing folder, and all missing directories of the dst path will be created.

The optional symlinks parameter specifies how to handle symbolic links. If symlinks has the value False or symlinks isn't specified, the linked files or folders themselves will be

30

inserted into the copied directory structure. If the symlinks value is True, only the links will be copied. If symlinks has the value False and the ignore_dangling_symlinks parameter is set to True, errors that occur if a symbolic link points to a nonexistent file will be ignored.

The ignore parameter expects a function that excludes certain files from copying. The ignore_patterns function is used to create such a function. The following example creates a function that ignores all file names ending in ".txt", and file names starting with "tmp":

```
>>> my_ignore_function = shutil.ignore_patterns("*.txt", "tmp*")
```

The function passed with the copy_function parameter is used for copying the files, where copy2 is the default.

The copytree function internally uses the copystat function to set the permissions of the created directories and files.

rmtree(src, [ignore_errors, onerror])

This deletes the entire directory structure under src. For ignore_errors, a truth value can be passed that determines whether errors occurring during deletion should be ignored or handled by the function passed for onerror. If ignore_errors isn't specified, any error that occurs will generate an exception.

If you specify onerror, it must be a function that expects three parameters:

- function
  A reference to the function that caused the error. This can be os.listdir, os.remove, or os.rmdir.
- path
  The path for which the error occurred.
- excinfo
  The return value of sys.exc_info in the context of the error.

Note

Exceptions raised by the onerror function won't get caught.

30.3.2   Archive Operations

For the following examples, we assume that the current working directory contains a directory called data, which is structured as shown in Figure 30.2.

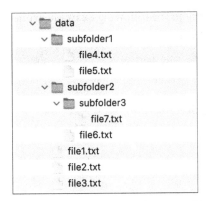

Figure 30.2 Sample Data for the Archive Functions

make_archive(base_name, format, [root_dir, base_dir, verbose, dry_run, owner, group, logger])

This function creates a new archive containing the files in the root_dir directory. If root_dir isn't specified, the files of the current working directory will be packed. The base_name parameter specifies the location and name of the archive file, but the file extension should *not* be included.

The desired format of the archive file is specified via the format parameter. You can get the available archive formats via the get_archive_formats function (described ahead).

A typical call of make_archive looks as follows:

```
>>> shutil.make_archive("test", "zip", "data")
'[...]/test.zip'
```

The unzip Unix program enables us to see that the archive contains all the files in the data directory:

```
$  unzip -v test.zip
Archive:  test.zip
 Length   Method    Size   Name
       2  Defl:N       4   file2.txt
       2  Defl:N       4   file3.txt
       2  Defl:N       4   file1.txt
       2  Defl:N       4   subfolder1/file5.txt
       2  Defl:N       4   subfolder1/file4.txt
       2  Defl:N       4   subfolder2/file6.txt
       2  Defl:N       4   subfolder2/subfolder3/file7.txt
```

If you want to pack only the files of a subdirectory of root_dir including the corresponding relative path, you can achieve this via the base_dir parameter.

We'll pack only the files in the subfolder2 subdirectory in the following example, while the relative path within the data directory will be preserved:

```
>>> shutil.make_archive("test2", "zip", "data", "subfolder2")
'[...]/test2.zip'
```

Again, we use unzip to check the contents of the archive:

```
$ unzip -v test2.zip
Archive:  test2.zip
 Length   Method    Size    Name
      2  Defl:N        4    subfolder2/file6.txt
      2  Defl:N        4    subfolder2/subfolder3/file7.txt
```

You can see that all files and folders in the subfolder2 directory have been packed, preserving the relative path to the data directory—namely, subfolder2.

For the technical and rarely used verbose, dry_run, owner, group, and logger parameters, we refer you to the Python documentation.

The function get_archive_formats returns a list of two-element tuples describing the available formats for creating archives:

```
>>> shutil.get_archive_formats()
[('bztar', "bzip2'ed tar-file"),
 ('gztar', "gzip'ed tar-file"),
 ('tar', 'uncompressed tar file'),
 ('xztar', "xz'ed tar-file"),
 ('zip', 'ZIP file')]
```

Each tuple in this list contains two strings: the name of the format and a short description.

The counterpart of get_archive_formats is provided by the get_unpack_formats function that lists the available formats for unpacking archives.

unpack_archive(filename, [extract_dir, format])

This function extracts the archive under the filename path into the extract_dir destination directory. If extract_dir isn't specified, the data will be extracted to the current working directory.

The format parameter can be used to specify the format of the archive. If no value is passed for format, then unpack_archive tries to determine the format of the archive based on the file extension.

30.4   Temporary Files: tempfile

If your programs need to process large amounts of data, it often doesn't make sense to keep all the data in the memory at once. For this purpose, you can use temporary files, which allow you to temporarily swap out data that isn't currently needed to the hard drive. However, temporary files are not suitable for storing data permanently.

For a convenient handling of temporary files, Python provides the tempfile module.

The most important function of this module is TemporaryFile, which returns an open file object associated with a new temporary file. The file is opened for read and write access in binary mode ("w+b"). We as users of the function don't need to bother about anything other than reading and writing our data. The module makes sure that the temporary file is created and also deletes it again when the file object is closed. In particular, this includes the implicit close when the file object is garbage collected.

Swapping a program's data to the hard drive represents a security risk because other programs could read the data and thus possibly gain access to security-relevant information. For this reason, TemporaryFile tries to remove the file from the file system immediately after its creation to hide it from other programs, provided this process is supported by the operating system. Also, a random string consisting of six characters is used for the file name, which makes it difficult for other programs to find out to which program a temporary file belongs.

Although in most cases you'll call TemporaryFile without parameters, let's take a look at the entire interface.

30.4.1   TemporaryFile([mode, [bufsize, suffix, prefix, dir])

The mode and bufsize parameters correspond to the parameters of the same name of the built-in open function (You can find more information about this in Chapter 6, Section 6.2.1). You can use suffix and prefix to customize the name of the new temporary file if necessary. What you pass for prefix will be placed before the automatically generated filename, and the value for suffix will be appended to the end of the filename. In addition, you can use the dir parameter to specify the folder in which the file should be created. By default, TemporaryFile automatically takes care of a location for the file.

To illustrate the use of TemporaryFile, here's a small example that first stores a string in a temporary file and then reads it back in:

```
>>> import tempfile
>>> with tempfile.TemporaryFile() as tmp:
...     tmp.write(b"Hello buffer")
...     tmp.seek(0)
...     data = tmp.read()
...     data
...
```

30

```
12
0
b'Hello buffer'
```

Note in this example that we had to pass a bytes string to the write method because the temporary file was opened in binary mode. If you want to write str objects to temporary files, you must open the file in "w" text mode or convert the strings to a bytes object using the encode method when saving.

If you don't want the temporary file to be hidden, you should use the NamedTemporaryFile function, which has the same interface as TemporaryFile and behaves the same except that the file is accessible for other programs.

30.4.2   tempfile.TemporaryDirectory([suffix, prefix, dir])

Using tempfile.TemporaryDirectory, you can create temporary folders using all means provided by the operating system to prevent unauthorized access to the temporary data. The interface of tempfile.TemporaryDirectory can be used in a similar way to tempfile.TemporaryFile.

The return value is the absolute pathname of the temporary folder:

```
>>> tempfile.TemporaryDirectory()
<TemporaryDirectory '/tmp/T/tmpf3ywpO3w'>
```

Chapter 31
Parallel Programming

This chapter will introduce parallel programming with Python, which allows multiple tasks to be executed simultaneously. Before we can start with the technical details and sample programs, we'll explain some terms and look at selected aspects how modern operating systems work.

> **Note**
>
> In this chapter, we consistently use f-strings for string formatting (see Chapter 12, Section 12.5.3) instead of the format method used in other chapters. In particular, this chapter also serves as a collection of examples for the use of f-strings in concrete applications.

31.1 Processes, Multitasking, and Threads

As users of modern computers, we are used to the fact that several programs[1] can be run simultaneously. For example, we write an email while in the background the latest vacation video is being converted to another format and a streaming service is playing our favorite song. Figure 31.1 shows a typical work session, with each box representing a running program. The length of the boxes along the time axis indicates how long the respective process is running.

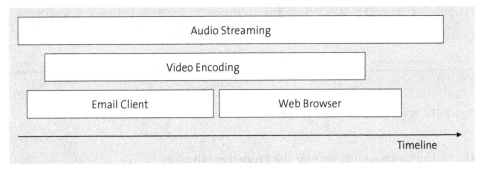

Figure 31.1 Several Processes Running Simultaneously

---

1 In the following sections, the terms *program* and *process* are used synonymously for a running program.

In fact, however, a processor can only perform exactly one task at a given time and not several tasks at the same time. Even on modern processors with more than one core or on computers with many processors, the number of programs that can be executed simultaneously is limited by the number of cores or processors. So how is it possible that the scenario described in the introduction also works on a computer with only one processor, which has only one core?

The trick behind this is very simple, because the limitation of the machine is cleverly hidden from the user by merely making them believe that several programs are running simultaneously. This is achieved in the following way. A program is allowed to exclusively use a processor just for a very short *time slice*. After such a time slice has elapsed, control is taken away from the program again, saving its current state. Then a time slice can be assigned to the next program. During the period when a program is waiting to be allocated a time slice, it's referred to as *sleeping*.

You can think of the work of a computer as waking up at breakneck speed each program that is running, allowing it to run for a short time, and then putting it back to sleep, before continuing with the next program. Due to the high speed of switching between processes, the user doesn't notice this. The management of the different processes and the allocation of the time slices is taken over by the operating system, which is therefore also called a *multitasking system*.

So the correct representation of our initial example should look more like Figure 31.2. Each small box symbolizes a time slice.

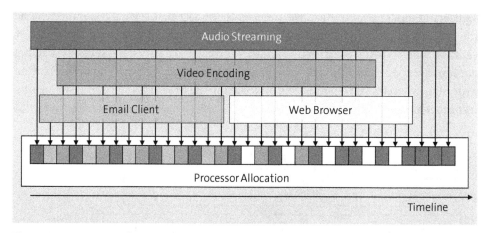

Figure 31.2 Processes Alternate, Not Run Simultaneously

31.1.1 The Lightweights among the Processes: Threads

Within a process itself, only one task can be executed at a time if the program is processed sequentially. In many situations, however, it's advantageous for a program to perform several operations simultaneously. For example, the user interface mustn't freeze during an elaborate calculation, but should display the current status, and the user must be able to cancel the calculation if necessary. Another example is a web server that must also be available for other requests while processing a client request.

It's possible to bypass the restriction to only one operation at a time by creating more processes. However, the creation of a process consumes a lot of resources, and the exchange of data between processes must also be handled because each process has its own memory that is protected from the other processes.

Another option to parallelize a program is provided by so-called threads. A *thread* is an individually executed sequence of operations within a process. By default, each process has exactly one thread that performs the execution of the program flow in that process.

Now, however, a process can also start several threads, which are then seemingly executed simultaneously by the operating system like processes. The advantage of threads over processes is that the threads of a process share their memory for global variables. So if a global variable is changed in one thread, the new value is also immediately visible for all other threads of the process.[2] In addition, managing threads is less expensive for the operating system than managing processes since the switch to another thread within the same process can keep parts of the context. This is why threads are also referred to as *lightweight processes*.

Figure 31.3 illustrates the threads in a process.

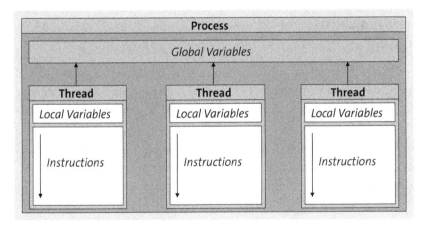

Figure 31.3 One Process with Three Threads

---

2 To avoid errors, such accesses in multiple threads must be specially secured with *critical sections*. We'll cover this topic in more detail later in Section 31.4.1 when discussing securing critical areas with lock objects.

> **Note**
>
> In CPython,[3] there is unfortunately currently no way to run different threads on different processors or processor cores for technical reasons. As a result, even Python programs that rely heavily on threading can only use a single processor or processor core.
>
> We'd like to leave the background of this circumstance aside at this point. You can find more information on the web by searching for "Global Interpreter Lock" (GIL).

31.1.2 Threads or Processes?

Whether you should use threads or processes for parallelization for your program depends on your requirements. For example, if you're developing a program that performs a lengthy calculation in the background while you still want the program's interface to respond to user input without delay, threads are a good choice. Likewise, threads are suitable for working with slow input/output interfaces such as network connections: while one thread is waiting for new data, another can process data already received.

The situation is different if your program has to process large amounts of data or perform complex calculations, so you want to use the entire available computing power of several processor cores. In this case, you're forced to use processes due to the previously mentioned limitation of CPython.

31.1.3 Cooperative Multitasking: A Third Way

So far, we've looked at two dominant approaches to parallel programming:

- *Threads* are parallel control flows within a process. This makes them lightweight and allows them to access shared memory. Due to the alternating execution of threads in time slices, accesses to shared data must be secured to guarantee their consistency.

- *Processes* are programs executed in parallel that operate in separate memory segments. This ensures the consistency of the data used by a process, but in return, communication between processes for data exchange must be taken care of separately.

Both threads and processes fall into the category of *preemptive multitasking*. This refers to approaches to parallel execution in which the operating system prematurely interrupts the execution of one thread or process in order to switch to another thread or

---

3 CPython refers to the reference implementation of Python. For an overview of alternative Python interpreters, see Chapter 40.

process. This fast switching realizes the quasi-parallel execution of threads and processes.[4]

An alternative to preemptive multitasking is *cooperative multitasking*. Here too, the system switches between the different control flows of a program to realize quasi-parallel execution, but it isn't the operating system that decides when to switch, but the program itself. The different control flows cooperate and inform each other when it's a suitable time to switch context — for example, when waiting for the response of an external computation or data access.

The collaborative approach makes it easy to ensure consistency of data shared by the different control flows. On the other hand, the programmer must explicitly take care of the cooperation. Python provides some tools here to make this as easy as possible.

31.2 Python's Interfaces for Parallelization

Python provides various interfaces for the parallel execution of program parts. It depends on the specific application which of the interfaces should be used (see Table 31.1).

Interface	Properties
concurrent.futures	Interface for executing threads and processes with a high degree of abstraction, low flexibility, and no synchronization capabilities
threading, multiprocessing	Interfaces for the execution of threads and processes with a lower degree of abstraction, high flexibility, and possibilities for synchronization
asyncio	Interface for cooperative multitasking

Table 31.1 Python's Interfaces for Parallelization

For simple tasks that can be performed independently and without data exchange, you can use the concurrent.futures module.[5] It provides a convenient interface that allows function calls to be executed in different threads or processes. In this context, it's assumed that each function call can be run independently of the others, whereby the order of the calls mustn't play any role and no data may be exchanged between the different function calls.

---

4 At this point, we'd like to point out again that on systems with multiple processors or multiple processor cores, a certain number of threads and processes may be executed genuinely in parallel.

5 The concurrent.futures module was introduced in Python 3.2. However, the futures module in the Python package index enables you to use this functionality also in older versions of Python.

The threading and multiprocessing modules, on the other hand, provide powerful tools for exchanging data between processes or threads in parallel programs in a secure manner. Internally, concurrent.futures uses the capabilities of the threading and multiprocessing modules, respectively, so it isn't a separate implementation but an additional abstraction layer.

The async and await keywords, as well as libraries such asyncio for the cooperative execution of specific tasks, form the basis of Python's support for implementing cooperative multitasking.

We'll first look at the more abstract concurrent.futures interface and later discuss selected problems of synchronizing multiple threads or processes in threading and multiprocessing. At the end of this chapter, we'll take a look at cooperative multitasking.

31.3 The Abstract Interface: concurrent.futures

For a case in which a program has to execute complex but independent tasks, the concurrent.futures module was developed. This module allows you to conveniently execute function calls in threads or processes.

The ThreadPoolExecutor and ProcessPoolExecutor classes are provided, whose instances represent a set of threads and processes respectively. Both classes implement a common interface—namely, that of an executor. An *executor* is used to process a sequence of tasks, whereby it can make use of several *workers*—that is, threads or processes.

The interface of an executor comprises the methods listed in Table 31.2.

Method	Description
submit(fn, [*args], {**kwargs})	Registers a new task with the executor. The task consists of calling the fn function with the args and kwargs parameters.
map(fn, [*iterables], {timeout})	Applies the fn function to all elements of the iterables iterable objects and creates an iterator over the results.
shutdown([wait, cancel_futures])	Instructs the executor to release all used resources as soon as the passed tasks have been processed.

Table 31.2 The Methods of the Executor Classes

You can think of an executor as the boss of a team of several workers, to whom you communicate via the submit method the tasks you want the team to do. The distribution of these tasks to the individual workers is handled by the executor.

When creating a new executor instance, we can specify the number of desired workers using the max_workers keyword parameter.

31.3.1   An Example with a futures.ThreadPoolExecutor

In the following example, we'll use a ThreadPoolExecutor to execute four calls of a simple example function in three threads:

```python
from concurrent import futures
from time import sleep, time

def test(t):
    sleep(t)
    print(f"I have waited for {t} seconds. Time: {time():.0f}")

e = futures.ThreadPoolExecutor(max_workers=3)
print(f"Start time:                          {time():.0f}")
e.submit(test, 9)
e.submit(test, 2)
e.submit(test, 5)
e.submit(test, 6)
print("All tasks started.")
e.shutdown()
print("All tasks completed.")
```

The test function generates a delayed output on the screen, where the t parameter can be used to specify the length of the delay. In the example, we have the executor call this function with various delays, which produces the following output:

```
Start time:                      1428830988
All tasks started.
I have waited for 2 seconds. Time: 1428830990
I have waited for 5 seconds. Time: 1428830993
I have waited for 6 seconds. Time: 1428830996
I have waited for 9 seconds. Time: 1428830997
All tasks completed.
```

The timestamps of the outputs prove that the function calls have been executed in parallel: the outputs for the wait times of 2, 5, and 9 seconds are exactly delayed by the respective waiting time after the start time. If the calls had been processed sequentially, the times would have added up.

An exception is the call for the wait time of 6 seconds, which appears on the screen only after 8 seconds as you can see by comparing the timestamps. The reason for this delay

31

is the number of worker threads of our executor. The executor internally manages a queue of tasks that have been submitted to it. This queue is processed in the same order in which the respective submit calls were made. In our example, the executor has three threads available to complete the four tasks. So first the call of the test function with the 9 parameter is started in a thread. After the calls with parameters 2 and 5 have been started in their own threads, the executor has reached the maximum number of workers we have defined. Thus, the call with parameter 6 can't occur until a worker thread has become available again. After 2 seconds the task with the shortest wait time terminates so that the call for parameter 6 is started with the corresponding delay.

Another interesting fact is the different behavior of the submit and shutdown methods: each submit call immediately returns control to the caller without waiting for the passed function to complete its work. Therefore the "All tasks started." output appears before the outputs of the test function. The shutdown call, on the other hand, blocks the execution of the caller until all tasks have been processed and then releases the resources used.

If the value False is passed for the wait parameter, shutdown also immediately returns control to the caller so that work can continue there without delay. The entire program is then nevertheless not terminated so long as work is still being carried out in the background. It's important to note that an executor can't accept any further tasks after shutdown has been called.

Therefore, if we replace the e.shutdown() line with e.shutdown(False) in the sample program, the output will change as follows:

```
Start time:                    1428829782
All tasks started.
All tasks completed.
I have waited for 2 seconds. Time: 1428829784
I have waited for 5 seconds. Time: 1428829787
I have waited for 6 seconds. Time: 1428829788
I have waited for 9 seconds. Time: 1428829791
```

As you can see, the output after calling e.shutdown now appears immediately on the screen, although there's still background work in process. Nevertheless, Python waits for the background processes that are still running so that any remaining output still occurs before the program terminates.

In Python 3.9, the shutdown method has been extended with the cancel_futures parameter. If the value True is passed for this parameter instead of the default value False, tasks that were not yet started at the time of the shutdown call will no longer be started. However, tasks already in progress will still be executed until termination in this case.

31.3.2   Executor Instances as Context Managers

The typical lifecycle of an executor instance is that it's created, tasks are assigned to it, and then it waits for the tasks to finish before finally being released.

Typically, an executor is used as a context manager via the with statement, which eliminates the need to explicitly call shutdown. The last part in our example can be replaced by the following with block:

```
print(f"Start time:                          {time():.0f}")
with futures.ThreadPoolExecutor(max_workers=3) as e:
    e.submit(test, 9)
    e.submit(test, 2)
    e.submit(test, 5)
    e.submit(test, 6)
    print("All tasks started.")
print("All tasks completed.")
```

When you use an executor as a context manager via with, the with block won't be exited until all assigned tasks are completed because the e.shutdown method is implicitly called without parameters.

31.3.3   Using futures.ProcessPoolExecutor

To use processes for parallelization instead of threads as in the previous example, the ThreadPoolExecutor class is replaced with ProcessPoolExecutor. In addition, you must make sure that the child processes won't start new processes recursively by themselves. The customized sample program then looks as follows:

```
from concurrent import futures
from time import sleep, time

def test(t):
    sleep(t)
    print(f"I have waited for {t} seconds. Time: {time():.0f}")

if __name__ == "__main__":
    print(f"Start time:                          {time():.0f}")
    with futures.ProcessPoolExecutor(max_workers=3) as e:
        e.submit(test, 9)
        e.submit(test, 2)
        e.submit(test, 5)
        e.submit(test, 6)
        print("All tasks started.")
    print("All tasks completed.")
```

31

In addition to using `ProcessPoolExecutor` instead of `ThreadPoolExecutor`, we make use of the `__name__` global variable to check if the Python file is executed directly and start the subprocesses only in this case. The reason is that the Python file in which the subprocesses are started must be importable by them as a module.[6] The value of the `__name__` global variable is `"__main__"` only if the file is executed directly with the Python interpreter. If, on the other hand, the file is imported as a module, it has a different value—namely, that of the module. This query thus prevents a subprocess from re-executing the code in the `if` block when the module is imported.

> **Note**
>
> Of course, an interactive session can't be imported from a subprocess. This leads to the fact that on Windows, for example, `ProcessPoolExecutor` can't be used in Python's interactive mode.

Now you're able to execute a function in parallel in different threads or processes. In the following section, we'll look at how you can access the return values of the parallel function calls.

31.3.4   Managing the Tasks of an Executor

The `test` function in the introductory example is of particularly simple design as it has no return value the caller could use. More interesting, however, are functions that return a value after a (possibly lengthy) calculation.

A Model Function for a Complex Calculation

As a model example, we'll now define a function that approximates the number π using the Wallis product.[7]

$$\frac{2}{1} \cdot \frac{2}{3} \cdot \frac{4}{3} \cdot \frac{4}{5} \cdot \frac{6}{5} \cdot \frac{6}{7} \cdot \frac{8}{7} \cdot \frac{8}{9} \cdots = \frac{\pi}{2}$$

The numerator always contains even numbers, which increase by 2 with every other factor. The denominator contains only odd numbers, which, with the exception of the first factor, also increase by 2 with every other factor.

We'll implement the `approximate_pi` function, which approximates π by multiplying the first n factors of Wallis Product:

---

6 This requirement results from how the subprocesses are initialized. For more details, please refer to the Python documentation.

7 The product is named after the English mathematician John Wallis (1616–1703), who discovered it in 1655.

```
def approximate_pi(n):
    pi_half = 1
    numerator, denominator = 2.0, 1.0
    for i in range(n):
        pi_half *= numerator / denominator
        if i % 2:
            numerator += 2
        else:
            denominator += 2
    return 2*pi_half
```

For example, with the parameter 1000 for n, the function produces the following output, where only the first two decimal places are correct:

```
>>> approximate_pi(1000)
3.140023818600586
```

As the value of n increases, better and better approximations of π are calculated, but this must also be paid for with more computing time. For example, a call with n= 30000000 takes about eight seconds on our test computer.

With approximate_pi, we thus have a sample function that fully utilizes a processor core and for larger values of n takes longer and longer for the calculation. In the following programs, approximate_pi serves as an example of a complex function whose runtime characteristics depend on the choice of the parameter value.

Now we'll run approximate_pi in multiple threads or processes.

Accessing the Results of the Calculation

In the introductory example, we used the submit method of an executor instance to enqueue new tasks to the executor. The submit method returns an instance of the futures.Future type with every call, which we have ignored so far. You can think of this instance as a pick-up ticket that allows you to check the status of the submitted task and collect the result after the calculation is complete. In the simplest case, we use the result method of the Future instance to get the result:

```
with futures.ThreadPoolExecutor(max_workers=4) as e:
    f = e.submit(approximate_pi, 10000000)
    print(f.result())
```

As output, we obtain the desired approximation of π using 10000000 factors in the Wallis product. The result method of a Future instance blocks the caller until the associated calculation is complete. If you have several tasks with different runtimes being performed at the same time, this may cause you to wait an unnecessarily long time for results that are already available:

```
with futures.ThreadPoolExecutor(max_workers=4) as e:
    f1 = e.submit(approximate_pi, 10000000)
    f2 = e.submit(approximate_pi, 100)
    print("f1:", f1.result())
    print("f2:", f2.result())
```

In this example, two calculations are performed, one taking significantly longer than the other. Nevertheless, the result of the calculation with n=10000000 is output first and only then does the result with n=100 follow:

```
f1: 3.1415924965090136
f2: 3.126078900215409
```

The concurrent.futures module provides functions to conveniently access the results of multiple calculations in the order of their completion.

concurrent.futures.as_completed(fs, [timeout])

The as_completed function creates an iterator that iterates over the results of the fs iterable of Future instances. The results are traversed in the order in which they become available. This allows the caller to immediately process a result once the respective calculation is complete:

```
N = (12345678,  123456,  1234,  12)
with futures.ThreadPoolExecutor(max_workers=4) as e:
    fs = {e.submit(approximate_pi, n): n for n in N}
    for f in futures.as_completed(fs):
        print(f"n={fs[f]:10}: {f.result()}")
```

In the example, we have executed the approximate_pi function with different parameters executed by a ThreadPoolExecutor with 4 threads. By using futures.as_completed, we get the following output, where the results of the shorter calculations are output first:

```
n=        12: 3.02317019200136
n=      1234: 3.1403210113038207
n=    123456: 3.1415799301866607
n=  12345678: 3.1415925263536626
```

We use the fs dictionary to remember the assignment of input parameters to the corresponding Future instance. Note that any iterable of Future instances can be passed to as_completed. In the above program, by using a dictionary we can easily access the number of factors used for each job after the calculation has finished. It's also interesting to note that, as above, we use the result method of the Future instances to query the result of the calculation. Because the futures.as_completed function returns only those Future instances whose computation has already been completed, result doesn't have to wait for the completion of the computation, but immediately returns the already determined value.

The timeout parameter can optionally be used to specify a time in seconds that futures.as_completed should wait for all results to be calculated. If after timeout seconds the last result is not yet calculated, a TimeoutError exception will be raised.

concurrent.futures.wait(fs, [timeout, return_when])

The wait function waits until the event specified by return_when has occurred or the timeout has expired. The return value is an instance that provides the done and not_done attributes. Here, done references the set of Future instances in fs that have been processed at the time of the event, while not_done contains the pending Future instances in a set.

The possible values for return_when are listed in Table 31.3.

Constant	Meaning
futures.FIRST_COMPLETED	The first task in fs has been completed.
futures.FIRST_EXCEPTION	The first task in fs raises an exception.
	If no exception is raised, wait until all tasks in fs have been processed.
futures.ALL_COMPLETED	All tasks in fs have been completed.

Table 31.3 Events Supported by futures.wait

By default, the function wait waits until all tasks are processed, as shown in the following example:

```
with futures.ThreadPoolExecutor(max_workers=4) as e:
    fs = {e.submit(approximate_pi, n): n for n in N}
    res = futures.wait(fs)
    for f in res.done:
        print(f"n={fs[f]:10}: {f.result()}")
```

Similar to as_completed, timeout can be used to specify a maximum time in seconds that wait will wait before returning control to the caller. The following example outputs the finished results every second until there are none left:

```
with futures.ThreadPoolExecutor(max_workers=4) as e:
    fs = {e.submit(approximate_pi, n): n for n in N}
    done = False
    while not done:
        res = futures.wait(fs, timeout=1.0)
        for f in res.done:
            print(f"n={fs[f]:10}: {f.result()}")
```

31

```
        del fs[f]
    done = (len(res.not_done) == 0)
```

By specifying a timeout, it's possible to ensure that the caller regains control at regular intervals while waiting for the next result.

> **Note**
>
> For both as_completed and wait functions, fs can also contain Futures instances that belong to different executor instances.

Executor.map(func, [*iterables], {timeout, chunksize})

The executor instances themselves have a map method that can be used to apply a function to all values in iterable objects, such as lists. Thus it behaves exactly like the built-in map function,[8] except that it executes the call of func for each element of the iterables in parallel in threads or processes using the executor.

The timeout parameter can be used to specify a time span in seconds that the processing of the function calls may take in total. If the calculation takes longer, a futures.TimeoutError exception will be raised. By default, the permitted computation time is unlimited.

Using chunksize, you can make sure that the elements of iterables are processed in blocks. For example, if a list of 100 elements is passed as iterables along with chunksize=20, 5 packages of 20 elements each will be processed per process. By default, a new process is started for each element. A value of chunksize different from 1 can greatly improve the processing speed in certain situations. Note that chunksize is only significant when using the ProcessPoolExecutor class.

Now we'll examine how the use of threads and processes affects the runtime of a program.

Calculations on Multiple Processors with ProcessPoolExecutor

The following example calls the approximate_pi function for a list of relatively large values for n, using a command line parameter to specify whether to use the built-in map or Executor.map function with threads and processes, respectively. The program calculates the runtime by calculating and outputting the difference between the start and end time.

```
from concurrent import futures
import sys
import time
```

---

8 The description of the built-in map function can be found in Chapter 17, Section 17.14.30.

```
def approximate_pi(n):
    ...


if __name__ == "__main__":
    start = time.perf_counter()
    N = (34567890, 5432198, 44444444, 22222222, 56565656,
        43236653, 23545353, 32425262)
    if sys.argv[1] == "threads":
        with futures.ThreadPoolExecutor(max_workers=4) as e:
            res = e.map(approximate_pi, N)
    elif sys.argv[1] == "processes":
        with futures.ProcessPoolExecutor(max_workers=4) as e:
            res = e.map(approximate_pi, N)
    else:
        res = map(approximate_pi, N)
    print(list(res))
    print(time.perf_counter() - start)
```

On an example computer with four processor cores, we obtained the following output, omitting the list of results:

```
$ python benchmark.py builtin
70.19322323799133
$ python benchmark.py threads
89.58459234237671
$ python benchmark.py processes
26.78869891166687
```

As you can see, running four worker processes is about 2.5 times faster than using the built-in map function. This is because the program is able to use four cores of the computer to speed up the calculation. Thus, the calculation actually ran in parallel on different processor cores.

At first glance, the longer runtime when running with four worker threads compared to the built-in map function is surprising. However, considering that only one thread can be executed at a time due to CPython's limitations, it becomes clear that a speed increase can't be expected. The fact that the threads variant is even slower is due to the additional effort required to manage the threads. In CPython, threads therefore are not suitable for speeding up complex calculations, but only to prevent the program from blocking.[9]

31

---

9 Several attempts have been made to improve CPython in this respect. Although it has not yet succeeded by the time this book is published, this may change in the future.

The futures.Future Class

So far, we've used instances of the futures.Future type only to read the results of executor tasks. However, futures.Future also provides a number of other methods to query the current state or to influence the execution.

Table 31.4 lists these methods.

Method	Description
cancel()	Attempts to cancel the task and returns True if successful, otherwise False.
cancelled()	Returns True if the task was cancelled, otherwise False.
running()	Returns True if the task is currently being executed, otherwise False.
done()	If the return value is True, the task was completed or canceled.
result([timeout])	Returns the result of the task, waiting for a maximum of timeout seconds.
exception([timeout])	Returns the exception raised in the task function, waiting for a maximum of timeout seconds. If the task is completed successfully, None is returned.
add_done_callback(fn)	Ensures that the fn function is called with the result of the task as soon as the result is available. The add_done_callback method can be called multiple times for different functions.

Table 31.4 Methods of an Instance of the futures.Future Type

31.4 The Flexible Interface: threading and multiprocessing

Now you can use the concurrent.futures interface to parallelize simple tasks using both threads and processes. If the tasks become more complex, such as when data must be exchanged or certain operations need to be synchronized, you need additional tools. These are provided by the threading and multiprocessing modules described in the following sections.

31.4.1   Threads in Python: threading

The threading module provides an object-oriented interface for working with threads.

Each thread is an instance of a class that inherits from threading.Thread. We now want to write a program that checks in multiple threads in parallel whether numbers entered by a user are prime numbers.[10] For this purpose, we'll define a PrimeNumberThread class that inherits from threading.Thread and expects the number to be checked as a parameter for the constructor.

The threading.Thread class contains a method called start that executes the thread. What exactly is to be executed is determined by the run method, which we override with the implementation of our prime number check. In the first step, the user should be able to enter numbers in a prompt, which are then checked. When the check is complete, the result is displayed on the screen. The program including the PrimeNumberThread class looks as follows:[11]

```python
import threading
class PrimeNumberThread(threading.Thread):
    def __init__(self, number):
        super().__init__()
        self.number = number
    def run(self):
        i = 2
        while i*i <= self.number:
            if self.number % i == 0:
                print(f"{self.number} is no prime "
                    f"as {self.number} = {i} * {self.number // i}")
                return
            i += 1
        print(f"{self.number} is prime")
my_threads = []
user_input = input("> ")
while input != "e":
    try:
        thread = PrimeNumberThread(int(user_input))
        my_threads.append(thread)
        thread.start()
    except ValueError:
        print("Wrong input!")
    user_input = input("> ")
```

---

10   A prime number is a natural number that has exactly two divisors. The first six prime numbers are therefore 2, 3, 5, 7, 11, and 13.

11   The algorithm used for the prime number check is very primitive and serves here only as an example of a CPU-intensive function.

```
for t in my_threads:
    t.join()
```

> **Note**
>
> This code should be executed in a Python console; it contains a weak point since differ-
> ent threads may print their results simultaneously leading to corrupt outputs. Espe-
> cially in development environments like IDLE, display errors may occur. We will tackle
> this problem in the next section.

Within the loop, the input is read by the user and a check is made to see if it's the "e"
keyword (for "end") to end the program. If something other than "e" was entered and
this input can be converted to an integer, a new instance of the `PrimeNumberThread` class
is created with the user input as a parameter and started with the `start` method.

The program also maintains a list called `my_threads` where all threads are stored. After
exiting the input loop, the program iterates over `my_threads` in a `for` loop and calls the
`join` method for each thread. This `for` loop ensures that the main program waits until
all started threads have been terminated because `join` interrupts the program execution until the thread for which it was called has been terminated.

A program run could then look as follows, with the partially delayed outputs showing
that calculations were actually performed in the background:

```
> 737373737373737
> 5672435793
5672435793 is not prime, as 5672435793 = 3 * 1890811931
> 909091
909091 is prime
> 10000000000037
> 5643257
5643257 is not prime, as 5643257 = 23 * 245359
> 4567
4567 is prime
10000000000037 is prime
737373737373737 is prime
> e
```

Securing Critical Sections with Lock Objects

A weakness of the program is that a thread can output the result after the calculation is
finished, while the user enters the next number to check. This may cause the user to
lose track of what they have already entered, as the following example shows:

```
> 10000000000037
> 5610000000000037 is prime
547
56547 is not prime, as 56547 = 3 * 18849
> end
```

In this case, the user wanted to examine the number 10000000000037 for its prime number property. Unfortunately, the thread that did the checking finished just as the user had already entered the first two digits 56 of the next number to be checked, 56547. This led to a "fragmentation" of the input and should of course be avoided.

To avoid such problems, a program can mark locations that are not allowed to run in parallel in multiple threads. Such sections are also referred to as *critical sections*. Critical sections are realized by so-called lock objects. The threading module provides the threading.Lock class to create such lock objects:

```
lock_object = threading.Lock()
```

Lock objects provide the two methods, acquire and release, which must be called respectively to enter or leave a critical section. If the acquire method of a lock object has been called, it's *locked*. If a thread calls the acquire method of a locked lock object, it must wait until the lock object has been released again via release. This technique prevents a critical section from being executed by multiple threads simultaneously.

Typically, lock objects are used in the following way:

```
lock_object.acquire()
# Here comes the critical code
lock_object.release()
```

To avoid having to write the enclosing calls of acquire and release every time, you can use lock objects as context managers via the with statement. The code shown previously can then be written more clearly in the following way:

```
with lock_object:
    pass # Here comes the critical code
```

We can now extend our sample program to include critical sections as follows, securing both user input and threaded output with the same lock object:

```
import threading
class PrimeNumberThread(threading.Thread):
    in_out_lock = threading.Lock()
    def __init__(self, number):
        super().__init__()
        self.number = number
```

```
    def run(self):
        i = 2
        while i*i <= self.number:
            if self.number % i == 0:
                with PrimeNumberThread.in_out_lock:
                    print(f"{self.number} is no prime "
                          f"as {self.number} = {i} * {self.number // i}")
                return
            i += 1
        with PrimeNumberThread.in_out_lock:
            print(f"{self.number} is prime")

my_threads = []
user_input = input("> ")
while user_input != "e":
    try:
        thread = PrimeNumberThread(int(user_input))
        my_threads.append(thread)
        thread.start()
    except ValueError:
        with PrimeNumberThread.in_out_lock:
            print("Wrong input!")
    with PrimeNumberThread.in_out_lock:
        user_input = input("> ")
for t in my_threads:
    t.join()
```

With this extension, it can no longer happen that a thread uncontrollably outputs its result while the user is making an input. Let's consider exactly how this works.

While the program waits for user input during the input function call, the Prime NumberThread.in_out_lock lock object is locked. At this point, if one of the running threads reaches a critical section in the run method, the with statement calls the acquire method of PrimeNumberThread.in_out_lock. Because the lock object is locked, this call blocks and the run method will pause its execution until the lock is released. As soon as the user has confirmed his input and the critical section in the while loop has been exited, the PrimeNumberThread.in_out_lock lock object will be released again so the run method can send its output to the screen.

The following section describes a particularly important application of critical sections.

Data Exchange between Threads with Critical Sections

The advantage of threads over processes is that they share the same global variables and can therefore easily exchange data. In particular, class attributes of the respective thread class or global variables are suitable for data exchange.

Still, there are a few pitfalls to be aware of when accessing a shared variable in multiple running threads.[12]

To illustrate the problem, let's consider a simple example where we start two threads that each add the number 1 to a shared counter variable 2000000 times:

```python
import threading

class MyThread(threading.Thread):
    counter = 0
    def run(self):
        for i in range(2000000):
            MyThread.counter += 1

A = MyThread()
B = MyThread()
A.start(), B.start()
A.join(), B.join()

print(MyThread.counter)
```

The shared counter is implemented as a class attribute of the MyThread class. After starting threads A and B and waiting with their join methods until their work has been completed, we output the value of the counter. Because 2000000 additions have been performed a total of two times, we expect the value 4000000 as output. Surprisingly, however, the program outputs the following value:

```
3542419
```

In fact, it seems that each call of the program outputs a different value. In 10 runs on our test computer, various values in a range from 2894816 to 3235044 were output.

Before we fix this problem in our program, let's first examine why this behavior occurs.

An Example of a Race Condition

As described in the introduction, concurrency in modern operating systems is achieved by providing threads[13] with small time slices to do their work. When such a time slice ends, the current state of the thread is saved and control is passed to the next thread.

---

12 The real art of parallel programming is to avoid these pitfalls. It's often difficult to keep track of the processes in parallel programs, which is why errors can easily creep in.

13 For the sake of clarity, we only refer to threads here. However, the described problem affects processes just as much when they work on shared data.

It now happens that the time slot of a thread ends exactly during the update of MyThread.counter because internally, the increase of the value consists of several steps. First, the value of MyThread.counter must be read, then a new instance must be created with the value incremented by one, which is linked to the MyThread.counter reference in the last step.

For example, if thread A is put to sleep when incrementing MyThread.counter before the new instance is created, thread B may be activated, which also wants to increment MyThread.counter. But because thread A hasn't yet calculated its new value of MyThread.counter and hasn't linked it to the reference, the newly activated thread B reads the *old* value of MyThread.counter and increments it. If thread A then becomes active again later, it increments the previously read value by one and assigns it to MyThread.counter. As a result, the value of MyThread.counter has only been incremented by one, even though both threads have each performed an addition.

Table 31.5 describes this scenario in detail.

Time Slice	Thread A	Thread B
1	Reads value from MyThread.counter— for example, 2.	*sleeps*
Time Slice of A Ends and B Is Activated		
2	*sleeps*	Reads value from MyThread.counter—in this case, also 2. Increments the value by 1. A new instance with the value 3 now exists in the memory. Binds the new instance to the MyThread.counter reference. Thus MyThread.counter refers to the value 3.
Time Slice of B Ends and A Is Activated		
3	Increments the value by 1. A new instance with the value 3 now exists in the memory. Binds the new instance to the MyThread.counter reference. Thus MyThread.counter refers to the value 3.	*sleeps*

Table 31.5 Problem Scenario when Accessing a Common Variable Simultaneously. The Time Slice Column Counts the Time Slices Specified by the Operating System.

This scenario explains why the final result can be smaller than the expected 400000. How often this problem occurs in one run of the program depends on how the operating system chooses the time slots of the two threads, which in turn depends on the system itself, the other programs that are running, and other unpredictable conditions. Such a scenario is referred to as a *race condition*.

It should be clear to you now that this unreliability renders our program completely worthless as the outcome depends dramatically on circumstances we can neither predict nor influence.

To solve the problem, we need to prevent one of the threads from starting to adjust the value of MyThread.counter when the other hasn't completed this step yet. As in the previous section, we can do this by securing the MyThread.counter increment line as a critical section with a lock object.

To do this, we need to modify the MyThread class as follows:

```python
class MyThread(threading.Thread):
    lock = threading.Lock()
    counter = 0
    def run(self):
        for i in range(200000):
            with MyThread.lock:
                MyThread.counter += 1
```

After this adjustment, our program returns the expected value of 400000 in each run.

Table 31.6 shows in detail how the critical section fixes the problem.

Time Slice	Thread A	Thread B
1	Reaches the with block. Locks the lock object with acquire via with. Reads value from MyThread.counter—for example, 2.	*sleeps*
Time Slice of A Ends and B Is Activated		
2	*sleeps*	Reaches the with block. The acquire method is called by with, while the lock object has already been locked. For this reason, B is put to sleep.

Table 31.6 Solving the MyThread.counter Problem with a Lock Object

Time Slice	Thread A	Thread B
B Was Put to Sleep by acquire and A Continues to Be Executed		
3	Increments the value by 1. A new instance with the value 3 now exists in the memory.	*sleeps*
	Binds the new instance to the MyThread.counter reference. Thus MyThread.counter refers to the value 3.	
	The lock object is released via release after leaving the with block.	
Time Slice of A Ends and B Is Activated		
4	*sleeps*	The lock object is automatically locked because in B the acquire method was called via with.
		Reads value from MyThread.counter—in this case, 3.
		Increments the value by 1. A new instance with the value 4 now exists in the memory.
		Binds the new instance to the MyThread.counter reference. Thus MyThread.counter refers to the value 4.
		The lock object is released via release after leaving the with block.

Table 31.6 Solving the MyThread.counter Problem with a Lock Object (Cont.)

You should make sure in your own programs that you protect all sections where problems can occur due to accesses from multiple threads by critical sections.

Inadequately secured programs with multiple threads may contain errors that are difficult to reproduce and localize. Thus, one challenge in parallel programming is to work around such problems.

Risks of Critical Sections: Deadlocks

If you use multiple lock objects, the program may get into a state that does not permit any thread to continue to run because two locked threads are waiting for each other. This is referred to as a *deadlock*.

The control flow described in Table 31.7 shows how a deadlock can occur. Here, A and B are two threads and M and L are two lock objects.

Time Slice	Thread A	Thread B
1	Locks the lock object L via L.acquire.	*sleeps*
Time Slice of A Ends and B Is Activated		
2	*sleeps*	Lock object M is locked via M.acquire.
Time Slice of B Ends and A Is Activated		
3	M.acquire is called. Since M is already locked, A is put to sleep.	*sleeps*
A Was Put to Sleep by M.acquire and B Continues to Be Executed.		
4	*sleeps*	Calls L.acquire, whereupon B is put to sleep as L is already locked.
A Was Locked by M.acquire and B by L.acquire		
5	*sleeps*	*sleeps*

Table 31.7 Sample Scenario of a Deadlock

At the end of this scenario, both threads are in the sleep state, waiting for a lock object to be released. But because the other thread has locked the lock object whose release is being waited for, the threads are never woken up. The program is therefore stuck in this deadlock state.

To conclude this section, we'll now provide a brief insight into the use of the multiprocessing module.

31.4.2   Processes in Python: multiprocessing

The multiprocessing module provides an object-oriented interface for managing multiple processes. The handling of multiprocessing is closely based on that of the threading module from Section 31.4.1, with the multiprocessing.Process class being the counterpart to the threading.Thread class.

As an example, we'll again consider the interactive prime number test, using processes for parallelization instead of threads:

```python
import multiprocessing

class PrimeNumberProcess(multiprocessing.Process):
    def __init__(self, number, in_out_lock):
        super().__init__()
        self.number = number
        self.in_out_lock = in_out_lock
```

```
def run(self):
    i = 2
    while i*i <= self.number:
        if self.number % i == 0:
            with self.in_out_lock:
                print(f"{self.number} ist no prime "
                      f"as {self.number} = {i} * {self.number // i}")
            return
        i += 1
    with self.in_out_lock:
        print(f"{self.number} is prime")

if __name__ == "__main__":
    my_processes = []
    in_out_lock = multiprocessing.Lock()
    user_input = input("> ")
    while user_input != "e":
        try:
            process = PrimeNumberProcess(int(user_input), in_out_lock)
            my_processes.append(process)
            process.start()
        except ValueError:
            with in_out_lock:
                print("Wrong input!")

        with in_out_lock:
            user_input = input("> ")
    for p in my_processes:
        p.join()
```

Compared to the thread version of the program, there are two main differences.

First, we need to make sure that any newly started process can import the file without causing the code for creating subprocesses to be run again. For this purpose, we use the __name__ variable to check whether the Python program has been imported or executed directly by the interpreter. If the module has been imported, the code in the if block won't be executed.[14]

Second, we can no longer use shared variables to exchange data between processes. This also applies to the lock object, which we've implemented in the thread version as a class attribute of the PrimeNumberThread class. We can work around the problem by creating a lock object in the main process, which we then pass as an additional param-

---

14 We already discussed this problem and solved it in the same way in Section 31.3 about
    concurrent.futures.

eter to the subprocesses. Python organizes the communication between processes to make locks work although the memory segments of the processes are separated.

31.5   Cooperative Multitasking

Cooperative multitasking represents a third way of parallel programming in Python, in addition to the `concurrent.futures` and `threading` or `multiprocessing` interfaces described so far. The central idea here is that functions working in parallel cooperate with each other.

The term *cooperation* is used here to express that cooperative functions, so-called *coroutines*, independently signal appropriate times at which they may be interrupted. This is especially the case when the function itself has to wait for an external event, such as a file access.

An instance that's running on a higher level and referred to as an *event loop* detects when a coroutine signals that it's waiting for an external event and can also detect when that event has arrived. This way, the event loop can use the wait time of a coroutine to let a concurrent coroutine compute. This form of cooperative multitasking can enable a very efficient concurrent execution of appropriate functions.

For the event loop to detect and associate the arrival of an external signal a paused coroutine is waiting for, special libraries for input/output operations are required. The standard library includes the `asyncio` module providing asynchronous implementations of common input and output tasks. In addition, the number of asynchronous libraries from third-party providers is growing steadily.

In the following sections, we'll first describe how cooperative functions can be defined and orchestrated in the context of an event loop. To do this, let's first look at a very simple example. Later, we'll deal with the options provided by the `asyncio` module and implement a first real sample application together. Toward the end of the section, we'll describe two additional fields of cooperative multitasking in greater detail: asynchronous comprehensions and asynchronous generators.

31

> **Note**
>
> The concept of cooperative multitasking was introduced in Python 3.7, making it a comparatively new language feature.

31.5.1   Cooperative Functions: Coroutines

The term *coroutine* refers to a function that signals when it's waiting for an external event, thus enabling its execution in the context of cooperative multitasking.

In the following sections, we'll define the sleep_print coroutine as a first example. Its task is to print text on the screen, then to go to sleep for a defined time, and finally print text again after waking up. The configured number of seconds n is always output in addition and also returned, so that screen outputs and return values can be attributed to a coroutine call at any time:

```python
import asyncio
async def sleep_print(n):
    print(f"I'll wait for {n} seconds ...")
    await asyncio.sleep(n)
    print(f"... I'm back (after {n} seconds)!")
    return c
```

The async keyword is placed before the already known def keyword, which introduces a function definition. This way, we specify that the following function definition is a coroutine.

The only other change compared to a conventional function definition is the use of the await keyword when calling the sleep coroutine. This keyword signals that the sleep_ print coroutine is waiting at this point for an external event—namely, the elapse of n seconds. This allows the control flow to be returned to the event loop, and the time of n seconds is available for concurrent coroutines.

To inform the event loop about the elapse of the configured time and to wake up the paused coroutine, we don't use the conventional sleep function of the time module, but its asynchronous counterpart from the asyncio module.

31.5.2   Awaitable Objects

Using the await keyword, a Python program can wait for the execution of a so-called *awaitable object*. A coroutine is an example of such an awaitable object:

```python
>>> async def coroutine():
...     await asyncio.sleep(1)
...
>>> coroutine
<function coroutine at 0x7fbf21a270e0>
>>> coroutine()
<coroutine object coroutine at 0x7fbf21286c20>
```

In the example, we define a short form of the sleep_print coroutine named coroutine. As we can easily verify in the interactive mode, this is a function object, just as if we hadn't used async and await. Unlike a conventional function, however, the coroutine isn't executed immediately by a call, but an awaitable `coroutine` object gets created. This object won't be executed until waited for using the `await` keyword.

An analogous behavior can be observed using the `sleep` routine from the `asyncio` module:

```
>>> asyncio.sleep
<function sleep at 0x7fbf212d8050>
>>> asyncio.sleep(1)
<coroutine object sleep at 0x7fbf219b7cb0>
```

A simple way to execute coroutines directly is provided by the `run` function from the `asyncio` module. This function initiates an event loop and starts the coroutine passed to it in this context. Note that concurrency isn't yet obtained in this simple way:

```
>>> asyncio.run(coroutine())
```

31.5.3 The Cooperation of Coroutines: Tasks

In the following sections, we'll use our first example centered on the `sleep_print` coroutine and combine several calls of `sleep_print` in a parent `program` coroutine:

```
import asyncio
async def sleep_print(n):
    print(f"I'll wait for {n} seconds ...")
    await asyncio.sleep(n)
    print(f"... I'm back (after {n} seconds)!")
    return n

async def program1():
    await sleep_print(5)
    await sleep_print(2)
    await sleep_print(1)
```

The `program1` coroutine does nothing other than wait for the execution of three differently parameterized `sleep_print` calls via `await`. The `program1` coroutine can be executed via the `run` function of the `asyncio` module in the context of an event loop:

```
asyncio.run(program1())
```

Among other things, the `sleep_print` coroutine outputs the number of seconds it had to wait before the screen outputs appear. From this information, we can see that the three calls of `sleep_print` were not executed in parallel:

```
I'll wait for 5 seconds ...
... I'm back (after 5 seconds)!
```

31

```
I'll wait for 2 seconds ...
... I'm back (after 2 seconds)!
I'll wait for 1 seconds ...
... I'm back (after 1 seconds)!
```

This is because a coroutine is processed sequentially. The await keyword signals the event loop that the coroutine may be interrupted at this point because it's waiting for an awaitable object. This means that the event loop may let other coroutines that were started concurrently compute at this point. However, the execution within a coroutine remains sequential even if it waits using await. So in the example, we first wait for the result of sleep_print(5), then for the result of sleep_print(2), and then for the result of sleep_print(1). This corresponds to a sequential execution of the three coroutines, but in the context of cooperative multitasking it would allow a concurrent coroutine to use the waiting phases for itself.

To execute coroutines concurrently, we need to encapsulate them in a *task*.[15] Such a task can be created using the create_task function of the asyncio module:

```python
async def program2():
    task1 = asyncio.create_task(sleep_print(5))
    task2 = asyncio.create_task(sleep_print(2))
    task3 = asyncio.create_task(sleep_print(1))
    await task1
    await task2
    await task3
```

First, the create_task function is used to create the task1, task2, and task3 tasks, which are themselves awaitable objects. This way, the three tasks are automatically registered for pending execution. The event loop decides when the execution takes place. In the next step, within the program2 coroutine, we'll use the await keyword to wait for the execution of the three tasks and thus the three calls of the sleep_print coroutine.

The resulting screen output shows that the calls were executed concurrently:

```
I'll wait for 5 seconds ...
I'll wait for 2 seconds ...
I'll wait for 1 seconds ...
... I'm back (after 1 seconds)!
... I'm back (after 2 seconds)!
... I'm back (after 5 seconds)!
```

---

15 Based on its concept, a *task* can be compared to a Future object in the context of concurrent.futures ().

> **Note**
>
> After a task is created via create_task, it gets registered for execution and will be executed regardless of whether and where we wait for its result. In rare use cases, it may make sense to create tasks and never wait for their result. Such an approach is referred to as *fire and forget*.
>
> It's important to note that a task that is not being waited on is terminated as soon as the execution of the calling coroutine has been completed.

Via the task object, which is returned when calling create_task, we gain access to the running task and can intervene in its execution or obtain information about the task after its execution.

task.cancel()

The cancel method allows you to cancel the execution of a running task. Within a running coroutine, an asyncio.CancelledError exception is raised in this case, which can also be caught and handled there to maintain a consistent state even in case of a cancellation.

> **Note**
>
> A coroutine can catch and ignore the asyncio.CancelledError exception. This effectively prevents a task from being aborted. This is possible, but should only be implemented in exceptional cases, if at all.

task.cancelled()

The cancelled method returns True if the task was cancelled via the cancel method and the running coroutine hasn't prevented this cancellation.

task.done()

The done method returns True if the execution of the task has finished and False otherwise. This may have been done via a cancellation using the cancel method. Alternative scenarios are the complete and error-free execution of the coroutine or the occurrence of an unhandled exception.

task.result()

The result method returns the return value of the coroutine running in the task. If the coroutine was terminated due to an unhandled exception, this exception is also raised by the result method.

31

31.5.4 A Cooperative Web Crawler

After shedding light on the concept of cooperative multitasking and looking at the definition of coroutines and their semantics based on a simple example, we now want to tackle a real-world use case of cooperative multitasking in this section.

Our goal is to write a simple web crawler. A *web crawler* is a program that autonomously browses through the internet via links and can discover and process web pages in this way. The computational effort required to process a web page is typically small; for example, it consists only of identifying links which is insignificant compared to the time a web crawler must wait for a response from the requested servers. This makes the example ideal for cooperative multitasking.

> **Note**
>
> The web crawler developed in this section serves as an example of cooperative multitasking in Python. Note that a robust web crawler must detect and adequately handle possible error cases, which we omit here in the interest of simplicity.
>
> For crawling web pages in a real-world use case, you can find comprehensive and easy-to-use third-party solutions such as *Scrapy* (*https://scrapy.org*).

Asynchronous Web Requests and File Accesses

Cooperative multitasking relies on coroutines interacting cooperatively with each other and signaling, for example, that they're waiting for an external input/output (I/O) operation. For this to happen when an external functionality is used, such as downloading a web page or accessing a file, you must use libraries that provide an asynchronous interface.

Because cooperative multitasking is a fairly recent addition to the Python language, the standard library provides only a small set of such asynchronous interfaces, which are bundled in the asyncio module. For the time being, we use third-party modules aiohttp for async HTTP requests and aiofiles for async file accesses. They can be installed via the conda and pip package managers:

```
$ conda install aiohttp aiofiles
$ pip install aiohttp aiofiles
```

A Crawler for Wikipedia Articles

To make the general use case of web crawling a bit more comprehensible for our example, we first want to restrict it to downloading a set of Wikipedia articles.

To do this, we define two coroutines, download and crawl, which can cooperatively download a set of articles using the aiohttp module:

```
import asyncio
import aiohttp
async def crawl(articles):
    async with aiohttp.ClientSession() as session:
        coroutines = [download(session, art) for art in articles]
        return await asyncio.gather(*coroutines)
```

The `crawl` coroutine is supposed to coordinate the download of a set of Wikipedia articles specified via the `articles` parameter. To do this, the `aiohttp` module allows you to first create a common `session` object that's shared across all requests.[16]

To create the session object, we'll use the asynchronous `with` statement (`async with`), which we'll look at in more detail in Section 31.5.6. For now, it's sufficient for us to note that an asynchronous `with` statement works like a regular `with` statement, the only difference being that when the context is entered and exited, coroutines are called respectively, which in turn may signal that they're waiting for an I/O operation.

After that, we'll create calls of the `download` coroutine for each article in `articles`, which we'll then start together with a `gather` call for concurrent execution. The `gather` function starts the coroutines passed to it as concurrent tasks and returns an awaitable object that can be used to wait for the return values of all started coroutines. In the example, we'll wait for all downloads to finish and return the list of individual results.

The `download` coroutine is called from within the `crawl` coroutine to perform the download of a single article. For this purpose, it receives the session object in the context of which the download is to be performed, and the article name, from which the URL can be composed.

```
async def download(session, article_name):
    url = f"https://en.wikipedia.org/wiki/{article_name}"
    async with session.get(url) as response:
        html = await response.text()
        print(f"I have downloaded {article_name}.")
        return html
```

In the context of another asynchronous `with` statement, an HTTP request is sent via the session object's get routine and its response is made available as `response`. Then the content of the server response, which contains the HTML code of the article, can be accessed via the `text` coroutine of the response object.

Once the `download` and `crawl` coroutines are defined, we can feed the `crawl` coroutine with a list of article names—in this case, articles on presidents of the United States—and initiate the cooperative download via `asyncio.run`:

---

16   For example, such a session object manages a pool of open TCP connections that can be reused for new requests. Creating a separate session object for each request is inefficient.

```
articles = [
    "George_Washington",
    "John_Adams",
    "Thomas_Jefferson",
    "James_Madison",
    "James_Monroe",
    "John_Quincy_Adams",
    "Andrew_Jackson",
    "Martin_Van_Buren",
    "William_Henry_Harrison"
]
htmls = asyncio.run(crawl(articles))
for article_name, html in zip(articles, htmls):
    with open(f"downloads/{article_name}.html", "w") as f_html:
        f_html.write(html)
```

Finally, as proof of successful execution, we'll write each article to an HTML file in the local working directory, which we can then view with a browser.[17]

A Wikipedia Crawler with a Queue

The initial approach to implementing a cooperative web crawler described in the previous section started one coroutine per Wikipedia article for its download and in this way was able to cooperatively organize the downloads of a fixed set of articles known in advance. But in a real-world use case for a web crawler, the web pages to be downloaded aren't known in advance as they result from the links found within downloaded web pages.

In this second attempt, we'd like to further approach this real-world use case and develop a cooperative web crawler that uses a queue to constantly feed a fixed number of download coroutines with new articles to be downloaded.

The concept of a *queue* is not limited to the use in cooperative multitasking, but describes a general approach to organizing data and processes. There are a number of *producers* that put data into the queue, and a number of *consumers* that get data from the queue and process it. In this context, the *first in, first out principle* applies: the data in a queue is read in the order in which the individual data items were put into the queue.

Let's first look at the implementation of the download coroutine, which represents the consumer reading article names from the queue and then performing the corresponding download:

---

17 Note that additional aspects of a web page, such as CSS styles and images, aren't downloaded, so the rendering of the local HTML file won't match the rendering of Wikipedia on the web.

```
import asyncio
import aiohttp
async def download(session, i, queue, html_dict):
    while True:
        article_name = await queue.get()
        url = f"https://en.wikipedia.org/wiki/{article_name}"
        async with session.get(url) as response:
            html_dict[article_name] = await response.text()
            print(f"Consumer {i} has downloaded {article_name}.")
        queue.task_done()
```

The consumer is passed a shared session object to perform the downloads in a shared context and an i index to later attribute screen outputs to a consumer. In addition, the queue and a dictionary for the downloaded HTML pages are passed. Note that in contrast to the use of threading, we don't need to protect writing to html_dict in any special way as coroutines can only be interrupted at defined points.

The consumer accesses the next article name in an infinite loop using the get method of the queue. This is a coroutine that, in the case of an empty queue, waits until a producer has put a new element in the queue. This is followed by the previously described download via the get coroutine of the session object and by adding the downloaded article to the result dictionary.

Once an element of the queue has been processed, this is signaled via the task_done method of the queue.

We first implement the producer as an ordinary find_articles function that puts a set of article names into the queue via the put_nowait method:[18]

```
def find_articles(queue):
    articles = [
        "George_Washington",
        "John_Adams",
        # ...
    ]
    for article_name in articles:
        queue.put_nowait(article_name)
```

The put_nowait and get_nowait methods work analogously to the put and get coroutines, the difference being that they don't wait in case of a full or empty queue, respectively.

In the first version of the web crawler, the crawl coroutine only had the task of starting a corresponding download coroutine for each article. In the modified variant with a

---

18 The examples are printed with abbreviated article lists; however, be sure to run them with a larger set of articles to observe the effects of the cooperative downloads.

queue, the queue is first instantiated and filled with presidents via the find_articles producer. After that, three[19] consumers are started, which process the queue item by item. Thus, a total of three downloads can be performed cooperatively at the same time using this approach:

```python
async def crawl():
    queue = asyncio.Queue()
    find_articles(queue)
    html_dict = {}
    async with aiohttp.ClientSession() as s:
        consumers = [asyncio.create_task(download(s, i, queue, html_dict))
                        for i in range(3)]
        await queue.join()
    for c in consumers:
        c.cancel()
    return html_dict
```

The join coroutine of the queue waits for all elements placed in the queue to be processed. Once that's done, we explicitly cancel the consumers, which are now endlessly waiting for new articles, via the cancel method and return the compiled result dictionary.

The example is executed in the same way as our previous approach:

```python
html_dict = asyncio.run(crawl())
for name, html in html_dict.items():
    with open(f"downloads/{name}.html", "w") as f_html:
        f_html.write(html)
```

Based on the screen outputs, you can see how consumers distribute the downloading of items among themselves. In the process, if some downloads take longer than others, it can happen that certain consumers process more items in total than others:

```
Consumer 1 has downloaded John_Adams.
Consumer 0 has downloaded George_Washington.
Consumer 0 has downloaded James_Monroe.
Consumer 1 has downloaded James_Madison.
Consumer 2 has downloaded Thomas_Jefferson.
Consumer 0 has downloaded John_Quincy_Adams.
Consumer 2 has downloaded Martin_Van_Buren.
Consumer 0 has downloaded William_Henry_Harrison.
Consumer 1 has downloaded Andrew_Jackson.
```

---

19 This is a freely selectable parameter.

A Wikipedia Crawler with a Queue and Multiple Producers

In the previous section, we significantly improved the practicality of the web crawler by distributing the articles to be downloaded to a freely configurable number of running download tasks via a queue. However, the behavior of the producer still needs improving because it needs to know all items in the queue before downloading can begin.

In this section, we'll implement another modification of the web crawler, where multiple producers can post items to the queue while other items are already being processed by consumers. To do this, we'll first write two producers—one for presidents and one for vice presidents:

```python
import asyncio
import aiohttp
import random

async def find_articles1(queue):
    articles = [
        "George_Washington",
        "John_Adams",
        # ...
    ]
    for article_name in articles:
        await queue.put(article_name)
        await asyncio.sleep(random.random())

async def find_articles2(queue):
    articles = [
        "Hubert_Humphrey",
        "Spiro_Agnew",
        # ...
    ]
    for article_name in articles:
        await queue.put(article_name)
        await asyncio.sleep(random.random())
```

The find_articles1 and find_articles2 producers iterate their respective (abbreviated) list of article names and put them into the queue using the put coroutine. They then go to sleep for a random period of less than a second before the next article name is placed in the queue. Both producers terminate after all presidents or vice presidents have been put into the queue.

No changes are necessary in the consumer compared to the last version of our web crawler, so we can jump directly to the crawl coroutine. Here, too, the changes are clear:

31

623

```
async def crawl():
    queue = asyncio.Queue(maxsize=3)
    html_dict = {}
    producers = [
        asyncio.create_task(find_articles1(queue)),
        asyncio.create_task(find_articles2(queue))
    ]
    async with aiohttp.ClientSession() as s:
        consumers = [asyncio.create_task(download(s, i, queue, html_dict))
                    for i in range(3)]
        await asyncio.gather(*producers)
        await queue.join()
    for c in consumers:
        c.cancel()
    return html_dict
```

First, for demonstration purposes, we limit the queue to a maximum size of three elements when it's instantiated via the maxsize parameter. This causes occasional waiting periods when calling the put coroutine within the producers. After that, the create_task function starts two tasks for the two producers.

After starting the consumers, we use a gather call to make sure that we'll first wait for the producers to finish before we use join to wait for the queue to be completely processed.

This variant of the web crawler can also be started by calling asyncio.run:

```
html_dict = asyncio.run(crawl())
for name, html in html_dict.items():
    with open(f"downloads/{name}.html", "w") as f_html:
        f_html.write(html)
```

Asynchronous File Access

Now we want to make one last modification to our cooperative web crawler. Up to this point, the aiohttp module was used to enable an asynchronous download of Wikipedia articles, which were then collected in a data structure and written to corresponding files in the working directory using conventional methods after the crawling was completed.

Now we want to change the program so that the writing of the result files also runs through an asynchronous interface, so that each result file can still be written by the consumer immediately after the download. For this purpose, we can use the third-party aiofiles module, which allows us to formulate a new consumer:

```python
import aiohttp
import aiofiles
async def download(session, i, queue):
    while True:
        article = await queue.get()
        url = f"https://en.wikipedia.org/wiki/{article}"
        async with session.get(url) as response:
            async with aiofiles.open(f"downloads/{article}.html", "w") as f:
                await f.write(await response.text())
                print(f"Consumer {i} has downloaded {article}.")
        queue.task_done()
```

The `aiofiles.open` coroutine can be used like the built-in `open` function, the difference being that the `read` and `write` methods of the generated asynchronous file object are coroutines that can be waited for to be executed within the `download` coroutine.

Also note in particular that the `html_dict` dictionary from the previous example is omitted. This change is also reflected in the updated `crawl` coroutine:

```python
async def crawl():
    queue = asyncio.Queue(maxsize=3)
    producers = [
        asyncio.create_task(find_articles1(queue)),
        asyncio.create_task(find_articles2(queue))
    ]
    async with aiohttp.ClientSession() as session:
        consumers = [asyncio.create_task(download(session, i, queue))
                        for i in range(3)]
        await asyncio.gather(*producers)
        await queue.join()
    for c in consumers:
        c.cancel()
```

By having consumers take care of writing the result files themselves, the effort required to run the web crawler is reduced to simply starting the `crawl` coroutine using `asyncio.run`:

```python
asyncio.run(crawl())
```

31.5.5   Blocking Operations in Coroutines

So far, we've agreed to always call only coroutines within coroutines—for example, within producers and consumers in the web crawler example—to ensure permanent cooperation of concurrent control flows.

If it is possible to implement an asynchronous program in this way, it should be done. Unfortunately, however, we can't always guarantee this and may be forced to execute blocking code within a coroutine for various reasons—for example:

- Longer CPU-bound calculations must be performed.
- An I/O operation must be performed for which an asynchronous interface such as the aiohttp or aiofiles module isn't available or can't be used.
- An existing implementation of the program must be called, one that hadn't been developed in the sense of cooperative multitasking.

Simply executing the blocking code within a coroutine will cause the entire event loop to block for the time of the blocking call. For this reason, the asyncio module provides the option to execute blocking code concurrently in a thread or process and wait for the result within a coroutine.

> **Note**
>
> Note that if blocking code is executed within a thread or process, you may need to take care of the thread safety of the data being processed.

As an example, let's take the web crawler developed in Section 31.5.4 and extend it with a fictitious processing function called process that allows for preprocessing the downloaded HTML code before it's stored in a result file. We won't implement real preprocessing but will simulate it via a call of the blocking time.sleep function and thus put the function to sleep so that it blocks for a random time of less than one second:

```python
import time
import random
def process(html):
    time.sleep(random.random())
    return html
```

Within the download coroutine, a loop reference to the running event loop can first be obtained via the get_event_loop function. This is needed to execute a blocking function call—in our case, process—in a separate thread using the run_in_executor coroutine of the event loop and wait for the result:

```python
async def download(session, i, queue):
    loop = asyncio.get_event_loop()
    while True:
        article = await queue.get()
        url = f"https://en.wikipedia.org/wiki/{article}"
        async with session.get(url) as response:
            html = await response.text()
            html = await loop.run_in_executor(None, process, html)
```

```
        async with aiofiles.open(f"downloads/{article}.html", "w") as f:
            await f.write(html)
            print(f"Consumer {i} has downloaded {article}.")
    queue.task_done()
```

The run_in_executor function can be passed a ThreadPoolExecutor or ProcessPoolExecutor instance (Section 31.3) via the first parameter in order to control whether the blocking function call should be executed in a thread or process. In the case of None, the default event loop behavior, ThreadPoolExecutor, is used.

Nothing has changed in the producers, the crawl coroutine, and the execution of the example via the run function:

```
asyncio.run(crawl())
```

31.5.6 Other Asynchronous Language Features

In the context of the cooperative web crawler developed step by step in Section 31.5.4, we already addressed the asynchronous with statement as a language extension for cooperative multitasking. In addition, you know the async and await keywords for defining coroutines and waiting for the execution of a coroutine, respectively.

In this section, we'd like to first catch up on the discussion of the asynchronous with statement and then discuss other language extensions that have been implemented with respect to cooperative multitasking.

Asynchronous with Contexts: async with

You already learned about the async with asynchronous with statement in Section 31.5.4. Basically, this statement behaves like the conventional with statement you know from Chapter 22, Section 22.1.

The conventional with statement ensures that an object acting as a context manager can be safely entered and exited:

```
with open("test.txt", "w") as f:
    f.write("Test")
```

In the example, the with statement ensures that the *test.txt* file is opened and closed again after complete execution of the statement body, especially even if exceptions occur. Internally, the with statement calls the __enter__ and __exit__ methods of the context manager, which implements its specific behavior for entering and exiting the context within these methods.

Because entering and exiting a context may require I/O operations, such as opening or closing files, suitable places to interrupt the coroutine may arise there. When entering and exiting an asynchronous context manager, the asynchronous with statement calls the `__aenter__` and `__aexit__` coroutines, which implement the specific behavior of the context manager in terms of cooperative multitasking:

```
async with aiofiles.open("test.txt", "w") as f:
    f.write("Test")
```

Using asynchronous `with` statements outside of coroutines isn't allowed.

Asynchronous Generators and Iterators: async for

So far, we've discussed coroutines that returned a result using a conventional `return` statement. In fact, coroutines may also contain the likewise conventional `yield` statement and thus become asynchronous generators. For more information on generators in the conventional sense, see Chapter 21, Section 21.1.

In the following example, we'll define an `async_range` asynchronous generator that iterates the numbers from 0 to n and simulates waiting for an I/O operation in each iteration step via a call of `asyncio.sleep`:

```
import asyncio
import random
async def async_range(n):
    for i in range(n):
        await asyncio.sleep(random.random())
        yield i
```

Such an asynchronous generator is a special case of an asynchronous iterator. For traversing an asynchronous iterator, Python supports the asynchronous `for` loop, a special loop construct that may only be used within coroutines:

```
async def coroutine(name, n):
    async for i in async_range(n):
        print(f"Current element of {name}: {i}")
```

> **Note**
> An asynchronous generator is the simplest way to implement an asynchronous iterator. An *asynchronous iterator* is basically an object that provides the `__aiter__` and `__anext__` coroutines that are implicitly used by the asynchronous `for` loop and implicitly provided via the definition of an asynchronous generator.

In the application, `for` and `async for` do not differ. The difference is that `async for` expects an asynchronous iterator and waits for the `__anext__` coroutine of the asynchronous iterator in each iteration step. Within this waiting time, coroutines running concurrently can run in the sense of cooperative multitasking.

We can directly observe the flow of the asynchronous iteration if we start two parallel executions of the `coroutine` coroutine and follow the individual iteration steps via the screen outputs:

```
async def main():
    await asyncio.gather(
        coroutine("Iterator 1", 10),
        coroutine("Iterator 2", 10)
    )
```

Starting the `main` coroutine is possible via `asyncio.run`:

```
asyncio.run(main())
```

It turns out that both coroutines are cooperatively executed concurrently. If we hadn't used an asynchronous `for` loop within `coroutine`, but a conventional `for` loop in combination with the built-in `range` function, concurrent execution wouldn't have been possible as the control flow between the iteration steps would never have been returned to the event loop.

> **Note**
>
> Analogous to the asynchronous `for` loop, there exist *asynchronous comprehensions*, the use of which doesn't differ from that of conventional comprehensions (see Chapter 12, Section 12.3.7 and Chapter 13, Section 13.1.6 and Section 13.2.1):
>
> ```
> lst = [i async for i in async_range(n)]
> ```

31.6   Conclusion: Which Interface Is the Right One?

In this chapter, you learned about the `concurrent.futures`, `threading`, `multiprocessing`, and `asyncio` modules that enable parallel programming in Python, providing interfaces at different levels of abstraction and with different approaches. In practice, the question arises as to which of the modules is most suitable for which use cases. In this section, we'd like to give you some basic recommendations to help you with this question.

31.6.1   Is Cooperative Multitasking an Option?

First you should decide if cooperative multitasking with `asyncio` is a viable option. This is usually the case when you develop a server or client that needs to perform many I/O-intensive operations in parallel. Because neither threads nor processes are created, cooperative multitasking is a very lightweight solution in these cases.

31

Note, however, that external libraries and also existing program code often don't support cooperative multitasking. In addition, cooperative multitasking in Python is a comparatively recent development, so support for older Python versions, if needed, may be difficult. The choice of cooperative multitasking is often a decision that strongly affects the fundamental design of a program.

31.6.2   Abstraction or Flexibility?

If you decide to use threads or processes, you should usually prefer the abstract concurrent.futures interface. This interface is considered to be a modern solution for parallel programming in Python and provides convenient solutions to parallel function execution.

The flexibility provided by threading and multiprocessing is rarely actually needed.

31.6.3   Threads or Processes?

Regardless of whether you choose the abstract or flexible interface, you have the choice of using threads or processes:

- You should opt for threads (via concurrent.futures or threading) if you're concerned with parallel execution of I/O-bound operations, such as handling user interactions during a blocking computation. Threads also allow for easy access to shared data structures.[20]

- You should opt for processes (via concurrent.futures or multiprocessing) if you're concerned with the true parallel execution of CPU-bound operations. In Python,[21] only processes allow for an accelerated execution of computations by using multiple CPU cores in parallel.

---

20 However, note the protection of write accesses, as described in Section 31.4.1.
21 To put it more precisely: in the reference interpreter, CPython.

Chapter 32
Data Storage

In the following sections, we'll look at the permanent storage of data in a wide variety of formats. This includes compressed archives, XML files, and databases, among others.

32.1 XML

The xml module of the standard library allows you to read and write *Extensible Markup Language (XML)* files. XML is a standardized description language that makes it possible to store complex, hierarchically structured data in a readable text format. XML can therefore be used very well for exchanging or storing data. Especially in the world of the internet, you can find many description languages based on XML, such as XHTML, RSS, MathML, and SVG.

So let's take a brief look at XML. The following simple XML file enables us to permanently store the contents of a Python dictionary:

```
<?xml version="1.0" encoding="UTF-8"?>
<dictionary>
    <entry>
        <key>Hello</key>
        <value>0</value>
    </entry>
    <entry>
        <key>world</key>
        <value>1</value>
    </entry>
</dictionary>
```

The first line of the file is the *XML declaration*. This optional specification identifies the XML version used and the encoding in which the file was saved. By specifying the encoding, in this case UTF-8, special characters such as German umlauts also can be processed correctly. For more information on encodings, see Chapter 12, Section 12.5.4 on strings.

In addition to the XML declaration, an XML document consists of *elements* that are defined using *tags*. Similar to a bracket, a tag has an opening and a closing variant. It thus represents a kind of group that can contain other tags. Each tag has a name, the *tag name*. To open a tag, this tag name is written in angle brackets. A closing tag consists of the tag name also written in angle brackets, with a slash added before the tag name. The following example shows an opening tag immediately followed by the corresponding closing tag:

```
<value></value>
```

Between an opening tag and the corresponding closing tag there can be text as well as other tags. In this way, a hierarchical structure can be created that is capable of representing even complex data records.

In addition, you can also specify *attributes* for a tag. Let's extend the previous example so that the data types of the keys and values of the dictionary are stored as attributes of the respective key or value tag:

```
<?xml version="1.0" encoding="UTF-8"?>
<dictionary>
    <entry>
        <key type="str">Hello</key>
        <value type="int">0</value>
    </entry>
    <entry>
        <key type="str">world</key>
        <value type="int">1</value>
    </entry>
</dictionary>
```

An *attribute* represents a key-value pair. In the example, each key and value tag is given a type attribute that can be used to specify the data type of the key or value. You must always enclose the value of an XML attribute in quotation marks.

> **Note**
>
> *Bodiless tags* are a special type of XML tags:
>
> ```
> <tag attr="value" />
> ```
>
> A bodiless tag is an opening and closing tag at the same time and consequently may only have attributes. Such a tag can't contain any text or other tags. An XML parser treats a bodiless tag as if `<tag attr="value"></tag>` were included in the XML file.

Like most other programming languages or XML libraries, Python provides various parsers for reading XML files. The term *parser* is not limited to XML, but generally refers to a program that performs a syntax analysis of certain data of a special format.

We can basically distinguish between two approaches to reading XML documents:

1. The document is read as a whole and processed into a class structure representing the tree hierarchy of the document. Content can't be processed until after the document has been completely read. This method enables random data access.

2. The document is read sequentially. Content can already be processed when the document hasn't been completely read yet. In addition, the document doesn't need to be fully loaded into the memory at any time.

For the first approach, the xml module provides the dom and ElementTree parsers. While dom implements the standardized *Document Object Model* (*DOM*) , which is available in equivalent form for many other programming languages, ElementTree provides an interface to XML files tailored to Python. For this reason, we'll only deal with ElementTree at this point.

For the second, sequential approach to an XML document, you can use the sax module of the xml package. You'll learn about this module in Section 32.1.2.

32.1.1 ElementTree

The xml.etree.ElementTree module reads an XML file in its entirety and processes the contained data into a tree structure. Thus, it allows you to access and modify individual elements of the XML file. Tags are represented in the resulting *element tree* by classes called *nodes*. The methods and attributes of these node classes enable you to read or modify the contained information.

This approach is especially interesting when random access to the XML data is required. *Random access* refers to a *selective access* to different, independent parts of the data record. The opposite of random access is sequential reading of the XML file. This approach is taken with the *Simple API for XML* (*SAX*) parser, described in Section 32.1.2.

Because the file is always read in its entirety to create the element tree, using Element Tree for large files is memory-intensive. In contrast, the competing SAX model sequentially reads small parts of the XML data and makes them immediately available for further processing. This approach requires less memory and allows parts of the stored data to already be used—for example, displayed—even when the file itself hasn't been fully read yet. However, random access to and manipulation of the XML data isn't possible with SAX.

The Element Tree

Let's now look at how the XML data is processed when we use ElementTree. To do this, we should look again at the previous example of an XML file:

```xml
<?xml version="1.0" encoding="UTF-8"?>
<dictionary>
    <entry>
        <key type="str">Hello</key>
        <value type="int">0</value>
    </entry>
    <entry>
        <key type="str">world</key>
        <value type="int">1</value>
    </entry>
</dictionary>
```

The `ElementTree` parser is used to process the XML data into a *tree*. A tree consists of *nodes* or *elements*, which are represented by instances of the class `Element`. Each of these node classes contains different references to neighboring nodes—namely:

- Its *parent*—the node directly above this node in the tree
- Its *children*—all nodes that are directly below this node in the tree
- Its *siblings*—all nodes that are directly adjacent to this node in the tree and have the same parent

Thus, each node of the tree contains references to all related surrounding nodes. In this way, the tree can be completely traversed and processed. The tree structure generated from the preceding example looks as shown in Figure 32.1.

The *root* of the element tree is an instance of the `ElementTree` class, which contains a hierarchy of `Element` instances, each with a tag name. Also, `Element` instances can have attributes and contain text.

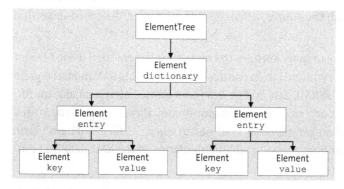

Figure 32.1 Generated Element Tree

Reading an XML File

At this point, we'll show you how you can use `ElementTree` on the basis of a simple example. To do this, let's recall again our sample file, the purpose of which was to represent the contents of a Python dictionary:

```
<?xml version="1.0" encoding="UTF-8"?>
<dictionary>
    <entry>
        <key type="str">Hello</key>
        <value type="int">0</value>
    </entry>
</dictionary>
```

The file consists of a top-level tag called dictionary, under which multiple entry tags may occur. Each entry tag contains two child tags named key and value, which together each represent a key-value pair of the dictionary. The data type of the key or the value is defined by the type attribute, which may occur with the key and value tags.

A program that uses ElementTree to load an XML file of this format looks as follows:

```
import xml.etree.ElementTree as ElementTree
types = {
    "int" : int,
    "str" : str
    }
def read_element(element):
    type = element.get("type", "str")
    try:
        return types[type](element.text)
    except KeyError:
        return element.text
def load_dict(filename):
    d = {}
    tree = ElementTree.parse(filename)
    tag_dict = tree.getroot()
    for entry in tag_dict:
        tag_key = entry.find("key")
        tag_value = entry.find("value")
        d[read_element(tag_key)] = read_element(tag_value)
    return d
```

First, the read_element function is implemented, which reads the type attribute from the Element instance of a key or value tag and converts the text enclosed by the respective tag to the data type specified by type. The content of the tag is then returned as an instance of the matching data type.

The main function load_dict of the sample program is passed the filename of an XML file and is supposed to process the data contained therein to a Python dictionary. To do this, the XML file is first prepared into a tree using the parse function of the ElementTree module. This function can be passed both a file name or an opened file object. After that, the `tag_dict` reference is assigned the root element of the tree to continue operating on it.

The following loop iterates over all child elements of the root element—that is, over all `entry` tags. In each iteration step, the first child elements with the `key` and `value` tag names are searched for and assigned to the `tag_key` and `tag_value` references. At the end of the loop, the `Element` instances of the respective `key` or `value` tags are passed through the `read_text` function, which converts the text contained in the tag body to an instance of the correct data type. The resulting instances are added to the result dictionary `d` as keys or values. Finally, the generated dictionary `d` is returned.

The dictionary read with `load_dict` from the XML file specified at the beginning looks like this:

```
>>> load_dict("dict.xml")
{'Hello': 0}
```

> **Note**
>
> Instead of reading the XML data from a file, the data can also be read from a string into an element tree using the `fromstring` method:
>
> ```
> >>> data = "<tag attr='value'/>"
> >>> ElementTree.fromstring(data)
> <Element 'tag' at 0x7f4762a31548>
> ```
>
> Note that in this case an `Element` instance is returned, not an `ElementTree` instance.

Writing an XML File

In the previous section, we described how you can read an XML file. Of course, the reverse problem must also be taken care of: data created in a program should be exported in an XML format.

To do this, an element tree must first be created. This can be done by reading a file or string as described previously. Alternatively, an element tree can also be created element by element:

```
>>> dictionary = ElementTree.Element("dictionary")
>>> entry = ElementTree.SubElement(dictionary, "entry")
>>> key = ElementTree.SubElement(entry, "key", {"type":"str"})
>>> key.text = "Hello"
>>> value = ElementTree.SubElement(entry, "value", {"type":"int"})
>>> value.text = "0"
```

First, an Element instance is created with the dictionary tag name, which acts as the root of the tree. The SubElement function then allows you to insert elements into the tree. For this purpose, the required parent element and the tag name must be passed. Optionally, a dictionary with attribute-value pairs can be passed.

Once an element tree has been constructed, the tostring function can be used. This function writes an Element instance with all its subelements in XML format into a string and returns it:

```
>>> ElementTree.tostring(dictionary)
b'<dictionary><entry><key type="str">Hello</key><value type="int">0</value></
entry></dictionary>'
```

Instead of exporting the data as a string, it also can be written directly to a file. For this purpose, you can use the write method, which can be passed a file name as well as an opened file object. In this case, however, an ElementTree instance must be created up front:

```
>>> et = ElementTree.ElementTree(dictionary)
>>> et.write("file.xml")
```

The optional second parameters of the tostring and write methods can be used to specify an encoding for writing.

Attributes of the Element Class

In the previous section, the text attribute of the created Element instances was accessed to specify the text they contain. There's a total of four of these attributes, which are briefly explained in Table 32.1.

Attribute	Description
attrib	References a dictionary that contains all XML attributes of the element as key-value pairs.
tag	References the tag name of the element.
tail	References the text in the XML file between the closing tag of the element and the next opening or closing tag.
text	References the text that's in the XML file between the opening tag of the element and the next opening or closing tag.

Table 32.1 Attributes of the Element Class

Each of these attributes can be both read and written.

Writing and Reading XML Attributes

The Element class defines the get and set methods to access its XML attributes:[1]

```
>>> value.get("type")
'int'
>>> value.set("type", "str")
>>> value.get("type")
'str'
```

The get method can be passed an optional default value that will be returned if the element doesn't have an attribute of the requested name.

Traversing an Element Tree

Basically, the Element class inherits all the properties of a list. So it's in particular possible to access child elements via an index. For this reason, the children of an Element instance can be iterated using a for loop:

```
>>> for e in entry:
...     print(e.tag)
...
key
value
```

Each element of an element tree also provides the iter method, which returns an iterator over all subordinate elements in the hierarchy, including the element on which the method is called. In this way, the element tree created in the previous sections also can be conveniently traversed:

```
>>> list(dictionary.iter())
[<Element 'dictionary' at 0x7f4762a31638>,
<Element 'entry' at 0x7f476187e278>,
<Element 'key' at 0x7f476187e188>,
<Element 'value' at 0x7f4762a314f8>]
```

The optional tag parameter can be used to restrict the iterator to elements with a specific tag name:

```
>>> list(dictionary.iter("value"))
[<Element 'value' at 0x7f4762a314f8>]
```

If an ElementTree instance is to be traversed, this can be done using the root element, which is accessible via the getroot method:

---

1 You shouldn't confuse this with the attributes of the Element class itself.

```
>>> et = ElementTree.ElementTree(dictionary)
>>> list(et.getroot().iter("value"))
[<Element 'value' at 0x7f4762a314f8>]
```

Finding Elements in the Tree Element

The Element class provides the find, findall, and findtext methods to search child elements according to specific criteria. The search criteria are defined by a so-called *path*. For this purpose, let's look at the following XML file:

```
<A>
    <B>
        <D>Hello</D>
    </B>
    <C>
        <E>
            <F>world</F>
        </E>
    </C>
</A>
```

We'll load this XML file into an ElementTree instance and then perform some search operations on element A:

```
>>> et = ElementTree.parse("test.xml")
>>> e = et.getroot()
```

First, we'll search for any tag name using the wildcard character * and the find method. The first matching element that's returned is element B:

```
>>> e.find("*")
<Element 'B' at 0x7f15ce584f10>
```

The find method searches only the direct children of the element for which it's called. Thus, a search for the tag name E leads to no result:

```
>>> e.find("E")
>>>
```

To search for elements that are located deeper in the XML hierarchy, we must pass a path describing the elements to search for, which also may contain wildcards:

```
>>> e.find("C/*/F")
<Element 'F' at 0x7f15ce58a050>
```

The findall and findtext methods work similarly to find, except that findall returns a list of all matching Element instances and findtext returns the text contained in the matching Element instance.

32

Inserting and Removing Elements

As previously described, an `Element` instance can be regarded as a list of its children, and it even inherits the functionality of a list. In particular, this concerns the possibility to extend it. Thus, child elements can be added to or removed from an `Element` instance using the `append`, `extent`, `remove`, and `clear` methods:

```
>>> x = ElementTree.Element("x")
>>> x.append(ElementTree.Element("y"))
>>> x.append(ElementTree.Element("z"))
>>> ElementTree.tostring(x)
b'<x><y /><z /></x>'
```

32.1.2   Simple API for XML

Unlike `ElementTree`, *SAX* doesn't create a complete representation of the XML file in the memory. It reads the file continuously and, by calling appropriate callback functions, notifies the programmer that, for example, an opening or closing tag has been read. This approach has one advantage: when loading very large XML files, parts that have already been read can be processed further, even though the file hasn't yet been read in its entirety.

But there are some drawbacks associated with the use of SAX. For example, in contrast to `ElementTree`, random access to individual elements of the XML data isn't possible. In addition, SAX doesn't provide any convenient way to modify or resave the XML data.

The reading of an XML file by a SAX parser—in SAX terminology, also referred to as a *reader*—is *event-driven*. This means that when creating the reader, the programmer must set up various *callback functions* and associate them with a specific *event*. If the event occurs when the XML file is read by the reader, the associated callback function is called and the code that the programmer intended for this purpose is executed. For example, an event can be the finding of an opening tag.

Thus, the SAX reader only provides the infrastructure for reading the XML file. The programmer alone decides whether and in what form the data is processed.

> **Note**
>
> The HTML description language for web pages is largely based on XML, but it provides a somewhat greater syntactic freedom.[2] For this reason, not every HTML document can be read with every XML parser.
>
> Especially for parsing HTML documents, the `html.parser` module is available in the standard library. The `HTMLParser` class contained there implements a SAX parser for HTML documents.

---

2 The newer XHTML standard, on the other hand, complies with the stricter XML rules.

Example

We now want to demonstrate the use of SAX with a simple example. For this purpose, we'll use the already known scenario: a Python dictionary has been saved in an XML file and is to be read by the program and converted back into a dictionary. The data has the following format:

```
<?xml version="1.0" encoding="UTF-8"?>
<dictionary>
    <entry>
        <key type="str">Hello</key>
        <value type="int">0</value>
    </entry>
</dictionary>
```

The following program, which uses a SAX reader, can process this file:

```python
import xml.sax as sax
class DictHandler(sax.handler.ContentHandler):
    types = {
        "int" : int,
        "str" : str
        }
    def __init__(self):
        self.result = {}
        self.key = ""
        self.value = ""
        self.active = None
        self.type = None
    def startElement(self, name, attrs):
        if name == "entry":
            self.key = ""
            self.value = ""
        elif name in ("key", "value"):
            self.active = name
            try:
                self.type = self.types[attrs["type"]]
            except KeyError:
                self.type = str
    def endElement(self, name):
        if name == "entry":
            self.result[self.key] = self.type(self.value)
        elif name in ("key", "value"):
            self.active = None
```

```
def characters(self, content):
    if self.active == "key":
        self.key += content
    elif self.active == "value":
        self.value += content
```

First, we create the `DictHandler` class, where we implement all the relevant callback functions—also referred to as *callback handlers*—as methods. The class must be derived from the `sax.handler.ContentHandler` base class.

One disadvantage of the SAX model is that we have to keep track of the current state after each step, so that the next time one of the callback functions is called, it's clear whether the text was read within the context of a `key` or a `value` tag, for example. For this reason, we create some attributes in the constructor of the class:

- `self.result` for the resulting dictionary
- `self.key` for the content of the currently considered key
- `self.value` for the content of the currently considered value
- `self.active` for the tag name of the tag that was last read
- `self.type` for the data type that's in the `type` attribute of a `key` or `value` tag

First, we implement the `startElement` method, which is called whenever an opening tag is read. The method is passed the tag name and the contained attributes as parameters. In the case of a `key` or `value` tag, `self.active` is modified accordingly and the `type` attribute of the tag is read.

The `endElement` method is called when a closing tag has been read. It's also passed the tag name as a parameter. In the case of a closing `entry` tag, we insert the current key-value pair that consists of `self.key` and `self.value` into the `self.result` dictionary. If a closing `key` or `value` tag is found, the `self.active` attribute is set back to `None` so that no more characters will be processed.

Finally, the `characters` method is called if characters were read that don't belong to a tag. The SAX reader doesn't guarantee that a contiguous text in the XML file will also result in a single call of `characters`. Depending on the name of the active tag, the read characters are appended to `self.key` or `self.value`.

Finally, the main `load_dict` function of the sample program is missing, in which the SAX parser is created and started:

```
def load_dict(filename):
    handler = DictHandler()
    parser = sax.make_parser()
    parser.setContentHandler(handler)
    parser.parse(filename)
    return handler.result
```

In the function body, the DictHandler class is instantiated and a SAX parser is created by the make_parser function of the xml.sax module. Then the parser's setContentHandler method is called to register the DictHandler instance with the included callback handlers. Finally, the parsing process is initiated by calling the parse method.

The dictionary read with load_dict from the XML file specified at the beginning looks like this:

```
>>> load_dict("dict.xml")
{'Hello': 0}
```

The ContentHandler Class

The ContentHandler class serves as the base class for custom SAX parsers and implements all SAX callback handlers as methods. To be able to use a SAX parser, a custom class must be implemented that inherits from ContentHandler and overrides the required callback handlers. An instance of a class derived from ContentHandler is expected by the setContentHandler method of the SAX parser. Table 32.2 lists the most important callback handlers that can be overridden in a class derived from ContentHandler.

Method	Description
startDocument()	Called once when the SAX parser starts reading an XML document
endDocument()	Called once when the SAX parser has completely read an XML document
startElement(name, attrs)	Called when an opening tag has been read
endElement(name)	Called when a closing tag named name has been read
characters(content)	Called when a text section has been read
ignorableWhitespace(whitespace)	Called when white space characters have been read

Table 32.2 Methods of the ContentHandler Class

32.2 Databases

The more data a program has to manage and the more complex the structure of this data becomes, the greater the programming effort required for the permanent storage and management of the data. In addition, tasks such as reading, writing, or updating data, which are required in many programs, have to be implemented again and again.

The solution to this problem is to insert an abstraction layer between the program using the data and the physical mass storage, the so-called *database*. The communication between the user program and the database takes place via a unified interface.

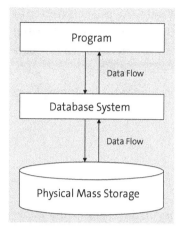

Figure 32.2 Database Interface

A database system accepts queries and returns all records that comply with the conditions of the queries. There are also queries, for example, to add data to the database or to change the structure of the database.

This chapter deals exclusively with *relational databases*, which organize a dataset into tables.[3] Queries to relational databases are typically formulated in a dedicated language: *Structured Query Language (SQL)*. SQL is too complex to describe exhaustively in this chapter. We'll only cover basic SQL commands here, which are necessary to illustrate the basic principle of databases and their application in Python.

SQL has been standardized and is supported by most relational database systems. Note that the systems often implement only subsets of the language and sometimes modify it slightly. For this reason, here we'll introduce you to the SQL variant used by SQLite, the default database in Python.

> **Note**
>
> In addition to the SQL query language, the database module interface is also standardized in Python. This has the pleasant side effect for the programmer that their code is executable with minimal adjustments on all database systems that implement this standard. The exact definition of this so-called *Python Database API Specification* can be found in PEP 249.

Before we dive into SQL itself, we'll create a small sample database and discuss which operations can be performed on it. We'll then implement this example using SQLite and the corresponding Python module `sqlite3`, covering parts of the SQL query language.

---

3 The *relational* descriptor goes back to the concept of relations in mathematics. In simple terms, a *relation* is an mapping between elements of two or more sets in the form of a table.

Imagine you had to manage the warehouse of a computer shipping company. You're responsible for ensuring that the delivered parts are stored in the correct location in the warehouse, and for each component the supplier, delivery date, and compartment number should be stored in the database. For customers who order their computers, the corresponding parts are reserved and are then no longer available for other customers. In addition, lists of all the company's customers and suppliers should be provided.

To create a database model for this scenario, you first create a table called *warehouse* that contains all the components located in the warehouse. For simplicity, assume that your warehouse is divided into compartments that are numbered consecutively. At the same time, each compartment can store only a single computer part.

A corresponding table with a few sample records for the warehouse could then look like Table 32.3 storing in addition the supplier and the reservation status.

Compartment Number	Serial Number	Component	Supplier	Reserved
1	26071987	Graphics card type 1	FC	0
2	19870109	Processor type 13	LPE	57
10	06198823	Power supply type 3	FC	0
25	11198703	LED fan	FC	57
26	19880105	Hard drive 10 TB	LPE	12

Table 32.3 Warehouse Table for Inventory

The *supplier* column contains the abbreviation for the supplying company, and the *reserved* column is set to 0 if the item in question hasn't yet been reserved by a customer. Otherwise, the field contains the customer number of the reserving customer. Only the occupied compartments are stored in the table so that all compartments for which no entry exists can be filled with new parts.

The detailed information about suppliers and customers is stored in two additional tables, called *suppliers* (see Table 32.4) and *customers* (see Table 32.5).

Short Name	Name	Phone Number
FC	FiboComputing Inc.	011235813
LPE	LettgenPetersErnesti	026741337
GC	Golden Computers	016180339

Table 32.4 Suppliers Table

Customer Number	Name	Address
12	James Everett	Madison Ave New York, NY 10003
57	Matt Aldwyn	24 Sunset Dr, Los Angeles, CA 90048
64	Steve Apple	2 Podmac St San Jose, CA 95014

Table 32.5 Customers Table

For you as a warehouse manager to benefit from this database, you must be able to manipulate the dataset. You need functions, for example, to add new customers and suppliers, update their data if and when they move, or remove them from your database if you wish. You also need to add new entries to the *warehouse* table and delete or adjust old ones. So to keep the database up to date, you need *add* and *delete* functions.

In addition, the database only becomes really useful when you can query the data it contains according to certain criteria. In the simplest case, for example, you want to request a list of all customers or suppliers or find out which compartments are currently occupied. However, you might also be interested to know whether the customer named Matt Aldwyn has reserved items and, if so, which items these are and where they are stored. Or you might want to know which components you need to reorder from the supplier with the telephone number 011235813 because the items are no longer available or have been reserved. These operations always *select* records according to certain criteria and return them to the calling user program.

After this theoretical preparation, we'll now turn to the implementation of the example in an SQLite database.

32.2.1   The Built-In Database in Python: sqlite3

SQLite is a simple database system that, unlike other systems, doesn't require a separate database server and stores the entire database in a single file. Despite this difference from other database systems, it provides a wide range of functionality and operates very efficiently in many use cases.[4] In addition, SQLite is capable to run on different systems, so it fits well into the multi-platform ecosystem of Python.

In Python, you first need to import the sqlite3 module to be able to use the database. You can then connect to a database file by calling the connect function, which returns a Connection object to the database:

```
import sqlite3
con = sqlite3.connect("warehouse.db")
```

---

4 For example, SQLite is used by Android and iOS and all major browsers (Firefox, Chrome, Safari).
   More use cases are provided on the SQLite website, see *https://www.sqlite.org/mostdeployed.html*.

The file extension can be freely chosen and has no influence on the functionality of the database. The preceding code causes the database, located in the *warehouse.db* file in the same directory as the program, to be read and connected to the Connection object. If there is no file named *warehouse.db* yet, an empty database is created under this name.

It often happens that you need a database only during the program run to manage or organize data without storing it permanently on the hard drive. For this purpose, you have the option to create a database in memory by passing the ":memory:" string to the connect method instead of a file name:

```
con = sqlite3.connect(":memory:")
```

To use the connected database, so-called *cursors* are used. You can think of a cursor as a current editing position within the database, similar to the flashing vertical line in a word processor. Those cursors enable us to modify or query records. There can be any number of cursors for a database connection. You can create a new cursor using the cursor method of the Connection object:

```
cursor = con.cursor()
```

Creating New Tables

Now we can send the first SQL statement to the database to create tables. For the creation of the *warehouse* table, the SQL statement looks as follows:

```
CREATE TABLE warehouse (
    ` compartment_number INTEGER, serial_number INTEGER, component TEXT,
      supplier TEXT, reserved INTEGER
)
```

> **Note**
> All uppercase words are components of the SQL language. However, SQL doesn't distin-guish between uppercase and lowercase, which is why we could have written every-thing in lowercase as well. For better readability, we'll always capitalize SQL keywords completely and lowercase names we assign throughout.

The INTEGER and TEXT strings after the column names specify the data type to be stored in the columns. It makes sense to define the compartment_number, serial_number, and reserved columns as integers and the component and supplier columns as character strings. SQLite defines several such data types for the columns of the database.

By default, Python data types are automatically converted to corresponding SQLite data types when written to an SQLite database. Table 32.6 shows the Python to SQLite data type conversion schema.

Python Data Type (Source Type)	SQLite Data Type (Target Type)
None	NULL
int	INTEGER
float	REAL
str	TEXT
bytes	BLOB

Table 32.6 SQLite Data Type Conversions when Writing Data

It's also possible to store other types of data in SQLite databases if appropriate conversion functions have been defined. How exactly this can be achieved is described when we talk about adapters and converters later in the chapter.

We now send the SQL statement to the database using the execute method of the cursor object:

```
cursor.execute("""CREATE TABLE warehouse (
    compartment_number INTEGER, serial_number INTEGER,
    component TEXT, supplier TEXT, reserved INTEGER)""")
```

We can create the tables for the suppliers and customers in the same way:

```
cursor.execute("""CREATE TABLE suppliers (
    short_name TEXT, name TEXT, phone_number TEXT)""")
```

```
cursor.execute("""CREATE TABLE customers (
    customer_number INTEGER, name TEXT, address TEXT)""")
```

Entering Data into the Tables

Next, we'll fill the still empty tables with sample data. To enter new records into an existing table, we use the INSERT statement, which looks as follows for the first sample record:

```
INSERT INTO warehouse VALUES (
    1, 26071987, 'Graphics card type 1', 'FC', 0
)
```

Inside the parentheses after VALUES, the values for each individual column are given in the same order in which the columns themselves were defined. As with all other database queries, we can use the execute method to submit the statement:

```
cursor.execute("""INSERT INTO warehouse VALUES (
    1, 26071987, 'Graphics card type 1', 'FC', 0)""")
```

When entering data records, however, you must keep in mind that the new data is not written to the database immediately after an INSERT statement has been executed, but is only stored in the memory for the time being. To make sure that the data really ends up on the hard drive and is thus permanently stored, you must call the commit method of the Connection object:

```
con.commit()
```

The commit method concludes a *transaction*. Transactions are chains of operations that must be fully executed in order to maintain the consistency of the database. Imagine that during a bank transfer, the money was debited from your account but not credited to the recipient due to an error. The rollback method can be used to undo all pending operations of the current transaction, i.e., all operations since the last commit call.

To ensure database consistency, you can guard critical database manipulations using a try-except statement and, if an error occurs, discard the changes in their entirety via rollback:

```
try:
    cursor = con.cursor()
    cursor.execute("""INSERT INTO warehouse VALUES (
        1, 26071987, 'Graphics card type 1', 'FC', 0)""")

    # This space can be used for other database manipulations

    con.commit()
except:
    print("A problem has occurred -> rollback")
    con.rollback()
    raise # Inform calling level about the error
```

Alternatively, you can use the Connection object as a *transaction manager* along with the with statement to secure critical areas. Here, the with statement automatically ensures that a commit is executed when all statements in the with block are successfully executed, and a rollback is executed in the event of an exception. However, exceptions that occur are passed on to the next higher level and must be caught there. The preceding example can be implemented via with as follows:

```
try:
    with con:
        cursor = con.cursor()
        cursor.execute("""INSERT INTO warehouse VALUES (
            1, 26071987, 'Graphics card type 1', 'FC', 0)""")
```

32

```
        # This space can be used for other database manipulations
except:
    print("A problem has occurred -> Automatic rollback")
    raise # Inform calling level about the error
```

You can learn more about the with statement in Chapter 22, Section 22.1.

To improve clarity, we'll omit the topics of error handling in the examples.

Secure Data Transfer

Usually the data we want to insert into the database won't be known before the program is run and therefore won't be in the source code as string constants. Instead, it will be user input or calculation results, which we then have in the memory as Python instances. At first glance, the format method for strings seems to be a suitable means for such cases, and the last INSERT statement could also have been assembled as follows:

```
>>> values = (1, 26071987, "Graphics card type 1", "FC", 0)
>>> "INSERT INTO warehouse VALUES ({}, {}, '{}', '{}', {})".format(*values)
"INSERT INTO warehouse VALUES (1, 26071987, 'Graphics card type 1', 'FC', 0)"
```

However, this method, which seems elegant at first glance, turns out to be a dangerous vulnerability upon closer inspection. Let's consider the following INSERT statement, which is supposed to insert a new supplier into the suppliers table:

```
>>> values = ("DR", "Danger Electronics",
...           "666'); There may be malicious code here")
>>> "INSERT INTO suppliers VALUES ('{}', '{}', '{}')".format(*values)
"INSERT INTO suppliers VALUES ('DR', 'Danger Electronics', '666'); There may be
malicious code here')"
```

As you can see, by having the value for the phone number contain the "'); " string, we have messed up the SQL query so that attempting to execute it would result in an error, causing the program to crash. By also including the text "There may be malicious code here", we have indicated that it may even be possible to manipulate a query in such a way that it results in valid SQL code, but a different operation than was intended (e.g., reading user data) is performed.[5]

> **Note**
>
> For security reasons, you should never use string formatting to pass parameters in SQL queries!

---

5 This form of attack on vulnerable programs is also referred to as *SQL injection*.

To pass parameters securely, you must write a question mark in the query string where the parameter should appear and pass a tuple with the appropriate values as the second parameter to the execute method:

```
values = ("DR", "Danger Electronics",
          "666'); There may be malicious code here")
sql = "INSERT INTO suppliers VALUES (?, ?, ?)"
cursor.execute(sql, values)
```

In this case, SQLite makes sure that the passed values are converted correctly and that no vulnerability can occur due to maliciously injected parameters.

Similar to string formatting, there is also the possibility to assign names to the parameters and to use a dictionary instead of the tuple instance for passing their values. To do this, you must write a colon in place of the question mark in the query string, followed by the symbolic name of the parameter, and pass the appropriate dictionary as the second parameter to execute:

```
values = {"short": "DR", "name": "Danger Electronics",
          "phone": "123456"}
sql = "INSERT INTO suppliers VALUES (:short, :name, :phone)"
cursor.execute(sql, values)
```

With this knowledge, we can elegantly and securely fill our tables with data:

```
for row in ((1, "2607871987", "Graphics card type 1", "FC", 0),
            (2, "19870109", "Processor type 13", "LPE", 57),
            (10, "06198823", "Power supply type 3", "FC", 0),
            (25, "11198703", "LED fan", "FC", 57),
            (26, "19880105", "Hard drive 10 TB", "LPE", 12)):
    cursor.execute("INSERT INTO warehouse VALUES (?,?,?,?,?)", row)
con.commit()
```

Structures like the for loop shown here, which perform the same database operation very often for different parameter sets each time, are common and provide potential for optimization. For this reason, cursor instances also contain the executemany method, which expects an operation template as the first argument. In addition, an iterable object containing the parameter sets for the individual operations has to be passed as the second argument. We use executemany to populate the suppliers and customers tables with data:

```
suppliers = (("FC", "FiboComputing Inc.", "011235813"),
             ("LPE", "LettgenPetersErnesti", "026741337"),
             ("GC", "Golden Computers", "016180339"))
cursor.executemany("INSERT INTO suppliers VALUES (?,?,?)",
                   suppliers)
```

```
customers = ((12, "James Everett",
              "Madison Ave New York, NY 10003"),
             (57, "Matt Aldwyn",
              "24 Sunset Dr, Los Angeles, CA 90048"),
             (64, "Steve Apple",
              "2 Podmac Str, San Jose, CA 95014"))
cursor.executemany("INSERT INTO customers VALUES (?,?,?)", customers)
con.commit()
```

Now you've learned how you can create databases and tables and populate them with data. In the next step, we'll deal with querying data.

Querying Data

To retrieve data from the database, you must use the SELECT statement. SELECT expects as parameters the columns you are interested and the name of the table you want to query, separated by commas. By default, all rows from the queried table will be returned. An additional WHERE clause enables you to select only certain records by specifying conditions for the selection. A simple SELECT statement is structured as follows:

```
SELECT <columnlist> FROM <tablename> [WHERE <condition>]
```

As indicated by the square brackets, the WHERE clause is optional and can be omitted.

For example, if you want to query the numbers of all occupied compartments[6] and their associated components, you should formulate the following query:

```
SELECT compartment_number, component FROM warehouse
```

Before we can query records from a database, it must have been loaded. To execute the following examples, you can continue with the database in memory that we created in the previous sections or load a database that's stored on the hard drive:

```
>>> con = sqlite3.connect("warehouse.db")
>>> cursor = con.cursor()
```

For issuing data queries, you can use the execute method of the cursor object. After that you can use cursor.fetchall to retrieve all data records your query returned:

```
>>> cursor.execute("SELECT compartment_number, component FROM warehouse")
>>> cursor.fetchall()
[(1, 'Graphics card type 1'), (2, 'Processor type 13'),
(10, 'Power supply type 3'), (25, 'LED fan'),
(26, 'Hard drive 10 TB')]
```

---

6 Note that only occupied compartments are represented in die database.

The return value of fetchall is a list containing a tuple with the values of the requested columns for each record.

With a suitable WHERE clause, you can limit the selection to the computer parts that aren't yet reserved:

```
>>> cursor.execute("""
...     SELECT compartment_number, component FROM warehouse WHERE reserved=0
... """)
>>> cursor.fetchall()
[(1, 'Graphics card type 1'), (10, 'Power supply type 3')]
```

You can also combine multiple conditions using logical operators such as AND and OR. This will help you determine, for example, which items supplied by *FiboComputing Inc.* have already been reserved:

```
>>> cursor.execute("""
...     SELECT compartment_number, component FROM warehouse
...     WHERE reserved!=0 AND supplier='FC'
... """)
>>> cursor.fetchall()
[(25, 'LED fan')]
```

Because it can be annoying to always specify the column names to be selected and you'll often want to execute queries over all columns, there is a shortened notation for this, where the column list is replaced by an asterisk:

```
>>> cursor.execute("SELECT * FROM customers")
>>> cursor.fetchall()
[(12, 'James Everett', 'Madison Ave New York, NY 10003'),
(57, 'Matt Aldwyn', '24 Sunset Dr, Los Angeles, CA 90048'),
(64, 'Steve Apple', '2 Podmac Str, San Jose, CA 95014')]
```

The order of the column values depends on the order in which the columns of the table were defined with CREATE.

As a final addition to the SELECT statement, let's look at queries over multiple tables, so-called *joins*. For example, say you want to query which components from the supplier with the phone number 011235813 are currently in the warehouse and in which compartments they are located.

A query over multiple tables differs from simple queries in that instead of the simple table name, a comma-separated list is specified that contains all the tables involved in the query. If columns are referenced, such as in the WHERE condition, the respective table name must also be specified. This also applies to the columns to be selected directly after SELECT. Our sample query concerns the *warehouse* and *suppliers* tables and can be formulated as a join as follows:

32

```
SELECT warehouse.compartment.number, warehouse.component, supplier.name
FROM warehouse, supplier
WHERE supplier.phone_number='011235813' AND
      warehouse.supplier=supplier.short_name
```

You can imagine the processing of such a join in such a way that the database joins each row of the warehouse table with each row of the supplier table with new data records and returns all rows of the resulting list in which the supplier.phone_number column has the value '011235813' and the warehouse.supplier and supplier.short_name columns match.

If you run the query with SQLite, you'll get the expected output:

```
>>> sql = """
...      SELECT warehouse.compartment_number, warehouse.component,
...          suppliers.name
...      FROM warehouse, suppliers
...      WHERE suppliers.phone_number='011235813' AND
...          warehouse.supplier=suppliers.short_name"""
>>> cursor.execute(sql)
>>> cursor.fetchall()
[(1, 'Graphics card type 1', 'FiboComputing Inc.'),
(10, 'Power supply type 3', 'FiboComputing Inc.'),
(25, 'LED fan', 'FiboComputing Inc.')]
```

Up to this point, using fetchall you've always loaded all the results of a query from the database at once and then output them collectively. However, this method is only suitable for relatively small amounts of data—first, because the program has to wait until the database has determined and returned all results, and second, because the entire result list is to be kept in memory. For operations that only require a single data record at a time like screen outputs, this is a waste of memory when the results are very large. For this reason, there is the possibility to query the data row by row—that is, always in small portions. This procedure makes sure you don't need to wait for the calculation of the complete result list, but can already start processing while the database is still processing the query. In addition, memory can be utilized more efficiently.

Using the fetchone method of the cursor class, we request one result tuple at a time. If all records of the last query have already been read, fetchone returns the value None. This allows large amounts of data to be read in a memory-efficient manner:

```
>>> cursor.execute("SELECT * FROM customers")
>>> while row := cursor.fetchone():
...      print(row)
(12, 'James Everett', 'Madison Ave New York, NY 10003')
(57, 'Matt Aldwyn', '24 Sunset Dr, Los Angeles, CA 90048')
(64, 'Steve Apple', '2 Podmac Str, San Jose, CA 95014')
```

Alternatively, you can use the iterator interface of the cursor class, which allows us to iterate over the result rows using for, as with a list:

```
>>> cursor.execute("SELECT * FROM customers")
>>> for row in cursor:
...     print(row)
(12, 'James Everett', 'Madison Ave New York, NY 10003')
(57, 'Matt Aldwyn', '24 Sunset Dr, Los Angeles, CA 90048')
(64, 'Steve Apple', '2 Podmac Str, San Jose, CA 95014')
```

Which of these alternatives to prefer is a matter of taste. However, the := operator (see Chapter 5, Section 5.4) is a fairly recent addition to the Python language. Hence, you have to stick to the iterator variant in case you are required to work with Python versions older than 3.8.

Data Types with SQLite

From the introductory part of this section, you already know about the way SQLite converts data when writing to the database. The corresponding conversion of SQLite data types to Python data types is described in Table 32.7.

SQLite Data Type (Source Type)	Python Data Type (Target Type)
NULL	None
INTEGER	int
REAL	float
TEXT	str
BLOB	bytes

Table 32.7 Type Conversion when Reading SQLite Databases

Essentially, this table raises two questions: How are other data types, such as lists or custom classes, stored in the database when only these types are supported? And how can we intervene in the conversion process when reading it from the database?

We'll answer the second question first.

Connection.text_factory

Each Connection instance created by sqlite3.connect has a text_factory attribute that refers to a function that's called whenever TEXT columns are read. The resulting tuple of the database query then contains the return value of this function. By default, the text_factory attribute is set to the built-in str function:

```
>>> con = sqlite3.connect("warehouse.db")
>>> con.text_factory
<class 'str'>
```

To achieve the exemplary goal of getting str instances for TEXT columns where all letters are capitalized, you can specify a custom text_factory function. This function must expect a single argument and return the converted value. The parameter is a bytes string containing the raw data from the database with UTF-8 encoding. So in this case, a simple function is sufficient, one that first converts the read value into a string and then uses the upper method to make all letters uppercase:

```
>>> def my_text_factory(value):
...     return value.decode("utf-8", "ignore").upper()
```

All you have to do now is set the text_factory attribute of the Connection object to your new callback function and enjoy the expected result:

```
>>> con.text_factory = my_text_factory
>>> cursor = con.cursor()
>>> cursor.execute("SELECT * FROM customers")
>>> cursor.fetchall()
[(12, 'JAMES EVERETT', 'MADISON AVE NEW YORK, NY 10003'),
(57, 'MATT ALDWYN', '24 SUNSET DR, LOS ANGELES, CA 90048'),
(64, 'STEVE APPLE', '2 PODMAC STR, SAN JOSE, CA 95014')]
```

To restore the original output behavior, simply assign the default value str to text_factory:

```
>>> con.text_factory = str
```

Connection.row_factory

Another attribute similar to text_factory for TEXT columns also exists for entire data records. The row_factory attribute can store a reference to a function that converts rows according to custom requirements. By default, the tuple function is used. As an example, we want to implement a function that provides us with access to the column values of a data record via the names of the respective columns. The result should look as follows:

```
>>> cursor.execute("SELECT * FROM customers")
>>> cursor.fetchall()
[{"customer_number": 12, "name": 'James Everett', "address": 'Madison Ave New
York, NY 10003'},
{"customer_number": 57, "name": 'Matt Aldwyn', "address": '24 Sunset Dr, Los
Angeles, CA 90048'},
{"customer_number": 64, "name": 'Steve Apple', "adress": '2 Podmac Str, San
Jose, CA 95014'}]
```

To achieve this, we need the `description` attribute of the `cursor` class, which gives us information about the column names selected by the query. The `description` attribute contains a sequence that of tuples with seven elements for each column, but we are only interested in the first one—namely, the column name:[7]

```
>>> con = sqlite3.connect("warehouse.db")
>>> cursor = con.cursor()
>>> cursor.execute("SELECT * FROM customers")
>>> cursor.description
(('customer_number', None, None, None, None, None, None),
('name', None, None, None, None, None, None),
('address', None, None, None, None, None, None))
```

As parameters, the `row_factory` function receives a reference to the cursor used for the query and the result row as a tuple.

Based on this knowledge, we can implement the `row_factory` function named `rows_dict` as follows:

```
def rows_dict(cursor, row):
    result = {}
    for columnno, column in enumerate(cursor.description):
        result[column[0]] = row[columnno]
    return result
```

> **Note**
>
> As a reminder, `enumerate` creates an iterator that returns a tuple for each element of the passed sequence that contains the index of the element in the sequence and its value. For more information, see Chapter 17, Section 17.14.13.

In practice, `row_factory` works as follows:

```
>>> con.row_factory = rows_dict
>>> cursor = con.cursor()
>>> cursor.execute("SELECT * FROM customers")
>>> cursor.fetchall()
[{'customer_number': 12, 'name': 'James Everett', 'address': 'Madison Ave New
York, NY 10003'},
{'customer_number': 57, 'name': 'Matt Aldwyn', 'address': '24 Sunset Dr, Los
Angeles, CA 90048'},
{'customer_number': 64, 'name': 'Steve Apple', 'address': '2 Podmac Str,  San
Jose, CA 95014'}]
```

---

7 The other six entries exist only for compatibility with the Python DB API and are always assigned the value `None`.

The sqlite3 module of Python already provides an extended row_factory named sqlite3.Row that processes rows in a similar way to our rows_dict function. Because sqlite3.Row is highly optimized and the column values can be accessed via the respective column name in a case-insensitive manner, you should prefer the built-in function to our example and only implement your own row_factory if you want to achieve something different.

After this short excursion to the factory functions, let's turn to the first of our two questions: How can we store any data type in SQLite databases?

Adapters and Converters

As you already know, SQLite supports only a limited set of data types. Consequently, we need to map all the other data types we want to store in the database to the existing ones. Due to their unlimited length, TEXT columns are best suited to store data of any type, so we'll limit ourselves to them in the following sections.

When encoding strings, we converted str instances to equivalent bytes instances using the encode method and recovered the original Unicode data using the decode method. Likewise, we'll now consider operations to first transform *any* data type into strings and then extract the original data back from the string. What we want to do is store the generated strings in the database and read them out again at a later stage.

Converting data types into a string is called *adaptation*, and recovering the data from this string is called *conversion*. Figure 32.3 illustrates this relationship using the example of the Circle class, whose attributes are the coordinates of the center of the circle Mx and My as well as the length of the radius R.

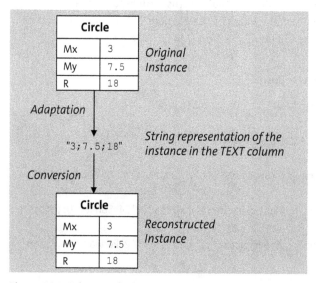

Figure 32.3 Schema of Adaptation and Conversion

A corresponding Circle class can be defined as follows:

```
class Circle:
    def __init__(self, mx, my, r):
        self.Mx = mx
        self.My = my
        self.R = r
```

Now we need to create an adapter function that turns Circle instances into strings.

We'll perform the conversion by creating a string that contains the three attributes of the circle, separated by semicolons:

```
def circle_adapter(k):
    return "{};{};{}".format(k.Mx, k.My, k.R)
```

For the database to know that we want to adapt Circle instances with this function, we need to register circle_adapter and associate it with the Circle data type. This is done by calling the sqlite3.register_adapter method, which expects the data type to be adapted as the first parameter and the adapter function as the second parameter:

```
>>> sqlite3.register_adapter(Circle, circle_adapter)
```

These steps allow us to store Circle instances in TEXT columns. However, the whole thing only becomes really useful when Circle instances are automatically generated again during the readout.

Thus, we still need to define the inverse function of circle_adapter—the converter—which restores the original Circle instance from the string. In our example, this turns out to be very simple:

```
def circle_converter(bytestring):
    mx, my, r = bytestring.split(b";")
    return Circle(float(mx), float(my), float(r))
```

Just like the adapter, the converter function must also be registered with SQLite, which we can achieve via the sqlite3.register_converter method:

```
>>> sqlite3.register_converter("CIRCLE", circle_converter)
```

Unlike register_adapter, register_convert expects a string as the first parameter, which assigns a name to the data type to be converted. By doing this, we have defined a new SQLite data type called CIRCLE, which we can use just like the built-in types for the columns of our tables. However, when connecting to the database, we need to tell SQLite that we want to use custom types. To do this, we pass an appropriate value to the connect method as the detect_types keyword parameter:

32

```
>>> con = sqlite3.connect(":memory:",
...                         detect_types=sqlite3.PARSE_DECLTYPES)
```

In the following sections, we'll demonstrate the definition and use of our new Circle data type in a small sample program:

```python
import sqlite3

class Circle:
    def __init__(self, mx, my, r):
        self.Mx = mx
        self.My = my
        self.R = r
    def __str__(self):
        return "Circle({}, {}, {})".format(self.Mx, self.My, self.R)

def circle_adapter(k):
    return "{};{};{}".format(k.Mx, k.My, k.R)

def circle_converter(bytestring):
    mx, my, r = bytestring.split(b";")
    return Circle(float(mx), float(my), float(r))

# Register adapters and converters
sqlite3.register_adapter(Circle, circle_adapter)
sqlite3.register_converter("CIRCLE", circle_converter)

# Here a sample database is stored in memory with
# a single-column table defined for circles
con = sqlite3.connect(":memory:",
                        detect_types=sqlite3.PARSE_DECLTYPES)
cursor = con.cursor()
cursor.execute("CREATE TABLE circle_table(k CIRCLE)")

# Write circle to database
circle = Circle(1, 2.5, 3)
cursor.execute("INSERT INTO circle_table VALUES (?)", (circle,))

# Read out circle again
cursor.execute("SELECT * FROM circle_table")

read_circle = cursor.fetchall()[0][0]
print(type(read_circle))
print(read_circle)
```

The output of this program is as follows, showing that read_circle is indeed an instance of the Circle class with the correct attributes:

```
<class '__main__.Circle'>
Circle(1.0, 2.5, 3.0)
```

Limitations

The SQLite database system has certain limitations compared to other databases. For example, a database is locked for read access while records are modified or added, which can be particularly impractical for web applications.

32.3 Compressed Files and Archives

Python's standard library provides functionality to process files that are compressed in various ways. For example, the gzip module of the standard library allows you to easily read and write files that are compatible with the zlib library.[8] Since you can work with other formats in a similar way to gzip, we limit our more detailed description to gzip and list which formats are also supported in Table 32.8.

The gzip module provides the function open, that can be used in a similar way as the built-in open function.

32.3.1 gzip.open(filename, [mode, compresslevel])

The gzip.open function returns an object that can be used like a normal file object.

The filename and mode parameters are equivalent to those of the built-in open function.

The last parameter, compresslevel, allows you to specify the degree to which the data should be compressed when written to the file. Allowed are integers from 0 to 9, where 0 is the worst compression level and 9 is the best. The higher the compression level, the more computing time is also required to compress the data. If the compresslevel parameter isn't specified, gzip uses the strongest compression by default:

```
>>> import gzip
>>> with gzip.open("testfile.gz", "wb") as f:
...     f.write(b"Hello world")
11
>>> with gzip.open("testfile.gz") as g:
...     g.read()
b'Hello world'
```

---

8 The zlib library is an open-source compression library used by the gzip Unix program, among others. For more information, visit the library's website at *http://www.zlib.net/*.

In the example, we write a simple `bytes` string to the testfile.gz file and then read it out again.

32.3.2   Other Modules for Accessing Compressed Data

There are other modules in Python's standard library that provide access to compressed data. Because these are very similar to the `gzip` module just presented, we won't provide any detailed descriptions here and instead refer you to the Python documentation.

Table 32.8 provides an overview of all modules that manage compressed data.

Module	Description
bz2	Provides convenient access to data compressed with the *bzip2* algorithm.
	In general, the compression of bzip2 is superior to that of zlib in terms of compression ratio.
gzip	Provides convenient access to data compressed with zlib.
lzma	Provides access to *LZMA*-compressed files in .xz and .lzma formats. The LZMA algorithm is characterized by its good compression rate and efficient decompression.
zlib	A low-level library that provides direct access to the functions of zlib. With it, among other things, it's possible to compress or decompress strings.
	The `gzip` module uses the `zlib` module internally.
zipfile	Provides access to *ZIP* archives, such as those created by the well-known WinZip program. Manipulation and creation of new archives is also possible.
tarfile	Implements functions and classes to read or write the *TAR* archives which are widely used in the Unix world.

Table 32.8 Overview of Python's Compression Modules

32.4   Serializing Instances: pickle

The `pickle` module provides functionality for *serializing* objects. Serialization means that a `bytes` object is created that stores all the information of the object so that it can be reconstructed later by a process referred to as *deserializing*.

Especially for storing Python instances into files or for transferring them, e.g., via a network connection, `pickle` is well suited. The following data types can be serialized or deserialized using `pickle`:

- None, True, False
- Numeric data types (int, float, complex, bool)

- `str`, `bytes`
- Sequential data types (`tuple`, `list`), sets (`set`, `frozenset`), and dictionaries (`dict`), so long as all their elements can also be serialized by `pickle`
- Global functions
- Built-in functions
- Global classes
- Class instances whose attributes can be serialized

Concerning classes and functions, you must note that such objects are stored only by their name when serialized. The code of a function or the definition of the class won't be stored. So, for example, if you want to deserialize an instance of a self-defined class, the class must be defined in the current context just as it was during serialization. If that's not the case, an `UnpicklingError` will be generated.

There are six formats in which `pickle` can store its data. Each of these formats has an identification number. Table 32.9 lists the available protocols and the version of Python from which onward each format can be used.

Version	Usable From	Remarks
0	–	ASCII format
1	–	Binary format
2	Python 2.3	Binary format
3	Python 3.0	Binary format
4	Python 3.4	Binary format, standard protocol
5	Python 3.8	Binary format

Table 32.9 Pickle Protocols

The `pickle` module provides its functionality via two interfaces: a function-based interface via the `dump` and `load` functions, and an object-oriented one with the `Pickler` and `Unpickler` classes.

To use `pickle`, the module must first be imported:

```
>>> import pickle
```

32.4.1   Functional Interface

pickle.dump(obj, file, [protocol])

The `pickle.dump` function writes the serialization of `obj` to the passed file object. To be able to do that, the passed file object must have been opened for write access.

The `protocol` parameter allows you to pass the `pickle` protocol version to use. The default value for `protocol` is 4. If you specify a binary format, the file object passed for `file` must have been opened in binary write mode:

```
>>> with open("pickle-test.dat", "wb") as f:
...     pickle.dump([1, 2, 3], f)
...     pickle.dump({"hello": "world"}, f)
```

For `file`, in addition to real file objects, you can pass any object that implements a `write` method with a `string` parameter such as `StringIO` instances.

pickle.load(file)

The `pickle.load` function loads the next serialized object, starting from the current read position of the `file` file object. In doing so, `load` independently recognizes in which format the data was saved.

The following example is based on the assumption that a file named *pickle-test.dat* exists in the current working directory, which contains a serialized list and a dictionary:

```
>>> with open("pickle-test.dat", "rb") as f:
...     print(pickle.load(f))
...     print(pickle.load(f))
[1, 2, 3]
{'hello': 'world'}
```

Again, you should make sure to open the files in binary mode if you use `pickle` protocols other than 0.

pickle.dumps(obj, [protocol])

The `pickle.dumps` function returns the serialized representation of `obj` as a `bytes` string, where the `protocol` parameter specifies the `pickle` protocol version to use. By default, the protocol version 4 is used:

```
>>> pickle.dumps([1, 2, 3])
b'\x80\x04\x95\x0b\x00\x00\x00\x00\x00\x00\x00]\x94(K\x01K\x02K\x03e.'
```

pickle.loads(string)

The `pickle.loads` function restores the object serialized in `string`. The protocol used for this is automatically detected, and superfluous characters at the end of the string are ignored:

```
>>> s = pickle.dumps([1, 2, 3])
>>> pickle.loads(s)
[1, 2, 3]
```

32.4.2   Object-Oriented Interface

When many objects are to be serialized into the same file, it's annoying to specify the file object and the protocol to be used each time dump is called. Using the Pickler and Unpickler classes, you can create instances that are bound to a file and a pickle protocol version which is then respected by all subsequent calls of the dump or load methods. In addition, by subclassing Pickler and Unpickler, you can extend their functionality, e.g., to transparently store or read data to or from an external data source like a database.

pickle.Pickler(file, [protocol])

The two file and protocol parameters have the same meaning as in the pickle.dump function. The resulting Pickler object has a method called dump, which expects an object to be serialized as a parameter.

All objects sent to the dump method are written to the file object passed when the pickler instance is created:

```
>>> with open("a_file.dat", "wb") as f:
...     p = pickle.Pickler(f, protocol=2)
...     p.dump({"first_name" : "Donald", "last_name" : "Duck"})
...     p.dump([1, 2, 3, 4])
```

pickle.Unpickler(file)

The counterpart to Pickler is Unpickler, which restores the original data from the passed file object. Unpickler instances have a parameterless method called load that reads the next object from the file each time. The protocol used is determined automatically.

The following example is based on the assumption that the file generated in the Pickler class example—*a_file.dat*—is located in the current working directory:

```
>>> with open("a_file.dat", "rb") as f:
...     u = pickle.Unpickler(f)
...     print(u.load())
...     print(u.load())
{'first_name': 'Donald', 'last_name': 'Duck'}
[1, 2, 3, 4]
```

32.5   The JSON Data Exchange Format: json

The *JavaScript Object Notation (JSON)* data format, originally developed for JavaScript, has become quasi-standard for simple data exchange, competing to a certain extent with XML. Unlike the XML markup language, JSON stores data in the form of valid

JavaScript code. Nevertheless, there are JSON parsers for all common programming languages—including Python, of course.

An object represented in JSON can be composed of the data types listed in Table 32.10, each of which has its counterpart with an identical meaning in Python.

JSON Data Type	Notation	Corresponding Python Data Type
Object	{}	dict
Array	[]	list
Number	12 12.34	int float
String	""	str
Value	true false null	bool bool NoneType

Table 32.10 Data Types in JSON and Their Counterparts in Python

Similar to dictionaries and lists, objects and arrays in JSON can contain further instances—in particular, further objects or arrays.

The standard library contains the json module, which can serialize Python instances to JSON format or create them from JSON format. To illustrate this, let's first create a data record that will be used in the following examples:

```
>>> entry = {
...     "first name": "Donald",
...     "last name": "Duck",
...     "address": [13, "Quack street", "Duckburg"],
...     "age": 81
... }
```

Similar to pickle, the json module provides the functions dump and dumps or load and loads, which store or load data. To be able to run the following examples, the json module must first be imported:

```
>>> import json
```

The dump function is passed a Python instance, which may consist of the data types listed in Table 32.10, and saves it to a file object that is opened for writing:

```
>>> with open("entry.json", "w") as f:
...     json.dump(entry, f)
```

Note that JSON is a human-readable data format. Thus, the file object doesn't have to be opened in binary mode as with `pickle`. Similar to `dump`, the `dumps` function returns the JSON representation of an instance as a string:

```
>>> s = json.dumps(entry)
>>> s
'{"first name": "Donald", "last name": "Duck", "address": [
13, "Quack street", "Duckburg"], "age": 81}'
```

The stored data can now be read again with the corresponding `load` and `loads` functions and converted back into a Python instance:

```
>>> with open("entry.json", "r") as f:
...     print(json.load(f))
{'first name': 'Donald', 'last name': 'Duck', 'address': [
13, 'Quack street', 'Duckburg'], 'age': 81}
>>> json.loads(s)
{'first name': 'Donald', 'last name': 'Duck', 'address': [
13, 'Quack street', 'Duckburg'], 'age': 81}
```

32.6   The CSV Table Format: csv

A widely used import and export format for databases and spreadsheets is the *comma-separated values* (*CSV*) format. CSV files are text files that contain data records in individual lines. Within the data records, the individual values are separated from each other by a delimiter such as the comma—hence the name.

For example, a CSV file that stores information about people and uses the comma as a separator might look as follows:

```
first name,last name,date of birth,place of residence,hair color
Howard,Hook,07/19/1980,Boston,Brown
Richard,Gold,09/19/1990,Detroit,Brown
Henry,Hawk,04/14/1959,Hartford,Dark blonde
Edith,Falcon,09/13/1987,Chicago,Black
Roger,Blackbird,03/25/1988,Miami,Light red
```

The first row contains the column headers, and all subsequent rows contain the actual data records.

Unfortunately, there is no standard for CSV files, so the delimiter, for example, may differ for different programs. This makes it difficult to read CSV files from different sources as the particular format of the exporting application must always be taken into account.

32

667

To be able to handle CSV files of various formats, Python provides the csv module. The csv module implements reader and writer classes that encapsulate read and write access to CSV data, respectively. With the help of so-called *dialects*, the format of the file can be specified. By default, there are predefined dialects for the CSV files generated by Microsoft Excel. The module also provides a class called Sniffer that can guess the dialect of a file.

You can view a list of all defined dialects via csv.list_dialects:

```
>>> import csv
>>> csv.list_dialects()
['excel', 'excel-tab', 'unix']
```

32.6.1   Reading Data from a CSV File with reader Objects

CSV files can be read using reader objects having the following constructor:

csv.reader(csvfile, [dialect], {fmtparam})**

The csvfile parameter must be a reference to a file object open for read access, from which the data is to be read.

With dialect, you can specify in which format the file to be read was written. To do this, you must pass a string contained in the list that csv.list_dialects returns. Alternatively, you can specify an instance of the Dialect class, which we'll describe in Section 32.6.2. By default, the value "excel" is used for dialect, and the files encoded with it use the comma as a delimiter.

You can specify a custom dialect using keyword arguments instead of an instance of the Dialect class. An example where we set the semicolon as a delimiter in this way looks as follows:

```
with open("file.csv") as f_csv:
    reader = csv.reader(f_csv, delimiter=";")
```

For an overview of dialects and possible values for fmtparam, see Section 32.6.2.

The reader class implements the iterator protocol and its instances can therefore be conveniently iterated in a for loop, for example. In the following example, we'll read the sample CSV file introduced before:

```
>>> with open("names.csv") as f_csv:
...     reader = csv.reader(f_csv)
...     for line in reader:
...         print(line)
['first name', 'last name', 'date of birth', 'place of residence', 'hair color']
```

```
['Howard', 'Hook', '07/19/1980', 'Boston', 'Brown']
['Richard', 'Gold', '09/19/1990', 'Detroit', 'Brown']
['Henry', 'Hawk', '04/14/1959', 'Hartford', 'Dark blonde']
['Edith', 'Falcon', '09/13/1987', 'Chicago', 'Black']
['Roger', 'Blackbird', '03/25/1988', 'Miami', 'Light red']
```

As you can see, for each line the reader returns a list with the values of each column. It's important that the column values are always returned as strings.

In addition to the standard reader, which returns lists, there is also DictReader, which creates a dictionary for each line that assigns the values of the respective line to the column headers.

```
>>> with open("names.csv") as f_csv:
...     reader = csv.DictReader(f_csv)
...     for line in reader:
...         print(line)
{'first_name': 'Howard', 'last_name': 'Hook', 'date_of_birth': '07/19/
1980', 'place_of_residence': 'Boston', 'haircolor': 'Brown'}
{'first_name': 'Richard', 'last_name': 'Gold', 'date_of_birth': '09/19/
1990', 'place_of_residence': 'Detroit', 'haircolor': 'Brown'}
[...]
```

csv.writer(csvfile, [dialect], {**fmtparam})

The constructor of the writer class expects the same arguments as the constructor of the reader class, except that the file object passed for csvfile must have been opened for write access.

The resulting writer object has the two writerow and writerows methods, which can be used to write single or multiple rows at once to the CSV file:

```
>>> data = (
...     ["Volvo", "P245", "130"], ["Ford", "Ecosport", "90"],
...     ["Mercedes", "CLK", "250"], ["Audi", "A6", "350"],
... )
>>> with open("cars.csv", "w") as f_csv:
...     writer = csv.writer(f_csv)
...     writer.writerow(["brand", "model", "horsepower"])
...     writer.writerows(data)
```

In the example, we create a new CSV file called *cars.csv*. We use the writerow method to write the column headers to the first line of the new file and then use writerows to write four sample records.

Similar to the DictReader class, there's also a DictWriter class, which can be created in almost the same way as the normal writer class, except that you have to pass a list of column headers in addition to the file object. For the writerow and writerows methods, DictWriter instances expect dictionaries as parameters, and the writeheader method is used to write the column headers to the CSV file. The following example creates the same CSV file as the previous one:

```
>>> data = ({"brand": "Volvo", "model": "P245", "horsepower": "130"},
...         {"brand": "Ford", "model": "Ecosport", "horsepower": "90"},
...         {"brand": "Mercedes", "model": "CLK", "horsepower": "250"},
...         {"brand": "Audi", "model": "A6", "horsepower": "350"})
>>> with open("cars.csv", "w") as f_csv:
...     writer = csv.DictWriter(f_csv, ["brand", "model", "horsepower"])
...     writer.writeheader()
...     writer.writerows(data)
```

32.6.2   Using Custom Dialects: Dialect Objects

The instances of the csv.Dialect class are used to describe the structure of CSV files. You shouldn't create Dialect objects directly, but use the csv.register_dialect function instead. Via register_dialect, you can create a new dialect and give it a name. This name can then be passed later as a parameter to the constructors of the reader and writer classes. Also, each registered name is included in the list returned by csv.get_dialects.

The register_dialect function has the interface described ahead.

csv.register_dialect(name, [dialect], {fmtparam})**

The name parameter must be a string that identifies the new dialect. With dialect, an already existing Dialect object can be passed, which is then linked with the corresponding name.

Most importantly, using the optional keyword arguments, you can specifiy the new dialect. The keyword parameters listed in Table 32.11 are allowed.

Name	Meaning
delimiter	Delimiter between column values. The default value is the comma, ",".
quotechar	A character to enclose fields that contain special characters such as the delimiter or newline character. The default value is the double quotes, '"'.

Table 32.11 Keyword Parameters for register_dialect

Name	Meaning
doublequote	A Boolean value specifying how the character specified for quotechar should be masked within fields themselves.
	If doublequote has the value True, quotechar will be inserted twice in succession. If the value of doublequote is False, the character specified for escapechar is written before quotechar instead.
	By default, doublequote has the value True.
escapechar	A character used to encode the delimiter within column values if quoting has the value QUOTE_NONE.
	With a doublequote value of False, escapechar is also used for encoding quotechar.
	By default, encoding is disabled, and escapechar has the value None.
lineterminator	Character used to separate the lines. By default, it's set to "\r\n".
	Note that this setting only affects the writer. All reader objects are unaffected by the lineterminator setting and always use "\r", "\n", or the combination of both as line separators.
quoting	Specifies if and when column values should be enclosed with quotechar.
	Valid values are as follows:
	■ QUOTE_ALL All column values are enclosed.
	■ QUOTE_MINIMAL Only the fields with special characters like line feeds or the separator for column values are enclosed.
	■ QUOTE_NONNUMERIC When writing, all nonnumeric fields are enclosed by quotechar. When reading, all unenclosed fields are automatically converted to float.
	■ QUOTE_NONE No enclosure with quotechar is made.
	■ By default, quoting is set to QUOTE_MINIMAL.
skipinitialspace	A Boolean value that specifies how to handle leading white spaces in a column value.
	A setting of True causes all leading white spaces to be ignored; a value of False causes the complete column contents to be read and returned.
	The default value is False.

Table 32.11 Keyword Parameters for register_dialect (Cont.)

32

As an example, let's register a new dialect called "my_dialect" that uses the tab character as a separator and encloses all fields with quotes:

```
>>> csv.register_dialect("my_dialect", delimiter="\t",
...                        quoting=csv.QUOTE_ALL)
```

We can now pass this new dialect to the constructor of the reader and writer classes and write and read our own CSV files this way.

Determining Dialects Automatically

The csv module provides the Sniffer class, which can be used to automatically generate the dialect of a CSV file from an extract. In the following example, we use Sniffer to determine the dialect of the *cars.csv* file from the previous examples:

```
>>> with open("cars.csv") as f_csv:
...     sample = f_csv.read(1024)
>>> dialect = csv.Sniffer().sniff(sample)
>>> dialect.delimiter
','
```

The sample program has correctly identified the delimiter as a comma. With the dialect thus created, it can now read the CSV file:

```
>>> with open("cars.csv") as f_csv:
...     reader = csv.reader(f_csv, dialect)
...     for row in reader:
...         print(row)
['brand', 'model', 'horsepower']
['Volvo', 'P245', '130']
['Ford', 'Ecosport', '90']
['Mercedes', 'CLK', '250']
['Audi', 'A6', '350']
```

The Sniffer class also contains a has_header method that determines whether or not the first row of the file contains column headers. In this example, it returns the value True:

```
>>> csv.Sniffer().has_header(sample)
True
```

> **Note**
>
> The Sniffer class uses heuristics to determine the dialect and check for column headers in the first row of the file. These heuristics can fail, so you should consider the returned values as qualified guesses and not as certain statements.

Chapter 33
Network Communication

Now that we've dealt in detail with the storage of data in files of different formats or databases, this chapter focuses on another important programming discipline: network communication.

Basically, the subject of network communication can be divided into several so-called *protocol layers*. Figure 33.1 shows a highly simplified version of the *OSI Model*,[1] which illustrates the hierarchy of the various layers.

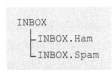

Figure 33.1 Network Protocols

The most rudimentary protocol is shown at the bottom of the graphic. This is the bare wire through which the data is transmitted in the form of electrical signals. Based on this, the more abstract protocols such as Ethernet and IP are implemented. Generally, protocols shown on higher levels in Figure 33.1 are more abstract and specialized compared to protocols on lower levels. The part that's actually interesting for application programmers begins above the IP protocol—namely, with the TCP and UDP transport protocols. We'll discuss both protocols in detail in the context of sockets in the following section.

The protocols built on top of TCP are the most abstract ones and therefore of particular interest to us. In this book, we'll cover the protocols listed in Table 33.1.

Protocol	Description	Module	Section
UDP	Basic connectionless network protocol	socket	Section 33.1.2
TCP	Basic connection-oriented network protocol	socket	Section 33.1.3

Table 33.1 Network Protocols

---

1 The OSI model was standardized by the International Organization for Standardization (ISO) in 1983 and also specifies what the protocols of the individual layers have to do.

Protocol	Description	Module	Section
HTTP	Transfer of text files such as web pages	`urllib` `requests`	Chapter 34, Section 34.4
FTP	File transfer	`ftplib`	Chapter 34, Section 34.5
SMTP	Sending of emails	`smtplib`	Chapter 35, Section 35.1
POP3	Retrieving emails	`poplib`	Chapter 35, Section 35.2
IMAP4	Retrieving and managing emails	`imaplib`	Chapter 35, Section 35.3

Table 33.1 Network Protocols (Cont.)

There are also abstract protocols based on UDP, such as the *Network File System* (*NFS*). However, we'll only cover TCP-based protocols in this book as they are the most interesting from the perspective of an application programmer.

We'll first give you a basic introduction to the low-level socket module in the first section of this chapter. It's worth taking a look at this module as it offers many network programming possibilities that are not accessible in the more abstract modules. In addition, you'll really learn to appreciate the convenience provided by abstract interfaces once you've become acquainted with the socket module.

The description of the socket API is followed by an introduction to the more sophisticated approach XML-RPC.

33.1   Socket API

The socket module of the standard library provides basic functionality for network communication. It implements the standardized *socket API*, which can also be found in similar form in many other programming languages.

The idea behind the socket API is that the program that wants to send or receive data via the network interface registers this with the operating system and receives from it a so-called *socket*. The program can then use this socket to establish a network connection to another socket. It doesn't matter whether the target socket is on the same computer, a computer on the local network, or a computer on the internet.

Let's start with some considerations about how a computer can be addressed in the complex world of a network. Every computer on a network, including the internet, has a unique IP address through which it can be addressed. An IP address is a string having a certain structure, e.g., *192.168.1.23*. Each of the four numerical values represents a byte and can therefore be between 0 and 255. In this case it's an IP address of a local network, which is indicated by the initial sequence *192.168*.[2]

But this isn't the end of the story. A single computer can be running several programs that want to send and receive data over the network interface at the same time, so for this reason, a network connection is also bound to a so-called *port*. The port allows you to address a specific program running on a computer with a specific IP address.

A port is a 16-bit number, so basically, 65,535 different ports are available. However, many of these ports are registered for protocols and applications and shouldn't be used for custom purposes. For example, ports 80 and 21 are registered for HTTP and FTP servers, respectively. In general, you can use ports from 49152 without hesitation.

Note that a firewall or router, for example, may block certain ports. So if you want to operate a server on your computer to which clients can connect via a certain port, you may have to enable this port with the corresponding software.

33.1.1 Client-Server Systems

The two communication partners of a network communication usually have different tasks. In the frequent case of client-server systems, one of the partners is the *server* that provides certain services, and on the other hand, there is the *client* that uses these services.

A server is accessible at a known address on the network and operates passively; that is, it waits for incoming connections. As soon as a connection request from a client arrives, a new socket is created to communicate with that particular client, provided the server accepts the request. Let's first take a look at *serial servers*, which are servers for which communication with the previous client must be completed before a new connection can be accepted. This is contrasted with the concepts of *parallel servers* and *multiplexing servers*, which we'll describe later.

The client represents the active communication partner. This means that it sends a connection request to the server and then actively uses its services.

The stages that a serial server and a client are in before, during, and after communication are illustrated by the flowchart in Figure 33.2. You can think of it as a blueprint for a serial server and its client.

First, the so-called *connection socket* is created in the server program. This is a socket designed solely to listen for incoming connections and accept them if necessary. No communication takes place over the connection socket. By calling the bind and listen

---

2 For simplicity, we are restricting ourselves to addresses conforming to the IPv4 specification in most examples. While having a different format than IPv4 addresses, addresses according to the more recent IPv6 standard can be used in a similar way. For details, please refer to Python's online documentation.

methods, the connection socket is bound to a network address and instructed to listen for incoming connection requests.

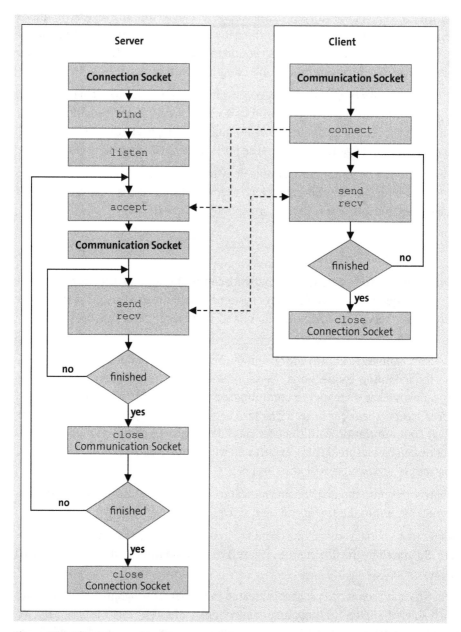

Figure 33.2 Client-Server Model

After a connection request has arrived and been accepted via accept, a new socket, the so-called *communication socket*, is created. Such a communication socket is used to handle the complete communication between server and client via methods like send or recv. A communication socket is only responsible for one connected client at a time.

As soon as the communication is finished, the communication socket is closed and possibly another connection is established. Connection requests that are not accepted immediately are buffered in the so-called *queue* and can be processed one after the other. Finally, the connection socket is also closed.

The structure of a client is comparatively simple. For example, there's only one communication socket that can be used to send a connection request to a specific server using the connect method. After that, similar to the server, the actual communication takes place via methods like send or recv. Once the communication has ended, the connection socket is closed.

Basically, two available network protocols can be selected for data transmission between server and client: UDP and TCP. In the following two sections, we'll implement small sample servers and clients for both of these protocols.

Note that the flowchart presented here refers to the connection-oriented and more common TCP protocol. The handling of the connectionless UDP protocol differs from this in some essential points, which will be described in the following section.

33.1.2 UDP

The User Datagram Protocol (UDP) network protocol was developed in 1977 as an alternative to TCP for the transmission of human speech. Characteristically, UDP is *connectionless* and *not reliable*. These two terms go hand in hand and mean, that no explicit connection is established between the communication partners, and, that UDP neither guarantees that sent packets arrive in the order in which they were sent nor that they arrive at all. Due to these limitations, however, comparatively fast transfers can take place with UDP because, for example, no packets have to be re-requested or buffered.

This makes UDP particularly suitable for multimedia applications such as VoIP, audio, or video streaming, where fast data transmission is important and minor transmission errors can be tolerated.

The sample project developed ahead consists of a server program and a client program. The client sends a text message via UDP to a specified address. The server program running there receives the message and displays it. Let's first look at the source code of the client:

```python
import socket
ip = input("IP address: ")
message = input("Message: ")
with socket.socket(socket.AF_INET, socket.SOCK_DGRAM) as s:
    s.sendto(message.encode(), (ip, 50000))
```

First, the call of the socket function creates a socket instance. Two parameters can be passed: the address type to be used and the network protocol to be used. The AF_INET and SOCK_DGRAM constants stand for Internet/IPv4 and UDP.

33

After that, two pieces of information are requested from the user: the IP address to which the message should be sent, and the message itself.

Finally, the message is sent to the specified IP address using the sendto method of socket, for which port 50000 is used. Note that messages to be sent must be passed to sendto as bytes strings or bytearray instances. In particular, this allows for the transfer of binary data.

The client program alone is useless so long as there is no matching server program on the other side that can receive and utilize the message. Note that UDP is connection-less, so the implementation is somewhat different from the flowchart of a server from Section 33.1.1. The source code of the server looks as follows:

```python
import socket
with socket.socket(socket.AF_INET, socket.SOCK_DGRAM) as s:
    s.bind(("", 50000))
    while True:
        data, addr = s.recvfrom(1024)
        print("[{}] {}".format(addr[0], data.decode()))
```

Again, a socket instance is first created and then bound to an address by calling the bind method. Note that this method gets an *address object* passed as a parameter. Whenever we talk about an address object in the context of sockets, we refer to a tuple with two elements: an IP address as a string and a port number as an integer.

Binding a socket to an address determines which internal interface the socket can use to receive packets. If no IP address is specified, this means that packets can be received via all addresses assigned to the server, such as via *127.0.0.1* or *localhost*.

After the socket has been bound to an address, data can be received. For this purpose, the recvfrom method (for *receive from*) is called in an infinite loop. The method waits until a packet is received and returns the read data along with the sender information as a tuple. Note that the received data is also returned in the form of a bytes instance.

The parameter of recvfrom identifies the buffer size and should be a power of two. The buffer size defines the maximum size of data that can be returned by one call of recvfrom. If a message to be received exceeds the buffer size, you can retrieve it bit by bit by calling recvfrom several times and concatenate the results.

33.1.3   TCP

The *Transmission Control Protocol* (*TCP*) isn't a competitor to UDP, but fills the gaps left open by UDP with its capabilities. Thus, TCP is primarily connection-oriented and reliable. *Connection-oriented* means that data packets are not simply sent to IP addresses, as with UDP, but that a connection is established up front and further operations are performed on the basis of this connection. *Reliable* means that with TCP, it isn't possible for packets to be lost, to arrive incorrectly, or to arrive in the wrong order, as is the case with UDP. Such occurrences are automatically corrected by the TCP protocol—for example, by re-requesting incomplete or erroneous packets.

For this reason, TCP is predominantly the first choice when it comes to a network communication. However, be sure to keep in mind that each packet that needs to be re-requested takes time, which can increase the latency of the connection.

In the following sections, we'll explain the use of TCP based on a small sample project. The idea is to create a rudimentary chat program where the client sends a message to the server, to which the server can reply. Thus, communication should always take place alternately. The source code of the server looks as follows:

```python
import socket
with socket.create_server(("", 50000)) as s:
    s.listen(1)
    while True:
        comm, addr = s.accept()
        while data := comm.recv(1024):
            print("[{}] {}".format(addr[0], data.decode()))
            message = input("Response: ")
            comm.send(message.encode())
        comm.close()
```

To create a connection socket for a TCP server, we use the create_server function, which combines creating and binding a TCP socket. Note that create_server expects an address object as a parameter, so the IP address and port specifications are combined in a tuple. By specifying an empty IP address, we bind the socket to all IP addresses of the server.

After that, the server is switched to passive mode by calling the listen method and instructed to listen for connection requests. Note that this method doesn't establish a connection yet. The passed parameter determines the maximum number of connection attempts to be buffered and should be at least 1.

In the subsequent infinite loop, the called accept method of the connection socket waits for an incoming connection request and accepts it. It returns a tuple whose first element is the communication socket that can be used to communicate with the connected client. The second element of the tuple is the address object of the connection partner.

After a connection has been established, a second infinite loop is initiated. In each iteration, we read a message via comm.recv from the connection partner and output the message text. If comm.recv returns an empty string, it means that the connection partner has terminated the connection. In such a case, the inner loop is aborted. When a real message has arrived, the server allows the user to enter a response and sends it via comm.send. We implement this logic using an assignment expression := (see Chapter 5, Section 5.4).

33

Now we need to take a closer look at the source code of the client:

```python
import socket
ip = input("IP address: ")
with socket.create_connection((ip, 50000)) as s:
    while message := input("Message: "):
        s.send(message.encode())
        response = s.recv(1024)
        print("[{}] {}".format(ip, response.decode()))
```

On the client side, the TCP connection socket s is created and connected by calling the create_connection function. The connection request can be accepted by the server via accept. If the connection is rejected, an exception will be raised.

The subsequent infinite loop works similarly to that of the server, with the difference that a message is first entered and sent, and then a response from the server is waited for. This puts the client and server into a rhythm where the server waits for a message whenever one is entered at the client and vice versa.

Consider it a challenge to extend the client and server into a usable chat program through threads,[3] for example. This could look like one thread listening to s.recv at a time and displaying incoming messages, and a second thread allowing the user to enter and send messages via input.

33.1.4   Blocking and Nonblocking Sockets

When a socket is created, it is by default in so-called *blocking mode*. This means that all method calls wait until the operation they trigger has been performed. Thus, a call of the recv method of a socket blocks the complete program until data has actually been received and can be read from the internal buffer of the socket.

In many cases, this behavior is desirable, but in a program with many connected sockets, for example, you don't want one of these sockets to block the entire program with its recv method just because no data has been received yet, while another socket has data ready for reading. To avoid such problems, the socket can be set to *nonblocking mode*. This affects various socket operations as follows:

- The recv and recvfrom methods of the socket object only return incoming data if it's already in the socket's internal buffer. As soon as the method has to wait for further data, it raises an OSError exception and thus returns the control flow to the program.

- The send and sendto methods send the specified data only if it can be written directly to the socket's output buffer. Occasionally it happens that this buffer is full and send or sendto would have to wait until the buffer can accept more data. In such a case, an

---

3   See Chapter 31.

OSError exception is raised in nonblocking mode, and the control flow is thus returned to the program.

- The connect method sends a connection request to the destination socket and doesn't wait for that connection to be established. By calling connect several times, it's possible to determine whether the operation is still being performed. If connect is called and the connection request is still running, an OSError exception is raised with the error message "Operation now in progress."

  Alternatively, in nonblocking mode, the connect_ex method can be used for connection requests. This method doesn't raise an OSError exception, but indicates a successful connection with a return value of 0. If errors occur during the connection, connect_ex also raises a corresponding exception.

A socket can be set to the nonblocking mode by calling its setblocking method:

```
s.setblocking(False)
```

In this case, method calls of the socket s would behave as described previously. Passing True to setblocking returns the socket to its initial blocking mode.

Socket operations are also called *synchronous operations* in blocking mode and *asynchronous operations* in nonblocking mode.

> **Note**
> It's possible to switch between blocking and nonblocking mode for a socket, even during operation. For example, you can use the connect method in blocking mode and then the read method in nonblocking mode.

33.1.5 Creating a Socket

This section describes the main ways to create a socket. In addition to the socket class already used in previous examples, these include the create_connection and create_server functions.

socket([family, type])

This function creates a new socket. The first parameter, family, identifies the address family and should be either socket.AF_INET for the IPv4 namespace or socket.AF_INET6 for the IPv6 namespace.

> **Note**
> *Internet Protocol version 6 (IPv6)* is the successor to the widely used IPv4 protocol, whose address space is now almost exhausted.

Python provides IPv6 support, for which it's usually sufficient to pass the constant AF_INET6 instead of AF_INET during socket instantiation. Some functions of the socket module are incompatible with IPv6, which we'll mention when discussing these functions.

IPv6 must be supported by the operating system in use. You can see if this is the case by looking at the socket.has_ipv6 Boolean variable.

The second parameter, type, identifies the network protocol to be used and should be either socket.SOCK_STREAM for TCP or socket.SOCK_DGRAM for UDP.

create_connection(address, [timeout, source_address])

This function connects via TCP to the remote peer identified by the address object and returns the socket object used to establish the connection. For the timeout parameter, a timeout value can be passed that will be taken into account when establishing the connection.

If an address object is passed for the source_address parameter, the socket object is bound to this address before the connection is established. The following call:

```
s = socket.create_connection((ip1,port1), timeout, (ip2, port2))
```

Is thus equivalent to this:

```
s = socket.socket(socket.AF_INET, socket.SOCK_STREAM)
s.settimeout(timeout)
s.bind((ip2, port2))
s.connect((ip1, port1))
```

The create_connection function can be used in conjunction with the with statement:

```
with socket.create_connection((ip, port)) as s:
    s.send(b"Hello world")
```

create_server (address, {family})

This function creates a TCP server bound to address and returns the connection socket created for it.

For the family parameter, the value socket.AF_INET or socket.AF_INET6 can be passed, depending on whether a connection is to be realized via IPv4 or IPv6.

33.1.6   The Socket Class

After a new instance of the socket class has been created by calling the socket or create_connection functions, it provides methods to connect to a second socket or to transfer data to the connection peer. Table 33.2 contains a description of the main methods of the socket class.

Note that the behavior of the methods differs in blocking and nonblocking modes. For more details, see Section 33.1.4.

Method	Description	Protocol
accept()	Waits for an incoming connection request and accepts it.	TCP
bind(address)	Binds the socket to address.	–
close()	Closes the socket. This means that no more data can be sent or received through it.	–
connect(address) connect_ex(address)	Connects to a server with at address.	TCP
getpeername()	Returns the address object of the connected socket. The address object is a tuple of IP address and port number.	TCP
getsockname()	Returns the address object of the socket itself.	–
listen()	Makes the socket listen for connection requests.	TCP
recv(bufsize)	Reads at most bufsize bytes of the data received at the socket and returns them as a string.	TCP
recv_into(buffer, [nbytes])	Like recv, but writes the read data to buffer instead of returning it as a bytes string. For example, a bytearray instance can be passed for buffer.	TCP
recvfrom(bufsize)	Like recv, but also returns the address object of the connection partner.	UDP
recvfrom_into(buffer, [nbytes])	Like recvfrom, but writes the read data to buffer instead of returning it as a bytes string. For example, a bytearray instance can be passed for buffer.	UDP
send(bytes) sendall(bytes)	Sends the bytes data to the connected socket.	TCP
sendto(bytes, address)	Sends the bytes data to a socket with the address address object.	UDP

Table 33.2 Methods of the Socket Class

33

Method	Description	Protocol
setblocking(flag)	Sets the socket to blocking or nonblocking mode.	–
getblocking()	Specifies whether the socket is in blocking or nonblocking mode.	–
settimeout(value) gettimeout()	Writes or reads the timeout value of the socket.	–

Table 33.2 Methods of the Socket Class (Cont.)

accept()

This method waits for an incoming connection request and accepts it. The socket instance must have been previously bound to a specific address and port by calling the bind method and must be expecting connection requests. The latter is done by calling the listen method.

The accept method returns a tuple whose first element is a new socket instance, also referred to as a *connection object*, which can be used to communicate with the connection peer. The second element of the tuple is another tuple containing the IP address and port of the remote socket.

bind(address)

This method binds the socket to the address. The address parameter must be a tuple of the form returned by accept.

After a socket has been bound to a specific address, it can be switched to passive mode, in the case of TCP, and wait for connection requests or, in the case of UDP, receive data packets directly.

connect(address) and connect_ex(address)

These methods connect to a server at address. Note that a socket must exist there waiting for connection requests on the same port for the connection to be established. The address parameter must be a tuple consisting of the IP address and the port number in the case of the IPv4 protocol.

The connect_ex method differs from connect only in that in nonblocking mode, no exception is raised if the connection isn't established immediately. The connection status is indicated via an integer return value. A return value of 0 means that the connection attempt was successful.

Note that for real errors that occur when trying to connect, exceptions will still be raised—for example, if the destination socket couldn't be reached.

listen(backlog)

This method puts a server socket into what is referred to as *listen mode*, which means that the socket listens for remote sockets that want to connect to it. After this method is called, incoming connection requests can be accepted via accept.

The backlog parameter sets the maximum number of buffered connection requests and should be at least 1. The largest possible value for backlog is defined by the operating system; usually, that's 5.

send(bytes) and sendall(bytes)

The method send sends the data bytes to the connected socket. The data has to be provided in form of a bytes string and number of bytes sent is returned. Note that in some circumstances, the data may not have been sent in full. In such a case, the application is responsible for resending the remaining data.

In contrast, the sendall method attempts to send the data until either the complete data record has been sent or an error has occurred. In the case of an error, a corresponding exception is raised.

settimeout(value) and gettimeout()

The method settimeout sets a timeout value for a socket. This value determines in blocking mode how long to wait for data to arrive or be sent. You can pass the number of seconds for value as a float or None.

The gettimeout method can be used to read the timeout value.

If a call of send or recv, for example, exceeds the maximum wait time, then a socket.timeout exception will be raised.

33.1.7   Network Byte Order

The nice aspect of standardized protocols such as TCP or UDP is that computers of many different types have a common interface through which they can communicate with each other. However, this common ground may stop behind the interface. For example, *byte order* is differs significantly among diverse systems. This byte order specifies the storage order of numbers whose memory representation requires more than one byte.

When binary data is transferred, it will cause problems if it's exchanged between two systems with different byte orders without conversion. However, the TCP protocol only guarantees that the bytes arrive in the order in which they were sent.

So long as you limit yourself to pure ASCII strings for network communication, no problems can occur, as individual ASCII characters never require more than one byte of memory. Moreover, connections between two computers of the same hardware platform are trouble-free. For example, binary data can be transferred between two x86 PCs without a problem.

But with a network connection, you usually want to transfer data without being bothered about the platform of the remote computer. For this purpose, the so-called *network byte order* has been defined. This is the byte order you must use for binary data on the network. To implement this network byte order in a useful way, the socket module contains four functions that either convert data from the host byte order to the network byte order (*hton*) or vice versa (*ntoh*).

Table 33.3 lists these functions and explains their meaning.

Alias	Meaning
ntohl(x)	Converts a 32-bit number from the network byte order to the host byte order
ntohs(x)	Converts a 16-bit number from the network byte order to the host byte order
htonl(x)	Converts a 32-bit number from the host byte order to the network byte order
htons(x)	Converts a 16-bit number from the host byte order to the network byte order

Table 33.3 Binary Data Conversion

Calling these functions may be redundant if the corresponding system already uses the network byte order.[4]

33.1.8 Multiplexing Servers: selectors

In most cases, a server isn't intended to serve only one client at a time, as was assumed in the previous examples for reasons of simplicity. Usually, a server has to manage a whole set of connected clients that are in different stages of communication. The question arises as to how something like this can be reasonably done in a single process — that is, without the use of threads.

Of course, you could switch all the sockets you use to nonblocking mode and take the management into your own hands. But this is only a solution at first glance as the blocking mode has an invaluable advantage: a blocking socket causes the program to go to sleep on a network operation until the operation can be performed. In this way, the processor load can be reduced.

In contrast, when using nonblocking sockets, we'd have to constantly iterate over all connected sockets in a loop and check if anything has happened—for example, if data is ready to be read. This approach, also called *busy waiting*, allows us to read multiple

---

4 By the way, the common x86 PC doesn't use the network byte order.

sockets quasi in parallel, but the program utilizes the processor much more because it's active for the entire period.

The selectors module allows you to manage several sockets in the same process and to wait for events arriving at these sockets. Such a server is referred to as a *multiplexing server*. The module defines the DefaultSelector class where sockets can be registered.

The following example writes a server that accepts and manages connections from any number of clients. These clients should be able to send multiple messages to the server, which will then display them on the screen. For the sake of simplicity, we don't include a server response option here:

```python
with socket.create_server(("", 50000)) as s:
    s.setblocking(False)
    s.listen(1)
    selector = selectors.DefaultSelector()
    selector.register(s, selectors.EVENT_READ, accept)
```

First, we'll create a nonblocking server socket in the usual way. This socket is then registered with a DefaultSelector instance along with an event. Possible events are EVENT_READ or EVENT_WRITE, which occur when data is ready to be read from a socket or when a socket is ready to be written to. The third parameter passed to the register method is a callback handler, which will be called in case of the event. In this case, we associate a READ event at the connection socket with the accept handler function that is to accepts an incoming connection:

```python
def accept(selector, sock):
    connection, addr = sock.accept()
    connection.setblocking(False)
    selector.register(connection, selectors.EVENT_READ, message)
```

The accept callback handler is passed the selector and the socket where the event occurred, which in this case is the connection socket. It then accepts the connection and attaches the event, that data is received at the resulting client socket, to the message handler function:

```python
def message(selector, client):
    message = client.recv(1024)
    ip = client.getpeername()[0]
    if message:
        print("[{}] {}".format(ip, message.decode()))
    else:
        print("+++ Connection to {} terminated".format(ip))
        selector.unregister(client)
        client.close()
```

33

The message handler function is also passed the selector and the relevant socket—in this case, the client socket. It then reads the received data and prints it as a message on the screen. For the sake of simplicity, again, we don't include a server response option.

If the connection was terminated by the client, recv returns an empty string. In this case, we need to call the unregister method of the selector to sign out this client socket. After that, the connection can be closed.

Finally, the multiplexing server must be put into operation. To do this, we call the selector's select method in an infinite loop, which blocks until one of the registered events has occurred:

```
while True:
    for key, mask in selector.select():
        key.data(selector, key.fileobj)
```

If an event occurs, select returns a tuple: (key, mask). Using the key instance, we can access the data associated with the event—in this case, the corresponding handler function. In addition, key.fileobj can be used to access the socket where the event occurred. The mask instance specifies which event specifically occurred. With the help of the binary AND, the EVENT_READ and EVENT_WRITE event types can be checked here.

For the sake of completeness, here is the source code of the client that matches this server:

```
import socket
ip = input("IP address: ")
with socket.create_connection((ip, 50000)) as s:
    while True:
        message = input("Message: ")
        s.send(message.encode())
```

This is pure socket programming, as we've already covered in the previous sections. Apart from possible latencies, the client doesn't notice whether it's being served by a serial or a multiplexing server.

33.1.9 Object-Oriented Server Development: socketserver

You can imagine that implementing a more complex server using the socket module can quickly become confusing and complicated. For this reason, the standard library of Python contains the socketserver module, which is intended to make it easier to write a server capable of serving multiple clients.

In the following example, the chat server from the previous section will be recreated using the socketserver module. For this purpose, a so-called *request handler* must first be created. This is a class derived from the socketserver.BaseRequestHandler base class.

Essentially, in this class, the handle method in which the communication with a client should take place must be overridden:

```python
import socketserver
class ChatRequestHandler(socketserver.BaseRequestHandler):
    def handle(self):
        addr = self.client_address[0]
        print("[{}] Connection established".format(addr))
        while True:
            s = self.request.recv(1024)
            if s:
                print("[{}] {}".format(addr, s.decode()))
            else:
                print("[{}] Connection closed".format(addr))
                break
```

Here the ChatRequestHandler class was created, which inherits from BaseRequestHandler. Later, each time a connection is established, the socketserver instance will create a new instance of this class and calls the handle method. The communication with the connected client then runs within this method. In addition to the handle method, the setup and finish methods can be overwritten, which are called either before or after the handle call.

In addition to the methods mentioned, the BaseRequestHandler base class defines the request attribute, through which information about a client's current request is accessible. For a TCP server, request references the socket instance used to communicate with the client. It can be used to send or receive data. When using the connectionless UDP protocol, request references a tuple containing the data sent by the client and the communication socket that can be used for the response.

The client_address attribute references an address tuple containing the IP address and port number of the client whose request is being handled by this BaseRequestHandler instance.

In the example, within the handle method, incoming data is read in an infinite loop. If an empty string was read, the connection is closed by the communication peer. Otherwise, the read string is output.

This completes the work on the request handler. What is missing now is the server that accepts incoming connections and instantiates the request handler in response:

```python
server = socketserver.ThreadingTCPServer(("", 50000), ChatRequestHandler)
server.serve_forever()
```

To create the actual server, we create an instance of the ThreadingTCPServer class. To do this, we pass the constructor an address tuple and the ChatRequestHandler request handler class we just created. By calling the serve_forever method of the ThreadingTCPServer instance, we instruct the server to accept all incoming connection requests from now on.

In addition to the serve_forever method, a server instance provides the handle_request method, which accepts and handles exactly one connection request. There is also a shutdown method for shutting down a server.

In addition to the ThreadingTCPServer class, other server classes can be instantiated, depending on how you want the server to behave. The interface is the same for all constructors.

TCPServer and UDPServer

These classes implement simple TCP or UDP servers. Note that these servers can only make one connection at a time. For this reason, the TCPServer class can't be used for our sample program.

ThreadingTCPServer and ThreadingUDPServer

These classes implement a TCP or UDP server that handles each request from a client in a separate thread, so the server can be in contact with multiple clients simultaneously. This makes the ThreadingTCPServer class ideal for the preceding example.

> **Note**
>
> The programmer is responsible for any resources shared by multiple threads. These may need to be backed up by *critical sections*.
>
> For more details on parallel programming, refer to Chapter 31.

ForkingTCPServer and ForkingUDPServer

These classes implement a TCP or UDP server that handles each request from a client in a separate process, so the server can be in contact with multiple clients simultaneously. The handle method of the handler request is executed in its own process, so it can't access instances of the main process.

33.2   XML-RPC

The *XML-RPC* standard[5] enables remote function and method calls via a network interface. From the programmer's point of view, remote functions can be called as if they belonged to the local program. The transfer of the function calls and especially the parameters and the return value are completely handled by the XML-RPC library so that the programmer only needs to call the functions.

---

5 For *XML remote procedure call.*

In addition to XML-RPC, there are other more or less standardized methods for remote function calls. But because XML-RPC is based on two existing standards, XML and HTTP, and doesn't introduce any new binary protocols, it's comparatively easy to implement and therefore available in many programming languages.

Since XML-RPC was developed independently of any particular programming language, it's possible to write the client and server in two different languages. For this reason, the XML-RPC specification had to agree on a lowest common denominator with regard to the peculiarities of certain programming languages and especially the available data types. You'll notice that you have to consider certain limitations when using a function with an XML-RPC-enabled interface.

In the following sections, we'll first look at how an XML-RPC server makes certain functions externally callable. We'll then turn our attention to the client side and clarify how such functions can be called.

33.2.1   The Server

To set up an XML-RPC server, the `xmlrpc.server` module is required. This module essentially contains the `SimpleXMLRPCServer` class, which sets up a corresponding server and provides methods for managing it. The constructor of the class has the interface described ahead.

SimleXMLRPCServer(addr, [requestHandler, logRequests, allow_none, encoding, bind_and_activate])

The only mandatory parameter is `addr`; it specifies the IP address and port to which the server will be bound. The information must be passed in a tuple of the form (`ip`, `port`), where the IP address is a string and the port number is an integer between 0 and 65535. Technically, the parameter is passed to the underlying `socket` instance. The server can bind itself only to addresses that are assigned to it. If an empty string is specified for `ip` in the tuple, the server is bound to all addresses assigned to the PC—for example, also to *127.0.0.1* or *localhost*.

You can specify a backend via the optional `requestHandler` parameter. In most cases, the default `SimpleXMLRPCRequestHandler` handler is sufficient. The task of this class is to convert incoming data back into a function call.

You can use the `logRequest` parameter to specify whether incoming function calls should be logged or not. The parameter defaults to `True`.

The fourth parameter, `allow_none`, allows `None` to be used in XML-RPC functions if `True` is passed here. Normally the use of `None` causes an exception because no such data type is provided in the XML-RPC standard. But because this is a common extension to the standard, `allow_none` is supported by many XML-RPC implementations.

The fifth parameter, encoding, can be used to specify an encoding for data transmission. By default, UTF-8 is used here.

The last optional parameter, bind_and_activate, determines whether the server should be bound to the address and activated directly after instantiation. This is interesting if you still want to manipulate the server instance before activating it, but is usually not needed. The parameter defaults to True.

Usually, the following call of the constructor is sufficient to instantiate a local XML-RPC server:

```
>>> from xmlrpc.server import SimpleXMLRPCServer
>>> srv = SimpleXMLRPCServer(("127.0.0.1", 1337))
```

Once an instance of the SimpleXMLRPCServer class has been created, it has methods that make certain function remotely callable. The main methods of a SimpleXMLRPCServer instance will be explained in the following sections.

s.register_function(function, [name])

This method registers the function object function for an RPC call. This means that an XML-RPC client connected to this server can call function through the network.

Optionally, the function can be given a different name by which it can be reached by the client. When you specify such a name, it can consist of any Unicode characters, even those that are not actually allowed in a Python identifier, such as a hyphen or a period.

s.register_instance(instance, [allow_dotted_names])

This method registers an instance for remote access. When the connected client calls a method of this instance, the call is routed through the special _dispatch method which must be defined by the instance as follows:

```
def _dispatch(self, method, params):
    pass
```

Each time a method is called remotely, _dispatch is invoked. The method parameter contains the name of the called method and params the parameters specified thereby.

A concrete implementation of the _dispatch method, which calls the actual method of the registered instance named method and passes the parameters, may look like the following:

```
def _dispatch(self, method, params):
    try:
        return getattr(self, method)(*params)
    except (AttributeError, TypeError):
        return None
```

This function returns None both if there is no method named method and if the method is called with the wrong number or otherwise inappropriate parameters.

> **Note**
>
> If you pass True for the optional allow_dotted_names parameter, periods are possible in the remote method call. This also allows you to call methods of attributes over the network. Be sure to note that this makes it possible for an attacker to access the program's global variables and potentially execute malicious code. You should set allow_dotted_names to True only within a local, trusted network.

s.register_introspection_functions()

This method registers the system.listMethods, system.methodHelp, and system.method Signature functions for remote access. These functions allow a connected client to obtain a list of all available functions and detailed information about individual ones.

For details on using the system.listMethods, system.methodHelp, and system.method Signature functions, see Section 33.2.2.

s.register_multicall_functions()

This method registers the system.multicall function for remote access. By calling the system.multicall function, the client can bundle multiple method calls. The return values of the method calls are also returned in bundles.

For details on how to use the system.multicall function, see Section 33.2.3.

Example

Now that the most important functions of the SimpleXMLRPCServer class have been explained, we're going to develop a small sample program at this point. The program is an XML-RPC server that provides two mathematical functions (more precisely, the calculation functions for the factorial and the square of an integer) that a connected client can call:[6]

```python
from xmlrpc.server import SimpleXMLRPCServer as Server
def fac(n):
    # Calculates the factorial of the integer n.
    res = 1
    for i in range(2, n+1):
        res *= i
    return res
```

---

6 This scenario makes perfect sense if you imagine the server running on a computer that is especially suited for these mathematical operations. Clients could then delegate these calculations to the server.

```
def square(n):
    # Calculates the square of the number n.
    return n*n
with Server(("", 50000)) as srv:
    srv.register_function(fac)
    srv.register_function(square)
    srv.serve_forever()
```

First, the two `fac` and `square` calculation functions are defined for the factorial and the square of a number, respectively. After that, an XML-RPC server listening on port 50000 is created. Then the functions just created are registered. Finally, the server is started by calling the `serve_forever` method and is now ready to receive and process incoming connection requests and method calls.

The server presented here is of course only one half of the sample program. In the following section, we'll discuss what an XML-RPC client should look like. Finally, at the end of the following section, we'll develop a client that can communicate with this server.

33.2.2   The Client

To write an XML-RPC client, the `xmlrpc.client` module of the standard library is used. This module mainly contains the `ServerProxy` class, which is used to communicate with an XML-RPC server. Here you can first see the interface of the constructor of the `ServerProxy` class.

ServerProxy(uri, [transport, encoding, verbose, allow_none, use_datetime])

This creates an instance of the `ServerProxy` class that's connected to the XML-RPC server described by the `uri` Uniform Resource Identifier (URI).[7]

In the second place, as with the `SimpleXMLRPCServer` class, a backend can be specified. The default classes of `Transport` for the HTTP protocol and `SafeTransport` for the HTTPS protocol should be sufficient for most use cases.

If the value `True` is passed for the fourth parameter, `verbose`, then the `ServerProxy` instance outputs all outgoing and incoming XML packets on the screen. This can be helpful for troubleshooting.

If you pass the value `True` for the last parameter, `use_datetime`, the `datetime` class of the standard library (Chapter 15, Section 15.2) is used instead of the `xmlrpc.client`-internal `DateTime` class for the representation of date and time information, which has a much larger range of functions.

---

7 A URI is the generalization of a URL.

The encoding and allow_none parameters have the same meaning as the parameters of the same name of the constructor of the SimpleXMLRPCServer class discussed at the beginning of the last section.

After instantiation, the ServerProxy class is connected to an XML-RPC server. This means in particular that you can call and use all functions registered with this server remotely, as they were methods of the ServerProxy instance. So no further special treatment is needed.

In addition, a ServerProxy instance includes three methods that provide further information about the available remote functions. Note, however, that the server must explicitly allow to call these methods. This can be done by calling the register_introspection_functions methods of the SimpleXMLRPCServer instance.

In the following sections, s is supposed to be an instance of the ServerProxy class.

s.system.listMethods()

This method returns the names of all remote functions registered with the XML-RPC server in the form of a list of strings. The listMethods, methodSignature, and methodHelp system methods aren't included in this list.

s.system.methodSignature(name)

This method provides information about the interface of the registered function with the function named name. The interface description is a string in the following format:

```
"string, int, int, int"
```

The first specification corresponds to the data type of the return value and all others to the data types of the function parameters. The XML-RPC standard permits that two different functions may have the same name, as long as they are distinguishable by their interface.[8] For this reason, the system.methodSignature method returns a list of strings rather than a single string.

Note that the system.methodSignature method has a deeper meaning only if the XML-RPC server is written in a language in which the function parameters are each bound to a data type. Such languages include C, C++, C#, and Java. If you call system.methodSignature on an XML-RPC server written in Python, the string "signatures not supported" will be returned.

s.system.methodHelp(name)

This method returns the docstring of the name remote function if one exists. If no docstring could be found, an empty string will be returned.

---

8 This is also called *function overloading*.

Example

The following code describes the use of a ServerProxy instance. The example implements a client matching the XML-RPC server of the previous section:

```
from xmlrpc.client import ServerProxy
cli = ServerProxy("http://127.0.0.1:50000")
print(cli.fac(5))
print(cli.square(5))
```

You can see that connecting to an XML-RPC server and executing remote functions requires only a few lines of code, making it almost as simple as if the functions were defined in the client program itself.

33.2.3 Multicall

The xmlrpc.client module contains a class called MultiCall. This class allows multiple function calls to be sent to the server in a bundle and instructs the server to return the return values in a bundle as well. This way, you can minimize the network load for frequent function calls.

The use of the MultiCall class is illustrated by the following example. The example requires a running server that provides the fac and square functions for remote access—exactly like the one we presented in Section 33.2.1. In addition, the server must allow the use of multicall by calling the register_multicall_functions methods:

```
from xmlrpc.client import ServerProxy, MultiCall
cli = ServerProxy("http://127.0.0.1:50000")
mc = MultiCall(cli)
for i in range(10):
    mc.fac(i)
    mc.square(i)
for result in mc():
    print(result)
```

First, we connect to the XML-RPC server as usual. Then we create an instance of the MultiCall class and pass the previously created ServerProxy instance to the constructor.

From then on, the bundled communication with the server runs via the MultiCall instance. For this purpose, the fac and square remote functions can be called as if they were local methods of the MultiCall instance. Note, however, that these method calls don't result in an immediate remote function call and thus don't return a value at this time.

In the example, fac and square are each called 10 times with consecutive integers.

By calling the MultiCall instance mc, all buffered remote function calls are sent together to the server. As a result, an iterator is returned that iterates over all return values in the order of the respective function call. In the sample program, we use the iterator in a `for` loop to output the results with `print`.

Especially when there are few return values, it makes sense to reference them directly:

```
value1, value2, value3 = mc()
```

Here it's assumed that three remote function calls have been made before, and accordingly there are three return values.

33.2.4   Limitations

The XML-RPC standard is not tailored to Python alone, but an attempt was made to find a lowest common denominator of many programming languages when drafting the standard, so that, for example, server and client can communicate with each other even if they were written in different languages.

For this reason, using XML-RPC comes with some limitations regarding the more complex or exotic data types of Python. For example, there is no representation of the `complex`, `set`, and `frozenset` data types in the XML-RPC standard. In addition, you can use `None` only if this was explicitly specified when instantiating the server or client class. Of course, this only means that instances of these data types can't be sent via the XML-RPC interface. Internally in the program, you can still use them. For example, if you try to send an instance of the `complex` data type as the return value of a function via the XML-RPC interface, an `xmlrpc.client.Fault` exception will be raised. Of course, it's still possible to send a complex number via an XML-RPC interface by transmitting the real and imaginary parts separately, each as an integer.

Table 33.4 lists all the data types provided in the XML-RPC standard and describes how you can use them in Python.

XML-RPC	Python	Notes
Boolean values	`bool`	—
Integers	`int`	32-bit Integers in the range from -2147483648 to 2147483647 can be used.
Floats	`float`	—
Strings	`str`	—
Arrays	`list`	Only XML-RPC-compliant instances may be used as elements in the list.
Structures	`dict`	All keys must be strings. Only XML-RPC-compliant instances may be used as values.

Table 33.4 Allowed Data Types for XML-RPC

33

XML-RPC	Python	Notes
Date/time	DateTime	The special data type xmlrpc.client.DateTime is used.[*]
Binary data	Binary	The special data type xmlrpc.client.Binary is used.
None	None	Only possible if the client was created with allow_none=True.
Floats with arbitrary precision	decimal.Decimal	–

[*] This is not the datetime data type from the datetime module of the standard library. However, the client be set up to automatically convert DateTime to datetime, as described in Section 33.2.2.

Table 33.4 Allowed Data Types for XML-RPC (Cont.)

It's possible to transmit instances of self-created classes. In such a case, the instance is converted into a *dictionary*, a structure in which the names of the contained attributes are represented as keys and the respective referenced instances as values. This happens automatically. Note, however, that the dictionary arriving on the opposite side is not automatically converted back into an instance of the original class.

We haven't yet encountered the last two data types listed in the table. These are data types contained in the xmlrpc.client module and are specifically tailored for use in the context of XML-RPC. The two DateTime and Binary data types mentioned are explained ahead.

The DateTime Data Type

The DateTime data type of the xmlrpc.client module can be used to send date and time information via an XML-RPC interface. Provided that the corresponding parameter was passed when instantiating the ServerProxy instance, an instance of the known datetime.date, datetime.time, or datetime.datetime data type can also be used directly instead of a DateTime instance.

When creating an instance of the DateTime data type, either one of the data types of the datetime module or a Unix timestamp as an integer can be passed:

```
>>> import xmlrpc.client
>>> import datetime
>>> xmlrpc.client.DateTime(987654321)
<DateTime '20010419T06:25:21' at 0x7f91671fb7f0>
>>> xmlrpc.client.DateTime(datetime.datetime(1970, 1, 1))
<DateTime '19700101T00:00:00' at 0x7f1d72595278>
```

You can safely send instances of the DateTime data type as a return value or a parameter via an XML-RPC interface.

The Binary Data Type

The Binary data type of the xmlrpclib module is used to send binary data via an XML-RPC interface. When instantiating the binary data type, a bytes string is passed that contains the binary data. These can be read again on the opposite side via the data attribute:

```
>>> import xmlrpc.client
>>> b = xmlrpc.client.Binary(b"\x00\x01\x02\x03")
>>> b.data
b'\x00\x01\x02\x03'
```

You can safely send instances of the binary data type as a return value or a parameter through an XML-RPC interface.

Chapter 34

Accessing Resources on the Internet

In this chapter, we'll look at the solutions Python provides for accessing resources on the internet. By this we mean, for example, downloading HTML documents or other files from web servers via HTTP or connecting to FTP servers to exchange files.

But first we'd like to provide an overview of the protocols and solutions in use before discussing a selection of the available solutions in detail.

34.1   Protocols

Two predominant protocols for data transfer exist on the internet: HTTP and FTP.

34.1.1   Hypertext Transfer Protocol

Hypertext Transfer Protocol (HTTP) is the protocol via which browsers and web servers communicate with each other to transfer web content. It's stateless and, together with the HTML and URL standards, represents the backbone of the modern internet. Nowadays, the protocol is often used in its encrypted variant, *Hypertext Transfer Protocol Secure (HTTPS)*.

Among other things, the HTTP protocol distinguishes between two main types of requests, which differ in whether and how data is transmitted from the client to the server:

- The most common method, *GET*, is used to retrieve a resource from a web server. Additional information can be sent to the server by encoding it in the URL. According to the standard, a GET request shouldn't cause server resources to be modified as in the case of a file upload, for example.

- The alternative *POST* method is suitable for transferring large amounts of data to a web server. The data isn't encoded in the URL as with GET, but is transferred as part of the request payload. The POST method is suitable, for example, for transferring form data on the web or for file uploads.

34.1.2   File Transfer Protocol

File Transfer Protocol (FTP) is a common protocol for file transfers on the internet. Unlike HTTP, it's *stateful*: this means that you first open a session with an FTP server and can then perform operations such as directory changes, uploads, or downloads within the context of this session.

34.2 Solutions

In Python, there's a bewildering variety of modules, both in the standard library and from third-party vendors, that provide access to resources on the internet.

34.2.1 Outdated Solutions for Python 2

First, the urllib module and its successor urllib2 from the standard library of Python 2 should be mentioned as they're still referred to again and again on the internet. With the change to Python 3, both modules have been removed from the standard library and are therefore no longer available in modern language versions.

34.2.2 Solutions in the Standard Library

With the switch to Python 3, the old urllib and urllib2 modules have been substantially reworked and merged into a new module called urllib. The name collision often leads to confusion, so always be aware of which language version is meant when talking about the urllib module. The urllib module represents the reference solution of the standard library for accessing resources on the internet under Python 3.

In addition, the ftplib and http modules are available in the standard library, which are suitable for direct communication with FTP or HTTP servers without additional abstraction layers.

34.2.3 Third-Party Solutions

In addition to the urllib module of the standard library, the third-party urllib3 and requests modules have been developed with the intention to make accessing resources on the internet as easy as possible. In this context, requests stands out: it's based on urllib3 and is now even recommended in the official Python documentation as a simple alternative to urllib. Note that urllib3 and requests only support access via HTTP, while urllib can also download files via FTP.

In the following sections, we'll first present requests as the simplest approach before turning to the urllib module of the standard library. Afterward, we'll discuss another solution for communicating with FTP servers in more complex use cases using the ftplib module of the standard library.

34.3   The Easy Way: requests

The third-party requests module enables you to access resources on the internet via HTTP and enjoys great popularity. It particularly impresses with its ease of use and can be installed via the conda and pip package managers:

```
$ conda install requests
$ pip install requests
```

The online documentation for requests can be found at *requests.readthedocs.io.*

34.3.1   Simple Requests via GET and POST

After the module is imported, it provides the get and post functions that can be used to send respective HTTP requests to a web server:

```
>>> import requests
>>> r_get = requests.get("https://www.python-book.com")
>>> r_post = requests.post("https://www.python-book.com")
```

The requests are executed directly by calling get or post and the response sent by the server is returned as a response object. The status_code and reason attributes of the response object allow us to first determine if the request was successful:

```
>>> r_get.status_code, r_get.reason
(200, 'OK')
>>> r_post.status_code, r_post.reason
(403, 'FORBIDDEN')
```

In this case, the POST request was rejected by the server, while the GET request was answered without any problem. We access the transmitted data content via the content and text attributes of the response object, where content contains the data as a bytes string and text decodes the data as text using the encoding indicated by the server:

```
>>> type(r_get.content)
<class 'bytes'>
>>> type(r_get.text)
<class 'str'>
>>> r_get.encoding
'utf-8'
```

The text attribute is also accessible for requests to download binary data, but is of little use. In this case, content should be used. If you want to save the downloaded data to a file in the local file system, you can do this independently of requests by writing to an open file object:

34

```
>>> with open("result.html", "wb") as f:
...     f.write(r_get.content)
```

> **Note**
>
> Besides GET and POST, requests also supports other HTTP request types like PUT,
> DELETE, HEAD, and OPTIONS. However, we won't go further into this at this point.

34.3.2   Web APIs

You can also use requests via get and post to access web APIs. In the following example,
we use Wikipedia's API to search for articles about Python:

```
>>> r_api = requests.get(
...     "https://en.wikipedia.org/w/api.php"
...     "?action=query&list=search&srsearch=Python&format=json"
... )
```

Note that wrapping the URL over multiple lines is done here for formatting reasons in
the book and isn't at all necessary when you use requests. Should the web server
respond to such a request with a response in JSON format, as is common with web APIs,
the response object provides the json method to deserialize it:

```
>>> r_api.json()
```

Additional data can be sent to the web server for GET or POST requests. While POST supports such *payloads* as part of the request itself, GET requires them to be encoded in the
URL. We used such an encoding of parameters in the URL in the previous example to
specify the search term for the Wikipedia search.

The get function also allows us to specify the data to be encoded in the URL via the
params parameter, avoiding the effort of manual encoding:

```
>>> r_api = requests.get(
...     "https://en.wikipedia.org/w/api.php",
...     params={
...         "action": "query",
...         "list": "search",
...         "srsearch": "Python",
...         "format":"json"
...     }
... )
>>> r_api.url
'https://en.wikipedia.org/w/api.php?action=query&list=search&srsearch=Python&
format=json'
```

It's recommended to specify the parameters via params as this method also takes special cases into account during encoding. For example, think of the & character in the search term.

For requests via POST, the data parameter can be used in addition to params in the same way to accommodate the payload in the message content:

```
>>> r_api = requests.post(
...     "https://en.wikipedia.org/w/api.php",
...     data={
...         "action": "query",
...         "list": "search",
...         "srsearch": "Python",
...         "format":"json"
...     }
... )
>>> r_api.url
'https://en.wikipedia.org/w/api.php'
>>> r_api.request.body
'action=query&list=search&srsearch=Python&format=json'
```

In this case, Wikipedia's web API supports both requests via GET and POST, and the transmission of parameters via URL encoding and message payload in the case of POST. This is a design decision by the API developers and needn't be the case for every web API.

This should suffice as an introduction to the requests module. In addition to the options shown here, requests offers a wealth of other features. These include the sending and receiving of cookies, the verification of SSL connections, and HTTP authentication. These topics are covered in the detailed online documentation for requests at *requests.readthedocs.io*.

34.4   URLs: urllib

A *Uniform Resource Locator* (*URL*) specifies a resource—for example, on the internet—by its location and the protocol to be used to access it.

The urllib package provides a convenient interface for handling resources on the internet. For this purpose, urllib contains the following modules (see Table 34.1).

Module	Description	Section
urllib.request	Contains functions and classes for accessing a resource on the internet	Section 34.4.1

Table 34.1 Modules of the urllib Package

Module	Description	Section
urllib.response	Contains the data types used in the urllib package	–
urllib.parse	Contains functions for the convenient reading, processing, and creation of URLs	Section 34.4.2
urllib.error	Contains the exception classes used in the urllib package	–
urllib.robotparser	Contains a class that interprets the *robots.txt* file* of a website	–

> * Programs that automatically crawl the internet usually first read a file called *robots.txt* in the root directory of the web server. There you can define which parts of the website may be searched.

Table 34.1 Modules of the urllib Package (Cont.)

The following sections describe the request and parse modules of the urllib package.

34.4.1   Accessing Remote Resources: urllib.request

The central function of the urllib.request module for accessing remote resources is urlopen, which is similar to the built-in open function except for the fact that a URL is passed instead of a file name. Also, no write operations can be performed on the resulting file object for obvious reasons.

In the following sections, we'll describe the most important functions contained in the urllib.request module in greater detail. To reproduce the examples, you must import the request module of the urllib package:

```
>>> import urllib.request
```

urllib.request.urlopen(url, [data, timeout], {cafile, capath})

The urlopen function accesses the network resource addressed by url and returns an open file object for that resource. Thus, the function enables you, for example, to download the source code of a website and read it like a local file.

For url, you can either specify a URL as a string or a request object. You can read more about request objects ahead. If no protocol such as http:// or ftp:// is specified for the URL, it's assumed that the URL references a resource on the local hard drive. For accesses to the local hard drive, you can also specify the file:// protocol.

The third optional parameter, timeout, is used to specify a time limit in seconds to be considered when accessing an internet resource. If this parameter isn't passed, a default value of the operating system will be used.

The optional keyword-only `cafile` and `capath` parameters allow you to provide certificates that are used by the `urlopen` function to authenticate itself to the remote peer. For `cafile`, a path to a file containing a certificate in *Privacy-Enhanced Mail* (*PEM*) format can be specified. You can use the `capath` parameter to specify a directory where the certificate files are located.

Transferring Parameters

If the protocol used is `http`, the optional `data` parameter of the `urlopen` function is used to pass POST parameters[1] to the resource. These POST values must be specially prepared using the `urlencode` function of the `urllib.parse` module:

```
>>> prm = urllib.parse.urlencode({"prm1": "value1", "prm2": "value2"})
>>> urllib.request.urlopen("http://www.python-book.com",
... prm.encode("ascii"))
<http.client.HTTPResponse object at 0x7fa3f74b4e48>
```

Besides POST, there's another method for passing parameters to a website: GET. With GET, the parameters are encoded directly in the URL:

```
>>> urllib.request.urlopen("http://www.python-book.com?prm=value")
<http.client.HTTPResponse object at 0x7fa3f74b4860>
```

Return Value

The file object returned by the `urlopen` function is a file-*like* object because it provides only a subset of the functionality of a real file object. Table 34.2 contains the main available methods of the file-like object and a short description.

Method	Description
`read([size])`	Reads `size` bytes from the resource and returns them as a `bytes` string. If `size` hasn't been specified, the complete content will be read.
`readline([size])`	Reads a line from the resource and returns it as a `bytes` string. If `size` has been specified, a maximum of `size` bytes will be read.
`readlines([sizehint])`	Reads the resource line by line and returns it as a list of `bytes` strings. If `sizehint` is specified, lines are read only until the total size of the lines read exceeds `sizehint`.

Table 34.2 Methods of the Returned File-Like Object

34

---

1 The HTTP protocol knows two types of parameter transfer: with POST, the data is sent invisibly for the user in the HTTP body, while with GET, it's encoded in the URL.

Method	Description
close()	Closes the opened object. After calling this method, no further operations are possible.
info()	Returns a dictionary-like info object containing meta information for the downloaded page.
geturl()	Returns a string with the URL of the resource.

Table 34.2 Methods of the Returned File-Like Object (Cont.)

Info Objects

The info method of the file-like object returned by urlopen provides an instance that contains various information about the network resource. This information can be accessed in the same way as a dictionary. Let's look at the following example:

```
>>> f = urllib.request.urlopen("http://www.python-book.com")
>>> d = f.info()
>>> d.keys()
['Server', 'Date', 'Content-Type', 'Content-Length', 'Connection', 'Vary',
'Strict-Transport-Security', 'X-Frame-Options', 'X-Content-Type-Options',
'Referrer-Policy', 'X-Xss-Protection', 'Accept-Ranges']
```

In the example, the internet resource http://www.python-book.com was accessed and the dictionary-like object containing information about the website was created by calling the info method. By using the keys method of a dictionary, all contained keys can be displayed. It depends on the protocol used what kind of information will be included. In caes of the HTTP protocol, the info object contains all the information sent by the server. For example, you can use the "Content-Length" and "Server" keys to read the size of the downloaded file in bytes and the identification string of the server software, respectively:

```
>>> d["Content-Length"]
'223290'
>>> d["Server"]
'nginx'
```

Request Objects

The urlopen function expects either a URL as a string or a so-called request object as first parameter. The latter is an instance of the Request class that allows you to specify the request properties in more detail:

```
>>> req = urllib.request.Request("http://www.python-book.com")
>>> f = urllib.request.urlopen(req)
```

For example, the request object can be used to modify the header sent with an HTTP request. In this way, for example, the browser identifier can be changed:[2]

```
>>> req = urllib.request.Request("http://www.python-book.com")
>>> req.add_header("User-agent", "My browser")
>>> req.header_items()
[('User-agent', 'My browser')]
>>> f = urllib.request.urlopen(req)
```

Installing Openers

When accessing remote resources, there are many special cases beyond the standard method discussed so far. For example, many servers require authentication. Another example is the use of a proxy server.

To realize this kind of more complex request, a separate so-called *opener* must be created and used. An opener is an instance of the OpenerDirector class that is responsible for accessing the resource described by the URL. There is a default opener that we've used implicitly in the previous examples.

An opener has one or more *handlers*, from which it selects the one suitable for a request. Each handler is designed for a specific use case:

```
>>> opener = urllib.request.OpenerDirector()
>>> opener.add_handler(urllib.request.HTTPHandler())
>>> opener.open("http://www.python-book.com")
<http.client.HTTPResponse object at 0x7f37b9334fd0>
```

In the example, an opener was created that has only the default HTTP handler. This opener can be used for a request via its open method. Alternatively, the opener can be installed, which will enable the urlopen function to use it as well:

```
>>> urllib.request.install_opener(opener)
```

Besides the standard HTTP handler, a number of other handlers are available. These include HTTPDefaultErrorHandler and HTTPRedirectHandler for handling errors and redirects in HTTP requests, ProxyHandler and ProxyBasicAuthHandler for using proxy servers, HTTPBasicAuthHandler and HTTPDigestAuthHandler for authentication to HTTP servers, and HTTPSHandler, FTPHandler, and FileHandler for HTTPS, FTP, and local file protocols, respectively.

34

---

2 Some websites use this identifier to exploit specific features of browsers or to exclude unsupported browsers. For this reason, it can be helpful to fake a known browser via the HTTP header.

34.4.2   Reading and Processing URLs: urllib.parse

The urllib.parse module contains functions that allow you to split a URL into its components or to reassemble these components into a valid URL.

To run the examples, you must first import the urllib.parse module:

```
>>> import urllib.parse
```

Escape Sequences

The quote function replaces special characters that mustn't appear as such in a URL with escape sequences of the form %xx, as they're allowed in URLs. With the optional safe parameter—a string—you specify characters that shouldn't be converted into an escape sequence:

```
>>> urllib.parse.quote("www.test.com/hello world.html")
'www.test.com/hello%20world.html'
```

The counterpart to quote is unquote:

```
>>> urllib.parse.unquote("www.test.com/hello%20world.html")
'www.test.com/hello world.html'
```

In addition to the quote_from_bytes and unquote_to_bytes functions for bytes strings, the quote_plus and unquote_plus functions exist, which behave like quote and unquote, but additionally replace a space in the URL with a plus sign (+). This is especially interesting in the context of HTML forms.

Breaking Up and Recomposing a URL

The urlparse function breaks a URL up into several parts. Basically, a URL can consist of six parts:[3]

```
scheme://netloc/path;params?query#fragment
```

The netloc section of the URL is also divided into four additional sections:

```
username:password@host:port
```

Except for the host specification in the netloc section, all specifications are optional and can be omitted.

The six components of the URL are returned as a tuple-like object with six elements. These most frequently used parts of the URL can be addressed via the indexes 0 to 5, just like a real tuple. In addition—and this distinguishes the returned instance from a tuple—all parts of the URL can be accessed via attributes of the instance. You can also

---

3 The params part of a URL is very rarely used.

use attributes to access the four parts of the netloc sections that aren't accessible via an index.

Table 34.3 lists all attributes of the return value of the urlparse function and briefly explains each of them. In addition, the corresponding index is given, provided that the associated attribute can also be addressed via an index. The attribute names match the names of the sections as used in the URL examples shown previously.

Attribute	Index	Description
scheme	0	The protocol of the URL, such as http or file.
netloc	1	The network location (netloc) usually consists of a domain name with subdomain and TLD.* Optionally, username, password, and port number can also be included in netloc.
path	2	A path specification that identifies a subfolder of the network location.
params	3	Parameters for the last element of the path.
query	4	Additional information can be transferred to a server-side script via the query string.
fragment	5	The fragment is also referred to as an *anchor*. A common example of an anchor is a jump mark within an HTML file.
username	–	The username specified in the URL, if available.
password	–	The password specified in the URL, if available.
hostname	–	The hostname of the URL.
port	–	The port number specified in the URL, if available.

* Top Level Domain

Table 34.3 Sections of a URL

In the following example, a complex URL will be broken up into its constituent parts:

```
>>> url = "http://www.example.com/path/to/file.py?prm=abc"
>>> parts = urllib.parse.urlparse(url)
>>> parts.scheme
'http'
>>> parts.netloc
'www.example.com'
>>> parts.path
'/path/to/file.py'
>>> parts.params
''
```

```
>>> parts.query
'prm=abc'
>>> parts.fragment
''
>>> parts.hostname
'www.example.com'
```

As a counterpart to urlparse, there's the urlunparse function, which generates a URL string from an iterable with six elements:

```
>>> url = ("http", "example.com", "/path/file.py", "", "", "")
>>> urllib.parse.urlunparse(url)
'http://example.com/path/file.py'
```

Note

The expression

```
urlunparse(urlparse(url)) == url
```

doesn't always evaluate to True because superfluous information, such as an empty fragment at the end of a URL, is lost when urlparse is called.

Breaking Up and Recomposing a Query String

The parse_qs and parse_qsl functions allow you to break up the query string of a URL into its components. The keys and values contained in the query string are returned as a dictionary (parse_qs) or list (parse_qsl):

```
>>> url = "http://www.example.com?hello=world&hello=blah&xyz=12"
>>> parts = urllib.parse.urlparse(url)
>>> urllib.parse.parse_qs(parts.query)
{'hello': ['world', 'blah'], 'xyz': ['12']}
>>> urllib.parse.parse_qsl(parts.query)
[('hello', 'world'), ('hello', 'blah'), ('xyz', '12')]
```

As a counterpart, the urlencode function generates a string from the key-value pairs of the query dictionary:

```
>>> urllib.parse.urlencode({"abc" : 1, "def" : "ghi"})
'abc=1&def=ghi'
```

Combining URLs

The urljoin function combines a base URL and a relative path specification:

```
>>> base = "http://www.test.com"
>>> relative = "path/to/file.py"
>>> urllib.parse.urljoin(base, relative)
'http://www.test.com/path/to/file.py'
>>> base = "http://www.test.com/hello/world.py"
>>> relative = "you.py"
>>> urllib.parse.urljoin(base, relative)
'http://www.test.com/hello/you.py'
```

You can see that urljoin doesn't simply concatenate the two components, but truncates filenames at the end of the base URL.

34.5   FTP: ftplib

The ftplib module allows an application to connect to an FTP server and perform operations on it. *FTP (File Transfer Protocol)* is a network protocol developed for file transfers in TCP/IP networks and is widely used on the internet. For example, file transfers to a web server are usually done via FTP.

The FTP protocol is very simple and consists of a set of human-readable commands. So basically, you could also communicate directly with an FTP server without interposing an abstracting library. Table 34.4 lists the most important FTP commands and briefly explains their meaning. You'll see that the ftplib uses a naming scheme that is based on these commands.

Command	Description
OPEN	Establishes a connection to an FTP server
USER	Transmits a user name to the FTP server for login
PASS	Transmits a password to the FTP server for login
CWD	Changes the current working directory on the FTP server (CWD for *change working directory*)
PWD	Returns the current working directory on the FTP server (PWD for *print working directory*)
DELE	Deletes a file on the FTP server (DELE for *delete*)
LIST LS	Transfers a list of all files and folders contained in the working directory
MKD	Creates a directory on the FTP server (MKD for *make directory*)
RMD	Deletes a directory on the FTP server (RMD for *remove directory*)

Table 34.4 FTP Commands

34

Command	Description
RETR	Transfers a file from the FTP server (RETR for *retrieve*)
STOR	Transfers a file from the client to the FTP server (STOR for *store*)
QUIT	Terminates the connection between server and client

Table 34.4 FTP Commands (Cont.)

The communication with an FTP server runs on two channels: on the *control channel* for sending commands to the server and on the *data channel* for receiving data. This separation of the command and transmission levels allows commands to be sent to the server even during an ongoing data transmission—for example, to abort the transmission.

Basically, a data transmission can proceed in two modes: In the *active mode*, the client requests a file and at the same time opens a port through which the file transfer then proceeds. This is contrasted with the *passive mode*, where the client instructs the server to open a port to perform the data transfer. This has the advantage that data transfers can also take place with clients that aren't directly addressable for the server because, for example, they're located behind a router or a firewall.

The ftplib module provides the FTP class that allows an application to connect to an FTP server and perform the operations supported there. So with this module, you can implement a full-fledged FTP client.

34.5.1   Connecting to an FTP Server

Already when instantiating the FTP class, a connection to an FTP server can be established. For this purpose, at least the address of the FTP server must be passed to the constructor as a string. The constructor of the FTP class has the interface described ahead.

FTP([host, user, passwd, acct, timeout, source_address], {encoding})

The constructor creates an instance of the FTP class connected to the FTP server host. When logging in to this server, the user name user and password passwd are used. The optional timeout parameter is used to set a timeout value in seconds for the connection request. If you don't specify timeout, a system default will be used.

The acct parameter (for *accounting information*) can be used to send further information to the FTP server, but this is usually not needed. With source_address, the source address to be used in the connection is specified as a tuple in the format (ip, port).

Alternatively, the FTP class can be instantiated without parameters. Then the connection is established using the connect and login methods, which must be passed the connection and login data respectively:

```
>>> import ftplib
>>> ftp = ftplib.FTP()
>>> ftp.connect("ftp.server.com")
'220 Server response'
>>> ftp.login("username", "password")
'230 Login successful.'
```

The connect method also supports the optional port and timeout parameters.

The connection to an FTP server can be terminated using the parameterless quit and close methods. Here, quit disconnects properly by sending a QUIT command to the server and waiting for its response, while close disconnects without notifying the server.

> **Note**
>
> The FTP class can be used as context manage, e.g., inside the with statement:
>
> ```
> with ftplib.FTP() as f:
>     f.connect("ftp.server.com")
>     f.login("username", "password")
> ```

To run the examples in the following sections, you must both import the ftplib module and create an FTP instance ftp that's connected to an FTP server of your choice.

34.5.2 Executing FTP commands

The FTP class defines methods for the most common FTP commands, as you'll see in the following sections. In addition, to communicate directly with the FTP server, there is a method called sendcmd, which sends a command as a string to the server and returns the server's response also as a string:

```
>>> ftp.sendcmd("PWD")
'257 "/" is the current directory.'
```

34.5.3 Working with Files and Directories

Similar to the commands described at the beginning that define the FTP protocol, there are methods of the FTP class that perform basic operations on files and directories. Table 34.5 summarizes the existing methods and briefly explains their meaning.

Method	Meaning
cwd(pathname)	Changes the current working directory to pathname.
delete(filename)	Deletes the filename file.

Table 34.5 File and Directory Operations on an FTP Server

Method	Meaning
mkd(pathname)	Creates the pathname directory.
mlsd([path])	Returns the contents of the current working directory or the path directory.
pwd()	Returns the path of the current working directory.
rename(fromname, toname)	Renames the file fromname to toname.
rmd(dirname)	Deletes the dirname server directory. The directory must exist and be empty.
size(filename)	Determines the file size of filename.[*]

[*] Note that the FTP command underlying this method, SIZE, is not standardized and thus not supported by all FTP servers.

Table 34.5 File and Directory Operations on an FTP Server (Cont.)

The mlsd method returns an iterable object containing the files and subdirectories of the path directory on the FTP server passed as parameters:

```
>>> for x in ftp.mlsd():
...     print("{}: {}".format(x[0], x[1]["type"]))
...
image.png: file
hello.txt: file
folder1: dir
folder2: dir
```

Each element in the directory is represented by a tuple with two entries containing the name and a dictionary with additional attributes. In the example, the value of the type attribute was output next to the file or folder name, which indicates whether it's a file or a directory.

34.5.4   Transferring Files

To exchange a file with an FTP server, two basic decisions must be made: the *direction* of the file transfer—a file can be sent or received—and the *transfer mode*. Each of the four possible combinations of these transfer parameters is represented by a method in the FTP class. The methods are called retrbinary, retrlines, storbinary, and storlines and are presented ahead.

The set_pasv method sets the FTP instance to active or passive mode, depending on the Boolean parameter passed. In the active state, the client must be accessible to the server; that is, it mustn't be located behind a firewall or router.

Note

The parameterless abort method interrupts a running data transfer. Depending on the server, such an interruption can only be performed at certain times.

---

retrbinary(cmd, callback, [maxblocksize, rest])

This method initiates a data transfer in binary mode. For this purpose, a corresponding FTP command must be passed as the first parameter, based on which the server starts a data transfer via the data channel. For a simple file transfer, the RETR *filename* command is used.

In the second place, a callback function object must be passed which must accept exactly one parameter. After each successfully transmitted block, this function is called. The transmitted binary data is passed as a parameter in the form of a bytes string.

The maxblocksize parameter sets the maximum size of the blocks into which the file will be divided for download.

The fourth, optional parameter, rest, is used to specify an offset in the file to be transferred, from which the server should send the file contents. This is useful, for example, to resume interrupted downloads without having to download parts of the file twice.

For the use of retrbinary, let's look at the following example:

```
>>> class Downloader:
...     def __init__(self):
...         self.data = bytes()
...     def __call__(self, data):
...         self.data += data
... image = Downloader()
... ftp.retrbinary("RETR image.png", image)
...
>>> len(image.data)
473831
```

The sample program downloads the *image.png* file from the current working directory of the FTP server and stores the binary data in the bytes string image.data. To avoid having to use a global reference to store the data, we created a Downloader class that can be called like a function using the __call__ magic method.

Alternatively, a LIST command can be issued via retrbinary. The directory content is also sent from the server via the data channel:

```
>>> def f(data):
...     print(data.decode())
...
>>> ftp.retrbinary("LIST", f)
drwxr-xr-x   3 peter   staff          96 Jul 17 09:27 folder1
drwxr-xr-x   3 peter   staff          96 Jul 17 09:28 folder2
-rw-r--r--   1 peter   staff          33 Jul 17 09:33 hello.txt
-rw-r--r--   1 peter   staff      684658 Jun 12  2020 image.png

'226 Transfer complete.'
```

retrlines(command, [callback])

This method initiates a file transfer in ASCII mode. To do this, you must pass an appropriate FTP command as the first parameter. For a simple file transfer, this would be RETR *filename*. However, it's also possible, for example, to transfer the contents of the working directory using a LIST command.

A file transfer in ASCII mode is done line by line. That is, the provided callback function is called after each completely transferred line. It receives the read line as a parameter. Note that the terminating newline character isn't passed.

If you haven't specified a callback function, the transferred data will be output:

```
>>> class Downloader:
...     def __init__(self):
...         self.lines = []
...     def __call__(self, line):
...         self.lines.append(line)
...
>>> text = Downloader()
>>> ftp.retrlines("RETR hello.txt", text)
'226 Transfer complete.'
>>> print("\n".join(text.lines))
This is the content of hello.txt
```

This sample program downloads the *text.txt* text file line by line and reassembles the downloaded lines in the text string into an overall text. Again, we use the callable Downloader class to save the intermediate results.

storbinary(command, file, [blocksize, callback, rest])

This method initiates a file upload. A corresponding FTP command must be passed as the first parameter. For a simple file upload, this command is STOR *filename*, where *filename* is the destination name of the file on the FTP server. As the second parameter, you have to pass a file object opened in binary mode, the content of which is to be uploaded.

Optionally, the maximum size of the data blocks in which the file will be uploaded can be specified as the third parameter, blocksize.

If for the fourth parameter, callback, the function object of a function expecting a single parameter is passed, this function will be called after each block sent. In this process, it receives the sent data as bytes string. The last parameter, rest, has the same meaning as in retrbinary.

The following sample program performs a binary file upload:

```python
with open("hello.png", "rb") as f:
    ftp.storbinary("STOR image.png", f)
```

The file is named *hello.png* in the local working directory, but is uploaded under the name *image.png*.

storlines(command, file, [callback])

This method behaves similarly to storbinary, the only difference being that the file is uploaded line by line in ASCII mode. The command, file, and callback parameters can be used as with storbinary.

Note that, as with storbinary, you must also have the file object passed for file opened in binary mode.

34

Chapter 35
Email

In this section, we'll introduce modules of the standard library that allow you to communicate with an email server—that is, to fetch email from it or to send email through the server.

An email is sent via a so-called *SMTP server*, with which communication is possible via a protocol of the same name. For this reason, in the first subsection we'll introduce the smtplib module of the standard library, which implements this communication protocol.

There are two common ways to download a received email: *POP3* and *IMAP4* protocols. Both can be used with the respective module, poplib or imaplib.

The last section will then describe the email module of the standard library, which allows any kind of file (usually images or documents) to be sent with an email via MIME encoding.

35.1 SMTP: smtplib

The *Simple Mail Transfer Protocol* (*SMTP*) is used to send an email via an SMTP server. SMTP is a text-based, human-readable protocol. Originally, SMTP didn't provide a way to authenticate the logged-in user, such as by user name and password. This quickly became unsustainable with the rapid development of the internet, so the SMTP protocol was extended accordingly, creating *Extended SMTP* (*ESMTP*). Table 35.1 lists and briefly explains the most important SMTP commands in the order in which they're used in an SMTP session.

Command	Description
HELO	Starts an SMTP session.
EHLO	Starts an ESMTP session.
MAIL FROM	Initiates the sending of an email. The sender address is added to this command.
RCPT TO	Adds a recipient to the email. (RCPT stands for *recipient*.)

Table 35.1 SMTP Commands

Command	Description
DATA	This command is used to specify the content of the email and finally send the email.
QUIT	Ends the SMTP or ESMTP session.

Table 35.1 SMTP Commands (Cont.)

The smtplib module essentially contains a class called SMTP. After this class has been instantiated, all further communication with the server runs through it.

35.1.1   SMTP([host, port, local_hostname, timeout, source_address])

When instantiating the SMTP class, the connection information to the SMTP server can optionally already be passed. The port only needs to be specified explicitly if it's different from the SMTP default port, 25.

The domain name of the local host can be passed as the third parameter. This is transmitted to the SMTP server as identification in the first command sent. If the local_ hostname parameter isn't specified, an attempt is made to determine the local host name automatically.

For the fourth parameter, you can pass a timeout value in seconds that will be taken into account when connecting to the SMTP server. If you don't specify timeout, a default value will be used.

With source_address, the source address to be used in the connection is specified as a tuple in the format (ip, port). To follow the examples in the following sections, you must first import the smtplib module, and an instance of the SMTP class named s must exist:

```
>>> import smtplib
>>> s = smtplib.SMTP("smtp.server.com")
```

Note

The SMTP class can be used with the with statement:

```
with smtplib.SMTP("smtp.server.com") as s:
    s.login("username", "password")
```

35.1.2   Establishing and Terminating a Connection

Establishing an SMTP connection is usually done in two steps: the actual connection and the login. In the smtplib module, these two steps are represented by the connect and login functions:

```
>>> s.connect("smtp.server.com", 25)
(220, b'The Message from the Server')
>>> s.login("username", "password")
(235, b'Authentication successful.')
```

The specification of the port with connect is optional and can be omitted if it's the SMTP default port, 25.

To terminate an SMTP connection, you must call the quit function.

35.1.3   Sending an Email

To send an email via SMTP, the sendmail function exists with the following interface:

```
sendmail(from_addr, to_addrs, msg, [mail_options, rctp_options])
```

Note that for this to work, the SMTP instance must be logged on to an SMTP server and, in most cases, authenticated.

The first two parameters contain the email addresses of the sender (from_addr) and a list of the email addresses of the recipients (to_addrs), respectively. An email address is a string of the following format:

```
Firstname Lastname <em@il.addr>
```

Alternatively, only the email address can be in the string.

As the third parameter, msg, you pass the text of the email. Other details such as the subject of the email can also be defined here. In Section 35.4, you'll learn exactly what this looks like and what options Python provides to create this header comfortably.

The sendmail method always returns a dictionary containing all recipients that were rejected by the SMTP server as keys and the respective error code with an error description as the value. When all recipients have received the email, the returned dictionary is empty.

> **Note**
>
> The text of an email may only consist of ASCII characters. To be able to send other characters and in particular also binary data, you can use the so-called *MIME encoding*, which we'll deal with in Section 35.4.

The optional mail_options and rcpt_options parameters can be used to pass a list of strings each containing options from the ESMTP standard. The options passed for mail_options are appended to the MAIL FROM command, while the options passed for rcpt_options are appended to the RCPT TO command.

35

35.1.4   Example

Now that you've learned about the main methods of an SMTP instance, here's a small example of connecting to an SMTP server to send two emails to different recipients:

```
>>> smtp = smtplib.SMTP("smtp.server.com", 25)
>>> smtp.login("username", "password")
(235, b'Authentication successful.')
>>> smtp.sendmail(
...     "Peter Kaiser <kaiser@python-book.com>",
...     "Johannes Ernesti <ernesti@python-book.com>",
...     "This is the text")
{}
>>> smtp.sendmail(
...     "Peter Kaiser <kaiser@python-book.com>",
...     ["ernesti@python-book.com", "kaiser@python-book.com"],
...     "This is the text")
{}
>>> smtp.quit()
(221, b'See you later')
```

For the first email, the full names of the sender and recipient were provided. The second example shows that the email address alone is also sufficient, and it demonstrates how an email can be sent to multiple recipients.

35.2   POP3: poplib

Now that we've used smtplib to explain how to send email through an SMTP server, in this section we'll describe the poplib module of the standard library. This module implements the *Post Office Protocol version 3 (POP3)* protocol. POP3 is a protocol used to view and retrieve emails stored on a POP3 server. The POP3 protocol thus competes with IMAP4, whose use with imaplib will be described in the next section.

Table 35.2 lists the most important POP3 commands and their meanings. The commands are in the same order in which they're used in a usual POP3 session.

Command	Description
USER	Transmits the user name for authentication on the server
PASS	Transmits the password for authentication on the server
STAT	Returns the status of the inbox, such as the number of new emails received

Table 35.2 POP3 Commands

Command	Description
LIST	Provides information about a specific email in the inbox
RETR	Transmits a specific email
DELE	Deletes a specific email
RSET	Cancels all pending deletions[*]
QUIT	Ends the POP3 session

[*] Delete operations are buffered and not executed until the end of the session.

Table 35.2 POP3 Commands (Cont.)

As with the smtplib module, the poplib module essentially contains the POP3 class, which must be instantiated before operations can be performed on a POP3 server. The interface of the constructor will be described in the following section.

35.2.1 POP3(host, [port, timeout])

The constructor of the POP3 class is passed the hostname of the server to connect to. Optionally, a port can be specified if it's to be different from the preset default port, 110. In addition, a timeout in seconds can be specified, which will be taken into account when connecting to the server.

To be able to execute the examples presented in the following sections, the poplib module must be imported and an instance of the POP3 class named pop must be present:

```
>>> import poplib
>>> pop = poplib.POP3("pop.server.com")
```

For most examples, this instance must also be connected to and authenticated with a POP3 server.

35.2.2 Establishing and Terminating a Connection

The instantiation of the POP3 class, which already connects to the destination server, is usually followed by an authentication step. For this purpose, the user and pass_ methods of the POP3 instance must be called:

```
>>> pop.user("username")
b'+OK USER accepted, send PASS'
>>> pop.pass_("password")
b'+OK Authentication succeeded'
```

> **Note**
>
> The preferred name for the password method, pass, is already assigned a keyword in Python. In such cases, an underscore is often appended to the name already being used.

After the password has been accepted by the server, the inbox may be accessed. The inbox will remain blocked for other login attempts until quit is called:

```
>>> pop.quit()
b'+OK '
```

35.2.3   Listing Existing Emails

After authenticating with a POP3 server, the emails stored there can be viewed and deleted. To do this, you can get an overview of the existing emails using the stat and list methods.

The stat method returns the status of the inbox. The result is a tuple with two integers—the number of messages contained and the size of the inbox in bytes:

```
>>> pop.stat()
(1, 623)
```

In this case, there's an email in the inbox and the total size of the inbox is 623 bytes.

The list method returns a list of the emails in the inbox. The return value of this method is a tuple of the following format:

```
(response, [b"mailID length", ...], datlen)
```

The tuple contains the server's response string as the first element and a list of bytes strings as the second one, each of which represents an email from the inbox. The string contains two specifications: the mailID is the sequential number of the email, a kind of index; and length is the total size of the mail in bytes. Regarding the index, you should note that all emails on the server are indexed consecutively, starting at 1:

```
>>> pop.list()
(b'+OK [...].', [b'1 623'], 7)
```

The first element of the tuple (response) doesn't contain the full response string from the server because the information that was prepared for the second element of the tuple was removed from response. To still be able to calculate the complete length of the server response, there's the third element of the tuple, datlen. This element references the length of the skipped information of the server's response. This would make `len(response)` + `datlen` equal to the total size of the response string actually sent by the server.

Optionally, you can specify the sequential number of an email about which more detailed information is to be returned. In this case, the method returns a bytes string of the format b"+OK mailID length":

```
>>> pop.list(1)
b'+OK 1 623'
```

35.2.4   Retrieving and Deleting Emails

The `retr` method can be used to retrieve an email. This method returns the contents of the email as a tuple that looks as follows:

```
(response, lines, length)
```

The first element of the tuple corresponds to the server's response string.[1] The second one is a list of bytes strings, each containing one line of the email, including the email header. The last element of the tuple is the size of the email in bytes.

In the following example, the email with the sequential number 1 is retrieved from the server:

```
>>> pop.retr(1)
(b'+OK 623 octets follow.', [...], 623)
```

Instead of the ellipsis, there would be a list of strings containing the lines of the full email.

In a similar way, deleting an email works via the `dele` method:

```
>>> pop.dele(1)
b'+OK '
```

> **Note**
> Note that most servers buffer delete commands and don't actually execute them until the `quit` method is called.
> In such a scenario, the `rset` method can be called to discard all pending deletions.

35.2.5   Example

The following sample program uses the `poplib` module to retrieve all emails from a POP3 server and display them on the screen:

---

1 The response string mentions "623 octets." The term *octets* ("groups of eight") refers to bytes.

```
import poplib
pop = poplib.POP3("pop.server.com")
pop.user("username")
pop.pass_("password")
for i in range(1, pop.stat()[0]+1):
    for line in pop.retr(i)[1]:
        print(line)
    print("***")
pop.quit()
```

First, an instance of the POP3 class is created and the program logs on to the POP3 server using the user and pass_ methods. The pop.stat()[0] expression returns the number of emails that are in the inbox. So in the for loop, all email indexes are traversed. The indexing of the emails in the inbox starts with 1.

In the inner loop, the current email with index i is downloaded by calling the method retr. The second element, the one with index 1 of the tuple returned by this method, contains a list with all the lines of the email content. This list is traversed in the loop and the current line is output in each case.

Note

For reasons of clarity, the sample program doesn't contain any error handling. In a finished program, you should check if the connection to the server could be established and if the authentication was successful.

35.3 IMAP4: imaplib

The imaplib module provides the IMAP4 class, which you use to connect to and communicate with an *Internet Message Access Protocol version 4* (*IMAP4*) server. The IMAP4 protocol is intended for managing emails on a mail server, similar to the POP3 protocol. Unlike POP3, with IMAP4 the emails mostly remain on the mail server, which has the advantage that you have full access to all archived emails from anywhere—even from a different device while you're on vacation, for example. Nowadays, most email providers offer both POP3 and IMAP4 access. Compared to POP3, IMAP4 supports commands for convenient management of emails on the server. For example, you can create subfolders and assort emails into them.

Unlike previous protocols such as FTP or POP3, IMAP4 is feature-rich, and although the protocol is still based on readable text messages, it's too complex to adequately describe in the style of the previous sections with a short table.

With IMAP4, emails can be sorted into different mailboxes. Here you can think of a *mailbox* as a directory that can contain emails, just as a folder contains files. The mailbox structure of the sample server used is shown in Figure 35.1.

```
INBOX
  ├─INBOX.Ham
  └─INBOX.Spam
```

Figure 35.1 Mailbox Structure of the Sample Server

There is a parent mailbox called INBOX and two child mailboxes, called INBOX.Ham and INBOX.Spam.

35.3.1   IMAP4([host, port, timeout])

To connect to an IMAP4 server, an instance of the IMAP4 class must be created. The constructor of this class can directly connect to an IMAP4 server with the hostname host using the port port. If the port parameter isn't specified, the default IMAP4 port, 143, is used. In addition, as of Python 3.9, a timeout in seconds can be specified, which is taken into account when connecting to the server.

Once an instance of the IMAP4 class has been created, it provides various methods to communicate with the connected server. Each method representing an IMAP4 command returns a tuple of the following form:

```
(status, [data, ...])
```

The resulting *status* tuple contains either "OK" or "NO", depending on whether the operation was successful or failed. The second element of the tuple is a list of the data the server sent in response. This data can be either bytes strings or tuples. If it's tuples, they have two elements each, both bytes strings:

```
(header, data)
```

The examples in the following sections are mostly based on the assumption that an IMAP4 instance im has been connected to an IMAP server:

```
>>> import imaplib
>>> im = imaplib.IMAP4("imap.server.com")
```

In most cases, the IMAP4 instance must also be authenticated with the server, which is covered in the following section.

35.3.2   Establishing and Terminating a Connection

If the IMAP4 instance hasn't already been connected to a server when it was created, this can be done using the open method. This method also has the parameters host and port, similar to the interface of the IMAP4 constructor.

In the second step, the login method is called to authenticate on the server. This method gets the user name and password passed as a string. You can terminate an existing connection using the logout method:

```
>>> im.login("username", "password")
('OK', [b'Logged in'])
>>> im.logout()
('OK', [b'Logged out'])
```

> **Note**
>
> The IMAP4 class is a context manager and can be used in a with statement:
>
> ```
> with imaplib.IMAP4("imap.server.com") as i:
>     pass
> ```
>
> When you exit the context, a logout is performed automatically.

35.3.3   Finding and Selecting a Mailbox

After connecting to an IMAP4 server, a mailbox must be selected to access the emails it contains. The list method returns the names of all mailboxes that match a given pattern. To do this, it's passed the base folder in which to search and the pattern to which the results must match. The passed pattern must be a string and usually contains fragments of a mailbox name, including a wildcard character (*):

```
>>> im.list(".", "*Ham")
('OK', [b'(\\HasNoChildren) "." "INBOX.Ham"'])
>>> im.list(".", "*am")
('OK', [b'(\\HasNoChildren) "." "INBOX.Ham"',
b'(\\HasNoChildren) "." "INBOX.Spam"'])
>>> im.list(".", "*")
('OK', [b'(\\HasNoChildren) "." "INBOX.Ham"',
b'(\\HasNoChildren) "." "INBOX.Spam"',
b'(\\Unmarked \\HasChildren) "." "INBOX"'])
>>> im.list(".", "NotExistingMailbox")
('OK', [None])
```

If no directory is passed, mailboxes of the main folder are returned. If you don't specify any pattern, all mailboxes contained in the respective folder will be returned.

Each entry of the result list is a bytes string and contains three pieces of information, each separated by a space: the so-called flags of the mailbox in parentheses, the directory of the mailbox, and the mailbox name, each in double quotes. In this example, the flags can be used to find out whether a mailbox contains child mailboxes (\HasChildren) or not (\HasNoChildren).

After a suitable mailbox has been found, it can be selected by calling the select method in order to perform further operations on it. You pass the name of the mailbox to be selected as the first parameter. The select method returns the number of emails contained in the selected mailbox:

```
>>> im.select("INBOX")
('OK', [b'2'])
```

No exception is raised if the requested mailbox doesn't exist. Instead, the error must be identified on the basis of the return value:

```
>>> im.select("INBOX.NonExistent")
('NO', [b'Mailbox does not exist, or must be subscribed to.'])
```

A selected mailbox can be closed using the close method.

35.3.4   Operations with Mailboxes

Besides selecting and closing, other operations can be performed with mailboxes, which are briefly summarized in Table 35.3. Each of these operations can be performed via a corresponding method of a connected IMAP4 instance and is passed one or several mailbox names as a string or a list of strings.

Method	Description
create(mailbox)	Creates a new mailbox named mailbox.
delete(mailbox)	Deletes the mailbox named mailbox.
rename(oldmailbox, newmailbox)	Renames the oldmailbox mailbox to newmailbox.

Table 35.3 Operations on Mailboxes

35

35.3.5   Searching Emails

The search method searches within the selected mailbox for emails matching one or several specified criteria. For this purpose, the method has the following interface:

```
search(charset, [*criteria])
```

Either the string "ALL" (all mails meet this criteria) or a string of the format "(FROM \"Johannes\")" can be used as a criterion. The second criterion is met for all emails written by a person called Johannes. The charset parameter specifies the encoding of the criteria strings. Usually this parameter isn't needed and None is passed.

The search method returns the IDs of the resulting emails as a list:

```
>>> im.search(None, '(FROM "Johannes")')
('OK', [b'1 2 3'])
>>> im.search(None, '(FROM "Johann")')
('OK', [b'1 2 3'])
>>> im.search(None, '(FROM "Johanninski")')
('OK', [b''])
```

35.3.6   Retrieving Emails

To retrieve emails, the fetch method exists with the following interface:

```
fetch(message_set, message_parts)
```

The message_set parameter must be a string containing the mail IDs of the emails to be downloaded. These can occur either individually in the string ("1"), as a range ("1:4" for mails numbered 1 through 4), as a list of ranges ("1:4,7:9" for mails numbered 1 through 4 and 7 through 9) or as a range with an undefined upper limit ("3:*" for all mails from mail number 3 onward).

The second parameter, message_parts, identifies which parts of the specified emails should be downloaded. A value of "(RFC822)" means the entire email should be downloaded, including the email header. With a value of "(BODY[TEXT])" only the text and with "(BODY[HEADER])" only the header of the email is downloaded:

```
>>> im.fetch("1", "(BODY[TEXT])")
('OK', [(b'1 (BODY[TEXT] {29}',
b'This is a test message\r\n'), b')'])
>>> im.fetch("1:2", "(BODY[TEXT])")
('OK', [(b'1 (BODY[TEXT] {29}',
b'This is a test message\r\n'), b')',
(b'2 (BODY[TEXT] {25}',
b'Another test message\r\n'), b')'])
```

In the case of a nonexistent mail ID, no exception is raised, but an empty result is returned. If the ID is invalid, a corresponding error message will be returned:

```
>>> im.fetch("100", "(BODY[TEXT])")
('OK', [None])
>>> im.fetch("NoID", "(BODY[TEXT])")
('NO', [b'Error in IMAP command received by server.'])
```

35.3.7   Example

In the following sample program, the `imaplib` module is used to connect to an IMAP4 server and display all emails contained in a specific mailbox. Here, the user has the option to select the mailbox. The source code of the sample program looks as follows:

```python
import imaplib
with imaplib.IMAP4("imap.hostname.com") as im:
    im.login("username", "password" )
    print("Existing mailboxes:")
    for mb in im.list()[1]:
        name = mb.split(b'"."')[-1]
        print(" - {}".format(name.decode().strip(' "')))
    mb = input("Which mailbox to display: ")
    im.select(mb)
    status, data = im.search(None, "ALL")
    for mailno in data[0].split():
        type, data = im.fetch(mailno, "(RFC822)")
        print("{}\n+++\n".format(data[0][1].decode()))
    im.close()
```

First, an instance of the `IMAP4` class is created and connected to an IMAP4 server. Then, using the `list` method, all the mailboxes contained in the main folder of the IMAP4 account are traversed and the names of the mailboxes are displayed on the screen. Note that the `list` method returns the names of the mailboxes with additional information. This information must be filtered out before the mailbox name can be displayed. Once the names have been displayed, the user is prompted to select one of the specified mailbox names.

The mailbox selected by the user is then also selected on the server via the `select` method. We pass the `"ALL"` string to the called `search` method afterward, which causes the mail server to return data about all emails in the selected mailbox.

We then iterate in a `for` loop over the list of mail IDs returned by `search` and download the respective email in its entirety using `fetch`. The downloaded mail will be output on the screen.

Finally, we close the selected mailbox via `close` and automatically terminate the connection to the server by exiting the `with` context.

No error handling was performed for this sample program either. In a finished program, both the connection request and the login and especially the user input should be checked.

35

35.4   Creating Complex Emails: email

In the previous sections, you learned how to send email through an SMTP server and how to download email from a POP3 or IMAP4 server. As you know, sending and receiving emails is based on pure ASCII protocols. Above all, this means that no binary data can be sent with these protocols. In addition, special characters that don't conform to the seven-bit ASCII standard cause problems.

To be able to send these types of characters or binary data, the *Multipurpose Internet Mail Extension* (*MIME*) standard was developed. It encodes special characters and binary data so that they can be sent as a sequence of pure ASCII characters. In addition, the MIME standard defines different file types and specifies a syntax that associates file attachments with a particular file type so that the files can be processed more easily at the recipient's end.

The corresponding email package of Python's standard library is very powerful, which is why only part of its functionality can be discussed here. First, we'll take a look at how you can create a simple ASCII email using email. Based on this, we'll move on to more complex MIME-encoded email.

35.4.1   Creating a Simple Email

The Message class of the email.message module serves as the base class for a new email. The following sample program shows how you can use it:

```
from email.message import Message
msg = Message()
msg.set_payload("This is my self-created email.")
msg["Subject"] = "Hello world"
msg["From"] = "Donald Duck <don@ld.com>"
msg["To"] = "Daisy Duck <d@isy.com>"
print(msg.as_string())
```

The output of the sample program—the generated email—looks as follows:

```
Subject: Hello world
From: Donald Duck <don@ld.com>
To: Daisy Duck <d@isy.com>

This is my self-created email.
```

First we create an instance of the Message class. The constructor of this class doesn't expect any arguments. The set_payload method adds a text to the email.

All that's missing now is the email header. To add it, the message instance can be accessed like a dictionary. This is how you can add the individual components of the header. The important elements are "Subject" for the subject, "From" for the sender, and "To" for the recipient of the mail.

Last but not least, the resulting email is written to a string via the as_string method and output.[2]

35.4.2   Creating an Email with Attachments

Earlier we announced that the email packet allows us to send binary data via email. The email.mime module is responsible for this. The following sample program creates an email and inserts an image file as an attachment:

```python
from email.mime.multipart import MIMEMultipart
from email.mime.image import MIMEImage
from email.mime.text import MIMEText
msg = MIMEMultipart()
msg["Subject"] = "Hello world"
msg["From"] = "Donald Duck <don@ld.com>"
msg["To"] = "Daisy Duck <d@isy.com>"
text = MIMEText("This is my self-created email.")
msg.attach(text)
with open("coffee.png", "rb") as f:
    image = MIMEImage(f.read())
msg.attach(image)
print(msg.as_string())
```

First, an instance of the MIMEMultipart class is created. This represents an email that can contain MIME-encoded binary data. As in the previous example, the subject, sender, and recipient are added to the email.

Then an instance of the MIMEText class is created to contain the plain text of the email. This instance is attached to the MIMEMultipart instance using the attach method.

And we'll do the same with the image: an instance of the MIMEImage class is created and filled with the binary data of the image. After that, we attach it to the email via attach.

Finally, the MIMEMultipart instance gets converted to a string by calling the as_string method, which can thus be sent as a pure ASCII email. The attachment is recognized by email programs as an image and then presented accordingly. The output of the example looks as follows:

```
Content-Type: multipart/mixed; boundary="===========0094312333=="
MIME-Version: 1.0
Subject: Hello world
From: Donald Duck <don@ld.com>
```

35

---

2 Using the smtplib module, the generated email string or Message instance can be sent directly.

735

```
To: Daisy Duck <d@isy.com>

--===============0094312333==
Content-Type: text/plain; charset="us-ascii"
MIME-Version: 1.0
Content-Transfer-Encoding: 7bit

This is my self-created email.
--===============0094312333==
Content-Type: image/png
MIME-Version: 1.0
Content-Transfer-Encoding: base64
```

iVBORwOKGgoAAAANSUhEUgAAAMgAAADICAIAAAAiOjnJAAAACXBIWXMAAA7EAAAOxAGVKw4bAAAg
AElEQVR4nIS8Sa9tXXYsFBFjzrXPucVXZwtnukC2ObvvGGR6FEeJ1wAghJPgxgOjSR+JPICHRgA4N
[...]

```
--===============0094312333==---
```

You can see that both the text and the image have been encoded in a similar way. The processing of the two sections for the text part of the email and for an image in the attachment is carried out by your mail program. The mime package also offers a corresponding functionality, which we'll talk about later.

Table 35.4 lists the available MIME data types.

MIME data type	Purpose
email.mime.application.MIMEApplication	Applications
email.mime.audio.MIMEAudio	Audio files
email.mime.image.MIMEImage	Graphic files
email.mime.message.MIMEMessage	Message instances
email.mime.image.MIMEText	Pure text

Table 35.4 Available MIME Data Types

When instantiating all these classes, you must pass the respective binary data or text that the corresponding instance should contain as the first parameter of the constructor. It's also important to note that all classes presented here are derived from the base Message class, meaning they contain the methods of this base class.

35.4.3   Reading an Email

Finally, we want to provide a short example of how a saved email can also be read again and automatically be converted to a Message instance. Let's look at the following example:

```
import email
mail = """Subject: Hello world
From: Donald Duck <don@ld.com>
To: Daisy Duck <d@isy.com>

Hello world
"""
msg = email.message_from_string(mail)
print(msg["From"])
```

In this sample program, an email is present in the form of a string and is read by the message_from_string function. This function returns a Message instance that we use for accessing the sender as an example:

```
Donald Duck <don@ld.com>
```

Alternatively, we could have used the message_from_file function to read the email from a file. We would then have had to pass an open file object to this function.

Chapter 36
Debugging and Quality Assurance

Debugging refers to the detection and elimination of errors, so-called *bugs*, in a program. For this purpose, a programmer usually deploys a *debugger*, a developer tool that allows you to monitor the flow of a program and stop it at certain points. When the program flow is stopped in a debugger, the current program state can be analyzed. In this way, errors can be found more quickly than by merely mentally going through the source code or analyzing program output.

Another aspect covered in this chapter is quality assurance. The quality of a piece of software can be evaluated according to many standards, such as its absence of errors or runtime efficiency.

In the first section, we'll focus on the topic of debugging in general. After that, we'll deal with quality assurance through automated tests and the creation of a runtime analysis.

36.1 The Debugger

Python comes with a program for debugging Python code, called *Python Debugger* (*PDB*). This debugger runs in a console window and is thus neither clear nor intuitive. For this reason, we've decided against discussing PDB here. If you're still interested in this debugger, perhaps because of its command-line-based user interface, you can find more information about it in the Python documentation.

Many modern development environments for Python include an extensive built-in debugger with a graphical user interface that makes debugging a Python program quite convenient. IDLE also offers a rudimentary graphical debugger, shown in Figure 36.1.

To enable the debugger in IDLE, you must select **Debug • Debugger** from the menu in the Python shell and then run the program you want to check for errors normally via **Run • Run Module**. In addition to the editor window, a window appears containing the currently executed line of code. Double-clicking this line will highlight it in the program code so that you'll always know where exactly you are in the program flow.

36

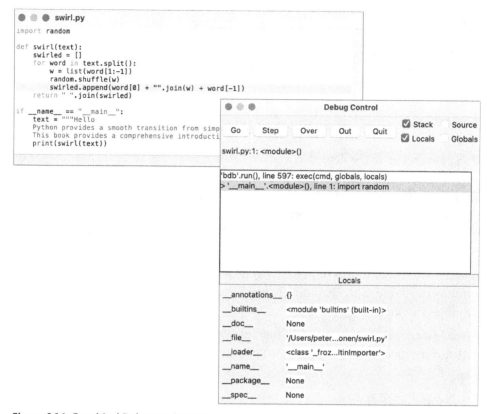

Figure 36.1 Graphical Debugger in IDLE

The basic principle of a debugger is to allow the programmer to run a program step by step, and in this way to get an accurate picture, line by line, of what changes have occurred and how they affect the program as it progresses. A debugging session usually starts with the programmer distributing so-called *breakpoints* in the program. When the debugger is started, the program is executed normally until the program flow hits the first breakpoint. At this point, the debugger stops the program flow and allows the programmer to intervene. Many debuggers also stop at the first program line immediately after startup and wait for further instructions from the programmer.

If the program flow has been stopped at a certain line in the source code, the programmer has several options to control the further program flow. These options, called *commands* ahead, are usually found in a prominent place in a toolbar for a graphical debugger as they represent the essential capabilities of a debugger:

- By using the *step over* command, you can make the debugger jump to the next source code line and stop there again.

- The *step into* command behaves similarly to *step over*, with the difference that step into also jumps into function or method calls, while these are skipped with step over.

- The *step out* command jumps out of the current function or method back to where it was called. Step out can thus be seen as a kind of inverse function of step into.

- The *run* command continues to execute the program until the program flow hits the next breakpoint or the end of the program occurs. Some debuggers allow a similar command to jump to a specific source code line or execute the program code up to the cursor position.

In addition to these commands, which can be used to control the program run, a debugger provides some tools, with the help of which the programmer can fully grasp the state of the stopped program. Which of these tools are available and what they are called varies from debugger to debugger, but we'd like to give you an overview of the most common tools here:

- The most basic tool is a list of all local and global references, including referenced instances that exist in the current program context. In this way, changes in value can be tracked and errors that occur can be detected more easily.

- In addition to the local and global references, the *call stack* is of interest. It lists the current call hierarchy so that it's possible to track exactly which function has called which subfunction. By clicking on a call stack entry, it's possible to jump to the corresponding line in the source code of the program.

- Especially with respect to the Python programming language, some debuggers provide an interactive shell that resides in the context of the stopped program and allows the programmer to conveniently modify references to intervene in the program flow.

- A so-called *postmortem debugger* can be considered along the lines of the previous point. In such a mode, the debugger won't stop the program until an uncaught exception has occurred. In the stopped state, the programmer again has a shell, plus the aforementioned tools to track down the error. This form of debugging is called *postmortem* because it's activated only after the actual error has occurred—that is, after the "death" of the program.

Based on this introduction to debugging techniques and with a little experimentation, you should have no problem getting to grips with the debugger of your favorite IDE.

Apart from the debugger itself, the standard library of Python also contains some modules that are especially important in the context of debugging, be it within the interactive Python shell of a debugger or completely detached from the debugger. These modules are described in the following sections.

36.2   Automated Testing

Python's standard library provides two modules for *test-driven development*, a type of programming in which many small sections of the program, referred to as *units*, are checked for errors by automated test runs. In test-driven development, the program is developed in small, self-contained steps until it passes all previous tests and all added tests again. This way, adding new code won't allow bugs to creep into old, already tested code.

In Python, the concept of *unit tests* that you may be familiar with is implemented in the unittest module. The doctest module makes it possible to place test cases within a docstring—for example, of a function. In the following sections, we'll first deal with the doctest module and then move on to the unittest module.

36.2.1 Test Cases in Docstrings: doctest

The doctest module allows you to create test cases within the docstring of a function, method, class, or module. The test is initiated when calling the testmod function contained in the doctest module. The test cases within a docstring aren't written in special language, but can be copied directly from a session in interactive mode into the docstring.

> **Note**
>
> Docstrings are also or mainly intended for the documentation of a function, for example. For this reason, you should keep the test cases in the docstring as simple and instructive as possible, so that the resulting docstring can also be used in the documentation of your program.

The following example explains the use of the doctest module using the fac function, which is supposed to calculate and return the factorial of an integer:

```
import doctest
def fac(n):
    """
        Calculates the factorial of an integer.

        >>> fac(5)
        120
        >>> fac(10)
        3628800
        >>> fac(20)
        2432902008176640000

        A positive integer must be passed.

        >>> fac(-1)
        Traceback (most recent call last):
```

```
          . . .
        ValueError: No negative numbers!
    """
    res = 1
    for i in range(2, n+1):
        res *= i
    return res
if __name__ == "__main__":
    doctest.testmod()
```

The docstring of the `fac` function first contains an explanatory text. Then follows—sep-arated from it by an empty line—an excerpt from Python's interactive mode, which contains function calls of `fac` with their return values. These test cases are traced when the test is executed and found to be either true or false.

These simple cases are followed—each introduced by a blank line—by another explan-atory text and an exceptional case in which a negative number was passed. Note that you can omit the stack trace of an occurring traceback in the docstring. The ellipsis characters written instead in the example are also optional.

The last test case hasn't been considered in the function yet, so it will fail in the test. To start the test, the `testmod` function of the `doctest` module must be called. Due to the fol-lowing `if` statement, this function is called whenever the program file is executed directly:

```
if __name__ == "__main__":
    doctest.testmod()
```

On the other hand, the test won't be performed if the program file is imported as a module by another Python program. In the provoked error case, the test result is as fol-lows:

```
**********************************************************************
File "fac.py", line 17, in __main__.fac
Failed example:
    fac(-1)
Expected:
    Traceback (most recent call last):
    ...
    ValueError: No negative numbers!
Got:
    1
**********************************************************************
1 items had failures:
    1 of   4 in __main__.fac
***Test Failed*** 1 failures.
```

Now we'll extend the fac function to raise the desired exception in case of a negative parameter:

```python
def fac(n):
    """
        [...]
    """
    if n < 0:
        raise ValueError("No negative numbers!")
    res = 1
    for i in range(2, n+1):
        res *= i
    return res
```

This change means that errors will no longer be displayed when the test is run again. To be precise: nothing will be displayed at all. This is because generally only failed test cases are output to the screen. If you also insist on the output of successful test cases, you should start the program file with the -v option (for *verbose*).

When using doctests, note that the defaults written in the docstrings are compared character by character with the output of the executed test cases. You should always keep in mind that the outputs of certain data types aren't always the same. For example, the entries of a set are in no guaranteed order. In addition, there is information that depends on the interpreter or other circumstances; for example, the identity of an instance corresponds internally to its memory address and will therefore naturally change when the program is restarted.

Another feature to watch out for is that a blank line in the expected output of a function must be indicated by the <BLANKLINE> string as a blank line acts as a separation between test cases and documentation:

```python
def f(a, b):
    """
    >>> f(3, 4)
    7
    <BLANKLINE>
    12
    """
    print(a + b)
    print()
    print(a * b)
```

To adapt a test case exactly to your needs, you can specify *flags*, settings that you can enable or disable. A flag is written as a comment after the test case in the docstring. If the flag is preceded by a plus sign (+), it will be enabled; if it's preceded by a minus sign

(-), it will be disabled. Before we get to a concrete example, we'll first introduce the three most important flags (see Table 36.1).

Flag	Meaning
ELLIPSIS	If this flag is set, the ... specification can be used for any output of a function. This way, variable information such as memory addresses or similar can be read over in larger outputs.
NORMALIZE_WHITESPACES	If this flag is set, white space characters won't be included in the result comparison. This is particularly interesting if you want to wrap a long result on several lines.
SKIP	This flag causes the test to be skipped. This is useful, for example, if you supply a number of examples in the docstring for documentation purposes, but only a few of them are to be included in a test run.

Table 36.1 Doctest Flags

In a simple example, we'll extend the doctest of the already known factorial function to compute the factorial of a relatively large number. Because it wouldn't make much sense to specify all digits of the result in the doctest, the number is to be specified in shortened form with the help of the ELLIPSIS flag:

```python
import doctest
def fac(n):
    """

    Calculates the factorial of an integer.

    >>> fac(1000) # doctest: +ELLIPSIS
    40238726007709373773543702...000
    >>> fac("Blah") # doctest: +SKIP
    'BlahBlah'
    """
    res = 1
    for i in range(2, n+1):
        res *= i
    return res
if __name__ == "__main__":
    doctest.testmod()
```

The setting of the flags has been highlighted in bold. As you can see, the example contains a second—obviously failing—test, but with the SKIP flag set. For this reason, a test run won't detect any error here.

Note that the testmod function in particular provides a wealth of options for using the test results in the program or adapting the process of testing to your needs. If you're interested in this, the Python documentation is a good place to start, as it describes the function in detail.

36.2.2   Unit Tests: unittest

The second module for test-driven development is called unittest and is also contained in the standard library. The unittest module implements the functionality of the JUnit module known from Java, which is the de facto standard for test-driven development in Java.

The difference from the doctest module is that with unittest, the test cases are defined outside the actual program code in a separate program file as regular Python code. This simplifies the execution of tests and keeps the program documentation clean. Conversely, however, more effort is involved in creating the test cases.

To create a new test case with unittest, you must create a class derived from the unittest.TestCase base class, in which individual test cases are implemented as methods. The following class implements the same test cases that we performed in the previous section using the doctest module. Here, the fac function to be tested must be implemented in the *fac.py* program file, which is imported as a module by the test program file:

```python
import unittest
import fac
class MyTest(unittest.TestCase):
    def testCalculation(self):
        self.assertEqual(fac.fac(5), 120)
        self.assertEqual(fac.fac(10), 3628800)
        self.assertEqual(fac.fac(20), 2432902008176640000)
    def testExceptions(self):
        self.assertRaises(ValueError, fac.fac, -1)
if __name__ == "__main__":
    unittest.main()
```

A class called MyTest was created that inherits from the unittest.TestCase base class. Two test methods named testCalculation and testExceptions have been implemented in the MyTest class. Note that the names of such test methods must start with test so that they are actually found and executed for testing later.

Within the test methods, the assertEqual and assertRaises methods are used, which cause the test to fail if the two specified values aren't equal or if the specified exception hasn't been raised.

To start the test run, the unittest.main function is called. The following conditional statement causes the unit test to be performed only when the program file is executed directly, and explicitly not when the program file has been imported as a module into another Python program:

```
if __name__ == "__main__":
    unittest.main()
```

To perform the test, the unittest.main function creates instances of all classes that exist in the current namespace and inherit from unittest.TestCase. Then all methods of these instances whose names begin with test are called.

In case of success, the output of the example looks as follows:

```
..
----------------------------------------------------------------------
Ran 2 tests in 0.000s

OK
```

The two dots at the beginning represent two successfully performed tests. A failed test would be indicated by an F.

In case of an error, the exact condition that led to the error would be specified:

```
.F
======================================================================
FAIL: testCalculation (__main__.MyTest)
----------------------------------------------------------------------
Traceback (most recent call last):
  File "test.py", line 7, in testCalculation
    self.assertEqual(fac.fac(5), 12)
AssertionError: 120 != 12


----------------------------------------------------------------------
Ran 2 tests in 0.001s

FAILED (failures=1)
```

The TestCase class additionally allows you to override the parameterless setUp and tearDown methods, which are executed before and after the calls of the individual test methods, respectively. Initialization and deinitialization operations can therefore be implemented in these methods. Exceptions raised in setUp or tearDown cause the current test to fail.

36

Basic Testing Methods

From the previous examples, you already know the `assertEqual` and `assertRaises` methods, which are used to implement the comparison underlying a test. The `TestCase` class defines a whole set of such methods, which are summarized in Table 36.2.

All these methods have the optional `msg` parameter, for which an error description can be specified, which is output in the event of a failed test. This parameter has been omitted from Table 36.2 for reasons of clarity.

Method	Tests For
`assertEqual(first, second)`	`first == second`
`assertNotEqual(first, second)`	`first != second`
`assertTrue(expr)`	`bool(expr) is True`
`assertFalse(expr)`	`bool(expr) is False`
`assertIs(first, second)`	`first is second`
`assertIsNot(first, second)`	`first is not second`
`assertIsNone(expr)`	`expr is None`
`assertIsNotNone(expr)`	`expr is not None`
`assertIn(first, second)`	`first in second`
`assertNotIn(first, second)`	`first not in second`
`assertIsInstance(obj, cls)`	`isinstance(obj, cls)`
`assertNotIsInstance(obj, cls)`	`not isinstance(obj, cls)`
`assertGreater(first, second)`	`first > second`
`assertGreaterEqual(first, second)`	`first >= second`
`assertLess(first, second)`	`first < second`
`assertLessEqual(first, second)`	`first <= second`

Table 36.2 Methods of the TestCase Class

Testing for Exceptions

The `TestCase` class contains the `assertRaises` and `assertWarns` methods, which can be used to test whether functions raise exceptions and warnings, respectively. They can be used with a functional interface:

```
assertRaises(exc, fun, *args, **kwds)
```

This tests whether the `fun` function object raises an exception of the `exc` type when executed with the `args` and `kwargs` parameters.

Alternatively, both `assertRaises` and `assertWarns` can create a context object:

```
with self.assertRaises(TypeError):
    pass
```

The advantage of this notation is that the code to be tested doesn't have to be encapsulated in a function.

Testing for Regular Expressions

To check strings, you can use the `assertRegex` and `assertNotRegex` methods, which are passed the `text` and `regex` parameters. Calling one of these functions checks whether `text` matches or doesn't match the `regex` regular expression. The `regex` regular expression can be passed both as a string and as an RE object:

```
self.assertRegex("Test", r"Te.t")
```

Likewise, there are the `assertWarnsRegex` and `assertRaisesRegex` methods, which work like their counterparts from the previous section, but check the text of the raised exception against a regular expression:

```
with self.assertRaises(TypeError, r"."):
    pass
```

36.3 Analyzing the Runtime Performance

Optimizing a program can take a lot of time. As a rule, the first step is to create an executable program that meets all the needed requirements, but doesn't yet necessarily place greater value on the optimization of the algorithm. This is mainly due to the fact that the actual bottlenecks are often only recognized when the program is finished, which means that a lot of time might have been invested in optimizing noncritical sections at an early stage.

To capture the runtime behavior of a Python program as accurately as possible, the three modules `timeit`, `profile`, and `cProfile` are part of the standard library of Python. These modules will be described in the following sections.

36

36.3.1 Runtime Measurement: timeit

The `timeit` module of the standard library allows you to measure exactly how long a Python program takes to execute. Typically, `timeit` is used to compare the runtime of two different algorithms for the same problem.

You'll certainly remember that in Chapter 17, Section 17.13, which was about functions, a recursive algorithm for calculating the factorial was given. We said that a runtime-optimized iterative algorithm is always more efficient compared to its recursive counterpart. In this section, we want to check this using the timeit module and additionally test by what percent the iterative variant can actually be executed faster.

To test the runtime of a Python code, the Timer class contained in the timeit module must be instantiated. The constructor of the Timer class has the interface described ahead.

Timer([stmt, setup, globals])

This creates an instance of the Timer class. The Python code to be analyzed can be passed to the constructor as the stmt parameter in string format. For the second parameter, setup, a string can also be passed containing the Python code needed to initialize stmt. Consequently, setup is also executed prior to stmt. Both parameters are optional and preset with the string "pass". The optional globals parameter can be used to pass a namespace as a dictionary in whose context the Python code to be analyzed is to be executed.

Once an instance of the Timer class has been created, it contains three methods, which are described ahead.

t.timeit([number])

This method first executes the setup code once and then repeats the code passed for stmt in the constructor number times. If the optional number parameter isn't specified, the code to be measured will be executed 1,000,000 times.

The function returns the time it took to execute the entire code (i.e., including all repetitions, but excluding the setup code). The value is returned in seconds as a float.

> **Note**
>
> To make the result as independent from external factors as possible, the garbage collection of the Python interpreter is disabled for the duration of the measurement. If garbage collection is an important part of your code to be included, you can re-enable it with the "gc.enable()" setup code after having imported the gc module.

t.repeat([repeat, number])

This method calls the timeit method repeat times and returns the results as a list of floats. The number parameter is passed to the timeit method with each call.

> **Note**
>
> It's usually not a good idea to average all values returned by repeat and output it as the average runtime. Other processes running on your system will distort the results of all measurements. Rather, you should take the smallest value in the returned list as the minimum runtime as this was the measurement with the least system activity.

t.print_exc([file])

If an exception is raised in the code to be analyzed, the analysis is aborted immediately and a traceback is issued. However, the stack trace of this traceback isn't always ideal as it doesn't refer to the actually executed source code.

To output a more meaningful stack trace, you can catch a raised exception and call the print_exc method. This method outputs a traceback on the screen that directly relates to the code being analyzed, making debugging easier. By specifying the optional file parameter, you redirect the output to a file object.

Example

We mentioned at the beginning that we'd use the timeit module to check by what percentage the iterative factorial computation is faster than the recursive one. To do this, we'll first import the timeit module and implement the two calculation functions:

```python
import timeit
def fac1(n):
    res = 1
    for i in range(2, n+1):
        res *= i
    return res
def fac2(n):
    if n > 0:
        return fac2(n-1)*n
    else:
        return 1
```

Then we create an instance of the Timer class for each of the two functions:

```python
t1 = timeit.Timer("fac1(50)", globals={"fac1":fac1})
t2 = timeit.Timer("fac2(50)", globals={"fac2":fac2})
```

Using the globals parameter, we first define the global namespace of the program under test so that the fac1 and fac2 functions can be accessed. At this point, we could also use the built-in globals function to provide the complete global namespace of the calling program to the program under test:

36

```
t1 = timeit.Timer("fac1(50)", globals=globals())
```

In the actual code to be analyzed, only the calculation of the factorial of 50 is triggered using the respective calculation function.

Finally, the runtime measurement is started with 1,000,000 repetitions and the respective result is output:

```
print("Iterative: ", t1.timeit())
print("Recursive: ", t2.timeit())
```

The output of the program is therefore:

```
Iterative:   3.3135700230195653
Recursive:   9.360691823996603
```

This means that the iterative algorithm is much faster than the recursive one. But this data isn't really representative yet because it could be that the test of the recursive function was slowed down by a process running in the system. For this reason, we'll start another test:

```
print("Iterative: ", min(t1.repeat(100, 10000)))
print("Recursive: ", min(t2.repeat(100, 10000)))
```

This time we run a test series that repeats a test with 10,000 individual repetitions 100 times and outputs the smallest of the results. The results are approximately congruent with those of the previous tests:

```
Iterative:   0.031242681987350807
Recursive:   0.09040119699784555
```

The absolute numerical values depend strongly on the system used. On a faster computer, they are correspondingly smaller.

> **Note**
>
> In addition to the object-oriented interface described here, the timeit module also provides a simplified functional interface that allows the timeit function to be called without first creating a Timer instance:
>
> ```
> timeit.timeit("fac1(50)", globals=globals(), number=1000)
> ```

36.3.2   Profiling: cProfile

To make a runtime analysis of a complete Python program, you can use a profiler. A *profiler* monitors an entire program run and lists in detail, after the program has ended, what percentage of the runtime was spent in which function. In this way, the programmer can identify the runtime bottlenecks of the program and start optimizing the program at sensible points.

The general rule is this: the higher the percentage of runtime spent in a particular function, the more time you should invest in optimizing that function.

> **Note**
>
> Since Python version 2.5, the cProfile profiler has been included in the standard library. This profiler implements the same interface as the profile profiler, but is written in C and not in Python. For this reason, the overhead of cProfile is smaller, and thus the timing measurements are better. We'll deal with the cProfile profiler here. But because it has the same interface as profile, the description is just as valid for the old profiler.
>
> The cProfile profiler may not be available for all Python interpreters. The pure Python counterpart profile, on the other hand, can be used anywhere.

There are two important functions in the cProfile module, which are described ahead.

run(command, [filename, sort])

This function executes the string passed as command and performs a detailed runtime analysis during execution. Usually, a function call of the main function of a larger program is passed for command.

The second, optional filename parameter can be used to specify a file path to which the result of the runtime analysis is written. If this parameter isn't specified, the result will be displayed on the screen. This result of the analysis is a tabular listing of all function calls. The next example demonstrates what this table looks like and how you need to read it.

The sort parameter controls what the results table should be sorted by. The values shown in Table 36.3 are possible.

Value	Sort by
"stdname"	Program file and function name—the default setting
"calls"	Number of calls of the function
"time"	Total time spent in the function
"cumulative"	Total time spent in the function and its subfunctions

Table 36.3 Possible Values for the Sort Parameter

runctx(command, globals, locals, [filename])

This function behaves like run, except that the globals and locals parameters can be used to specify the global and local context in which command is executed. For the globals and locals parameters, a dictionary can be passed as returned by the built-in globals and locals functions.

Example

The following is a runtime analysis for a small sample program. For this purpose, we'll first look at the source code of the program:

```python
import math
def calc1(n):
    return n**2
def calc2(n):
    return math.sqrt(n)
def calc3(n):
    return math.log(n+1)
def program():
    for i in range(100):
        calc1(i)
        for j in range(100):
            calc2(j)
            for k in range(100):
                calc3(k)
program()
```

There are three small functions called calc1, calc2, and calc3 in the program, each of which is passed an integer as a parameter, then applies a mathematical operation to that number and returns the result. In the main program function, there are three nested loops, each iterating over all integers from 0 to 99 and calling one of the three calculation functions. The question we want to solve with the help of the profiler is where an optimization of the program would be particularly worthwhile and where it would be superfluous.

The profiler is integrated into the program as follows:

```python
import cProfile
# Sample program
cProfile.run("program()")
```

Here, # Sample program stands for the code of the previous sample program. The program() code line of the sample program is now superfluous. Running the runtime analysis provides the following result:

```
    2020104 function calls in 0.576 seconds

 Ordered by: standard name

  ncalls  tottime  percall  cumtime  percall filename:lineno(function)
       1    0.000    0.000    0.576    0.576 <string>:1(<module>)
     100    0.000    0.000    0.000    0.000 test.py:10(calc1)
   10000    0.002    0.000    0.003    0.000 test.py:12(calc2)
 1000000    0.203    0.000    0.407    0.000 test.py:14(calc3)
       1    0.166    0.166    0.576    0.576 test.py:16(program)
       1    0.000    0.000    0.576    0.576 {built-in method builtins.exec}
 1000000    0.204    0.000    0.204    0.000 {built-in method math.log}
   10000    0.001    0.000    0.001    0.000 {built-in method math.sqrt}
       1    0.000    0.000    0.000    0.000 {method 'disable' of '_lsprof.
Profiler' objects}
```

Each line of this table refers to a function of the sample program. The column labels of the table may not be very clear, so let's explain them briefly:

- ncalls stands for the number of calls of the function.

- tottime stands for the total time in seconds spent in the function. This doesn't include calls of subfunctions.

- percall stands for the quotient of tottime and ncalls.

- cumtime stands for the total time in seconds spent in the function. Calls of subfunctions are included.

- percall stands for the quotient of cumtime and ncalls.

- filename:lineno(function) stands for the function name, including the program file and the line where the function is located in the source code.

The table displayed by the profiler provides a good overview of where the time-critical functions of the program are located. In this case, the calc3 function stands out, being called a total of 1,000,000 times and accounting for a whopping 70% of the runtime. The calc2 function, on the other hand, which is called up 10,000 times, accounts for only 0.5% of the total runtime. The remaining runtime is spent in the main program function, except for a vanishingly small percentage in calc1.

Admittedly, this result could have been estimated from the program. Each loop iterates over 100 numbers and calls the corresponding function in each iteration step. Thus, the innermost function is called 100^3 or 1,000,000 times. The runtime percentages of the calc3 and calc2 functions are also about a factor of 100 apart. Any fluctuations result from the fact that different calculations are performed.

Although this example seems somewhat artificial, the approach can be applied to a larger, time-sensitive project. In the case of our example, the focus will be on optimiz-

36

ing the `calc3` function as it strongly dominates with 1,000,000 calls and a runtime share of 70%.

Note

In the example, the `cProfile` profiler was imported as a module in a Python program and started by calling the `run` function for a part of this program.

Via the -m command line option of the Python interpreter, it's also possible to run the profiler for a Python program in its entirety without having to modify the program code:

```
$ python -m cProfile program.py
```

36.3.3   Tracing: trace

In the previous section, we described what Python can do to examine a program using a profiler. This works very well in the specific example we used, but it also has a major drawback: the profiler works at the function level. This means that only the runtime of entire functions gets measured. But it's often the case that, even within a larger function, there are parts that are neglectable in terms of runtime and parts that are very runtime-intensive. In such a case, we can use to another tool: the tracer.

A *tracer*, available in Python via the `trace` module, monitors a program run, recording how many times each line of code in the program has been executed. Such a *coverage analysis* is performed for two main reasons:

- With the help of a coverage analysis, lines of code can be identified that are called particularly frequently and are therefore possibly particularly runtime-intensive. Those lines could then be specifically optimized. Note, however, that a tracer doesn't measure the actual runtime of a line of code, but only how many times that line was executed in the program flow.

- Often, for security-relevant programs, a coverage analysis must be submitted to prove that every line of code was executed at least once during a test. In this way, we try to avoid, for example, the autopilot program of an airplane failing because a case occurs that wasn't thought of while testing the software.

In this section, we want to perform the coverage analysis to identify runtime-critical points in a program. To do this, we'll create a slightly modified version of the sample program from the previous section. *Modified* here means that the code was written without subfunctions:

```python
import math
def program():
    for i in range(100):
        i**2
```

```
    for j in range(100):
        math.sqrt(j)
        for k in range(100):
            math.log(k+1)
```

The coverage analysis is performed using the trace module. This requires the following additional code:

```
import trace
import sys
tracer = trace.Trace(ignoredirs=[sys.prefix, sys.exec_prefix], trace = 0)
tracer.run("program()")
r = tracer.results()
r.write_results(show_missing=True, coverdir="result")
```

First, an instance of the Tracer class is created which is passed two keyword parameters. The ignoredirs parameter is used to pass a list of directories whose contained modules aren't to be included in the coverage analysis. In this case, we don't want to pass any modules from the standard library, so we add the corresponding sys.prefix and sys.exec_prefix directories. We set the second parameter, trace, to 0; otherwise, every line executed during the program run will be printed on the screen.

Then, as with the profiler, we execute the run method of the Trace instance, passing the Python code to be executed. After the tracer has finished, the results can be retrieved via the results method of the trace instance. We don't want to process the results further in this case, so we save them to the hard drive using the write_results method. Here we use the coverdir parameter to specify the subdirectory where the results should be stored. If the value True is passed for the show_missing parameter, lines of code that were never executed during the program run are marked with an arrow.

The result is saved in the result subfolder as a text file with the file name modulename.cover, where *modulename* is replaced with the name of your tested module.

In the example, the result looks as follows:

```
        import trace
>>>>>> import sys
>>>>>> import math
>>>>>> def program():
  101:     for i in range(100):
  100:         i**2
10100:         for j in range(100):
10000:             math.sqrt(j)
1010000:             for k in range(100):
1000000:                 math.log(k+1)
>>>>>> tracer = trace.Trace(
>>>>>>     ignoredirs = [sys.prefix, sys.exec_prefix],
```

```
>>>>>>      trace = 0)
>>>>>> tracer.run("program()")
>>>>>> r = tracer.results()
>>>>>> r.write_results(show_missing=True, coverdir="result")
```

You'll see that the results are prepared into an easily readable file. Basically, the file is divided into two columns: on the right, there's the source code of the program, while the left-hand side indicates the number of times each line of code was called. The arrows (>>>>>>) in the left-hand column indicate lines of code that were never executed during the monitored program run.

> **Note**
>
> At first it may seem confusing that the line for i in range(100): is executed 101 times in total, although the loop counts from 0 to 99. This is due to the fact that the control flow, after processing the 100th iteration, visits the for statement once again to check whether the loop has terminated. After the 101st run of the loop header, the control flow exits the loop.
>
> The values 10100 and 1010000 in rows 7 and 9 of the coverage analysis can be explained in the same way.

Chapter 37
Documentation

If you distribute your programs and modules to users and other developers, good documentation is very important. Without a reasonable description, even the best program is worthless as it's too much work to infer the functionality from the source code alone or to guess it by trial and error.

Programmers often find writing documentation a nuisance because it takes a relatively large amount of time without improving the programs themselves. For this reason, there are many modules and programs in the Python world that haven't been sufficiently documented.

However, there are tools and methods that make writing documentation as easy as possible. In this section, we'll look pydoc, which can be used to document Python programs based on their source code. The pydoc tool analyzes the program text and collects in particular the information from so-called *docstrings*. The collected information is processed and exported as a HTML file.

37.1 Docstrings

The basis for the help texts displayed by the help function are special comments in the source code, also called *docstrings* (short for *documentation strings*). Docstrings are meant to describe functions, modules, or classes. These descriptions can be read and displayed by external tools or by the help function we've mentioned earlier. In this way, documentation can be easily generated from the comments.

The following two examples show a class and a function, each documented with a docstring. Note that a docstring must always be placed at the beginning of the function or class body to be recognized as a docstring. A docstring also can be used in other places, but then it can't be assigned to a class or function and thus works only as a block comment:

```
class MyClass:
    """Example of docstrings.

    This class shows how docstrings are
    used.
    """
```

37

```
    pass

def MyFunction():
    """This function does nothing.

    Seriously, this function really does nothing.
    """
    pass
```

To be able to use the docstring internally in the program, each instance has an attribute called __doc__, which contains its docstring. Note that function objects and imported modules are also instances:

```
>>> print(MyClass.__doc__)
Example of docstrings.

    This class shows how docstrings are
    used.
>>> print(MyFunction.__doc__)
This function does nothing.
    Seriously, this function really does nothing.
```

You can also comment a module via a docstring. The docstring of a module must be located at the beginning of the corresponding program file and is also accessible via the __doc__ attribute. For example, the docstring of the math module of the standard library can be read as follows:

```
>>> import math
>>> print(math.__doc__)
This module provides access to the mathematical functions
defined by the C standard.
```

The built-in help function generates a help page from the docstrings contained in an object and displays it in interactive mode:

```
>>> import math
>>> help(math)
```

Figure 37.1 shows the help page generated by the preceding example.

As soon as you start implementing larger programs in Python, you should add docstrings to functions, methods, classes, and modules. Not only does this help with the programming itself, but also with the later creation of program documentation, which can be generated partly automatically from the existing docstrings.

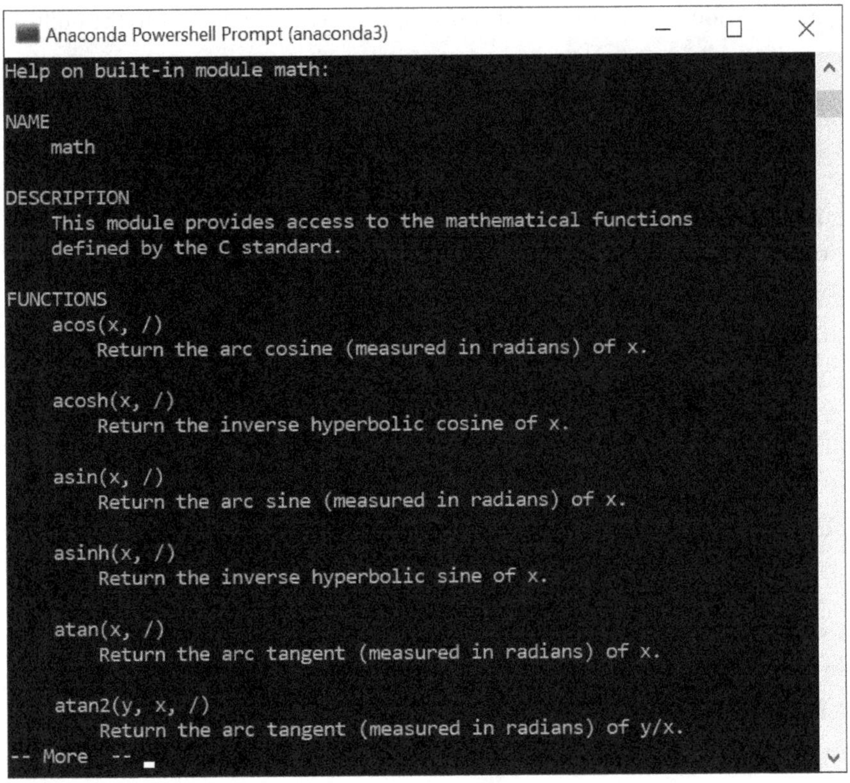

```
Anaconda Powershell Prompt (anaconda3)                    —    □    ×

Help on built-in module math:

NAME
    math

DESCRIPTION
    This module provides access to the mathematical functions
    defined by the C standard.

FUNCTIONS
    acos(x, /)
        Return the arc cosine (measured in radians) of x.

    acosh(x, /)
        Return the inverse hyperbolic cosine of x.

    asin(x, /)
        Return the arc sine (measured in radians) of x.

    asinh(x, /)
        Return the inverse hyperbolic sine of x.

    atan(x, /)
        Return the arc tangent (measured in radians) of x.

    atan2(y, x, /)
        Return the arc tangent (measured in radians) of y/x.
-- More  --
```

Figure 37.1 Help Page Generated by help Function

37.2   Automatically Generated Documentation: pydoc

The pydoc module of the standard library contains a script called pydoc or pydoc3, which is used to automatically generate program documentation.

> **Note**
>
> On Windows, the pydoc script may not be entered in the system path for executable files. In this case, you'll find it in the *Tools* subfolder of the Python installation.

In the simplest case, you call pydoc with the modules you want to document as parameters. A prerequisite for successful documentation generation is that the passed modules can be imported by Python. The modules must therefore be located in the local working directory or in one of the directories entered in sys.path. As an example, we'll now generate the documentation of the time module of the standard library:

```
$ pydoc time
```

37

761

This call generates documentation and displays it in the console, similar to the built-in help function.[1]

Alternatively, you can specify a path to the program file to be documented:

```
$ pydoc /path/to/module.py
```

In addition to a module or program, pydoc can also create documentation for individual elements of a program, such as for individual classes, functions, or methods. For this purpose, the corresponding name is specified as a parameter:

```
$ pydoc time.sleep
```

Displaying the generated documentation directly in the shell is only one of the possible display formats supported by pydoc. The -w option can be used to save the documentation in HTML format:

```
$ pydoc -w time
```

The generated *time.html* file can be viewed in a web browser. Instead of saving the documentation in HTML format first, you can use the -b option to start a web server that provides a module overview. In this overview, you'll find modules of the standard library, as well as modules located in the local working directory:

```
$ pydoc -b
```

The documentation page provided by the web server is automatically opened in the system's default browser. In addition, you can use the -n and -p options to specify the hostname and port, respectively, under which the web server should be started:

```
$ pydoc -b -n localhost -p 3000
```

---

1 By the way, the built-in help function uses pydoc internally to generate the displayed help texts.

PART V
Advanced Topics

In the fifth and final part of this book, we cover selected topics in detail, discussing both solutions offered by the standard library and third-party solutions that go beyond it, if needed. The topics covered in this part include the distribution of Python projects, programming graphical user interfaces, scientific computing with Python, and interfacing Python with other programming languages.

At the end of this part, you'll find Chapter 44, where we present short, informative sections about modules that would be too small or too insignificant for their own chapter. These modules are often intended for a very specific purpose and are accordingly kept simple. The final chapter is Chapter 45, where we explain the differences between Python generations 2.x and 3.x.

Chapter 38
Distributing Python Projects

It's likely that you have already written one or two stand-alone Python programs in the course of this book. You may even have already written a program or module in Python that could be useful to other users. At this point, the question arises how to adequately publish a Python program or module. Ideally, it should be done in such a way that the user doesn't need to be an expert to install it.

First, we'll summarize the existing approaches to distributing Python packages, then we'll discuss the third-party setuptools package in detail in Section 38.2. After that we discuss the creation of EXE files in Section 38.3, and the package managers pip and conda in Section 38.4. Finally, in Section 38.5, we'll highlight another important aspect of creating distributions: the localization of programs.

38.1 A History of Distributions in Python

Software distribution is about providing the relevant data—for example, libraries, executables, source code—in a *distribution* or *package* that's convenient for the user to install. We basically distinguish between two types of distributions:

- A *source distribution* doesn't contain any precompiled data, but only the source code of the provided software. This source code must be compiled on the user's side. The advantage of a source distribution is that it can be used unchanged on all supported platforms.

- A *binary distribution* contains a compilation of the software. For this reason, binary distributions are usually platform-dependent, so custom distributions must be created for many destination platforms. The advantage of a binary distribution is its ease of installation: the included files just need to be copied to the right place in the system. In particular, no build step is necessary.

The Python world is teeming with a bewildering variety of approaches to generating distributions. In the following sections, we'll present the most important ones of these approaches.

38.1.1   The Classic Approach: distutils

The distutils package is a now-obsolete solution that was included in the standard library up to Python 3.10 and has been the standard for distributing Python software for a long time. To create a distribution, an installation script called *setup.py* is created that describes the properties of the distribution. This includes, for example, metadata such as the author or license and a list of files to be included in the distribution. Running the installation script can create a source or binary distribution:

- A source distribution contains the setup.py installation script, which can be used in this case to install the software on the target system.
- A binary distribution is created in the form of a Windows installer or an RPM package for certain Linux distributions.

The major drawback of the distutils package was that dependencies between distributions couldn't be taken into account. Not least because of this, it has become obsolete nowadays due to more comprehensive solutions such as setuptools and has no longer been part of the standard library since Python 3.10.

38.1.2   The New Standard: setuptools

The setuptools third-party package is based on distutils, so it's used in a similar way and is compatible with distutils installation scripts. However, it surpasses its predecessor's feature set in several important ways, which has now made it the new standard in Python software distribution.

With setuptools, so-called *Python wheels* can be created. These are special distributions that contain additional metadata; in particular, dependencies to other wheels can be described. Python wheels can be identified by their *.whl* file extension.

> **Note**
>
> In addition to wheels, Python developers occasionally come across *Python eggs*. This distribution format has become obsolete with the introduction of standardized wheels.

38.1.3   The Package Index: PyPI

The Python Package Index (PyPI) is a collection of Python packages maintained by the Python Software Foundation and is available at *pypi.python.org*. You can also add your own packages to the PyPI after registration.

The packages listed in PyPI can be conveniently downloaded and installed using the pip package manager. In the process, the package manager installs or updates dependencies as necessary. In Section 38.4.1, we'll describe how pip works in more detail.

38.2   Creating Distributions: setuptools

To create a distribution using the setuptools package, the following steps are generally required:

- Writing your module or package[1]
- Writing the *setup.py* installation script
- Creating a source distribution or a binary distribution

These steps will be described in detail in the following sections.

> **Note**
>
> In general, you can use setuptools to create distributions of not only modules or packages, but also extensions. Such extensions can later be imported like a module or package, but unlike normal modules or packages, they are written in a different programming language—usually C or C++. In Chapter 40, Section 40.3.3, we will describe the use of setuptools in connection with extensions.

38.2.1   Installation

Because setuptools is a third-party package that isn't included in the standard library, it must be installed before you can build and install distributions. This can be done conveniently via the Anaconda package manager *conda*:

```
$ conda install setuptools
```

Alternatively, if you don't use Anaconda, the setuptools package can be installed via the Python package manager *pip*:

```
$ pip install setuptools
```

38.2.2   Writing the Module

Remember that there's a difference between a module and a package. Whereas a *module* consists of only one program file, a *package* is a folder that can contain several submodules or subpackages. You can recognize a package by the *__init__.py* program file in the package directory. The distinction between the terms *module* and *package* will play a role when we create the installation script.

At this point, let's develop the sample module, which will form the basis of all the descriptions in this chapter. This is a very simple module that demonstrates the basic

---

1 Actually, this is not a step in creating a distribution; nevertheless, it's obviously an indispensable requirement. You can also package multiple modules and/or packages into a common distribution. You'll learn more about this in the course of this section.

functionality of setuptools. Comments about more complex distributions containing packages, for example, have been added at the respective places throughout the text.

The purpose of the sample module is to modify any text so that it reads like the following one:

> *Accroding to a stduy of Cmabridge Uinverstity, it dosne't matetr in wichh odrer the ltetres ouccr in wdros.*
>
> *The olny improtnat apscet is taht the frist and lsat leettr are in the rghit psiotoin. The rset can be ttolaly wnorg, and it can be raed wtiohut any porelbm.*
>
> *Tihs is so bcesuae the haumn biarn deons't read ecah lteetr idnvidialuly, but the wrod as a wlohe.*

The module provides a function called swirl_text, which obtains a string and returns it "swirled" in such a way that only the first and last letter remain safely in place:

```python
import random
def swirl_text(text):
    list = []
    for word in text.split():
        w = list(word[1:-1])
        random.shuffle(w)
        list.append(word[0] + "".join(w) + word[-1])
    return " ".join(list)
```

The function iterates in a loop over all words contained in the passed string. At each iteration, the substring to be swirled is extracted from the respective word. This ensures that the first and last letters won't be included in this substring. The shuffle function of the random module is used to swirl the letters. Finally, the swirled string, the initial letter, and the final letter are merged and appended to the list of generated words, list. At the end, this word list is combined into a text and returned.

For simplicity, the function assumes a benign input string. This means in particular that the string shouldn't contain any punctuation signs.

We now want to create a distribution of the swirl module so that other Python programmers can also make use of this extremely powerful tool as easy as possible.

38.2.3   The Installation Script

The first step toward distributing your own module is to create an *installation script*. This is a Python program file called *setup.py*, which will later be used to create the distribution. Also, the installation of a source distribution on the user's side is done by calling this program file.

In the example, only the setup function of the setuptools module needs to be called in the installation script:

```
from setuptools import setup
setup(
    name="swirl",
    version="1.0",
    author="Mickey Mouse",
    author_email="mickey@mouse.com",
    py_modules=["swirl"]
)
```

To this function we pass various keyword parameters that contain information about the module. In addition, the function is passed all program files that should belong to the distribution via the py_modules parameter. This way, it's also possible to provide several self-written modules in one distribution.

In fact, that's all there is to it. This program file can now be used to install the module on any machine with Python installed or to create a distribution of the module. We'll explain later how this works in detail, but first we want to take a look at the setup function.

setuptools.setup({arguments})

The setup function of the setuptools package must be called in the *setup.py* program file and triggers the desired installation process. To do this, you must pass various keyword parameters to the function that provide information about the module or package. Table 38.1 lists the most important possible arguments and briefly clarifies their meaning.

Unless otherwise specified, the respective parameters are strings.

Parameter Name	Description
author	The name of the author.
author_email	The author's email address.
data_files	A list of tuples that can be used to include additional files in the distribution.
description	A short description of the distribution.
download_url	The URL where the distribution can be downloaded directly.
ext_modules	A list of setuptools.Extension instances containing the names of all Python extensions to be compiled and included in the distribution.
license	The license for the distribution.

Table 38.1 Possible Keyword Parameters for Setup

38

Parameter Name	Description
long_description	A detailed description of the distribution.
maintainer	The name of the package manager.
maintainer_email	The email address of the package manager.
name	The name of the distribution.
package_data	A dictionary that can be used to include files belonging to a package in the distribution.
package_dir	A dictionary that can be used to include packages in subdirectories in the distribution.
packages	A list of strings containing the names of all packages to be included in the distribution.
py_modules	A list of strings containing the names of all Python modules to be included in the distribution.
script_name	The name of the installation script to be used in the distribution. This parameter defaults to sys.argv[0], which is the name of the script that is currently running.
scripts	A list of strings containing the names of all script files to be included in the distribution.
url	The URL of a website with further information about the distribution.
version	The version number of the distribution.

Table 38.1 Possible Keyword Parameters for Setup (Cont.)

Distributing Packages

If your project consists of one or more packages instead of individual modules, you must specify the names of all packages to be included in the distribution using the packages keyword parameter:

```python
from setuptools import setup
setup(
    [...]
    packages=["package1", "package2", "package1.subpackage1"]
)
```

In this case, the package1 and package2 packages, which must be located in the root directory, will be included in the distribution. In addition, the subpackage1 package will be included, which is inside the package1 package. You can certainly include packages via packages as well as individual modules via py_modules in the distribution.

Often there is an **src** or **source** folder in the main folder besides the installation script, which then contains the modules or packages of the distribution. To make such a subfolder known in the installation script, you must pass the `package_dir` keyword parameter when calling `setup`:

```
from setuptools import setup
setup(
    [...]
    package_dir={"": "src"},
    packages=["package1", "package2", "package1.subpackage1"]
)
```

This places the program directory ("") on the `src` directory. You can also specify this for individual packages. For example, you can use another entry in this dictionary with the key "package3" and the value "path/to/my/package/package3" to include a third package that is located in a different directory than the `package1` and `package2` packages. After that, `package3` can be added to the distribution via the `packages` list. Subpackages of `package3` then also no longer need to be addressed via the full path.

Alternatively, the `find_packages` function can be used to automatically enter all packages in the package directory:

```
from setuptools import setup, find_packages
setup(
    [...]
    packages=find_packages()
)
```

Distributing Script Files

In addition to modules and packages, other files may belong to your project and should therefore also find a place in the distribution. First, this includes simple script files, which, for example, implement tools related to your package. The difference between a module and a script file is that the module itself doesn't execute any Python code but only provides functions or classes, while a script file contains an executable program. The `distutils` package installs script files into a directory where they can be executed system-wide.[2]

Such script files can be passed by the `scripts` keyword parameter when calling `setup`. For `scripts`, as for other parameters, a list of strings must be passed, each containing a file name.

38

---

2 On Windows, this is the **Scripts** subfolder of the Python installation; on Linux, it's the */usr/bin* directory.

A small service performed by the setuptools package with respect to script files is to automatically adjust the shebang line to the operating system on which the distribution is installed.

Distributing Resources

The next category of additional files are resources required by and included in specific packages. For example, package1 requires the *hello.txt* and *world.txt* files. In such a case, these files can be passed via the package_data keyword parameter as a dictionary:

```
setup(
    [...]
    packages=["package1", "package2", "package1.subpackage1"],
    package_data={"package1": ["hello.txt", "world.txt"]}
)
```

Instead of specifying each file individually, wildcards can also be used. Thus, the value ["*.txt"] would include all text files located in the directory of the package1 package.

> **Note**
>
> You should always separate folders in a path with a single slash (/). The setuptools package then takes care of the correct "translation" of the path into the format of the respective operating system.

Dependencies

If your software has dependencies on other packages, you can specify them using the install_requires keyword parameter:

```
setup(
    [...]
    install_requires=['package>=1.0']
)
```

In this case, the installation of the software requires the installation of the package package in a version not older than 1.0. If the installation is done with a package manager like pip or Easy Install, the package package can be downloaded and installed automatically from PyPI, if it's available there.

If a dependency on a package not included in the package index is required, you can use the dependency_links keyword parameter to specify a list of URLs to search for unknown packages.

38.2.4   Creating a Source Distribution

Once you've written the installation script, you can use it to create a source distribution of your software. To do this, you must go to the directory where the installation script is located and run it using the sdist argument:

```
$ python setup.py sdist
```

This command creates the source distribution in the dist subfolder according to the naming scheme *ProjectName-Version.Format*. You can specify the format of the archive using the --formats option. It's also possible to create a distribution in multiple archive formats:

```
$ python setup.py sdist --formats=zip,gztar
```

Possible values are zip for a ZIP archive (*.zip*), gztar for a gz-compressed TAR archive (*.tar.gz*), bztar for a bz2-compressed TAR archive (*.tar.bz2*), xztar for an xz-compressed TAR archive (*.tar.xz*), ztar for a z-compressed TAR archive (*.tar.Z*), and tar for an uncompressed TAR archive (*.tar*). If the --formats option isn't specified, a ZIP archive is created on Windows and a gz-compressed TAR archive is created on Unix systems.

All files that were entered in the installation script are included in the archive. In addition, a file named *README* or *README.txt* is automatically included in the archive if one exists in the same folder as the installation script.

The resulting archive—the source code distribution—then can be published and distributed. The user who downloads this distribution can install your module or package as described in Section 38.2.6.

38.2.5   Creating a Binary Distribution

Besides a source code distribution, creating a binary distribution is of particular interest because it involves the lowest installation overhead. Conversely, however, it means more work for you as different formats for binary distributions may have to be created for different operating systems. The most prominent of these formats is a Windows installer, but RPM packages for RPM-based Linux distributions[3] and Python wheels can also be created.

Note that in addition to a binary distribution, you should always publish a source distribution of your project as there are operating systems that can't make use of either an RPM package or a Windows installer.

To create a binary distribution, the installation script is called with the arguments listed in Table 38.2.

38

---

3 These include Red Hat, Fedora, SUSE, and Mandriva.

Argument	Meaning
bdist_rpm	Creates an RPM package for specific Linux systems
bdist_egg	Creates a Python egg
bdist_wheel	Creates a Python wheel*

* This requires the wheel package from the package index in addition to setuptools.

Table 38.2 Possible Arguments of the Installation Script

Because all the information needed to create the binary distribution has already been specified in the installation script, creating a binary distribution is done with a simple call of *setup.py*:

```
$ python setup.py bdist_wheel
```

> **Note**
>
> So long as your project consists of pure Python modules—that is, it doesn't include packages or extensions—the installation file for Windows also can be generated on other operating systems, such as Linux. However, as soon as packages or extensions are included, you must use a Windows system.

38.2.6 Installing Distributions

Now that you have the basic tools for creating binary and source code distributions, let's talk about using the distributions themselves.

We don't need to say much about a binary distribution here because the installation procedure is the same as usual on the operating system in question. Wheels can be installed using a package manager like pip; Section 38.4.1.

To install a source distribution, you must also call *setup.py*:

```
$ python setup.py install
```

When the *setup.py* program file is executed with the install argument, it installs the distribution into the Python environment that exists on the system. Note that this may require administrator or root privileges, depending on the system.

> **Note**
>
> The distribution will be installed into the system's default Python third-party libraries directory. If you don't want this, you can specify a target directory via the --prefix option:
>
> ```
> $ python setup.py install --prefix="path/to/target_directory"
> ```

38.3   Creating EXE files: cx_Freeze

The setuptools package can be used to create distributions from Python projects, which can then be installed on the target system in the context of an existing Python environment. Especially on Windows, it's sometimes useful to deliver a program as a simple executable that runs without further prerequisites even on systems where no Python environment is installed. Such a distribution can be created with the third-party cx_Freeze module.

38.3.1   Installation

Because cx_Freeze is a third-party package, it must be installed before you can use it. This can be done via the Anaconda package manager conda:

```
$ conda install -c conda-forge cx_Freeze
```

Alternatively, if you don't use Anaconda, cx_Freeze can be installed via the Python package manager pip:

```
$ pip install cx_Freeze
```

If you use Linux, an installation may also be possible via the package manager of your Linux distribution.

For more information, please visit the project website at *https://cx-freeze.readthedocs.io/*.

> **Note**
>
> Depending on your operating system and the Python version you use, cx_Freeze is installed via pip as a source distribution and thus requires a compatible C++ compiler installed on the system. For this reason, we recommend installing cx_Freeze via Anaconda.

38.3.2   Usage

In this section, we use the cx_Freeze module to create an executable from a small sample program. Here you can first see the source code of the sample program:

```python
import sys
if len(sys.argv) > 2:
    print("Result: {}".format(int(sys.argv[1]) + int(sys.argv[2])))
```

This is a simple program that adds two numbers passed as arguments and outputs the result.

38

There are two ways to use the cx_Freeze module: via the cxfreeze[4] script, which must be passed the path to the program file to be processed as an argument, or alternatively in combination with setuptools. To do this, we write the following *setup.py* program file in the context of the sample program shown previously:

```
from cx_Freeze import setup, Executable
setup(
    [...]
    executables=[Executable("calc.py")]
)
```

Instead of the ellipsis [...], usually additional parameters for the setup function are provided, which can be used, for example, to specify the name of the program or the email address of the author (Section 38.2.3). To create an executable file with cx_Freeze, the executables keyword parameter must be specified. For this purpose, a list of Executable instances is passed, each representing an executable to be created.

Once the installation script is ready, the executable file can be generated. To do this, the *setup.py* installation script must be called with the build argument:

```
$ python setup.py build
```

Then the configured executables will be created automatically. In doing so, cx_Freeze generates the native formats for the respective operating system. For example, it isn't possible to create a Windows executable on Linux.

After the installation script has finished, you'll find the *dist* subfolder in the program directory, which contains the finished distribution of your Python program. This contains not only the executable file itself, in this case, *calc.exe*, but also other files needed for the program. For example, the Python interpreter is stored in the *python311.dll* DLL[5] and the required parts of the standard library are stored in the *library.zip* archive.

38.4   Package Manager

A *package manager* is a utility that automatically downloads and installs software components on demand. In doing so, a package manager must be able to know and resolve dependencies between software packages to enable the user to install them as smoothly as possible.

A package manager always works in combination with a *package source*, often referred to as a *repository* or *package index*, from which it obtains the software components and

---

4 On Windows and macOS, you can find cxfreeze in the *Scripts* subdirectory of the Python installation. On Linux, cxfreeze is usually installed in the global system executable directory.

5 The abbreviation DLL stands for *Dynamic Link Library*.

information about versioning and dependencies. A package manager is helpful for both users and providers of software:

- A user can install software with a simple and standardized procedure without having to worry about dependencies him or herself.
- A vendor only needs to add the software package to the package source and doesn't need to bother about system- or user-specific installation solutions.

For the installation of Python packages, you can use the pip and conda package managers, which will be described in the following sections.

38.4.1 The Python Package Manager: pip

In the previous sections, PyPI was mentioned frequently. This is an archive of hundreds of thousands Python packages that can be found at *pypi.python.org*. To be able to use this huge archive of Python software adequately, there is, among other things, the *pip package manager*,[6] which can not only download and install individual packages from PyPI, but also resolve dependencies.

The pip package manager is itself included in PyPI and can be downloaded and installed as a source distribution via *pypi.python.org/pypi/pip*.

After the installation, packages can be installed in a shell using the pip command:

```
$ pip install package
```

In this case, the package named package is searched for in PyPI and will be installed, provided it exists. For package, a local path to a Python wheel can also be specified. An installed package can be removed again in a similarly easy way:

```
$ pip uninstall package
```

The pip list command can be used to list all currently installed packages with version numbers. The pip show command provides information about an installed package:

```
$ pip show matplotlib
Name: matplotlib
Version: 3.1.1
Summary: Python plotting package
Home-page: https://matplotlib.org
Author: John D. Hunter, Michael Droettboom
[...]
```

Using pip, you can install Python software conveniently, particularly on systems that don't provide their own package managers, such as Microsoft Windows.

---

6 The name *pip* can be read as a recursive acronym for "pip installs packages."

> **Note**
>
> Many operating systems, including most Linux distributions, contain a package manager that handles the installation and management of programs. To prevent pip from interfering with such a package manager, the `--user` option is available:
>
> ```
> $ pip install --user matplotlib
> ```
>
> If you specify this option, pip installs the package into the local user directory.

> **Note**
>
> If you get an error message indicating that you don't have access rights ("permission denied") when installing a package with pip on Windows, you should try starting the command prompt or PowerShell, where you can run pip with administrator rights.

38.4.2 The conda Package Manager

If you use the Anaconda Python distribution, the conda package manager is also available in addition to pip, which you can use to conveniently install Python packages. One advantage of conda over pip and other package managers is that it can install and manage other programs besides Python packages. It also ensures that the packages and programs installed by conda are available in versions that match each other.

The conda package manager offers extensive functionality[7] that goes far beyond our requirements in the context of this book. It's available in a command line version or in a graphical variant. Here, we'll focus on some basic functionalities in the command line version.

To use conda, you must open a command line via the **Start** menu item **Anaconda Prompt** on Windows and a shell on Linux or macOS.

> **Note for Linux or macOS**
>
> If you haven't set Anaconda's Python interpreter as the default Python during installation, as described in Chapter 2, Section 2.2, you must first run the following command:
>
> ```
> $ export PATH=/home/your_user/anaconda3/bin:$PATH
> ```
>
> Where `/home/your_user/anaconda3` is the path where you installed Anaconda.

You can then execute conda within the command line or shell. For example, the following call will return the currently installed version of conda:

---

7 For example, it provides mechanisms that install different versions of Python and packages in parallel and switch between the installed versions conveniently. For more information, you should refer to the documentation on conda at *https://docs.conda.io*.

```
$ conda --version
```

A typical call of conda has the following structure:

```
$ conda command arguments
```

Similar to pip, there are commands for installing and uninstalling Python packages, among other things. Table 38.3 shows a selection of the available commands.

Command	Description
info	Displays information about the installation of conda
help	Outputs a description of how you can use conda
search	Searches for packages by their name
list	Displays all installed packages
install	Installs packages
remove	Uninstalls packages
update	Updates packages

Table 38.3 Some of the Commands of conda

As an example, we'll use the py-spy package, that you can use to analyze the runtime behavior of your programs.[8] First, we'll use the search function of conda to search for the package. We don't need to specify the exact name of the package; a part of the name is enough:

```
$ conda search py-s
Loading channels: done
No match found for: py-s. Search: *py-s*
# Name                      Version          Build  Channel
[...]
py-spy                      0.3.11      h55d743e_1  pkgs/main
[...]
```

The output informs us that conda has found a py-spy package related to the request. For each package that has been found, the combinations of the version of the package and the version of the Python interpreter required for the package are displayed.

You can use the following command to install the latest version of py-spy for the currently selected Python interpreter:

---

8 We do not describe py-spy in this book any further. However, you might want to have a closer look at this useful tool.

```
$ conda install py-spy
[...]
The following NEW packages will be INSTALLED:

  py-spy                pkgs/main/osx-64::py-spy-0.3.11-h55d743e_1
Proceed ([y]/n)?
```

Before the installation starts, conda lists the package to be installed and its dependencies to be installed as well and asks for confirmation. To confirm the installation, acknowledge the last question by pressing ⌈Enter⌋. If you then display the list of installed packages, py-spy will be included:

```
$ conda list
[...]
py-spy                    0.3.11                h55d743e_1
[...]
```

To remove the package again, you can use the remove command:

```
$ conda remove py-spy
```

In some use cases, you need a specific version of a package. This can be achieved using conda by adding an equal sign after the package name, followed by the required version number:

```
$ conda install py-spy=0.3.11
```

Of course, this way you can only install the versions available in the database of conda.

> **Note**
>
> In practice, you should always use the latest available version of a piece of software, unless there's a valid reason for using an old version.

The conda-forge Repository

By default, conda searches the official package sources of Anaconda and installs the package versions available there. For very new packages or package versions it happens that there is no corresponding package in the official repository yet. In addition, there are packages that are not important enough to be included in the official repository.

A remedy in such situations can be provided by the community-organized project *conda-forge*,[9] where many additional packages and package versions for conda are available. To install a package from conda-forge, you can use the channel parameter of

---

9 See *http://conda-forge.org/*.

conda. For example, at time of printing of this book, version 4 of the package django, which we describe in Chapter 42, was not available in the official Anaconda package sources. However, it could already be installed via conda-forge:

```
$ conda install --channel conda-forge django=4.0.6
```

Many of the packages provided by conda-forge are of high quality, so you can find a valuable source of up-to-date software there. Nevertheless, we recommend preferring the official Anaconda package sources if you find a package there in the version you need, because here, in addition to the community, a company pays attention to the quality.

38.5 Localizing Programs: gettext

The gettext module of the standard library is useful for the internationalization and localization of Python programs. *Internationalization* refers to the process of abstracting the user interface of a program so that it can be easily adapted to other linguistic or cultural environments. *Localization* is the process of adapting the program to the conditions of a particular country or region. Note that the gettext module is limited to the translation of strings. Other differences, such as date formats or currency symbols, aren't taken into account.

The gettext module is based on the *GNU gettext API*,[10] which is widely used as part of the GNU project and provides tools for the localization of a program. The module allows you to use an interface that is similar to the GNU gettext API. In addition, there is a somewhat more abstract, object-oriented interface compared to the GNU gettext API, which we'll refer to in this section.

First, a few words about how the localization of a program works. The programmer writes his or her program in which the user interface is created in English. To localize the program, each string to be output is sent through a so-called *wrapper function*. This is a function that expects the nonlocalized English string as a parameter and returns the appropriate translation.

Internally, gettext uses different language compilations for translation. These are binary files that contain the translation of the program into one specific language at a time. These binary files are called MO files because of their file extension *.mo*. How these files are created is, among other things, the content of the next section.

38.5.1 Example of Using gettext

Internationalization always plays a role when a program is made available to a large group of users. It's a common procedure, especially in open-source projects, to publish the program originally in only one or two languages; further translations are later cre-

---

10 See *http://www.gnu.org/software/gettext/*.

ated by the users and sent to the author. For this to work, the programmer should at least ensure the translatability of the program.

At this point, we'll show you how to use gettext on the basis of a small sample program. The source code of the sample program looks as follows:

```python
import gettext
import random
trans = gettext.translation("myprogram", "locale", ["de"])
trans.install()
values = []
while True:
    w = input(_("Please enter a value: "))
    if not w:
        break
    values.append(w)
print(_("The random choice is {}").format(random.choice(values)))
```

The program itself is no big deal: it reads strings from the user until one of these strings is empty—that is, until the user has pressed ⌜Enter⌟ without making any input. Then the program randomly selects one of these strings and outputs it. So with this program, for example, a randomly selected person in a group could be designated as the driver for the upcoming Saturday night. Interaction with the user is in English only, but every string that is output is sent through a function called _ up front.

> **Note**
>
> In the print output at the end of the sample program, the _ function is called for a placeholder-containing string before this placeholder is replaced by dynamic content. This is important as otherwise no translation can take place.

The really interesting parts of the program are the two lines after the import statements:

```python
trans = gettext.translation("myprogram", "locale", ["de"])
trans.install()
```

Here a so-called translation object is created. This is an instance that ensures the translation of all strings into a specific language. To create such an object, the gettext.translation function is called. This function gets a freely selectable name, the so-called *domain*, as its first parameter. The second parameter is the subdirectory where the translations are located, and finally the third parameter is a list of languages. In the above example, we use "de" for the German language.[11] The translation object then translates into the first language from the list for which a language compilation can be found.

---

11   *Deutsch* means *German* in German.

By calling the `install` method of the translation object, it installs its internal translation method as the _ function in the local namespace. This will translate all strings that call the _ function into the language represented by the translation object, if a translation is available.

Note

It's possible to create several translation objects and install different ones during the program. Strings are then translated using the currently installed translation object.

38.5.2 Creating the Language Compilation

To create the *language compilation*, you must first create a list of all the strings to be translated. These are all those that are sent through the _ function before output. As it would be an unreasonable amount of work to create this list manually, Python contains a program called *pygettext.py*[12] that does exactly that job for you. The program creates a *PO file*. This is a human-readable variant of the MO file format. This PO file then is translated by translators into different languages. This can be done manually or by using various tools available for this purpose. The PO file created for the sample program looks as follows:[13]

```
[...]
#: main.py:9
msgid "Please enter a value: "
msgstr "Bitte geben Sie einen Wert ein: "
#: main.py:13
msgid "The random choice is {}"
msgstr "Die Zufallswahl ist {}"
```

Instead of the ellipsis, the file contains information such as the author, the software used, and the encoding of the file.

---

12 On Windows, you can find the *pygettext.py* program in the *Tools/i18n* subfolder of your Python installation. On Unix-based operating systems, such as Linux, the program file should be in the system path and directly executable. Your Linux distribution may install the *pygettext.py* program of Python 3 under a modified name, such as *pygettext3.py*, to allow parallel installation of Python 2 and 3.

13 Only the German language contents of the file have been written in manually. The rest was generated automatically using pygettext.

A translated PO file is compiled into binary MO format by the *msgfmt.py* program,[14] which is also included with Python. A finished language compilation must be located in the following folder in order to be found as such by gettext:

Program directory/subfolder/Language/LC_MESSAGES/Domain.mo

The name of the directory subfolder is specified when the gettext.translate function is called and was *locale* in our example. This directory must contain another directory for each existing language, which in turn must have an *LC_MESSAGES* subdirectory. The language compilation itself must have the domain specified in the program as its name.

Thus, in our sample program, the language compilation must be located in the following directory:

Program directory/locale/de/LC_MESSAGES/myprogram.mo

If the language compilation isn't available, a corresponding exception is raised when the gettext.translation function is called:

```
Traceback (most recent call last):
  [...]
FileNotFoundError: [Errno 2] No translation file found for domain: 'myprogram'
```

If the language compilation is in place, you'll notice when you run the program that all strings have been translated into German:

```
Bitte geben Sie einen Wert ein: Donald Duck
Bitte geben Sie einen Wert ein: Daisy Duck
Bitte geben Sie einen Wert ein: Scrooge McDuck
Bitte geben Sie einen Wert ein:
Die Zufallswahl ist Donald Duck
```

---

14 On Windows, you can find the *msgfmt.py* program in the *Tools/i18n* subfolder of your Python installation. On Unix-based operating systems such as Linux, the program file should be located in the system path and be directly executable. Here, the same note applies as for *pygettext.py*.

Chapter 39
Virtual Environments

The pip package manager makes it easy to install third-party Python modules along with their dependencies. The installation is then usually done for the Python interpreter installed in the system, and the installed package is available to any Python program from then on.

Let's suppose we were to develop two Python programs A and B on the same system, each with very different requirements. In such (quite common) scenarios, there are multiple conceivable reasons that a simple, system-wide installation of all dependencies of A and B could be an issue:

- The dependencies of A and B could be mutually exclusive—for example, via different version requirements—making simultaneous installation impossible.

- Installing a dependency required for A could change the behavior of B in a way we don't want.

- A dependency of A might be experimental or unsafe, so we don't want to make it available system-wide.

- We may be concerned that future updates of dependency packages we make for B will disrupt the functionality of A, which is particularly important to us.

For such use cases, Python provides the concept of virtual environments. A *virtual environment* is a directory that contains its own Python interpreter and pip package manager. Python programs can be run and Python packages can be installed in this directory without affecting the system-wide installation of Python.

In this way, a virtual environment can be set up for each of the imaginary Python programs A and B mentioned previously, in which the respective dependencies of A and B are installed completely independently of each other in the appropriate versions.

> **Note**
>
> We'll first look at the venv module in Section 39.1, which allows you to set up and use a virtual environment within a shell.
>
> Especially for Windows users, the graphical user interface of *Anaconda Navigator* for managing virtual environments is much more convenient. Development environments such as *PyCharm* (see Section A.5.1 in the appendix) also provide such a graphical interface.

39

In Section 39.2, we'll briefly review the management of virtual environments in Anaconda.

39.1 Using Virtual Environments: venv

A virtual environment named test_environment can be created using the venv module of the standard library:

```
$ python -m venv test_environment
```

This command creates a *test_environment* directory that contains the new virtual environment. Within this directory, the *bin* subfolder contains the executable components relevant to the virtual environment, including the Python interpreter and the pip package manager.

39.1.1 Activating a Virtual Environment

Aside from the fact that a virtual environment was created, nothing else happened. A Python program would still run in the context of the system-wide Python installation at this point. To use a virtual environment, it must first be *activated*.

To activate a virtual environment on Windows, you must run the activate script in the *Scripts* subdirectory of the virtual environment:

```
$ test_environment\Scripts\activate
```

On Linux and macOS,[1] the script can be found in the *bin* subdirectory. With the additional source command, we enable the script to modify the environment variables of the currently running shell:

```
$ source test_environment/bin/activate
```

39.1.2 Working in a Virtual Environment

The activate script of the virtual environment sets all Python-specific environment variables of the current shell to reference the Python installation of the virtual environment. In this way, the virtual environment can be used in the current shell as if it were the system-wide Python installation. In particular, Python packages can be installed via pip:[2]

```
(test_environment) $ pip install setuptools
```

---

1 More precisely, in the Bash and Zsh shells common on Linux and macOS.
2 By the way, a separate installation of setuptools isn't necessary in virtual environments because the package is already installed when the environment is created.

The (test_environment) annotation is used in most shells to indicate which virtual environment is currently being used after the activation script is executed. Python programs can also be executed in virtual environments as usual:

```
(test_environment) $ python test.py
```

In this case, the execution takes place in the context of the virtual environment—that is, in particular, in the context of the packages installed there.

39.1.3   Deactivating a Virtual Environment

You can leave a virtual environment using the deactivate command. This has been made universally available on both Windows and Linux via the activate script within the running shell, so a simple execution is all that's required:

```
(test_environment) $ deactivate
```

The command changes all Python-specific environment variables of the current shell back to referencing the system-wide Python installation. To permanently remove a virtual environment, it suffices to delete the directory where it's located.

> **Note**
>
> In addition to the venv module of the standard library for using virtual environments, the third-party virtualenv module is also very popular. For more information on virtualenv, you can visit *https://virtualenv.pypa.io*.

39.2   Virtual Environments in Anaconda

Anaconda also supports the creation and management of virtual environments. This can either be done via the graphical *Anaconda Navigator* or within a shell, similar to the usage of venv. An Anaconda environment can be created via the conda create command:

```
$ conda create --name test_environment2
```

This command doesn't create the environment as a folder in the local working directory, but in a central collection of virtual environments organized by Anaconda. Activating and deactivating an environment involves the same semantics as working with venv and is done via conda activate and conda deactivate respectively:

```
$ conda activate test_environment2
$ conda deactivate
```

39

A major advantage of Anaconda is that it can also create virtual environments that use a version of the Python interpreter that differs from the system installation, whereupon all required packages are automatically downloaded from the Anaconda package index:

```
$ conda create --name test_environment3 python=3.10
```

These defaults can also be made when configuring virtual environments via the graphical user interface in Anaconda Navigator. Especially because of the easier handling, we recommend the use of Anaconda on Windows.

> **Note**
>
> Many developers make their Python programs directly executable on Unix-based operating systems using a shebang line (see Chapter 4, Section 4.1.1). If your program needs to run in the context of an Anaconda environment test_environment, the shebang line can be adjusted accordingly:
>
> ```
> #!/usr/bin/env conda run -n test_environment python
> ```
>
> This shebang line makes the program run in the context of the enabled test_environment environment using Anaconda. Note that Anaconda must be contained in the system path for this to work.

Chapter 40
Alternative Interpreters and Compilers

In the previous chapters, we have always regarded the Python language and its interpreter as a single entity. Implicitly, we have referred to the Python language in combination with its *reference implementation*, the CPython interpreter. This quibble becomes relevant only in this chapter, where we discuss alternative interpreters and compilers.

In addition to CPython, a number of other interpreters and compilers exist that implement the Python language. Some approaches are limited to a subset of the language's scope, while others extend the language.

Often the development of an alternative interpreter is driven by a desire for more efficient program execution, as the CPython reference implementation focuses on simplicity and extensibility, possibly at the expense of efficiency.

Other alternative interpreters and compilers base their approach on the desire for interoperability between Python and other programming languages.

In the following sections, we'll describe some of the most important alternative interpreters and compilers and demonstrate their advantages with some examples.

40.1 Just-in-Time Compilation: PyPy

A Python interpreter worth mentioning in the context of optimization is *PyPy*,[1] which, unlike CPython, contains *a just-in-time (JIT) compiler*. Such a JIT compiler translates particularly frequently executed parts of a running program into machine code to make them more efficient. Because the compilation only takes place at runtime, information about the current program run can be taken into account during optimization, which can't be incorporated in the case of *ahead-of-time compilation*. JIT compilation is particularly useful for CPU-intensive programs.

40.1.1 Installation and Use

Like CPython, PyPy is licensed under the free MIT license and can be downloaded from the project website at *http://www.pypy.org*, where you can also find further installation instructions.

---

1 By the way, PyPy itself is written in Python.

If you use Linux, an installation may also be possible via the package manager of your Linux distribution.

> **Note**
>
> To start a Python program in PyPy from a shell, the `pypy` or `pypy3` command is used, depending on the type of your installation:
>
> ```
> $ pypy program.py
> ```
>
> Also note that the language version currently supported by PyPy doesn't necessarily have to be at the same level as the reference implementation, CPython. For this reason, Anaconda also downgrades the Python interpreter installed in the environment during installation, if necessary.

40.1.2   Example

To demonstrate the strengths of PyPy, we'll use the following short sample program that sums the numbers from 0 to 10000000 with alternating signs:

```
result = 0
for n in range(10000000):
    result += (-1)**n * n
```

This sample program can be executed about four times faster with PyPy than with CPython.

Of course, the runtime gain depends heavily on the type of program being executed. An I/O-bound program—for example, one that mainly performs disk accesses—can hardly be accelerated by JIT compilation. Also, programs where most of the runtime takes place in efficiently implemented external libraries, such as in elaborate NumPy calculations (see Chapter 43), may benefit little from PyPy.

40.2   Numba

The *Numba* project aims to provide an easy-to-use *JIT compiler* for numeric Python code. Numba is not a separate interpreter, like PyPy is, but a function decorator[2] that translates the decorated function completely or partially into the C or CUDA programming language and then executes it directly on the CPU or the GPU. This allows Numba to execute certain types of functions, in some cases considerably faster.

The Numba JIT compiler is most suitable for the accelerated execution of numerical calculations. In simplified terms, this refers to code that consists of mathematical

---

2 For more information on function decorators, see Chapter 23.

calculations and loop constructs. More complex language elements and libraries that aren't directly supported by Numba can still be used, but they reduce the expected run-time gain as these pieces of code must be executed in the Python interpreter without JIT compilation.

For mathematical calculations, Numba provides direct support for large parts of the NumPy library (see Chapter 43) for scientific computing.

> **Note**
>
> The language scope supported by Numba for JIT compilation is limited, especially with respect to exception handling. The online documentation at *numba.pydata.org* provides an overview of the language constructs that can be compiled and accelerated with Numba.

40.2.1 Installation

If you use the Anaconda Python distribution, you can install Numba via the conda package manager:

```
$ conda install numba
```

Alternatively, an installation from the Python package index via the pip package manager is also possible:

```
$ pip install numba
```

If you use Linux, an installation may also be possible via the package manager of your Linux distribution. For more information and alternative installation options, you should visit the project's website at *numba.pydata.org*.

> **Note**
>
> Installing Numba via pip may fail if there are conflicts with system-wide installed components. For this reason, we recommend installation via Anaconda.

40.2.2 Example

The outstanding feature of Numba is its ease of use. To compile and potentially accelerate a function using Numba, it's sufficient to import the numba module and apply the numba.jit function decorator. In the following example, this was done for a function called approximate_pi to determine the number π via the Wallis product:[3]

---

3 See also Chapter 31, Section 31.3.4.

```
import numba
@numba.jit
def approximate_pi(n):
    pi_half = 1
    numerator, denominator = 2.0, 1.0
    for i in range(n):
        pi_half *= numerator / denominator
        if i % 2:
            numerator += 2
        else:
            denominator += 2
    return 2 * pi_half
```

For more details on how a function decorator works, see Chapter 23. The approximate_pi function compiled using Numba can be executed over 60 times faster in the example than its pure Python counterpart without numba.jit.

Note

Numba has the potential to massively speed up functions with intensive numerical calculations. However, the JIT compilation itself also takes some time. The use of Numba is therefore only worthwhile if the function in question is called very frequently or calculates for a long time.

To exclude JIT compilation during a time measurement with timeit, the function can be executed once via the setup parameter prior to the time measurement for compilation:

```
import timeit
timeit.timeit("approximate_pi(1000)",
    setup="approximate_pi(1000)", globals=globals())
```

The numba.jit decorator used in the example compiles the sections of the function that are covered by Numba's feature set, and it automatically falls back to execution in the Python interpreter for other sections of the function, or for the entire function if necessary. In particular, it isn't directly obvious which parts of a function are compiled and which aren't.

The alternative numba.njit decorator forces a compilation of the whole function. The compilation raises an exception if language elements are used that aren't supported by Numba.

40.3   Connecting to C and C++: Cython

Cython isn't an alternative interpreter, but a programming language in its own right that's essentially compatible with Python and is compiled to C. In this way, a convenient mode of interoperability between Python and C programs is created.

Basic use cases for Cython are, on the one hand, compiling and accelerating the execution of an existing Python program and, on the other hand, easily combining Python code with external code written in C or C++.

> **Note**
>
> Note that a basic knowledge of the C programming language is assumed for understanding this section.

40.3.1   Installation

If you use the Anaconda Python distribution, you can install Cython via the conda package manager:

```
$ conda install cython
```

Alternatively, an installation from the Python package index via the pip package manager is also possible:

```
$ pip install cython
```

If you use Linux, you can also install Cython via the package manager of your Linux distribution, if necessary. For more information and alternative ways to install, you can visit the project's website at *cython.org*.

> **Note**
>
> Cython requires that a C compiler is installed on your system, which is often the case on Linux and macOS. But if problems occur when compiling Cython code, they can be solved, if necessary, by installing the compilers supplied in Anaconda for Linux or macOS:
>
> ```
> $ conda install gxx_linux-64
> $ conda install clangxx_osx-64
> ```
>
> On Windows, you must install the *C++ Build Tools*, which can be downloaded as part of the *Build Tools for Visual Studio*, available at *visualstudio.microsoft.com*.

40

40.3.2   The Functionality of Cython

As mentioned at the beginning, Cython is a standalone programming language that is almost entirely compatible with Python. This means that, with a few exceptions, any Python code is also valid Cython code.

The Cython compiler translates Cython code into the C programming language, which can then be further translated into machine code using a C compiler. The binary can be imported like a module via the `import` statement, but it's executed natively on the target system and thus has the potential to be many times more performant. Such modules are also referred to as *extensions*.

Cython extends the Python language scope in that C data types can be defined and used in addition to Python data types, and it enables their use in the control structures of the language.

In total, Cython thus offers solutions for three use cases:

- Due to the compatibility between Python and Cython, unmodified Python code can be compiled to a Cython extension that runs natively on the target system. This is usually accompanied by a gain in runtime efficiency.

- By using data types from C and C++, Cython provides the option to bypass Python's duck typing and to develop in a statically typed way. For example, if the compiler knows which data types can be passed in a function interface, more efficient code can be generated.

- The option to use data types from C and C++ also allows you to work directly with libraries written in C or C++.

In the following sections, we'll describe a short example for each of the three use cases. Note here that the Cython language is very extensive and we can't provide a complete introduction. For more information, refer to the online documentation at *cython.org*.

40.3.3   Compiling a Cython Program

As a first example, we want to turn an existing Python module into a compiled extension using Cython. To do this, we'll first implement the *bubble sort* naive sorting method in Python and save it as *sort_python.py*:

```python
def sort(values):
    for i in range(len(values)):
        for j in range(i):
            if values[i] < values[j]:
                values[i], values[j] = values[j], values[i]
```

In addition, we'll store the same code as Cython code in a Cython program file named *sort_cython.pyx*. Note that in this example we don't need to make any changes to the program as any Python code is also valid Cython code.

The Setup Script

Next we'll add a setup script that specifies via the cythonize function that the *sort_cython.pyx* Cython code should be built into an extension using the Cython compiler:

```
from setuptools import setup
from Cython.Build import cythonize
setup(
    ext_modules = cythonize("sort_cython.pyx", language_level=3)
)
```

For more details about setup scripts, see Chapter 38 about distributing Python projects. By calling the setup script with the build_ext argument, the extension can be built:

```
$ python setup.py build_ext --inplace
```

The optional --inplace argument makes sure that the extension is built in the local working directory and can be imported directly from there, which is helpful in this example.

After the creation, the extension is available in the working directory as *sort_cython.so* on Linux and macOS and as *sort_cython.pyd* on Windows. Sometimes additional information like the system architecture or the Python version is included in the file name.

> **Note**
>
> Similar to building via build_ext, you can use the bdist_wheel argument to create a wheel distribution of the extension suitable for publishing the extension:
>
> ```
> $ python setup.py bdist_wheel
> ```

Importing a Cython Extension

The created extension can now be imported and used like an ordinary Python module:

```
>>> import sort_cython
>>> values = [1, 7, 4, 2]
>>> sort_cython.sort(values)
>>> values
[1, 2, 4, 7]
```

In the sample programs accompanying the book, you will find not only the Python and Cython implementations of our sorting method discussed here, but also a program that compares the runtimes of the individual implementations. This way, you can evaluate the runtime gain achieved by Cython with your hardware and software setup.

40

We will also implement a variant that uses the external function qsort below. Keep in mind that qsort runs considerably faster than our reference implementation due to a significantly more efficient sorting algorithm.

40.3.4   A Cython Program with Static Typing

A programming language is *statically typed* if it requires that data types of variables must already be fixed at compile time. Static typing has the potential to be more efficient because data-type-based optimizations can be performed at compile time and additional code paths to handle possible data type alternatives can be omitted.

Using Cython, selective sections of a Python program can be statically typed by explicitly using C data types.

The *sort_cython.pyx* Cython code can be extended as follows to restrict it to a use with a sequence of 32-bit integer values:

```
def sort(int[:] values):
    cdef int tmp
    for i in range(len(values)):
        for j in range(i):
            if values[i] < values[j]:
                values[i], values[j] = values[j], values[i]
```

The changes compared to the pure Python implementation are clear:

- In the function interface, int[:] is used to declare that a memory view of 32-bit integer values (the int C data type) is passed for values. Such a memory view can be created automatically from the bytes, bytearray, and array.array Python data types and from NumPy arrays (see Chapter 43).

- In the second line, we use the Cython cdef keyword to explicitly declare the tmp intermediate variable as a 32-bit integer as well.

Note that the code is now no longer valid Python code due to the Cython syntax. We call the modified *sort_cython2.pyx* extension, and it can be generated via a setup script of the same name as the previous Cython extensions.

When calling the sort function from the sort_cython2 extension, we must make sure to pass a compatible data type. We achieve this, for example, using the sequential array data type from the module of the same name, where we specify the data type of the elements via the "i" argument when instantiating:

```
>>> import array
>>> import random
>>> import sort_cython2
>>> values = array.array("i", range(10))
>>> random.shuffle(values)
```

```
>>> values
array('i', [0, 4, 6, 8, 1, 9, 2, 5, 7, 3])
>>> sort_cython2.sort(values)
>>> values
array('i', [0, 1, 2, 3, 4, 5, 6, 7, 8, 9])
```

The statically typed sort_cython2 variant runs many times faster than the source program, which was written in pure Python. Note that for this runtime gain, we calculate with fixed 32-bit integer values instead of the flexible int Python base data type.

40.3.5 Using a C Library

In the last step, we want to modify our sample program to use the qsort function from the C standard library instead of our own implementation of the bubblesort sorting method. The example shows how Cython enables the simple connection of C libraries:

```
from libc.stdlib cimport qsort

cdef int compare(const void* a, const void* b) nogil:
    return (<int*>a)[0] - (<int*>b)[0]

def sort(int[:] values):
    qsort(&values[0], len(values), sizeof(int), compare)
```

The program consists of three main components: the inclusion of the qsort function from the C standard library, the definition of a comparison function that is used by qsort to compare two elements, and the definition of the sort function that can be called afterward from within a Python program. We'll describe each of these three components in detail in the following sections.

Importing the qsort Function from the C Standard Library

In Cython, the import of functions and data types from Cython headers[4] is done via the from/cimport statement, which is to be used in a similar way to the from/import statement of Python.

It's important to note here that C headers can't be automatically converted to Cython headers and that C headers can't be directly included in a Cython program. In this case, we take advantage of the fact that Cython already provides ready-made declarations for the standard C and C++ libraries, so that one line is sufficient to import qsort:

```
from libc.stdlib cimport qsort
```

If such ready-made Cython headers aren't available, each function and data type from a C header that is to be used in a Cython program must be previously declared in

40

---

4 A Cython header has the .pxd file extension.

Cython. This is done using the `cdef extern from` statement, in which first the C header is specified and then, one level indented, the Cython declarations matching the C header.

Here it isn't necessary to declare the complete contents of the C header in Cython; it's sufficient to declare the functions and data types that are actually to be used in the program. For the sorting example, a Cython declaration of the `qsort` function from the *stdlib.h* C header[5] may look as follows:

```
cdef extern from "<stdlib.h>" nogil:
    void qsort (void *array, size_t count, size_t size,
                int (*compare)(const void *, const void *))
```

The `nogil` keyword specifies that the *Global Interpreter Lock (GIL)* may be released for calling the `qsort` function. This is a synchronization mechanism in the reference interpreter CPython that ensures that only one interpreter thread is executed at a time.

Defining the Comparison Function

The `compare` function is a callback called by the `qsort` function to compare two elements. Based on these comparisons, `qsort` sorts the passed array. This allows the `compare` function to be implemented in pure C without the need to include Python data types. Such a function can be defined in Cython using the `cdef` keyword:

```
cdef int compare(const void* a, const void* b) nogil:
    return (<int*>a)[0] - (<int*>b)[0]
```

The a and b elements to be compared are passed as `void` pointer due to the interface of the `qsort` function. These are first converted to `int` pointers using the Cython syntax, `<int*>`. After that a dereferencing is done via the `[0]` array access.[6] The `compare` function returns the difference of the values a and b and thus works as a simple comparison function for integers in the way it's expected by the `qsort` function.

Calling qsort

Finally, we define the `sort` function analogously to the previous examples. This means the `qsort` function is called according to its interface:

```
def sort(int[:] values):
    qsort(&values[0], len(values), sizeof(int), compare)
```

The `&values[0]` Cython syntax, which we use to get a pointer to the contents of a memory view, is worth highlighting. Furthermore, the `sizeof` operator known from C can also be used in Cython.

---

5 The angle brackets around the filename of the C header indicate that it's a header to be found in a system directory, as opposed to a header in the local working directory.
6 Unlike C, Cython doesn't support explicit syntax for dereferencing pointers.

When running the example, you'll notice that the runtime has once again decreased significantly compared to the previous implementations. On the one hand, this is due to the fact that we have swapped out algorithms to an external optimized C library; on the other hand, qsort uses a much more efficient sorting procedure compared to our previous naive approach.[7]

40.4   The Interactive Python Shell: IPython

The open-source IPython project is developing an alternative Python shell that offers several advantages over the classic interactive mode. Apart from a wealth of helpful tools that facilitate interactive work with Python, the concept of IPython separates the shell from the underlying Python interpreter. This separation makes interesting applications possible, such as an architecture for interactive parallel computing in Python (we won't cover that here, however).

40.4.1   Installation

For users of the Anaconda Python distribution, IPython is already preinstalled or can be postinstalled if required using conda as follows:

```
$ conda install ipython
```

Also, IPython is included in PyPI and can be installed via the pip package manager:

```
$ pip install ipython
```

If you use Linux, an installation may also be possible via the package manager of your Linux distribution.

For more information on IPython, you should visit the project website at *https://www.ipython.org*.

40.4.2   The Interactive Shell

IPython can be launched via the ipython command, and then it presents itself in an interactive shell similar to the interactive mode of CPython:

```
Python 3.10.5 (main, Jun 23 2022, 17:15:25) [Clang 13.1.6 (clang-1316.0.21.2.5)]
Type 'copyright', 'credits' or 'license' for more information
IPython 8.4.0 -- An enhanced Interactive Python. Type '?' for help.
In [1]:
```

40

---

7 The name qsort comes from the *quick sort* sorting algorithm. However, no specific implementation is prescribed in the C standard.

Tab Completion

Probably the most convenient of the improvements introduced in the IPython interactive shell is *tab completion*. When pressing ⌨Tab, IPython tries to complete the current input, which works particularly well for methods and attributes. If the completion isn't clear, IPython provides a list of possibilities:

```
In [2]: import sys
In [3]: sys.path<TAB>
sys.path                sys.path_hooks              sys.path_importer_cache
```

Information about Instances

By appending a question mark, IPython outputs detailed information about an instance. This contains, among other things, the data type and a possible docstring:

```
In [4]: x = "test"
In [5]: x?
Type:        str
String form: test
Length:      4
Docstring:
str(object='') -> str
str(bytes_or_buffer[, encoding[, errors]]) -> str
[...]
```

You can obtain even more detailed information about an instance by appending a second question mark: x??.

Input History

As in the interactive mode, IPython keeps an input history that can be scrolled through using the ⌨Up and ⌨Down arrow keys. In contrast to the interactive mode, each input is assigned an index, which is written in square brackets in the prompt:

```
In [6]:
```

In this case, the next entry in the history would be assigned index 6. Old entries can be executed again via their index. For this purpose, the %rerun magic function is used: it can rerun individual indexes as well as entire ranges of the input history. First, we'll run some sample inputs that we'll want to repeat later:

```
In [6]: x = "test"
In [7]: x *= 2
In [8]: x
Out[8]: 'testtest'
```

Due to the %rerun magic function, the inputs with indexes between 6 and 8 can then be executed again without having to enter them a second time:

```
In [9]: %rerun 6-8
=== Executing: ===
x = "test"
x *= 2
x
=== Output: ===
Out[9]: 'testtest'
```

The %history magic function works like %rerun and displays the relevant parts of the input history without re-executing them.

Magic Functions

As shown in the previous section, the IPython shell provides the user with so-called magic functions,[8] all of which start with a percentage sign so that they don't interfere with regular identifiers. Table 40.1 lists the main magic functions available and explains their meaning.

Magic function	Meaning
%cd	Switches the current working directory
%debug	Starts the interactive IPython debugger
%edit	Starts an external editor for code entry
%history	Displays the input history
%load	Loads external program code into the current environment
%logstart	Starts logging of the entered commands
%logstop	Stops logging of the entered commands
%lsmagic	Lists the available magic functions
%macro	Creates a macro from parts of the input history
%matplotlib	Determines how matplotlib plots should be handled
%pdef	Outputs the interface of a callable object
%pfile	Outputs the file in which an object was defined
%prun	Executes a printout in the profiler[*]

Table 40.1 Magic Functions in IPython

40

---

8 Not to be confused with Python's magic methods (see Chapter 19, Section 19.11).

Magic function	Meaning
%pwd	Outputs the current working directory
%recall	Executes a previous input once again
%save	Saves entered commands to a file
%time	Executes an expression and measures its runtime
%timeit	Executes an expression multiple times and generates runtime statistics from it

* For more details on profiling in Python, see Chapter 36, Section 36.3.

Table 40.1 Magic Functions in IPython (Cont.)

You can also display a help page for the magic functions via an attached question mark, which explains their use.

40.4.3 The Jupyter Notebook

Jupyter Notebook, formerly IPython Notebook, is a web application for the interactive use of Python in the browser. A notebook document consists of a sequence of *cells*. There are four basic types of cells:

- *Code cells* contain Python code that can be edited and re-executed at any time.
- *Markdown cells* contain formatted text for description. They can also contain LaTeX formulas, for example.
- *Raw cells* contain unformatted text.
- *Heading cells* contain headings to structure the document.

Installation

You can install Jupyter Notebook conveniently via the conda and pip package managers:

```
$ conda install -c conda-forge notebook
$ pip install notebook
```

Alternatively, the more comprehensive web development environment *JupyterLab* built on top of Jupyter Notebook can be installed:

```
$ conda install -c conda-forge jupyterlab
$ pip install jupyterlab
```

For more information, visit the project website at *https://jupyter.org*.

Jupyter Notebook

You can use the `jupyter notebook` command to start a web server that runs Jupyter Notebook. This will automatically start a browser with the notebook. A saved notebook document can then be loaded in the displayed list. Alternatively, you can use the **New •
Python 3** menu item to create a new notebook document for Python 3.

The document shown in Figure 40.1 contains three code cells in which the `factorial` function is defined and evaluated twice. Within a code cell, you can write your Python code as you would in an editor. Pressing Shift+Enter executes the entered code in its entirety. Alternatively, you can use the **Play** button in the menu.

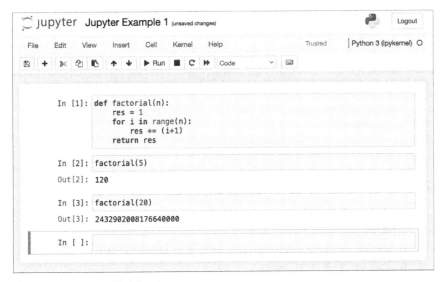

Figure 40.1 Jupyter Notebook

It's possible to change the factorial function afterward without any problem. Cells dependent on this can then be selected and executed again by pressing Shift+
Enter.

Between the code cells we can insert markdown cells to describe the executed code. The **Insert** menu item can be used to insert new code cells, which can then be turned into markdown cells via the selection list in the menu bar.

Within markdown cells, you can use the Markdown formatting language to format the text. For example, text enclosed in double asterisks (**text**) is written in bold. In addition, the LaTeX math environment is supported: a mathematical formula can be written between a pair of single or double dollar signs, which is then displayed graphically. The code for the formula shown in Figure 40.2 is `$$\text{factorial}(n) = \prod_{i=1}^n i$$`.

Particularly interesting is the use of Jupyter Notebook in combination with the `matplotlib` module, which you read about in Chapter 43. If in-line mode has been

40

set up via the %matplotlib magic function, matplotlib plots will also be integrated into the notebook (see Figure 40.3).

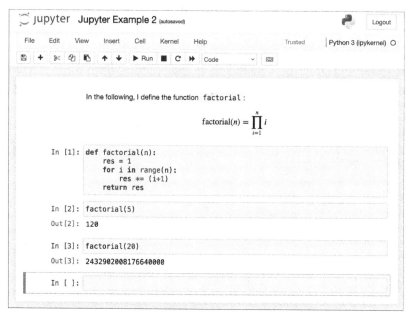

Figure 40.2 Notebook with Markdown Cells

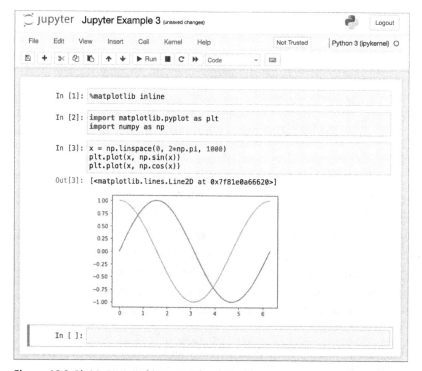

Figure 40.3 Plot Integrated into Notebook Document

Chapter 41
Graphical User Interfaces

Having dealt exclusively with console applications up to now—that is, programs that have a purely text-based interface to the user—the tingling in our fingers and thus the urge to step to a graphical user interface (GUI) can no longer be suppressed. In contrast to the text-oriented interface of console applications, programs with a graphical interface are more intuitive to use, more graphically appealing, and generally perceived as more modern. Above all, a GUI consists of *windows*. Within these windows, you can place any kind of controls. *Controls*, often referred to as *widgets*, are individual control units that make up the GUI as a whole. For example, a button or a text field is a control.

Both the terminology and the implementation of a GUI depend very much on which library, also referred to as a *toolkit*, is used. For this reason, we'll first describe various toolkits that can be used with Python; we won't get to the actual programming of a GUI until we reach the second section. At that point, we'll first cover the tkinter module, which uses the *Tk toolkit* and is included in the standard library. After that, we'll present a project-oriented introduction to the more comprehensive and contemporary *Qt framework* using *PySide6*.

41.1 Toolkits

A toolkit is a library that can be used to create programs with a GUI. In addition to some platform-dependent toolkits, such as Microsoft Foundation Classes (MFC) or Windows Forms for Windows, platform-independent toolkits such as Qt, GTK, and wxWidgets are particularly useful in connection with Python. These toolkits are mostly written for C (GTK) or C++ (Qt, wxWidgets), but can also be accessed with Python via so-called *bindings*. In the following sections, we'll list and briefly explain the most important Python bindings for GUI toolkits.

41.1.1 Tkinter (Tk)

Website: *http://wiki.python.org/moin/TkInter*

The *Tk toolkit* was originally developed for the *Tool Command Language* (*Tcl*) and is the only toolkit included in the standard Python library. The tkinter module (Tk interface)

41

allows you to write Tk applications and thus offers an interesting opportunity to provide smaller applications with a GUI for which the user doesn't need to install additional libraries at a later time. An example of a Tk program is the IDLE development environment, which is included with every Python version.

After an introduction of the most common toolkits in the context of Python, we'll introduce you to programming GUIs with tkinter in Section 41.2.

41.1.2 PyGObject (GTK)

Website: *https://pygobject.readthedocs.io*

The *GIMP Toolkit* (*GTK*) was originally developed for the graphics program GIMP and today is one of the most widespread cross-platform toolkits along with Qt. Both the toolkit itself and the PyGObject Python bindings are released under the GNU Lesser General Public License (LGPL) and can be downloaded and used free of charge.

GTK is the basis of the free GNOME desktop environment and therefore enjoys great popularity, especially among Linux users. Although it was actually written for C, GTK is object-oriented from the ground up and can therefore be used well with Python.

41.1.3 Qt for Python (Qt)

Website: *https://www.qt.io/qt-for-python*

Qt is a comprehensive framework developed by the Qt Company, which evolved from the Norwegian Trolltech company, and it includes both a GUI toolkit and non-GUI functionality. The thoroughly object-oriented C++ framework is the basis of the free K Desktop Environment (KDE) and for this reason is as widespread and popular as GTK.

Under the name Qt for Python, the Qt Company meanwhile develops the official Python PySide6 binding for the framework. Previously, the PyQt bindings by third-party provider Riverbank Computing[1] were very popular. Unlike PyQt, PySide6 is officially supported by the Qt developers at the Qt Company and is available under the terms of the LGPL.

PyQt and PySide6 are highly compatible, so it's often sufficient to modify the import statements to make a PyQt program executable under PySide6. However, this API compatibility is not complete and is not guaranteed for the future.

Both Qt itself and the Python PySide6 bindings are available under a dual license system. For software released under the GPL or LGPL, Qt and PySide6 can also be used under the terms of the General Public License (GPL) and LGPL. In addition, there is a license model for commercial use. Qt is used for many commercial projects, including, for example, Google Earth, Mathematica, and the Linux versions of Skype and Spotify.

---

1 See *https://riverbankcomputing.com*.

41.1.4   wxPython (wxWidgets)

Website: *http://www.wxpython.org*

WxWidgets, formerly wxWindows, is a free GUI toolkit whose first version was released back in 1992. Accordingly, the toolkit is highly developed and available for all common platforms. Especially in terms of Python, wxWidgets is popular and well documented. One of the goals of the wxWidgets project is to best reflect the look and feel of the various platforms on which the toolkit can run. This is achieved in particular by the fact that wxWidgets doesn't use its own widgets, but instead uses the routines of the respective platform for this purpose. Both wxWidgets and wxPython are constantly under active development.

41.2   Introduction to tkinter

Now that we've introduced the various GUI toolkits for which Python bindings are available, let's turn our attention to programming GUIs. For this purpose, the standard library includes the `tkinter` module, which can be used to program graphical interfaces with the Tk toolkit. The `tkinter` module is the only way to write a GUI in Python without installing third-party libraries, so it's worth taking a look at `tkinter` and its capabilities.

> **Note**
>
> If you run the following sample programs in an Anaconda environment under Linux, it may happen that the system fonts usually used aren't available and so-called bitmap fonts may be used instead. This leads to an unsightly, too small display of the dialogs, especially on high-resolution monitors.
>
> Because there's no easy solution to this problem, we advise using your Python system installation to run the sample programs instead of Anaconda in these cases.

41.2.1   A Simple Example

To get started using `tkinter`, we'd like to present and then describe a simple sample program. The program brings a dialog to the screen that prompts the user to enter their name. In addition, the program features a button to reverse the entered name, such that the letters appear in reverse order. Another button ends the dialog. The graphic in Figure 41.1 shows what the GUI will look like later. The left side shows the GUI before clicking the **Reverse** button and the right after clicking it.

41

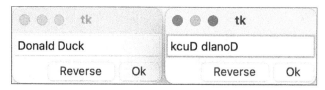

Figure 41.1 First GUI

This sample program is based on the following source code:

```python
import tkinter
class MyApp(tkinter.Frame):
    def __init__(self, master=None):
        super().__init__(master)
        self.pack()
        self.createWidgets()
    def createWidgets(self):
        self.nameEntry = tkinter.Entry(self)
        self.nameEntry.pack()
        self.name = tkinter.StringVar()
        self.name.set("Your name...")
        self.nameEntry["textvariable"] = self.name
        self.ok = tkinter.Button(self)
        self.ok["text"] = "Ok"
        self.ok["command"] = self.quit
        self.ok.pack(side="right")
        self.rev = tkinter.Button(self)
        self.rev["text"] = "Reverse"
        self.rev["command"] = self.onReverse
        self.rev.pack(side="right")
    def onReverse(self):
        self.name.set(self.name.get()[::-1])
```

First, the tkinter module is imported and a class is created that inherits from tkinter.Frame. The Frame base class represents a *frame widget*. This is a widget that is invisible by default and has no significant functionality; it represents the starting point for a custom widget or dialog. We use the Frame widget as a container for the widgets of the dialog.

In the constructor of MyApp, the constructor of the base class and the pack method are called. This method registers the widget for which the method was called with the so-called *packer*. The packer then arranges the registered widgets on the surface according to the programmer's wishes. In particular, the positions of the widget elements are usually not specified by fixed coordinates, but determined dynamically by the packer.

The createWidget method is called last in the constructor and has the task of initializing the widgets needed for our dialog. To do this, we first create an instance of the tkinter.Entry class that represents an input field. This is then applied to the surface via pack. After that, an instance of the tkinter.StringVar class is created under the name self.name, which we can later use to read or modify the text entered in the self.nameEntry input field. Initially, we set the text to Your name... and register the control variable with the Entry widget. This is done by setting the textvariable key of the entry instance, similarly to a dictionary.

In the further course of the function, we create the two buttons that are to be available in the dialog in a similar way. For a button, the text (for the button label) and command options can be set in a similar way as for an entry widget. The command option is used to specify a function that will be called when the user has clicked the button. In the case of the **OK** button, we set the command attribute to the quit method. This method comes from the Frame base class and terminates the dialog.[2]

When calling the pack methods of the two buttons in the sample program, you see a way to tell the packer the desired position for a widget. So, for example, you can use the side keyword parameter to specify whether the widget should be left- or right-justified. Of course, this isn't the only possible specification. You'll learn about more possibilities in the course of this chapter.

Finally, the implementation of the onReverse function follows, which is called when the user has clicked on the self.rev button. Here, the text entered in the input field is read via the self.name control variable, reversed, and written back into the input field.

We've now created a class that represents the dialog. What's still missing is the code that instantiates the class and displays the dialog. Here's how to do it:

```
root = tkinter.Tk()
app = MyApp(root)
app.mainloop()
```

First, an instance of the tkinter.Tk class is created to represent the dialog frame. We then instantiate the MyApp application class, passing the Tk instance as the parent instance. Calling mainloop in the third line displays the dialog. The method blocks until the dialog is terminated.

So much for the first introductory Tk program. In the following sections, we'll take a look at important aspects of Tk, such as the concept of control variables and the packer. After that we'll describe the most important widgets.

41

---

2 If you run the example in the IDLE development environment, the dialog may not close. In this case, you should try to run the example directly.

41.2.2   Control Variables

In the introductory example, we used control variables to implement the data exchange between the program and user interface. A *control variable* is bound to a specific piece of information for a widget, such as the text of an input field, and always contains the value the widget is currently displaying. Conversely, the control variable can be used to change the corresponding information about the widget from within the program.

It's clear that control variables don't necessarily have to be strings; for example, think of a widget for entering an integer. Python's basic data types can't be used as data types for control variables. This is because the widget associated with a control variable needs to be notified when the value of the variable changes. This isn't possible with the basic data types. Here you have to draw on special data types of the tkinter module. Table 41.1 lists all available types.

Data Type	Corresponding Python Type
tkinter.BooleanVar	bool
tkinter.DoubleVar	float
tkinter.IntVar	int
tkinter.StringVar	str

Table 41.1 Data Types for Control Variables

All these data types inherit from the tkinter.Variable base class, whose constructor has the interface described in the following section.

Variable([master, value, name])

A master widget can be specified via the master parameter. This is especially useful if you use multiple Tk instances at the same time. If only one Tk instance exists, it will be automatically used as the master widget and the master parameter doesn't need to be specified.

For the value parameter, a value can be specified that the created instance should store. The value passed here is converted to the data type of the control variable. Note that a failed conversion isn't noticeable until the get method is called.

After instantiation, a control variable provides the get and set methods to access the value stored in it:

```
>>> t = tkinter.Tk()
>>> v = tkinter.StringVar(value="Hello world")
>>> v.get()
'Hello world'
```

```
>>> v.set("Blah Blah")
>>> v.get()
'Blah Blah'
```

Note that an exception is raised only when get is called if the variable stores an invalid value, while a call of the set method with an invalid value is silently ignored.

Note

An interesting feature of control variables is that they can be used by multiple widgets at the same time. In this way, simple connections can be made between the contents of the widgets.

Thus, in the introductory sample program, the self.name control variable can be assigned to the self.rev button in addition to the self.nameEntry input field:

```
self.rev["textvariable"] = self.name
```

In this way, the name entered in the input field is immediately adopted as the button's label.

41.2.3   The Packer

A GUI consists of a set of widgets arranged in a meaningful structure in the dialog. Theoretically, it's possible to define the position of each widget "by hand." However, this approach would be problematic because the programmer usually isn't interested in the exact coordinates of the widgets, but rather wants to specify the structure in which they should be arranged. In addition, the programmer would have to handle resizing of the dialog him or herself, for example, and move or resize the widgets as necessary.

Tk provides the so-called *packer*, which is responsible for the task of arranging the widgets in the dialog. The programmer only needs to specify a structure for the dialog in the form of instructions for the alignment of a widget.

The widgets of a dialog are arranged hierarchically in Tk, which is similar to other toolkits. This means that each widget has a parent. Also, each widget may contain any number of children. In Tk terminology, a parent is called a *master* and a child is called a *slave*. The hierarchy of widgets in the sample program at the beginning of this chapter is illustrated in Figure 41.2.

The hierarchy of widgets is important for understanding how the packer works. This is because it arranges the children within their parents and in turn arranges the parents along with the children within their respective parents. So it makes sense to encapsulate widgets so that they can be arranged together by the packer. For this purpose, programmers often use the Frame widget.

41

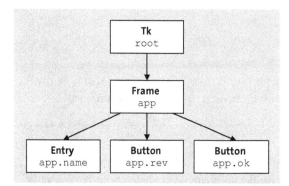

Figure 41.2 Hierarchy of Widgets in the Sample Program

As already mentioned, the packer can be given a layout according to which it has to arrange the widgets. In the sample program, we achieved this by passing the side keyword parameter with the value "right" when calling the pack method of the two buttons. The packer places widgets with this layout statement right-aligned in the GUI. In the following sections, we want to demonstrate how the packer works using the now well-known sample program as an example.

The packer always works in a rectangular window pane (outlined in black in the following images). Initially, if no widget has been "packed" yet, this is the entire window (see Figure 41.3).

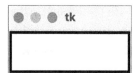

Figure 41.3 Mode of Operation of the Packer: Step 1

First, the Entry widget is packed without specifying the layout. In such a case, the packer arranges the widgets vertically. So the Entry widget is placed all the way at the top and across the full width of the dialog (see Figure 41.4).

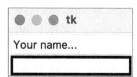

Figure 41.4 Mode of Operation of the Packer: Step 2

What's interesting is what happens to the workspace, which will be reduced in size and will no longer include the widget packed last. So once a widget has been placed, it won't be moved back and forth based on layout specifications of later widgets.

Next, the buttons are inserted into the remaining workspace. These have the layout statement "right-justified" and are therefore placed horizontally from the right-hand edge of the dialog. They occupy the full height of the workspace as they are placed horizontally, leaving a residual workspace on the left where the packer can place any additional widgets (see Figure 41.5).

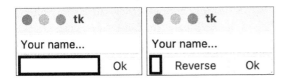

Figure 41.5 Mode of Operation of the Packer: Step 3

So much for the general mode of operation of the packer. In Table 41.2, you can take a closer look at the layout statements that can be given to the packer in the form of keyword parameters when calling the pack method.

Parameter	Possible Values	Meaning
after	Widget	The widget should be packed after the specified widget.
anchor	"n", "ne", "e", "se", "s", "sw", "w", "nw", "center"	If the area allocated to the widget is larger than the widget, anchor can be used to specify the orientation of the widget within this area. The possible values are the compass directions and "center".
before	Widget	The widget should be packed before the specified widget.
expand	bool	Specifies whether the position of the widget should be adjusted when the master widget is enlarged (see Figure 41.7).
fill	"x", "y", "both", "none"	The size of the widget will be adjusted when the master widget is enlarged. The size can be adjusted horizontally, vertically, completely, or not at all (see Figure 41.7).
in	Widget	Inserts the widget into the specified master widget.
ipadx ipady	int	Pixel size for the horizontal or vertical inner padding.
padx pady	int	Pixel size for the horizontal or vertical outer padding.

Table 41.2 Layout Statements

41

Parameter	Possible Values	Meaning
side	"left", "right", "top", "bottom"	The side of the workspace where the widget will be inserted. A widget placed on the left- or right-hand side occupies the entire height, and a widget placed on the top or bottom occupies the entire width of the workspace. You can achieve more differentiated layouts using a Frame widget.

Table 41.2 Layout Statements (Cont.)

Padding

You've certainly already noticed that the dialog we created in our sample application looks quite strange. This is because the widgets are placed directly next to each other without any space in between. Using so-called *paddings*, you can define the size of this space and thus achieve a less squat dialog appearance.

Basically, there are two types of padding: outer and inner. *Outer padding* describes the distance between widgets. This value is passed to the pack method using the padx and pady keyword parameters. The value here must be an integer corresponding to the required spacing in pixels. Figure 41.6 shows the dialog with each widget having been given an outer padding of five pixels.

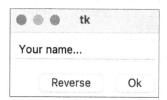

Figure 41.6 Padding in Use

Inner padding is a spacing specification within a widget. Slave widgets[3] included in this widget respect this padding and are placed further inside accordingly. This type of padding is especially useful for Frame widgets. The inner padding can be specified in the same way as the outer padding via the ipadx and ipady keyword parameters.

Behavior upon Enlargement of the Master Widget

Figure 41.7 shows the effects of the fill and expand layout statements based on an example.

---

3 *Slave widget* is the Tkinter terminology for a child widget. For example, in the interface shown, the input field is a slave of the parent Frame widget.

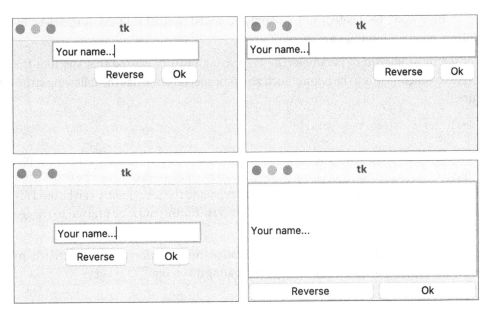

Figure 41.7 Fill and Expand Layout Statements

The upper-left image shows the behavior of the dialog without further layout statements when the window is enlarged. To the right, the fill="both" layout statement was used, at the bottom left expand=True, and finally at the bottom right the combination of expand and fill. The layout statements were always passed equally for all pack calls, including the pack call for the parent Frame widget.

41.2.4   Events

When writing a Tk application, the control flow is passed to the Tk framework by calling the mainloop method after the application class is created and instantiated. The question arises in what way we can respond to user input—for example, if we have no real control over the program and the graphical interface at all. For this reason, a number of events are defined in Tk. For example, an event is a keystroke or mouse click by the user. Using the bind method of a widget, we can bind a self-defined method to an event. A method bound to an event is called by the Tk framework whenever the corresponding event occurs, such as when the user presses a special key.

Binding Events

The bind(event, func, [add]) method of a widget binds the func function to the event event. For func, a function object must be passed, which expects exactly one parameter, the so-called *event object*. This function is called the *event handler*. If the value True is passed for the add optional parameter and there are already other functions bound to

41

event, they won't be deleted; func will only be added to the list of event handlers. By default, previous bindings are overwritten.

For the most important parameter, event, a string must be passed that specifies the event to which func is to be bound. Such an event specification has the following structure:

```
"<modifier-modifier-type-detail>"
```

The two modifier entries in the event specification are optional and allow, for example, a mouse click with the Shift key pressed and a normal mouse click to be considered separately. The type entry identifies the event type, and the detail entry can be used for a more detailed specification, such as which mouse button must be pressed to trigger the event.

For example, the following bind call causes a call of the f function to be triggered whenever the user left-clicks in the widget while holding down the Shift key:

```
widget.bind("<Shift-ButtonPress-1>", f)
```

Alternatively, an event can be bound for all widgets of the application at once. For this purpose, the bind_all method is used, which has the same interface as bind:

```
widget.bind_all("<Shift-ButtonPress-1>", f)
```

The bind and bind_all methods return a function ID that can be used to reference the established connection. This is especially important if event bindings are to be removed again. This is done using the unbind and unbind_all methods. Both functions are passed an event string and cancel all connections existing with this event:

```
widget.unbind("<Shift-ButtonPress-1>")
widget.unbind_all("<Shift-ButtonPress-1>")
```

The unbind method also can be passed a function ID to unbind a concrete event.

In the following sections, we'll go into more detail about the elements of the event string.

Event Modifier

Let's start with the values that can be used for the modifier entries in the event specification. As already demonstrated with an example, these are additional conditions under which the type event must occur—for example, entering an "a" while holding down the Ctrl key. The most important modifiers are listed and explained in Table 41.3.

Attribute	Meaning
Alt, Control, Shift, Lock	When the event occurs, the specified key ([Alt], [Ctrl], [Shift] or [Capslock]) must be pressed.
Buttonx Bx	The mouse button x must be pressed when the event occurs. The number x specifies which button is meant: 1 stands for the left, 2 for the middle,[*] and 3 for the right mouse button. Other mouse buttons are numbered consecutively.
Double Triple	The event must occur twice or three times in quick succession, such as a double-click.

[*]   The scrolling wheel counts as the middle mouse button. If there is neither a scrolling wheel nor a real middle mouse button, clicking the left and right mouse buttons at the same time counts as clicking the middle mouse button.

Table 41.3 Modifier

Event Types

Now that we've taken care of the modifiers, we'll discuss the type entry of the event specification. The available event types are listed and explained in Table 41.4. If a detail argument is required, this will also be mentioned.

Note that a widget may need to have the input focus to receive a specific event.

Event	Meaning
KeyPress Key	The user has pressed a key. The event can be restricted to a specific key via the detail entry in the event specification.[*]
KeyRelease	The user has released a key. Here you can use the same detail specifications as for KeyPress.
ButtonPress	The user has pressed a mouse button over the widget.[**] In the detail entry of the event specification, the number of a mouse button can be specified to limit this. Here 1 corresponds to the left, 2 to the center, and 3 to the right mouse button.
ButtonRelease	The user has released a mouse button. Here too, the detail entry in the event specification can be used to specify which mouse button is meant.

Table 41.4 Events

41

Event	Meaning
Motion	The user has moved the mouse over the widget. The Buttonx modifier can be used to specify that a particular mouse button should be pressed while the user moves the mouse.
Enter, Leave	The user has entered or left the widget area with the mouse pointer.
FocusIn, FocusOut	The widget gained or lost the input focus.
Expose	The widget was completely or partially hidden by other windows and was retrieved by the user. In this case, parts of the widget may need to be redrawn.
Destroy	The widget was destroyed.
Configure	The widget has changed its size or position.
MouseWheel	The user has moved the mouse wheel.

* The following, mostly self-explanatory values are possible here: Alt_L, Alt_R, BackSpace, Cancel, Caps_Lock, Control_L, Control_R, Delete, End, Escape, F1-F12, Home ("Pos1"), Insert, Left, Up, Right, Down, Next ("Page down"), Num_Lock, Pause, Print, Prior ("Page up"), Return, Scroll_Lock, Shift_L, Shift_R, and Tab. In addition, a single character can be specified.

** The widget over which the mouse button was pressed gets a "subscription" to mouse events, so to speak. Specifically, this means that the release and motion events will be sent to this widget even if the mouse is over another widget in the meantime. Only releasing the button will cancel this "subscription".

Table 41.4 Events (Cont.)

Event Handler

After an event is triggered, the associated event handler is called. This handler is then passed an event object—more precisely, a tkinter.event instance—that contains more detailed information about the event that occurred. Table 41.5 lists and explains the most important attributes of the event object. Note that depending on the triggered event, only some of the attributes are useful.

Attribute	Meaning
char	Contains the entered character as a string. Valid for KeyPress and KeyRelease.
delta	Indicates how far the user has moved the mouse wheel. The sign indicates the direction of rotation. Valid for MouseWheel.

Table 41.5 Attributes of the Event Object

Attribute	Meaning
focus	Indicates whether the widget over which the mouse is located has the input focus or not. Valid for Enter and Leave.
height, width	Contains the new height or width of the widget in pixels. Valid for Configure and Expose.
keycode, keysym	Contains the keycode or the symbolic name of the pressed key. Valid for KeyPress and KeyRelease.
time	Contains an integer timestamp describing the time of the event. It's the time elapsed since system startup in milliseconds.
type	Contains the integer identifier of the event type.
widget	References the widget in which the event occurred.
x, y	Contains the X or Y coordinate of the mouse pointer in pixels. This specification is relative to the upper-left corner of the widget.
x_root, y_root	Contains the X or Y coordinate of the mouse pointer, but this time relative to the upper-left-hand corner of the screen. Valid for ButtonPress, ButtonRelease, KeyPress, KeyRelease, and Motion.

Table 41.5 Attributes of the Event Object (Cont.)

Example

This concludes the introduction to the main event types. Now we'll present a sample program that illustrates the use of events. The graphical interface of the program contains a label, a widget that displays only a text, an input field, and a button that can be used to close the dialog. The program is supposed to receive certain events sent to the input field and confirm the receipt of the event by a corresponding message in the label:

```python
import tkinter
class MyApp(tkinter.Frame):
    def __init__(self, master=None):
        super().__init__(master)
        self.pack()
        self.createWidgets()
        self.createBindings()
    def createWidgets(self):
        self.label = tkinter.Label(self)
        self.label.pack()
```

41

```
            self.label["text"] = "Please send an event"
            self.entry = tkinter.Entry(self)
            self.entry.pack()
            self.ok = tkinter.Button(self)
            self.ok.pack()
            self.ok["text"] = "Exit"
            self.ok["command"] = self.quit
        def createBindings(self):
            self.entry.bind("Duckburg", self.eventDuckburg)
            self.entry.bind("<ButtonPress-1>", self.eventMouseClick)
            self.entry.bind("<MouseWheel>", self.eventMouseWheel)
        def eventDuckburg(self, event):
            self.label["text"] = "You know the secret password!"
        def eventMouseClick(self, event):
            self.label["text"] = "Mouse click at position " \
                                 "({},{})".format(event.x, event.y)
        def eventMouseWheel(self, event):
            if event.delta < 0:
                self.label["text"] = "Please move the mouse wheel"\
                                     " in the right direction."
            else:
                self.label["text"] = "Thank you very much."
```

First, as usual, the three widgets of the application are initialized in the createWidgets method, which is called by the constructor. After that, the createBindings method is called, which is responsible for registering the event handlers. This method takes three events into consideration: typing the Duckburg string, clicking the left mouse button, and moving the mouse wheel. Note that all three events refer to the entry field—the Entry widget. For example, only mouse clicks above this entry field are registered as an event.

This is followed by the eventDuckburg, eventMouseClick, and eventMouseWheel event handler methods. The eventMouseWheel method benefits from the fact that the sign of event.delta indicates the direction in which the mouse wheel was moved.

We haven't yet discussed the use of the label widget in detail, but it's obvious that you can set the "text" key to change the text it displays. A more detailed discussion of this widget can be found in the following section.

Note

On Windows, a movement of the mouse wheel triggers the MouseWheel event associated in this sample program. On Linux, the two directions of the mouse wheel are interpreted as alternative buttons 4 and 5 of the mouse. A movement of the mouse wheel here triggers one of the following events: ButtonPress-4 or ButtonPress-5.

> The online resources for this book (available at *www.rheinwerk-computing.com/5566*) contain a variant of the sample program that works on Windows as well as Linux.

Finally, the code that shows the dialog is still missing. But compared to the previous sample program, it hasn't changed:

```
root = tkinter.Tk()
app = MyApp(root)
app.mainloop()
```

Figure 41.8 shows the sample program.

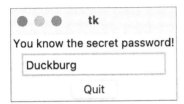

Figure 41.8 Sample Program with Events

This concludes the introduction to the world of events. In the following sections, we'll describe the different types of widgets you can use in tkinter applications.

41.2.5   Widgets

Now that we've covered the basics of Tk, you'll learn about the widgets that are available and how you can use them. Table 41.6 lists all the Tk widgets described in this chapter.

Widget	Meaning
Widget	The base class of all widgets.
Button	A button.
Canvas	A widget for drawings and graphics.
Checkbutton	A widget that can be either enabled or disabled.
Entry	A one-line input field.
Label	A widget for labels.
LabelFrame	A widget for labeled frames.
Listbox	A list of entries.

Table 41.6 Widgets Explained

41

Widget	Meaning
Menu	A context menu.
Menubutton	A button that displays a context menu when clicked.
OptionMenu	A button that displays a selection list when clicked.
Radiobutton	A widget that can be either enabled or disabled. Within a group, only exactly one radio button may be activated.
Scrollbar	A bar that allows a user to scroll through oversized widgets.
Spinbox	A widget for setting a numerical value.
Text	A multiline input field.

Table 41.6 Widgets Explained (Cont.)

Note

The sample programs presented for each widget are abbreviated to illustrate the basic principle. The online resources for this book contain more detailed and executable versions of the sample programs.

The Widget Base Class

The tkinter.Widget class is the base class of all widgets and provides basic functionality. First, this includes the winfo methods (for *widget info*), which you can use to find information about a widget, such as its position. Table 41.7 describes the main winfo methods. For this purpose, we assume that w is a widget.

Interface	Meaning
w.winfo_children()	Returns a list of the subwidgets of w
w.winfo_class()	Returns the name of the widget class of w as a string
w.winfo_geometry()	Returns the position and the dimension of the w widget in relation to the parent widget as a string of the format "BxH+X+Y"
w.winfo_height() w.winfo_width()	Returns the height or width of the w widget in pixels
w.winfo_pointerx() w.winfo_pointery() w.winfo_pointerxy()	Returns the X, Y coordinate of the mouse pointer or a tuple of both coordinates in relation to the upper-left-hand corner of the screen

Table 41.7 Methods of winfo

Interface	Meaning
w.winfo_rootx() w.winfo_rooty()	Returns the X or Y position of the w widget in relation to the upper-left-hand corner of the screen
w.winfo_screenheight() w.winfo_screenwidth()	Returns the height or width of the screen in pixels
w.winfo_x() w.winfo_y()	Returns the X or Y coordinate of the w widget in relation to the parent widget

Table 41.7 Methods of winfo (Cont.)

As you already know from previous examples, you can configure a widget. For this purpose, you can access configuration keys as in a dictionary:

```
w["width"] = 200
w["height"] = 100
```

Alternatively, widgets can be configured when you instantiate them. For this purpose, the required settings can be passed to the respective constructor as keyword parameters:

```
frame = tkinter.Frame(width=200, height=200)
```

Many widgets have width and height keys for the width and height of the widget;[4] padx and pady for horizontal and vertical padding; state for the state of the widget;[5] and foreground and background for the foreground and background color.

The other keys provided by a widget depend on its type and can't be covered exhaustively in this chapter. In the following sections, you'll learn about the main widget types included in tkinter.

Button

An instance of the tkinter.Button class represents a *button widget* and corresponds to a button in the GUI. You've already seen how to use a button in the sample program. It's important to set the text and command options after instantiating the button class; these are used to specify the button's label and the handler function. The handler function is called by the Tk framework when the user has clicked the button:

```
class MyApp(tkinter.Frame):
    def __init__(self, master=None):
        super().__init__(master)
```

41

---

4 Width and height are specified in pixels and character widths and line heights, respectively, depending on the control.
5 Possible values here include, for example, "enabled", "disabled", and "active".

```
        self.pack()
        self.ok = tkinter.Button(self)
        self.ok["text"] = "label"
        self.ok["command"] = self.handler
        self.ok.pack()
    def handler(self):
        print("Button pressed")
```

After setting up the ok button, the handler method is always called when the user clicks the button.

Check Button

The *check button*, also referred to as a *checkbox*, is a widget related to the button. A check button consists of a small box and a label and can be in one of two states: enabled and disabled. The user can change the state by clicking the small box. The activated state of a check button is indicated by a check mark or a cross in the box (see Figure 41.9).

Figure 41.9 Check Button in Use

Creating and using a check button is very simple and works similarly to a button. In addition, however, a control variable must be created for the current state of the check button:

```
check = tkinter.Checkbutton(master)
check["text"] = "Hello world"
checked = tkinter.BooleanVar()
checked.set(True)
check["variable"] = checked
check.pack()
```

Once the check button has been instantiated, a label can be specified via the text option. Then, using the variable option, a control variable is assigned for the state of the check button. Finally, the check button is brought to the GUI by calling the pack method.

As is the case with a button, the command option can be used to specify a handler function called by the Tk framework when the user changes the state of the check button. Within this handler function, the current status of the check button can then be queried via the checked control variable.

Check buttons often don't appear alone, but represent groups of settings whose individual elements can be activated or deactivated independently of each other. The following more complex sample program shows how multiple check buttons can be created and their events processed by a common handler function:

```python
class MyApp(tkinter.Frame):
    def __init__(self, master=None):
        super().__init__(master)
        self.pack()
        self.names = ("Donald Duck", "Scrooge McDuck", "Gladstone Gander")
        self.checks = []
        self.vars = []
        for name in self.names:
            var = tkinter.BooleanVar()
            var.set(False)
            check = tkinter.Checkbutton(self)
            check["text"] = name
            check["command"] = self.handler
            check["variable"] = var
            check.pack(anchor="w")
            self.checks.append(check)
            self.vars.append(var)
    def handler(self):
        x = " and ".join(
            [name for name, var in zip(self.names, self.vars) if var.get()]
        )
```

For each entry of the self.names tuple, a check button and a control variable are created and stored in the self.checks and self.vars lists, respectively. Each created check button is assigned the common handler handler function. In this handler, the built-in zip function is used to iterate over tuples of names and corresponding control variables to output those names whose checkboxes were selected by the user.

Radio Button

Like a check button, a *radio button* is a widget that can be activated or deactivated through a user click. The special feature of the radio button is that you can define a group of radio buttons within which exactly one of the radio buttons is always activated. Here, the radio buttons form a group that shares the same control variable. In the following sample code, the user is allowed to choose the capital of a G7 state:

```python
class MyApp(tkinter.Frame):
    def __init__(self, master=None):
        super().__init__(master)
        self.pack()
```

41

```
            self.selection = ["Berlin", "London", "Ottawa",
                              "Paris", "Rome", "Tokyo", "Washington DC"]
            self.city = tkinter.StringVar()
            self.city.set("Paris")
            for a in self.selection:
                b = tkinter.Radiobutton(self)
                b["text"] = a
                b["value"] = a
                b["variable"] = self.city
                b["command"] = self.handler
                b.pack(anchor="w")
        def handler(self):
            print(self.city.get())
```

First, a list of all cities to be available for selection and a control variable are created. This variable will later always contain the name of the city currently selected by the user. At the beginning, Paris is selected.

Then we iterate over all cities in a loop and create a radio button for each city. In this case, the following options are set: text for the label, value for the value the control variable takes when the radio button is selected, variable for the control variable, and command for the handler function. As with the check button, this handler function is called whenever the user modifies the selection.

Figure 41.10 shows the GUI of this sample program.

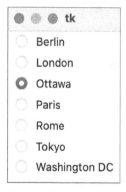

Figure 41.10 A Lot of Radio Buttons

Entry

An *entry widget* is a one-line input field where the user can write any text. The following sample code creates an Entry widget and writes text into it:

```
class MyApp(tkinter.Frame):
    def __init__(self, master=None):
        super().__init__(master)
```

```
        self.pack()
        self.entryVar = tkinter.StringVar()
        self.entryVar.set("Hello world")
        self.entry = tkinter.Entry(self)
        self.entry["textvariable"] = self.entryVar
        self.entry.pack()
        self.entry.bind("<Return>", self.handler)
    def handler(self, event):
        print(self.entryVar.get())
```

An Entry widget and a control variable are instantiated. Then the control variable is set to a value and linked to the input field. Once the input field has been passed to the packer, we connect the Return event, which is triggered when the [Enter] key is pressed in the input field, to a handler function that outputs the current contents of the input field. The GUI of this sample program is shown in Figure 41.11.

Figure 41.11 Entry Widget

Label

A *label widget* is a very simple widget whose only task is to display a text in the GUI. The following sample program shows how you can use the Label widget:

```
class MyApp(tkinter.Frame):
    def __init__(self, master=None):
        super().__init__(master)
        self.pack()
        self.label = tkinter.Label(self)
        self.label["text"] = "Hello world"
        self.label.pack()
```

After instantiating the tkinter.Label class, the text option is used to change the label's caption and the label is finally passed to the packer. Instead of using the text option, we could also have defined a control variable via the textvariable option at this point and applied the required text to it.

The GUI of this sample program is not very spectacular, but it's shown in Figure 41.12.

Figure 41.12 Label in Use

41

LabelFrame

A *label frame widget* is a special variant of the Frame widget and is used to group widgets. LabelFrame draws a labeled frame around its child widgets. In the following sample program, a label frame is added to the check button example:

```python
class MyApp(tkinter.Frame):
    def __init__(self, master=None):
        super().__init__(master)
        self.pack()
        self.names = ("Donald Duck", "Scrooge McDuck", "Gladstone Gander")
        self.group = tkinter.LabelFrame(self)
        self.group["text"] = "Duckburg"
        self.group.pack()
        self.checks = []
        self.vars = []
        for name in self.names:
            var = tkinter.BooleanVar()
            var.set(False)
            check = tkinter.Checkbutton(self.group)
            check["text"] = name
            check["command"] = self.handler
            check["variable"] = var
            check.pack(anchor="w")
            self.checks.append(check)
            self.vars.append(var)
    def handler(self):
        print(" and ".join(
            [name for name, var in zip(self.names, self.vars) if var.get()])
        )
```

Using the LabelFrame widget is limited to instantiating the tkinter.LabelFrame class, specifying the text option for the frame label, and creating the child widgets. The GUI created in this example is shown in Figure 41.13.

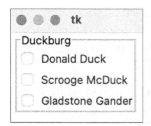

Figure 41.13 Label Frame Widget

Listbox

A *list box* is a widget that represents a list of entries. Depending on the application, the user may select or modify one or more entries. In the simplest case, a list box can be created as follows:

```python
class MyApp(tkinter.Frame):
    def __init__(self, master=None):
        super().__init__(master)
        self.pack()
        self.entries = ["Berlin", "London", "Ottawa", "Paris",
                        "Rome", "Tokyo", "Washington DC"]
        self.lb = tkinter.Listbox(master)
        self.lb.insert("end", *self.entries)
        self.lb.pack()
```

First we create the self.entries list, which contains the entries we want to write to the list box later. Then an instance of the tkinter.Listbox class is created and packed. Finally, for each desired entry, we call the insert method of the list box, which appends the respective entry to the end of the list box.

The list box generated by this source code is shown in Figure 41.14.

Figure 41.14 A List Box Example

The entries of a list box are numbered consecutively starting from 0. The entries can be accessed via this index. For this purpose, the Listbox class defines a set of methods, summarized in Table 41.8. Some of the methods are passed a first index and an optional last index. If last is specified, the method applies to all entries with an index between first and last. If last is not specified, it refers exclusively to the element with the first index. Instead of concrete indexes, the "end" string can also be passed for first and last.

41

Method	Meaning
curselection()	Returns a list with the indexes of the currently selected entries.
delete(first, [last])	Deletes one or more entries.
get(first, [last])	Returns one or more entries as a string.
insert(index, [*elements])	Inserts one or more entries as specified by elements at the index position in the list box.
selection_clear(first, [last])	Deselects one or more entries.
selection_includes(index)	Indicates whether an entry is selected.
selection_set(first, [last])	Selects one or more elements.
size()	Returns the number of entries.

Table 41.8 Methods of a List Box

The sample program for the list box described previously was static. The user could select an entry from the list box, but nothing happened. The following sample program shows how you can respond to a change in the user selection. To do this, we create the following application class:

```
class MyApp(tkinter.Frame):
    def __init__(self, master=None):
        super().__init__(master)
        self.pack()
        self.entries = ["Berlin", "London", "Ottawa", "Paris",
                        "Rome", "Tokyo", "Washington DC"]
        self.lb = tkinter.Listbox(self)
        self.lb.pack(fill="both", expand="true")
        self.lb["selectmode"] = "extended"
        self.lb.insert("end", *self.entries)
        self.lb.bind("<<ListboxSelect>>", self.selectionChanged)
        self.lb.selection_set(0)
        self.label = tkinter.Label(self)
        self.label.pack()
        self.selectionChanged(None)
```

In the constructor, a list box is first created and filled with the already known city names. The user should be able to select any set of cities. This behavior corresponds to the extended value of the selectmode configuration key. Other possible values are single, browse, and multiple.

Then we connect a handler method to the so-called virtual event <<ListboxSelect>>. A virtual event is a special event that can only be used with a specific widget type. The <<ListboxSelect>> event is called whenever the user has changed the selection in the list box.

Then the first element of the list box is selected as the only one and a label widget is created. Finally, the selectionChanged handler method is called to add meaningful text to the label widget. The selectionChanged method looks as follows:

```
def selectionChanged(self, event):
    self.label["text"] = "We are going to: " + ", ".join(
        (self.lb.get(i) for i in self.lb.curselection()))
```

Each time the user changes the selection in the list box, this method is called. Here the indexes of the selected entries are read and the corresponding city names are identified and written into the label, separated by commas.

The GUI created with this sample program is shown in Figure 41.15.

Figure 41.15 List Box with User Interaction

Menu

In a more complex GUI, there is often a *menu bar* directly below the title bar of a dialog, which contains several menus. A *menu* is a button that allows the user to access a list of additional commands. Usually, for example, in the **File** menu, you can find the **Save** and **Save As** commands. The following sample program shows how you can equip a tkinter dialog with a menu:

```
class MyApp(tkinter.Frame):
    def __init__(self, master):
        super().__init__(master)
        self.pack()
        self.menuBar = tkinter.Menu(master)
        master.config(menu=self.menuBar)
        self.fillMenuBar()
    def fillMenuBar(self):
        self.menuFile = tkinter.Menu(self.menuBar, tearoff=False)
```

```
        self.menuFile.add_command(label="Open", command=self.handler)
        self.menuFile.add_command(label="Save", command=self.handler)
        self.menuFile.add_command(label="Save as", command=self.handler)
        self.menuFile.add_separator()
        self.menuFile.add_command(label="Quit", command=self.quit)
        self.menuBar.add_cascade(label="File", menu=self.menuFile)
    def handler(self):
        print("Hello world!")
```

The tkinter.Tk instance that forms the basis of every tkinter application contains a menu option that can be used to set a menu bar. This can be done within the constructor of the MyApp class, where the tkinter.Tk instance can be accessed via the master parameter. There, the menu bar is first created as tkinter.Menu instance and ultimately entered as a menu bar via the menu option.

The fillMenuBar method, which can be called from the constructor, has the task of filling the newly created menu bar. To do this, we first create a menu, which is henceforth available under the name menuFile. The tearoff parameter can be used to control whether it should be possible to detach the menu. This behavior is inappropriate for most desktop environments and was therefore not allowed. However, you can nevertheless experiment with this setting.

Then menu items are added to the menu via the add_command method. These are given a label and a handler function (command), which is called in the same way as the handler function of a button when the user has selected the respective menu item. In this example, the handler method is called, which demonstrates that the sample program works by outputting a text. Only for the **Exit** menu item is self.quit entered as a handler method to terminate the application.

The add_separator method can be used to insert a separator line into the menu in order to visually group related menu items by category as well.

Finally, the add_cascade method adds the new menu under the **File** title to the menu bar.

The GUI of the sample program is shown in Figure 41.16.

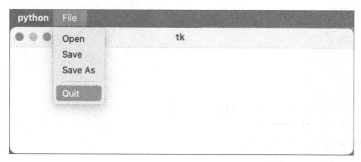

Figure 41.16 Menu Bar

This simple example can be extended even further: in addition to the add_command method for adding a simple menu item and add_separator method for adding a separator, a Menu instance also has the add_checkbutton and add_radiobutton methods. These two methods allow you to use radio buttons and check buttons in a menu. The options that specify the radio or check buttons in more detail are passed as keyword parameters to the methods (see Figure 41.17).

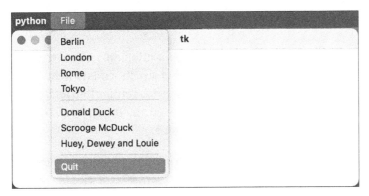

Figure 41.17 More Complex Menu Bar

Menu Button

A *menu button* is a button that displays a menu when the user clicks it. The following sample code shows how such a widget can be used:

```python
class MyApp(tkinter.Frame):
    def __init__(self, master):
        super().__init__(master)
        self.pack()
        self.mb = tkinter.Menubutton(self, text="Hello world")
        self.menu = tkinter.Menu(self.mb, tearoff=False)
        self.menu.add_checkbutton(label="Donald Duck")
        self.menu.add_checkbutton(label="Scrooge McDuck")
        self.menu.add_checkbutton(label="Huey, Dewey, and Louie")
        self.mb["menu"] = self.menu
        self.mb.pack()
```

First, an instance of the tkinter.Menubutton class is created. The label of the menu button is defined by the text option. After that, we create the menu that can be displayed when clicking the menu button. This is a tkinter.Menu instance that can be created and used as in the previous section.

Finally, the menu is bound to the menu button via the menu option, and the menu button is passed to the packer. The resulting GUI is shown in Figure 41.18.

The menu button label doesn't change regardless of the item selected in the menu.

41

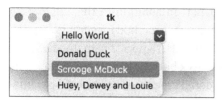

Figure 41.18 Menu Button in Use

Option Menu

In the case of the menu button described in the previous section, we noticed that the button's label doesn't change automatically when the user selects a menu item. However, this behavior is often required. A widget that behaves this way is often referred to as a *dropdown list*. In the Tk framework, this widget is called an *option menu*. The following code shows how you can use the OptionMenu widget:

```
class MyApp(tkinter.Frame):
    def __init__(self, master):
        super().__init__(master)
        self.pack()
        self.lst = ["Linux", "macOS", "Windows"]
        self.var = tkinter.StringVar()
        self.var.set("Linux")
        self.op = tkinter.OptionMenu(self, self.var, *self.lst,
                                     command=self.handler)
        self.op.pack()
    def handler(self, text):
        print(text, self.var.get())
```

After creating a list of items required for the dropdown list and a control variable, we instantiate a tkinter.OptionMenu instance, passing both the control variable var and the list of items. Note that the list of entries is unpacked, since the entries must be passed as positional parameters.

The command keyword parameter is used to specify a handler function that will be called when the user has changed the selection. Unlike the handler functions from the previous examples, in this case handler is passed the text of the new selection. In the handler function, we output the name of the new selection twice: once by passing the parameter and another time by reading the control variable. Both variants should always provide the same name.

The GUI generated by the sample program is shown in Figure 41.19.

Figure 41.19 Option Menu Widget in Use

To be able to respond to a selection of the user, the command option can be used again. This option can be used to specify a handler function that will be called by the Tk framework whenever the user makes a selection. The handler function must accept one parameter: the text of the currently selected element.

Scrollbar

It often happens that the contents of a widget, such as the entries of a list, need more space than is provided by the widget. For those cases, certain widget types allow to include a so-called *scrollbar*. The following example shows how you can use a scrollbar in conjunction with a list box:

```python
class MyApp(tkinter.Frame):
    def __init__(self, master):
        super().__init__(master)
        self.pack()
        self.lb = tkinter.Listbox(self)
        self.lb.pack(side="left")
        self.sb = tkinter.Scrollbar(self)
        self.sb.pack(fill="y", side="left")
        self.lb.insert("end", *[i*i for i in range(50)])
        self.lb["yscrollcommand"] = self.sb.set
        self.sb["command"] = self.lb.yview
```

First, a list box and a scrollbar are created and arranged in the GUI so that the scrollbar appears to the right of the list box. Then the list box is filled with the squares of the numbers between 0 and 50. What is missing now is the connection between the scrollbar and the list box: currently we've only created two widgets that are independent of each other.

To bind the scrollbar to the list box, we first set the yscrollcommand option of the list box to the set method of the scrollbar. This allows for automatic adjustment of the scrollbar when the list box entries are scrolled using the arrow keys or the mouse wheel. Then the command option of the scrollbar is set to the yview method of the list box. Now it's also possible to scroll the list box with the scrollbar.

41

The GUI generated in the preceding example is shown in Figure 41.20.

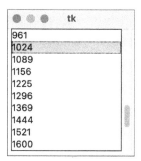

Figure 41.20 List Box with Attached Scroll Bar

Instead of the `yscrollcommand` option and the `yview` method, we could have used the `xscrollcommand` option and the `xview` method to implement a horizontal scrollbar.

The ability to attach a scrollbar demonstrated here works not only with `Listbox` widgets, but also with `Canvas`, `Entry`, `Spinbox`, and `Text` widgets.

Spinbox

A *spinbox* is a widget in which a user can enter an integer. In addition, the user can correct the entered number up or down using two buttons on the edge of the widget. The following code snippet demonstrates the use of a spinbox:

```
s = tkinter.Spinbox(master)
s["from"] = 0
s["to"] = 100
s.pack()
```

The spinbox is instantiated, then the `from` and `to` options are used to set the limits within which the stored number may move. In this example, no number greater than 100 or less than 0 may be entered. You can see the spinbox created in the example in Figure 41.21.

Figure 41.21 Spinbox in Action

Instead of specifying two limits using the `from` and `to` options, you can specify the allowed values concretely. This is done via the `values` option:

```
s = tkinter.Spinbox(master)
s["values"] = (2,3,5,7,11,13,19)
s.pack()
```

In this case, the user can select one of the prime numbers between 2 and 19 in the spinbox. The order in which the numbers appear in the spinbox is given by the order of the values in the tuple. There doesn't have to be a connection to the actual ordering of the numbers.

If the values the spinbox can accept are specified concretely, data types other than `int` can also be used:

```
s["values"] = ("A", "B", "C")
```

In this example, the user can use the spinbox to select one of the three letters.

Text

So far, you've only seen one way to get single-line text input from the user via the `Entry` widget. The *Text* widget allows you to display or have the user type a multiline, formatted text.

The following example shows how you can use the `text` widget to display formatted text:

```python
class MyApp(tkinter.Frame):
    def __init__(self, master):
        super().__init__(master)
        self.pack()
        self.text = tkinter.Text(master)
        self.text.pack()
        self.text.tag_config("o", foreground="orange")
        self.text.tag_config("u", underline=True)
        self.text.insert("end", "Hello world\n")
        self.text.insert("end", "This is a long orange text\n", "o")
        self.text.insert("end", "And it is even underlined", "u")
```

First, the `text` widget is instantiated and packed. After that, we define so-called *tags*, which later allow us to format the text to be displayed. In this case, we define the o tag for orange text and the u tag for underlined text.

Then we add three lines of text each to the end of the text contained in the widget. The first line of text should be displayed unformatted, the second in orange color, and the third one underlined. Figure 41.22 shows how the text is displayed.

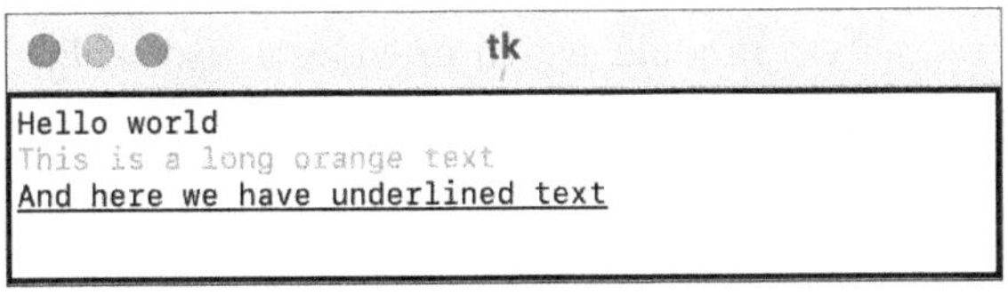

Figure 41.22 Text Widget

41

By default, the user is allowed to modify the text displayed in the text widget. The following example shows how to respond to user input in the text widget and read the entered text:

```python
class MyApp(tkinter.Frame):
    def __init__(self, master):
        super().__init__(master)
        self.pack()
        self.text = tkinter.Text(master)
        self.text.pack()
        self.text.bind("<KeyRelease>", self.textChanged)
    def textChanged(self, event):
        print("Text:", self.text.get("1.0", "end"))
```

Unlike the entry widget, a text widget doesn't allow you to set up a control variable for the text it contains. This is because the text widget also requires formatting instructions for the text to be displayed. These would have to be replicated in a string control variable in a cumbersome way using special code sequences.

Instead of a control variable, the text widget provides the get method, which can be used to read the text displayed in the widget. This is the plain text; any formatting instructions are lost when they're read using get.

In the sample program, an event handler has been set up for the KeyRelease event. This is triggered whenever the user releases a key while the text widget has the input focus. Note that we use the KeyRelease event, not KeyPress. If we used the KeyPress event, our event handler would be called before the character entered by the user was entered into the text widget.

In the textChanged event handler, we call the get method of the text widget. This method is passed two indexes that indicate which part of the text is to be read. In this case, we're interested in the entire text contained in the widget and specify the indexes 1.0 and end. The 1.0 index reads as "first row, zeroth character." Note that the indexing of the rows starts at 1, while that of the columns, the characters, starts at 0. So the 1.0 index denotes the first character of the text displayed in the widget. The end index, of course, denotes the last character of the text contained in the widget.

It's possible to connect a horizontal or vertical scrollbar with a text widget. This is done in the same way as the listbox widget via the xscrollcommand and yscrollcommand options. You can find an example of this in the earlier discussion of the scrollbar. In Section 41.2.7, we'll describe the scrolledtext module, which provides a text widget already equipped with scrollbars.

41.2.6   Drawings: The Canvas Widget

The *Canvas* widget is a widget that displays any kind of graphics. For example, you can use the Canvas widget to draw a diagram or to display an image. In the following sample program, the Canvas widget is used to draw a circle and two lines:

```python
class MyApp(tkinter.Frame):
    def __init__(self, master):
        super().__init__(master)
        self.pack()
        self.cv = tkinter.Canvas(self, width=200, height=200)
        self.cv.pack()
        self.cv.create_oval(50, 50, 150, 150, fill="orange", width=3)
        self.cv.create_line(50, 150, 150, 50, width=3)
        self.cv.create_line(50, 50, 150, 150, width=3)
```

First, we create a square Canvas widget with a side length of 200 pixels. In this canvas, we can then draw basic geometric shapes using the create methods of the widget. In this case, we use the create_oval and create_line methods to draw a circle and two lines, respectively.

The create methods are each passed two coordinate pairs as first parameters. These specify the position at which the shape is to be drawn. The coordinate information refers to the local coordinate system in the Canvas widget, whose origin is in the upper-left-hand corner of the widget as shown in Figure 41.23. The positive Y-axis of this coordinate system points down. So the (50, 100) coordinate pair denotes the point that is 50 pixels to the right and 100 pixels below the top-left-hand corner of the widget.

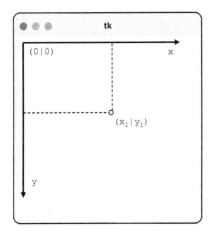

Figure 41.23 Tkinter Coordinate System

The create_oval method is passed the upper-left-hand and lower-right-hand corners of the rectangle surrounding the ellipse. Thus, the position and shape of the ellipse are completely described. The `create_line` method gets the start and destination point of the line.

In addition, the `create` methods can be passed options as keyword parameters that specify the appearance of the drawn shape. In this case, the `fill` option for the fill color and `width` option for the pen thickness are set.

The drawing generated by this code is shown in Figure 41.24.

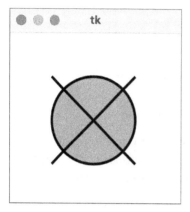

Figure 41.24 Drawing in a Canvas Widget

In the following sections, we'll discuss the `create` methods provided by the Canvas widget and show you examples where necessary.

create_arc(x1, y1, x2, y2, {**kw})

The `create_arc` method adds a portion of the ellipse defined by the x1, y1, x2, and y2 coordinates to the Canvas widget. Options can be passed as keyword parameters. Two important pieces of information are determined by these options: the part supposed to be drawn and the shape it should have.

The `style` option may be set to the `"pieslice"`, `"chord"`, or `"arc"` string and determines the appearance of the ellipse section. Figure 41.25 shows the results of three calls of `create_arc` where only the `style` option was modified.

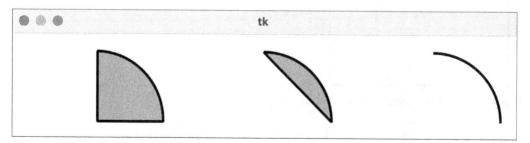

Figure 41.25 From Left to Right: pieslice, chord, and arc

To specify the part of the ellipse to be drawn, you need the start and extent options. The start option can be used to determine the angle from which the section to be drawn begins. The extent option is also an angle and denotes the extent of the section. The angles are measured in degrees and are traced counterclockwise. The start and extent options are preset with 0.0 and 90.0 respectively.

The fill and outline options allow you to specify the fill or outline color of the ellipse. Colors are specified as strings in the format "#RRGGBB", where the individual components stand for the hexadecimal red, green, and blue components, respectively. The width option sets the pen thickness.

create_image(x, y, {**kw})

The create_image method allows you to display an image in a Canvas widget. We'll explain how this works with the following sample program:

```
class MyApp(tkinter.Frame):
    def __init__(self, master):
        super().__init__(master)
        self.pack()
        self.cv = tkinter.Canvas(self, width=800, height=600)
        self.cv.pack()
        self.img = tkinter.PhotoImage(file="coffee.png")
        self.cv.create_image(0, 0, image=self.img, anchor="nw")
```

First, the *coffee.png* image is loaded using the tkinter.PhotoImage class. Note that the PhotoImage class supports only PNG, GIF, and PPM/PGM graphic formats.[6] After that, the loaded image is drawn into the Canvas widget at position (0,0) by calling the create_image method. We use the image option to tell create_image which graphic we want to draw.

The second specified option, anchor, determines the relationship of the passed coordinate pair to the drawn graphic. The value "nw" passed in the example means that at the (x,y) position in the local coordinate system of the Canvas widget, the upper-left-hand corner of the image should be located. The anchor option defaults to "center", so if we hadn't specified it, the center of the image would be at point (x,y).

The GUI generated by the sample program looks like the one shown in Figure 41.26.

41

---

6 If you need more graphic formats, you should look into the third-party Pillow library, which provides a class compatible with PhotoImage and is described in Chapter 44, Section 44.8.

Figure 41.26 Graphic in the Canvas Widget

create_line([*coords], {**kw})

The create_line method draws a polyline into the Canvas widget. For this purpose, it's passed an arbitrary number of coordinate pairs as positional parameters. The options that can be used to define the properties of the polyline are passed as keyword parameters. In the following example, we draw the *House of Santa Claus*[7] using a single call of the create_line method:

```python
class MyApp(tkinter.Frame):
    def __init__(self, master):
        super().__init__(master)
        self.pack()
        self.cv = tkinter.Canvas(self, width=200, height=200)
        self.cv.pack()
        points = (10, 140,    90, 60,    10, 60,
                  50, 10,    90, 60,    90, 140,
                  10, 140,    10, 60,    90, 140)
        self.cv.create_line(*points, width=3)
```

The result of this sample program is shown in Figure 41.27.

Note that the polyline drawn with the create_line method isn't necessarily closed, even if that's the case in the example. This is a distinguishing feature from the otherwise similar create_polygon method.

---

7 In Germany *Das Haus vom Nikolaus* is a well-known game for children who are challenged to draw the whole sketch without lifting the pen and without drawing any of the lines more than a single time.

Figure 41.27 House of Santa Claus (German: Das Haus vom Nikolaus)

create_oval(x1, y1, x2, y2, {**kw})

The `create_oval` method draws an ellipse. The position and shape of the ellipse are determined by points `(x1, y1)` and `(x2, y2)`, which indicate the upper-left and lower-right corner points of the rectangle enclosing the ellipse. Figure 41.28 shows an ellipse drawn using `create_oval`, including the enclosing rectangle and the position of the two corner points.

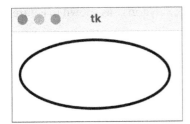

Figure 41.28 Ellipse in the Canvas Widget

You can pass the same options to the `create_oval` method as to the `create_line` method.

create_polygon([*coords], {**kw})

The `create_polygon` method draws a polygon into the `canvas` widget. The polygon is defined by its vertices, which are passed in the form of any number of coordinate pairs. In the following sample program, we use the `create_polygon` method to draw a triangle filled with orange color:

```python
class MyApp(tkinter.Frame):
    def __init__(self, master):
        super().__init__(master)
        self.pack()
        self.cv = tkinter.Canvas(self, width=200, height=200)
        self.cv.pack()
```

41

```
points = (10, 10,
          90, 50,
          10, 90)
self.cv.create_polygon(*points, width=3,
                       fill="orange", outline="black")
```

The resulting polygon looks like the one shown in Figure 41.29.

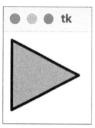

Figure 41.29 Triangle Made with create_polygon Method

You can see that the passed points are connected. In addition, the surface is closed by a connection between the first and the last point and can be filled. The create_polygon method is also capable of drawing and filling nonconvex polygons,[8] as shown in Figure 41.30.

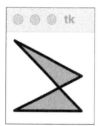

Figure 41.30 Nonconvex Polynomial

In this case, the list of points from the previous example has been extended by the point (90, 90).

create_rectangle(x1, y1, x2, y2, {**kw})

The create_rectangle method draws a rectangle into the canvas widget. The rectangle is defined by the upper left-hand corner (x1, y1) and the lower-right-hand corner (x2, y2).

---

8 A *nonconvex polygon* is a polygon that contains two points whose connecting line is not completely inside the polygon. Nonconvex polygons are often called concave, which, strictly speaking, is wrong: a *concave polygon* is a polygon whose complement is convex.

The only difference from create_ellipse is that not the ellipse enclosed by the described rectangle is drawn, but the rectangle itself. The possible options correspond to those of the create_ellipse method. Therefore, no further examples are necessary.

create_text(x, y, {**kw})

The create_text method allows you to write any text into a canvas widget. By default, the text is written centered at the position determined by x and y. This behavior can be changed via the anchor option.

This is demonstrated by the following sample program:

```python
class MyApp(tkinter.Frame):
    def __init__(self, master):
        super().__init__(master)
        self.pack()
        self.cv = tkinter.Canvas(self, width=200, height=200)
        self.cv.pack()
        self.font1 = ("Arial", 12, "italic")
        self.font2 = ("Courier New", 12, "bold italic")
        self.font3 = ("Comic Sans MS", 12, "bold")
        self.cv.create_text(55, 30, text="Python ", font=self.font1)
        self.cv.create_text(55, 50, text="Python ", font=self.font2)
        self.cv.create_text(55, 70, text="Python ", font=self.font3)
```

After creating the canvas widget, three tuples are created, each defining a font type. For details on how to find the fonts available on the current system, see Section in Section 41.2.7. At this point, we'd like to focus on the fact that the first element of the tuple contains the font name, the second the font size, and the third element can contain further specifications such as bold or italic.

After specifying the fonts, we call the create_text method three times, each time with a different font. The text to be written is specified using the text option, and the font type is specified using the font option. The sample program generates the GUI shown in Figure 41.31.

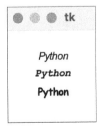

Figure 41.31 Text in a Canvas Widget

create_window(x, y, {kw})**

The create_window method allows you to place widgets inside a Canvas widget. The widget is drawn to the position specified by x and y, taking into account any value passed for the anchor option. The widget itself must be instantiated up front and is specified via the window option.

The following sample program combines a small drawing and a widget to create a menacing GUI:

```python
class MyApp(tkinter.Frame):
    def __init__(self, master):
        super().__init__(master)
        self.pack()
        self.cv = tkinter.Canvas(self, width=200, height=200)
        self.cv.pack()
        self.cv.create_oval(10, 10, 190, 90, fill="red", width=3)
        self.b = tkinter.Button(None, text="Self Destruction")
        self.cv.create_window(100, 50, window=self.b)
```

The source code should be self-evident and generates the GUI shown in Figure 41.32.

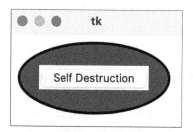

Figure 41.32 Button Embedded in a Canvas Widget

Well, you don't have to click the button if you don't want to . . .

41.2.7 Other Modules

Finally, we'd like to give you an overview of other modules included in the tkinter package as these cover some quite interesting areas and in some respects facilitate working with the Tk framework. In the following sections, we'll describe the scrolledtext, filedialog, font, and messagebox modules.

tkinter.scrolledtext

In the section about the Text widget, we said that it's possible to provide a Text widget with a vertical scrollbar via the yscrollcommand option. However, since such a vertical scrollbar is common requirement, it would be cumbersome if we had to write the code each time to instantiate and bind the scrollbar.

For this purpose, the scrolledtext module is available in the tkinter package, which provides the ScrolledText widget. This widget behaves like a Text widget but comes with a vertical scrollbar by default so that the programmer doesn't have to bother with it anymore.

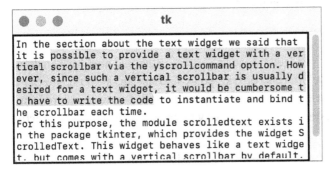

Figure 41.33 ScrolledText widget

Internally, the ScrolledText widget consists of a Text widget, a scrollbar, and a Frame widget that includes the other two widgets. You can access the scrollbar and Frame widget via the vbar and frame attributes of the ScrolledText widget.

Note that the ScrolledText widget doesn't offer a horizontal scrollbar by default. You have to create and link it yourself, just like with the Text widget.

tkinter.filedialog

When you program GUIs, there are *standard dialogs* that are made for certain questions to the user that are asked over and over again. Such standard dialogs have the advantage for the programmer that there is no need to come up with a self-designed dialog. The advantage for the user is that he isn't constantly confronted with different GUIs for the same question, but always finds the same familiar dialog. It's also possible to use the standard dialogs of the operating system or desktop environment in the Tk framework.

An important class of standard dialogs is the file dialog, which prompts a user to select files or folders from the hard drive, be it to load them into the program or save content to it. File dialogs are needed all the time.

The filedialog module of the tkinter package provides ready-made file dialogs. Usually, a function call is sufficient to integrate the dialog into your own application. Table 41.9 describes the functions provided by the filedialog module.

41

Function	Standard Dialog For
askdirectory({**options})	The selection of a directory
askopenfilename({**options})	The selection of a file to open
asksaveasfilename({**options})	The selection of a location for a file to save

Table 41.9 Standard Dialogs in the tkinter.filedialog Module

tkinter.font

In the description of the Canvas widget in Section 41.2.6, you learned how you can draw any text into the Canvas widget. In this context, you could use an option to specify a font that should be used to write the text. At that point, we used some standard fonts that are available on every system. There was no way to find out which fonts were actually available to us.

The font module of the tkinter package provides a solution to this problem in the form of the families function. This function returns a tuple containing the names of all fonts you can use, for example, in connection with the font option when calling the create_text method of the canvas widget. The families function doesn't require you to pass any parameters to it.

Apart from this function, the font module also contains a Font class whose description would go beyond the scope of this introduction. You can find more information about it, for example, in the interactive help of tkinter.font.

tkinter.messagebox

The messagebox module of the tkinter package allows you to display so-called message boxes via a simple function call. A *message box* is a small window containing a message to the user. It can be used to inform the user about an error or to ask them a question. There are several types of message boxes—for example, one that displays a corresponding icon for an error message in addition to the message, or one that offers **Yes** and **No** buttons with which the user can answer a question posed in the message.

The messagebox module provides a set of functions through which different types of message boxes can be created and displayed. These functions all have the same interface and can be used as in the following example:

```
import tkinter.messagebox
tkinter.messagebox.askokcancel("sample program",
    "The installation of 'virus.exe' is about to be started.")
```

This message box can be closed using the **OK** and **Cancel** buttons. The return value of the function indicates which of the buttons the user has clicked. The function returns True if the user closed the message box using the **OK** button, and False if the user clicked **Cancel**.

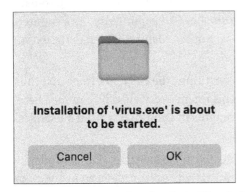

Installation of 'virus.exe' is about to be started.

Cancel   OK

Figure 41.34 Message Box Created with askokcancel

Apart from askokcancel, the functions listed in Table 41.10 are available.

Function	Buttons	Return Value
askokcancel	**OK** **Cancel**	True False
askquestion	**Yes** **No**	"yes" "no"
askretrycancel	**Retry** **Cancel**	True False
askyesno	**Yes** **No**	True False
askyesnocancel	**Yes** **No** **Cancel**	True False None
showerror	**OK**	"ok"
showinfo	**OK**	"ok"
showwarning	**OK**	"ok"

Table 41.10 Message Boxes in the tkinter.messagebox Module

41

41.3   Introduction to PySide6

In the previous section, we described the `tkinter` module, which can be used to write Tk GUIs in Python. The big advantage of `tkinter` is that it's included in the standard library and thus doesn't need to be installed separately. However, Tk is no longer up-to-date and is more suitable for writing prototypes or smaller GUI applications. As a counterpart to Tk, this section provides you with a project-oriented introduction to the extensive Qt framework.

We've already provided an overview of what constitutes the Qt[9] framework, and thus the PySide6 Python bindings, in Section 41.2. This rough overview will be refined here, where we'll take a look at the concepts and strengths of Qt primarily from a technical point of view.

For this purpose, in the next section we'll first deal with the question of where and how Qt and PySide6 can be obtained and installed. After that, we'll give you an overview of the basic concepts of the Qt framework.

41.3.1   Installation

Because PySide6 is a third-party package, it must be installed before you can use it. This can be done conveniently via the Anaconda package manager conda, if it hasn't already been installed by default:

```
$ conda install -c conda-forge pyside6
```

Alternatively, if you don't use Anaconda, PySide6 can be installed via the Python package manager pip:

```
$ pip install pyside6
```

If you're a Linux user, an installation may also be possible via the package manager of your Linux distribution.

41.3.2   Basic Concepts of Qt

As an introduction to programming with Qt or PySide6, this section provides an overview of the main concepts and strengths of the Qt framework.

License

Qt and PySide6 are subject to a dual license system. Projects that you develop with the provided free versions of Qt and PySide6 may only be released under a license that is

---

9 The name Qt is pronounced like *cute*.

also free—for example, the GPL. To be allowed to publish a commercial program, you must pay a license fee.

Scope

You'll already have noticed that we've referred to a *framework* rather than a toolkit in the context of Qt. This is due to the fact that the majority of the classes contained in the Qt framework have nothing to do with programming GUIs, but provide useful functions elsewhere. For example, the Qt framework contains classes for working with XML data or for network communication. While many of these classes are effectively redundant in combination with the standard library of Python, they add significant value in programming languages such as C++ that don't have such extensive standard libraries.

Signals and Slots

One of the biggest differences from other GUI toolkits is the signal-and-slot principle that Qt uses to allow individual objects to communicate with each other. Every event that occurs in a Qt object, such as when a button is clicked, sends a *signal* that can be received by connected *slots*. Signals and slots are more flexible than the overloading of methods used in other toolkits for communication.

For more details on the signal-and-slot principle, see Section 41.4.

Layouts

The Qt framework supports *layouts* in the GUI of a program. Using a layout, widgets can be automatically positioned in relation to each other. This group of widgets then can be moved or resized together without losing their relative alignment.

For more information on layouts, see Section 41.3.3.

Drawing Functions

Qt provides extensive functionality for drawing in the GUI. Thus, Qt allows drawing a wide variety of shapes with a wide variety of types of fill or line style. In addition, Qt provides capabilities for transforming drawings using transformation matrices, which enables amazing effects and sets Qt apart from many other GUI toolkits. Likewise, Qt allows reading and writing many graphic formats, including, most importantly, the SVG vector format.

For more details on drawing using Qt, see Section 41.6.

The Model-View Concept

Qt implements the *model-view concept*, which allows for the separation of form and content. Thus, in Qt you can store the data that a program processes in its own class structure, separate from the functionality that displays the data. In this way, the overall

41

program structure becomes clearer, and the independent further development and reuse of individual components are facilitated.

For more details on the model-view concept, see Section 41.7.

QML

With QML, Qt contains a scripting language based on CSS that enables the design of GUIs and the creation of simple program logic on an abstract level.

Tools

The next outstanding area of Qt centers on the included tools. A Qt installation usually includes the Qt Designer, Qt Assistant, and Qt Linguist programs. Qt Designer is a program for the comfortable design of GUIs. We'll return to this program later in this chapter.

The Qt Assistant and Qt Linguist programs, which are also included, aren't described in this book. It should only be mentioned here that Qt Assistant is a tool for reading the Qt help and Qt Linguist is a tool for localizing Qt applications.

Documentation

The last point to mention is the documentation of the Qt framework, which is either included with your Qt installation or can be found on the internet at *https://doc.qt.io/ qtforpython*. The Qt documentation is very comprehensive and contains a large number of examples.

41.3.3   Development Process

In this section, we'll describe the complete development process of a simple Qt application. We'll build on the knowledge gained here later when we move on to a more complex application.

The sample program we develop in this section is a form that reads some personal data from the user.

The Dialog

In this example, the user's first name, last name, date of birth, and address are to be read and saved. In addition, the user is supposed to accept the general terms and conditions of our pseudoportal and be able to optionally order a catalog.

Based on these prerequisites, we can create a *dialog* in the next step. A dialog is a single window of a GUI and contains multiple widgets. A *widget* is a single control or operating element of the GUI. A widget can contain any number of child widgets, so-called children. In the dialog shown in Figure 41.35, for example, the input fields, which are themselves also widgets, are subordinate to the **Personal Data** grouping widget.

Figure 41.35 shows the main dialog of our first application and explains the names and meanings of each widget.

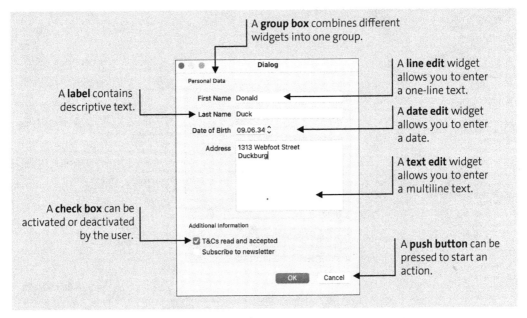

Figure 41.35 Different Widgets of the Main Dialog

Now we can start creating the dialog. Qt provides a convenient development tool for this purpose, the Qt Designer. With the help of Qt Designer, even complex dialogs can be edited without any problem.

Qt Designer can be started from a shell or, on Windows, from the Anaconda prompt using the designer command:

```
$ designer
```

After launching the designer, you will be offered the possibility to load template. In this case, we decide to use the **Dialog without Buttons** template, which provides a completely empty dialog. After that, Qt Designer presents itself as shown in Figure 41.36.

The Qt Designer workspace can be roughly divided into three areas:

- In the middle you'll find your dialog template, which is still empty at this point.
- On the left-hand side, there's a list of all available widgets. To add one of these widgets to the dialog, you can select it and drag it onto the dialog. Once a widget has been added to the dialog, it can be positioned or resized as per your requirements.
- On the right-hand side, you can edit the properties of the currently selected widget.

41

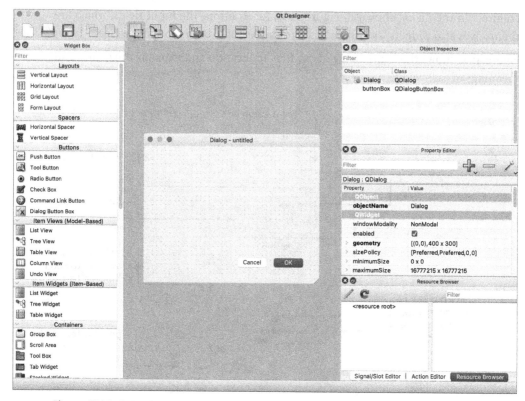

Figure 41.36 Qt Designer

Let's start by placing **OK** and **Cancel** buttons in the dialog. To do this, you must drag two buttons from the list on the left and place them in the dialog. The labels of the buttons can be changed by double-clicking the current text. To make the **OK** button the default button of the dialog, you must change the `default` property of the button in the list on the right to `true`. Then you should drag two group boxes onto the dialog and adjust the size and position according to your requirements. You can adjust the title of a group box by double-clicking the current text (see Figure 41.37).

Basically, you could add more widgets to the dialog now by placing them in one of the two groups. This automatically makes them child widgets that are positioned absolutely in their respective group. To make the child widgets adjust automatically when the main dialog is resized, we'll create a layout for them. To create a layout, you must select all the widgets that should belong to it and choose one of the buttons from the layout toolbar (see Figure 41.38).

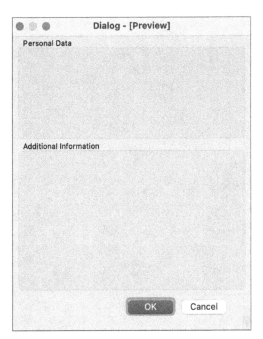

Figure 41.37 Dialog with Group Boxes

Figure 41.38 Layout Toolbar

Clicking the first icon arranges the widgets horizontally, clicking the second icon verti-cally. The following two icons create a splitter between the widgets, which can later be moved by the user. Another interesting feature is the fifth button, which arranges the selected widgets in a table. Clicking the last icon dissolves an existing layout.

With the help of layouts, the absolute arrangement of group boxes or buttons shown previously can be turned into a full-fledged dialog, whose elements automatically adapt to a change in size. For this purpose, the two buttons, including a spacer for the left-hand edge, are arranged horizontally. The group boxes and button layout are then arranged vertically in a parent layout (see Figure 41.39).

In a similar way, the other widget of the planned dialog can be inserted and provided with layouts. To edit the text of the `label` widgets, you must double-click the current text, just as you would for a group box. In the designer, the finished dialog looks like the one shown in Figure 41.40.

41

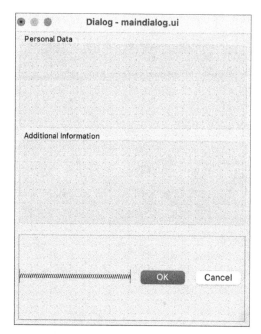

Figure 41.39 Basic Layout

Figure 41.40 Finished Layout

With this, the dialog is outwardly designed, but one important thing is still missing: each widget needs a name by which it can be addressed later in the program. You can define this name in Qt Designer. To give a widget a new name, you need to select it, right-click to open the corresponding context menu, and select the **Change object-Name** menu item.

Table 41.11 lists the names assigned in the example for all important widgets. Widgets that exist only for layout reasons, such as the group boxes and labels, don't need to be named because no operations will be performed on them later.

Widget	Name
The dialog itself	`Maindialog`
The "First Name" line edit widget	`first_name`
The "Last Name" line edit widget	`last_name`
The "Date of Birth" date edit widget	`date_of_birth`
The "Address" text edit widget	`address`
The "T&Cs read and accepted" checkbox widget	`tncs`
The "Subscribe to newsletter" checkbox widget	`newsletter`
The "OK" button widget	`buttonOK`
The "Cancel" button widget	`buttonCancel`

Table 41.11 Names of the Important Widgets

Once all names have been assigned, the layout of the main dialog is finished and can be saved in the project directory. In the case of this sample program, the dialog is to be saved under the file name *maindialog.ui*.

The Program

The dialog stored in a *.ui* file can be converted to a Python class using the `pyside6-uic` program provided with PySide6. This class can then be imported and used by a program. The `pyside6-uic` program is passed the path to the *.ui* file as a command line parameter and outputs the Python class created from it to the screen by default. To redirect the output to a program file, you can use the `-o` command line option:

```
$ pyside6-uic -o maindialog.py maindialog.ui
```

To use the prepared dialog, we create the *program.py* program file. The simplest program, which displays the main dialog and performs no other operations, starts by importing PySide6 and the `Ui_maindialog` dialog class, created using `pyside6-uic`, from the *maindialog.py* program file in the local working directory:

41

```
import sys
from PySide6 import QtWidgets
from maindialog import Ui_Maindialog
```

Note that though the Ui_maindialog class defines all the widgets needed to display the dialog in the user interface, it isn't by itself a dialog in the sense of the Qt framework. For this reason, we create our own MyDialog class derived from QDialog to represent the actual dialog:

```
class MyDialog(QtWidgets.QDialog):
    def __init__(self, parent=None):
        super().__init__(parent)
        self.ui = Ui_Maindialog()
        self.ui.setupUi(self)
```

Within the constructor of MyDialog, the constructor of the base class is called first. We then instantiate the Ui_Maindialog class and have the MyDialog instance set up by calling the setupUi method, as described by Ui_Maindialog. In particular, the widgets of the dialog are also created and positioned in this process:

```
if __name__ == "__main__":
    app = QtWidgets.QApplication(sys.argv)
    dialog = MyDialog()
    dialog.show()
    sys.exit(app.exec())
```

To execute the program, an instance of the QApplication class is created, which provides the framework of an application with a GUI. This includes, for example, the main loop of the application. The sys.argv command line parameters are passed to the constructor of the QApplication class. Each Qt application can have only one QApplication instance at a time, regardless of how many dialogs are to be displayed later.

After creating the framework for the Qt application, the main dialog can be created by instantiating the MyDialog class. The show method inherited from the QDialog base class makes the dialog visible. Last but not least, the main event loop must be started by the exec method of the QApplication instance. Because we don't want to perform any further operations at the moment after the dialog has been closed by the user, we pass the return value of app.exec directly to sys.exit, thus terminating the sample program. The program blocks after calling app.exec until the user closes the main dialog.

This simple sample program will be usefully extended in the following sections. For example, the values entered by a user are to be read and written to the console window that exists next to the user interface. Adding the necessary changes to our example program, we'll explain the signal-and-slot concept of Qt next.

41.4 Signals and Slots

When writing a program with a GUI, you apply the principle of event-driven programming. This principle doesn't provide for a program to be processed sequentially from top to bottom, but instead, when certain events occur, it executes a section of code that was intended by the programmer for that event. The application of event-driven programming is necessary in the case of a GUI because here the user controls the program and not the other way round, as was the case with a console application. The user controls the program by their inputs, which arrive as events in the program. When and in which order the user makes the entries is not predetermined by the program.

In Qt, two techniques of event-driven programming can be found: one is events, and the other is signals and slots. You'll learn about both techniques in the following sections.

Each widget in the GUI is represented internally in the program by an instance of a corresponding Qt class. Each of these classes provides *event handlers*, methods that the programmer can override in a derived class to execute their own code when a special event occurs. Event handlers are used for only a few events, but they occur frequently. An example of such an event is the paintEvent, which occurs whenever the contents of a widget need to be redrawn. The widget responds to the event by executing its event handler. This can happen very frequently in some circumstances. For an example of implementing an event handler, see Section 41.6 in the context of the drawing functionality of Qt.

In addition to events, the Qt framework provides *signals and slots* for handling events. This central concept for communicating Qt objects is perhaps the biggest differentiator between Qt and other GUI toolkits.

A *signal* is sent by a widget when a certain event, such as a user input, has occurred. There are predefined signals for each widget in Qt for most use cases. In addition, it's possible to send your own signals to self-determined events.

To receive a signal, a *slot* must be set up. A slot is a function or method that is called whenever a specific signal is sent. To do this, a slot must be connected to a signal. It's possible to connect one slot with several signals and vice versa.

In the following sections, the example from the previous section will be extended to a useful application. This application is supposed to output the data entered by the user in the dialog to the console window opened in parallel, provided that the user confirms the entries by clicking the **OK** button. When the user clicks **Cancel**, no data should be output:

```
import sys
from PySide6 import QtWidgets, QtCore
from maindialog import Ui_Maindialog
```

```
class MyDialog(QtWidgets.QDialog):
    def __init__(self, parent=None):
        super().__init__(parent)
        self.ui = Ui_Maindialog()
        self.ui.setupUi(self)
        # Set up slots
        self.ui.buttonOK.clicked.connect(self.onOK)
        self.ui.buttonCancel.clicked.connect(self.onCancel)

    def onOK(self):
        # Read data
        print("First name: {}".format(self.ui.first_name.text()))
        print("Last name: {}".format(self.ui.last_name.text()))
        print("Address: {}".format(self.ui.address.toPlainText()))
        date = self.ui.date_of_birth.date().toString("MM.dd.yyyy")
        print("Date of birth: {}".format(date))
        if self.ui.tncs.checkState():
            print("T&Cs accepted")
        if self.ui.newsletter.checkState():
            print("Subscribed to newsletter")
        self.close()

    def onCancel(self):
        print("Too bad")
        self.close()
```

In the constructor of the MyDialog dialog class, the clicked signals for the **OK** and **Cancel** buttons are connected to the slots onOk and onCancel provided for them. The clicked signals are triggered whenever the user clicks the button. The signals a widget provides are contained as attributes in the corresponding widget instance. To connect a signal to a slot, the connect method of the signal is called and the slot is passed as a parameter. In the sample program, the clicked signals of the ui.buttonOK and ui.buttonCancel buttons are connected to the onOK and onCancel slots. From now on, these slots will be called whenever the user clicks the associated button.[10]

Note

In this case, the connected signals are parameterless. There are more complex signals that pass one or more parameters. In such a case, the connected slot must also expect a corresponding number of parameters.

---

10 This convenient process of connecting signals and slots isn't possible in this way in the Qt C++ framework. If you're already familiar with Qt, you should know that the classic variant of connecting signals and slots also works with PySide6, but it has the drawback that the C++ interface of the signals must be specified.

In the onOK method, the user's input is to be read from the various widgets of the main dialog. Each of these widgets is represented by an instance of a corresponding Qt class. We've previously set the names of these instances in Qt Designer. You can see which widget got which name in Table 41.11 from Section 41.3.3.

It is possible to read the content of the widgets. How this is done varies from widget to widget. For example, the contents of a QLineEdit widget can be accessed using the text method. It's also worth mentioning that the date method of the date_of_birth QDateEdit instance returns the stored date not directly in the form of a string, but in the form of a QDate instance. This must be converted to a string by calling the toString method. Finally, after all data has been read and output, the dialog is closed by calling the close method.

In the second slot, onCancel, no further operations are necessary apart from closing the dialog:

```
app = QtWidgets.QApplication(sys.argv)
dialog = MyDialog()
dialog.show()
sys.exit(app.exec())
```

The code that instantiates the application and dialog class and starts the main event loop is the same code that did its job in the previous sample program.

> **Note**
>
> As the example demonstrates, even a Python program with a GUI on Windows still opens a console window that can be written to using print.
>
> This may be desirable in some cases, but is often disruptive if communication with the user is to happen entirely through the graphical interface. If you don't want a console window to open, you can change the Python program file extension from .py to .pyw. Then all output to the console will be suppressed and no console window will be opened.

41.5   Important Widgets

Now that we've started working with Qt based on a small sample program, this section introduces the main widget classes provided by Qt. In this context, we'll provide a concise introduction for each widget as well as a table listing the most important methods and signals.

41

41.5.1   QCheckBox

The QCheckBox class represents a checkbox in the GUI. A *checkbox* is a widget that can be either activated or deactivated by the user and is independent of other checkboxes in its meaning (see Table 41.12).

Method	Description
checkState()	Returns the state of the checkbox. Valid states are QtCore.Qt.Checked, QtCore.Qt.Unchecked, or QtCore.Qt.PartiallyChecked.
setCheckState(state)	Sets the state of the checkbox. Here you can set the states that will be returned by checkState.
Signal	**Description**
stateChanged(int)	Sent when the user changes the state of the checkbox. The new state is passed as a parameter.

Table 41.12 Important Methods and Signals of QCheckBox

41.5.2   QComboBox

The QComboBox class represents a combo box, also known as a dropdown menu, on the GUI (see Table 41.13).

Method	Description
addItem([icon], text)	Adds an element named text to the combo box. Optionally, a QIcon instance can be passed to display an icon next to the name.
clear()	Deletes all elements of the combo box.
currentIndex() currentText()	Returns the index or the name of the selected element.
setModel(model)	Sets QAbstractItemModel.*
setView(itemView)	Sets QAbstractItemView.
Signal	**Description**
currentIndexChanged(int)	Sent when the selected element changes. The index of this element is passed as a parameter.

* For more details on Qt's model-view architecture, see Section 41.7.

Table 41.13 Important Methods and Signals of QComboBox

41.5.3 QDateEdit, QTimeEdit, and QDateTimeEdit

The QDateEdit, QTimeEdit, and QDateTimeEdit classes represent widgets that read a date or time from the user. A calendar is displayed to the user for input.

The methods in Table 41.14 relate to handling dates in QDateEdit and QDateTimeEdit widgets. The setMinimumTime, setMaximumTime, minimumTime, maximumTime, setTime, and time methods work in a similar way for time specifications in QDateTimeEdit and TimeEdit widgets.

Method	Description
setMinimumDate(date) setMaximumDate(date)	Sets the smallest or largest possible date. For date, a QDate or a datetime.date instance can be passed.
minimumDate() maximumDate()	Returns the smallest or largest possible date as a QDate instance.
setDate(date)	Sets the date displayed in the widget.
date()	Returns the selected date as a QDate instance.
Signal	**Description**
dateChanged(QDate)	Sent when a new date is selected.
dateTimeChanged(QDateTime)	Sent when a new date or time is selected.
timeChanged(QTime)	Sent when a new time has been selected.

Table 41.14 Important Methods and Signals of QDateEdit

41.5.4 QDialog

The QDialog class represents a dialog in the GUI. A dialog can be used like any other widget class, the difference being that dialogs can't be embedded in other widgets.

Basically, there are two types of dialogs—modal and nonmodal dialogs:

- A *modal dialog* is a dialog that places itself in the foreground of the application and takes the input focus. The user can't operate other dialogs of the application while a modal dialog is open. Thus, a modal dialog can be used for an important communication with the user, which is essential for the further program run.

- The counterpart to this is the *nonmodal dialog*. If a dialog isn't opened modally, it can be operated in parallel with the rest of the application. A well-known example of a nonmodal dialog is the **Find and Replace** dialog in a word processing program, where it must be possible for the user to make changes in the main window while the dialog is open.

To display a dialog modally, you must call the exec method. This method blocks the program flow until the user closes the dialog. The return value of exec indicates in which form the dialog was terminated. In this context, one of the two QtCore.Qt.

41

Accepted and QtCore.Qt.Rejected constants is returned, the first representing an exit from the dialog via the **OK** button and the second representing an exit via the **Cancel** button. Within the dialog class, the accept and reject methods can be called to exit the dialog with the corresponding return value.

A nonmodal dialog can be displayed using the show method. This method returns immediately without waiting for the dialog to end, thus allowing parallel processing of the dialog and the main application.

41.5.5   QLineEdit

The QLineEdit class represents a single-line input field in the GUI.

Method	Description
setText(text)	Sets the text of the input field.
text()	Returns the text of the input field.
Signal	**Description**
textChanged(QString)	Sent when the text of the input field has been changed.

Table 41.15 Important Methods and Signals of QLineEdit

41.5.6   QListWidget and QListView

The QListWidget and QListView classes represent widgets for displaying lists. Whereas QListWidget is a classic widget, QListView uses the model-view architecture. For an introduction to the concept of model-view programming using the QListView widget, see Section 41.7. QListWidget is used whenever creating a model-view architecture for the data to be displayed would require disproportionately much work and the flexibility that a model-view architecture provides isn't needed.

Method	Description
addItem(label)	Adds an item named label to the end of the list.
currentItem()	Returns the currently selected item as a QListWidgetItem instance. You can find the name of the item using the text method of the item.
Signal	**Description**
currentItemChanged(QListWidgetItem, QListWidgetItem)	Sent when a new item is selected. The newly selected item and the previously selected item are passed as parameters.

Table 41.16 Important Methods and Signals of QListWidget

41.5.7   QProgressBar

The QProgressBar class represents a progress bar in a GUI. A progress bar shows the progress of a lengthy operation. The QProgressBar widget doesn't allow any interaction with the user.

Method	Description
setMinimum(minimum) setMaximum(maximum)	Sets the lower or upper integer limit of the value range.
setValue(value)	Sets the current value to be displayed. The passed value must be an integer and must be within the specified limits.
setOrientation(orientation)	Sets the orientation of the progress bar. Possible values are QtCore.Qt.Horizontal and QtCore.Qt.Vertical for horizontal and vertical orientation respectively.

Table 41.17 Important Methods of QProgressBar

41.5.8   QPushButton

The QPushButton class represents a button in the GUI. A button is a labeled widget the user can click to trigger an action.

Method	Description
setText(text)	Sets the label of the button
Signal	**Description**
clicked()	Sent when the user has clicked on the button

Table 41.18 Important Methods and Signals of QPushButton

41.5.9   QRadioButton

The QRadioButton class represents a radio button in the GUI. A radio button is used to let the user make a selection from several given choices. All radio buttons of a dialog that have the same parent widget belong to one group. Within a group, only one radio button can be activated at a time. If the user activates another one, the previously activated one will be deactivated. To accommodate multiple groups of radio buttons in the same dialog, they must have different parent widgets. For this purpose, the frame widget, represented by the QFrame class, is suitable, which corresponds to an invisible frame in the widget.

41

Method	Description
isChecked()	Returns the state of the radio button
Signal	**Description**
toggled()	Sent when the radio button has been activated or deactivated

Table 41.19 Important Methods and Signals of QRadioButton

41.5.10   QSlider and QDial

The QSlider class represents a slider in the GUI which is similar to a slide control, like the kind you might know from a mixing desk, for example. Basically, a slider is used to let the user select an integer value that must be within a certain range. The QDial class works similarly to QSlider, but it corresponds to a knob instead of a slider.

Method	Description
setMinimum(minimum) setMaximum(maximum)	Sets the lower or upper integer limit of the value range.
setValue(value)	Sets the current value to be displayed. The passed value must be an integer and must be within the specified limits.
value()	Returns the currently set value.
setOrientation(orientation)	Sets the orientation of the slider. Possible values are QtCore.Qt.Horizontal and QtCore.Qt.Vertical for horizontal and vertical orientation respectively.
Signal	**Description**
valueChanged()	Sent when the set value of the slider or the knob has been changed.

Table 41.20 Important Methods and Signals of QSlider and QDial

41.5.11   QTextEdit

The QTextEdit class represents a multiline input field in the GUI. The user can write any text in such an input field.

Method	Description
setPlainText(text)	Sets the text of the input field
toPlainText()	Returns the text of the input field
Signal	**Description**
textChanged()	Sent when the text of the input field has been changed

Table 41.21 Important Methods and Signals of QTextEdit

41.5.12 QWidget

The QWidget class is the base class of all widgets and implements much of the cross-widget functionality. In general, widgets can be divided into two varieties:

- The most common case is a child widget. A *child widget* is positioned in relation to its *parent widget* and can't extend beyond the edges of the parent widget.

- A widget without a parent widget is a *window*. Theoretically, any instance of a class derived from QWidget can serve as a window—for example, a button or a checkbox. Practically, however, this makes little sense, and only more suitable classes such as QDialog are used as windows.

Table 41.22 lists the most important event handlers that are called when various events occur. To set up an event handler, you can derive a class from QWidget directly or from another widget class and implement the corresponding method there.

Event	Description
paintEvent(event)	Called when the widget needs to be redrawn. The method is passed a QPaintEvent instance.
resizeEvent(event)	Called when the widget has been resized. A QResizeEvent instance is passed to the method.
mousePressEvent(event)	Called when the user clicks on the widget with the mouse. A QMouseEvent instance is passed to the method.
mouseMoveEvent(event)	Called when the user moves the mouse while holding down a mouse button. Using the setMouseTracking method, the widget can be set to call the method even if the user moves the mouse without holding down a button.
keyPressEvent(event)	Called when the widget has the input focus and the user presses a key. If the key is pressed for a long enough time, the keyPressEvent method is called multiple times. A QKeyEvent instance is passed.

Table 41.22 Events of a Widget

41

41.6 Drawing Functionality

In the previous sections, we introduced the Qt framework using a small sample program and then discussed the most important widgets. This section covers the topic of drawing in Qt. The topic of the final section on Qt will then be the model-view architecture.

When you create your own widget—that is, define a class that inherits from a widget or directly from QWidget—you have the option to draw any content into the widget yourself. This is especially useful when an application wants to display content in a widget for which there's no prebuilt class available in the Qt framework. This can be, for example, a diagram or a specific graphic.

In the following sections, we'll first look at the basics of drawing in Qt and then bring some simple shapes, such as a circle or a rectangle, onto the screen.

The sample classes presented in the following sections should be considered in the context of the following code:

```python
from PySide6 import QtWidgets, QtGui
import sys

class MyWidget(QtWidgets.QWidget):
    def __init__(self, parent=None):
        super().__init__(parent)

if __name__ == "__main__":
    app = QtWidgets.QApplication(sys.argv)
    widget = MyWidget()
    widget.show()
    sys.exit(app.exec())
```

We'll only reimplement the MyWidget class in each of the sections. To create an executable Qt program from these examples, the presented class must be inserted into the context shown here.

41.6.1 Tools

To be able to draw inside a widget, the paintEvent event handler must be implemented. This is a method called by the Qt framework whenever the widget needs to be partially or completely redrawn. This happens, for example, when the application window was partially hidden or minimized and was brought to the foreground by the user. The paintEvent method is passed an instance of the QPaintEvent class that contains, among other things, the area of the widget to be redrawn.[11]

Within the paintEvent method, a painter must be created that is used to perform the drawing operations. A *painter* is an instance of the QtGui.QPainter class. A basic widget that implements the paint event and creates a painter looks as follows:

```
class MyWidget(QtWidgets.QWidget):
    def __init__(self, parent=None):
        super().__init__(parent)
    def paintEvent(self, event):
        painter = QtGui.QPainter(self)
```

For drawing, there are two basic tools in Qt besides the painter: the pen and the brush.

Pen is an instance of the QtGui.QPen class. If you want to use a pen, that must be made known to the painter using the setPen method. Basically, a pen is used for drawing lines, such as for outlines of certain figures. For this purpose, a pen needs three main pieces of information: the line color, the line thickness, and the line style. You can create a pen as follows:

```
pen = QtGui.QPen(QtGui.QColor(255,0,0))
```

The constructor of the pen is passed an instance of the QColor class to specify the color of the pen—in this case, red.[12] Once a pen has been created, its line width and line style can be set using the setWidth and setStyle methods, respectively:

```
pen.setWidth(7)
pen.setStyle(QtCore.Qt.DashLine)
```

The integer passed to the setWidth method corresponds to the line thickness in pixels that a line drawn with this pen will later have on the screen. The setStyle method can be passed various constants, each of which defines a particular line style. A selection of these constants is shown in Table 41.23.

Constant	Description
QtCore.Qt.SolidLine	A solid line. This is the default setting and doesn't need to be set explicitly.
QtCore.Qt.DashLine	A dashed line.

Table 41.23 Line Styles for a Pen

---

11 In our simple examples, we will always redraw the entire graphic when calling the paintEvent method. However, the more complex and elaborate a graphic is, the more likely you should redraw only the area specified by the QPaintEvent instance.

12 An RGB color specification consists of three individual values between 0 and 255. The first value specifies the red, the second the green and the third the blue component of the color.

Constant	Description
QtCore.Qt.DotLine	A dotted line.
QtCore.Qt.DashDotLine	A line alternately dashed and dotted.

Table 41.23 Line Styles for a Pen (Cont.)

The second important tool for drawing is the *brush*, which is used to fill areas. Like a pen, a brush first specifies the fill color. Similar to the pen, you can create a brush as follows:

```
brush = QtGui.QBrush(QtGui.QColor(0,0,255))
```

The color value, in this case blue, is also passed to the constructor of the brush in the form of a QColor instance. Once the brush has been created, a style can also be set using the setStyle method. Here, for example, you can set hatching, color gradients, or textures—but we won't go into this in greater detail here.

In general, pens and brushes must be selected before they can be used. For this purpose, the setPen or setBrush methods of the painter are called with the respective QPen or QBrush instance as a parameter. A subsequent drawing operation is then performed with the selected tools. You can select only one brush and one pen at a time.

41.6.2   Coordinate System

Before we start drawing, we need to think about the coordinate system used in Qt. This is based on other GUI toolkits and is shown in Figure 41.41.

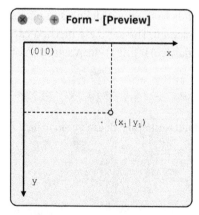

Figure 41.41 Qt Coordinate System

The origin of the coordinate system is in the upper-left-hand corner of the widget, and the Y-axis points downward, unlike the Cartesian coordinate system used in mathematics. The unit of the coordinate system is the pixel.

Each widget has its own local coordinate system whose origin is always relative to the widget's position in its upper-left-hand corner. This has the advantage that a drawing doesn't need to be adjusted when the widget is changed in its position on the screen or within another widget.

41.6.3 Simple Shapes

The Qt framework provides a set of abstract drawing operations that allow you to draw simple geometric shapes, such as a rectangle or an ellipse. Basically, drawing operations are implemented as methods of the QPainter class.

Let's start by drawing a rectangle. For this purpose, we use the drawRect method of a painter. Before we can draw a rectangle, we need to create and select a pen for the edge of the rectangle and a brush for the fill:

```python
class MyWidget(QtWidgets.QWidget):
    def __init__(self, parent=None):
        super().__init__(parent)
        self.pen = QtGui.QPen(QtGui.QColor(0,0,0))
        self.pen.setWidth(3)
        self.brush = QtGui.QBrush(QtGui.QColor(255,255,255))
    def paintEvent(self, event):
        painter = QtGui.QPainter(self)
        painter.setPen(self.pen)
        painter.setBrush(self.brush)
        painter.drawRect(10, 10, 130, 130)
```

In the constructor of the MyWidget class, a pen and brush are created, which will be used to draw the rectangle. In this case, it's a black pen with a thickness of three pixels and a white brush. In the paintEvent method, the two tools are selected after the painter has been created. After that, a rectangle is painted on the screen using drawRect. The parameters passed indicate, in order, the X coordinate of the upper-left-hand corner, the Y coordinate of the upper-left-hand corner, the width of the rectangle, and the height of the rectangle. All values are specified in pixels.

On the screen, we can see the rectangle—or, more precisely, a square (see Figure 41.42).

Similarly, other figures can be drawn whose shape is described by specifying an enclosing rectangle. For example, you only need to change the drawRect method name to draw a rectangle with round corners (drawRoundRect) or an ellipse (drawEllipse).

41

Figure 41.42 Square Drawn with drawRect

To resize one of these figures to fit the widget, the parameterless `rect` method of a widget class can be used, which returns the dimensions of the widget as a `QRect` instance.[13] This way it's possible, for example, to fill the entire widget with a shape.

In addition to these three basic shapes, a number of other methods exist for drawing special shapes. Table 41.24 provides an overview of the most important of these methods, which aren't discussed further in this chapter.

Method	Description
drawArc(x, y, w, h, a, alen)	Draws an open arc with the start angle a and the span angle alen. The other parameters specify the surrounding rectangle. *Open* in this case means that the two ends of the arc aren't connected by a line.
drawChord(x, y, w, h, a, alen)	Draws a closed arc. *Closed* means that the two ends of the arc are connected by a line.
drawConvexPolygon(point, ...)	Draws a convex polygon.* Either one QPolygon instance or any number of QPoint instances can be passed.
drawLine(x1, y1, x2, y2)	Draws a line from (x1, y1) to (x2, y2).
drawLines(line)	Draws a polyline. This can be passed as a list of QPoint instances.

Table 41.24 Methods of a Painter

---

13 The QRect class describes a rectangle and contains, among other things, the parameterless methods x, y, width and height, which can be used to access the coordinates of the upper left corner and the dimensions of the rectangle.

Method	Description

`drawPie(`
    `x, y, w, h, a, alen`
`)`
	Draws a section of an ellipse colloquially known as a *piece of a pie*.

`drawPolygon(point, ...)`	Draws any polygon. This method is more general than `drawConvexPolygon`.

* A *polygon* is an area bounded by a finite number of connected straight line segments. A surface is called *convex* if the connecting line between every two points in the surface passes completely within the surface. A nonconvex polygon is much more complex to represent than a convex one.

Table 41.24 Methods of a Painter (Cont.)

41.6.4   Images

In addition to drawing basic geometric shapes, the Qt framework allows images of various formats to be loaded from the hard drive and displayed using a painter via the QImage class.[14] The following sample program loads the *coffee.png* image and displays it using the drawImage method of the painter:

```
class MyWidget(QtWidgets.QWidget):
    def __init__(self, parent=None):
        super().__init__(parent)
        self.image = QtGui.QImage("coffee.png")
        self.target = QtCore.QRect(10, 10, 810, 610)
        self.source = QtCore.QRect(0, 0, self.image.width(),
                                   self.image.height())
    def paintEvent(self, event):
        painter = QtGui.QPainter(self)
        painter.drawImage(self.target, self.image, self.source)
```

In the constructor of the MyWidget widget class, an instance of the QImage class is first created by specifying the path of the image to be loaded. After that, two rectangles named self.source and self.target are created. The self.target rectangle specifies the rectangle in the widget where the image should be drawn. The self.source rectangle corresponds to the section of the image that is to be drawn in the process. In this case, the source rectangle encloses the entire image.

The widget created with this code looks like the one shown in Figure 41.43.

---

14   Qt can handle the file formats BMP, GIF, JPG and PNG, among others.

Figure 41.43 Image in a Widget

41.6.5 Text

Now that you can draw both geometric shapes and graphics in a widget, what's missing is drawing text—for example, to label diagrams.

To draw text in a widget, you can use the drawText method of a painter. In the following example, the text Hello World is centered in the widget:

```
class MyWidget(QtWidgets.QWidget):
    def __init__(self, parent=None):
        super().__init__(parent)
        self.font = QtGui.QFont("Helvetica", 16)
        self.pen = QtGui.QPen(QtGui.QColor(0,0,255))
    def paintEvent(self, event):
        painter = QtGui.QPainter(self)
        painter.setPen(self.pen)
        painter.setFont(self.font)
        painter.drawText(self.rect(), QtCore.Qt.AlignCenter, "Hello World")
```

In the constructor of the MyWidget class, an instance of the QFont class is first created. This class represents a font in a specific size. In addition, a pen is created that specifies the font color in which the text is to be written.

As before, we must first create a painter in the paintEvent method. After that, setFont and setPen are used to select the font and pen. Then the text is drawn by calling the drawText method. The method is passed a rectangle as the first parameter and an alignment specifier within that rectangle as the second parameter. The text to be written is passed as the third parameter. To position the text within the specified rectangle, several constants can be combined using the binary OR operator (|). The most important of these constants are listed and briefly explained in Table 41.25.

Constant	Alignment
QtCore.Qt.AlignLeft	Left
QtCore.Qt.AlignRight	Right
QtCore.Qt.AlignHCenter	Horizontally centered
QtCore.Qt.AlignTop	Top
QtCore.Qt.AlignBottom	Bottom
QtCore.Qt.AlignVCenter	Vertically centered
QtCore.Qt.AlignCenter	Horizontally and vertically centered

Table 41.25 Constants for Positioning Text

The widget created with this code is shown in Figure 41.44.

Figure 41.44 Text Drawn via drawText

There is a second, simplified variant of using drawText. In this context, there are also three parameters that are passed: the X and Y coordinates to which the text is to be written, and a string containing the text. In the sample program shown previously, say that the call of drawText is replaced by the following line of code:

```
painter.drawText(0, 16, "Hello World")
```

The text will then appear in the upper-left-hand corner of the window. Note that the coordinates passed in the second variant of drawText reference the lower-left-hand corner of the text, so the text can't be written at position 0/0. The value of 16 pixels passed as the Y coordinate corresponds to the selected font size, which is why the text appears directly below the top border of the widget.

41

41.6.6 Eye Candy

It was mentioned at the beginning that the Qt framework stands out from the mass of GUI toolkits in terms of its drawing functionality, among other things. Admittedly, the basics described so far for drawing in a Qt widget are important, but they are also not particularly impressive. Functions for drawing basic geometric shapes, images, and text can be found in this or similar ways in many other toolkits. For this reason, in this chapter we want to bring some aspects of Qt's drawing functionality to the forefront and present them as "eye candy." The aspects of drawing in Qt described here serve as a demonstration of the drawing functionality and are intended to provide keywords you can use to dig deeper into the Qt documentation later.

The executable source code for the examples shown can be found in the online resources for this book.

Gradients

Apart from a flat coat of paint, a brush can also fill an area with more complex textures. For example, the inside of a rectangle can be filled with a gradient, as shown in Figure 41.45.

Figure 41.45 Gradient with QLinearGradient

To create a brush that fills areas with a gradient, you must first create an instance of a *gradient* class. This type of class contains all the information needed to draw a gradient. There are three different gradient classes, each describing its own type of gradient (see Table 41.26).

Class	Description
QtGui.QConicalGradient	Describes a conical color gradient. The result resembles the top view of a cone.
QtGui.QLinearGradient	Describes a linear color gradient. Such a widget was used in the sample widget in Figure 41.45.
QtGui.QRadialGradient	Describes a circular color gradient.

Table 41.26 Gradient Classes

After creating an instance of a gradient class with the required information about the gradient, it can be passed as a parameter to the constructor of a brush. A brush created in this way can then be used to fill an area with a gradient.

Transparency

The Qt framework supports *alpha blending* for both a brush and a pen. This refers to drawing partially transparent structures. Figure 41.46 shows two overlapping semi-transparent circles.

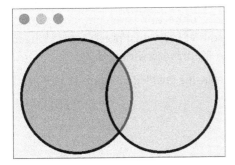

Figure 41.46 Alpha Blending

To use alpha blending, it's sufficient to pass a QColor instance with a transparency value when creating a brush or a pen. This transparency value is passed to the QColor constructor as the fourth parameter. Integer values between 0 (completely transparent) and 255 (opaque) are possible here.

These options for displaying transparencies can also be used in conjunction with the color gradients for interesting effects (see Figure 41.47).

Figure 41.47 Transparency Effect

41

This sample widget displays an image overlaid by a rectangle. The inside of this rectangle has been drawn with a gradient brush. The target color of this gradient is completely transparent.

Antialiasing

If you look again at the sample widget with the two overlapping, partially transparent circles, you'll notice that you can see the individual pixels that make up the outline of the circles. The circles don't look very appealing because of this. In many cases, these or similar such drawings should look "clean." For this purpose, there is a technique called *anti-aliasing*, which you may have heard about in connection with computer games. Anti-aliasing smoothes the edges of a drawing so that individual pixels are no longer visible. The Qt framework provides basic support for drawing with antialiasing.

You can see the transparency example with antialiasing enabled in Figure 41.48.

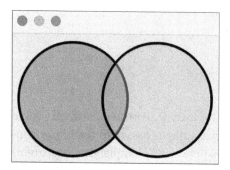

Figure 41.48 Antialiasing

To activate antialiasing in a painter, you can use the following code line:

```
painter.setRenderHints(QtGui.QPainter.Antialiasing)
```

Here, `painter` is a `QPainter` instance.

Transformations

Another useful feature provided by Qt is referred to as *transformations*, which can be applied to any shape to be drawn using transformation matrices. A transformation matrix is represented by the `QMatrix` class.

In the example in Figure 41.49, first a figure was created. As this is not a prefabricated shape, the figure must be assembled into a single unit with the help of a so-called painter path, an instance of the `QPainterPath` class. The shape of this example consists of two lines and a Bezier curve.[15]

---

15   A Bézier curve is a curve described by a mathematical function with—in the case of a cubic Bézier curve—four parameters. Bézier curves can also be drawn in many graphics programs.

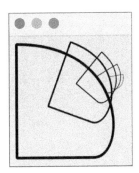

Figure 41.49 Matrix Transformations

Once both the transformation as a `QTransform` instance and the painter path have been created, the transformation can be applied to the painter and the resulting transformed painter path can finally be drawn. In the example, the transformation was changed again and again in five iteration steps and the resulting figure was drawn in each case.

41.7   Model-View Architecture

With version 4, the *model-view architecture* was introduced into the Qt framework. The basic idea of this type of programming is to separate shape from content. In terms of Qt, this means that classes containing data should be separated from classes displaying that data. Thus, there is a *model class*, which provides a known interface for the stored data, and a *view class*, which accesses the data via the model class and displays it in the GUI. It's not assumed that the data is actually stored in the model class, only that the model class provides methods to access the data. The data itself can be located in a database or file.

Splitting the program logic into model and view classes has the advantage of making the program simpler and better structured overall. In addition, changes in the data representation don't result in the need to adjust the display class. Conversely, the model class doesn't care in what shape the data it provides gets displayed on the screen.

The relationship between the model and view classes is illustrated in Figure 41.50.

The Qt framework provides some classes that help the programmer to create a model-view architecture. Among them are base classes for both model and view classes. In the following sections, we'll describe a rudimentary address book application as an example of a model-view architecture.

41

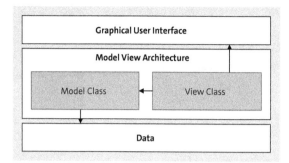

Figure 41.50 Model-View Architecture

41.7.1   Sample Project: An Address Book

In this section, we'll give you a hands-on introduction to programming a model-view architecture using a simple sample program. For this purpose, we'll use a graphical address book that reads several address records from a text file at startup and then displays them graphically on the screen. Internally, the datasets are read and processed by a model class. A view class then takes care of displaying the data.

In the first step, we focus on reading and displaying the data. After that, other aspects of model-view programming in Qt will be introduced via extensions to the sample program. The preliminary application developed in this section is shown in Figure 41.51.

Figure 41.51 Address Book

The address data is to be read from a file of the following format:

```
Donald Duck
don@ld.com
1313 Webfoot Street
```

Duckburg
01234/313

Scrooge McDuck
scrooge.mcduck@aol.com
The Money Bin, Killmotor Hill
Duckburg
0190/123456
[...]

The address data is thus stored line by line in a file. Two entries in the address book are separated by a blank line in the source file. Apart from the fact that the name of the person to whom the entry belongs is in the first line of the entry, there are no other requirements for formatting the data.[16]

The address book represents a sample implementation for a model-view architecture:

- The *model class* has the task of reading the source file with the address data and providing an interface through which this data can be accessed.

- The *view class* accesses the data stored in the model class and then presents it in a suitable form on the screen. Because the address book is basically a list of address entries, we can use the QListView base class of the Qt framework here, which provides the basic functionality for displaying model data with a list structure. If the structure of the data were different, the QTreeView or QTableView base class could be used, which visualizes a tree-like or tabular structure of the data, respectively.

Figure 41.52 represents the program structure graphically.

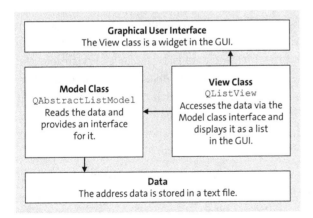

Figure 41.52 Model-View Architecture of the Sample Program

41

---

16 In fact, the file format is rather unsuitable for the presented purpose, because, for example, there is no efficient way for the program that reads the file to assign the individual partial information of the entry, for example, to filter out the e-mail address. However, the file format is used here because of its simplicity.

The source code of the model class is located in the *model.py* program file and looks as follows:

```python
from PySide6 import QtCore
class Model(QtCore.QAbstractListModel):
    def __init__(self, filename, parent=None):
        super().__init__(parent)
        self.dataset = []
        # Load record
        with open(filename) as f:
            lst = []
            for line in f:
                if not line.strip():
                    self.dataset.append(lst)
                    lst = []
                else:
                    lst.append(line.strip())
            if lst:
                self.dataset.append(lst)
    def rowCount(self, parent=QtCore.QModelIndex()):
        return len(self.dataset)
    def data(self, index, role=QtCore.Qt.DisplayRole):
        return self.dataset[index.row()]
```

The Model class is defined, which inherits from the QtCore.QAbstractListModel base class. This base class implements the basic functionality of a model class for a record with a list structure.

In the constructor of the Model class, the address data is loaded from a text file of the format described previously. For this purpose, the filename of this file is passed to the constructor. Because the file format in which the data is available is very simple, the import process is also comparatively simple and doesn't need to be explained in further detail. It's important, however, that the individual entries of the address book get stored internally within the class in a list that's referenced by the self.dataset attribute. Each entry of this list is in turn a list of strings corresponding to the lines of the entry.

At the end of the class definition, two more methods are defined that must be implemented by each model class. These methods form the interface through which the view class can later access the data stored in the model class.

The rowCount method must return the number of elements as an integer that the record contains. The parent parameter passed in the process is irrelevant at this point.

The data method is called by the view class to access a specific element of the dataset. The index parameter determines that element. However, index is not an integer, but a

QModelIndex instance. The numeric index can be accessed via the row method of this instance.

The view class that matches the model class is contained in the *view.py* program file and looks as follows:

```
class View(QtWidgets.QListView):
    def __init__(self, model, parent=None):
        super().__init__(parent)
        self.delegate = ViewDelegate()
        self.setItemDelegate(self.delegate)
        self.setModel(model)
        self.setVerticalScrollMode(QtWidgets.QListView.ScrollPerPixel)
```

The View class is derived from the QListView base class. This base class provides the functionality needed to graphically display a list-like data set. Alternatively, the QTreeView or QTableView class could have served as a base class if a tree-like or tabular structure would have been better for displaying the data.

The constructor of the View class is passed an instance of the Model class just defined, the contents of which are to be displayed graphically. However, to actually display the data, another class is needed, the so-called *delegate*. A delegate, which we'll describe after the view class, is assigned to the view class via the setItemDelegate method. The delegate class contains the drawing routines for an element of the data record.

Finally, the model is imported using setModel and the scroll mode is set to *pixel by pixel*, which is rather a cosmetic matter. In the normal state, the QListView widget always moves the content by whole entries when scrolling, which doesn't look nice with large entries.

What we still need to describe is the delegate class that carries out the drawing of the entries. For this purpose, it can access the dataset via the interface of the model class. In the image that illustrated the model-view architecture of the sample program at the beginning, the delegate class was omitted for simplicity reasons. We want to make up for this here and show in Figure 41.53 how the delegate class integrates into the model-view architecture.

The delegate class positions itself as a helper class between the view and model classes. The view class calls the paint method of the delegate class for each entry in the dataset and assembles the ListView widget from the individual drawings, which is displayed in the GUI. As with the view and model classes, there is a base class in the Qt framework from which a self-defined delegate class must be derived.

To adequately draw an entry, the delegate class can access the data record through the interface provided by the model class. Of course, the view class itself can also read data from the data record in this way.

41

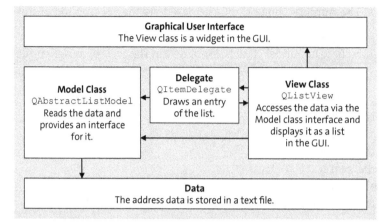

Figure 41.53 Model-View Architecture of the Sample Program

In the following sections, the sample program will be extended by the still missing delegate class. This class is defined in the same program file as the view class. Because the delegate class is comparatively extensive, we'll describe it method by method:

```python
from PySide6 import QtWidgets, QtGui, QtCore
class ViewDelegate(QtWidgets.QItemDelegate):
    def __init__(self, parent=None):
        super().__init__(parent)
        self.frame_pen = QtGui.QPen(QtGui.QColor(0,0,0))
        self.title_text_pen = QtGui.QPen(QtGui.QColor(255,255,255))
        self.title_color = QtGui.QBrush(QtGui.QColor(120,120,120))
        self.text_pen = QtGui.QPen(QtGui.QColor(0,0,0))
        self.title_font = QtGui.QFont("Helvetica", 10, QtGui.QFont.Bold)
        self.text_font = QtGui.QFont("Helvetica", 10)
        self.row_height = 15
        self.title_height = 20
        self.outer_padding = 4
        self.inner_padding = 2
        self.text_padding = 4
```

In the constructor of the ViewDelegate class, the attributes that are important for drawing an address entry are initialized. These include, on the one hand, the drawing tools with which the address entry is to be drawn and, on the other hand, constants that define reference values for drawing an entry. To illustrate which attribute is intended for what, let's visualize once again what an entry will look like in the program (see Figure 41.54).

Figure 41.54 Address Book Entry

Table 41.27 lists all attributes of the ViewDelegate class, with short descriptions of their meanings.

Attribute	Description
frame_pen	The pen used to draw the thin black frame around the entry
title_text_pen	The pen used to write the title
title_color	The brush used to draw the gray rectangle under the title
title_font	The font in which the title is written
text_pen	The pen used to write the address data
text_font	The font in which the address data is written
row_height	The height of an address data line in pixels
title_height	The height of the title in pixels
outer_padding	The distance of an entry from the dialog border and from other entries in pixels
inner_padding	The distance between the gray rectangle under the title and the border of the entry in pixels
text_padding	The distance of the text from the border of the entry on the left-hand side in pixels

Table 41.27 Attributes of the ViewDelegate Class

That's all for the constructor. Let's now turn to the sizeHint method, which must be implemented by every delegate class:

```python
def sizeHint(self, option, index):
    num = len(index.data())
    return QtCore.QSize(170, self.row_height*num + self.title_height)
```

The method is called by the view class to obtain the height and width of a single item. Two parameters are passed to it: option and index.

41

For the `option` parameter, an instance of the `QStyleOptionViewItem` class is passed, which can contain various statements on what style the item should be drawn in. Because these formatting statements may also affect the dimensions of an entry, they are also passed to the `sizeHint` function. In our sample program, the `option` parameter isn't relevant and won't be explained further.

The second parameter, `index`, specifies the element whose dimensions are to be returned. For `index`, an instance of the `QModelIndex` class is passed. Most important is the data method of the `QModelIndex` instance, which can be used to access the data of the entry.

The implementation of the `sizeHint` method calculates the width and height of an entry and returns the values as a `QSize` instance. The width is a constant 170 pixels.[17]

The following `paint` method must be implemented by a delegate class and is called whenever a single entry needs to be redrawn. Only one entry is drawn per paint call:

```python
def paint(self, painter, option, index):
    frame = option.rect.adjusted(self.outer_padding, self.outer_padding,
                        -self.outer_padding, -self.outer_padding)
    frame_title = frame.adjusted(self.inner_padding, self.inner_padding,
                        -self.inner_padding+1, 0)
    frame_title.setHeight(self.title_height)
    frame_title_text = frame_title.adjusted(self.text_padding, 0,
                                self.text_padding, 0)
    dataset = index.data()
    painter.save()
    painter.setPen(self.frame_pen)
    painter.drawRect(frame)
    painter.fillRect(frame_title, self.title_color)
    # Write title
    painter.setPen(self.title_text_pen)
    painter.setFont(self.title_font)
    painter.drawText(
        frame_title_text, QtCore.Qt.AlignLeft | QtCore.Qt.AlignVCenter,
        dataset[0]
    )
    # Write address
    painter.setPen(self.text_pen)
    painter.setFont(self.text_font)
    for i, entry in enumerate(dataset[1:]):
        painter.drawText(
            frame_title.x() + self.text_padding,
```

---

17 This is a simplification of the example program. Alternatively, the width of the entry can be calculated using the longest line. To do this, use the `width` method of a `QFontMetrics` instance.

```
            frame_title.bottom() + (i+1)*self.row_height,
            entry
        )
    painter.restore()
```

The `paint` method is passed the three `painter`, `option`, and `index` parameters. For the `painter` parameter, a `QPainter` instance is passed that is to be used for drawing. The two `option` and `index` parameters have the same meaning as in the `sizeHint` method.

In the `paint` method, some rectangles are calculated first, which are used to draw the entry afterward. Note that `option.rect` describes the drawing area for the entry in terms of a `QRect` instance. All drawing operations should therefore be aligned with this rectangle. The created local references have the meanings listed in Table 41.28.

Attribute	Description
frame	The rectangle around which the thin black frame is drawn
frame_title	The rectangle of the title line highlighted in gray
frame_title_text	The rectangle in which the text in the title bar will be written

Table 41.28 Local References in the Paint Method

Once the local references have been created, the state of the painter is saved using `save` so that it can be restored at the end of the method using `restore`. A painter passed as a parameter should always be returned to its initial state after the drawing operations have been performed; otherwise, unwanted side effects could occur in higher-level functions.

Then, using the painter's `drawRect` and `fillRect` methods, the frame around the entry and the grayed-out title bar are drawn. Now only the labels are missing. For this purpose, we first select the appropriate font and the required pen using `setFont` and `setPen`. The title line of the entry is written in the `frame_title_text` rectangle, left-aligned and vertically centered with the bold `title_font` font and a white pen.

The `drawText` method of the painter can be called in several variants. For example, it's possible (as with the title line) to pass a rectangle and a alignment specifier within that rectangle, or (as with the entry address lines) to specify directly the coordinates to which the text is to be written.

Last but not least, let's take a look at the main program, which is located in the *program.py* program file:

```
from PySide6 import QtWidgets
import sys
import model
import view
```

41

```
if __name__ == "__main__":
    m = model.Model("addressbook.txt")
    app = QtWidgets.QApplication(sys.argv)
    list = view.View(m)
    list.resize(200, 500)
    list.show()
    sys.exit(app.exec())
```

After the local `model` and `view` modules have been imported, an instance of the `Model` class is created, representing the data record from the *addressbook.txt* file.

The `View` class is the only widget in the application that also serves as a window. Before displaying the widget using `show`, we set its size to a reasonable value (200 pixels wide and 500 pixels high) by calling the `resize` method.

When the main program is executed, you can see that the `QListView` base class of the view class actually takes care of subtleties such as scrolling entries or resizing them when they are resized (see Figure 41.55).

Figure 41.55 Scrolling in the Address Book

41.7.2   Selecting Entries

After the address data has been displayed as a list, the question arises in which form user interactions can be implemented. In this section, the sample program will be extended to allow the user to select an entry from the address book. In the following section, we'll then describe how you can edit entries.

The basic structure of the sample program doesn't have to be changed much for this. Strictly speaking, the selection was already possible in the last sample program, but we've only drawn all entries of the list alike so far. So what's still missing is the graphical highlighting of the selected entry.

The address book with a selected entry is shown in Figure 41.56.

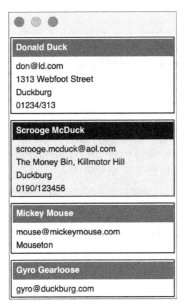

Figure 41.56 Selected Entry in the Address Book

The selected entry differs from the other entries in the color of the title bar and its background. Instead of gray, these areas are drawn in blue for selected entries. For this purpose, we first create a new brush in the constructor of the delegate class with the required shades of blue as the color:

```
def __init__(self, parent=None):
    super().__init__(parent)
    [...]
    self.title_color_selected = QtGui.QBrush(QtGui.QColor(0,0,120))
    self.background_color_selected = QtGui.QBrush(QtGui.QColor(230,230,255))
    [...]
```

Now, only when drawing an entry, in the `paint` method, it must be distinguished whether the entry to be drawn is the currently selected one or not. This can be determined by the `state` attribute of the `QStyleOptionViewItem` instance that's passed when the `paint` method is called for the `option` parameter.

So we change the drawing of the gray title rectangle to the following code:

```
if option.state & QtWidgets.QStyle.State_Selected:
    painter.fillRect(frame, self.background_color_selected)
    painter.fillRect(frame_title, self.title_color_selected)
else:
    painter.fillRect(frame_title, self.title_color)
```

41

This code must be placed before drawing the thin black frame:

```
painter.setPen(self.frame_pen)
painter.drawRect(frame)
```

Those were the steps necessary to allow the user to select an entry of the address book.

41.7.3   Editing Entries

Now that we've looked at how you can display address data in a `QListView` widget and extended the sample program to allow an entry to be selected by the user, the obvious question is whether we can also allow the user to edit a data record. While it isn't as simple as allowing selection in the previous section, the model-view architecture of Qt also provides a convenient interface for editing an entry.

Later in the program, editing an entry will look as shown in Figure 41.57.

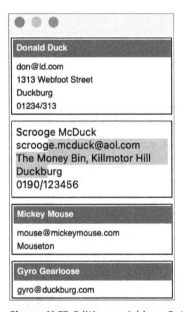

Figure 41.57 Editing an Address Entry

To enable the editing of entries, the individual entries of the data record must first be explicitly marked as editable by the model class. To do this, the model class must implement the `flags` method:

```
def flags(self, index):
    return (QtCore.Qt.ItemIsSelectable | QtCore.Qt.ItemIsEditable
                                       | QtCore.Qt.ItemIsEnabled)
```

This method is called whenever the QListView widget wants to get more detailed information about the entry specified by the QModelIndex instance, index. In our case, regardless of the index of the entry, the ItemIsSelectable, ItemIsEditable, and ItemIsEnabled flags are returned, representing selectable, editable, and enabled entries. By default—that is, if the flags method isn't implemented—each item receives the ItemIsSelectable and ItemIsEnabled flags.

In addition to the flags method, the model class is supposed to implement the setData method, which has the task of transferring the entries changed by the user to the data record:

```
def setData(self, index, value, role=QtCore.Qt.EditRole):
    self.dataset[index.row()] = value
    self.layoutChanged.emit()
    return True
```

The index of the changed entry and the changed content of this entry are passed to the method. The additional role parameter should not interest us further at this point. In the body of the method, the old entry of the self.dataset stored in the model class is replaced by the modified one. After that, the layoutChanged signal is sent, which causes the view class to completely rebuild the display. This is useful because the user's changes may have changed the number of lines and thus the height of the respective entry.

These are all the changes that must be made to the model class to allow the editing of an entry. However, the delegate class must also implement some additional methods. These are createEditor, setEditorData, updateEditorGeometry, setModelData, and eventFilter, which are described ahead.

The createEditor method is called when the user double-clicks on an entry to edit it. The createEditor method must return a widget that will be displayed instead of the corresponding edit entry:

```
def createEditor(self, parent, option, index):
    return QtWidgets.QTextEdit(parent)
```

The method is passed the already known option and index parameters, which specify the entry to be edited. In addition, the widget to be entered as the parent widget of the editor widget is passed for parent. In this case, we create a QTextEdit widget where the user should edit the entry.

The setEditorData method is called by the QListView widget to fill the widget created by createEditor with content:

```
def setEditorData(self, editor, index):
    editor.setPlainText("\n".join(index.data()))
```

41

To do this, the method is passed the editor widget in the form of the editor parameter and the familiar index parameter, which specifies the entry to be edited. In the method body, the data of the entry to be edited is read and joined to a single string using join. This string is then written to the QTextEdit widget by calling the setPlainText method.

The updateEditorGeometry method is called by the QListView widget to let it set the size of the editor widget:

```python
def updateEditorGeometry(self, editor, option, index):
    frame = option.rect.adjusted(self.outer_padding, self.outer_padding,
                                 -self.outer_padding, -self.outer_padding)
    editor.setGeometry(frame)
```

The method is passed the known option and index parameters plus the instance of the editor widget. In this case, we use setGeometry to give the editor widget the same size the corresponding entry would have had if it had been drawn normally.

The setModelData method is called when editing has been done by the user to read the changed data from the editor widget and pass it to the model class:

```python
def setModelData(self, editor, model, index):
    model.setData(index, editor.toPlainText().split("\n"))
```

The method is passed both the editor widget and the model class in the form of the editor and model parameters. In addition, a QModelIndex instance is passed that specifies the edited entry. In the method, the text of the QTextEdit widget is read and divided into individual lines. After that, the setData method of the model class created earlier is called.

Chapter 42

Python as a Server-Side Programming Language on the Web: An Introduction to Django

In today's World Wide Web, technology is drastically different from its beginnings. The purely informative network of static HTML pages has developed into an interactive exchange platform based on which practically anything is possible. You can shop on the internet, book your next vacation, follow the news, maintain your social contacts in chats or on community sites, or help design knowledgebases like Wikipedia.

All these new possibilities the internet owes essentially to the programs that generate web pages dynamically with the required data. For a long time, web programming was mainly a domain for the PHP scripting language,[1] which has prevailed in the past due to a lack of alternatives. Scripting languages in general are particularly suitable for programming web applications because the development times are often considerably shorter due to the lower technical complexity compared to low-level programming languages, so that new functions can be implemented quickly and less code is required for the same functionality. In addition, especially for programs on the web, execution speed is often less important as most of the time is usually spent while transferring data through the relatively slow connection between the server and the client.

Nowadays, PHP is no longer the only server-side programming language that meets these criteria. Alongside PHP, languages such as Perl, Java, Ruby, and, in particular, Python have joined the ranks.

To meet the special requirements that arise in the development of dynamic websites, so-called web frameworks are used. The purpose of these frameworks is to relieve the programmer of the repetitive tasks that arise when creating dynamic web pages.

These tasks include the following:

- Communicating with the web server
- Generating HTML output via template systems
- Accessing databases

---

1 PHP, a recursive abbreviation of PHP: Hypertext Preprocessor, is a scripting language designed for embedding in HTML pages. The syntax of PHP is based on the C programming language. Almost every hosting service today offers support for PHP scripts.

42

Ideally, the developer no longer needs to worry about the specifics of the database and the server, but can focus on implementing the functions of his application.

There are many web frameworks for Python available, all of which have their advantages and disadvantages. We'll cover the Django framework in this book, which stands out for its feature set, elegance, and widespread use. Django is a mature framework that was first released in 2005. It's available free of charge under the BSD license and is especially designed for the development of complex database-driven applications.

Due to the large scope of Django, we'll only be able to provide basic knowledge about it in this chapter. But there's a lot of useful documentation about Django available on the internet. You're especially encouraged to visit the project website, *http://django-project.com/*, which provides detailed descriptions.

To familiarize you with the basics of Django, we'll now implement a small web application that can manage news articles. Moreover, it will be possible for visitors to the site to make comments on individual articles.

42.1   Concepts and Features of Django

Django is based on the model-view concept, which was introduced in Chapter 41, Section 41.6 about Qt. A typical Django application defines a data model, which is automatically managed by Django in a database. The output for end users is handled by so-called views, which can access the data model.

Currently, Django supports the MySQL, MariaDB, Oracle, SQLite3,[2] and PostgreSQL databases. The web developer can entirely do without any technical details such as the SQL query language when dealing with the data models. Their job is just to tell Django which database it has to use. The database layout is defined via Python code, while Django manages the communication with the database.

As a special treat for the web developer, Django automatically creates an administration interface based on the model definition to manage the model's data.

Django distinguishes between projects and applications. A *project* is a website as a whole, which may include, for example, a news page, a forum, and a guestbook. *Applications* (also referred to as *apps*) are responsible for realizing the functions of a project. So the example project would have three applications: a news application, a forum application, and an application for the guestbook.

Django is based on the principle of *loose couplings* for all parts of the web application. This means that as much as possible can be developed independently, so that the individual parts can be used on other sites. In particular, it should be possible to use applications in different projects easily without having to significantly adapt the code.

---

2 SQLite3 is included as a module in Python's standard library and can be used immediately without any special configuration.

Another principle of Django is *don't repeat yourself* (or DRY). In practice, the implementation of this principle ensures, for example, that Django uses the definition of data objects on the one hand to manage the database, and on the other hand to provide an administration interface.

42.2   Installing Django

In this section, we'll describe the installation of the `django` module, which is needed to develop Django applications. To learn how to make ready-made applications available to the public on a web server, see the Django documentation at *http://www.django-project.com* or contact your hosting service.

Django is in active development and is constantly being improved and extended. At the time of this book's printing, version 4.0 of Django is included in the Anaconda distribution, which we refer to in the context of this chapter.

The Anaconda Python distribution provides a package for Django that you can install using conda, as described in Chapter 38, Section 38.4.2:[3]

```
$ conda install django
```

To install a concrete version of Django, you can specify it as follows:[4]

```
$ conda install django=4.0.6
```

Installation via pip or, if you are on Linux, via the package manager of your distribution is also possible. In any case, you should pay attention to which version of Django is installed because due to intensive further development, it can't be guaranteed that the examples will still work with later Django versions.

Once you've successfully completed the installation, you should be able to import the `django` module into Python:

```
>>> import django
>>> django.get_version()
'4.0.6'
```

We'll use the `django-admin` program provided by Django in this tutorial. For this reason, you should also check that the program is found by your operating system. To do that, you must run the following command in a console:

---

3 It is possible that the official package repository for conda does not yet contain the latest version. In such a case you can resort to pip or *conda-forge*, see Chapter 38, Section 38.4.2.

4 At the time of writing this book, this was the most recent Django version. You should check the website to see which version is up-to-date when you install Django.

42

```
$ django-admin version
4.0.6
```

The program should then print the Django version number and exit. Now we can venture into our first Django project.

42.3   Creating a New Django Project

Before we can start working with Django, we need to create a project folder that contains the configuration of our project. Django provides the django-admin tool for this purpose. The following command in the command line creates the project structure:

```
$ django-admin startproject news_site
```

The news_site string is the desired name of the new project. After the successful execution of django-admin, a new folder structure with the project files exists on the hard drive (see Figure 42.1).

Figure 42.1 Folder Structure of a Fresh Django Project

As you can see, two nested directories with the name of the project, **news_site**, have been created. The inner directory contains the actual project, while the outer directory is used for administration.

Table 42.1 explains the meanings of the individual files.

File Name	Purpose
news_site/__init__.py	The file is empty by default and is only necessary so that the project can be imported as a Python module.
	Every Django project must be a valid Python module.
news_site/settings.py	This file stores all settings for our project. This includes in particular the configuration of the database.

Table 42.1 Meaning of the Files in a Django Project

File Name	Purpose
news_site/urls.py	This is where you define which addresses should be used to access the pages of our project.
news_site/wsgi.py *news_site/asgi.py*	These files are needed to use the project with a WSGI- or ASGI-compatible web server.[*]
manage.py	The *manage.py* program is used to manage a project. For example, it enables you to update the database or run the project for debugging.

[*] Web Server Gateway Interface (WSGI) and Asynchronous Server Gateway Interface (ASGI) are specifications that standardize the communication of Python programs with a web server.

Table 42.1 Meaning of the Files in a Django Project (Cont.)

Now we can start working on the project.

42.3.1   The Development Web Server

The fresh project structure can already be tested in this state. To facilitate Django application development, the framework provides a simple web server. This server constantly monitors the changes you make to your application code and automatically reloads the changed parts of the program without the need to restart it.

You can start the development web server from the manage.py management program by passing the runserver parameter. Before you execute the command, you must go to the **news_site** project directory. On Windows, the python command is omitted at the beginning of the following example, provided you have associated *.py* files with Python:[5]

```
$ cd news_site
$ python manage.py runserver
Watching for file changes with StatReloader
Performing system checks...

System check identified no issues (0 silenced).
[...]
Starting development server at http://127.0.0.1:8000/
Quit the server with CONTROL-C.
```

As you can see from the output, the development server can be reached at the address *http://127.0.0.1:8000/*. In the browser, the page looks as shown in Figure 42.2.

42

---

5 You can ignore the warning concerning the unapplied migrations at this point.

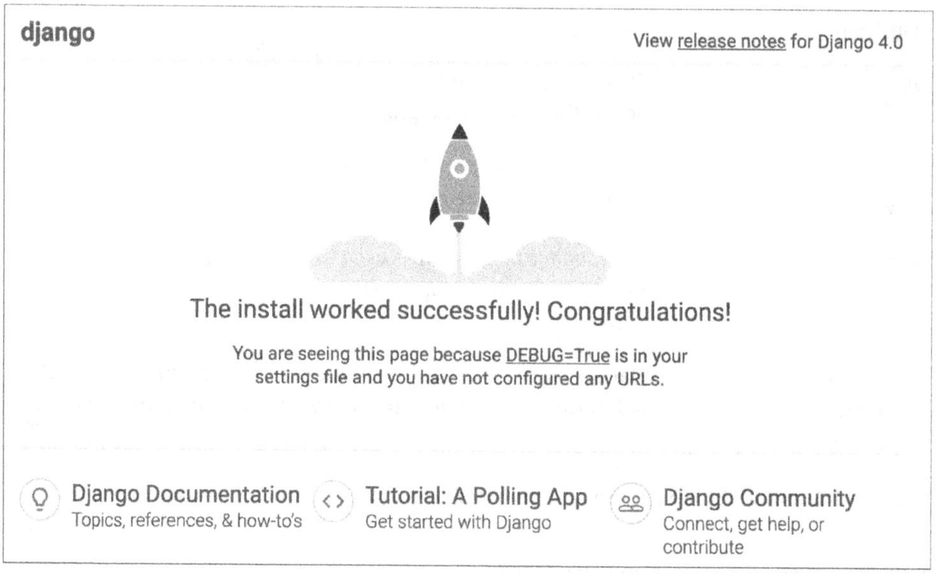

Figure 42.2 Output of the Empty Project in the Browser

> **Note**
>
> Django's development web server is intended for web application development only and should never be used for a public site. You should use mature web servers, such as Apache, for production use of your web applications. For instructions on configuring Apache with Django, see the Django documentation.

42.3.2 Configuring the Project

Before we can use the project in a way that makes sense, it must first be configured. To do that, we open the *settings.py* file in a text editor. That's a simple Python module that configures Django via global variables. But it also contains very specific settings we aren't interested in here.

In the first step, we'll focus on the settings that affect Django's database. In the file, you'll find a block of the following type:

```
DATABASES = {
    'default': {
        'ENGINE': 'django.db.backends.sqlite3',
        'NAME': BASE_DIR / 'db.sqlite3',
    }
}
```

The DATABASES dictionary defines the databases to be used with the Django project. In this context, another dictionary with the database configuration is assigned to the name of each database. In a project that uses only one database, there's only the mandatory `'default'` entry.

The value for the `ENGINE` key specifies the database driver used. Django provides the drivers listed in Table 42.2.[6]

Database driver	Database
django.db.backends.sqlite3	SQLite3
django.db.backends.mysql	MariaDB (from version 10.2) and MySQL (from version 5.7); requires, for example, `mysqlclient`
django.db.backends.postgresql	PostgreSQL (from version 9.5); requires `psycopg2`
django.db.backends.oracle	Oracle Database Server (from version 19c); requires `cx_Oracle`

Table 42.2 Database Drivers Provided by Django. It Might Be Necessary to Add Third-Party Modules.

The other specifications define the parameters of the database. For SQLite3 in the example, the `NAME` parameter specifies the path to the database file. Other parameters are `HOST`, `PORT`, `USER`, and `PASSWORD`, which can be used to specify access to a database server—for example, with MySQL or PostgreSQL.

Because SQLite comes with Python by default and therefore no additional modules need to be installed when using SQLite, our sample project will use a SQLite database. For this purpose, we'll leave the two settings relevant for SQLite—`ENGINE` and `NAME`—as in the default configuration, which creates the database file in the same directory as *manage.py*.

You should also check if the language of Django is set to US English. This can be done via the `LANGUAGE_CODE` variable:

```
LANGUAGE_CODE = 'en-us'
```

For reasons of simplicity, we'll also disable Django's support for time zones by adjusting the `USE_TZ` variable:

```
USE_TZ = False
```

With this done, the basic settings are in place and we can start the development of our Django application.

42

---

6 In addition to these included drivers, there are other drivers provided by other vendors.
   For more information on this, please visit *https://docs.djangoproject.com/en/4.0/ref/databases/#third-party-notes*.

42.4   Creating an Application

A project represents just the framework for a website. The actual functionality is implemented by the applications that are integrated into the project. Just as for projects, Django provides a tool for creating the basic framework of an application.

To create a news application, we'll use a console to go to the project directory where the *manage.py* file is located and execute the following command (the `python` at the beginning can be omitted on Windows):

```
$ python manage.py startapp news
```

The program creates a new folder named *news* in the project directory, which contains another directory and several files (see Figure 42.3). Here, `news` is the name of the new application.

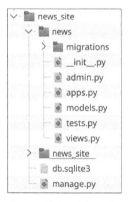

Figure 42.3 Folder of a New Django Application

For us, the first two files of interest are *models.py* and *views.py*, which are used to implement Django's underlying model-view concept (see Figure 42.4).

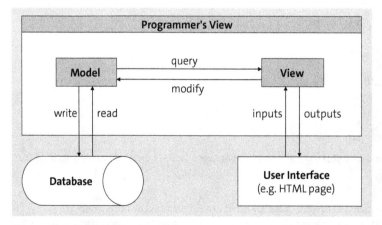

Figure 42.4 Model-View Concept

The so-called *model* defines the structure of the data in the database. Models also provide a convenient interface for accessing the stored data. How the actual communication with the database takes place isn't relevant to the programmer. They can use the model's interfaces when handling the data without having to bother about technical details such as SQL statements.[7] The database itself remains "hidden" from them because they "see" it only indirectly through the model. In particular, all required tables are automatically created in the database based on the model definition.

The so-called *view* takes care of the preparation of the data for the user. It can access the models and read and modify their data. The view doesn't care what the user interface looks like. The task of the views is only to determine the data requested by the user, to process them and then to pass them to a so-called *template*, which is responsible for the actual display. We're going to deal with templates later.

42.4.1   Importing the Application into the Project

We still need to let Django know that our newly created application should be imported into the news_site project. To do this, we add the news application to the INSTALLED_APPS tuple in *settings.py*:

```
INSTALLED_APPS = [
    'django.contrib.admin',
    'django.contrib.auth',
    'django.contrib.contenttypes',
    'django.contrib.sessions',
    'django.contrib.messages',
    'django.contrib.staticfiles',
    'news',
]
```

The INSTALLED_APPS list contains the import names of all applications used by the project. You're probably wondering why our empty project already contains some applications. Django imports these applications by default because they're actually needed in every project.

42.4.2   Defining a Model

Next, we define a data model for the news application. The data model contains a Python class for each type of data record in the application. These classes must be derived from the models.Model base class in the django.db package and define the properties of the datasets and their links to each other.

---

7 Of course, you can also send your own SQL commands to the database in case Django's model interface isn't sufficient for a specific case. In practice, however, you'll only need to make use of this feature in exceptional cases.

The sample model for the news application defines one model class for articles and one for visitor comments. We write the definition in the *models.py* file, which then contains the following:

```python
from django.db import models

class Article(models.Model):
    title = models.CharField(max_length=100)
    timestamp = models.DateTimeField()
    text = models.TextField('Article text')

class Comment(models.Model):
    article = models.ForeignKey(Article, on_delete=models.CASCADE)
    author = models.CharField(max_length=70)
    text = models.TextField('Comment text')
```

The attributes of the records are specified via class members, where each attribute must be an instance of a special field type[8] of Django. The properties of the attributes are specified via the parameters of the field type constructors.

The Article class has a CharField named title that has a maximum length of 100 characters. The CharField field type is used to store texts of limited length. The timestamp attribute is intended to specify the publication time of each article and uses the DateTimeField field type intended for time specifications. Finally, the attribute named text stores the actual article text. The TextField field type used can store texts of any length.

The two author and text attributes of the Comment class store the name of the visitor who wrote the comment and the comment text itself.

The article attribute is used to establish a relationship between the articles and comments.

42.4.3   Relationships between Models

There can be several comments for one article and each comment refers to one article. The ForeignKey field type specifies a *one-to-many relation*, which means that there is exactly one article for a comment.

The on_delete parameter to be specified when instantiating ForeignKey specifies the behavior of the model in case the foreign key is deleted from the database. The models.CASCADE behavior selected in the example makes sure that when an article is deleted, the associated comments will also be deleted.

---

8 Django provides field types for many use cases. Here, we'll focus on those field types that are relevant for the sample project.

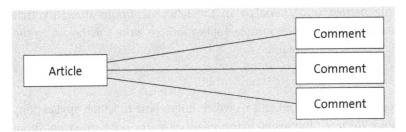

Figure 42.5 One-to-Many Relation for Article and Comment

In addition to one-to-many relations, Django also supports *many-to-many relations* and *one-to-one relations*, which we won't describe any further here.

42.4.4   Transferring the Model to the Database

Now that we've created the application, inserted it into the project, and defined its data model, we can create the associated database. To do this, let's look at Django's mechanism for synchronizing the database layout with the data model.

During development with Django, you specify the database layout indirectly through the models you define in the *models.py* file. Therefore, changes from *models.py* must be transferred to the database so that the database layout fits your models. In particular, inconsistencies arise when you change a model without adjusting the database accordingly.

In the example, we've created the Article and Comment models in the *models.py* file. However, the database of the project is still empty. Let's do away with this inconsistency now.

To conveniently transfer changes to the data model into the database, Django provides migrations. A *migration* is a Python program that describes changes to the data model. Django provides commands that generate these migrations automatically, so you as a programmer don't need to bother about the technical details.[9] We'll use the following command to create the migration for the initial database layout for the news application, omitting the python command at the beginning on Windows.

```
$ python manage.py makemigrations news
Migrations for 'news':
  news/migrations/0001_initial.py:
    - Create model Article
    - Create model Comment
```

42

---

9 However, it's explicitly intended that the programmer must manually adjust migrations if Django's automatisms should ever be insufficient.

Now there's a file named *0001_initial.py* in the *news/migrations* directory that describes the database layout of the sample application. To write this layout to the database, we use the migrate command:

```
$ python manage.py migrate
```

The longish output of the command tells us which migrations to which applications have been executed. We aren't interested in the details here. The only important thing is that we have now created a database that fits the data model.

Note

The concept of migration is very powerful and allows you to conveniently change the database layout afterward or even to undo changes.

The workflow is as follows:

1. You modify your data model in the *models.py* file.
2. You create a migration using the $ python manage.py makemigrations command.
3. You transfer the changes to the database via $ python manage.py migrate.

You can find more information about this in the Django documentation under the *Migrations* keyword.

The sample project is now initialized, so let's turn to managing articles and comments.

42.4.5   The Model API

In this section, you'll learn about the model API, which you can use to access your model's data. The manage.py program can be started with the shell parameter in a shell mode where we can use the models in an interactive Python shell.

Creating Data Records

First, we want to use the shell to write a news article into the database:

```
$ python manage.py shell
>>> from news.models import Article, Comment
>>> from datetime import datetime
>>> m = Article(title='Our First Article',
...             timestamp=datetime.today(),
...             text='Traditionally, the first article says "Hello World".')
>>> m.save()
```

With this simple code, a new article was created and stored in the database. Because both the project and the application are simple Python modules, we can import them via an import statement.

To create new records, we just need to instantiate the associated model class. The constructor of the model class expects keyword parameters for all attributes of the dataset. It's also important to note that for each column value, Django expects a value with a data type that matches the column definition. For this reason, the datetime.datetime type must be imported to handle dates. For the text columns, you can use strings.

You can access the attributes of a model instance in the usual way and also modify them via assignments:

```
>>> m.title
'Our First Article'
>>> m.title = "Hello World"
>>> m.save()
>>> m.id
1
```

With the last query, m.id, we access the model's id column that was automatically inserted by Django. As m is the first entry, m.id has the value 1.

We can add comments directly above the respective article. By binding the Comment class to the article, each Article instance gets a comment_set attribute that provides access to the comments of the article:

```
>>> m2 = Article(title='Django Survey',
...              timestamp=datetime.today(),
...              text='How do you like this framework?')
>>> m2.save()
>>> c1 = m2.comment_set.create(author='Jeff', text='Great!')
>>> c2 = m2.comment_set.create(author='Bill', text='Fantastic!')
>>> m2.comment_set.count()
2
>>> m2.save()
```

Now there's a second article in our news table, which already has two comments. The first m2.save() is required because an id column value isn't generated by the database to associate comments with the data record until it's saved.

There's one more unattractive peculiarity in our model that we should get rid of. Take a look at what Python outputs when we print an Article instance:

```
>>> m2
<Article: Article object (2)>
```

This form of representation isn't very useful as it doesn't provide any information about the content of the object. You can specify the __str__ magic method in the *models.py* file of each class, which should return a meaningful representation of the object's

42

content. We modify the *models.py* file in such a way that the __str__ methods of the Article and Comment classes each return the identifying text attribute:

```
class Article(models.Model):
    ...
    def __str__(self):
        return self.title


class Comment(models.Model):
    ...
    def __str__(self):
        return "{} says '{}'".format(self.author, self.text)
```

For the changes to take effect for the Python shell, you must restart it via python manage.py shell. To do this, simply exit the Python interpreter with the exit() function call and then restart it. Don't forget to import the model classes and datetime again after the restart.

If you now generate an article in the new shell, you can also have it output in a meaningful way:

```
>>> m = Article(title='New: Nice Outputs',
...              timestamp=datetime.today(),
...              text='Finally, the outputs look really nice.')
>>> m
<Article: New: Nice Outputs>
>>> m.save()
```

You should equip all your model classes with a __str__ method if possible as Django often draws on it to output information on data records.

Querying Data Records

By now you know how to add new records to the database of a Django project. However, just as important as creating new records is querying records from the database. To access the data records already contained in the database, each model class provides a class attribute called objects, whose methods allow the convenient reading of data:

```
>>> Article.objects.all()
<QuerySet [<Article: Hello World>,
           <Article: Django Survey>,
           <Article: New: Nice Outputs>]>
```

The all method of `Article.objects` allows us to have a list[10] returned with all articles in the database. Of particular interest are the `get` and `filter` methods of the `objects` attribute, which can be used to determine specific records that meet certain conditions. The desired conditions are passed as keyword parameters in the queries. If more than one condition is specified, Django automatically links them with a logical AND.

With `get`, you can query individual data records. If the required conditions apply to more than one record, `get` will raise a `MultipleObjectsReturned` exception. If no matching record is found, `get` acknowledges this with a `DoesNotExist` error. We use `get` to read the survey article from the database:

```
>>> survey = Article.objects.get(title='Django Survey')
>>> survey.comment_set.all()
<QuerySet [<Comment: Jeff says 'Great!'>,
           <Comment: Bill says 'Fantastic!'>]>
```

As you can see, not only does Django read the corresponding data record from the database, it also creates a matching instance of the associated `Model` class, which can then be used as if we had just created it.

Field Lookups

We can also use the `filter` method to read multiple records at once, so long as they match the passed criteria:

```
>>> Comment.objects.filter(article__id=2)
<QuerySet [<Comment: Jeff says 'Great!'>,
           <Comment: Bill says 'Fantastic!'>]>
```

In this query, Django returns all `Comment` records associated with an `article` whose `id` attribute has the value 2. This type of query is possible because Django is able to "follow" links even across multiple tables. The double underscore is considered a separation between object and subobject, similar to the dot in Python syntax. This type of condition transfer is also supported by `get`.

The double underscore can be used to refine normal conditions in addition to querying across links from different model classes. This is done by following a keyword parameter with the double underscore by a specific name. For example, you can use the following `filter` call to determine all surveys whose `text` attribute starts with the string `'Now'`:

```
>>> Article.objects.filter(text__startswith='Finally')
<QuerySet [<Article: New: Nice Outputs>]>
```

---

10 The return value of `all` is not a list in the sense of an instance of the `list` data type. In fact, an instance of Django's own `QuerySet` data type is returned, but it behaves outwardly similar to `list` instances.

This type of refined query is referred to as *field lookup* in Django. All field lookups are passed to the `filter` method in the form `attribute__lookuptype=value`. Django defines many and sometimes very specific field lookup types, which is why Table 42.3 should only be understood as a rough overview.

Field Lookup Type	Explanation
exact	Checks if `attribute` is exactly equal to `value`. This is the default behavior if no field lookup is specified.
contains	Checks whether `attribute` contains `value`.
gt	Checks if `attribute` is greater than `value` (gt: *greater than*).
gte	Checks whether `attribute` is greater than or equal to `value` (gte: *greater than or equal*).
lt	Checks if `attribute` is less than `value` (lt: *less than*).
lte	Checks if `attribute` is less than or equal to `value` (lte: *less than or equal*).
in	Checks if `attribute` is in the list passed for `value`—for example, `Article.objects.filter(id__in=[3, 2])`.
startswith	Checks if the value of `attribute` starts with `value`.
endswith	Checks if the value of `attribute` ends with `value`.
range	Checks if `attribute` is in the range defined by the two-element tuple `value`: `Article.objects.filter(id__range=(1, 3))`.
regex	Checks if the `attribute` matches the regular expression `value`.
iexact, icontains, istartswith, iendswith, iregex	Behaves like the respective field lookup type without a leading i. The comparison is not case-sensitive.

Table 42.3 An Overview of the Most Important Field Lookup Types

Queries on Result Sets

The `filter` method returns an instance of the `QuerySet` data type. The special thing about the `QuerySet` data type is that you can execute the methods for database access on its instances. In this way, subsets of query results can be generated very conveniently.

As an example, we first determine the set of all comments whose associated article contains the word survey in its title. Then we extract from the set the articles whose text is 'Great!':

```
>>> c = Comment.objects.filter(article__title__regex='Django Survey')
>>> c
<QuerySet [<Comment: Jeff says 'Great!'>,
           <Comment: Bill says 'Fantastic!'>]>
>>> c.filter(text='Great!')
<QuerySet [<Comment: Jeff says 'Great!'>]>
```

Of course, you can also call the filter method of the first result directly without having to create the intermediate set c:

```
Comment.objects.filter(article__title__regex='.*survey.*').filter(
    text='Great!')
```

You should familiarize yourself with the model API by playing around with it before reading on. It's a key component of using Django.

42.4.6 The Project Gets a Face

Now, the project has progressed to the point where a database of news stories and comments has been created. In this section, we'll deal with the "face" of our site—that is, what we want the site visitor to see.

You probably remember the diagram for building the model-view architecture from the section introducing Django.

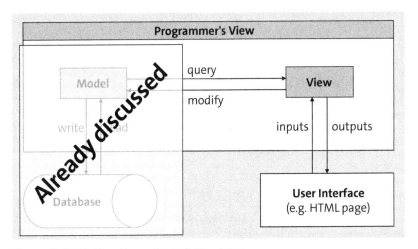

Figure 42.6 We Now Know the Left-Hand Part

42

909

Figuratively speaking, we've worked our way from left to right exactly up to the center as we've already dealt with models and databases, but not with views and the user interface. So now we'll take care of the right-hand side of the schema.

Views

A *view* is a simple Python function that returns what should be displayed in the visitor's browser. You can freely select the exact data to be displayed. A view can return HTML source code, for example, but plain text or even binary files such as images or PDF files are also possible. Usually, you want to define a separate view for everything you want to display on a website.

Our sample project will have two views: one to display an article overview and one to display a single article, including its comments. The view function for the article overview gets the name `articles`, and the other will be named `articles_detail`.

Because we want to focus on the basic handling of views in this section, we'll use a normal text output. In the following section we'll then show how you can also conveniently generate HTML source code.

The views of an application are usually stored in the *views.py* file. A *views.py* file containing a simple view function `articles` for the text output of the articles looks as follows:

```python
from django.shortcuts import render
from django.http import HttpResponse

from.models import Article, Comment


def articles(request):
    rows = []
    for m in Article.objects.all():
        rows.append("Article: '{}' from {}".format(
            m.title, m.timestamp.strftime('%d.%m.%Y at %H:%M')))
        rows.append('text: {}'.format(m.text))
        rows += ['', '-' * 30, '']
    response = HttpResponse('\n'.join(rows))
    response['Content-Type'] = 'text/plain'
    return response
```

At the beginning, we import the two model classes from the news application of the project. We then import a class called HttpResponse from the django.http module, which we use in our views to return the result.

Django passes the articles view function a parameter called request, with which we can access certain information about the query. We'll need request only in the next section.

Inside articles, we manage a list called rows, which stores all text rows of the result. In a for loop, we iterate over all the articles in the database that we read with the model API and insert five rows for each article in the rows list.

At the end, we create an instance of the HttpResponse data type, whose constructor we pass the concatenation of rows as a parameter. It's important that we use the [] operator to set the 'content type' of the output with 'text/plain' to plain text, because otherwise there'll be display problems in the browser.[11]

Before we can view the result of this work in the browser, we need to tell Django at which address the view should be accessible.

Defining Addresses

If you've already created web pages yourself, you're probably used to being able to access your programs (such as *index.php*) and other files (such as image files) directly through their address on the server. For example, if an *index.php* file is located in the *my_page/scripts/* directory relative to the root directory of the web server at the address *http://www.myserver.com*, you can access it using the address *http://www.myserver.com/my_site/scripts/index.php*.

Django takes a different approach by abstracting completely from the server's folder structure. Instead of taking the addresses of the real files on the server for public access, you can specify yourself the address through which a certain part of the page should be accessible. Each view can be addressed individually and can be linked to any address.

Addresses are configured using so-called *paths* in configuration files named *urls.py*. In general, the project itself and each of the applications have their own *urls.py* file. In such a file, a variable called urlpatterns is defined, which contains a list with all addresses of the project. The address details themselves are tuples with two elements, where the first element contains the regular expression for the address and the second element contains the information about the linked view. The *news_site/urls.py* file for the project, which already contains an address specification for the articles view, looks like this:

```
from django.urls import include, path
from django.contrib import admin

urlpatterns = [
    path('articles/', include(('news.urls', 'news'), namespace='news')),
    path('admin/', admin.site.urls),
]
```

42

---

11   The [] operator of HttpResponse instances can be used to set any kind of HTTP header data.

At this point, we're only interested in the following line:

```python
path('articles/', include(('news.urls', 'news'), namespace='news'))
```

Here we specify that an address that starts with `'articles/'` after the server address[12] should be processed further in the `news.urls` module. This module is located in the *news/urls.py* file, which we fill with the following content:

```python
from django.urls import path
from . import views

urlpatterns = [
    path('', views.articles, name='articles'),
]
```

The rule for the `''` path specifies that an empty address should return the result of the previously defined `articles` function.

If we now call the address *http://127.0.0.1:8000/articles* in a browser, an overview of the articles actually appears, as shown in Figure 42.7.[13]

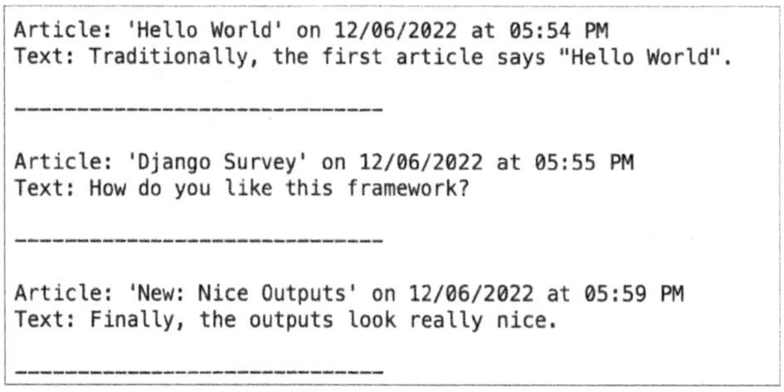

```
Article: 'Hello World' on 12/06/2022 at 05:54 PM
Text: Traditionally, the first article says "Hello World".

--------------------------------

Article: 'Django Survey' on 12/06/2022 at 05:55 PM
Text: How do you like this framework?

--------------------------------

Article: 'New: Nice Outputs' on 12/06/2022 at 05:59 PM
Text: Finally, the outputs look really nice.

--------------------------------
```

Figure 42.7 First Example Django Page in the Browser

The resolution of the address is done according to the following schema: The web server was asked for the address *http://127.0.0.1:8000/articles/*, which is composed of the server address, `'http://127.0.0.1:8000/'`, and the path on the server, here `'articles/'`. For the resolution, the *urls.py* file in the project directory is searched for a rule that matches the `'articles/'` path. In our case, this is the first rule from the following line:

```python
path('articles/', include(('news.urls', 'news'), namespace='news')),
```

Django then removes the part of the relative address that belongs to the rule and looks for a matching rule in the `'news.urls'` module for the rest. Because there's nothing left

---

12   A leading circumflex ensures that the regular expression must be at the beginning of the string to match.

13   If you haven't already done so, you need to start the Django development web server with `python manage.py runserver`.

after removing `'articles/'` from the relative address, the rule from the *news/urls.py* file, which searches for the empty string with `''`, will now match.

By removing parent address parts in this way, applications can work with relative addresses without having to know the parent structure.

> **Note**
>
> The parameter values for `namespace` and `name` aren't important at the moment. They'll be used later in connection with the generation of addresses.

Parameterized Addresses

We now also want to make the detail page of each article available to the user. It would be extremely unattractive to define a separate view function for each article, because on the one hand we would inflate the program code and on the other hand we would limit the number of possible articles by the number of view functions we implement.

It's therefore much more elegant if we define a view function that can display any article. Which article is requested concretely is to be specified by a parameter, which contains the `id` of the desired article.

Django supports parameter passing for views via a custom syntax inside the path string allowing us to extract parts from a string and give them names. In addition, we can specify what data type each value should be converted to.

To make the individual articles accessible via addresses such as *http://www.myserver .com/articles/1/* and *http://www.myserver.com/articles/2/*, we add the following entry to the *news/urls.py* file:

```
path('<int:article_id>/', views.articles_detail, name='articles_detail'),
```

When a visitor to the site accesses the address *http://www.myserver.com/articles/2/* now, Django first finds the matching entry `'articles/'` in the *news_site/urls.py* file. After truncating the beginning of `'articles/'`, the string `'2/'` remains, for which Django then searches for a suitable rule in the *news/urls.py* file. This can be found with the expression `'<int:article_id>/'` converting the string `'2'` to an integer and assigning it to the name `article_id`.

Now Django calls the view function `news.views.articles_detail`, passing a keyword parameter `article_id` with the value 2 in addition to the `request` parameter.

A URL rule may well include multiple such placeholder, as the following example shows:[14]

```
path('<int:a>/<str:b>/<int:c>', views.view_fct, name='ex')
```

---

14 Besides the conversion to integer values, other variants are supported, shown here with the example of str. Details can be found in the Django documentation under the keyword *path converters*.

A request for the address *http://www.server.com/articles/99/something/1337/* with this rule results in the call view.view_fct(request, a=99, b='something', c=1337). Here we have assumed that the rule is located in the *news/urls.py* file.

The articles_detail View Function

Now we implement the articles_detail view function by writing the following to the *views.py* file:

```python
from django.http import HttpResponse, Http404
from.models import Article, Comment

def articles(request):
    ...

def articles_detail(request, article_id):
    try:
        m = Article.objects.get(id=article_id)
    except Article.DoesNotExist:
        raise Http404

    rows = [
        "Title: '{}' from {}".format(
            m.title, m.timestamp.strftime('%d.%m.%Y at %H:%M')),
        'Text: {}'.format(m.text),
        '', '-' * 30,
        'Comments:', '']
    rows += ['{}: {}'.format(c.author, c.text)
                for c in m.comment_set.all()]
    response = HttpResponse('\n'.join(rows))
    response['Content-Type'] = 'text/plain'
    return response
```

We also import the Http404 exception to send an error to the visitor's browser if it calls a nonexistent article. At every call of the view, the value for the article_id parameter is passed as it is specified in the address,. In a try/except statement, we try to output the appropriate article, and if unsuccessful, generate the preceding Http404 error.

If the article could be read successfully from the database, we store the text lines for the user page in the rows list and also generate outputs for all comments of the article using a list comprehension.

Finally, we wrap it all up in the usual way in a HttpResponse instance and return the result.

The output generated by articles_detail now looks as shown in Figure 42.8 for the URL *http://127.0.0.1:8000/articles/2/*.

```
Title: 'Django Survey' on 12/06/2022 at 05:55 PM
Text: How do you like this framework?

--------------------------------
Comments:

Jeff: Great!
Bill: Fantastic!
```

Figure 42.8 Example of Article Detail Page

Shortcut Functions

If you develop web applications, you'll very often find similar patterns in your code. For example, it's very common to retrieve a record from the database and, if it doesn't exist, generate a Http404 error.

To avoid having to type the same code every time and thereby artificially inflating your source code, Django provides so-called *shortcut functions* that carry out frequently needed tasks for you. The shortcut functions are located in the django.shortcuts module and can be imported via import.

For example, to retrieve a record from the database and raise a Http404 exception if it fails, you can use the shortcut function get_object_or_404. This function has almost the same interface as the get method of the model API, the only exception being that the model class of the data record being searched must be passed as the first parameter.

This turns the try/except statement into a one-line:

```
from django.shortcuts import get_object_or_404
m = get_object_or_404(Article, id=article_id)
```

Django defines a number of other shortcut functions we won't describe here. See the Django documentation for a detailed description of all available shortcuts.

42.4.7 Django's Template System

Our views implemented so far are still far from ideal: First, they are visually unappealing because only plain text is output. Second, they're generated directly from string constants in the view function. Particularly the second aspect needs improving as it's one of the main goals of Django to make the components of a project as independent of each other as possible. Ideally, the view function only takes care of processing the parameters and retrieving and formatting the data. The generation of the output for the browser should be delegated to another system that really only cares about the output.

This is where so-called *templates* come into play, which specialize in generating appealing output from transferred data. Basically, templates are files that contain placeholders. If a template is called with certain values for the placeholders, the placeholders will be replaced by those very values and as a result you'll obtain the expected output. In

42

addition to simple placeholder substitutions, Django's template system also supports control structures such as conditional statements and loops.

Before we turn to the definition of templates themselves, we'll first describe the import of templates in view functions.

Django encapsulates its template system in the django.template submodule. With the loader class of this module, we can load a template file and create a new template object from it. The values for the placeholders in the template are passed via a so-called *context*, which can be created using the RequestContext class.

Importing Templates in View Functions

In Django, a template is represented by a file. Where this file is stored is important so that Django's template system can find it. By default, Django searches in subdirectories named *templates* in all application directories. For example, templates for the news application should be stored in the *news_site/news/templates/news* directory.

We therefore save the template for the overview page of our news application under the path *news_site/news/templates/news/articles.html*.

Before filling the template with content, we adjust the articles view function to use the new template:

```
from django.http import HttpResponse
from django.template import loader

from.models import Article, Comment

def articles(request):
    template = loader.get_template('news/articles.html')
    context = {'articles' : Article.objects.all()}
    return HttpResponse(template.render(context))
```

This adjustment has essentially shrunk the articles view function to three lines.[15]

With the get_template method of the loader class, we load the desired template. Then we create a context that links the list of all articles with the 'articles' placeholder. We generate the final output of the template for the generated context using the render method and pass everything as a parameter to HttpResponse. Changing the context type to 'text/plain' isn't necessary because the templates will now generate HTML code.[16]

Now we can turn to the *articles.html* template itself.

---

15 You can take the position that such simply designed view functions are superfluous. Django provides so-called generic views for this purpose. For more details, see the Django documentation.

16 Of course, you can also write templates that continue to generate plain text output.

> **Note**
>
> You're probably wondering why we created another directory named *news* inside the *news/templates* directory instead of storing the template directly in *news/templates*.
>
> This directory structure prevents ambiguities from arising in a project when you use multiple applications that have templates with the same name. Let's assume that the project has another application named `congestions`, which provides information about the current traffic and also uses a template file called *articles.html*. In this case, the name `'articles.html'` is no longer unique, while the names `'news/ articles.html'` and `'congestions/articles.html'` still are.

The Template Language of Django

Django implements its own language for defining templates. This is designed in such a way that any output data type can be generated with it, as long as it can be expressed as text. So it's up to you whether you generate plain text, HTML source code, XML documents, or other text-based file types.

The *articles.html* template contains the following template code in the example:[17]

```
<h1>News Overview</h1>

{% for m in articles %}
  <div class="container">
    <div class="headline">
      <div class="title">{{ m.title|escape }}</div>
      <div class="timestamp">
        {{ m.timestamp|date:'Y.m.d' }} at
        {{ m.timestamp|time:'H:i' }}
      </div>
      <div style="clear: both"></div>
    </div>
    <div class="text">
      {{ m.text|escape|linebreaksbr }}
      <div class="link_bottom">
        <a href="{% url 'news:articles_detail' m.id %}">Details</a>
      </div>
    </div>
  </div>
{% endfor %}
```

---

17 Note that important HTML elements have been deliberately omitted here for the sake of clarity, which means that the HTML code no longer conforms to the standards. Of course, you should only generate valid HTML files in your own programs.

42

Basically, the template shown here is a simple HTML file supplemented by special instructions of the template language. In the example, all places where Django's template language is used have been printed in bold.

Let's now take a closer look at the marked areas.

Outputting Variables

The output of elements of the used context is done via double curly brackets. For example, {{ articles}} outputs the context variable articles, and {{ m.title }} accesses the title attribute of the n context variable. As you can see, the dot can also be used in the output to access the attributes of context variables.

However, accessing attributes is just a special application of the dot operator in Django's template language. When Django encounters a specification like {{ variable.member }} while processing a template, it determines the data in the following way:

1. First, it tries to access a value with variable['member'], like a dictionary.
2. If this fails, an attempt is made to read the value with variable.member.
3. If this fails again, it tries to interpret member as a list index by reading a value with variable[member]. (Of course, this only works if member is an integer.)
4. If all these attempts fail, Django takes the value set in *settings.py* under TEMPLATES['OPTIONS']['string_if_invalid']. By default, this is an empty string.

Because of this procedure, for example, the expression {{ articles.0 }}, which is invalid as Python code, is also permitted to access the first element of the articles context variable.

If the evaluation according to the this schema results in a callable instance, it gets called and its return value is output. For example, if the context variable has a something method, its return value will be output by {{ variable.something }} in the template.

Filters for Variables

You can customize the replacement of context variables using filters. A *filter* is a function that can process a string. To apply a filter to the value of a variable, you add a vertical bar followed by the filter name after the variable name:

{{ variable|filter }}

It's also possible to connect several filters one after the other by separating them with a vertical bar:

{{ variable|filter1|filter2|filter3 }}

In this line of code, filter1 is applied first to the value of variable, the result is passed to filter2, and its return value would finally be processed with filter3.

Some filters can also be passed parameters. To do this, the filter name is followed by a colon, followed by a string with the parameter:

```
{{ variable|filter:'parameter'}}
```

Here, this was applied to adjust the output of the timestamp.[18]

Django implements a large number of such filters. Table 42.4 explains the filters used in the example.

Filter	Meaning
escape	Replaces the characters <, >, &, ", and ' with appropriate HTML encodings
linebreaksbr	Replaces all linefeeds with the HTML tag ` `, which creates a new line
date	Formats a date with the format specified by the passed parameter
time	Formats a time with the format specified by the passed parameter

Table 42.4 Some Filters in Django

By the way, you can also define your own filters. Information about this and a detailed overview with all Django filters can be found in the documentation.

Tags

Django's template language uses *tags*, which allow you to manage the control flow within a template. Each tag has the structure {% tag_name %}, where tag_name depends on the respective tag.

There are also tags that enclose a block. Such tags have the following structure:

```
{% tag_name parameter %}
    Tag content
{% endtag_name %}
```

There are tags that can be used to map control structures such as conditional output or repeated output of a block.

The if block can be used to output a certain part of the template only if a condition is met:

```
{% if visitor.has_birthday %}
    Welcome and Happy Birthday!
{% else %}
    Welcome to our site!
{% endif %}
```

---

18   The format for date and time formatting is based on the date PHP function and therefore differs from the format of the strftime function in the time module of the standard library. For more information on this, refer to the Django documentation.

If `visitor.has_birthday` evaluates to `True`, the visitor to the page is wished a happy birthday. Otherwise they'll be greeted normally. Of course, the `else` branch can also be omitted.

Complex logical expressions can also be formed as conditions:

```
{% if condition1 and condition2 or condition3 %}
    condition1 and condition2 apply and/or condition3 applies
{% endif %}
```

In addition to conditional statements, there's also an equivalent to Python loops: the `for` tag. The `for` tag is closely based on the Python syntax and can be used as follows:

```
{% for name in names %}
    {{ name }} is a great name
{% endfor %}
```

Of course, this loop works only if the context variable `names` refers to an iterable object.

If `name` had the value `['Colin', 'Luke', 'Cathy']`, then the template shown previously would produce the following output:

```
Colin is a great name.
Luke is a great name.
Cathy is a great name.
```

Creating Addresses

Django is able to automatically generate addresses for the pages of your project. This is done using the `url` tag, which we used in the example to create links to the detailed pages of the articles:

```
{% url 'news:articles_detail' m.id %}
```

The `'news:articles_detail'` specification identifies the page to be called according to the `<namespace>:<view-name>` schema. In Section 42.4.6, under Defining Addresses, we linked all the rules of the *news/urls.py* file within the *news_site/urls.py* file via `namespace='news'` to the `'news'` namespace. This means Django looks there for a rule called `'articles_detail'`. We also defined a corresponding rule that expects a parameter for the `id` of the article. This enables Django to generate the appropriate address, using the `m.id` value for the `article_id` parameter.

If you use this mechanism, you don't need to explicitly specify the addresses to sub-pages of the project in templates, but you can use the names of the corresponding URL rules. Therefore, to change the addressing in your project afterward, you can centrally adjust the rules in the *urls.py* files without having to edit all templates.

Template Inheritance

It often happens that many pages of a web application have the same basic structure, such as a header or navigation. But if each page has its own template, this basic framework would have to be included in all templates, leading to unnecessary code duplication.

To solve this problem, you can define the basic structure of the page in a central template and derive the actually needed templates from it.

Assuming that the template in the *base.html* file contains the basic framework of the web page, another template can be derived from it using the extends tag:

```
{% extends 'base.html' %}
```

As a consequence, the entire content of *base.html* will be inserted into the inheriting template. In order for a requesting template to be able to determine the content of the resulting page itself, a template can define so-called blocks via the block tag. A block is a place within a template that's given a name and can be provided with concrete content by inheriting templates.

Let's take a look at two sample files. First, *base.html*:

```
---------- Header ------------
{% block content %}default content{% endblock %}
---------- Footer ------------
```

When you output this template with Django, the block tag will simply be ignored and replaced with its contents:

```
---------- Header ------------
default content
---------- Footer ------------
```

It gets interesting when we let another template inherit from *base.html*. Let's look now at *inheriting_template.html*:

```
{% extends 'base.html' %}
{% block content %}Hello, I have inherited!{% endblock %}
```

The output of *inheriting_template.html* then looks as follows:

```
---------- Header ------------
Hello, I have inherited!
---------- Footer ------------
```

Of course, the basic framework of a page isn't the only application for template inheritance. You can use inheritance whenever multiple templates are based on a common structure.

42

Knowing this, we can now create an appealing HTML template structure for the web project. We'll store the basic structure of the page, including the *Cascading Style Sheets* (*CSS*),[19] in a *base.html* file. The *base.html* file has the following content. For the sake of clarity, some parts have been omitted:

```html
<!DOCTYPE html>
<html>
<head>
  <title>Our Django Page</title>
  <style type="text/css">
    /* This is where the CSS styles go */
  </style>
</head>
<body>
  <div id="content">
    <h2>{% block title %}Django Sample Page{% endblock %}</h2>
    {% block content %}
    {% endblock %}
  </div>
</body>
</html>
```

The template defines a simple HTML page in which there are two template blocks: title and content. These blocks are now to be filled with content by the inheriting templates for the article overview and the article details.

In our example, we assume that our news_site web project will consist of several applications that all share the same basic framework. For this reason, it makes sense to store the *base.html* template file in a central location so that all applications can access it. To do this, we create a *templates* subdirectory in the *news_site/news_site* directory. Just as before with templates for the news application, we create a subdirectory named *main* in this template directory, in which we store the central templates of the project, such as *base.html*. You can see the resulting directory structure in Figure 42.9.

Now we have to make sure that Django finds the *main/base.html* template in the central template directory. For this purpose, we adjust the TEMPLATES setting in the *settings.py* file as follows:

```python
TEMPLATES = [
    {
        # Other settings
        'DIRS': [BASE_DIR / "news_site/templates"],
        # More other settings
```

---

[19] CSS is a formatting language used, for example, for customizing the output of HTML pages.

```
        },
]
```

Figure 42.9 Directory Structure with Main Template

Now we'll change the *articles.html* file of the news application so that it inherits from *main/base.html* and fills the title and content blocks:

```
{% extends 'main/base.html' %}
{% block title %}News Overview{% endblock %}
{% block content %}
    {% for m in articles %}
        <div class="container">
          <div class="headline">
            <div class="title">{{ m.title|escape }}</div>
            <div class="timestamp">
              {{ m.timestamp|date:'Y.m.d' }} at
              {{ m.timestamp|time:'H:i' }}
            </div>
            <div style="clear: both"></div>
          </div>
          <div class="text">
```

```
            {{ m.text|escape|linebreaksbr }}
            <div class="link_bottom">
              <a href="{% url 'news:articles_detail' m.id %}">Details</a>
            </div>
          </div>
        </div>
    {% endfor %}
{% endblock %}
```

Once you've saved the files, you can view the result in your browser at the URL *http://127.0.0.1:8000/articles/* (see Figure 42.10).[20]

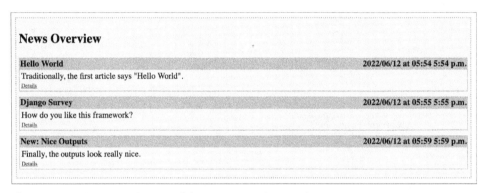

Figure 42.10 Nice HTML Output of the First Example Template

If you click the **Details** link, you will of course still be taken to the dull text view of the respective article. To change this, we also need to adjust the articles_detail view function:

```
from django.http import HttpResponse, Http404
from django.shortcuts import render, get_object_or_404
from django.template import RequestContext, loader

from.models import Article, Comment

def articles(request):
    ...

def articles_detail(request, article_id):
    template = loader.get_template('news/articles_detail.html')
    article = get_object_or_404(Article, id=article_id)
    return HttpResponse(template.render({'article' : article}))
```

---

20 The complete *base.html* file including all CSS styles is part of the online resources for this book (available at *www.rheinwerk-computing.com/5566*).

Note the newly added import of get_object_or_404.

To complete the HTML output, the only thing missing is the template for the detail page of the articles, which we place in the same directory as *articles.html* under the name *articles_detail.html*:

```
{% extends 'main/base.html' %}
{% block title %}
  News details for entry {{ article.id }}
{% endblock %}
{% block content %}
  <div class="container">
    <div class="headline">
      <div class="title">{{ article.title|escape }}</div>
      <div class="timestamp">{{ article.timestamp }}</div>
      <div style="clear: both"></div>
    </div>
    <div class="text">
      {{ article.text|escape|linebreaksbr }}
    </div>
  </div>
  <div class="container">
    <div class="headline">Comments</div>
    {% if article.comment_set.count %}
      <table>
      {% for c in article.comment_set.all %}
        <tr class="comment_line">
          <td class="column_header">{{ c.author }}:</td>
          <td>{{ c.text|escape|linebreaksbr }}</td>
        </tr>
      {% endfor %}
      </table>
    {% else %}
      No comments
    {% endif %}
  </div>
  <div class="link_bottom">
    <a href="{% url 'news:articles' %}">Back</a>
  </div>
{% endblock %}
```

In the browser, for example, the result can be viewed under the URL *http://127.0.0.1: 8000/articles/2/* and will then appear as shown in Figure 42.11.

42

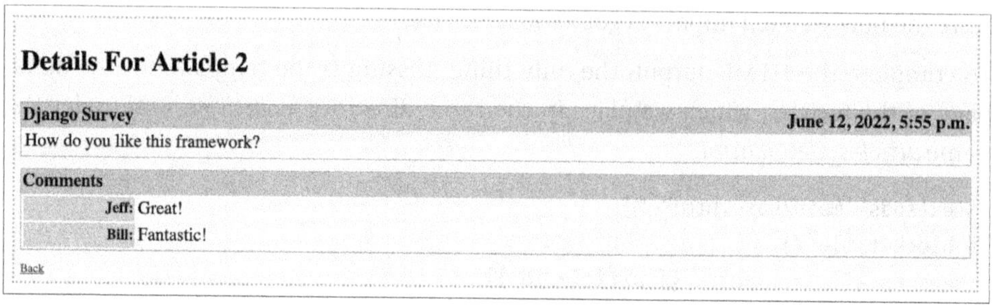

Details For Article 2

Django Survey	June 12, 2022, 5:55 p.m.
How do you like this framework?	

Comments

Jeff: Great!

Bill: Fantastic!

Back

Figure 42.11 Detail Page of an Article with Two Comments

You'll certainly have noticed that the two articles and articles_detail views have a very similar structure: first a template is loaded, then the context dictionary is created, and finally an HTTPResponse object is returned that contains the return value of template.render.

To make the program code more compact, Django provides a shortcut function named render for such cases. With render we can shorten the two view functions once again:

```python
from django.shortcuts import render

def articles(request):
    return render(request, 'news/articles.html',
        context={'articles' : Article.objects.all()})

def articles_detail(request, article_id):
    article = get_object_or_404(Article, id=article_id)
    return render(request, 'news/articles_detail.html',
        context={'article' : article})
```

The render shortcut function is passed the path to the desired template as the second parameter and the context as the third parameter.

We're now at the stage where we can produce appealing output with little effort. This project is thus almost complete. The only thing missing is the ability for visitors to the site to comment on the news.

42.4.8   Processing Form Data

To make a dynamic web application truly interactive, users must be able to contribute to the content of the page in addition to simply navigating the page. This often happens via guest books, forums, or comment functions.

On the technical side, these functionalities require an interface to transfer data from the user's browser to the server application.

For this purpose, the HTTP protocol provides two methods that enable the so-called argument transfer. The difference between the two transfer methods is that data transmitted with *GET* is appended directly to the address of the respective page and is thus immediately visible to the user, while the *POST* method transmits data invisibly to the user in the background.

Both methods work with named placeholders, which are usually linked to data by HTML forms.

A Form for Submitting Comments

We'll provide a form on the detail page of each news item where the visitor can enter new comments on the displayed news. The form will have two text fields: one for the visitor's name and one for the comment itself. In the browser, it should later look like as shown in Figure 42.12.

Figure 42.12 Comment Form

We'll choose POST as the transfer method for the entered data to avoid overcrowding the address bar. Saving the new comments will be handled by the articles_detail view function, which is passed a POST parameter called save_comment when the form is submitted. In addition, the form should have a field for error output in case the user has entered too little information.

The template for the form definition then looks as follows:[21]

```
<div class="container">
  <div class="headline">New comment</div>
  <span class="error">{{ error }}</span>
  <form method="post" action="">
    {% csrf_token %}
    <input type="hidden" name="save_comment" value="1"/>
    <table>
      <tr class="comment line">
        <td class="column identifier">Your name:</td>
        <td><input type="text" name="visitor_name"
                   value="{{ visitor_name }}"/></td>
```

---

21 This part is inserted at the bottom of the *articles_detail.html* file. The complete template file can be found in the online resources for this book.

```
        </tr>
        <tr class="comment line">
          <td class="column identifier">Comment:</td>
          <td>
            <textarea name="comment_text">{{ comment_text }}</textarea>
          </td>
        </tr>
      </table>
      <input type="submit" value="Submit" />
  </form>
</div>
```

As you can see in the `<form method="post" action="">` line, when the form is sent, the article detail page itself is called. In addition, the values of the `visitor_name` and `comment_text` text fields are passed as POST data.[22]

If errors occur when saving a comment, an article can be set by the view function via the `error` context variable. To ensure that the user's entries aren't lost in such a case, the text fields can be provided with initial values by the view via the `username` and `comment` context variables.

Accessing POST and GET Variables in View Functions

As you already know, Django passes each view function a parameter called `request`. This parameter contains information about the request and in particular the GET and POST parameters. For this purpose, `request` has two attributes called `GET` and `POST` that provide access to the parameters by their names as in a dictionary.

Based on this information, we can extend the `articles_detail` view function as follows (the elements in the listing that aren't yet known will be explained afterward):

```python
from django.http import HttpResponseRedirect

def articles_detail(request, article_id):
    article = get_object_or_404(Article, id=article_id)

    if 'save_comment' in request.POST:
        name = request.POST.get('visitor_name', '')
        text = request.POST.get('comment_text', '')

        if name and text:
            comment = article.comment_set.create(
                author=name, text=text)
```

---

22 The `{% csrf_token %}` tag is used to protect against *cross-site request forgery* (*CSRF*), a common attack on websites. But we won't go into further detail about this here. You should use this tag in all forms.

```
        comment.save()
        return HttpResponseRedirect('.')

    else:
        return render(request, 'news/articles_detail.html',
            context={'article': article,
                        'error': 'Input your name and a comment.',
                        'visitor_name' : name, 'comment_text' : text})

    return render(request, 'news/articles_detail.html',
        context={'article' : article})
```

At the beginning of the function, we read the article in question from the database as before or return a Http404 error. Then we use the in operator to check if 'comment.save' has been passed via POST to save a new comment if necessary. If 'comment.save' wasn't passed, the if block is omitted and the detail page is displayed.

When a new comment is to be saved, we read the entered name and comment text from request.POST. Then we check if something has been entered in both text fields. If an entry is missing, the detail page is displayed again in the else branch, with a corresponding error text being output. By setting the visitor_name and comment_text context variables to the previously passed values, any input made by the user is not lost, but reappears in the text fields, as shown in Figure 42.13.

Figure 42.13 Form with Incorrect Input

If the two name and text variables have valid values, we create a new comment object in the database. However, in this case we use the HttpResponseRedirect class to redirect the visitor to the detail page instead of outputting a template. The reason for this is simple. If a visitor has posted a new comment and has now landed back on the details page, they could use their browser's refresh function to reload the page. But when a page is refreshed, both GET and POST data are retransmitted. Therefore, with each page reload, the same comment would be saved again. By indirect redirection using HttpResponseRedirect, we solve this problem: now the POST and GET variables are discarded.

You can import HttpResponseRedirect via import from the django.http module.

This makes the sample project fully functional: articles can be browsed and commented on. However, it lacks a way for the site operator to conveniently manage the articles. Therefore, to conclude, let's look at Django's capabilities to automatically generate the administration interface for a web application.

42.4.9   Django's Admin Control Panel

A time-consuming task in the creation of a web application is the development of an *administration interface* or *admin control panel* (ACP). ACPs are tools that allow site operators to manage page content without having to modify the program code or access the database directly.

For example, the ACP should be able to add new articles to the news page and edit or delete old ones. Likewise, it should be possible to manage comments.

Basically, an ACP is a separate web application that can be used to edit all the data of the application being administered. The development effort is correspondingly high.

The good news for you as a budding Django developer is that you don't need to bother much about programming ACPs in your projects. Django creates a comfortable and convenient administration interface almost automatically, so you're spared the hassle of implementing it yourself. You only need to make small changes to the configuration of the project.

Creating an Admin User

Because the administration interface isn't intended for public access, we must first create a privileged user. To do this, we use a command line to navigate to the directory where your project's *manage.py* file is located. In the example, this is the outer *news_ site* directory. There we call manage.py with the createsuperuser parameter (on Windows, python can be omitted at the beginning of the line):

```
$ python manage.py createsuperuser
Username (leave blank to use 'user'): admin
Email address: someone@myserver.com
Password:
Password (again):
Superuser created successfully.
```

The program will ask for the desired username and email address of the administrator. In addition, a password must be assigned with which the administrator can log in to the ACP later.

Using Django's ACP

Now we can start Django's development web server and open the ACP at *http://127.0.0.1:8000/admin/*, which greets us with the login dialog shown in Figure 42.14.[23]

After logging in, the default ACP view is shown as in Figure 42.15, with Django offering user management functions by default, which we won't describe any further here.

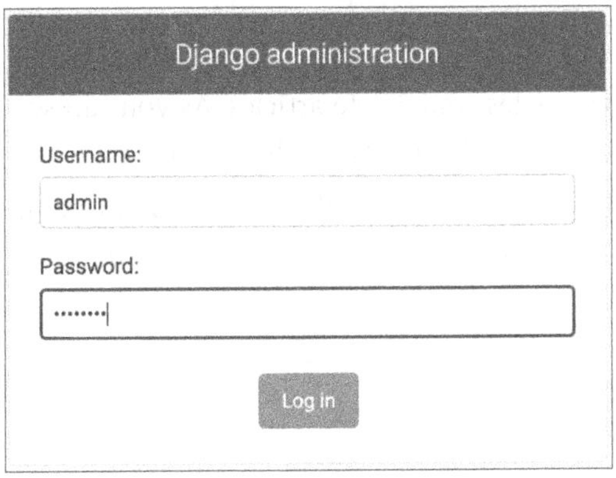

Figure 42.14 Django's Login to the Administration Area

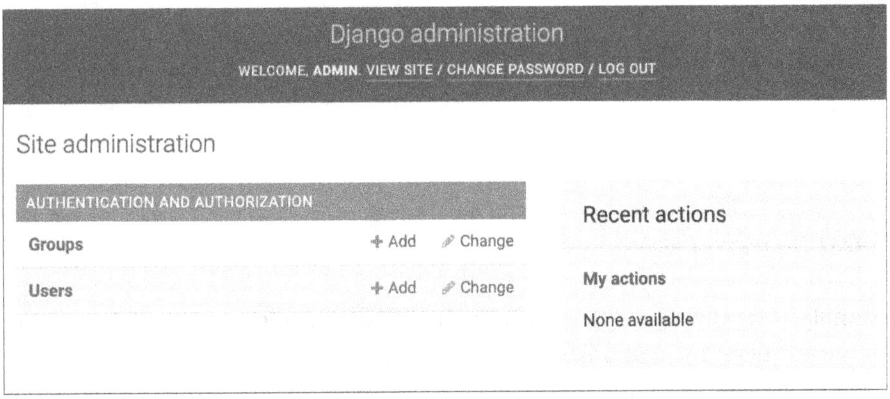

Figure 42.15 Django ACP Home Page

For news articles and comments to be editable as well, we need to configure Django accordingly. To do this, we register the `Article` model with the admin page by modifying the *news/admin.py* file as follows:

```
from django.contrib import admin
from.models import Article

admin.site.register(Article)
```

---

23   The address of the ACP is set in the *news_site/urls.py* file like all other addresses. Django has a corresponding entry inserted by default, as you saw in Section 42.4.6.

When you now reload the ACP in your browser, there's a new **Article** entry to edit the entries of the articles (see Figure 42.16).

Figure 42.16 ACP Entry for Editing Articles

Now you can modify any article, add new articles, and delete articles. As you can see, Django uses the __str__ method of the Article model to display the articles.

Because the handling of the ACP is intuitive, we'll merely modify an article as an example. By clicking the **Articles** link, we get to the overview of all articles, as shown in Figure 42.17.

> ## Select article to change
>
> **ADD ARTICLE +**
>
> Action: [— — — ▼] [Go]   0 of 3 selected
>
> ☐ ARTICLE
>
> ☐ **New: Nice Outputs**
>
> ☐ **Django Survey**
>
> ☐ **Hello World**
>
> 3 articles

Figure 42.17 Overview of All Articles in ACP

For example, if we click the article with the text **Django Survey**, we'll be taken to the editing view. There, for demonstration purposes, we'll change the title to "Django Framework Survey" (see Figure 42.18).

After clicking the **Save** button in the bottom-right-hand corner, the article with its new text is saved in the database and we'll return to the article overview.

As an interesting feature, Django stores its change history for each data record; that is, it stores the date and time as well as who made what change to the data. This additional feature is especially useful when many users have access to the administration page and you want to keep track of the changes made. The changes to a particular data record can be retrieved using the **History** button.

You should keep in mind what a great benefit this service from Django provides: based on a simple model definition, the entire database and even the associated management tool are generated. This work would have otherwise cost you hours.

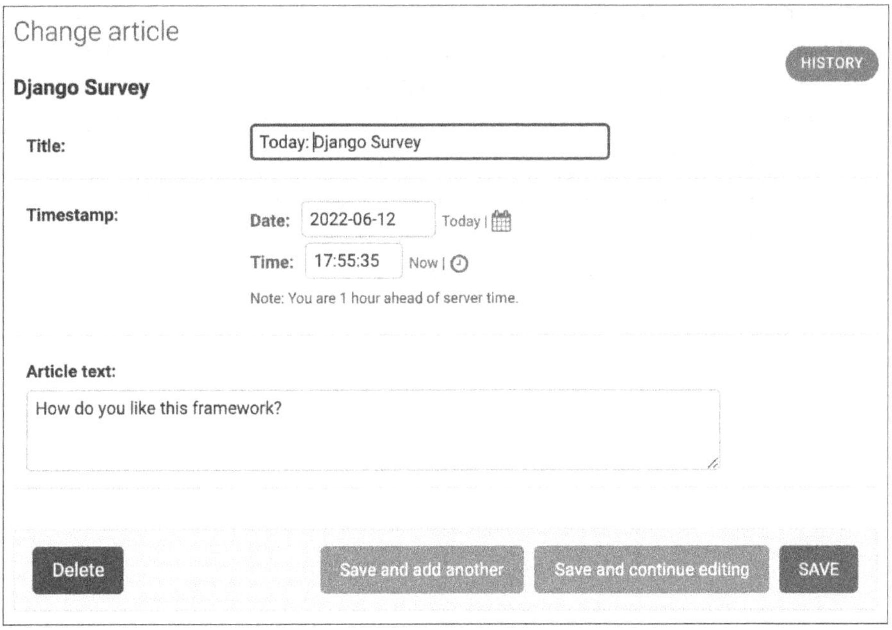

Figure 42.18 Editing an Article

Customizing the Admin Control Panel

In practice, the standard layout of Django's ACP often isn't ideally adapted to the workflows of administrators. For example, if we want to make the comments on our articles changeable in the ACP, we can add a `admin.site.register(comment)` line to the *news/admin.py* file, but then we'd have a list of all comments, just as with the articles, without taking into account the affiliation to the respective article. It's much more natural to edit the comments together with the related article.

Fortunately, Django provides extensive options to customize the ACP according to the developer's requirements. The described extension for editing comments can be implemented by modifying the *news/admin.py* file as follows:

```python
from django.contrib import admin
from.models import Article, Comment

class CommentInline(admin.TabularInline):
    model = Comment
    extra = 1

class ArticleAdmin(admin.ModelAdmin):
    inlines = [CommentInline]

admin.site.register(Article, ArticleAdmin)
```

When registering a model for the ACP, you can also pass a class that affects the appearance of the ACP page. This class inherits from the admin.ModelAdmin class and is implemented in the example via ArticleAdmin. Within this class, the layout of the ACP page is now controlled via class attributes. In the example, we use the inlines attribute to include the article comments *inline*—that is, directly on the page. The value for inlines is a list containing all desired elements to be embedded. In the example, it has only the CommentInline entry. The CommentInline class inherits from admin.TabularInline, which embeds the entries as a table. The value of extra determines how many empty entries for creating new comments should be displayed among the already existing comments. So in the example, only an empty entry is displayed.

The result of this customization is shown in Figure 42.19.

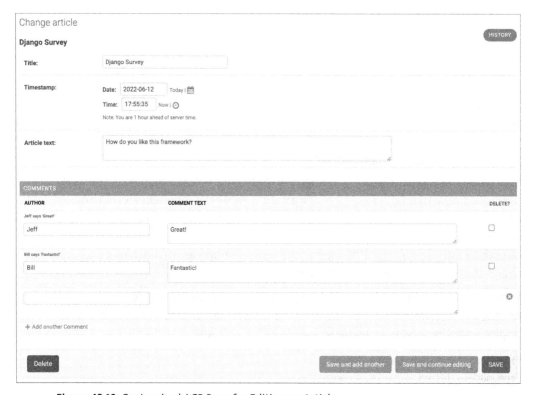

Figure 42.19 Customized ACP Page for Editing an Article

This example is only to be understood as a first glance. Django provides other extensive customization options for the ACP, which are beyond the scope of this introductory chapter.

This also makes the administration interface of our sample application fully functional. If you want to deepen your Django knowledge to include more advanced techniques, we recommend the excellent online documentation on the Django website at *http://djangoproject.com*.

Chapter 43
Scientific Computing and Data Science

In recent years, Python has become the dominant programming language in data science. This is partly due to a number of common and popular third-party modules for scientific computing and data record handling, which we'd like to introduce in this chapter.

The numpy and scipy modules presented here can be used, for example, to solve equations and optimization problems, calculate integrals, and perform statistical calculations or simulations. The results can be visualized via the matplotlib module. The capabilities are comparable to environments such as MATLAB or Scilab. Finally, we'll describe the pandas module as a comprehensive solution for analyzing, manipulating, and visualizing large data records.

The calculations are carried out internally by accelerated routines so that efficient software can be written by using these modules.

In this chapter, we don't present an exhaustive explanation of the manifold capabilities of numpy, scipy, matplotlib, and pandas, but rather introduce the basic use of the modules on the basis of a simple example. In addition, at the end of the chapter you'll find an overview of the structural design of scipy as well as further examples for the use of the numpy.ndarray data type.

The goal of this chapter is to provide an overview of whether numpy, scipy, matplotlib, and pandas are useful for your specific programs. After reading this introduction, you'll be able to make specific use of the online documentation.

Table 43.1 contains a short description of the four modules.

Module	Description
numpy	Provides the flexible ndarray data type for multidimensional arrays, which can be used to perform extensive calculations efficiently.
scipy	Implements diverse mathematical operations based on numpy.
matplotlib	Visualizes data graphically. The developers' declared goal is to produce high-quality graphics that can be used in scientific publications, for example.
pandas	Enables efficient work with large datasets—for example, for analysis, manipulation, or visualization.

Table 43.1 Modules for Numerical Calculations and Visualization

43

The modules aren't included in the standard Python library and must therefore be installed separately. You'll learn how to do that in the following section.

43.1   Installation

Because numpy, scipy, matplotlib, and pandas are third-party packages, they must be installed before you can use them. This can be done via the Anaconda package manager:

```
$ conda install numpy scipy matplotlib pandas
```

If you use Anaconda, the packages are usually preinstalled by default. Alternatively, if you don't use Anaconda, the packages can be installed via the Python package manager:

```
$ pip install numpy scipy matplotlib pandas
```

If you're a Linux user, an installation may also be possible via the package manager of your Linux distribution.

Further information on manual installation and the respective online documentation can be found on the projects' websites:

- *https://www.numpy.org*
- *https://www.scipy.org*
- *https://www.matplotlib.org*
- *https://pandas.pydata.org*

43.2   The Model Program

We'll use a simple model program. For the function $f(x) = x^3 - 10\,sin(x) - 4$, it calculates the derivative and an antiderivative numerically and displays them graphically in the interval [-3,3].

Using this model program, we'll explain typical procedures for working with numpy, scipy, and matplotlib:

```
import numpy as np
import scipy as sp
import matplotlib as mpl
import matplotlib.pyplot as plt
import scipy.misc
import scipy.integrate
def f(x):
    return x**3 - 10*np.sin(x) - 4
```

```
def df(x):
    return sp.misc.derivative(f, x)
@np.vectorize
def F(x):
    return sp.integrate.quad(f, 0, x)[0]
X = np.linspace(-3, 3, 200)
Y = f(X)
Y1 = df(X)
Y2 = F(X)
plt.plot(X, Y, linewidth=2, label="$f$")
plt.plot(X, Y1, linewidth=2, linestyle="dashed", label="$f'$")
plt.plot(X, Y2, linewidth=2, linestyle="dotted", label="$F$")
plt.legend()
plt.show()
```

Figure 43.1 shows the resulting graphic.

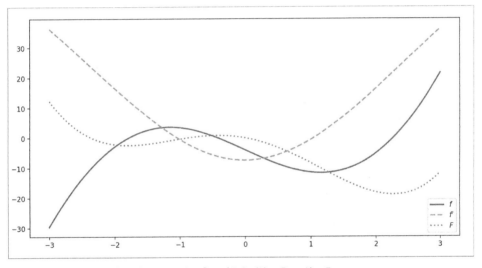

Figure 43.1 Function f with Derivative f' and Primitive FunctionF

This simple sample program already shows the most important features you should keep in mind when working with numpy, scipy, and matplotlib. We'll now describe the individual parts of the program.

43.2.1   Importing numpy, scipy, and matplotlib

In the first four lines, we import the numpy, scipy, and matplotlib modules and give them short names:

937

```
import numpy as np
import scipy as sp
import matplotlib as mpl
import matplotlib.pyplot as plt
```

This way of importing the modules has proved itself in practice and was therefore introduced as a convention. In the examples used in this chapter, we'll always assume that the modules have been imported in this way, and we recommend that you follow this convention in your own programs as well.

Following the basic `import` statements, the `scipy.misc` and `scipy.integrate` modules are loaded as well.

Because `scipy` is very extensive, it doesn't make sense for each program to import all functions at once. For this reason, `scipy` is divided into several packages that must be imported when needed. In our example, we use the `derivative` function from the `scipy.misc` package to calculate the derivative. We determine the primitive function using the `quad` function from the `scipy.integrate` package.

An overview table of the structure of `scipy` can be found in Section 43.3.2.

43.2.2 Vectorization and the numpy.ndarray Data Type

After the `import` statements, functions f, df, and F are defined, which evaluate the function f, its derivative f', and a primitive function F.

For working with `numpy` and `scipy`, it's important that the f, df, and F functions work not only for single numbers but for whole arrays of numbers. An *array* is an ordered sequence of similar objects, usually numbers. Before we go into the interaction of arrays and functions, we'll briefly describe the basic handling of arrays.[1]

To create an array, you can use the `numpy.array` function, to which you pass a list of the desired elements of the array, for example:

```
>>> a = np.array([0.5, 1, 2, 3])
>>> a
array([0.5, 1. , 2. , 3. ])
```

The special aspect of instances of the `numpy.ndarray` data type is that you can calculate with them as with numbers. The operations are performed element by element:[2]

---

1 You'll learn more about the handling of arrays later in Section 43.3.1.

2 If A is a two-dimensional array and x is a one-dimensional array, A*x does *not* cause a matrix-vector multiplication as is common in linear algebra. For matrix-vector multiplication, you can use `numpy.dot` or the `ndarray.dot` method: `np.dot(A,x)` or `A.dot(x)` respectively. In addition, Python 3.5 introduced the @ operator so that A@x can be written instead of `np.dot(A,x)` in newer versions of Python.

```
>>> a+a
array([1., 2., 4., 6.])
>>> a*a
array([0.25, 1.  , 4.  , 9.  ])
>>> a**3
array([ 0.125, 1.  , 8.  , 27.  ])
>>> 4*a
array([ 2., 4., 8., 12.])
```

In addition to arithmetic operations, functions can also be applied to arrays by inserting each element of the array into the function and combining the results as a new array.

For example, we can apply the f function from the sample program to the a array:

```
>>> f(a)
array([ -8.66925539, -11.41470985,  -5.09297427,  21.58879992])
```

Here the values $f(0.5)$, $f(1)$, $f(2)$, and $f(3)$ are calculated, stored in a new array, and returned.

This principle of applying the same operation to an entire array of numbers is called *vectorization*. If a function can process arrays in addition to numbers, it's also referred to as *being vectorized*.

The functions of the math module of the Python standard library, such as sin, cos, tan, or exp, aren't vectorized, so numpy and scipy offer their own vectorized versions of these functions. In the example, we therefore use the numpy.sin function instead of math.sin, which is able to calculate the sine values for an array of numbers.

Based on this information about arrays and vectorization, you can understand the next two lines of the model program:

```
X = np.linspace(-3, 3, 100)
Y = f(X)
```

First, the numpy.linspace function generates a new array X to which the f function is subsequently applied element by element. The calculated function values are stored in the Y array.

Using numpy.linspace, you can create an array with a specified number of elements that all have the same spacing. The first two parameters of numpy.linspace define the largest and the smallest element of the array. For example, the following call creates an array with five elements in the interval from -1 to 1:

```
>>> np.linspace(-1,1,5)
array([-1. , -0.5,  0. ,  0.5,  1. ])
```

43

So, in the model program, we create an array containing 100 numbers from the interval -3 to 3 and calculate the corresponding value of the f function for each of these numbers.

The following line, Y1 = df(X), then determines the derivative of f at the points stored in the X array. When defining df, we take advantage of the fact that the scipy.misc.derivative function is vectorized and therefore also works with an array as a parameter.

Vectorizing Nonvectorized Functions Using numpy.vectorize

If a function like f or df is composed of vectorized operations only, the result is also vectorized again automatically, though there are also cases where vectorization isn't automatically guaranteed. But you don't have to think about the best way to vectorize a function yourself: numpy offers a handy tool for that.

As an example, let's consider a function called clip_positive, which should return the value of a number if it's positive, and 0 if the number has a negative value. A possible implementation of this function is as follows:

```
>>> def clip_positive(x):
...     if x > 0: return x
...     else: return 0
>>> clip_positive(10)
10
>>> clip_positive(-5)
0
>>> clip_positive(2)
2
```

We also want to pass arrays to this function as the value for x so that a new array is created that contains the entry itself for positive entries of x and the value 0 for negative entries. However, the way the function is implemented now, it doesn't work for arrays because case discrimination in this form can't be applied to arrays.

The solution is the numpy.vectorize function decorator,[3] which adapts a function so that it accepts arrays as parameters in addition to single numbers:

```
>>> @np.vectorize
... def clip_positive(x):
...     if x > 0: return x
...     else: return 0
>>> clip_positive(10)
array(10)
>>> clip_positive(-5)
array(0)
```

---

3 For more information on using the function decorators, .

```
>>> b = np.array([4, -3, 0.7, -10, 8])
>>> clip_positive(b)
array([4. , 0. , 0.7, 0. , 8. ])
```

As you can see, the `clip_positive` function now works with both single numbers and entire arrays as parameters. However, an array is also created now if a number was passed for the x parameter. This isn't a problem because arrays of length 1 behave like numbers and can therefore be used as such in further calculations.

With this knowledge, we can understand the implementation of function F in the model program. The following snippet repeats the definition from the program:

```
@np.vectorize
def F(x):
    return sp.integrate.quad(f, 0, x)[0]
```

The `scipy.integrate.quad` function expects the function to be integrated as the first parameter. The two subsequent parameters are used to specify the integration limits. The return value of `scipy.integrate.quad` is a tuple consisting of two elements, where the first entry is an approximation of the integral and the second entry is an upper limit for the approximation error:

```
>>> sp.integrate.quad(f, 0, 4)
(31.463563791363885, 7.668063971742951e-13)
```

Thus, for x, the F function returns the integral over f from 0 to x—that is:

$$F(x) = \int_0^x f(t)dt$$

Thus, according to the fundamental theorem of calculus, F is an antiderivative of f. The `numpy.vectorize` function decorator extends the function to use arrays as parameter values.

The Y2 = F(X) line of the model program determines the values of a primitive function of f at the locations stored in the X array.

> **Note**
>
> The vectorized functions of numpy and scipy are implemented with hardware acceleration and are therefore very efficient. If you vectorize a function using numpy.vectorize, this speed advantage will be lost.
>
> You should therefore try to use the fast routines of numpy and scipy for runtime-critical functions as much as possible.

43

43.2.3   Visualizing Data Using matplotlib.pyplot

Now that the required data has been calculated, let's display it graphically. We'll use the `matplotlib.pyplot` module, which is based on the drawing interface of MATLAB.

You can think of this interface as a blank sheet of paper to which new graphical elements are added by calls of functions from the `matplotlib.pyplot` module. Once the drawing is finished, the result is displayed on the screen using the `matplotlib.pyplot.show` function.

The most important function is `matplotlib.pyplot.plot`, which can be used to visualize any data. In the simplest case, you pass a list of numbers to the `plot` function:

```
>>> plt.plot([1, 3, 5, 2, 1, 4, 6, 7, 3])
[<matplotlib.lines.Line2D object at 0x7f3c5e0947f0>]
>>> plt.show()
```

These numbers are now interpreted as function values, where the indexes of the list, such as 0, 1, 2, …, 8 are interpreted as corresponding values on the x-axis. Linear interpolation is performed between the specified function values so that the individual data points are connected by straight lines. Figure 43.2 illustrates the result.

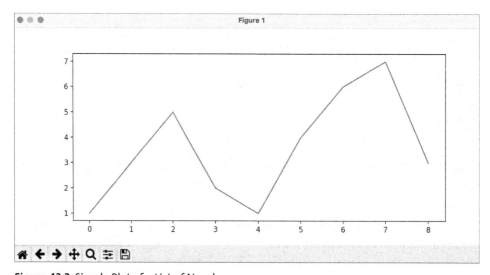

Figure 43.2 Simple Plot of a List of Numbers

The toolbar at the top of the window provides a number of operations to modify the graphic. In addition, the graphic can be saved in different graphics formats (e.g., PNG, PS, EPS, PDF, or SVG).

Usually you want to specify the values on the x-axis belonging to the function values explicitly and not have them determined automatically via the indexes. For this purpose, you must pass two lists or arrays to the `plot` function, where the first parameter contains the x-values and the second parameter contains the corresponding y-values.

For example, to draw a period of the sine function, we first create an array containing data points in the interval [0,2π] with numpy.linspace and then apply the numpy.sin function to it. We then pass the results on to plot:

```
>>> X = np.linspace(0, 2*np.pi, 200)
>>> Y = np.sin(X)
>>> plt.plot(X, Y)
[<matplotlib.lines.Line2D object at 0x7f3c5d495e80>]
>>> plt.show()
```

The result is shown in Figure 43.3.

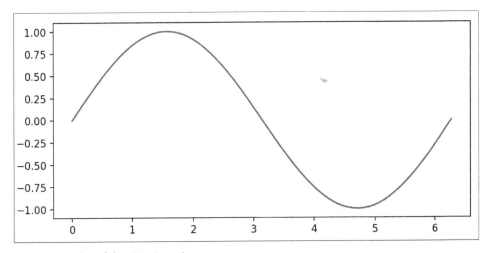

Figure 43.3 Plot of the Sine Function

If you want to display several functions in one graphic, you can call plot several times before the result is displayed using show, as is done in the model program.

Additional parameters of the plot function can be used to adjust the appearance of the graphic. The following snippet shows the commands used to generate the graphical output in the model program. We use the linewidth parameter to adjust the thickness of the lines and change the appearance of the lines via linestyle. The label parameter can be used to assign a string to each plot, which is displayed in the plot legend. Calling the legend function makes the legend visible:

```
plt.plot(X, Y, linewidth=2, label="$f$")
plt.plot(X, Y1, linewidth=2, linestyle="dashed", label="$f'$")
plt.plot(X, Y2, linewidth=2, linestyle="dotted", label="$F$")
plt.legend()
plt.show()
```

Note

For text specifications such as a legend, the LaTeX syntax for formatted output can be used. In this example, the surrounding dollar signs denote a mathematical formula. For more details on formatted output, see the `matplotlib` online documentation.

The final result is shown in Figure 43.4.

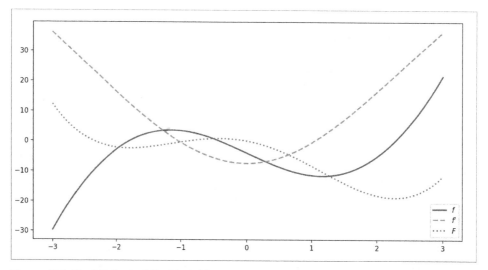

Figure 43.4 Final Output of the Model Program

The `matplotlib` module is capable of generating and designing complex 2D and 3D visualizations. In particular, it has extensive export capabilities to use the visualizations in scientific papers, for example.

The available options go far beyond the introduction presented here. We refer you to the online documentation at *http://www.matplotlib.org* for more information.

43.3   Overview of the numpy and scipy Modules

This section provides tips for practical work with the `numpy.ndarray` data type. We also provide an overview table of the submodules of `scipy`.

43.3.1   Overview of the numpy.ndarray Data Type

The core of `numpy` and `scipy` is the `numpy.ndarray` data type, which can manage multi-dimensional arrays. We'll therefore teach you the basics of using `numpy.ndarray` in this chapter. This introduction is meant as a first start and doesn't cover all the options provided by `numpy.ndarray`.

For further information, refer to the online documentation for numpy at *https:// www.numpy.org*.

The Shape and Data Type of an Array

An *array* is a collection of several similar elements in a single unit, where the elements can be accessed via integer indexes. We'll limit ourselves to one- and two-dimensional arrays in the examples in this chapter for the sake of clarity.

Each array has a *shape* and a *data type*. Here, the shape specifies the dimensions of the array, while the data type specifies what kind of data the elements of the array can store. Both the shape and the data type must be specified when the array is created and can't be changed afterward.

The structure of arrays resembles that of nested list instances. However, arrays are optimized to handle a large number of similar data objects efficiently. A list, on the other hand, can manage references to any data object resulting in more overhead and thus reduced performance compared to the array.

Table 43.2 lists the most important available data types for elements of numpy.ndarray instances.[4]

Name	Description of Possible Values
numpy.bool	Boolean values (True or False), each stored internally as one byte
numpy.int	Integers, using 32 or 64 bits for storage, depending on the platform
numpy.float	Double precision floats for which 64 bits of memory are used
numpy.complex	Complex numbers, where both real and imaginary parts are stored as 64-bit floats

Table 43.2 Overview of NumPy's Most Important Data Types

In addition to these basic types, there are a number of other types that behave in the same way as the basic data types but consume a different amount of memory.

For example, int8 denotes a type that can store integers fitting in one byte, i.e., eight bits. For details on these types, please refer to the online documentation for numpy.

When creating arrays, you should always make sure to specify the correct type; otherwise, inaccuracies may occur if the selected data type can't represent the range of values you want to work with.

---

4 The data types have the same names as Python's built-in numeric data types because they can store similar values. Nevertheless, they are special data types for using numpy.

Creating Arrays and Basic Properties

In the model program from the previous section, one-dimensional arrays were created using the numpy.array and numpy.linspace functions, as shown in the following example:

```
>>> np.array([-1, 4, -5, 7])
array([-1,  4, -5,  7])
>>> np.linspace(0, 1, 11)
array([0. , 0.1, 0.2, 0.3, 0.4, 0.5, 0.6, 0.7, 0.8, 0.9, 1. ])
```

Each array has a dtype attribute that stores the data type of the array:

```
>>> x = np.array([-1, 4, -5, 7])
>>> x.dtype
dtype('int64')
>>> y = np.array([-1, 4, -5.2, 7])
>>> y.dtype
dtype('float64')
```

As you can see, the selected data type depends on which values were passed to the numpy.array function. In this context, numpy always chooses a type that's as simple as possible and can store all passed values. This can be an unwanted limitation if an array is to store other values after its creation. For example, the x array of the preceding example can't store floats.

To explicitly specify the data type of an array, you can pass a dtype keyword parameter to most array creation functions:

```
>>> x = np.array([-1,4,-5,7], dtype=np.float64)
>>> x
array([-1.,  4., -5.,  7.])
>>> x.dtype
dtype('float64')
```

The shape as the second basic property of an array is stored in the shape attribute:

```
>>> x.shape
(4,)
```

The shape attribute stores a tuple, which in turn stores the number of components for each dimension of the array. In the example, the x array therefore has one dimension with four components.

To create an array with multiple dimensions, you can pass a nested structure of iterable objects to the numpy.array function. In the simplest case, this is a list that contains other lists:

```
>>> b = np.array([[1,2], [3,4], [5,6]])
>>> b
array([[1, 2],
       [3, 4],
       [5, 6]])
>>> b.shape
(3, 2)
```

In this example, an array with two dimensions—a *matrix*—is created that contains the elements of the passed lists row by row.

There are a number of special functions that can be used to create arrays of a particular shape. Table 43.3 provides a brief overview of some of these functions.

Name	Description
array(object)	Creates an array from the data referenced by object. Often, object is a reference to a nested list.
linspace(start, stop, num)	Creates an array containing num equidistant data points from start to stop (each inclusive).
empty(shape)	Creates an array with the shape dimensions. The shape parameter is a tuple that contains the number of desired components for each dimension. The values of the array aren't initialized, so they may contain arbitrary numbers.
eye(N, [M, k])	Creates a two-dimensional array with N rows and M columns, containing zeros everywhere except the main diagonal. The value 1 is set on the main diagonal. The k parameter can be used to shift the diagonal. If the M parameter isn't specified, an array with N rows and N columns is created.
ones(shape)	Creates an array of the shape shape whose elements all have the value 1.
zeros(shape)	Creates an array of the shape shape whose elements all have the value 0.
diag(v, [k])	Creates an array that has the values of the v sequence on the main diagonal and whose other elements are filled with 0. The k parameter can be used to shift the diagonal, which should take the values of v.

Table 43.3 Some of the Functions for Creating Arrays

43

As an example, say we want to create a 9×9 matrix that has values from 1 to 9 on the main diagonal and 5 on the two secondary diagonals. All other values should be set to 3:

```
>>> M = 3*(np.ones((9,9)) - np.eye(9,9))
>>> M += 2*(np.eye(9,9,1) + np.eye(9,9,-1))
>>> M += np.diag(range(1,10))
```

To do this, we first create a matrix M with np.ones and np.eye, which has the value 3 everywhere except for the main diagonal. Then we add the value 2 to the two secondary diagonals using np.eye to arrive at the desired 5. Finally, using np.diag, we create a diagonal matrix with the values from 1 to 9 on the main diagonal and add them to M to obtain the final result:

```
>>> M
array([[1., 5., 3., 3., 3., 3., 3., 3., 3.],
       [5., 2., 5., 3., 3., 3., 3., 3., 3.],
       [3., 5., 3., 5., 3., 3., 3., 3., 3.],
       [3., 3., 5., 4., 5., 3., 3., 3., 3.],
       [3., 3., 3., 5., 5., 5., 3., 3., 3.],
       [3., 3., 3., 3., 5., 6., 5., 3., 3.],
       [3., 3., 3., 3., 3., 5., 7., 5., 3.],
       [3., 3., 3., 3., 3., 3., 5., 8., 5.],
       [3., 3., 3., 3., 3., 3., 3., 5., 9.]])
```

This procedure of assembling more complex arrays using prefabricated blocks is characteristic of using numpy.ndarray.

Accessing the Elements of an Array

The individual elements of an array can be accessed via an index, as is the case with lists. Slicing also works for one-dimensional arrays, similar to slicing for lists:[5]

```
>>> a = np.array([-1,4,-5,7])
>>> a[2]
-5
>>> a[2:]
array([-5,  7])
```

Because numpy.ndarray is a mutable data type, the values of an array can be changed even after creation:

```
>>> a[2] = 1337
>>> a
array([  -1,    4, 1337,    7])
```

---

5 There are even more advanced slicing options for arrays with more than two dimensions. For details, refer to the online documentation for numpy.

```
>>> a[0:2] = [-20, -20]
>>> a
array([ -20,   -20, 1337,     7])
```

If an array has several dimensions, the indexes for individual elements consist of several numbers:

```
>>> a = np.zeros((5,5))
>>> a[0,1] = 1
>>> a[3,2] = 2
>>> a[1,3] = 3
>>> a
array([[0., 1., 0., 0., 0.],
       [0., 0., 0., 3., 0.],
       [0., 0., 0., 0., 0.],
       [0., 0., 2., 0., 0.],
       [0., 0., 0., 0., 0.]])
```

Slicing also works with multidimensional arrays by specifying a range for each dimension. In this way, you can, for example, selectively change individual blocks of a matrix:

```
>>> a[0:3,0:3] = 5*np.ones((3,3))
>>> a[3:,3:] = 11
>>> a
array([[ 5.,   5.,   5.,   0.,   0.],
       [ 5.,   5.,   5.,   3.,   0.],
       [ 5.,   5.,   5.,   0.,   0.],
       [ 0.,   0.,   2.,  11.,  11.],
       [ 0.,   0.,   0.,  11.,  11.]])
```

You can assign a number to an entire block, as shown in the second line of the preceding example. In this case, each entry of the block in question is assigned the value 11.

In the same way, it's possible to extract a part from an existing matrix:

```
>>> b = a[1:4,1:4]
>>> b
array([[ 5.,   5.,   3.],
       [ 5.,   5.,   0.],
       [ 0.,   2.,  11.]])
```

However, care must be taken here: matrices a and b share the same data, so changes to matrix b will also affect matrix a and vice versa. To copy a part of a matrix, you can use the copy() method of the numpy.ndarray data type. The following example extracts the same range from a as the previous example, but this time the data is copied:

```
>>> b = a[1:4,1:4].copy()
```

43

In Table 43.4, we provide an overview of a selection of attributes and methods of the numpy.ndarray data type. There, a is an instance of numpy.ndarray.

For the sake of clarity, some parameter lists have been simplified. For a complete list, please refer to the online documentation.

Name	Description
Attributes	
a.shape	Describes the shape of the array a as a tuple.
a.ndim	Specifies the number of dimensions of the array a.
a.size	Specifies the total number of elements of the array a.
a.itemsize	Specifies how many bytes each individual element of the array a consumes in memory.
a.dtype	Describes the data type of the elements of the array a.
a.nbytes	Specifies the memory in bytes that the elements of a consume in total.
a.real	Returns an array containing the real parts of the elements of a as elements.
a.imag	Returns an array containing the imaginary parts of the elements of a as elements.
General methods	
a.tolist()	Creates a nested list containing the elements of a.
a.dump(file)	Writes the a array into the file file object in such a way that it can be read again afterward with the pickle module. For more details about the pickle module, see Chapter 32, Section 32.4.
a.astype(dtype)	Creates a copy of the a array. The elements of the resulting array have the dtype data type.
a.copy()	Creates a copy of the a array.
a.fill(value)	Sets all elements of a to value.
Methods for Resizing	
a.reshape(shape)	Returns an array of the passed shape containing the same data as a. Shares the returned array and its data with a.
a.resize(new_shape)	Changes the shape of a in place to new_shape.

Table 43.4 Selection of Attributes and Methods of the numpy.ndarray Data Type

Name	Description
`a.transpose()`	Returns an array containing the values of a mirrored at the main diagonal. Here, the returned array and a share the same data.
`a.flatten()`	Copies the elements of the a array into an array with one dimension by concatenating the data from multiple dimensions.
`a.ravel()`	Like a.`flatten`, except that no copy is created, so the returned array shares the data with a.
Calculation Methods	
`a.argmax()`	Returns the index of an element of a that has the largest value in a.
`a.max`	Returns the largest value in a.
`a.argmin()`	Returns the index of an element of a that has the smallest value in a.
`a.min()`	Returns the smallest value in a.
`a.clip(min, max)`	Returns an array where the values of a have been limited by min and max.
`a.conj()`	Creates a new array from the a array via a complex conjugation of all elements.
`a.sum()`	Returns the sum of all elements of a.
`a.mean()`	Returns the mean value of all elements in a.
`a.var()`	Calculates the variance of all elements of a.
`a.std()`	Calculates the standard deviation of all elements of a.
`a.prod()`	Returns the product of all elements of a.
`a.all()`	Returns True if the truth values of all elements of a are True. If that's not the case, it returns False.
`a.any()`	Returns True if there is an element in a whose truth value is True. Otherwise, it returns False.

Table 43.4 Selection of Attributes and Methods of the numpy.ndarray Data Type (Cont.)

The skillful handling of the `numpy.ndarray` data type requires some practice. But once you get used to the peculiarities of vectorization, you can write very compact and efficient programs with it.

43

43.3.2   Overview of scipy

The scipy module provides a number of submodules for specific types of calculations. Table 43.5 gives an overview of the modules that are available and what functionalities they provide.

For more detailed information on these modules, refer to the online documentation for scipy at *http://www.scipy.org.*

Submodule	Description
cluster	Provides cluster analysis functions to categorize data records.
constants	Provides mathematical and physical constants.
fftpack	Provides functions for the discrete Fourier transform (implemented with the fast Fourier transform). Differential operators and convolutions are also provided.
integrate	Provides functions that approximate integrals numerically. Both function objects and lists of discrete function values can be integrated. In addition, there are functions that can be used to numerically solve ordinary differential equations in one or more dimensions.
interpolate	Provides functions for interpolation. Among other things, polynomial interpolation (Lagrange and Taylor) as well as splines in one and several dimensions are supported.
io	Provides convenience functions that read and write data from various formats. Supported are data of the MATLAB and IDL programs as well as the Matrix Market File format and Arff files. It can also read and write data in NetCDF format and WAV sound files.
linalg	Provides functions from linear algebra. These include functions for solving linear equations, calculating eigenvalues and eigenvectors, and standard decompositions of matrices (e.g., LU, Cholesky, SVD). In addition, matrix functions such as the matrix exponential function are implemented and functions for generating special matrices (e.g., the Hilbert matrix) are provided.
misc	Provides general functions that don't fit into any of the other categories. These include, for example, functions for calculating the factorial or numerical differentiation.

Table 43.5 Submodules of scipy

Submodule	Description
ndimage	Provides functions with which image data can be processed. There are filter and interpolation functions as well as functions for morphology and analysis.
odr	Implements regression routines for orthogonal regression, which can also be used to compensate for measurement errors in the independent variables.
optimize	Provides functions for solving extreme value problems and finding zeros. Problems in one and multiple dimensions with and without constraints are supported.
signal	Provides functions for signal processing. These include, for example, filter and convolution functions as well as B-splines and wavelets.
sparse	Provides functions for efficient handling of sparse matrices.
spatial	Provides functions for answering range queries (k-d tree). In addition, a class for Delaunay triangulation is also provided.
special	Provides a set of special functions, such as the gamma function or orthogonal polynomials.
stats	Provides multiple statistical functions and probability distributions.
weave	Allows embedding C/C++ code into Python programs.

Table 43.5 Submodules of scipy (Cont.)

In addition to the modules included in scipy, there are a number of other modules that, for various reasons, aren't part of the standard scipy package. These modules are grouped under the name *SciKits* and can be downloaded from *http://scikits.appspot.com*.

43.4   An Introduction to Data Analysis with pandas

In this section, we want to look at the pandas library for representing, analyzing, manipulating, and visualizing data records. The pandas library enjoys great popularity wherever structured, tabular data records have to be processed. Not least because of pandas, Python and its ecosystem have become the reference environment in the emerging data science field. Together with NumPy and SciPy, pandas is one of the Python libraries that account for Python's wide use in scientific applications.

The installation of pandas can be done via pip or conda and is described in Section 43.1. For more information, please visit the pandas website at *https://pandas.pydata.org*.

43

The pandas library provides two main data types that allow for working with data records organized in tables:

- A series is an indexed sequence of values. For example, each column or row of a tabularly organized data record can be considered individually as a series instance.

- A DataFrame is a two-dimensional data structure with row and column indexes and thus represents a complete tabular data record.

Basically, you can think of working with data records in pandas as working with Excel tables or with tables in relational databases like SQLite (see Chapter 32, Section 32.2.1). In particular, we can visualize, analyze, manipulate, and combine larger amounts of data. To this end, we'll describe a few examples in the following sections.

To use pandas, the library must be imported. Similar to NumPy, its short name, pd, has become commonly used:

```
>>> import pandas as pd
```

In this section, we'll present a purely project-based introduction to working with pandas based on a simple sample data record. However, this introduction can't do justice to pandas in terms of its complexity and scope. So you should consider the following introduction as a first pandas sample project that explains the basics and the terminology on which you can build a more in-depth study of pandas if you're interested.

43.4.1   The DataFrame Object

As a first simple example, we'll create a data record describing four US cities with millions of inhabitants, with the record containing name, state, and population properties (see Table 43.6).

Name	State	Population
New York	New York	8,253,213
Los Angeles	California	3,970,219
Chicago	Illinois	2,677,643
Houston	Texas	2,316,120

Table 43.6 Exemplary Data Record of US Megacities

To be able to process the data record in pandas, it must be represented as a DataFrame instance. To do this, we instantiate a DataFrame and pass a dictionary with its contents:

```
>>> df = pd.DataFrame({
...     "City": ["New York", "Los Angeles", "Chicago", "Houston"],
...     "State": ["New York", "California", "Illinois", "Texas"],
...     "Population": [8253213, 3970219, 2677643, 2316120],
... })
```

The dictionary that describes the data record when the DataFrame is created maps the column names of the data record as keys and the column contents as values. In interactive mode, a DataFrame can be output at any time so that we can get a convenient overview of its structure:

```
>>> df
          City        State  Population
0     New York     New York    8253213
1  Los Angeles   California    3970219
2      Chicago     Illinois    2677643
3      Houston        Texas    2316120
```

It turns out that the DataFrame reflects the structure of the data record from Table 43.6. In addition, a numerical row index was automatically assigned.

In addition to the output of the data record itself, we request the number of stored rows via the built-in len function, the data types of the individual columns via the dtypes attribute, and the column index via the columns attribute:

```
>>> len(df)
4
>>> df.dtypes
City          object
State         object
Population     int64
dtype: object
>>> df.columns
Index(['City', 'State', 'Population'], dtype='object')
```

Each column of a data record has a consistent data type. In the example, we can see from the dtypes attribute that the "City" and "State" columns have the object data type for generic string content, while the Population column has automatically been assigned the int64 data type for integers due to its content.

43.4.2   Selective Data Access

In the previous section, we created a sample data record in the form of a DataFrame instance and thus took the first step toward using pandas. In this section, we want to build on this and describe how we can access individual elements or entire subsections

43

955

of the data record. Keep in mind that we are working with a very small data record for clarity reasons. However, the methods presented can be readily applied to very large real-world data records.

We have already indicated that two indexes are automatically created when the DataFrame instance is created:

- The *column index* assigns a unique identification for each column of the data record. By default, we simply use the column name here.

- The *row index* assigns a unique identification for each row of the data record. By default, the rows are numbered consecutively starting at 0.

Accessing Data via the Column Index

Using the column index, we can access individual columns of the data record. This access is similar to that of a dictionary:

```
>>> df["City"]
0        New York
1     Los Angeles
2         Chicago
3         Houston
Name: City, dtype: object
```

Individual columns are not represented as DataFrame instances, but as Series instances:

```
>>> type(df["City"])
<class 'pandas.core.series.Series'>
```

Provided that the column name fulfills the conditions of a Python identifier, pandas also allows for a short form of column access via attributes of the DataFrame instance:

```
>>> df.City
0        New York
1     Los Angeles
2         Chicago
3         Houston
Name: City, dtype: object
```

Instead of accessing a single column, we can also "cut out" a set of columns from the data record. To do this, we specify a list of relevant column names when accessing columns instead of a single column name:

```
>>> df[["City", "Population"]]
          City  Population
0     New York     8253213
```

```
1   Los Angeles     3970219
2       Chicago     2677643
3       Houston     2316120
```

In this case, the result is returned as a `DataFrame` instance, even if only one column was cut out.

Index-Based Row and Column Access: loc

The `loc` attribute of a `DataFrame` instance provides a flexible way to selectively access row and column contents of the data record, basically using the associated row or column index. The methods described in the previous section for column access via the column index can be understood as shorthand for a corresponding access via the `loc` attribute.

To extract a row of the data record, we access the `loc` attribute of the `DataFrame` instance with the corresponding row index:

```
>>> df.loc[1]
City          Los Angeles
State          California
Population        3970219
Name: 1, dtype: object
>>> type(df.loc[1])
<class 'pandas.core.series.Series'>
```

When you access a single row, it's returned as a `series` instance. Similar to the column access, we can also cut out multiple rows from the data record:

```
>>> df.loc[[1,3]]
          City        State  Population
1   Los Angeles  California     3970219
3       Houston       Texas     2316120
>>> type(df.loc[[1,3]])
<class 'pandas.core.frame.DataFrame'>
```

When we cut out multiple rows, the result is returned as a `DataFrame` instance, analogous to the column access.

The `loc` attribute also enables slicing (see Chapter 12, Section 12.2.5) to slice out all rows between a start index and an end index. To do this, we use the same syntax that is used for slicing lists:

43

```
>>> df.loc[1:3]
          City        State   Population
1  Los Angeles  California     3970219
2      Chicago     Illinois     2677643
3      Houston       Texas     2316120
```

> **Note**
>
> Note that pandas includes the final index row in the result when slicing via loc. This makes slicing here subtly different from conventional slicing for lists (see Chapter 12, Section 12.2.5).

In addition to the simple row access, loc also allows for combined access to row and column ranges. In particular, individual cells or specific cell ranges can be cut out of the data record in this way. For combined row and column access, the required specifications of the row and column ranges are written separated by a comma:

```
>>> df.loc[3, "City"]
'Houston'
```

Here, the previously discussed access variants can be combined without any problem:

```
>>> df.loc[[1,3], "City"]
1     Los Angeles
3         Houston
Name: City, dtype: object
>>> df.loc[1:3, "City":"Population"]
          City        State   Population
1  Los Angeles  California     3970219
2      Chicago     Illinois     2677643
3      Houston       Texas     2316120
```

A single colon can be used to cut out entire rows and columns:

```
>>> df.loc[3, :]
City          Houston
State           Texas
Population    2316120
Name: 3, dtype: object
>>> df.loc[:, "City"]
0       New York
1    Los Angeles
2        Chicago
3        Houston
Name: City, dtype: object
```

Note that the result of the access operation via `loc` may have a different data type depending on the degree of restriction. When you cut out individual cells, the cell contents are returned in their correct data type. If individual row or column ranges are cut out, the result is returned as a `Series` instance. For more complex sections that span multiple rows or multiple columns, we obtain the result as a `DataFrame`:

```
>>> type(df.loc[1, "City"])
<class 'str'>
>>> type(df.loc[:, "City"])
<class 'pandas.core.series.Series'>
>>> type(df.loc[:, :])
<class 'pandas.core.frame.DataFrame'>
```

Custom-Defined Row Indexes

In the previous accesses to rows of the `df` data record, we implicitly used pandas to automatically assign a sequential numeric row index. When creating a `DataFrame` instance, we can also define our own row index using the optional `index` parameter:

```
>>> df2 = pd.DataFrame({
...      "City": ["New York", "Los Angeles", "Chicago", "Houston"],
...      "State": ["New York", "California", "Illinois", "Texas"],
...      "Population": [8253213, 3970219, 2677643, 2316120],
... }, index=["i1 ", "i2", "i3", "i4"])
>>> df2
            City        State  Population
i1      New York     New York    8253213
i2   Los Angeles   California    3970219
i3       Chicago     Illinois    2677643
i4       Houston        Texas    2316120
```

The element access examples we discussed earlier can be easily applied as well to the `df2` data record with a custom-defined index:

```
>>> df2["i2":"i4"]
            City        State  Population
i2   Los Angeles   California    3970219
i3       Chicago     Illinois    2677643
i4       Houston        Texas    2316120
```

Alternatively, you can also determine a column to be the index column using the `set_index` method:

```
>>> df2 = df2.set_index("City")
```

The record modified in this way then allows row access via the city name:

43

959

```
>>> df2
               State  Population
City
New York       New York    8253213
Los Angeles  California    3970219
Chicago         Illinois    2677643
Houston           Texas    2316120
>>> df2["Los Angeles":"Houston"]
               State  Population
City
Los Angeles  California    3970219
Chicago         Illinois    2677643
Houston           Texas    2316120
```

A combination of several columns can also be used for the row index.

A desirable property for an index is *uniqueness*—that is, the property that each row of the data record can be addressed by a unique index value.[6] Note that by default pandas doesn't check whether the assigned row index is unique. A row access via a nonunique index may cause a combination of several rows to be unexpectedly returned.

Position-Based Row and Column Access: iloc

In the previous section, we introduced the loc attribute, which provides a flexible way to access portions of a data record based on row and column indexes. In this section, we want to briefly describe the iloc attribute, which provides a similar kind of access, but purely position-based:

```
>>> df.iloc[0, 1]
'New York'
>>> df.iloc[:, 1]
0      New York
1    California
2      Illinois
3         Texas
Name: State, dtype: object
```

For the access via iloc, rows and columns are numbered consecutively starting at 0 and can be addressed via this position-based index. Apart from this difference, the access via iloc works in the same way as the access via loc, which is why we won't provide any additional examples here.

---

6 With this in mind, we should also question again the choice of the city name as the index column in the example. For example, consider that the data could contain Springfield, Kentucky, and Springfield, Illinois.

Note

Note that when you use slicing in `iloc`, unlike slicing in `loc`, the final index of the slice won't be included in the result. In this context, slicing in pandas behaves exactly like slicing in lists (see Chapter 12, Section 12.2.5).

43.4.3   Deleting Rows and Columns

Now that we've dealt with accessing parts of the data record, we'd like to describe how you can delete entire rows and columns from the record.

For this purpose, the `drop` method of a record is used, which deletes rows in its default parameterization. To do so, you must pass the index of the row to be deleted or a list of indexes of the rows to be deleted to the method:

```
>>> df.drop(0)
          City        State  Population
1  Los Angeles  California     3970219
2      Chicago     Illinois     2677643
3      Houston        Texas     2316120
>>> df.drop([0, 2])
          City        State  Population
1  Los Angeles  California     3970219
3      Houston        Texas     2316120
```

The `drop` method doesn't remove elements from an existing `DataFrame` instance, but returns the manipulated record as a copy.

The deletion of columns is also done by the `drop` method, which must be informed via the additional `axis=1` argument that the columns of the data record are to be considered:

```
>>> df.drop("State", axis=1)
          City  Population
0     New York     8253213
1  Los Angeles     3970219
2      Chicago     2677643
3      Houston     2316120
```

43.4.4   Inserting Rows and Columns

To experimentally test the extension of a pandas data record, we'll first create a second `df2` data record, with four additional cities:

43

```
>>> df2 = pd.DataFrame({
...     "City": ["Phoenix", "Philadelphia", "San Antonio", "San Diego"],
...     "State": ["Arizona", "Pennsylvania", "Texas", "California"],
...     "Population": [1708127, 1578487, 1567118, 1422420],
... })
```

The concat function creates a record resulting from the concatenation of the records passed to it as parameters. In addition, we use the ignore_index parameter to specify that new row indexes should also be assigned for the newly inserted content instead of taking them from the source data record:

```
>>> pd.concat([df, df2], ignore_index=True)
            City         State  Population
0       New York      New York     8253213
1    Los Angeles    California     3970219
2        Chicago      Illinois     2677643
3        Houston         Texas     2316120
4        Phoenix       Arizona     1708127
5   Philadelphia  Pennsylvania     1578487
6    San Antonio         Texas     1567118
7      San Diego    California     1422420
```

To string together the columns of multiple records, the axis=1 argument is specified in the same way as for the drop method from the previous section:

```
>>> pd.concat([df, df2], axis=1)
```

Of course, such a means of concatenation makes little sense in the context of our example.

43.4.5   Logical Expressions on Data Records

Beyond the index-based access methods, pandas provides the option to cut out rows of a record that meet certain content criteria, similar to accessing a relational database. To be able to formulate appealing examples, we use the append method described previously to define a richer data record, df3:

```
>>> df3 = pd.concat([df, df2], ignore_index=True)
```

In the following example, we'll use the > comparison operator to identify cities with populations greater than 3,000,000:

```
>>> df3["Population"] > 3000000
0     True
1     True
2     False
```

```
3     False
4     False
5     False
6     False
7     False
Name: Population, dtype: bool
```

The result of such a logical expression is a data record that contains, for each cell considered, the evaluation of the logical expression for that cell. In the example, we've restricted ourselves to the column with the number of inhabitants and compared the values contained there with the limit of 3,000,000. As you can see, the result contains the entry True twice, corresponding to the two largest cities, New York and Los Angeles, while the condition for all other cities was evaluated as False.

Similar to NumPy (see Chapter 38, Section 38.3), we can again use the Boolean result of a condition applied to a pandas data record in the access, and thus cut the rows of the data record that match the condition:

```
>>> df3[df3["Population"] > 3000000]
        City       State  Population
0    New York    New York    8253213
1  Los Angeles  California    3970219
```

The & and | operators, which are normally used for the bitwise AND and the bitwise OR, can be used to logically link conditions. In this way, we can identify those cities that have more than two million inhabitants and are additionally not located in Texas:

```
>>> df[(df["Population"] > 2000000) & (df["State"] != "Texas")]
        City       State  Population
0    New York    New York    8253213
1  Los Angeles  California    3970219
2     Chicago    Illinois    2677643
```

Note that the parentheses around the single conditions are necessary because of the operator precedence.

43.4.6   Manipulating Data Records

So far, we've dealt with read accesses to DataFrame instances, learning about the loc and iloc attributes in particular. In this section, we want to use pandas to manipulate a data record. Before we venture into the topic of manipulation, we'll create a copy of the df3 data record that we can edit per our requirements:

```
>>> df4 = df3.copy()
```

43

Basically, the way manipulating a data record works is that we first restrict ourselves to the area of the record we want to manipulate and then apply an operation to that sub-area. In this way, we can, for example, double the population of each city:

```
>>> df4["Population"] *= 2
>>> df4
            City          State  Population
0       New York       New York    16506426
1    Los Angeles     California     7940438
2        Chicago       Illinois     5355286
3        Houston          Texas     4632240
4        Phoenix        Arizona     3416254
5   Philadelphia   Pennsylvania     3156974
6    San Antonio          Texas     3134236
7      San Diego     California     2844840
```

Also, other arithmetic operations and especially many NumPy functions can be applied here to entire rows or columns of pandas data records. In the following example, we'll replace the content of each entry in the state column with the respective two-letter state abbreviation:

```
>>> df4["State"] = ["NY", "CA", "IL", "TX", "AZ", "PA", "TX", "CA"]
>>> df4
            City State  Population
0       New York    NY    16506426
1    Los Angeles    CA     7940438
2        Chicago    IL     5355286
3        Houston    TX     4632240
4        Phoenix    AZ     3416254
5   Philadelphia    PA     3156974
6    San Antonio    TX     3134236
7      San Diego    CA     2844840
```

Instead of replacing the entire column, we can also replace cells based on their contents—for example, to reenter Texas instead of TX:

```
>>> df4.loc[df4["State"] == "TX", "State"] = "Texas"
>>> df4
            City  State  Population
0       New York     NY    16506426
1    Los Angeles     CA     7940438
2        Chicago     IL     5355286
3        Houston  Texas     4632240
4        Phoenix     AZ     3416254
```

```
5   Philadelphia    PA      3156974
6    San Antonio  Texas     3134236
7      San Diego    CA      2844840
```

With such replacement operations on the row or column level, a replacement can also be performed by taking into account the respective index. In the following example, we'll replace New York with Dallas by first creating a Series instance for Dallas and then performing the assignment:

```
>>> df4.loc[0] = pd.Series({
...     "City": "Dallas",
...     "State": "Texas",
...     "Population": 1343266
... })
>>> df4
           City  State  Population
0         Dallas  Texas    1343266
1    Los Angeles     CA    7940438
2        Chicago     IL    5355286
3        Houston  Texas    4632240
4        Phoenix     AZ    3416254
5   Philadelphia     PA    3156974
6    San Antonio  Texas    3134236
7      San Diego     CA    2844840
```

If a column should be missing during such an assignment, the value NaN (for *not a number*) is assigned to the corresponding cell. Additional existing columns will simply be ignored.

43.4.7   Input and Output

An essential aspect of working with data records is the ability to read data records from different data formats and to save the data again after manipulation. A DataFrame instance can be stored very easily in different data formats, with an individual method dedicated to each data format:

```
>>> df3.to_html("cities.html")
>>> df3.to_csv("cities.csv")
>>> df3.to_json("cities.json")
>>> df3.to_excel("cities.xlsx")
```

43

> **Note**
>
> For exporting and importing a data record to and from the XLSX format of Microsoft Excel, in addition to the installation of pandas, the openpyxl package is required, which can be installed via conda and pip:
>
> ```
> $ conda install openpyxl
> $ pip install openpyxl
> ```

Analogous to exporting data records into different data formats, existing data records can be read from several formats and made available as a DataFrame instance:

```
>>> df5 = pd.read_html("cities.html")
>>> df5 = pd.read_csv("cities.csv")
>>> df5 = pd.read_json("cities.json")
>>> df5 = pd.read_excel("cities.xlsx")
```

In the examples shown here, the data was loaded from an HTML table, a CSV file (see Chapter 32, Section 32.6), a JSON file (see Chapter 32, Section 32.5), and an XLSX file from Microsoft Excel. In addition, pandas supports a large number of other file formats for import and export, including in particular common file formats for storing tabular data records such as HDF5.

43.4.8 Visualization

A strength of pandas that should be emphasized here is the convenient possibility to visualize data records and thus to get a quick overview of data. For this purpose, you can use the plot method of a DataFrame instance, which, depending on the parameterization, can generate quite different plots. In the following sections, we compare the population figures of the cities in the df3 data records in the form of a bar chart:

```
>>> df3.plot(x="City", y="Population", kind="barh")
```

> **Note**
>
> If you run the examples in an interactive Python shell, you must call the show function of Matplotlib to have the plots displayed:
>
> ```
> >>> import matplotlib.pyplot as plt
> >>> plt.show()
> ```
>
> If you work in Jupyter Notebook, you can have pandas plots displayed automatically by executing the following line in a cell (see also Chapter 40, Section 40.4.3):
>
> ```
> % matplotlib inline
> ```

When calling the `plot` method, we specify which columns of the data record should be used for the two axes of the visualization (parameters x and y) and which type the visualization should have (parameter `kind`). The created visualization is shown in Figure 43.5.

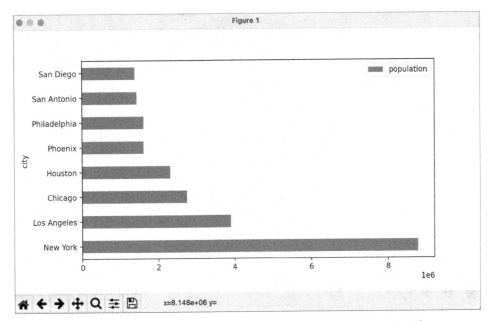

Figure 43.5 Compilation of the Population Figures of Large US Cities Created with the Help of pandas

If we don't make an explicit specification for the x-axis of the plot, pandas will use the index column, so the following combination of specifying a new index column and visualizing without explicitly specifying the x-axis will produce the same result as in Figure 43.5:

```
>>> df3.set_index("City").plot(kind="barh")
```

We have the option to create various types of plots via the `kind` parameter, including line charts (`line`), horizontal and vertical bar charts (`barh` and `bar`), histograms (`hist`), box plots (`box`), pie charts (`pie`), and scatter diagrams (`scatter`).

As an alternative to the bar chart, the data record can also be visualized as a pie chart:

```
>>> df3.set_index("City").plot(y="Population", kind="pie", legend=False)
```

The result is shown in Figure 43.6. Note that pandas creates the visualizations using Matplotlib (Section 43.2.3) and also passes specified keyword parameters to the same.

43

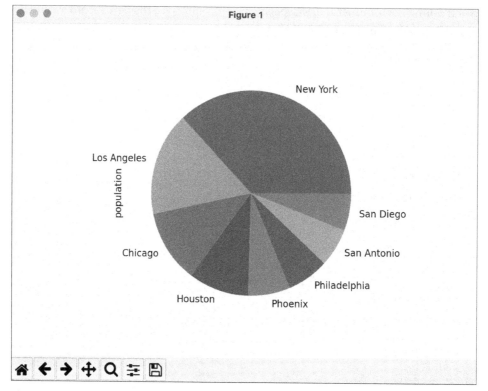

Figure 43.6 Distribution of Population Figures among the 10 Largest US Cities

This concludes the introduction to the possibilities of processing and visualizing data records in Python using the pandas library. Note that this section can only be considered as an introduction to pandas and its large set of features. Feel encouraged to use this introduction as a springboard for a deeper study of pandas and the related data science ecosystem in Python.

Chapter 44
Inside Knowledge

This chapter is a collection of thematically independent, smaller modules that can be useful in your everyday programming work. It's worth reading the following sections and keeping the presented modules in mind.

44.1   Opening URLs in the Default Browser: webbrowser

The webbrowser module can be used to open a website in the default browser of the system currently in use. The module essentially contains the open function, which is explained ahead.

The open(url, [new, autoraise])function opens the URL in the system's default browser. For the new parameter, an integer between 0 and 2 can be passed. Here, a value of 0 means that the URL should be opened in an existing browser window if possible; 1 means that the URL should be opened in a new browser window; and 2 means that the URL should be opened in a new tab of an existing browser window if possible. The default setting of the parameter is 0.

If the value True is passed for the autoraise parameter, an attempt is made to bring the browser window with the open URL to the foreground. Note that many systems do this automatically:

```
>>> import webbrowser
>>> webbrowser.open("https://www.python-book.com", 2)
True
```

44.2   Interpreting Binary Data: struct

When a file is read in binary mode, the file contents arrive in the program as a sequence of bytes. A byte consists of eight bits and thus represents a number between 0 and 255. Values that don't fit into this number space are represented by a sequence of bytes.

In Chapter 6, Section 6.4.3, we binary-read a graphic in bitmap file format to get the height, width, and color depth of the image. As image dimensions can exceed 255 pixels, the height and width of the image are stored in bitmap format by a sequence of four bytes.

44

Python's standard library contains the struct module, which takes care of interpreting byte sequences for us. The preceding example can be written using the struct module as follows:

```python
from struct import unpack
with open("coffee.bmp", "rb") as f:
    f.seek(18)
    values = unpack("iiHH", f.read(12))
    print("Width:", values[0], "px")
    print("Height:", values[1], "px")
    print("Color depth:", values[3], "bpp")
```

First, the reading position is set to the 18th byte. After that, we read the following 12 bytes in one go and pass them together with a format description to the unpack function of the struct module. The unpack function decomposes the byte sequence according to the format description and joins the single values. The tuple returned by unpack contains the interpreted values.

Table 44.1 lists the most important format specifications along with their size and the Python data type they are converted to.

Specification	Data Type	Size	Signed
c	bytes	1 byte*	—
b	int	1 byte	Yes
B	int	1 byte	No
?	bool	1 byte	—
h	int	2 bytes	Yes
H	int	2 bytes	No
i	int	4 bytes	Yes
I	int	4 bytes	No
l	int	4 bytes	Yes
L	int	4 bytes	No
q	int	8 bytes	Yes
Q	int	8 bytes	No
e	float	2 bytes	Yes
f	float	4 bytes	Yes

Table 44.1 Format Specifications for Unpack

Specification	Data Type	Size	Signed
d	float	8 bytes	Yes
s	bytes	–	–

* The c format specification stands for a single character, while s represents a string of any length.

Table 44.1 Format Specifications for Unpack (Cont.)

Aside from the unpack function, the struct module contains the following other functions that we'll briefly describe:

- **pack(fmt, [*values])**
  This function is the counterpart to unpack. It encodes the passed values into a byte sequence using the fmt format specifications:

```
>>> import struct
>>> struct.pack("iif", 12, 34, 5.67)
b'\x0c\x00\x00\x00"\x00\x00\x00\xa4p\xb5@'
```

- **pack_into(fmt, buffer, offset, [*values])**
  This function works like pack, but writes the encoded data to the bytearray instance buffer at the offset position.

- **unpack_from(fmt, buffer, [offset])**
  This function works like unpack, but it reads the data of the byte sequence only from the offset position. With the help of unpack_from, the seek call can be saved in the bitmap example shown previously.

- **calcsize(fmt)**
  This function returns the size of the byte sequence that would result from calling pack with the fmt format specification.

44.3 Hidden Password Entry

The getpass module enables the convenient entry of a password via the keyboard. The functions included in the getpass module are explained ahead. To run the examples, you must first import the module:

```
>>> import getpass
```

44.3.1 getpass([prompt, stream])

The getpass function reads an input from the user as input does and returns it as a string. The difference from input is that getpass is intended for entering passwords.

44

This means that the user's input using getpass is covert; that is, it isn't displayed in the console.

The optional prompt parameter can be used to specify the text that prompts the user for the password. The parameter is preset with "Password: ". For the second optional parameter, stream, a file-like object can be passed in which the prompt request will be written. This works only on Unix-based operating systems; on Windows, the prompt parameter is ignored:

```
>>> s = getpass.getpass("Your password please: ")
Your password please:
>>> print(s)
This is my password
```

44.3.2 getpass.getuser()

The getuser function returns the name with which the current user has logged into the operating system:

```
>>> getpass.getuser()
'Username'
```

44.4 Command Line Interpreter

The cmd module provides a simple and abstracted interface for writing a line-based command interpreter—cmd. A line-based command interpreter is an interactive console in which commands are entered line-by-line and interpreted immediately after the input has been confirmed. The interactive mode is a well-known example of such a command interpreter. In a separate project, cmd could be used for an administrator console, for example.

The cmd module contains the Cmd class, which can be used as a base class for your own command interpreters and provides a rough framework for doing so. Because Cmd is meant to be a base class, it makes no sense to instantiate the class directly. The following sample project uses the Cmd class to create a rudimentary console. The console should support a total of four commands—date to output the current date, time to output the current time, timer to initialize and read a stopwatch, and exit to exit the console:

```
import cmd
import time
class MyConsole(cmd.Cmd):
    def __init__(self):
        super().__init__()
        self.prompt = "==> "
```

```python
    def do_date(self, prm):
        d = time.localtime()
        print("Today is {}-{:02}-{:02}".format(d[0],d[1],d[2]))
        return False
    def help_date(self):
        print("Outputs the current date")
    def do_time(self, prm):
        z = time.localtime()
        print("It is {:02}:{:02}:{:02}".format(z[3], z[4], z[5]))
        return False
    def do_timer(self, prm):
        if prm == "start":
            self.startTime = time.perf_counter()
        elif prm == "get":
            print("{} seconds have passed".format(
                        int(time.perf_counter() - self.startTime)))
    def do_exit(self, prm):
        print("Goodbye")
        return True
```

In the example, we defined the MyConsole class, which is derived from cmd.Cmd. In the constructor of the class, we initialize the base class and set the self.prompt attribute. This attribute comes from the base class and references the string that should prompt a user for a command.

To implement a command in a cmd.Cmd console, we can simply create a do_command method, replacing command with the name of the relevant command. In this sense, you'll find the do_date, do_time, do_timer, and do_exit methods for the three available commands in the MyConsole class. Each of these methods is called when the command is entered by the user and is passed the string that the user wrote after the command as the only parameter. The sample implementation of the methods is very simple and needn't be explained in detail here.

It's important that a command method uses the return value to indicate whether the console should accept other commands after this command. If the method returns False, further commands will be accepted. If the return value is True, the command loop will be terminated. The return value False of some methods is superfluous in the preceding example as a function or method without a return value implicitly returns None and the truth value of None is False. Nevertheless, the corresponding return statement is included in the source code for demonstration purposes.

In addition to the command methods, there is a help_date method as a sample implementation of the interactive help provided by the cmd.Cmd class. When a user enters a question mark or the help command followed by a command name, the help_command

44

method is called with the corresponding command name. It then outputs a short explanatory text for the respective command.

To turn the preceding code into a full-fledged program, the class must be instantiated and the command loop started by calling the `cmdloop` method:

```
console = MyConsole()
console.cmdloop()
```

After starting the program, by `==>` the user is prompted to enter a command. A sample session in the console looks as follows:

```
==> date
Today is 2022-07-17
==> time
It is 7:26:50
==> time
It is 7:26:54
==> timer start
==> timer get
5 seconds have passed.
==> exit
Goodbye
```

The help texts of the commands can be displayed as follows:

```
==> help date
Outputs the current date
==> ? date
Outputs the current date
==> help
Documented commands (type help <topic>):
==========================================
date
Undocumented commands:
=======================
exit  help  time
```

The `help` command without parameters outputs a list of all documented and undocumented commands of your console.

The sample program presented here is intended as a simple way to use the `Cmd` class. In addition to the function shown here, the class provides further options to adapt the behavior of the console exactly to your needs.

44.5   File Interface for Strings: io.StringIO

The io module of the standard library contains the StringIO class, which provides the interface of a file object, but internally operates on a string.

This is useful, for example, if a function expects an open file object as a parameter to write to, but you would rather have the written data in the form of a string. Usually a StringIO instance can be passed here so that the written data can be reused as a string afterward:

```
>>> from io import StringIO
>>> pseudofile = StringIO()
```

The constructor can optionally be passed a string containing the initial contents of the file. From now on, the returned instance referenced by pseudofile can be used like a file object:

```
>>> pseudofile.write("Hello world")
11
>>> print(" Hello world", file=pseudofile)
```

Besides the functionality of a file object, an instance of the StringIO class provides an additional method called getvalue, through which the internal string can be accessed:

```
>>> pseudofile.getvalue()
'Hello world Hello world\n'
```

Just like a file object, a StringIO instance can be closed by calling the close method when it's no longer needed:

```
>>> pseudofile.close()
```

> **Note**
>
> Instances of the StringIO type can be used as context manages inside a with statement, see Chapter 22:
>
> ```
> >>> with StringIO() as pseudofile:
> ...      pseudofile.write("Hello world")
> ...      print(" Hello world", file=pseudofile)
> ...      pseudofile.getvalue()
> 11
> 'Hello world Hello world\n'
> ```
>
> This is necessary to make the StringIO type a fully featured drop-in replacement for file objects. However, since StringIO instances do not handle open files, connections, or similar resources, the close method merely frees memory. As a result, it is not as important to ensure calling close for StringIO as it is for other context managers, e.g., file objects.

44

44.6   Generators as Consumers

In Chapter 21, Section 21.1, you learned about generators. Generators are special functions that return multiple values in succession so that iteration can be performed over them.

An example is the following generator, which generates the first n square numbers:

```
def square_generator(n):
    for i in range(1,n+1):
        yield i*i
for q in square_generator(3):
    print(q)
```

This sample program outputs the numbers 1, 4, and 9 on the screen. Each for loop uses the iterator protocol, so the second for loop in the example is semantically equivalent to the following program:

```
g = square_generator(3)
try:
    while True:
        v = next(g)
        print(v)
except StopIteration:
    pass
```

Here, a generator instance g is created first, and then the next value is read with next(g) until a StopIteration exception is raised—that is, until no more values are left. In this case, the generator delivers values to the caller, without the caller being able to pass on any information to the generator; the generator acts as a producer and the caller as a consumer of the data.

There's a way in Python to reverse this relationship so that a generator can receive data from the caller and thus become a consumer. For this purpose, a generator has a send(value) method that sends a value to a generator instance. In the generator, a value sent in this way can be received by reading the return value of the yield statement. The following sample program implements a consuming generator that outputs all received values via print:

```
def printer():
    while True:
        value = (yield)
        print(value)

p = printer()
next(p)
```

```
p.send(87)
p.send("Test")
p.send([4,3,2])
```

The program generates the following output:

```
87
Test
[4, 3, 2]
```

After defining the `printer` generator function, a generator instance is created with `p = printer()`, and the `next(p)` call runs the generator instance to the first `yield`. This is necessary because data can only be sent to a generator instance if it's waiting at a `yield` statement. Now we send the value `87` to the generator using `p.send(87)`, which causes the generator to resume its work where it was interrupted by `yield`—that is, in the `value = (yield)` line. It's now crucial that the `yield` statement accept the sent value so that after executing the line the `value` reference points to `87`. Then the output occurs and the loop starts over, causing the generator to relinquish control to the calling level and wait at `yield`.

If the return value of the `yield` statement is used, the statement must be enclosed in parentheses. The parentheses can be omitted only if the `yield` statement is the only operand on the right-hand side of an assignment, but even then it's good style to use parentheses anyway. Examples of valid `yield` statements include the following:

```
def yield_can_only_be_inside_def_blocks():
    a = yield
    a = yield 5
    a = (yield) + 10
    print((yield))
    function(10, (yield 20))
```

The following examples show `yield` statements that aren't allowed:

```
def yield_can_only_be_inside_def_blocks():
    a = yield + 10
    print(yield)
    function(10, yield 20)
```

Note

If you use subgenerators with `yield from`, the values sent using `send` are passed through to the lowest nested subgenerator.

44

44.6.1   A Decorator for Consuming Generator Functions

To make a consuming generator function run automatically to the first yield when it's generated, you can use the following consumer decorator. If printer is decorated with consumer in this example, the explicit next(p) call will be omitted:

```python
def consumer(f):
    def h_f(*args, **kwargs):
        gen = f(*args, **kwargs)
        next(gen)
        return gen
    return h_f


@consumer
def printer():
    while True:
        value = (yield)
        print(value)
```

This decorator eliminates the need to explicitly call next(p) after the generator has been created.

44.6.2   Triggering Exceptions in a Generator

From the calling level, exceptions can be raised in a generator function by passing them to the throw method of the generator instance. Within the generator function, the exception then occurs at the yield statement where the generator was stopped.

The following example uses this option to include information about the internal state of a generator in the traceback in case of an error:

```python
def generator(n):
    for i in range(1,n+1):
        try:
            yield i*i
        except Exception as e:
            raise Exception("Error at index {}".format(i))


g = generator(100)
next(g)
next(g)
g.throw(ValueError)
```

The example results in the following output:

```
Traceback (most recent call last):
  File "gen.py", line 4, in generator
    yield i*i
ValueError

During handling of the above exception, another exception occurred:

Traceback (most recent call last):
  File "gen.py", line 11, in <module>
    g.throw(ValueError)
  File "gen.py", line 6, in generator
    raise Exception("Error at index {}".format(i))
Exception: Error at index 2
```

> **Note**
>
> If you use subgenerators with yield from, the exceptions raised with throw are passed
> through to the deepest nested subgenerator.

44.6.3   A Pipeline as a Chain of Consuming Generator Functions

One area of applying consuming generator functions is the construction of pipelines
by concatenating individual building blocks. As an example, you can consider a pipeline that processes a signal—that is, a sequence of numerical values. There are two
types of building blocks:

1. Filter blocks that can receive numbers and pass them to another block

2. Output blocks that can receive numbers and don't pass them on, but, for example,
   output them on the screen

In the following program, we'll implement the two filter_lift(stage, target) and
filter_average(window, target) filter blocks:

```python
@consumer
def filter_lift(stage, target):
    while True:
        target.send(stage + (yield))


@consumer
def filter_mean(window, target):
    values = []
    while True:
        values.append((yield))
        if len(values) >= window:
            target.send(sum(values)/window)
```

44

```
        values.pop(0)

@consumer
def output():
    while True:
        print((yield))

p = output()
f = filter_lift(10, p)
f = filter_mean(2, f)

for d in [1, 3, 2, 4, 2, 1]:
    f.send(d)
```

The filter_lift block adds the stage number to each received value and sends the result to the target consumer. In the second block, filter_mean, the mean value of the last values received in window is passed to target. For this purpose, the last values are stored in the values list.

The output generator function is a simple output block that prints each received value on the screen.

The following lines are used to build a signal processing pipeline of three blocks:

```
p = output()
f = filter_lift(10, p)
f = filter_mean(2, f)
```

If a value is now sent into the pipeline in the for loop with f.send(d), it will first be processed by filter_mean. Once enough values have been collected by filter_mean (2 in this example), their mean value is sent on to filter_lift, where it's increased by 10 and sent to output, where the value is finally output.

Thus, the sample program generates the following output:

```
12.0
12.5
13.0
13.0
11.5
```

You can extend this example by defining more filter or output blocks and connecting them in different orders to form a pipeline.

44.7 Copying Instances: copy

As you already know, in Python an assignment only creates a new reference to the same instance instead of creating a copy of the instance.

In the following example, s and t reference the same list, as the comparison with is reveals:

```
>>> s = [1, 2, 3]
>>> t = s
>>> t is s
True
```

This approach doesn't always behave as intended because changes to the list referenced by s also affect t due to side effects and vice versa.

For example, if a method of a class returns a list that's also used within the class, the list can also be modified via the returned reference, which is usually not what we want:

```
class MyClass:
    def __init__(self):
        self.list = [1, 2, 3]
    def get_list(self):
        return self.list
    def show_list(self):
        print(self.list)
```

If we now use the get_list method to return a reference to the list, we can use a side effect to modify the list attribute of the instance:

```
>>> instance = MyClass()
>>> lst = instance.get_list()
>>> lst.append(1337)
>>> instance.show_list()
[1, 2, 3, 1337]
```

To prevent this, the get_list method should return a copy of the internally managed list instead of the list itself.

This is where the copy module comes in, which is designed to create real copies of an instance. For this purpose, copy provides two functions: copy.copy and copy.deepcopy. Both methods expect the instance to be copied as a parameter and return a reference to a copy of it:[1]

---

1 Of course, a list can also be copied by means of slicing. However, the copy module allows copying any instance.

```
>>> import copy
>>> s = [1, 2, 3]
>>> t = copy.copy(s)
>>> t
[1, 2, 3]
>>> t is s
False
```

The example shows that although t contains the same elements as s, it still doesn't reference the same instance as s, so the comparison with is is negative.

The difference between copy.copy and copy.deepcopy can be found in the handling of references that contain the instances to be copied. The copy.copy function creates a new list, but the references within the list still point to the same elements. With copy.deepcopy, on the other hand, the instance itself is copied and then recursively all instances referenced by it.

We illustrate this difference with a list containing another list:

```
>>> lst = [1, [2, 3]]
>>> lst2 = copy.copy(lst)
>>> lst2.append(4)
>>> lst2
[1, [2, 3], 4]
>>> lst
[1, [2, 3]]
```

As expected, attaching the new element 4 to lst2 doesn't change the instance referenced by lst. But if we change the [2, 3] inner list, this will affect both lst and lst2:

```
>>> lst[1].append(1337)
>>> lst2
[1, [2, 3, 1337], 4]
>>> lst
[1, [2, 3, 1337]]
```

The is operator shows the reason for this behavior—lst[1] and lst2[1] are the same instance:

```
>>> lst[1] is lst2[1]
True
```

If we use copy.deepcopy instead, the list is copied including all contained elements:

```
>>> lst = [1, [2, 3]]
>>> lst2 = copy.deepcopy(lst)
>>> lst2[1].append(4)
>>> lst2
```

```
[1, [2, 3, 4]]
>>> lst
[1, [2, 3]]
>>> lst[1] is lst2[1]
False
```

Both the manipulation of lst2[1] and the is operator show that lst2[1] and lst[1] are different instances.

Now we can modify the sample MyClass class so that the get_list method returns a copy of the internally managed list:

```
class MyClass:
    def __init__(self):
        self.list = [1, 2, 3]
    def get_list(self):
        return copy.deepcopy(self.list)
    def show_list(self):
        print(self.list)
```

If we now run the same test code as shown previously with the new class, the unwanted side effect is gone:

```
>>> instance = MyClass()
>>> lst = instance.get_list()
>>> lst.append(1337)
>>> instance.show_list()
[1, 2, 3]
```

We use deepcopy here so that the list attribute is protected from side effects even if there are modifiable elements in the list.

> **Note**
>
> There are data types that aren't actually copied by both copy.copy and copy.deepcopy, but only referenced one more time. These include module objects, methods, file objects, socket instances, and traceback instances.

> **Note**
>
> When copying an instance using the copy module, the object is created in the memory one more time. This takes up more memory and computing time than a simple allocation. For this reason, you should use copy only when you actually need a real copy.

44

44.8 Image Processing: Pillow

The third-party Pillow library enables the processing of raster graphics in Python.

Pillow is a fork[2] of the *Python Imaging Library* (*PIL*) for Python 2, which isn't developed much further. One of Pillow's goals is to remain as compatible as possible with PIL.

At this point, we'll provide an introduction to using Pillow based on an example. It covers loading and saving image files, cropping portions of an image, geometric transformations, and applying and writing filters.

44.8.1 Installation

Because Pillow is a third-party package, it must be installed before you can use it. This can be done via the Anaconda package manager:

```
$ conda install pillow
```

Alternatively, if you don't use Anaconda, Pillow can be installed via the Python package manager:

```
$ pip install pillow
```

If you're a Linux user, installation may also be possible via the package manager of your Linux distribution.

For more information, please visit the project website at *https://python-pillow.org*.

44.8.2 Loading and Saving Image Files

The basic functionality of an image-processing library is to load and save image files. This works in Pillow via the open method of the Image class:

```
>>> from PIL import Image
>>> coffee = Image.open("coffee.png")
```

The properties of the loaded image are available through attributes of the resulting Image instance:

```
>>> coffee.format
'PNG'
>>> coffee.size
(800, 600)
>>> coffee.mode
'RGB'
```

---

2 A *fork* is a project that was created as a spin-off from another project.

You can display an image via the show method:

```
>>> coffee.show()
```

For this purpose, Pillow saves the graphic to a temporary directory and uses the operating system's methods for displaying image files (see Figure 44.1).

Figure 44.1 Pillow Can Display Loaded Images Directly, Using the Tools of the Operating System

Analogous to open, the save method is available for saving loaded image files. The file format is determined on the basis of the specified file extension. In this case, we save the opened PNG image as a GIF file:

```
>>> coffee.save("coffee.gif")
```

Pillow supports BMP, EPS, GIF, IM, JPEG, JPEG 2000, MSP, PCX, PNG, PPM, SPIDER, TIFF, WebP, and XBM formats. There's also partial support for a number of other formats, which can be read, but not written.

44.8.3   Accessing Individual Pixels

The load method of an open Image instance can be used to access the pixel matrix underlying the image:

44

```
>>> px = coffee.load()
>>> px[100, 100]
(151, 163, 175)
>>> px[100, 100] = (255, 255, 255)
```

To access a particular pixel, its coordinates[3] are written in square brackets after the px pixel matrix instance. In this case, the color value of the pixel with coordinates (100, 100) is equal to (151, 163, 175). The color value can be changed, which affects the underlying coffee image.

44.8.4   Manipulating Images

Pillow provides a lot of options to manipulate images. In the following sections, we'll briefly describe the most important of these operations, including predefined transformations or filters, based on examples.

Cutting Out Parts of an Image

An Image instance provides the crop method, which can be used to cut out parts of an image:

```
>>> cup = coffee.crop((50, 275, 450, 575))
```

The desired portion of the image is specified in the form of a tuple with four values. The first two values set the coordinates of the upper-left-hand corner, while the last two values set the coordinates of the lower-right-hand corner in pixels. The section cut out in this example thus starts at position (50, 275) and is 400 pixels wide and 300 pixels high.

The result of a crop call is returned as an Image instance and also can be displayed using show (see Figure 44.2).

Figure 44.2 Cropped Portion of the Image

---

3   The specifications refer to the local image coordinate system whose origin is in the upper-left-hand corner of the image.

Merging Images

Regardless of whether it was cut from an image or loaded independently, an Image instance can be pasted into a second Image instance. In the following example, we'll create a new Image instance of the appropriate size, and then use the paste method to paste the cup portion cut out in the previous section twice:

```
>>> two_coffee = Image.new("RGBA", (800, 300))
>>> two_coffee.paste(cup, (0, 0, 400, 300))
>>> two_coffee.paste(cup, (400, 0, 800, 300))
>>> two_coffee.show()
```

The static method new of the Image class creates a new image of the specified size—in this case, 500 pixels wide and 250 pixels high. The color space of the image also is specified—in this case, RGBA.[4] The resulting image of the paste operations is shown in Figure 44.3.

Figure 44.3 Merging Images

Geometric Image Transformations

Pillow supports a number of operations for the geometric transformation of Image instances. This includes, for example, scaling an image:

```
>>> small_coffee = coffee.resize((400, 400))
```

In this case, the coffee sample image is resized to 400 × 400 pixels and compressed and returned as a new Image instance.

A second class of image transformations involves reflections and rotations by integer multiples of 90 degrees. Such transformations don't change the image geometry and are referred to as *transpositions* in Pillow. A transposition can be performed using the transpose method of an Image instance:

---

4 This means that the color value of a pixel is composed of its red, green, and blue components. In addition, there is an alpha component that specifies the transparency value of a pixel. Pillow supports a number of other color spaces besides RGBA.

44

```
>>> trans1 = small_coffee.transpose(Image.Transpose.FLIP_LEFT_RIGHT)
>>> trans2 = small_coffee.transpose(Image.Transpose.FLIP_TOP_BOTTOM)
>>> trans3 = small_coffee.transpose(Image.Transpose.ROTATE_90)
>>> trans4 = small_coffee.transpose(Image.Transpose.ROTATE_180)
>>> trans5 = small_coffee.transpose(Image.Transpose.ROTATE_270)
```

Figure 44.4 shows the results of the individual transposition operations in a merged image.

Figure 44.4 Geometric Transpositions: Vertical and Horizontal Mirroring, Plus 90-, 180-, and 270-Degree Rotations

Rotations by integer multiples of 90 degrees are convenient because they leave the image geometry unchanged. Of course, you can also rotate images with Pillow as you like. For this purpose, you can use the rotate method:

```
>>> coffee.rotate(30).show()
```

In this case, the geometry of the image also is preserved. Free spaces created by the rotation are filled with the default background color of the image—in this case, black (see Figure 44.5).

Alternatively, the expand keyword parameter can be used when calling rotate to specify that the image dimensions should be adjusted to the rotated image:

```
>>> coffee.rotate(30, expand=True).show()
```

Figure 44.5 Rotation of 30 Degrees

Predefined Image Filters

The ImageFilter module contains a set of predefined filter functions that can be applied via the filter method of an Image instance. In this way, for example, a Gaussian Blur filter can be superimposed on an image:

```
>>> from PIL import ImageFilter
>>> coffee.filter(ImageFilter.GaussianBlur(10)).show()
```

This filter calculates the color value of each pixel based on the color values of the pixels in its vicinity. The degree of the resulting blur can be varied via the environment size; in this case, the environment size is 10 pixels. The result is shown in Figure 44.6.

In addition to the GaussianBlur filter shown here, the ImageFilter module contains the following filter classes: UnsharpMask for an unsharp mask, Kernel for a convolution operation, and RankFilter, MedianFilter, MinFilter, and MaxFilter for simple environment-based filters.

In addition, the preconfigured and therefore parameterless BLUR, CONTOUR, DETAIL, EDGE_ENHANCE, EDGE_ENHANCE_MORE, EMBOSS, FIND_EDGES, SMOOTH, SMOOTH_MORE, and SHARPEN filters are included in ImageFilter, which can also be applied via filter:

```
>>> coffee.filter(ImageFilter.FIND_EDGES).show()
```

Figure 44.6 GaussianBlur filter

Custom Pixel Operations

As described in the previous section, Pillow contains a number of predefined filters. Using the point method of an image instance, you can write simple filter functions yourself. These filters may only refer to the pixel itself and not to its surroundings. The point method is passed a function object that's called for each color component of each pixel and can change them:

44

```
>>> coffee.point(lambda i: 0 if i < 125 else 255).show()
```

In this example, a threshold filter is applied that decides between full intensity (value 255) and no intensity (value 0). This decision is made independently for each color component. The result corresponds to a maximum contrast setting and is artistically valuable, as Figure 44.7 shows.

Figure 44.7 Custom-Defined Pixel Operation

Image Enhancements

In addition to the filters already mentioned in the ImageFilter module, there's the ImageEnhance module, which contains a number of classes that can improve various aspects of an image, such as brightness or contrast:

```
>>> from PIL import ImageEnhance
>>> enhancer = ImageEnhance.Contrast(coffee)
>>> enhancer.enhance(0.5).show()
```

First, an instance of the Contrast class is created with the image to be processed. This instance can then be used to apply different contrast settings. For this purpose, the enhance method of the enhancer instance is called with the contrast value. A value less than 1 decreases the contrast of the output image, while a value greater than 1 increases the contrast.

In a similar way, you can use the following enhancement filters: Color for color balance, Brightness for brightness, and Sharpness for sharpness.

Drawing Operations

Pillow supports basic drawing operations that can be used to add simple geometric shapes to an image. Also, text can be written in images. The ImageDraw and ImageFont Pillow modules are required for this:

```
>>> from PIL import ImageDraw
>>> draw = ImageDraw.Draw(coffee)
>>> draw.rectangle((50, 275, 450, 575), outline=(255,255,255,255))
>>> coffee.show()
```

First, an instance of the ImageDraw class must be created, which then can be used to draw into the image specified during instantiation—for example, to draw a white rectangle. In addition to the rectangle method, you can use the drawing methods summarized in Table 44.2.

Method	Description
arc	Draws an open arc
chord	Draws a closed arc
ellipse	Draws an ellipse
line	Draws a line
pieslice	Draws a pie slice
point	Draws a point or a pixel
polygon	Draws a polygon
rectangle	Draws a rectangle
text	Draws a text

Table 44.2 Drawing Methods of ImageDraw

The ImageFont class can be used to write text in an open image. To do this, a font must be loaded via the truetype method and instantiated in a font size—in this case, 40 point. After that, text can be written into the image using the text method of an ImageDraw instance:

```
>>> from PIL import ImageFont
>>> font = ImageFont.truetype("Arial.ttf", 40)
>>> draw.text((175, 225), "delicious", font=font, fill=(255,255,255,255))
>>> coffee.show()
```

44

You can see the combined result of the previous two examples in Figure 44.8.

Figure 44.8 Drawing Functionality in Pillow

44.8.5   Interoperability

Pillow allows you to conveniently edit image files and, after editing, either save them or display them using the methods of the operating system. In addition, Pillow can interact with various GUI toolkits to achieve the simplest possible representation of an Image instance in a GUI. For this purpose, you have the ImageQt class for interoperability with PySide2 or PyQt:

```
>>> from PIL import ImageQt
>>> coffeeQt = ImageQt.ImageQt(coffee)
```

Or you have the ImageTk class for interoperability with Tkinter:

```
>>> from PIL import ImageTk
>>> from tkinter import Tk
>>> root = Tk()
>>> coffeeTk = ImageTk.PhotoImage(coffee)
```

The classes mentioned inherit from their corresponding counterparts, QtGui.QImage and tkinter.PhotoImage respectively, and can therefore be used directly in the context of PySide2/PyQt and Tkinter respectively.

Chapter 45
From Python 2 to Python 3

The Python programming language is in continuous development and has undergone many changes since the release of version 1.0 in January 1994. In this chapter, we'll describe the development of the Python language. We'll start with version 2.0, which was released in 2000.

Following this, the big jump to version 3.0 will be described in greater in detail. Because Python 2 is still being used today, you should be aware of the existing differences.

Table 45.1 lists the innovations of the individual Python versions that are important from a user's point of view. This list is not exhaustive as the changes are too numerous to reproduce here in full.

For a comprehensive listing of all changes in a Python version, see the section titled "What's New in Python x.y" of the online documentation at *https://docs.python.org*.

Version	Year	Major Innovations
2.0	2000	■ The `unicode` data type for Unicode strings. ■ List comprehensions. ■ Augmented assignments. ■ Garbage collection for cyclic references.
2.1	2001	■ The `__future__` module. ■ Comparison operators can be overloaded individually. ■ The `import` statement also works case-sensitive on Windows and macOS.
2.2	2001	■ Nested namespaces. ■ New-style classes allow for inheriting built-in data types. ■ Multiple inheritance. ■ Properties. ■ The iterator concept. ■ Static methods and class methods. ■ Automatic conversion of the `long` and `int` data types.
2.3	2003	■ The `set` data type (initially within the `sets` module, as of 2.4 as a built-in data type). ■ Generator functions. ■ The `bool` data type.

Table 45.1 Evolution of the Python Language

Version	Year	Major Innovations
2.4	2004	■ Generator expressions. ■ Function and class decorators. ■ The `decimal` module.
2.5	2006	■ Conditional expressions. ■ The relative `import` statement. ■ Unification of the `try-except-finally` statement. Previously, `except` and `finally` branches couldn't be used together.
2.6	2008	Version 2.6 was developed at the same time as 3.0 and includes the new features from version 3.0, which don't affect the backward compatibility of the language: ■ The `with` statement. ■ The `multiprocessing` package. ■ A new syntax for string formatting. ■ `print` becomes a function. ■ Literals for numbers in the octal and binary systems.
2.7	2010	Version 2.7 is the latest version of Python 2 and includes some of the new features of Python 3.1 and 3.2: ■ Dictionary comprehensions and set comprehensions. ■ The `argparse` module.
3.0	2008	Changes that aren't also included in version 2.6: ■ Many built-in functions and methods now return iterators instead of lists. ■ The `long` data type disappears. ■ The `bytes` data type for binary data. ■ The `str` data type now stores only Unicode strings. ■ Dictionary comprehensions. ■ Keyword-only parameters. ■ The `nonlocal` statement. ■ A literal for the `set` data type. ■ Many modules of the standard library were removed, renamed, or modified.
3.1	2009	■ The `OrderedDict` data type in the `collections` module. ■ The `bit_length` method of the `int` data type. ■ The automatic numbering of placeholders in string formatting. ■ A new algorithm for the internal representation of `float` values.

Table 45.1 Evolution of the Python Language (Cont.)

Version	Year	Major Innovations
3.2	2011	■ The *.pyc compilations are now collected in a subdirectory called __pycache__. ■ Many modules of the standard library were extended.
3.3	2012	■ The yield from syntax. ■ The u "string" syntax is allowed again. ■ The exception hierarchy was revised.
3.4	2014	■ Comprehensive integration of pip. ■ The enum module.
3.5	2015	■ The @ operator for matrix multiplication. ■ Coroutines with async and await.
3.6	2016	■ The f literal for formatted strings. ■ A syntax for the annotation of variables. ■ Asynchronous generators and comprehensions.
3.7	2018	■ The built-in function breakpoint. ■ Functions in time with nanosecond resolution.
3.8	2019	■ The := operator for assignment expressions. ■ Support for positional-only parameters in function and method interfaces. ■ Self-documenting expressions in f-strings.
3.9	2020	■ The zoneinfo module for time information in local time zones. ■ The | unification operator for dictionaries. ■ Speed improvements in CPython.
3.10	2021	■ The distutils package is classified as deprecated. ■ Structural pattern matching.
3.11	2022	■ Speed improvements in CPython. ■ Exception Groups and except*. ■ Tracebacks with more detailed information about the error location

Table 45.1 Evolution of the Python Language (Cont.)

In the following sections, we'll describe the drastic version jump from Python 2 to Python 3. The special thing about version 3.0 is that it's no longer backward compatible with older Python versions. This means that a program written for Python 2 most likely won't run under Python 3. The break with backward compatibility allowed Python developers to remove long-dragged-along ugliness and inconsistency from the language, releasing an all-around renewed version of Python.

45

All in all, the changes introduced with Python 3.0 are not dramatic, but it takes some getting used to in order to switch from Python 2 to Python 3. For this reason, in this chapter we'll provide a clear description of the main differences between Python 2 and 3.

Python 3 contains a tool called 2to3 that makes it easy to convert a larger project from Python 2 to 3 by automatically converting large parts of the source code. We'll explain how you can use this program in the second section.

45.1   The Main Differences

This section explains the main differences between Python versions 2 and 3.

> **Note**
>
> Python 3 also introduced many subtle changes—for example, to the interfaces of many modules in the standard library—which can't all be explained here for obvious reasons. Answers to such detailed questions can be found in the online documentation on the Python website at *http://www.python.org/*.

45.1.1   Input/Output

In terms of input/output, there are two noticeable changes that can be explained quickly.

The print keyword from Python 2 was replaced by a built-in function of the same name. As a rule, only parentheses need to be added around the expression to be output (see Table 45.2).

Python 2	Python 3
>>> **print** "Hello world" Hello world	>>> **print**("Hello world") Hello world
>>> **print** "ABC", "DEF", 2+2 ABC DEF 4	>>> »print«("ABC", "DEF", 2+2) ABC DEF 4
>>> **print** >>f, "files"	>>> **print**("files", file=f)
>>> **for** i **in** range(3): ... print i, ... 0 1 2	>>> **for** i **in** range(3): ... print(i, end=" ") ... 0 1 2

Table 45.2 Print Is Now a Function

For more information, especially on the keyword parameters of the built-in print function, see Chapter 17, Section 17.14.

The second noticeable change to input/output concerns the built-in input function. The input function from Python 3 corresponds to the raw_input function in Python 2. There's no equivalent for the input function from Python 2 in Python 3 as a built-in function, but its behavior can be emulated using eval (see Table 45.3).

Python 2	Python 3
>>> input("Your value: ") Your value: 2**5 32	>>> eval(input("Your value: ")) Your value: 2**5 32
>>> raw_input("Your value: ") Your value: 2**5 '2**5'	>>> input("Your value: ") Your value: 2**5 '2**5'

Table 45.3 Comparing input versus raw_input

These were the two changes that required the most familiarization in terms of screen output and keyboard input, respectively.

45.1.2   Iterators

Although Python 2 already supports the iterator concept, many functions commonly used to iterate a collection of elements return a list instance containing all elements, such as the prominent range function. Usually, however, this list is only iterated in a for loop, so it is pointless to construct it as a whole in many cases. This can be done more elegantly and with less memory consumption by using iterators.

For this reason, many of the functions and methods that return a list in Python 2 return an iterator tailored to the circumstances in Python 3. To transfer these objects into a list, they can simply be passed to the built-in list function.

Thus, for example, the range function in Python 3 behaves just like the xrange function in Python 2. A call of list(range()) in Python 3 is equivalent to the range function in Python 2 (see Table 45.4).

Python 2	Python 3
>>> xrange(5) xrange(5)	>>> range(5) range(0, 5)
>>> range(5) [0, 1, 2, 3, 4]	>>> list(range(5)) [0, 1, 2, 3, 4]

Table 45.4 range Now Returns an Iterator

45

Apart from range, the built-in map, filter, and zip functions are affected by this change and now return an iterator. The keys, items, and values methods of a dictionary now return a view object, which is also iterable. The iterkeys, iteritems, and itervalues methods of a dictionary and the built-in xrange function from Python 2 no longer exist in Python 3.

45.1.3   Strings

Probably the most fundamental change in Python 3 is the reinterpretation of the str data type. In Python 2 there are two data types for strings: str and unicode. While the former can be used to store any byte sequence, the latter was responsible for Unicode text.

In Python 3, the str data type is exclusively for text and is comparable to the unicode data type in Python 2. For storing byte sequences, Python 3 provides the bytes and bytearray data types, where bytes is an immutable data type and bytearray is a mutable data type. In Python 3, neither the u literal for Unicode strings nor the unicode data type exists.

The bytes and str data types are more clearly delineated in Python 3 than is the case with the str and unicode data types in Python 2. For example, it's no longer possible to concatenate a string and a bytes string without explicit encoding or decoding.

Table 45.5 lists the differences between str in Python 2 and str in Python 3 as an example.

Python 2	Python 3

>>> u = u"I am Unicode"
>>> u
u'I am Unicode'
>>> u.encode("ascii")
'I am Unicode'
	>>> u = "I am Unicode"
	>>> u
	'I am Unicode'
	>>> u.encode("ascii")
	b'I am Unicode'

>>> a = "I am ASCII"
>>> a.decode()
u'I am ASCII'
	>>> a = b"I am ASCII"
	>>> a.decode()
	'I am ASCII'

>>> "abc" + u"def" u'abcdef'	>>> b"abc" + "def" Traceback (most recent call last): [...] TypeError: can't concat bytes to str

Table 45.5 Strings in Python 2 versus Python 3

The stronger delineation of str and bytes in Python 3 has implications for the standard library. For example, you can only use bytes strings for network communication. It's also important to note that the type of data read from a file now depends on the mode in which the file was opened. The difference between binary and text mode in Python 3 is thus of interest even on operating systems that don't distinguish these two modes at all by themselves.

> **Note**
>
> To reduce the effort to convert code between Python 2 and Python 3, the u"hello" notation for strings is allowed again as of Python 3.3. It has no special meaning, but is equivalent to "hello".

45.1.4   Integers

Python 2 provides two data types for storing integers: int for numbers in the 32- or 64-bit number range and long for numbers of any size. In Python 3, there's only one such data type, called int, but it behaves like long from Python 2. The distinction between int and long is essentially irrelevant for a programmer even in Python 2 as the two data types are automatically converted into each other.

A second change was made with respect to the division of integers. In Python 2, an integer division is performed in this case, so the result is again an integer. In Python 3, the result of dividing two integers is a float. Here, the // operator is used for integer division (see Table 45.6).

Python 2	Python 3
>>> 10 / 4 2	>>> 10 / 4 2.5
>>> 10 // 4 2	>>> 10 // 4 2
>>> 10.0 / 4 2.5	>>> 10.0 / 4 2.5

Table 45.6 Integer Division in Python 2 versus Python 3

45.1.5   Exception Handling

Minor syntactic changes were made with regard to raising and catching exceptions. The old and the new syntax are contrasted by means of an example in Table 45.7.

45

Python 2	Python 3
```try: raise SyntaxError, "Help" except SyntaxError, e: print e.args```	```try: raise SyntaxError("Help") except SyntaxError as e: print(e.args)```

Table 45.7 Exception Handling in Python 2 versus Python 3

It should be noted that the syntax used in the example for Python 3 concerning raising the exception also works in Python 2. However, the syntax specified in Python 2 was removed from the language for Python 3.

45.1.6   Standard Library

With Python 3, the standard library has also been thoroughly cleaned up. Many modules that had hardly been used were removed; others were renamed or combined with others into packages. Table 45.8 lists the most important modules that were renamed in Python 3.

Python 2	Python 3
ConfigParser	configparser
cPickle	_pickle
Queue	queue
SocketServer	socketserver
repr	reprlib
thread	_thread

Table 45.8 Renamed Modules of the Standard Library

Most of the modules listed here aren't addressed in this book because they are very specific. However, you can find more information about them in the online documentation for Python.

In addition to renamed modules, some thematically related modules have been combined into packages. These are listed in Table 45.9.

Package in Python 3	Modules from Python 2
html	HTMLParser, htmlentitydefs

Table 45.9 Combined Modules of the Standard Library

Package in Python 3	Modules from Python 2
http	httplib, BaseHTTPServer, CGIHTTPServer, SimpleHTTPServer, Cookie, cookielib
tkinter	Apart from turtle, all modules that have something to do with Tkinter
urllib	urllib, urllib2, urlparse, robotparse
xmlrpc	xmlrpclib, DocXMLRPCServer, SimpleXMLRPCServer

Table 45.9 Combined Modules of the Standard Library (Cont.)

45.2 Automatic Conversion

To simplify the migration from Python 2 to Python 3 even for larger projects, there is a tool in the Python 3 distribution called 2to3, which we'll introduce in this section. You can find the 2to3 tool in the *Tools/scripts* subdirectory of your Python distribution.

> **Note**
>
> The 2to3 module is considered deprecated as of Python 3.10 due to the parsing technology used and isn't expected to be available in Python 3.13 anymore.
>
> Based on 2to3, extensive third-party libraries such as modernize, future, and six have been established to assist in the smooth transition of a codebase from Python 2 to Python 3.
>
> These libraries share the common approach of creating a codebase that can be executed under both Python 2 and Python 3 by converting as automatically as possible. This can serve as an interim version to a final porting to Python 3, or as a permanent base if Python 2 and Python 3 are to be supported simultaneously.

The use of 2to3 is exemplified by the following Python 2 sample program:

```python
def get_input(n):
    lst = []
    for i in xrange(n):
        try:
            z = int(raw_input("Please enter a number: "))
        except Exception, e:
            raise ValueError("This is not a number!")
        lst.append(z)
    return lst
try:
    res = get_input(5)
```

45

```
    print res
except ValueError, e:
    print e.args[0]
```

This program reads five numbers from the user using the get_input function and outputs a list filled with these numbers. If the user enters something that's not a number, the program exits with an error message. You can see immediately that this program can't be executed under Python 3 in this way. The calls of xrange, raw_input, and the two except statements prevent this.

Already with the 14 lines of source code shown here, it's tedious to make the code compatible with Python 3 by hand. Imagine this work for a larger project! But fortunately, we have 2to3. We call 2to3 once with the name of the Python program to convert as the only parameter. The result looks as follows:

```
--- test.py (original)
+++ test.py (refactored)
@@ -1,15 +1,15
 def get_input(n):
     lst = []
-    for i in xrange(n):
+    for i in range(n):
         try:
-            z = int(raw_input("Please enter a number: "))
-        except ValueError, e:
+            z = int(input("Please enter a number: "))
+        except ValueError as e:
             raise ValueError("This is not a number!")
         lst.append(z)
     return lst
 try:
     res = get_input(5)
-    print res
-except ValueError, e:
-    print e.args[0]
+    print(res)
+except ValueError as e:
+    print(e.args[0])
```

By default, the conversion program doesn't modify your specified source code files, but only produces a diff expression. This is a special description language for the differences between two pieces of text. You can include this diff expression in your source file using the patch Unix program, for example. Alternatively, you can use the -w command switch to allow the 2to3 script to directly modify the specified source file. The original Python 2 code is saved as *filename.py.bak*. When 2to3 is fed with the -w switch and the sample source code shown earlier, the converted code looks like this afterward:

```
def get_input(n):
    lst = []
    for i in range(n):
        try:
            z = int(eval(input("Please enter a number: ")))
        except Exception as e:
            raise ValueError("This is not a number!")
        lst.append(z)
    return list
try:
    res = get_input(5)
    print(res)
except ValueError as e:
    print(e.args[0])
```

You'll see that the problem areas mentioned at the beginning have been changed, and you'll notice that the translated code is executable under Python 3.

Instead of a single program file, you can also pass a list of files or folders to the 2to3 script. If you've passed a folder, any source file contained in it or one of its subfolders will be converted.

Finally, we'd like to talk about the most important command line switches you can use to customize the behavior of 2to3 according to your needs (see Table 45.10).

Switch	Alternative	Description
-d	--doctests_only	If this switch is set, only the doctests contained in the specified source file will be converted to Python 3. By default, doctests won't be touched. You can find more information about doctests in Chapter 36, Section 36.2.1.
-f FIX	--fix=FIX	With this option, you specify which fixes should be applied. A *fix* is a specific replacement rule, such as replacing xrange with range.
-x NOFIX	--nofix=NOFIX	The counterpart of -f. Here you determine which fixes may not be applied.
-l	--list-fixes	By setting this switch, you'll get a list of all available fixes.

Table 45.10 Command Line Options for 2to3

45

Switch	Alternative	Description
-p	--print-function	If this switch is set, print statements won't be converted. This is useful if you've already written print like a function in Python 2 or included the corresponding print_function future import.
		The 2to3 program can't decide on its own whether or not to parenthesize a print statement.
-w	--write	If this switch is set, the changes will be written directly to the examined source file. A backup will be created under filename.py.bak.
-n	--nobackups	If this switch is set, the creation of the backup file will be omitted.

Table 45.10 Command Line Options for 2to3 (Cont.)

Appendix A

A.1 Reserved Words

Table A.1 contains words that mustn't be used as identifiers because they correspond to a keyword.

and	continue	finally	is	raise
as	def	for	lambda	return
assert	del	from	None	True
async	elif	global	nonlocal	try
await	else	if	not	while
break	except	import	or	with
class	False	in	pass	yield

Table A.1 List of Reserved Words

A.2 Operator Precedence

Table A.2 specifies the precedence of all syntax elements that can occur in a valid Python expression. This list includes the operator precedence already defined in Chapter 10, Section 10.2.

Operator	Usual meaning
(...),	Parentheses in arithmetic expressions
[...], {...}	Literals for tuples, lists, sets and dictionaries
[...], {...}	Comprehensions
x[...]	Access to elements of a sequence
x.	Access to attributes and methods
x(...)	Function and method calls
await x	Await expression
x ** y	yth power of x
+x	Positive sign
-x	Negative sign
~x	Bitwise complement of x

Table A.2 Complete Operator Ranking

Operator	Usual meaning
x * y	Product of x and y
x / y	Quotient of x and y
x % y	Remainder for integer division of x by y
x // y	Integer division of x by y
x @ y	Matrix multiplication of x and y
x + y	Addition of x and y
x - y	Subtraction of x and y
x << n	Bitwise shift by n places to the left
x >> n	Bitwise shift by n places to the right
x & y	Bitwise AND between x and y
x ^ y	Bitwise exclusive OR between x and y
x | y	Bitwise nonexclusive OR between x and y
x < y	Is x smaller than y?
x <= y	Is x smaller than or equal to y?
x > y	Is x greater than y?
x >= y	Is x greater than or equal to y?
x != y	Is x unequal to y?
x == y	Is x equal to y?
x is y	Are x and y identical?
x is not y	Are x and y not identical?
x in y	Is x located in y?
x not in y	Is x not located in y?
not x	Logical negation
x and y	Logical AND
x or y	Logical OR
... if ... else	Conditional expression
lambda	Lambda expression
x := y	Assignment expression

Table A.2 Complete Operator Ranking (Cont.)

A.3 Built-In Functions

Python contains a large number of built-in functions, which have been introduced at various points in the book for didactic reasons. Therefore, we haven't provided any list of all built-in functions in the book so far. Table A.3 lists all built-in functions, along with a short description and a note about where in the book the function is explained in detail. Note that the functions in this table are specified without parameter signatures.

Built-in function	Description	Section
__import__	Imports a module or package.	Chapter 18, Section 18.4
abs	Calculates the absolute value of a number.	Chapter 17, Section 17.14.1
all	Checks if all elements of a sequence return True.	Chapter 17, Section 17.14.2
any	Checks if at least one element of a sequence returns True.	Chapter 17, Section 17.14.3
ascii	Creates a printable string describing the passed object. Special characters are masked so that the output contains only ASCII characters.	Chapter 17, Section 17.14.4
bin	Returns a string representing the passed integer as a binary number.	Chapter 17, Section 17.14.5
bool	Generates a Boolean value.	Chapter 11, Section 11.6 Chapter 17, Section 17.14.6
bytearray	Creates a new bytearray instance.	Chapter 12, Section 12.5 Chapter 17, Section 17.14.7
bytes	Creates a new bytes instance.	Chapter 12, Section 12.5 Chapter 17, Section 17.14.8
breakpoint	Stops the program flow and starts the integrated PDB command line debugger at the position of the function call.	–
callable	Indicates whether an instance is callable.	–
chr	Returns the character with a given Unicode code point.	Chapter 17, Section 17.14.9

Table A.3 Built-In Functions in Python

Built-in function	Description	Section
classmethod	Creates a class method.	Chapter 19, Section 19.7
complex	Generates a complex number.	Chapter 11, Section 11.7 Chapter 17, Section 17.14.10
delattr	Deletes a specific attribute of an instance.	Chapter 19, Section 19.9.1
dict	Creates a dictionary.	Chapter 17, Section 17.14.11
dir	Returns a list of all attributes of an object.	–
divmod	Returns a tuple with the result of an integer division and the remainder. divmod(a, b) is equivalent to (a // b, a % b).	Chapter 17, Section 17.14.12
enumerate	Returns an enumeration iterator for the passed sequence.	Chapter 17, Section 17.14.13
eval	Evaluates a Python expression.	Chapter 17, Section 17.14.14
exec	Evaluates a Python expression.	Chapter 17, Section 17.14.15
filter	Allows you to filter out certain elements of a list.	Chapter 17, Section 17.14.16
float	Generates a float.	Chapter 11, Section 11.5 Chapter 17, Section 17.14.17
format	Formats a value with the specified format specification.	Chapter 17, Section 17.14.18
frozenset	Creates an immutable set.	Chapter 13, Section 13.2 Chapter 17, Section 17.14.19
getattr	Returns a specific attribute of an instance.	Chapter 19, Section 19.9.1
globals	Returns a dictionary with all references of the global namespace.	Chapter 17, Section 17.14.20
hasattr	Checks whether an instance has a certain attribute.	Chapter 19, Section 19.9.1
hash	Returns the hash value of an instance.	Chapter 17, Section 17.14.21

Table A.3 Built-In Functions in Python (Cont.)

Built-in function	Description	Section
help	Launches the built-in interactive help of Python.	Chapter 17, Section 17.14.22
hex	Returns the hexadecimal value of an integer as a string.	Chapter 17, Section 17.14.23
id	Returns the identity of an instance.	Chapter 7, Section 7.1.3 Chapter 17, Section 17.14.24
input	Reads a string from the keyboard.	Chapter 17, Section 17.14.25
int	Generates an integer.	Chapter 11, Section 11.4 Chapter 17, Section 17.14.26
isinstance	Checks whether an object is an instance of a specific class.	Chapter 19, Section 19.9.2
issubclass	Checks whether a class inherits from a given base class.	Chapter 19, Section 19.9.2
iter	Creates an iterator object.	Chapter 21, Section 21.2.5 Chapter 21, Section 21.2.9
len	Returns the length of a given instance.	Chapter 17, Section 17.14.27
list	Creates a list.	Chapter 17, Section 17.14.28
locals	Returns a dictionary containing all references of the local namespace.	Chapter 17, Section 17.14.29
map	Applies a function to each element of a list.	Chapter 17, Section 17.14.30
max	Returns the largest element of a sequence.	Chapter 17, Section 17.14.31
min	Returns the smallest element of a sequence.	Chapter 17, Section 17.14.32
next	Returns the next element of the passed iterator.	Chapter 21, Section 21.2.5
oct	Returns the octal value of an integer as a string.	Chapter 17, Section 17.14.33
open	Creates a file object.	Chapter 6, Section 6.4.1
ord	Returns the Unicode code of a given character.	Chapter 17, Section 17.14.34

Table A.3 Built-In Functions in Python (Cont.)

Built-in function	Description	Section
pow	Performs a power operation.	Chapter 17, Section 17.14.35
print	Outputs the passed objects on the screen in other output devices.	Chapter 17, Section 17.14.36
property	Creates a managed attribute.	Chapter 19, Section 19.5.2
range	Creates an iterator that can be used for counting.	Chapter 17, Section 17.14.37 Chapter 21, Section 21.2.5
repr	Returns a string representation of an instance.	Chapter 17, Section 17.14.38
reversed	Creates an iterator that iterates backward through an iterable object.	Chapter 17, Section 17.14.39
round	Rounds a number.	Chapter 17, Section 17.14.40
set	Creates a set.	Chapter 13, Section 13.2 Chapter 17, Section 17.14.41
setattr	Sets a specific attribute of an instance to a specific value.	Chapter 19, Section 19.9.1
sorted	Sorts an iterable object.	Chapter 17, Section 17.14.42
staticmethod	Creates a static method.	Chapter 19, Section 19.6
str	Creates a string.	Chapter 12, Section 12.5 Chapter 17, Section 17.14.43
sum	Returns the sum of all elements of a sequence.	Chapter 17, Section 17.14.44
tuple	Creates a tuple.	Chapter 12, Section 12.4 Chapter 17, Section 17.14.45
type	Returns the data type of an instance.	Chapter 7, Section 7.1.1 Chapter 17, Section 17.14.46
vars	Returns the x.__dict__ dictionary if an instance x is passed. Without argument, vars is equivalent to locals.	–
zip	Combines several sequences into tuples—for example, to iterate them with a for loop.	Chapter 17, Section 17.14.47

Table A.3 Built-In Functions in Python (Cont.)

A.4   Built-In Exceptions

Python also contains a set of built-in exception types. These exceptions are raised by functions of the standard library or by the interpreter itself. They are built-in, which means they can be used at any time in the source code. Table A.4 lists the built-in exception types and common circumstances in which they occur. The inheritance hierarchy is indicated by the indentation depth of the type name.

Exception Type	Appearance
BaseException	Base class of all built-in exception types (see Chapter 20, Section 20.1.1)
SystemExit	When exiting the program via sys.exit. This exception doesn't cause a traceback.
KeyboardInterrupt	When exiting the program via a key combination (usually Ctrl + C).
GeneratorExit	When terminating a generator.
Exception	Base class of all "normal" exceptions. Also, all self-defined exception types should inherit from exception.
StopIteration	When calling the next method of an iterator, if no next element exists.
ArithmeticError	Base class of exception types for errors in arithmetic operations.
FloatingPointError	In case of a failed floating point operation.
OverflowError	For an arithmetic calculation whose result is too large for the data type used.
ZeroDivisionError	For a division by zero.
AssertionError	In case of a failing assert statement (see Chapter 20, Section 20.2).
AttributeError	When accessing an attribute that doesn't exist.
BufferError	In case of a failed operation on a buffer data type.
EOFError	If the built-in input function gets an end-of-file (EOF) signal without being able to read data first.
ImportError	In case of a failed import statement.

Table A.4 Hierarchy of Built-In Exception Types

Exception Type	Appearance
ModuleNotFoundError	When an import statement fails because no module with the specified name exists.
LookupError	Base class of exception types for errors on key or index accesses.
IndexError	In case of a sequence access with an invalid index.
KeyError	In case of a dictionary access with an invalid key.
MemoryError	When there isn't enough memory available to perform an operation.
NameError	When an unknown local or global identifier is used.
UnboundLocalError	When a local reference is used in a function or method before it's been assigned an instance (see Chapter 17, Section 17.11.5).
OSError	For system-related errors.
BlockingIOError	When an operation set as nonblocking, such as an access to a socket, would block.
ChildProcessError	When an operation on a child process has failed.
ConnectionError	For connection-related errors.
BrokenPipeError	For write accesses to a pipe whose other end has been closed.
ConnectionAbortedError	In the event of an aborted connection attempt by the remote party.
ConnectionRefusedError	In the event of a connection attempt rejected by the remote party.
ConnectionResetError	In case of a connection reset by the remote party.
FileExistsError	When trying to create an existing file.
FileNotFoundError	When trying to access a file that doesn't exist.
InterruptedError	When a system call was interrupted by a signal.
IsADirectoryError	When trying to perform a file operation on a directory.
NotADirectoryError	When trying to perform a directory operation on a file.

Table A.4 Hierarchy of Built-In Exception Types (Cont.)

Exception Type	Appearance
PermissionError	When the access rights required for an operation don't exist.
ProcessLookupError	When a process couldn't be found.
TimeoutError	When a time limit is exceeded by a system operation.
ReferenceError	When accessing an object that has already been released by the garbage collection.
RuntimeError	In case of an error that isn't covered by any of the other exception types.
NotImplementedError	Base classes raise this exception from methods that must be implemented by a derived class.
SyntaxError	In case of a syntax error in the program or in a code passed to exec or eval.
IndentationError	Base class of exception types for errors caused by an incorrect indentation of the source code.
TabError	In case of incorrect mixing of tabs and spaces for indentation.
SystemError	In case of an internal error in the Python interpreter.
TypeError	In case of an operation on an instance of a data type unsuitable for it.
ValueError	In case of an operation on an instance that has a suitable type but an unsuitable value.
UnicodeError	In case of incorrect encoding or decoding of Unicode characters.
UnicodeDecodeError	In case of a Unicode-specific error in a decoding.
UnicodeEncodeError	In case of a Unicode-specific error in an encoding.
UnicodeTranslateError	In case of a Unicode-specific error in a translation.
Warning	Base class of warning types.
DeprecationWarning	When using a functionality that's classified as deprecated.

Table A.4 Hierarchy of Built-In Exception Types (Cont.)

Exception Type	Appearance
PendingDeprecationWarning	When using a functionality classified as deprecated in the future.
RuntimeWarning	In circumstances that could lead to runtime errors, such as version differences.
SyntaxWarning	In case of a syntax that's problematic but valid.
UserWarning	Base class for self-defined warnings.
FutureWarning	When using functionalities that will change in future versions.
ImportWarning	In case of problems caused by the integration of a module.
UnicodeWarning	For Unicode-specific problems.
BytesWarning	For bytes-specific problems.
ResourceWarning	In case of problems with the use of resources.

Table A.4 Hierarchy of Built-In Exception Types (Cont.)

A.5 Python IDEs

Most of the sample programs in this book are limited in scope and can be written easily using a simple text editor with only rudimentary Python support. For larger projects, it's advisable to use a comprehensive *IDE*. Such a development environment usually provides convenient features that simplify programming in Python, such as code completion, intelligent help functions, and a graphical integration of the PDB Python debugger. An up-to-date overview of all Python IDEs listing their advantages and disadvantages can be found on the web at *https://wiki.python.org/moin/IntegratedDevelopmentEnvironments*. At this point, we'd like to briefly present the most interesting IDEs to help you decide which to use.

A.5.1 PyCharm

Website: *http://www.jetbrains.com/pycharm*

Operating Systems: Windows, Linux, macOS

License: Open source (Community Edition) or commercial (Professional Edition)

PyCharm is the IDE written in Java by the Czech company *JetBrains*. Even in the free *Community Edition*, it provides comprehensive IDE functionalities like code inspection with intelligent help and a graphical debugger. In addition, PyCharm enables the convenient management of virtual environments and integrates version control systems such as *Git* or *SVN*. The commercial *Professional Edition* also provides numerous features in the area of databases and web development with various Python frameworks, including Django.

Due to its number of features and their comfortable use, the Community Edition of PyCharm is perfectly suitable for everything from Python programming for beginners to professional development. In particular, the intelligent code helpers allow many errors to be detected before the program is executed.

A.5.2   Visual Studio Code

Website: *https://code.visualstudio.com/*

Operating Systems: Windows, Linux, macOS

License: Open source

With *Visual Studio Code*, often abbreviated as *VS Code*, Microsoft has released a lightweight, language-independent code editor that can be extended for various programming languages via its distinctive plug-in interface. For the development of Python programs, *Microsoft Python Extensions* are required, which are automatically offered to the developer for installation when working on a Python program.

With the installation of the Python extensions, Visual Studio Code can be used as a full-fledged Python IDE and then provides, in particular, an interactive debugger, intelligent code helpers, virtual environment management, and the offer of many other plug-ins.

Visual Studio Code enjoys great popularity among developers and is especially recommended to users looking for a lightweight IDE they can tailor to their individual needs.

A.5.3   PyDev

Website: *http://www.pydev.org*

Operating Systems: Windows, Linux, macOS

License: Open source

The *Eclipse* IDE was originally developed by IBM for Java, but it can be extended by plug-ins for many programming languages. Among the abundance of available Eclipse plug-ins, *PyDev* is an Eclipse plug-in that turns Eclipse into a Python IDE.

The PyDev plug-in provides code completion, syntax checking, and many other conveniences. In addition, PyDev contains an extensive built-in Python debugger that can also handle threads in a useful way. As part of the commercial project called *LiClipse*, a version of PyDev independent of Eclipse is also offered.

A.5.4 Spyder

Website: *https://www.spyder-ide.org/*

Operating Systems: Windows, Linux, macOS

License: Open source

The *Spyder* development environment targets the use of Python in scientific computing. Similar to MATLAB or Jupyter Notebook (see Chapter 40, Section 40.4.3), Spyder divides the code into cells that can be executed independently in blocks. The integrated IPython console can display plots and formulas graphically, allowing comfortable work with libraries such as matplotlib and SymPy.[1] In addition, Spyder provides an intelligent help function, as well as graphical interfaces for debugging and profiling Python applications.

---

1 SymPy is a Python library for symbolic computing. For more information, visit *http://www.sympy.org*.

Appendix B
The Authors

  Johannes Ernesti and **Peter Kaiser** received their doctorates in mathematics and computer science, respectively, from the Karlsruhe Institute of Technology (KIT).

They have been developing Python software professionally and privately for more than 20 years, currently as part of their research in neural machine translation at DeepL.

This book served as the basis for several trainings in companies and universities. At KIT, a Python lecture based on this book has been held annually since 2015.

Index

E

F

J

K

Z

- Your complete guide to backend programming with JavaScript

- Install the Node.js environment and learn to use core frameworks

- Debug, scale, test, and optimize your applications

Sebastian Springer

Node.js

The Comprehensive Guide

If you're developing server-side JavaScript applications, you need Node.js! Start with the basics of the Node.js environment: installation, application structure, and modules. Then follow detailed code examples to learn about web development using frameworks like Express and Nest. Learn about different approaches to asynchronous programming, including RxJS and data streams. Details on peripheral topics such as testing, security, performance, and more, make this your all-in-one daily reference for Node.js!

834 pages, pub. 08/2022
E-Book: $44.99 | **Print:** $49.95 | **Bundle:** $59.99
www.rheinwerk-computing.com/5556